The Wadsworth Special Educator Series

THE FOLLOWING SPECIAL EDUCATION TITLES
ARE NEW FOR 1998 FROM WADSWORTH PUBLISHING

- Special Education Issues Within
  the Context of American Society
  Susan M. Benner, Ed.D., University of Tennessee
  ISBN: 0-534-25230-3

- Promoting Learning for Culturally
  and Linguistically Diverse Students
  Russell M. Gersten, Ph.D., University of Oregon
  Robert T. Jiménez, Ph.D., University of Illinois
  ISBN: 0-534-34417-6

- Transition from School to Adult Life, Second Edition
  Frank R. Rusch, Ph.D., University of Illinois
  Janis G. Chadsey, Ph.D., University of Illinois
  ISBN: 0-534-34432-1

Special Education Issues Within the Context of American Society

SUSAN McLEAN BENNER
University of Tennessee

Wadsworth Publishing Company
I(T)P® An International Thomson Publishing Company

Belmont, CA • Albany, NY • Bonn • Boston • Cincinnati • Detroit • Johannesburg • London • Madrid
Melbourne • Mexico City • New York • Paris • Singapore • Tokyo • Toronto • Washington

*This book is dedicated to I. Ignacy Goldberg, and the other members of the
Department of Special Education faculty at Teachers College, Columbia University
in the late 1970s who took in a southerner and introduced her to many new
perspectives toward disabilities, education, religion, politics, and life.*

Education Editor: Joan Gill
Assistant Editor: Valerie Morrison
Marketing Manager: Jay Hu
Project Editor: John Walker
Print Buyer: Barbara Britton
Permissions Editor: Veronica Oliva

Production: Matrix Productions Inc.
Photo Researcher: Sarah Evertson
Copy Editor: Donald Pharr
Cover: Jeanne Calabrese
Compositor: Thompson Type
Printer: Malloy Lithography

COPYRIGHT © 1998
By Wadsworth Publishing Company
A Division of International Thomson Publishing Inc.
I(T)P® The ITP logo is a registered trademark under license.

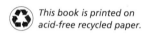 *This book is printed on
acid-free recycled paper.*

Printed in the United States of America
1 2 3 4 5 6 7 8 9 10

For more information, contact Wadsworth Publishing Company, 10 Davis Drive, Belmont, CA 94002, or
electronically at http://www.thomson.com/wadsworth.html

International Thomson Publishing Europe
Berkshire House 168-173
High Holborn
London, WC1V 7AA, England

Thomas Nelson Australia
102 Dodds Street
South Melbourne 3205
Victoria, Australia

Nelson Canada
1120 Birchmount Road
Scarborough, Ontario
Canada M1K 5G4

International Thomson Publishing GmbH
Königswinterer Strasse 418
53227 Bonn, Germany

International Thomson Editores
Campos Eliseos 385, Piso 7
Col. Polanco
11560 México D.F. México

International Thomson Publishing Asia
221 Henderson Road
#05-10 Henderson Building
Singapore 0315

International Thomson Publishing Japan
Hirakawacho Kyowa Building, 3F
2-2-1 Hirakawacho
Chiyoda-ku, Tokyo 102, Japan

International Thomson Publishing Southern Africa
Building 18, Constantia Park
240 Old Pretoria Road
Halfway House, 1685 South Africa

Library of Congress Cataloging-in-Publication Data

Benner, Susan, M.
    Special education issues within the context of American society / by Susan M. Benner.
        p.   cm.
    Includes bibliographical references and index.
    ISBN 0-534-25230-3
    1. Special education—Social aspects—United States.
  2. Handicapped children—Education—United States. 3. Children of minorities—Education—
United States. 4. Educational sociology—United States.   I. Title.
LC3981.B46   1997
371.9'0973—dc21

97-18651
CIP

Contents

Preface

Special education as a field has grown tremendously over the past 25 years. During this period of enormous growth, the field has had a reciprocal relationship with American society—both influencing and being influenced by the larger society. Special educators and parents of children with disabilities rode the crest of the Civil Rights Movement to establish a legal mandate for a free appropriate public education for all children. Passage of the Individuals with Disabilities Education Act, formerly known as the Education of All Handicapped Children Act of 1975, has proven to be a watershed event in the history of special education. Powerful political forces and precedent-setting litigation throughout the country enabled this piece of legislation to become law. Implementation and interpretation of the law has, in turn, been influenced by the economic, social, and political ebb and flow of the country. We cannot separate the issues that face special educators from the context in which the issues arise. The educational system in this country operates within the economics of the times, political forces that influence federal policies, religious and ethical standards, and scientific advances in medicine and technology.

We may find that our views toward educational practices fluctuate as we adjust our contextual perspective. For example, when focused on a child with severe emotional disabilities who would most appropriately be served at an expensive residential facility, we can champion the cause. However, when we learn that the cost of providing this program to one child could have provided daily transportation for every child in the school district for the entire school year, we realize that choices and priorities might not always be easy decisions. Ethical dilemmas between the good of the individual versus the good of the group perpetually haunt us. We can see a parallel example in public health policies toward child vaccinations. A normal, healthy infant receiving the prescribed round of vaccinations, has a toxic reaction, resulting in brain damage. The child's parents and her teachers, viewing the tragedy from the perspective of the 1990s, question why these vaccinations were really necessary. Public health officials, who set vaccination policies, are aware that there are risks involved, and, inevitably, a small number of healthy babies will be permanently damaged through the course of administering these vaccinations. They also know historical statistics on the numbers of deaths and disabilities that these diseases caused prior to the availability of the vaccinations and that they have not been eradicated worldwide. A far greater percentage of children would face danger without the vaccinations than the numbers put at risk through vaccinations. Thus, from the parent's and teacher's view, a needless tragedy has occurred. From the perspective of the public health officials, while the damage to a single child is certainly a tragedy, it is far from needless; but rather, it is an unfortunate part of the program serving the common good.

The text is designed to provide multiple perspectives toward current issues in special education—without dictating solutions. However, the reader is cautioned that even the process of selecting which perspectives to include in this book was not a bias-free process. There is always another way to look at it! Each chapter begins with an introduction that provides a general overview of the topic and defines the focus of the chapter. In the remaining portions of each chapter two issues are presented for discussion and debate. These are divided somewhat loosely into an introductory section containing relevant statistics, research findings, historical information, and other "facts" followed by a decision-point that presents arguments for two differing interpretations of the facts. These argument sections are intended to present plausible conclusions and interpretations of the facts, and are highly subjective in nature. Readers are urged to argue and debate the points, and add additional perspectives, facts, and biased conclusions to the issues at hand. Readers will find that decisions they make linked to issues in the first parts of the book have a substantial impact on other issues raised later in the text. The material must be offered in a somewhat linear fashion, with the understanding that the issues ultimately become mutually dependent and fully integrated into all others.

The text is divided into three main parts. In Part One, the foundations of the special education system are covered. This material includes debates that have been in the field for many years (e.g., the use of categories and labeling of children for services; overidentification of minorities as disabled) that continue to hold significance to the field as well as newer concerns that we are now confronting (e.g., inclusion of students with severe disabilities in general education settings). Part Two deals with basic assessment and instructional practices in special education. Radical ideas, such as the elimination of standardized testing in the eligibility process, are evident throughout these discussions. Curriculum development is addressed as well as instructional practices and the relationship between research and application of new techniques in our classrooms. Part Three addresses broader political and societal concerns that have particular relation to education and people with disabilities. It begins with the mundane matter of paying for special education and advances forward to far deeper concerns focused on the nature of our society and its future. The moral systems to which we adhere, the quality of life we seek for ourselves and others, and the meaning behind popular phrases such as family values are linked back to special education and the lives of persons with disabilities. These chapters were by far the most troubling to write and left the author with many unanswered questions. Presenting the dilemmas is far easier than finding the answers.

Regarding the language used in this text a final note is necessary. The terms used to refer to individuals who receive special education services have been evolving since the inception of the concept. Most recently the phrase "handicapped children" has been deemed insulting and inappropriate, and the language of all federal legislation has been converted to phrases such as "individuals with disabilities." I am a willing supporter of this shift in terminology, and have adhered to it in all new writing. Some of the source materials and quotes may, however, use the older term. At the time these materials were written, the authors certainly were not intending to be insulting; and no meaning should be attributed to that usage other than that the materials were written prior to the conversion to people-first language and the replacement of handicapped with disabled.

Acknowledgments

The development of this text has extended over a four year period of time with the help and support of many individuals. First and foremost I wish to thank my family who has always encouraged and supported my writing efforts and tolerated the messes I created while working on this text.

I would like to thank the authors of Chapter 4, Laurence J. Coleman and Marie E. Peine for their contributions to the text on issues focused on the equities and/or inequities of schooling practices for high-ability learners. I would also like to express gratitude to my colleagues at the University of Tennessee, Laurence J. Coleman, J. Amos Hatch, and Sharon L. Judge, as well as several doctoral students for their critiques and discussion of draft revisions of Chapters 10 and 12 during a research study group. The time and attention they focused on these materials provided me with vital feedback in developing the final versions of these chapters. Likewise, I wish to express my gratitude to Charlotte Duncan for her editorial assistance with the later drafts of every chapter, particularly her assistance in verifying accuracy and completeness of the reference sections. I also extend a word of thanks to my secretary, Vicki Church, who always proves to be an excellent source of support and help. And finally, I wish to thank the reviewers: Professor Chuck Atkinson, Western Washington University; Professor Patricia Carlson, Iowa State University; Professor Karen B. Cole, Northern Illinois University; Professor Ken Howell, Western Washington University; Professor Elliott Lessen, Northern Illinois University; Professor Sheldon Maron, Portland State University; Professor Kathleen Marshall, University of South Carolina; Professor Diane Schwartz, Hofstra University; Professor Debbie Voltz; University of Louisville, Professor Pat Willott, Wheelock College.

I would also like to express my appreciation of Vicki Knight who served as editor to the project through the initial stages of manuscript development. She helped me conceptualize the project and analyze the reviewer comments. Likewise, I am appreciative of the reviewers who provided essential critique of earlier, less structured drafts of the text. Their positive suggestions for structuring and organization provided critical assistance that enabled me to bring the project to its conclusion. I also wish to thank Joan Gill, who served as editor during the latter stages of the project, her assistant, Valerie Morrison who took care of many of the last minute details necessary to meet deadlines, and John Walker, who guided the book through production. My final thanks go to Merrill Peterson of Matrix Productions who transformed the manuscript into a book and Sarah Evertson of Image Quest who provided photographs.

✧

PART I

Special Education and Related Services: Who Are They For, and Where Do They Take Place?

Since the passage of the Individuals with Disabilities Education Act (IDEA) and the establishment of parallel state laws, there have been substantial discussions and debates over what special education and related services actually entail and who can and should be deemed eligible for them. Some might even contend that all children are special and worthy of the benefits (?) of such programs.

Part One includes four chapters that touch on the structural issues facing educators today. The issues of eligibility and standards for placement in special education have always received substantial critique. Congressional hearings and moves to dramatically alter the eligibility criteria, including the elimination of categories, are constantly under discussion. Clearly, there is a need to establish positive educational solutions to the dilemmas presented by those children who face extreme poverty, those who have a non-English speaking heritage, and those for whom special education has become a form of racial or cultural discrimination. What those solutions should be is not so clear. Juxtaposed to these concerns is the need to ensure that all students have appropriate educational enhancements that can provide the necessary support in the achievement of potential.

1

Classification and Eligibility

INTRODUCTION

The special education system in place today is far different from that which was available prior to 1975. There was no nationwide categorical listing of disabling conditions that entitled children to a free appropriate public education. Individual states had their own policies toward students with disabilities, and categorical terms varied across state borders. In the wake of the federal mandate in 1975 to provide a free appropriate public education for all children with disabilities, personnel in the educational system immediately faced the task of defining who was eligible for the designated special education and related services across all states. The initial legislation, Individuals with Disabilities Education Act of 1975 (IDEA),[1] included a specific list of disabling conditions that entitled students with those conditions to receive the mandated benefits in the least restrictive environment. Subsequent amendments to this law (e.g., IDEA, 1990) have included additions and adjustments to the categorical listing. Federal definitions were established for the various categories, but each state was required to adopt its own definitions and establish specific criteria of eligibility for each of

---

1. Originally titled as Education of All Handicapped Children Act (1975), this legislation was retroactively renamed Individuals with Disabilities Act to eliminate the use of the word *handicapped* and to adhere to "people-first" wording in the title.

these conditions. For a child to reap the benefits of IDEA, he or she must be assessed and found to have one or more of the designated conditions and, as a result thereof, need special education. Although adaptations are required for some additional conditions under Section 504 of the Rehabilitation Act of 1973, a general nondiscrimination protection, children with such conditions are not offered all the rights and privileges included in IDEA.

Some of the disability categories listed in IDEA have been extremely difficult to define, triggering an evolving series of definition revisions. For example, defining *learning disabilities* has proven very controversial, and numerous organizations and commissions have struggled over the years to develop an acceptable definition. Recently, the confusion surrounding this category and its relationship with the medical diagnosis of attention deficit with hyperactivity disorder (ADHD) has increased. Mental retardation is another category that has had multiple definition revisions during the twentieth century, including some since the original passage of IDEA in 1975. The changes have significantly altered both the eligibility criteria and the assessment practices associated with this classification, putting a far greater emphasis on adaptive behavior in both the home and the school environment. However, the most significant change in the definition of *mental retardation* occurred prior to the passage of IDEA and included a "miraculous cure" for approximately 13% of the population. In 1973, the performance criteria on intelligence tests was lowered from scores below one standard deviation from the mean on an individual IQ test to scores below two standard deviations. Such changes are an inevitable part of an evolving field and can be considered as healthy alterations. Yet such changes also cast doubt and concern over our legalistic assumptions of the precision of our definitions, eligibility criteria, and accuracy of assessment.

Innumerable historical and contextual factors and educational practices have influenced and are influenced by the categories of disability recognized in IDEA. When the legislation was new, a consistent categorical listing for special education eligibility for all participating states had to be in place in a relatively short period of time. Untested ideas had to be implemented as school personnel sought appropriate testing instruments, qualified personnel in special education and related services, and suitable instructional materials. Policies and procedures regarding the formation of multidisciplinary teams, the writing of individual education plans (IEPs), and the inclusion of parents in the decision-making process all had to be developed in compliance with the new state and federal laws. With the maturation of the field, widely available tests and instructional materials for each disability identified in the law have appeared on the commercial market. Other conditions that never made the list, such as minimal brain dysfunction and social maladjustment, seem to have gone by the wayside and have been replaced by the legitimized terms used in the legislation. Therefore, the evolution of the field has been reflected, in large measure, by the roles and values afforded to our categories of disabilities. The remainder of this section further elaborates on the historical context of the disability conditions and the power the categories hold in allowing one to receive the rights stipulated in IDEA.

Historical Context

When the federal and state laws mandating a free appropriate public education were first implemented, many children had been excluded from public education. Some were kept in institutions, considered uneducable and even untrainable: unfit to remain in our open communities. Others were placed on waiting lists for places in limited special education classrooms but grew up before their turns ever arrived. Still others plodded through their years in school unidentified and unserved. These children were often labeled stupid or lazy rather than being certified as having a disability, as might occur today. IDEA and subsequent state laws were intended to address the needs of all—the unserved, the underserved, and the previously unidentified. In order to ensure that school personnel could not say to any child with a legitimate need for special education and related services, "These laws do not apply to you," a specific list of conditions specifying who is entitled to special education services was included in the legislation. However, this categorical approach proved to be controversial even before its adoption and triggered slogans such as "Label jars, not children." Innumerable studies on the effects of labeling, including the now classic studies reported by Hobbs (1975), became a part of our growing research base. The debate still continues on the merits and detriments of labeling students.

The categories became the foundation for the establishment of special education programs and placement of students. For example, programs for students who were diagnosed as mildly retarded were distinct from those serving children with learning disabilities, which were separate from programs designed for students who were emotionally disturbed. Children who had no more in common than that they each had some type of physical disability were put together in classes, regardless of age or cognitive ability. An eight-year-old who was severely retarded might be in the same class with a fourteen-year-old who was of normal intelligence simply because both had some degree of cerebral palsy. At the outset, children served through IDEA were not mixed by category, although placement in the least restrictive environment was always a component of the law. Thus, students with all types of disabilities were supposed to be served in the least restrictive environment, but not mixed with one another. Residential schools serving students with hearing impairments or visual impairments were established long before the passage of IDEA. However, prior to the federal mandate to offer all children a public education, a child who was both hearing impaired and mentally retarded often had nowhere to go. Such children would be rejected by programs serving students with hearing impairments as well as by school-based mental retardation programs. The children would often be placed in institutions serving a population with mental retardation, where programming needed by persons with hearing impairments would not necessarily be available. The primary condition of disability became the overriding factor in placement decisions, but its determination was and remains a rather subjective process.

Teaching licensure programs that paralleled these categorical conditions were established throughout the country. Staffing and child placement were almost exclusively related to the diagnostic decision about the student. The diagnostic condition was assumed to imply the programming needs of the child. Teacher

Congressional action sets the stage for students with disabilities to find their place in public education.

training included a series of courses specifically covering the nature and needs of and instructional approaches for children by disability. Again, age and other variables, such as cultural background, distance from a school, or family resources, were treated as though they were of far less importance than the child's diagnostic category. A shortage of licensed teachers and category-specific placement spaces created serious compliance problems for school administrators. In the strictly categorical system, if a class for learning disabled (LD) students were full but a class for educable mentally retarded (EMR) students still had spaces available in a neighborhood school, and the next child needing services from that neighborhood was diagnosed as learning disabled, she would have nowhere to be placed. If there were an LD class across town with space in it, that became the placement of choice, thus removing her from the neighborhood school and her friends for the sake of her diagnosis. The expanding numbers of eligible students, categorical service delivery, and the need to provide services in the least restrictive environment (including proximity to one's neighborhood) became persistent conflicts. Concurrently, special educators recognized that there were overlaps and at least some consistency in instructional methods appropriate for use with students across categories. The other variables, particularly age appropriateness and neighborhood, increased in influence in placement decisions while disability conditions diminished. States began collapsing areas of teacher licensure as well as mixing students with various disabilities within the same classroom or resource program.

The delivery of services no longer typically follows the strict categorical delineations for the high-incidence disabilities associated with mild educational handicaps. Within an elementary school, resource/consultant special educators serve the majority of students who have been identified as eligible for services due to such mild problems, *regardless* of diagnosis. The exceptions may be those children with speech disorders, visual impairments, or hearing impairments who

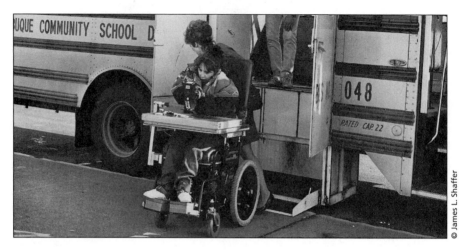

Transportation is only one of the many related services provided to students with disabilities.

are often assigned to itinerant specialists for some of their educational needs. Additionally, residential schools for students with sensory impairments remain a preferred choice for some with these conditions. However, for the other mild conditions, once a child has been deemed eligible for special education, his eligibility category becomes somewhat secondary to planning an effective instructional program for him. Learning style, individual strengths and needs, cultural heritage, and age all contribute to programming more than the diagnostic condition might contribute. Yet the categorical conditions remain a substantial component of the law. The inconsistencies between categorical eligibility for services, the cross-categorical or noncategorical nature of most special education programs, and mixed patterns of teacher licensure reflect the contradictions and inconsistencies regarding the value and significance of disability categories.

Entering the System

Determination of exactly who fits into each category is based upon both state and federal definitions and certification criteria. Ysseldyke (1987) noted the weight of this classification system, describing it as an activity that is "at the root of nearly everything that occurs in special education" (p. 253). Professional organizations, student groups used in research studies, parent support groups, and teacher licensure patterns have all reflected this categorical system. It has been a widely tolerated system, if not a fully accepted one. It has been credited with aiding communication among professionals and parents, offering relief and understanding to parents and teachers who are seeking some explanation of a child's difficulties, and guiding the direction of program planning. It has also been criticized as rigid, incomplete, and confusing. The act of labeling is denounced as causing more harm than benefit, serving to set limits on children rather than protecting them from frustrations and unnecessary failure. Throughout IDEA reauthorization negotiations, the categorical system is always subject to heated discussion and debate. It has not been required for infants, toddlers, and preschoolers, for the general diagnosis of developmental delay is sufficient to offer services to children in this age range. Further, recent reauthorization changes to IDEA now permit the use of this nonspecific category through the early elementary grades, presuming that the child does meet the eligibility criteria for at least one categorical condition.

Even with these alterations and adjustments, the categorical system and eligibility standards remain as substantial components of special education policy. The establishment of eligibility consumes much of the available special education resources in time and personnel devoted to diagnostic assessments. For some children, this assessment process produces little other than their ineligibility for special education, an outcome that can be confusing both to teachers and to parents. Since the classification system is one through which a student enters into the world of special education, many decisions are based on the findings of eligibility assessments. Questions are posed and answered based on the definitions and certification criteria for each of the disability conditions. The system relies on the assumptions that the meanings provided for the disability conditions are precise, that the test instruments designed to determine eligibility are accurate, and that appropriate programming for students is built upon the diagnostic information (Lovitt, 1993). The accuracy of these assumptions is at the heart of the debate regarding the categorical system.

As the availability of special education services and the use of diagnostic categories, such as learning disabilities, has expanded, parental awareness has increased concurrently. Parents today often initiate a request for a screening for learning disabilities or respond cooperatively when educators make such a request. The learning disability explanation might become so attractive to some parents that they resist all other considerations in analyzing school-related problems. As Pollak (1985) notes, "It may be increasingly common, especially among more affluent and educated parents somewhat conversant with learning disability-related problems and terminology, and dissatisfied with their child's academic progress, to assume that some kind of learning disability is the cause" (p. 490). However, the conviction with which some such parents hold to their identification and explanation of their child's struggles in school can become a serious obstacle to redefining the problem more consistently with the assessment findings. Pollak emphasizes the enigma this situation can create when family systems and/or individual psychodynamics are prematurely removed from consideration.

Evaluators may unwittingly become partners with the parents, who are actively or covertly seeking a learning disability diagnosis. The professional, assigned to the case by the school or hired by the parents, may not be thoroughly familiar with the child, hidden parental agendas, or dysfunctional patterns of interactions common between the child and other family members. The diagnosis of a learning disability becomes a mask for other, possibly more significant issues inherent in the parent–child relationship. The parents can resist focusing on more painful considerations about the causes of and implied treatments for the child's problems once the child-based disability is established. Should such potentially harmful misuses of the present system be considered as repairable limitations of a basically functional eligibility system or further evidence of the need for radical reform, including the elimination of categorical definitions that are in use today?

Focus of Discussion

The focus of this chapter is on the classification system used in special education and the tensions between categorical eligibility and cross-categorical or noncategorical delivery of services, with an expanding number of students being deemed eligible and others appearing to fall through the eligibility cracks. The critical issues discussed in this chapter relate to two basic dilemmas. The first contrasts the potentially damaging effects of labeling and the relationship of categories to educational efficacy. The second issue focuses on the conflicting tension between the ever-increasing special education population and the numbers of students facing school failure who are ineligible for services under the present categorical system.

CATEGORICAL LABELING
AND EDUCATIONAL EFFICACY

The issue of labeling is far from new, yet it continues as an unsettled point of debate. Special education labels create opportunities for students to receive educational support services that are not otherwise available to them. They influence the attitudes students have about themselves as well as attitudes others hold toward them (Budoff & Siperstein, 1982; Coleman, 1983; Dickie, 1982; Feldman, Kinnison, Jay, & Harth, 1983; Fogel & Nelson, 1983; Rolison & Medway, 1985; Smith, Osborne, Crim, & Rhu, 1986; Sutherland, Algozine, Ysseldyke, & Freeman, 1983; Taylor, Smiley, & Ziegler, 1983). As they become a part of a student's developing self-concept, they may have a lifelong impact for the individual. Although disability-specific classrooms for high-incidence mild disabilities are no longer the predominant special education delivery model, specific disability conditions continue to influence the nature of special education services. For example, students identified as learning disabled most likely receive services while maintaining identity and full participation in the general educational program. Others, who come to be classified as mentally retarded or emotionally disturbed, tend to be further removed from the general educational curriculum, even though their programs may include some contact with the mainstream. The sense of responsibility for the education of the eligible student has typically rested with special educators, as has the determination of an altered curriculum.

Differential effects of the labels are also seen in parental reactions. The label of emotional disturbance might leave parents feeling guilty and ashamed, whereas the learning disability label might create the opposite effect, relieving the burden of guilt and blame from student, teacher, and parent. Crowell (1993) noted an unusually low incidence of emotional disturbance and behavioral disorders in Mississippi. When he asked special education teachers why this pattern was occurring, they indicated that parental objection to the label was the primary explanation for the low referral rate. The reaction to a child's diagnosis of hearing impairment for parents who are deaf themselves might actually be positive, whereas hearing parents would more likely express concern and anxiety about the child's condition. The focus of this debate is on the necessity of the label in order for a child to be considered eligible for services and the distinctiveness of each of the labels in planning and delivering services. The most difficult issues evolve around perceived inconsistencies and inaccuracies in the labels' use and the relevance of diagnostic labels to the placement and instructional practices employed with many students in the special education conglomerate today.

Precision and Stability of Labels

Stability of and accuracy in diagnosis are vital elements of consideration in the debates regarding categorical labeling. Singer, Palfrey, Butler, and Walker (1989) explored the variation in special education classifications across five major metropolitan school districts. They identified the many factors influencing this variability, determining that there was substantial differentiation in referral practices, effectiveness and vigor of child-find programs, psychometric standards and guidelines for certification, personnel participating in evaluation committees, strength of professional and special interest groups, level of cooperation with parents who initiate requests for services, availability and costs of services, acceptability of certain categorical diagnoses, and history of litigation and legal action. In spite of these many variables, Singer's group points out that the variability apparent in the application of the categories to students exceeds what could reasonably be anticipated. They compared the functional levels in areas such as speaking, academic ability, and social skills of students with the same labels across five different districts. The results indicated that within districts, classification patterns are consistent, particularly for students with observable or low-prevalence/high-severity conditions, such as hearing impairments. When they projected how the students would fare if moved to another district, they determined that although a majority would have retained the same classification, many would have experienced a change in diagnosis. Those who were classified as emotionally disturbed were most likely to be reclassified as learning disabled or mentally retarded. The second group most likely to be reclassified were those who were identified as mentally retarded. A consistent pattern was seen in the reclassification of 35% of the students with physical/multiple handicaps as mentally retarded. This finding seemed to be tied to district policy regarding the designation of a primary condition when cognitive impairments are present. Within districts, the group that appeared to be the least stable, serving the role of category of last resort, was that of learning disabilities.

Wolman, Thurlow, and Bruininks (1989) reviewed the records of 523 students with mild conditions that included learning disabilities, behavior disorders, educable mentally handicapped, and speech impairment. Of these high school students, 24% had been classified into at least two categories while in school. The classification most often involved in reclassifications was that of learning disabilities, with a rate of 18%. Halgren and Clarizio (1993) have more recently reported the substantial changes that are evident in special education classifications over time. In nearly four out of five cases, students identified with a speech/language impairment had had a change. Changes were also apparent across other disability labels, and infrequent only among the most severely impaired.

Halgren and Clarizio also reported that out of a sample of 654 students who were in special education, 21.9% were terminated and 16.3% reclassified when reevaluations occurred. The category most often associated with termination was speech/language impairment, with a 54.7% rate of termination. Other termination figures were 10.7% for sensory-motor disabilities, 10% for learning disabilities, and 5% for emotional disturbance. No terminations were associated with mild or severe mental retardation; however, reclassifications were most often associated with mild mental retardation (39.3%). Other categorical reclassification rates were speech/language impairment (22.9%), emotional disturbance (16.7%), sensory-motor disabilities (14.3%), learning disabilities (11.4%), and severe mental retardation (5.1%). Highest rates of reclassification were found at the preschool level (24.7%) and lowest rates at the secondary level (11%). Those who were reclassified had significantly lower IQ scores than those who were terminated.

In citing a variety of other research in this area, Halgren and Clarizio point out the wide variance researchers have reported in reclassification and termination rates. They speculate as to the causes of the inconsistent findings, including the unreliability of special education diagnoses, variability of settings studied (urban, suburban, rural), the length of the follow-up period for the study, severity of disability, lack of common definitions across states, socioeconomic differences in samples, access to compensatory educational programs, limited services available in middle and secondary schools, and increased accuracy of diagnosis following a period of special education services for the child.

Instructional Differentiation

In the initial years of implementation of IDEA, emphasis was placed on the differential instructional needs of children as defined by their disability. Research designed to evaluate the correlation of instructional needs to disability and the efficacy of special education in general was commonly found in the professional literature. The findings, while always subject to interpretation, were not supportive of either treatment effects by disability or special education in general. Bender, Scott, and McLaughlin (1993) report that none of the research related to trait by treatment confirms differing curricular needs among specific disability groups. These findings might indicate the lack of correlation between disability and instructional needs, or they might suggest other concerns, such as poor delivery of special education.

Within the walls of special education, there is evidence of a lack of individualization. Wesson and Deno (1989) analyzed IEPs of students with mild handicaps who were served through resource rooms and found that there was very little differentiation in them, with each child's IEP appearing similar to those of her classmates. These findings are consistent with those of Ysseldyke, O'Sullivan, Thurlow, and Christenson (1989), who found little difference in the instruction received by students with three different categorical labels of mild disability. Smith's (1990) conclusion, after a decade of related research, is that the IEP is "nonviable and impractical" (p. 12). Allington and McGill-Franzen (1988) have reported that special education teachers as well as teachers in Chapter One reading programs find and adopt their favorite routines, employing them as children present themselves for instruction, group after group. The children are then obligated to "conform to the routine if they are to be successful" (p. 90). As the teachers employed their routines, the obligation to analyze individual student needs for instructional planning did not occur.

Nevertheless, there is a strong research base documenting specific effective instructional strategies. Wang (1989) uses the term "adaptive instruction" to refer to "an alternative educational approach designed to achieve the overall goal of enabling each student to experience schooling success through a systematic process of making instructional accommodations that meet the unique learning characteristics and needs of individual students" (pp. 100–101). The types of adaptations to which Wang is referring include mastery learning, cooperative teams, individual tutorials, and large- and small-group instruction. These methods of teaching in themselves do not represent anything that would be inappropriate for any child. The emphasis is on individual needs, not those of a diagnostic category. The debate remains about the extent the diagnosis reveals the appropriate instructional strategies.

The literature provides an extensive supply of studies that target the efficacy of a particular strategy or approach in particular settings. Fister and Kemp (1993) summarize the research validating five strategies for learning, including precision teaching, the use of study guides, cooperative learning, self-management, and graphic organizers. Findings were reported as positive and used to argue that we need to teach these proven strategies to students with learning problems. Although each of these techniques was effective with the majority of students participating in the studies on the variables measured (typically, student success), no concern was expressed or possible explanations offered for the lack of success by a fairly large percentage of participating students. For example, Fister and Kemp (1993) use results finding that nearly 70% of the students participating in precision teaching improved to extol the benefits of each of these strategies. For 70% of the population, then, we might really have something that offers a key to successful learning, although not unique to students with disabilities. For the remaining approximately 30%, some will receive no benefit from the strategy, and some (13% worsened), it seems, will regress. Where does the problem lie—within the child, within the strategy, within the interaction between the child and the strategy? The act of drawing the correct conclusion can involve reflective analytical teaching based on teacher flexibility and familiarity with multiple instructional approaches. In practice, a choice might simply reflect the teacher's preferred routine. The notion that teachers get trained in and adopt preferred routines and expect students to adapt to them is consistent with research findings that document the efficacy of particular programs.

Once research documenting the benefits of an approach with some students is available, that approach is typically then presented to teachers as the *one* to use, contrary to the spirit of individualized matching of instructional approaches to student characteristics. Because an approach is received well by those being trained, who willingly embed the new information into their preferred routines, it has established content validity. However, we can predict that some students will not be successful with the new procedures, and teacher reactions to these individuals may reflect their commitment either to routines or to individualization of instruction. In some instances the preferred instructional routines of supervisors may even prevent classroom teachers from accommodating individuals for whom the routines are ineffective.

There have been some recent attempts to document the efficacy of providing all students with the same instruction (e.g., Pinnell, 1989; Slavin, Madden, Karweit, Levermon, & Dolan, 1990). Jenkins, Jewell, Leicester, O'Connor, Jenkins, and Troutner (1994) even took on the notion of ability grouping for reading instruction as an issue worthy of reconsideration. They note the research-based characteristics that consistently differentiate low–ability reading groups from high-ability reading groups. The low groups tend to receive less reading instruction, have less time on-task, read less material, and work on lower order decoding and drill work than on meaning and higher order learning. Thus, the nature of the instruction between upper and lower reading groups differs regardless of whether the instruction is located in the general classroom, led by the classroom teacher, or is based in a pull-out program, led by a special educator or reading specialist. Jenkins et al. conducted a field test in which students from special education and Chapter One and all general students were heterogeneously grouped and taught using the same instructional materials. Students participating in the study who were receiving special education were classified as learning disabled ($n = 52$), mildly retarded ($n = 3$), and seriously behavior disordered ($n = 3$). The instruction encompassed an integrated language arts and reading program, involved the support personnel (special education and Chapter One teachers) to provide tutorial support, and offered cross-age peer tutoring to those needing extra supports. They discovered that the tutoring was insufficient for some and instituted a limited pull-out fifteen- to twenty-minute daily program of intense decoding work for those students. They determined that gain scores on several achievement and behavioral measures were indicative of the experimental school students' superior performance over those at the control school. However, since all data are presented as means, it is unknown if all experimental students made moderate gains in excess of the control students or some made tremendous gains, while others showed little or no progress, and a few actually experienced a regression. Jenkins et al. provided a predetermined identical intervention for each child identified as needing additional help with decoding. From the positive results of their "field test," they could at least argue in favor of nonability grouping, although they could not refute the need for, nor claim the effectiveness of, their instruction for *every* student.

Proposition One

Specific criteria defining who is eligible for special education and the mandates stipulated in IDEA are essential to ensure an equal educational opportunity for all children. Without such criteria, states and local education agencies would be free to dismiss from their rolls those children who placed the heaviest burden on the educational system or those who were simply viewed as lazy or worthless by educators. The current system has proven flexible and open to continued alterations, enabling it to be a viable tool for the field.

Decision Point 1.1: Retention or Elimination of Categories

Arguments for Proposition One Although the disability-specific conditions in use today are not always mutually exclusive, distinct categories, they do provide a useful system of organization for special education services. They offer a starting point for teachers, parents, and children alike when school difficulties seem to be overwhelming. The listing of categorical conditions in IDEA is not intended to be the definitive word on what constitutes a disability that warrants access to special education and related services. Rather, the listing is the best current thinking in the field on how to avoid the exclusion of any child needing special education from receiving appropriate services. The fluidity and functionality of the list have been supported and maintained over time through periodic changes in the terms used and definitions of the included conditions. For example, when mandated services were extended downward to three-year-olds, the adoption of developmental delay as a suitable category was included to avoid premature labeling of children. The application of this general category for young children in the primary grades has also been accepted as a legitimate practice when more precise labeling seems inappropriate or harmful.

The fact that changes have occurred to the accepted list of disability conditions over the years is evidence of its usefulness as a malleable tool for the field. The list does not dictate to the field what is and is not possible. When inconsistencies, omissions, limitations, or harmful effects are evident and attributed to originating from the listing of disability conditions included in IDEA, change is possible. The addition of traumatic brain injury and autism as specific conditions occurred because students with these conditions were considered as inaccurately labeled by any of the other existing categories and ill served by the other labels. On the other hand, educational handicaps associated with attention deficit with hyperactivity disorder were felt to be adequately addressed by the available list. The careful delineation of seriously emotionally disturbed as a disability category has helped reduce the confusion between the presence of a disability warranting special education and related services and the social and behavioral problems some children display in school settings.

Precision and Stability of Labels The fact that children seem to vary in time as to their qualifications for certain labels need not indicate that diagnoses are inaccurate or lack value and meaning. Stability of labels throughout a lifetime is not relevant to a child in third grade who is struggling to read and write, unable to keep up with her class, and beginning to feel the effects of constant frustration and failure on her self-esteem and ability to interact with her peers. Rather, she and her parents need advice and support on how best to enable her to achieve greater success in school. The determination of her need for glasses, a hearing aid, adapted instructional approaches, an altered set of goals, a modified curriculum, or an effective means of coping with any learning disabilities that may be present is vital to her educational future and could even change its course. The process begins with the identification of any disability condition. From there, further decisions about her educational program can be made. Whether she retains the categorical label placed upon her at the initial referral or not, whether she is served in a program that is disability-specific or not, she has received the initial attention and consideration of a multidisciplinary team that has focused its attention on her educational needs. Many possible causes of her problems have been eliminated in the diagnostic process, even if the final solutions to her educational difficulties take longer to discover than the initial prognosis indicated. By fifth grade, the child may no longer fit any of the disability categories or be more appropriately given a new diagnosis. Our system allows for change and even includes policies that indicate change can be expected, as indicated by the required periodic reevaluation of every child served.

The figures reported by Halgren and Clarizio (1993) and others regarding reclassification and termination provide clear evidence of the fluidity and effectiveness of the categorical system. Termination of eligibility could be considered one of the intended outcomes of special education. If we can take a child who is experiencing difficulty in school due to a learning disability, offer adaptive instructional approaches, teach the student some coping skills, and offer an individualized educational program, we should be able to reduce the discrepancy between his potential and actual achievement. If it is reduced sufficiently, the student may no longer meet the required discrepancy criteria. The characteristics (e.g., visual processing deficit, central auditory processing disorder, hyperactivity, impulsivity) that may have led to the diagnosis could still be present in the child, but his ability to function in school has been altered. His need for special education may have been eliminated.

A child's loss of eligibility for the label is the greatest success for the special education teacher, not an indication of the instability of the diagnostic process or the subjectivity of categories. If a child, through intervention, maturation, or improved personal adjustment, comes to lose the behavioral characteristics that initiated a special education referral and diagnosis, it does not mean the label was inaccurate, unnecessary, or harmful. Indeed, such findings could be used to argue the benefits of labeling in that the problem gets identified and addressed, and improvements in child functioning result. A child facing serious emotional difficulty may meet the criteria for seriously emotionally disturbed and be placed in an expensive residential treatment center. The hopes for this student may center on his ability to benefit from the available therapies, with some vision of his returning to his community, his home school, and the mainstream of the educational system. The fact that diagnostic labels may not be permanent supports the notion that many conditions can improve through intervention and need not be viewed as lifelong disabilities. Labels are temporarily useful tools in describing a child's present functioning and are not intended to be indicators of lifelong conditions or even predictors of the future. The fact that people misunderstand or misuse them does not mean that they hold no value or need to be eliminated, rather that teachers and others need to have a greater understanding of their uses and limitations.

Instructional Differentiation Some of the categories, particularly learning disabilities and serious emotional disturbance, are criticized as being highly imprecise and subjective. These complaints, coupled with the variation evident in diagnostic practices throughout the nation, are real issues. However, these limitations of the categorical system are not comparable to the profound differences in recommendations and programming implied by some of the labels. It is obvious that it would be fruitless to treat a chronically tantruming child who had virtually no language skills as if he were emotionally disturbed when, in fact, the child had a significant hearing loss. The child's hearing impairment would go untreated while inappropriate exploration of adjustment difficulties were pursued. Likewise, mislabeling a child who has a serious emotional disorder as learning disabled inappropriately shifts the emphasis on treatment needs from emotional adjustment to instructional approaches. In such as case, both the student and the teacher seem to be set up for chronic failure since the underlying problem is not a basic processing disorder but one of underlying emotional disturbance.

There are real distinctions between the categories listed in IDEA and differences in educational interventions based on those distinctions. Lovitt (1993) has noted some positive consequences of the categorical diagnosis and placement practices "might be that those individuals who were specifically identified and accordingly grouped stay in school longer, get more out of school while they are in it, and live more productive lives when they leave it than they would have had they not been specially dealt with" (pp. 51–52). Historically, the categorical approach was used for educational placement and programming to the exclusion of other considerations about children (e.g., chronological age, proximity of classes to one's neighborhood, appropriate levels of instruction), and it created very inappropriate groups for many children. This substantial flaw in the system, which no longer exists as a prevailing method of placement for students with disabilities, remains as a futile argument against the categorical system. The rigidity and inflexibility of the system were caused by policies and procedures regarding placements and teacher licensure, not the diagnostic categories themselves. The needed changes have resulted in placement practices today that offer far greater choices and opportunities for children with disabilities than ever before. The appropriate application of disability-specific instructional interventions need not be limited to settings exclusively for single types of students.

Argument Summary Our system of eligibility for special education is based on the presence of a disability within a child. The cause of the disability is of no consequence when considering the child's rights and needed educational interventions, but its nature does unquestionably influence the type of interventions needed. Although the categorical system is not without limitations or problems, it has proven amendable as needed over time. The categorical conditions associated with eligibility should not be blamed when they are misused or misunderstood, or when other related policies (e.g., placement practices, teacher licensure) create restrictions for students. The categories listed in IDEA are tools for us to use as we seek to meet the educational needs of students with disabilities, not arbitrary pigeonholes to which we must limit ourselves and our children. The categorical approach offers a means of organizing an otherwise overwhelming task, monitoring schools, establishing accountability for special education services, and focusing attention on individual children through the diagnostic process.

Arguments for Proposition Two   Special education exists to offer educational services to students with disabilities, but far too much of our effort goes into the determination of eligibility according to arbitrary, subjective categorical criteria. Once the initial eligibility hurdle is behind a child, services begin, and the diagnostic files take on little consequence for the actual interventions that occur for many children. Teachers assigned to work with special education students may even be unaware of and unconcerned about their students' diagnoses but desperately need specific instructional techniques recommended for them. The uselessness of many diagnostic reports for classroom teachers struggling to identify effective intervention strategies is real.

The recent acceptance of "developmental delay" as a suitable term to use for young children in the classification process appears to be a move in the right direction, but it does not reflect real change. It is merely an attempt to retain the categorical structure while creating the appearance of reform and change. In fact, children must continue to meet specific eligibility criteria for one of the listed disability conditions, but the label need not be used. The deemphasis on categorical identification is on paper only. Resources and time will still be devoted to finding a label for every child, even though those labels might not be used in conversations with the parents or in communications with classroom teachers.

The foundation of the entire eligibility and classification system was challenged when Fuchs, Fuchs, Benowitz, and Barringer (1987) attacked the use of norm-referenced tests on children with handicaps. While some tests have been restandardized since their article appeared in *Exceptional Children,* the point that students are being evaluated on instruments in which they were specifically excluded from the norming sample remains—a practice counter to basic psychometric principles. The diagnostic process for many students includes an individual intelligence test as the pivotal piece of information. Sabatino and Vance (1993) speak to the need to move away from this practice and the whole notion of a list of conditions that make one eligible for special education. First, they note that general education should be able to provide its own tutorial and remedial services, not relying on special education to pick up the responsibility for every child experiencing difficulties in school. Special education should offer "cognitive re-education of students with cognitive dysfunction" (p. 31).

> **Proposition Two**
> The ambiguity and confusion, the inconsistencies across school systems in defining eligibility, and the ever-expanding list of categories all point to the need to radically alter the existing categorical structure. The labeling system established as a part of IDEA should be replaced by one reflecting the noncategorical and cross-categorical programming practices in place in special education today.

The emphasis in special education can be more appropriately placed on determining the most effective interventions for children rather than on making arbitrary distinctions between labels. For example, it is of little benefit to contend that a child has a learning disability rather than a language impairment, to debate the distinctions between emotional disturbance and behavior disorders, or whether a child with an IQ bordering on the mental retardation eligibility criterion can be certified as learning disabled. In 1978 in England, educators "formally recognized that to categorize children's difficulties under fixed headings was both artificial and unhelpful to the children, their parents and their teachers" (Feiler & Thomas, 1988, p. 19). Indeed, "any shortcomings in the resources available to help the child" (p. 19) should be acknowledged, not just child deficits.

The categorical system of eligibility is not only flawed; it is also extremely expensive. Rueda (1989), citing Shepard and Smith, noted that in Colorado the cost of an initial determination of eligibility due to a learning disability was nearly the same as that of all personnel costs for the provision of special education instruction and support services for the average pupil. Further, it routinely required twenty-one hours of assessment to determine the diagnosis—a substantial amount of lost instructional time. The increasing costs of special education coupled with the inefficiency of the categorical eligibility assessment system for students with mild high-incidence conditions will certainly keep this issue before us until changes are made (Bender et al., 1993).

Precision and Stability of Labels The instability and imprecision of the special education classification system is readily apparent in the figures reported by Halgren and Clarizio (1993) and others. How can educational diagnosticians face parents, teachers, and children and claim to have an explanation for educational problems in the form of a child-based disability and two years later claim that said disability is no longer evident? How is it possible that a child has a learning disability in one state but becomes seriously emotionally disturbed after his parents move to a new state? Was the move really that traumatic for the child? Wang and Reynolds (1985) reported one instance in which a successful special education program was eliminated because the resulting declassification of students reduced the availability of special education funds for the school district. Effective instructional techniques, it seems, can "cure" a child of his disability. Perhaps the children never had a "disability" but clearly profited from the appropriate educational interventions provided to them. The logic that we must label the child in order to offer him needed services reflects the current system but must be challenged directly, not merely accepted as a necessary evil. If we accept the fact that the system, flawed throughout, necessitates the labeling of children prior to allowing them access to services, the ends become justification for the means, and no real challenges to the system are possible.

Some would, in fact, argue that the labels are "'social constructions,' as opposed to fixed stable entities that provide information about within-child characteristics" (Rueda, 1989, p. 123). Unfortunately, they are treated as far more than the temporary labels based on locally specific meanings as might be more appropriate as indicated by the reclassification data. The categories rely on a system of diagnosis that was built around labels and serves to give them credibility. The tests that have appeared on the market, which were developed specifically to identify the listed conditions, are now used as proof that these conditions exist. The instability of student performance in the assessment process is interpreted as evidence of the effectiveness of interventions, inconsistency of a student's abilities, or deterioration of a student's condition—anything but a lack of meaning attributed to the expensive labeling process. We have marketed to ourselves and the educational establishment this diagnostic fraud.

Consideration must be given to the idea that the disability label was never really needed. For example, when a language disorder is evident, it need not be necessary to arbitrate whether the child be certified as language impaired and served by the speech/language therapist as opposed to learning disabled and served by the special educator. The current system demands that much effort and attention be placed on such an initial decision. Yet the stability of those decisions is very limited. Children could be better served through a process involving the identification of their educational needs rather than their diagnostic labels. The number of irrelevant, expensive intelligence test administrations that offer virtually no insights for instructional interventions for the classroom teacher, could be dramatically reduced, if not eliminated, by deemphasizing or altogether abandoning the current labeling process. An assessment of a student's motivation to master tasks might be of far greater value to a teacher planning interventions than the IQ score and far cheaper and simpler to ascertain (Benner, 1992).

A system that deemphasizes labels need not abandon the important role that diagnosis and analysis of assessment findings can play in the process of identifying effective interventions. Unquestionably, sensory impairments must be specifically diagnosed, as must any other medical conditions that might trigger symptoms confused as behavioral problems, such as Tourette's Syndrome. Indeed, the system currently in place offers no guarantees that such errors are avoided. In some instances, rapid diagnosis and treatment are critical to the prevention of secondary disabilities, as evidenced in the screening procedures for PKU in newborn nurseries. A speech/language therapist may be the most appropriate professional to intervene when a child has a voice disorder, but she must defer to the surgeon when a physical condition is present that is causing the problem or to the mental health expert if it is psychological in nature. However, these important uses of diagnostic procedures and categorization need not be used to force our acceptance of a labeling system that is highly inaccurate, ineffective, and of little or no value to many children identified as having one of the high-incidence disability conditions.

Instructional Differentiation The only conclusion to be drawn from the research on trait by treatment interaction (Bender et al., 1993) is that noncategorical service-delivery models are more appropriate than those based on categorical distinctions. In fact, since the mid-1980s the available literature has overwhelmingly supported the notion of noncategorical delivery of services for students with mild educational problems (Morsink, Thomas, & Smith-Davis, 1987). The negative research findings continue while the federal system of classification remains virtually unchanged in the 1990s. The logic of the system is based on flawed concepts of homogeneity, placement, and instruction (Lovitt, 1993). The assumptions of the categorical system are that individuals can be accurately diagnosed as having any of the approved conditions through appropriate assessment processes and that they are then best served in programs especially designated for such types. By virtue of the disabling conditions, appropriate instructional programming can be defined and provided for the children with similar conditions. There is no other justification for the efforts put into differentiating between students with high-incidence conditions, and the instructional differentiation justification has proven untrue. Yet each period of reauthorization of IDEA triggers a group of hopeful advocates pushing for their favorite condition to achieve the status of being specified in the law. Publishing companies watch these movements astutely, ready to offer up the necessary tests, instructional tools, and teacher-training materials before the ink authorizing the latest approved condition and its need for unique services is dry. If the instruction is the same, certainly the bureaucracy surrounding placement in these specialized systems would be hard to justify. Allington and McGill-Franzen (1989) recommend the merger of all instructional efforts for low-achievement students and the elimination of all categorical programs and specialist teachers in order to reduce class size for everyone. Such seems worthy of experimentation.

Argument Summary The flaws in the categorical approach to special education eligibility are systemic, not minor incidentals that can be addressed through a series of refinements designed to keep a basically well-designed system functioning smoothly. Cosmetic adjustments that appear to constitute change, such as the use of developmental delay for young children, offer no significant improvement and may slow the process of creating real change by appearing to address the problems inherent in the system. The wasting of dollars for irrelevant diagnostic testing continues, as does the classification and reclassification of children. Disagreements about diagnosis breed disputes over professional responsibilities and designated interventions. Students cross state lines and are metamorphosized into new disability conditions. A system that dropped the emphasis on labeling and replaced it with an emphasis on the pursuit of effective intervention strategies could prove far more acceptable to parents, more understandable to teachers, and far friendlier to students needing special education services. Such radical change is likely to be resisted by all who have a stake in the existing categorical structure, whether that stake be professional status or commercial investment. The fact is that labels are not needed to offer an appropriate education for children. The existing system must not be allowed to restrict our vision of how services could become accessible to the intended group of students without the necessity of categorical boxes being placed around children.

ELIGIBILITY AND GAPS IN THE SYSTEM

Not only has the list of eligible classifications been expanding, but specific definitions and eligibility criteria have changed as well. In some instances, the changes have restricted or reduced the number of children eligible for services (e.g., mental retardation); in other cases, the changes have resulted in increases in the numbers of eligible students, such as learning disabilities (U.S. Department of Education, 1995). The high-incidence disabilities of mental retardation, learning disability, and seriously emotionally disturbed, and the popular medical diagnosis of ADHD have been targeted to further detail the issues linked to the classification system and the gaps that some argue are created by it. Although some of the concerns expressed here may have less application to low-incidence categories, such as hearing or visual impairment, they are intended to focus on the eligibility system as a whole as well as the specific categories discussed.

Changing Definitions

In 1973 a substantial change in the numbers of students eligible for the diagnostic label mental retardation and the meaning of that label occurred when the intellectual functioning criteria was altered. Concurrently, in the definition an increased emphasis was placed on adaptive behavior. This emphasis has continued to be highlighted in the current American Association of Mental Retardation (AAMR Ad Hoc Committee on Terminology and Classification, 1992) definition, which specifically lists adaptive skill areas in which limitations occur. Included as a part of this definition are four assumptions considered essential to its application. They address the importance of cultural and linguistic diversity, the context of community environments, and the need to consider all individuals as possessing strengths and personal abilities, capable of improving in performance, regardless of diagnosis and severity of problems. In addition, there is a radically altered subclassification system that abandons the four levels of mental retardation (mild, moderate, severe, profound), upon which many teacher-training programs and delivery-system models have been based. The new subclassification system is based on the intensity and pattern of support system the individual requires (intermittent, limited, extensive, and pervasive). Eligibility determination for this definition is intended to rely less on standardized intelligence testing and more on functional assessments linked to context and environment. However, these changes espoused by AAMR are slow in coming into the educational system. State disability definitions and certification criteria, teacher licensure standards, and teacher-training programs are each controlled by bureaucracies that must react over time to the changed definition and subclassification system. The interrelated nature of these systems necessitates that any changes in one be confirmed and supported by the others, further lengthening the time required for reform.

Learning disabilities is a far newer category than mental retardation but has probably seen as many definition changes and triggered more debates on who should be included or excluded. The evidence of brain damage, the absence of brain damage, hyperactivity, hypoactivity, the interplay of cultural and socioeconomic factors, and racial discrimination within the ranks of special education have all been controversial issues associated with defining the term. Typical eligibility criteria require that a child demonstrate a significant discrepancy between potential and achievement. However, variability as to what constitutes such a discrepancy and testing policies used in the process of identifying a discrepancy mean that some students are considered learning disabled in one state or district and not so in another (U.S. Department of Education, 1995). Ysseldyke (1987) noted that in 1984, thirteen states had chosen to use a modified version of the federal definition of learning disabilities, eleven developed their own definition, one was using a definition developed by the National Joint Committee on Learning Disabilities, two offered noncategorical services not requiring a specific definition for LD, and twenty-four had adopted the federal definition. The numbers of students served through this category have grown far more than any envisioned in 1975, when it was first established as a federal category of disability, moving from 23.8% of the population of students with disabilities in 1976 to 51.1% in 1992–1993 (U.S. Department of Education, 1995).

ADHD, a condition that is not included specifically in the list of categories covered by IDEA, is significantly influencing the field of special education as well. The 1995 edition of the *Diagnostic and Statistical Manual of Mental Disorders* (DSM-IV-R, American Psychiatric Association, 1995) offers more specificity than previous descriptions of the condition, yet it remains confusing for many. Reid, Maag, and Vasa (1994) offer a sharp criticism of current decision making regarding ADHD, citing the lack of research surrounding the disorder and the unchallenged assumptions inherent in the definition. They argue that ADHD "cannot be reliably differentiated from other disorders in terms of etiology, response to treatment, course, or relation to external referents other than symptoms by which it is purported to be defined" (p. 200). They also point out that ADHD is much more prevalent in the United States than in other countries. For example, children in the United States are fifty times more likely to be diagnosed with ADHD than children in either Britain and France. The diagnostic scales rely on the imprecision and subjectivity of terms such as "fidgets," "talks excessively," and other opinion-based and tolerance-related descriptors. Reid et al. (1994) also tackle the reasonableness of the conclusion that ADHD has a biological etiology based on the fact that children respond favorably to stimulants: "Yet this belief is as logically inchoate as the statement that behaviors indicative of juvenile delinquency (e.g., aggression, vandalism) are biologically based because 'afflicted' youngsters would respond 'favorably' to Thorazine" (p. 203). They further note the absurdity of the tautological relations of the biological etiology and the symptoms of ADHD: "Like its predecessor MBD [minimal brain dysfunction], you have ADHD because you exhibit the symptoms and you exhibit the symptoms because you have ADHD" (p. 203).

However, other researchers (e.g., Lerner, Lowenthal, & Lerner, 1995; Burcham, Carlson, & Milich, 1993; Fiore, Becker, & Nero, 1993; and Zentall, 1993) find the term and diagnostic criteria helpful for many children in our society today. The inclusion of the term in the *DSM* came only after much thought and research into the viability of the syndrome (McBurnett, Lahey, & Pfiffner, 1993). The diagnostic criteria might be deemed subjective, but the diagnosis is not intended to be derived from a single person's opinion but a pattern of behavior displayed throughout a child's life. When parents, coaches, scout leaders, teachers, and relatives all concur that a child "fidgets" abnormally, the consistency of the information gives it meaning. For such children and their parents, the diagnosis of ADHD and ensuing treatments can reverse a downward spiral of frustration and ever-increasing school failure. With the diagnosis comes a rational explanation of the child's patterns of behavior and possible treatments to diminish the effects of the condition.

The syndrome and its proposed inclusion in the list of disabilities in IDEA triggered a great deal of discussion, both in support of its viability as a distinct disability category and in opposition to it as a recognized condition requiring special education. The final decision for exclusion was based on the rationale that children so diagnosed who required special education would meet the established criteria for one of the already existing conditions, such as learning disabled, speech impaired, or seriously emotionally disturbed, or could be classified as other health impaired (Council for Exceptional Children, 1993). If adaptations short of formal special education services are needed, schools are required to make such accommodations in accordance with Section 504 of the Rehabilitation Act.

Another group whose status as "disabled" and, therefore, eligibility for the rights and privileges stipulated in IDEA has been hotly contested is students characterized as socially maladjusted or conduct disordered. In fact, this group is specifically excluded from services unless they qualify for the seriously emotionally disturbed classification or fall far enough behind in school to qualify as learning disabled. Nelson, Rutherford, Center, and Walker (1991) note the discrepancy between federal prevalence estimates for serious emotional disturbance, which range between 1.2% and 2% of the school population, and actual numbers of students receiving services through the serious emotional disturbance label, which is less than 1% of public school students. These figures might suggest that children projected to need services as a result of serious emotional disturbance are going unserved. They might also indicate that the label is unfavorable and avoided, but services are still provided by using other, more acceptable labels (Crowell, 1993). The debate remains on whether many children who desperately need special education are unfairly and arbitrarily excluded from this group or the category is in danger of becoming a safe haven for juvenile delinquents hoping to avoid punishment for their disruptive or aggressive behaviors in school.

Including and Excluding Groups from Special Education

Increases in the eligible population have significantly raised the costs of special education. A greater percentage of educational funding goes into special education than ever before; therefore, greater attention is being turned to eligibility policies as administrators seek ways to hold down costs. Between the late 1970s and late 1980s, the number of children served with the label specific learning disabilities nearly doubled—jumping from approximately 1.2 million to 2 million (Kirk, Gallagher, & Anastasiow, 1993). By 1992–1993, 2,366,494 children receiving special education were labeled with specific learning disabilities, and the figure rose an additional 3.3% in 1993–1994 to 2,444,020 (U.S. Department of Education, 1995). Similarly, in the period between the late 1970s and late 1980s, the category of serious emotional disturbance saw an increase—from 300,000 to 400,000 (Kirk et al., 1993). The figures for serious emotional disturbance have continued this pattern of increase, making a 3.1% jump between 1992–93 and 1993–94 (U.S. Department of Education, 1995). Current figures indicate slight increases for the speech/language impaired diagnosis, with a 1.1% rise in the population served between 1992–93 and 1993–94 (U.S. Department of Education, 1995). The category of mental retardation saw a reduction from 900,000 to 600,000 between the 1970s and 1980s (Kirk et al., 1993), but this dramatic reduction has leveled off, with 1993–1994 figures at 553,992, actually an increase of 4.1% over the previous year (U.S. Department of Education, 1995). As would be expected, substantial increases were seen in the newest categories of traumatic brain injury (33.7% increase) and autism (21.3%) between 1992–93 and 1993–94. The other health impaired category took a similar leap, with a 26.1% annual increase, attributed directly to the increased number of children diagnosed with ADHD (U.S. Department of Education, 1995). It is doubtful that these numbers reflect real changes in the functioning of students; they are, instead, indicative of adjustments in educators' definitions and eligibility criteria for each of the terms. Eligibility criteria control access to special education but cannot control the characteristics and behaviors present in the population.

The following scenario makes the point. A general classroom teacher struggles to teach a child whose tested IQ falls between 70 and 80. When she seeks help from special education, she is told that the child's IQ is too high for him to be considered mentally retarded but too low for him to qualify for services as learning disabled. Another child, the teacher has been told by the parents, has ADHD and is taking medication to increase his attention span and reduce his distractibility and impulsivity. The child is not a discipline problem but continues to struggle with his assignments. When the child is referred for a special education evaluation, he is diagnosed as other health impaired; and the teacher is given monthly consulting services from a special educator on techniques to use with him. Another child, who is constantly disruptive and bullying other children, is a constant challenge for the teacher. When the teacher seeks help from special educators for this child, the referral and evaluation may reveal little that she did not already know. A full report describing the child as having behavioral problems might be provided, but since no evidence of serious emotional disturbance was found, the child is deemed ineligible for services. Three other children in the class have been diagnosed as having specific learning disabilities and receive direct support services from a resource teacher five days a week. The teacher is grateful for the support for these three, but wonders why there is no better support for the others. Have the eligibility categories and criteria come to interfere with serving students with special needs, or has the provision of special education for some led classroom teachers to expect help with every single challenging child with whom they come in contact? Do we need to tighten the eligibility criteria and keep the percentage of students served through special education under control, or do we need to loosen or even drop the criteria altogether to provide services for all who need help?

Decision Point 1.2:
Retention or Elimination of Eligibility Standards

Arguments for Proposition One Special education is subject to much criticism today, from friends and supporters as well as those who would be considered less sympathetic to the cause of educating students with disabilities. The magnitude of its growth has far exceeded anything anticipated in 1975, when IDEA was first enacted. Although the elimination of waiting lists, the children rejected from our schools as unworthy of an education, the neglect and misunderstanding of pupils with psychological processing disorders, and the ridicule of children with speech impairments or emotional problems are not the pervasive realities they were as recently as the early 1970s, we have new problems. For every school-related difficulty that a child experiences, someone is quick to suggest that a child-based factor, such as a learning disability, must be the root cause. Emotional disturbance is viewed by some as a means by which disruptive students can avoid accountability, and special education is little more than a loss of standards. Drugs become the intervention of choice when a child is more active or impulsive than the adults around the child think she ought to be. The criticisms directed toward special education must be considered with great care by those in the field who wish to preserve its intended purposes and avoid its destruction rather than be dismissed as antiquated voices from the past or radical conservatives of the present, unworthy of serious consideration and debate.

The first step in this process of self-reflection should be the thorough review of eligibility criteria with an eye toward reducing the number of students receiving special education to capture only those who have a disability, not simply all who are experiencing difficulty in school. Allowing the numbers of students served to mushroom has resulted in fewer services for those children who have legitimate disabilities, fueling the arguments of critics that it wastes resources, lowers standards, and reduces educational opportunities for the more capable (Merrow, 1996). Definitions of disabilities and eligibility criteria must be designed to restrict the numbers of students who qualify for services, not open the doors to every child. This distinction needs to occur not for cost-containment purposes, but to maintain the integrity and intended purpose of special education.

Proposition One

Special education is not a system intended to address all the problems of all the children in America's schools today. It has a specific mission to address the needs of students *with disabilities* and must retain that focus. Eligibility standards must remain and services must be restricted to only those children who have a disability. Without retention of its intended focus, special education will become merely one more in the myriad of educational offerings that have no distinct purpose or value.

Changing Definitions The changes in definitions associated with the high-incidence conditions of mental retardation, learning disabilities, and serious emotional disturbance have created a variety of problems for the field. In the case of mental retardation and serious emotional disturbance, the definition adjustments served to make the categories more restrictive. These restrictions have left some children who previously would have qualified for services ineligible. Indeed, these restrictions are based on the fact that the children so labeled should include only those who have a disability, not just school adjustment problems or a rate of learning a bit slower than average. On the other hand, the vagueness associated with definitions of learning disabilities, combined with the concurrent restrictions on mental retardation and serious emotional disturbance, has resulted in dramatic increases in the numbers of children so identified. Although mental retardation and serious emotional disturbance have been narrowed to prevent overuse of these labels, specific learning disabilities has become the catch-all category with fewer and fewer restrictions. To add even more to the overall numbers, children identified as ADHD are now expanding the rolls of special education and are classified as other health impaired or as one of the high-incidence disability categories (Reid et al., 1994).

Social and political pressures have twisted the broad category of learning disabilities into an all-encompassing umbrella term from which it is harder to exclude children than it is to include them. Obviously, students who are achieving at a rate two or more years behind their apparent ability levels are facing problems in school. The extent to which those problems can be specifically attributed to a child-based psychological processing disorder is another matter. With no real measures to determine the presence or absence of such disorders, substantial debate on what constitutes evidence of them, and educational interventions that rely primarily on coping with rather than curing them, educational diagnosticians have come to use the discrepancy formula as the basis for diagnosis. With a sufficient discrepancy between potential and achievement, virtually any child can technically qualify. This situation has resulted from our inability to set limits on who should be included in this catch-all condition. A child may even be labeled learning disabled to avoid unpleasant confrontations with parents who insist on the diagnosis. In addition, it may be used in preference to less socially accepted labels because there is a teacher with suitable credentials and services are available, or for many other compromising reasons. The field has jeopardized the meaning of this label by permitting its inclusiveness. Not every child who is behind in school should be considered learning disabled. Those who have the most to lose from the misuses of this label are the small percentage of the population for whom the label was intended. The restrictions set in place for mental retardation and emotional disturbance must likewise be used to close the door into special education via a learning disability diagnosis for children who do not have a real disability. Currently, to gain entry into the system, it is serving as a loophole to enable the students excluded from the other categories. The restrictions on the other categories are circumvented through the openness of the learning disability category, thus preventing general educators from assuming a sense of responsibility for and obligation to children who have mild learning or adjustment problems.

Including and Excluding Groups from Special Education Arguments abound regarding the numbers of children who appear to be unfairly excluded from special education. In particular, children diagnosed as ADHD, those who have behavior problems or display social maladjustments, and others with IQ scores too high for the diagnosis of mental retardation and generally too low to demonstrate a sufficient discrepancy between potential and performance to qualify as learning disabled have advocates who argue for their need for special education. The debate must not be whether the educational needs of all children should be met. Obviously, they should be. However, the question remains as to whether special education is the right vehicle to meet those needs.

Some contend that special education services could be used more for prevention of serious emotional disturbances if restrictions on children served were loosened. The fact is that special education is intended to serve students with disabilities, not prevent them from occurring. If the field engaged in prevention programs for all disabilities, the nature and extent of services would be far different from the educational services in place today. Prevention programs for child abuse, alcoholism, middle ear infections, and bike and auto accidents are just a sample of the types of programs that would need to be provided. All such programs are worthy but are not within the realm of special education. The social supports and behavioral standards used in general education must address the needs of more than just the model child, compliant and eager to learn; however, the temptation to accept responsibility for all children who display behavioral problems and bring them into the special education fold only weakens our ability to provide the intensity and quality of programs needed for students with real disabilities. Children considered socially maladjusted may be socialized into what is considered a deviant cultural group, with behaviors and attitudes contrary to those accepted by the mainstream (Nelson et al., 1991). There is no reason to believe that such individuals are emotionally disturbed, because they do conform their behavior to their own reference group. However, "the behavior patterns considered 'normative' of this deviant culture have been termed 'delinquent' or 'antisocial' by educators, sociologists, psychologists, and criminologists" (Nelson et al., 1991, p. 408). It could be argued that even when a student has behaviors consistent with a peer group, if the entire peer group's standards are not normal or accepted by the mainstream culture, each of the members of that peer group stands outside the norms and expectations of society. Their chosen lifestyles will put them at high risk to engage in criminal activity, be rejected by the legitimate side of society, and close off their options to become normal, contributing members of the mainstream society. Although these students should be identified and served through a prevention model of education rather than be processed through the judicial system down the road, *they are not disabled.* Since they are not disabled, they should not receive special education services. Affording all the members of gangs protection from punishment because they are socially maladjusted is not equivalent to holding a child with schizophrenia guiltless for sudden outbursts that might include physical harm to others.

There are students who do not meet the criteria for the serious emotional disturbance diagnosis, who may not affiliate with a deviant peer group, but who may exhibit antisocial or delinquent behaviors. These behaviors may result from very specific environmental and social factors, such as chaotic conditions in the home, parental substance abuse, difficulties with school work, problems associated with social relationships, or family poverty and dependence on welfare (Kauffman, 1989). Students struggling to cope with such conditions may gravitate toward socially deviant groups, experience downward cycles of poor school performance, and choose to become school dropouts. Is it reasonable to take a child who may have begun his life without love and affection, security and nurturance, structure and discipline and label him as emotionally disturbed when he acts out? Could *educational* interventions have prevented his troubles had they been available to him? The intertwining of social conditions, political perspectives, racial and ethnic concerns, and the quality of available educational programs is real.

Argument Summary Special education as a field is not intended to address every problem posed by our society as children progress through the educational system. Some children will come to school hungry or poorly clothed. Some will lack the self-confidence to tackle unfamiliar tasks with eagerness and enthusiasm. Personalities and temperaments of children trigger both positive and negative reactions from their teachers. Parental support and values toward education are not the same in every home. Many immigrant children, unfamiliar with the English language, are in American schools today. Many children, feeling emotional pain as their parents divorce, will need an outlet for their confusion and hurt. Indeed, every child is a unique person with individual needs and abilities. Every child deserves to have parents and teachers who will support and assist her in developing educational goals and plans to achieve those goals. However, not every child will have such support. This fact of life leads some to the conclusion that special education should take everyone in who needs help, regardless of the source of the problem. Certainly our educational system must have in place the means of addressing a wide array of problems and issues confronting children today, but special education must not attempt to assume this comprehensive role. The purpose of special education is to provide an appropriate educational support system specifically for children with disabilities. We must retain that focus by clearly restricting the population we serve, serving it well, and avoiding the temptation to tackle every other social or personal problem challenging American schools today. Rather, we must work collaboratively with compensatory program personnel, educational guidance counselors, bilingual educators, general education teachers and administrators, social workers, and parents to offer as cohesive a program as possible. Special education is one piece of the puzzle and should not attempt to become the entire puzzle.

Arguments for Proposition Two What does it mean to get a child into the special education system? It can mean that a child must demonstrate failure, not just the danger signs, before access is allowed. It can mean that administrators bend the rules to get a child certified just for the sake of getting some services, not because the disability is an accurate, meaningful diagnosis. It always means that child must assume a label and all the ramifications of such labeling. After the label is placed on the child, she has a right to a free appropriate public education. Surely that right existed without the necessity of a label being placed on the child. The concept of identifying supports and helping students who are experiencing educational difficulties without the complications of assessment, diagnosis, certification of an educational disability, and assignment of a label is inherent in the support team process stipulated in IDEA. The introduction of the support team process into the practice has not really opened the doors of special education services to needy students and anxious teachers, but it does offer the potential for a new conception of services and eligibility. If it became more than just another step in the referral process, the entire system could be converted to a model of support teaming for students with educational problems rather than one controlled by the eligibility gatekeepers.

Administrators and diagnosticians alike seem to be at a loss on how to contain special education growth while maintaining an acceptable level of services using the current categorical system of eligibility. Lawsuits are threatened when children are deemed ineligible. School administrators are accused of intentionally restricting eligibility criteria to save on costs, instead of being viewed as advocates for the best educational opportunities for all. Adversarial relationships between the administrators and parents and teachers naturally follow. Teachers are frustrated when children for whom they seek help do not qualify for services, yet others in their classes might have IEPs requiring more instructional or testing modifications than they consider ethical or appropriate. The tangled confusion surrounding eligibility can set a negative tone before special educators have even begun their work with a family.

The requirements of the system become the argument for the retention of the system—a seriously flawed line of reasoning. It is argued that children must be labeled in order to qualify for services as well as for school systems to receive the cost benefits associated with serving students with disabilities. Algozzine (1991) wonders about the relationship between funding and numbers served. He goes on to challenge the logic that labeling is a necessary element of our funding system when evidence fails to support it as an effective practice. Under the categorical system, when a child is struggling in school and a special education referral is made, the most important issue becomes eligibility, not educational needs.

> **Proposition Two**
> If special educators were free to provide assistance for those who need it, rather than for those who are eligible for it, all would benefit. The model of services could shift from one of diagnosis and treatment to a far greater emphasis on prevention and intervention. Special educators must not abandon their responsibility for children who are now caught in the eligibility cracks but who desperately need supports to remain in school and complete an educational course of study.

Were a support system to become easier to move in and out of, with less mystery shrouding the eligibility process, we might see less stigmatization associated with the delivery of special education and better instructional services.

The United States already sits near the top in comparisons with other countries in percentages of total populations between ages six and seventeen registered as having special needs (Pijl & Meijer, 1994). The U.S. percentage is 9%, only lower than Denmark (13%), in a comparison study involving six countries. Italy, England and Wales, and Sweden all had lower than 3% referred, with the Netherlands falling between 4 and 7 percent. But the numbers cannot be isolated from other aspects of the approach to special education. Although Denmark has a higher percentage of students receiving special education services, the situation is not equivalent to that in the United States. Labels and special education do not carry the same meaning and impact in Denmark. Pijl and Meijer (1994) note that "In Denmark special services are provided—and—discontinued—relatively easily, and so many students receive these services for short periods that the label is of less significance there" (p. 122). The support team concept could provide the avenue for such a transformation of special education within the United States. The numbers of children actually needing to be diagnosed with a particular disability could then be just those with conditions for which the diagnosis would hold direct benefit to the child and family or teaching staff, such as hearing loss, neurological impairments, psychotic conditions, and so forth. Mild school-related problems, social adjustment difficulties, and similar fluctuating conditions warranting timely interventions to prevent secondary disabilities or failure in school could all be considered worthy of attention and effort by support teams without the lengthy eligibility trail. Categorical conditions and definitions could take a background role in the overall delivery system rather than one of prominence and control.

Changing Definitions The single major disability category showing the greatest decline over the past two decades has been mental retardation. The changes in the definition of mental retardation have produced this substantial drop, not any change in child behaviors or functioning. The dramatic drop is evidence of the power of the definition change. It was intentionally altered to exclude many children who seemed to have been unfairly labeled and restricted in their educational and employment opportunities. In particular, the change has reduced the racial bias of the label associated with the use of standard IQ tests in the diagnostic process (Jones, 1983). Children are no longer given the lifelong stigma of the

mental retardation label when their score on an intelligence test is lower than average but more attributable to differences in life experiences than to intellectual
potential. The fact remains that not all humans have the same intellectual capacities, but the practice of designating large numbers of students as retarded merely
because they performed poorly on a particular IQ test has been reduced, if not
eliminated. The label, for many children considered mildly retarded, had come
to be symbolic of racial prejudice and injustice, not educational benefit and opportunity. However, with the loss of the label came the loss of services. It was appropriate to drop the label for these children, but their need for educational
supports did not disappear as dramatically as did their disability. Without the
label, the children are the same, struggling academically just as they did when
they wore the labels. These children would be best served by having a support
system in place that did not necessitate the identification of any child-based deficit
for eligibility. The practices of either abandonment or relabeling with inappropriate diagnoses could end.

　　While the mental retardation category has been dropping, the categories of
specific learning disabilities, emotional disturbance, and other health impairments have been on the rise. The debates over the definition of learning disabilities and the need for special education for students with ADHD, which have
occurred in a period characterized by a highly litigious society, seem to have
opened the eligibility standards up far broader than originally anticipated. It is
time to stop the squabble over precisely which children display the characteristics
worthy of these labels and which ones have some of the traits, but are not deemed
sufficiently impaired to receive a ticket into special education. The labels have
been so overused as to have lost any real meaning. One of the newest federal categories used in special education is that of traumatic brain injury. Does the establishment of such a category necessarily lead to the notion that these children can
now be better served because there is a label unique to their condition? Will they
be clustered together in classes, or will their "unique" educational needs be met
through a variety of settings? Can we continue establishing new categories as dissatisfaction grows with the existing categories?

Including and Excluding Groups from Special Education The use of the categorical
approach to special education can be blamed for children being diagnosed as having conditions that they do not and never have had. A child displaying serious
difficulties in the classroom must receive one of the approved diagnoses in order
to receive special education services. Diagnosticians then operate from a closed
field, limiting their considerations about the child to "the list." Sabatino and
Vance (1993) report of a case in which a child received innumerable diagnoses
and ineffective treatments prior to finally being identified as having a postneuro-
logical impairment. The case involved a seven-year-old boy who, in spite of an
IQ over 120 and academic achievement at a third-grade level, was repeating first
grade for the second time. He appeared to prefer working and playing in isolation, and his teacher found him to be highly inconsistent in his ability to learn.
He would have extended periods in which no problems were displayed, adjusting
well to peers, school assignments, and the classroom environment, only to ex-

plode into an emotional storm for no apparent reason. After approximately ten to fifteen minutes of such behavior, he would appear apathetic and nonresponsive for another fifteen to thirty minutes. His diagnoses and treatments that offered no benefit included ADHD, treated with Ritalin at maximum dosages; unconscious anger and associated poor ego strength and lack of personal integrity necessary for self-control, treated with a year of play therapy; and serious emotional disturbance, treated by placement in a self-contained classroom for disruptive children with a rigorous classroom engineering system. The fact that the child had had spinal meningitis accompanied by a high fever that lasted several days when he was four was consistently overlooked. An appropriate treatment plan and educational system were finally developed that allowed the boy to fit in well in a general class and achieve high marks. The case might be argued as documenting the need for the traumatic brain injury category. Better it should be given a broader application and used to argue against the categorical approach that limited the child's range of diagnoses and treatments in the first place.

With the changes in definitions and eligibility for special education have come new responsibilities for general education teachers. Classroom teachers are now expected to accommodate their instructional programs for children with IQs down to 70 without the assistance of special education. Whereas the children with IQs between 70 and 85 who were once labeled mentally retarded were not well served by the label (Jones, 1983), they are even less well served by their current status—ineligible for any special education. The loss of eligibility has taken away their right to IEPs and the educational adjustments available planned out through the IEP process. In some cases, teachers have been persistent enough and educational diagnosticians clever enough to find alternate disability categories through which the child could be made eligible for services (e.g., language impaired). These children do not need a new label. They simply need to have their educational needs met.

The exclusion of students considered socially maladjusted from the benefits and services associated with IDEA reflects the irrational logic upon which the categorical system of eligibility is based. Mild problems must become severe before treatments can begin. Social maladjustment has been described as a profoundly limiting social disability, requiring a long-term supportive environment in the treatment process (Kauffman, 1989). The full implications of the establishment of such an eligibility category for social maladjustment and conduct disorders under our present system are unknown, but it could be anticipated that addition of the category would substantially increase the number of eligible students. The debates associated with disciplinary restrictions for students with disabilities would greatly increase, as suggested by Neel and Rutherford (1981) over a decade ago. Today the issue of disciplinary restrictions looms larger than ever before.

Nelson et al. (1991) dispute our ability to differentiate between seriously emotionally disturbed and socially maladjusted students in a reliable, meaningful way. Although acknowledging "that not all students should qualify for services that are expensive and in short supply" (p. 411), they argue that the needs of these students must be recognized. Their academic deficits, lack of interest in their own academic performance, poor peer relationships, and lack of social competence all contribute to place the students at high risk for educational failure or eventual placement in special education as seriously emotionally disturbed. Nelson et al. argue that the needs of these students should be addressed through prereferral interventions before eligibility for special education programs is considered. However, if such interventions prove insufficient, they assert that there must be more options to serve such children.

Argument Summary Tightening the restrictions on eligibility would only trigger more lawsuits and frustrated teachers, but broadening the eligibility criteria under the current system would only exacerbate an already problematic situation. Definitions have changed, and eligibility criteria have changed, but the only real change has been in which label has been attached to a child and increased confusion over eligibility issues. Having force-fit children into the existing categories over the years, we can now recognize the flaws in the system and begin learning how to make the system work for us through a support team concept. The notion of prereferral interventions through support teams can offer the beginnings of a whole new approach to the provision of special education services. The notion that such services must be restricted to a distinct group of students who are disabled denies the realities of human functioning. Although some conditions are clearly present or absent (e.g., genetic disorders, loss of hearing), many others occur on a continuum (e.g., mental retardation, emotional disturbance, learning disabilities). Rather than continuing to struggle over how far up or down the continuum an individual must be to have access to special education, we should devise a comprehensive system of services that allows all to benefit without the burden of labels. Educational programs with distinct missions, such as service to students with disabilities, should be designed as fully integrated components of the education enterprise, not segregated appendages in competition for dollars with the very programs for which they are intended to offer support services.

CLOSING THOUGHTS

Since the extent to which specialized instruction has, in fact, been in use in special education settings is subject to question, the lack of clear documentation regarding the efficacy of special education programs neither confirms nor refutes the benefits of specialized instruction. The merits of the cases for and against specialized instruction are limited by the quality of current and past practices in special education.

We have placed substantial emphasis on the categorical eligibility of students in special education and attempted to match them to instructional approaches by disability. It has been difficult to defend the continuation of these categorical distinctions for instruction, with the exception of those students with sensory impairments who might have a specific need for alternative forms of written or oral communication. Yet the task of attempting the individualization of literally all instruction, with no advance organizers or clustering of students according to their needs, would probably require an individual tutor focused on each individual student over the course of the day. Learner characteristics that have been reported as correlates to learning include task involvement, energy deployment, autonomy, time on task, and resource use and decision making (Wang & Lindvall, 1984). Yet our classification systems and instructional models do not address such variables. Perhaps we are matching instruction on the wrong characteristics—diagnostic labels based on standardized test performance rather than functioning within classroom settings. Variables that have been proposed that might be of more relevance to instructional planning than diagnostic information include positive, nondisruptive behavior; appropriate activity level; attitudes toward school and teachers; motivation for continual learning; attributions for success and failure; levels of general academic knowledge and knowledge in specific subject matter areas; self-regulatory and self-control strategies; comprehension monitoring; positive strategies for coping with failure; and positive strategies to aid the generalization of concepts (Wang, 1989). The list reads like a guide to critical variables for success in the general classroom. Students who are successful in general education would not require specialized instruction directed at these concerns, whereas students with disabilities would need such focused instruction.

REFERENCES

AAMR Ad Hoc Committee on Terminology and Classification. (1992). *Mental retardation: Definition, classification, and systems of support*. Washington, DC: American Association on Mental Retardation.

Algozzine, B. (1991). Observations to accompany analyses of the *Tenth Annual Report to Congress. Exceptional Children, 57*, 271–275.

Allington, R., & McGill-Franzen, A. (1989). Different programs, indifferent instruction. In D. K. Lipsky & A. Gartner (Eds.), *Beyond separate education: Quality education for all* (pp. 75–98). Baltimore: Paul H. Brookes.

American Psychiatric Association. (1995). *Diagnostic and statistical manual of mental disorders* (4th ed., rev.). Washington, DC: Author.

Bender, W. N., Scott, K., & McLaughlin, P. J. (1993). A model for noncategorical service delivery for students with mild disabilities. In R. C. Eaves & P. J.

McLaughlin (Eds.), *Recent advances in special education and rehabilitation* (pp. 127–145). Boston: Andover Medical Publishers.

Benner, S. M. (1992). *Assessing young children with special needs: An ecological perspective*. New York: Longman.

Budoff, M., & Siperstein, G. N. (1982). Judgments of EMR students toward their peers: Effects of label and academic competence. *American Journal of Mental Deficiency, 86*, 367–371.

Burcham, B., Carlson, L., & Milich, R. (1993). Promising school-based practices for students with attention deficit disorder. *Exceptional Children, 60*, 174–180.

Coleman, J. M. (1983). Handicapped labels and instructional segregation: Influences on children's self-concepts versus the perceptions of others. *Learning Disability Quarterly, 6*, 3–11.

Council for Exceptional Children. (1993). The ADD controversy—What did CEC say? *Exceptional Children, 60,* 181–182.

Crowell, A. R. (1993). Contrasting perspectives on programming for students with emotional disturbance and behavioral disorders in Mississippi. *Behavioral Disorders, 18,* 228–230.

Dickie, R. F. (1982). Still crazy after all these years: Another look at the question of labeling and noncategorical conceptions of exceptional children. *Education and Treatment of Children, 5,* 355–363.

Education for All Handicapped Children Act (EHA), 20, U.S.C., sections 1400 et seq. and amendments.

Feiler, A., & Thomas, G. (1988). Special needs: Past, present and future. In G. Thomas & A. Feiler (Eds.), *Planning for special needs: A whole school approach* (pp. 5–31). Oxford, UK: Basil Blackwell.

Feldman, D., Kinnison, L., Jay, R., & Harth, R. (1983). The effects of differential labeling on professional concepts and attitudes toward the emotionally disturbed/behaviorally disordered. *Behavioral Disorders, 8,* 191–198.

Fiore, T. A., Becker, E. A., Nero, R. C. (1993). Educational interventions for students with attention deficit disorder. *Exceptional Children, 60,* 163–173.

Fister, S., & Kemp, K. (1993). Translating research: Classroom application of validated instructional strategies. In R. C. Eaves & P. J. McLaughlin (Eds.), *Recent advances in special education and rehabilitation* (pp. 107–126). Boston, MA: Andover Medical Publishers.

Fogel, L. S., & Nelson, R. O. (1983). The effects of special education labels on teachers' behavioral observations, checklist scores, and grading of academic work. *Journal of School Psychology, 21,* 241–251.

Fuchs, D., Fuchs, L. S., Benowitz, S., & Barringer, K. (1987). Norm-referenced tests: Are they valid for use with handicapped students? *Exceptional Children, 54,* 263–271.

Halgren, D. W., & Clarizio, H. F. (1993). Categorical and programming changes in special education services. *Exceptional Children, 59,* 547–555.

Hobbs, N. J. (1975). *The futures of children.* San Francisco: Jossey-Bass.

Individuals with Disabilities Education Act of 1990, 20, U.S.C., Chap. 3 (1990).

Jenkins, J. R., Jewell, M., Leicester, N., O'Connor, R. E., Jenkins, L. M., & Troutner, N. M. (1994). Accommodations for individual differences without classroom ability groups: An experiment in school restructuring. (1994) *Exceptional Children, 60,* 344–358.

Jones, P. E. (1983). Special education and socioeconomic retardation. *Journal for Special Educators, 19,* v–ix.

Kauffman, J. M. (1989). *Characteristics of behavior disorders of children and youth* (4th edition). Columbus, OH: Merrill.

Kirk, S. A., Gallagher, J. J., & Anastasiow, N. J. (1993). *Educating exceptional children.* Boston: Houghton Mifflin.

Lerner, J. W., Lowenthal, B., & Lerner, S. R. (1995). *Attention deficit disorders: Assessment and teaching.* Pacific Grove, CA: Brooks/Cole.

Lovitt, T. C. (1993). Recurring issues in special and general education. In J. I. Goodlad & T. C. Lovitt (Eds.), *Integrating general and special education* (pp. 49–71). New York: Macmillan.

McBurnett, K., Lahey, B. B., & Pfiffner, L. (1993). Diagnosis of attention deficit disorders in DSM-IV: Scientific basis and implications for education. *Exceptional Children, 60,* 108–117.

Merrow, J. (1996). What's so special about special education? *Education Week, 48,* 38. (May 8, 1996)

Morsink, C. V., Thomas, C. C., & Smith-Davis, J. (1987). Noncategorical special education programs: Process and outcomes. In M. C. Wang, M. C. Reynolds, & H. J. Walberg (Eds.), *Handbook of special education: Research and practice: Learner characteristics and adaptive education* (Vol. 1, pp. 287–309). New York: Pergamon.

Neel, R. S., & Rutherford, R. B. (1981). Exclusion of the socially maladjusted from services under PL94-142. In F. H.

Wood (Ed.), *Perspectives for a new decade: Education's responsibility for seriously emotionally disturbed and behaviorally disordered youth* (pp. 79–84). Reston, VA: Council for Exceptional Children.

Nelson, C. M., Rutherford, R. B., Center, D. B., & Walker, H. (1991). Do public schools have an obligation to serve troubled children and youth? *Exceptional Children, 57,* 406–415.

Pijl, S. J., & Meijer, C. J. W. (Eds.). (1994). Analysis of findings. In C. J. W. Meijer, S. J. Pijl, & S. Hegarty (Eds.), *New perspectives in special education* (pp. 113–124). New York: Routledge.

Pinnell, G. S. (1989). Reading recovery: Helping at-risk children learn to read. *Elementary School Journal, 90,* 161–183.

Pollak, J. M. (1985). Pitfalls in the psychoeducational assessment of adolescents with learning and school adjustment problems. *Adolescence, 20,* 479–493.

Reid, R., Maag, J. W., & Vasa, S. F. (1994). Attention deficit hyperactivity disorder as a disability category: A critique. *Exceptional Children, 60,* 198–214.

Reid, R., Maag, J. W., Vasa, S. F., & Wright, G. (1994). Who are the children with attention deficit-hyperactivity disorder? A school-based survey. *Journal of Special Education, 28,* 117–137.

Rolison, M. A., & Medway, F. J. (1985). Teachers' expectations and attributions for student achievement: Effects of label performance pattern, and special education intervention. *American Educational Research Journal, 22,* 561–573.

Rueda, R. (1989). Defining mild disabilities with language-minority students, *Exceptional Children, 56,* 121–128.

Sabatino, D. A., & Vance, H. B. (1993). Describing the cognitive aspects of intelligence. In R. C. Eaves & P. J. McLaughlin (Eds.), *Recent advances in special education and rehabilitation* (pp. 30–48). Boston: Andover Medical Publishers.

Singer, J. D., Palfrey, J. S., Butler, J. A., & Walker, D. K. (1989). Variation in special education classification across school districts: How does where you live affect what you are labeled? *American Educational Research Journal, 26,* 261–281.

Slavin, R. E., Madden, N. A., Karweit, N. L., Livermon, B. J., & Dolan, L. (1990). Success for all: First-year outcomes of a comprehensive plan for reforming urban education. *American Educational Research Journal, 27,* 255–278.

Smith, R. W., Osborne, L. T., Crim, D., & Rhu, A. H. (1986). Labeling theory as applied to learning disabilities: Survey findings and policy suggestion. *Journal of Learning Disabilities, 19,* 195–202.

Smith, S. (1990). Individualized education programs in special education: From intent to acquiescence. *Exceptional Children, 57,* 6–14.

Sutherland, J. H., Algozine, B., Ysseldyke, J. E., & Freeman, S. (1983). Changing peer perceptions: Effects of labels and assigned attributes. *Journal of Learning Disabilities, 16,* 217–220.

Taylor, R. L., Smiley, L. R., & Ziegler, E. W. (1983). The effects of labels and assigned attributes on teacher perceptions of academic and social behavior. *Education and Training of the Mentally Retarded, 18,* 45–51.

U.S. Department of Education. (1991). *Thirteenth Annual Report to Congress on the Implementation of the Individuals with Disabilities Education Act.* Washington, DC: Office of Special Education Programs.

U.S. Department of Education. (1995). *Seventeenth Annual Report to Congress on the Implementation of the Individuals with Disabilities Education Act.* Washington, DC: Office of Special Education Programs.

Wang, M. C. (1989). Adaptive instruction: An alternative for accommodating student diversity through the curriculum. In D. K. Lipsky & A. Gartner (1989) (Eds.), *Beyond separate education: Quality education for all* (pp. 99–120). Baltimore: Paul H. Brookes.

Wang, M. C., & Lindvall, C. M. (1984). Individual differences and school learning environments. In E. W. Gordon (Ed.), *Review of research in education*

(Vol. 11, pp. 161–226). Washington, DC: American Educational Research Association.

Wang, M. C., & Reynolds, M. C. (1985). Avoiding the "Catch 22" in special education reform. *Exceptional Children, 51,* 497–502.

Wesson, C. L., & Deno, S. L. (1989). An analysis of long term instructional plans in reading for elementary resource room students. *Remedial and Special Education, 10,* 21–28.

Wolman, C., Thurlow, M. L., & Bruininks, R. H. (1989). Stability of categorical designations for special education students: A longitudinal study. *Journal of Special Education, 23,* 213–222.

Ysseldyke, J. E. (1987). Classification of handicapped students. In M. C. Wang, M. C. Reynolds, & H. J. Walberg (Eds.), *Handbook of special education: Research and practice: Learner characteristics and adaptive education* (Vol. 1, pp. 253–271). New York: Pergamon.

Ysseldyke, J. F., O'Sullivan, P. J., Thurlow, M. L., & Christenson, S. L. (1989). Qualitative differences in reading and math instruction received by handicapped students. *Remedial and Special Education, 10,* 14–20.

Zentall, S. S. (1993). Research on the educational implications of attention deficit hyperactivity disorder. *Exceptional Children, 60,* 143–153.

2

Special Education
and Cultural Diversity
in America

INTRODUCTION

Children with disabilities come from all types of families, regardless of socioeconomic status, cultural heritage, language spoken in the home, or racial composition. However, certain factors undeniably put a child at higher risk to have a disability. In some instances, such as is the case with genetic disorders, the statistical probability of a child having a specific disorder can be calculated based on family history, genetic testing, environmental factors, and other pertinent variables. Once born, a child faces many additional risks. Such risks include trauma resulting from automobile, boat, roller blade, or bicycle-related accidents; injury resulting from violent crime; injury from swimming and diving accidents; secondary complications of childhood illnesses; as well as the chronic problems of malnutrition, abuse, neglect, and poverty. For children living in middle-class suburbs, the risk of disability due to violence is far lower than is such risk for the child living in an inner-city area known for drugs and gangs. The extent to which these differences in risk factors are associated with the equitable provision of services to students with disabilities or the abuse of special education as a means of segregating the "undesirables" is at issue.

Some risks to children can be lowered. Children who are placed in child-restraint devices in automobiles or wear helmets while biking or roller blading stand far less risk of permanent neurological injury than those who do not use such equipment. The adherence to recommended vaccination schedules for young children lowers their risk of serious illnesses that might result in permanent disabilities. These protections require knowledge and understanding of their importance, access to needed resources, as well as initiative and follow-through on the part of parents. Parents new to the United States, those who have limited proficiency in English, and ones with limited access to medical resources may fail to provide their children such protections. Further, other risk factors directly linked to poor performance in school are not so easily remedied. Students who face racial prejudice in their schools may find themselves at high risk of being considered less capable than those who are preferred by school personnel. For those who speak a language other than English, their poor communication skills might be erroneously treated as evidence of limited cognitive ability. Homeless or migrant children may never even receive any education, much less education that is free from biased peers and teachers.

The risk factors influencing students' ability to be successful in education today weave in and out of their personal lives. The five key indicators linked to children and youth who are considered to be educationally disadvantaged are (a) living in a poverty household, (b) minority/racial group identity, (c) living in a single-parent family, (d) having a poorly educated mother, and (e) having a non-English language background (Natriello, McDill, & Pallas, 1990). Not all children falling into any one or more of these categories are doomed to educational failure, but of the children who do poorly in schools, these factors are most frequently prevalent. The problem becomes confounded when the interactive nature of the indicators is considered.

The traditional role of the educational system does not include the capacity to alter these variables or their psychological and developmental implications. For example, although schools might offer support groups for children who come from single-parent families, provide programs targeted toward the reduction of teen pregnancy, or furnish reduced-price or free meals to children living in poverty, the system itself does not have the direct mission of reducing the number of children coming from single-parent families, addressing the sexual habits of teens, or eliminating poverty in our society. For students from poverty backgrounds, compensatory programs are available that are intended to help reduce the impact of poverty on educational progress, not directly reduce poverty. Furthermore, for a child who has entered the United States speaking another language, the educational choices available have been closely tied to fluctuating political attitudes toward the use of non-English instruction of children in American schools. The issues encompass such broad concerns as cultural identity, religious and sexual mores, rates of immigration and political responses to refugees fleeing to the United States, availability of employment for both Americans and immigrants, and biological heritage.

Changing Demographic Patterns

Shifting patterns of population growth are apparent throughout the country today. Continued immigration and variable birth rates are changing the racial and cultural ratios in the public schools. The increasing ethnic and racial diversity is evident in the 1990 census and other data sources (Williams, 1992). One

These young children hope to find an education to match their parents' dreams.

fifth of our population growth of the 1980s has been attributed to legal immigrants, who numbered 500,000 per year. However, an estimated additional 200,000 illegal immigrants per year also enter the country. The Hispanic population had reached 21 million at the 1990 census, a 44% increase since 1980. Whereas these figures indicate that Hispanics are the fastest growing single group, the category of "other" races (mostly Asians) increased more, with a growth rate of 65% during the 1980s. African Americans still remain approximately 12% of the total population, but Caucasians have dropped from 86% of the population to 84%.

Williams further notes that African Americans, Hispanics, and Asians are projected to make up one fourth to one third of the total U.S. population by the year 2000. These projections are based on current rates of population increase, which for the Caucasian population is 14% while African Americans are increasing at a rate of 39% and other minorities at 56%. The current patterns can be projected into the future by consideration of average age, with Caucasians having an average age of thirty-one years, African Americans having an average of twenty-five, and Hispanics having an average of only twenty-two. The implications for future childbearing are apparent. This national shift is foreshadowed in our largest urban counties and some nonmetropolitan counties where the shift has already taken place, and no single ethnic or racial group is a majority. All of the nation's twenty-five largest city school systems had "majority minorities" by the late 1980s. Minority enrollments of 20% or greater in K–12 programs are already evident in thirty-three states. Over the period of the late 1980s, minority enrollment increased in forty-four states (Williams, 1992). These patterns of change apparent in the 1990 census will likely prevail and strengthen when the 2000 census is recorded.

Poverty affects approximately one quarter of the children born in the United States today (Feistritzer, 1987). The same groups continue to fall into the high-risk categories. The overwhelming majority (90%) of the increase in children

Teachers are often from a different cultural heritage than their students.

born into poverty occurs in households headed by a female African American or a female Hispanic. The rate of infant mortality for African American children is twice that of Caucasian infants, and the risk of neurological impairment is nine times greater. Hispanics have the highest rates of poverty, with 39 out of every 100 Hispanic children considered to be living in poverty. Additionally, they experience high dropout rates, with an overall rate of 37% not completing high school (Orum, 1986). The Hispanic dropout rate in urban areas is particularly high, with a rate of 80% in New York City (Grossman, 1995). African Americans and Native Americans also have high dropout rates, with the highest reported rates being 90% for Native Americans in Alaska and 70% for the same group in California. Migrant students also face a high dropout rate, estimated between 45% and 57% (Grossman, 1995). Considering the variables mentioned previously as most likely to be correlated with school failure, such populations of students are certainly vulnerable. Poverty is even linked to poor progress within special education, regardless of ethnic background of the student. When students with disabilities were divided into four groups according to socioeconomic status, the poorest quartile had the highest dropout rate of 26.7%, whereas the top quartile dropout rate was lowest, at 6.7% (Grossman, 1995).

Bilingual Childrenin the Educational System

The demographic statistics indicate a substantial increase in the numbers of students in school in the United States who would be considered as language minorities. The children who are bilingual or who are not able to use English fluently do present a unique challenge to general educators as well as special educators. Special educators have a responsibility to serve students with disabilities rather than those with cultural differences. However, there is a point at which these two circumstances will overlap and/or may begin to have a reciprocal relationship. The child whose primary language is something other than English and whose family members continue to speak another language will face additional educational hurdles not present for the child whose native language is English, regardless of the level of poverty, quality of health care, number of adults and children living in the household, or any other factor. There will inevitably be children with learning disabilities, mental retardation, speech/language impairments, emotional disorders, and every other disability who happen not to speak English. The identification and delivery of services to such children cannot necessarily be accomplished through the usual channels. Additionally, there is an inherent danger in the diagnostic process for these students. Just as disabilities must be identified so that services can be provided, they must not be inaccurately assumed to have disabilities that are not there. That it is not right to label a student as mentally retarded or learning disabled based on the fact that the child is unfamiliar with the English language or American culture is generally supported by all educators. Yet these students may find themselves unable to compete in the regular educational track without accommodation to their unique needs. As a result, some may find themselves inaccurately labeled as disabled. Figueroa and Ruiz (1993) provide a descriptive list of the various children present in our schools today who are referred to special education, including (a) some who temporarily stop speaking while adjusting to a new language; (b) those who use "I don't know" as a coping mechanism; (c) the "Ping-Pong" kids, who prematurely exit bilingual programs only to return after failing in an English-only setting; (d) some who develop limited proficiency in both languages, neither sufficient for academic progress; (e) those who lose their initial language but return to their native home and eventually return to the United States with no language; and (f) the "immersion victims," who receive decontextualized drill in English-as-a-second-language classes.

In some instances, school personnel may avoid referrals of limited-English-proficiency children whom they suspect might have disabilities into special education because of their inability to offer appropriate services to them. These multiple scenarios leave little doubt that a simple answer that addresses everyone's needs to the dilemmas associated with educating the bilingual child will not be found in one package.

Attempts to provide special education to language-minority students who have experienced difficulties in school have been accompanied by at least four chronic problems: "inappropriate assessment procedures and tools, inaccurate differential diagnosis (inability to separate language and culture from learning problems), lack of effective instructional interventions, and inappropriate placements" (Rueda, 1989, p. 121). While acknowledging the impact that cultural and linguistic differences can have in association with learning problems, Rueda emphasizes the need to consider these issues in the broader context of special education. Approaches to the education of language-minority students that have been identified in the literature represent three broad categories that Rueda has identified as the system-maintenance approach, the system-improvement approach, and the system-restructure approach. The first, system maintenance, is based on the maintaining of existing eligibility criteria, a categorical delivery system, and continuation of autonomous administration of special education, regular education, and bilingual education. A more popular approach is that of system improvement. Supporters of this approach agree that reform is needed in assessment practices and that distinctions between learning disabilities and language problems associated with the acquisition of a second language must be established. Child behaviors must be understood in terms of patterns of behavior routinely associated with the acquisition of a second language that are similar to inappropriate classroom behaviors of English-speaking students. Both of these approaches are predicated on the assumption that "once 'true' cases of a disability have been identified, there is little questioning of established categories, and a general acceptance of the professional boundaries that divide special education, regular education, and bilingual education" (Rueda, 1989, p. 125).

Those calling for system restructuring would include the bilingual educational system in the need for reform and restructuring of the general and special educational systems. Rueda cites a major criticism of the present system for those holding this view is targeted at existing assessment procedures that may isolate a child from her context and cultural experiences. The ultimate result of comprehensive restructuring would be the elimination of the existing eligibility and classification system, which would be replaced by a single educational system that would have built-in support and assistance for any student with poor achievement. Other reformers might prefer to keep separate administrative structures while providing delivery systems that rely on inclusion-based programs for all students with mild disabilities.

Comments from Grossman (1995) on the beliefs of teachers of limited-English-proficient students reflect the incompleteness that some teachers feel that the present structures offer limited-English-proficiency students with disabilities. They are forced to choose between linguistically appropriate education services and special education not matched to the students' linguistic needs. The schools appear unable to provide special education and related services personnel capable of providing bilingual assessment and instructional services for many students; therefore, they choose not to make referrals. Only in districts where services are available, and only for children whose languages can be covered, are bilingual special education referrals made.

The role of educators who teach language-minority students can be described as requiring a choice between striving toward assimilation of the students into American culture or as striving toward the development of a second cultural identity for them (Cummins, 1989). The extent to which schools should pursue the accommodation to or assimilation of ethnicity is a source of contention. Cummins argues that teachers who hope to expand a student's linguistic and cultural repertoires as contrasted with those who hope to replace them offer empowerment to their students.

Maintenance of cultural identity allows students to bring the positive aspects of their culture to their educational experience. Strong education values that prevail in an original culture can counteract the poor attitudes toward school that dominate in some American groups. Students who have a strong cultural identity have more self-esteem and self-confidence than those who reject their own cultural background. Expectations that students assimilate into American culture can force a conflict of values and lifestyles with parents and extended family members. The damage that assimilation might do to these family relationships could impede student learning and attitude far more than the difficulties caused by the retention of cultural identity.

Others contend that assimilation offers greater opportunity for students to merge into the mainstream of U.S. society as they reach adulthood. The American culture is based upon an integration of many cultures. Additionally, there are many subcultures of ethnic groups within the United States that add to the richness and diversity of the country, all of whom must come together as citizens of the same country. Grossman (1995) has identified various arguments used to dispute the necessity of accommodating cultural differences in special education programs. Since there is no concept of a monolithic culture within the United States, it would be pointless to set groups apart when a continuum of differences is more reflective of reality. Within designated groups, such as Asian/Pacific Island Americans, Hispanic Americans, or African Americans, there appear to be many differences, yet when compared to European Americans, these groups may find many similarities within their own ethnic identities. The accommodation of specific cultural needs of the wide variety of different students found in many school systems today would be virtually impossible. In some parts of the country a single school district may have upwards of one hundred different language/culture groups. Even if accommodation were philosophically preferred, a single teacher really could not be expected to teach every group represented in her class in a unique fashion particular to their distinct cultural needs. Further, the use of overgeneralized assumptions and stereotypes about culturally different students by European American teachers could actually be misleading and prejudicial. It is not assumed that all Anglo children are the same in regard to the strength of their religious beliefs, punctuality, responsibility and work ethic, morals, and so forth. Yet the making of such assumptions about other groups seems to be encouraged by some in their quest for cultural accommodations.

The debate extends into the special education arena. Logic in the arguments varies. For example, the notion of accommodation to cultural differences in children can actually be considered discriminatory in and of itself. Nondiscrimination holds to the principle that all children are treated fairly and equally, not differentially according to racial or cultural generalizations. The differential treatment of students from non-European American groups could result in lower expectations and standards based on prejudicial negative cultural stereotyping. Further, European American students would perceive these differences as preferential treatment or even presume their teachers had different (lower) expectations of the non-European Americans. The debates over Ebonics offer a practical example.

Assimilation could be argued as the best opportunity for students to grow into successful Americans. There are not separate standards and laws for adults from different cultures. The educational system has the responsibility to prepare all of its future citizens to fit within the same nation, not innumerable mini-nations, free to set their own laws, languages, and morality. Students do grow into adults who must make their way in the mainstream culture. Creating an atmosphere that fosters a strong, separate cultural identity for young people could make the adjustments that will be required of them as adults simply harder. Yet many parents prefer that their children maintain a strong ethnic pride and connection to an ethnic community (Villegas, 1994). These parents "do not want success to come at the expense of personal alienation from, and marginalization within, their own ethnic community" (p. 352). Thus, the meanings of data and the logic of political preferences have many angles for viewing.

Family–Professional Communication and Cultural Understanding

Disability, special education, and psychological assessments all have culturally bound meanings. Within the context of mainstream American society, special education laws have developed over time in response to demands and expectations of the people. For recent immigrants and others who may not feel themselves a part of this mainstream society, these laws and the educational regulations associated with them may have far different meanings than they do for the advocacy groups that helped get them passed. Harry (1992) documents the confusion and misunderstanding for Hispanic families that can surround the diagnosis and labeling process associated with special education. In a case study Harry uses to illustrate her points, she notes that a diagnosis of retardation was understood by the family to mean crazy—something that caused a great deal of distress to the child as well as to the mother. As the cycle continued, this child eventually grew up and had her own daughter who was also considered retarded. Both generations of Puerto Rican mothers never understood why these ablebodied girls, able to speak in two languages, were considered "retardado." Meaningful communication between educators and non-English speaking families with varying cultural backgrounds will not occur merely through the assurances that accurate translations of American policies and standards are provided.

Although the original legislation passed in 1975 required much better communication with and inclusion of parents in decisions, there has been no requirement that services be family focused. Such a mandate does now exist for programs receiving federal funds to serve the birth-to-three population. Professionals in the field of early childhood special education now focus much of their attention on improved communication with and understanding of families. For example, Sontag and Schacht (1994) interviewed 536 families to investigate parental perceptions regarding their need for and sources of information, the nature of their participation in early intervention, and the cultural differences related to ethnicity. Ethnic representation included white (not Hispanic) 75%, Hispanic 15%, American Indian 5%, black 2%, and Asian 3% (portions consistent with the state in which the study was conducted). Results did indicate significant differences among white, American Indian, and Hispanic parents in two categories—parent information needs and sources of information, and parent participation and preferences in early intervention. Both the Hispanic and American Indian parents were less involved in coordinating services for their children, reported a higher need to know how to obtain services, and were less involved with other parents of special needs children than the white group. The reasons for these differences can only be speculated.

The "proper" relationship between parents and professionals may be viewed quite differently for persons with differing cultural beliefs. It is ironic to consider the well-trained American early childhood special educator seeking to offer a family-focused service model and trying to defer to parents who have been equally well trained within their culture to revere professionals whose wisdom and advice they would prefer to follow. Both might come away from a meeting frustrated and disappointed, primarily due to unspoken cultural expectations.

A critical issue for the family is the extent to which they seek assimilation into the American culture and value system and how much they prefer to retain separateness and cultural affiliations. For example, some Mexicans come into the United States as migrant workers, planning to return to Mexico, whereas other Mexican immigrants prefer to settle in the United States permanently. Their interest in assimilation and motivation to encourage their children to become comfortable with American culture will not be the same (Grossman, 1995). This issue is one that has a profound impact on the family as well as the student. Cummins (1989) describes what some decry as the outcome for parents when assimilation is sought. They retain a powerless status and receive reinforcement of their internalized inferiority. Parental illiteracy and lack of interest in their children's education become the simplistic explanations for their children's failures in school. Although the parents might be quite eager to support their children, they may not know how to help their children academically and feel excluded by the school. Such may particularly be the case for upwardly mobile low-income families who hope to become a part of the U.S. middle class (Grossman, 1995).

The responsibility of classroom teachers to develop an understanding of and value the cultural mores of a group can also be debated. Chamberlain and Medinos-Landurand (1991) note the difficulties that can arise from cultural insensitivity. First, they point to the dangers of misperceptions, citing work by Deyhle. For example, Navajo students do not share a common understanding of what a test is with contemporary Anglo second-graders, who understand that it is a time to try to do one's best. They note that we can create difficulties through cross-cultural stereotyping, referring to work by Tannen to illustrate the point. Since Athabaskan Indians consider conversation with strangers to be inappropriate, others who meet them might describe these Native Americans as "sullen, uncooperative, or even stupid" (p. 115). However, from the other perspective, the Western Apache (also from the Athabaskan group), "noting the willingness of Anglos to talk when meeting strangers, stereotype these Anglos as ridiculously garrulous and hypocritical" (p. 115). Another potential danger that Chamberlain and Medinos-Landurand discuss is that of miscommunication. The previously presented case of the "retardado" Puerto Rican girl is a very real example of such danger.

The final danger mentioned by Chamberlain and Medinos-Landurand (1991) is that of assessment bias. This bias involves extrinsic factors, such as child-rearing practices, the value of competition in the student's culture, and response styles. The intrinsic factors that may be present in assessment instruments themselves "include the use of culture-bound stimuli, background knowledge not accessible to the student, language and conceptual differences, and selection practices for determining normative samples" (p. 116). To further elaborate their points, Chamberlain and Medinos-Landurand describe a variety of cultural variables that might prove particularly troubling for school-age children, including (a) cooperation versus competition; (b) time (as in speed and punctuality); (c) polychronic versus monochronic orientation (as in doing more than one thing at a time, or maintaining a singular focus); (d) bodily movements; (e) proximity; (f) touching; (g) eye contact; (h) gender; (i) individual versus family orientation; (j) verbal and nonverbal communication norms; (k) fate versus individual responsibility; (l) perceptual style; and (m) cognitive style. The nature of these variables is such that they will certainly influence how a child performs in the classroom as well as on both formal and informal assessments. Thus, the attitudes of school personnel, teachers, administrators, and psychologists toward their responsibility to investigate and understand such variables for students in their system will have the power to change the educational experience of those children positively or negatively.

Yet is it reasonable for school personnel to be expected to know cultural details about every conceivable group they might encounter, or provide a bilingual teacher for every possible foreign language, including Hmong and Tigrinya? In consideration of the health care profession, Groce and Zola (1993) suggest a compromise position for health care workers regarding health beliefs and practices that may be equally applicable to teachers. It is predicated on the acknowledgment that everyone's personal beliefs and practices are based on their own cultural heritage and that it is simply not realistic to expect individuals to become familiar with the minute details of numerous specific cultures. They suggest that health care workers should simply assume that there are culturally based variations in basic beliefs and become familiar with how such beliefs might affect health practices. If a teacher determined to study Hispanic culture to better understand a future unknown student who might be of Hispanic origin, she should be forewarned. Although the label "Hispanic" has come to be considered as one cohesive group, it, in fact, represents dozens of differing cultural groups that do not always hold to identical beliefs and practices regarding child rearing or disabilities. Such is the case for every other racial or ethnic grouping, geographic region, and subculture. Sensitivity to cultural differences does not require full knowledge of all cultures but serves as a constant reminder that miscommunication can occur unintentionally.

In addition to the many cultural mores and behavioral patterns, there are issues linked to the beliefs regarding disability that affect attitudes (Groce & Zola, 1993). First is the perceived cause of disability. In some cultures the birth of a child with impairments is considered a form of punishment, whereas in other instances the child himself is considered to be "evil," to be avoided. "Bad blood" may be the preferred explanation of inherited disorders for some, whereas witchcraft may offer the needed explanation for others. Where beliefs in reincarnation are strong, a disability is associated with previous transgressions. Although children who are disabled are therefore avoided and viewed negatively, they are encouraged to lead virtuous lives for the sake of their future lives. In some instances, particularly throughout Latin America and Southeast Asia, chronic illness and disability are associated with an imbalance of the elements within the body. The belief then follows the logic that the burden of responsibility for the disability lies with the affected individual. Both the cause and the cure are in the hands of the individual. Failure to reestablish one's own equilibrium and good health further confound the individual's troubles.

The second issue associated with cultural differences regarding disability is related to the expectations for survival. The allocation of scarce resources in a futile attempt to intervene in the life of the child who is severely disabled and with a poor prognosis for survival would be considered sheer waste for some (see chapters 10 and 11 for further discussion of this issue). On the other hand, anticipation of a miracle through divine intervention can seriously interfere with a family's ability to engage in long-term planning regarding the education and treatment of a child with severe disabilities. A final issue correlated with disabilities and culture is one linked to the social and gender roles considered appropriate for children and adults with disabilities. Gender bias may even play a role when families make decisions regarding the use of resources and energy in the educational programming of children with disabilities. For example, Chinese males with disabilities may be considered worthy of intervention, whereas similar intervention for disabled females might be viewed as a poor investment of resources. Both children are loved and cared for, but because the male has a greater likelihood of a more productive livelihood, he is afforded more intervention towards development of skills.

Groce and Zola (1993) illustrate the misunderstandings possible when the dominate culture's views are assumed to be held by all with a case in which a family who had recently immigrated to the United States from southern Italy strongly rejected the suggestion that their twenty-two-year-old retarded daughter move into a neighborhood group home. The underlying cause proved to be based on beliefs associated with supervision of unmarried females, not the disability. The obligation of the new immigrant to adjust to the systems and authority of the chosen country is juxtaposed with the system's need to offer flexibility and cultural sensitivity to its newest members. The provision of services to children who have disabilities within this population and those who might appear to have problems due to their language difficulties does require consideration of these many issues.

Minorities and Eligibility for Special Education

A historical review of practices related to eligibility for special education services and related litigation documents a pattern of racial and cultural discrimination. Have practices changed since the 1970 *Diana v. State Board of Education* (*Diana v. State Board of Education*, 1970) and 1972 *Larry P. v. Riles* (*Larry P. v. Riles*, 1979) cases? California was forced to stop the practice of using intelligence tests biased in favor of middle-class children. However, other states continue using these and similar tests with all children, including those for whom the California courts established them to be culturally unfair. At the same time, however, criteria used to diagnose the presence of mental retardation were dramatically altered in order to reduce the racial discrimination associated with this disability condition. Nevertheless, there is continued evidence of a statistical overrepresentation of minorities in certain special education categories. The overrepresentation coupled with the changing demographic patterns within the United States makes the issue of minority eligibility practices even more significant.

Educational statistics do confirm the frequency with which minority children are placed in special education settings (Grossman, 1995). For example, Chinn and Hughes (1987) report that there is a tendency for Hispanic students to be overrepresented in special education and other remedial programs. They are particularly likely to have a diagnosis of learning disabled. At the same time, this group is underrepresented in programs for gifted and talented students. However, African Americans remain the most consistently overrepresented minority in special education programs, constituting 54% of the children diagnosed with mild mental retardation (Williams, 1992). The African American enrollment in programs for students with mental retardation and emotional disturbance is twice the level that would be expected from census data. Native Americans and Native Alaskans are overrepresented in programs serving the learning disabled while underrepresented in programs for gifted and talented students. However, there are two minority groups that do stand out against the pattern of poverty and overrepresentation in special education—Asians and Pacific Islanders. Both appear to be underrepresented in special education and overrepresented in gifted and talented programs (Williams, 1992) and programs for the speech impaired (Grossman, 1995).

The issue has a unique twist to it in that it involves inclusion of a disproportionate percentage of culturally diverse students rather than the traditional discriminatory pattern of exclusion. However, from another perspective it could be considered exclusion from the general educational programs that lead to the best educational and employment opportunities following high school graduation. Such seems at least an arguable conclusion, given that in the *Larry P.* trial Judge Peckham described the special education program as both "inferior" and "dead end." However, the question of quality and benefits of special education is not specifically linked to the racial discrimination issue, since all of special education is targeted for criticism, not just its services to minorities.

Focus of Discussion

Even the choice of words (e.g., Native Americans versus Indians) used to describe the groups of children targeted for discussion in this chapter may stir emotions and cause readers to infer certain biases of the author toward the issues (Grossman, 1995). Others may identify groups that were not specifically and directly addressed and presume a slight. In fact, the words chosen have been considered as the most descriptive, providing an emphasis on the characteristics of the children most relevant to a discussion of their educational needs, not necessarily for their political significance. In regard to the omission of some groups, the reader is encouraged to consider the spirit of the issues raised rather than the need to separately address every group that might have concerns related to the themes of this chapter. The two chapter issues relate to the determination of special education eligibility for students who are from minority populations, and the implications of the homogeneity of our teaching force for the education of a diverse society.

MISREPRESENTATION OF MINORITIES IN SPECIAL EDUCATION PROGRAMS

There are disproportionate numbers of minority and limited-English-proficient students in special education programs, with higher percentages served as disabled and fewer such students served in gifted and talented programs. In this regard, Grossman (1995) has described three major educational problems experienced by poor and non-European American students: (a) misrepresentation, including overenrollments and underenrollments in special education programs; (b) culturally inappropriate services, characterized as poorly matched to socioeconomic and geographic factors; and (c) linguistically inappropriate services for students who are limited-English-proficient or who speak a nonstandard English. The disproportionate presence of minority students in special education programs is not debated; however, its significance is hotly contested. The extent to which current assessment and eligibility criteria reflect biased practices, and the motives of educators who have tolerated (and encouraged, some might argue) the pattern, reflects the best long-term interests of students who come from backgrounds widely different from mainstream middle-class America is at issue.

Harry (1992) espouses the social constructionistic nature of mild disabilities as they are currently defined. She uses this position as a basis to argue that "any deviance classification is based on the values and expectations of a society in a particular era" (p. 35). She goes on to contend that IDEA and its associated medical model for service delivery deny the ambiguity and variability, giving the educational notion of disability an appearance of far more objectivity than is actually the case. We accept "the belief that a child's failure to master certain skills is indicative of an objectively identifiable intrinsic deficit" (p. 35). Although Harry acknowledges that the law addresses the importance of unbiased assessment, she sees that there is a high degree of actual subjectivity when students from culturally diverse backgrounds are targets of assessments. She questions the presumed direct link to the presence of a child-based disability and poor school performance, particularly for non-European American students.

School Performance and Its Personal Meaning

In the past, even with similar assessment results, students who were poor, African American, Hispanic American, or Native American found themselves labeled as having mental retardation, emotional disturbance, or behavioral problems, as contrasted to European American middle-class children, who would be placed in programs for students with learning disabilities when facing problems in school (Grossman, 1995). The labels used to certify students as disabled have evened out somewhat across racial and ethnic lines, but the disproportionate percentages of minorities placed in special education remain. The pursuit of a dividing line between special and general education for minority students is a rather elusive target, surrounded by an intensity of debate. Harry (1992) describes the approach to that dividing line for underachieving minority students as the meeting point of general and special education, where those who have been described as having "mental withdrawal—grade retention—drop out syndrome" make the transition from "normalcy" to "disability." The role of special education as serving or blaming the child for his difficulties within the educational system is at the crux of the debate. Is special education the system to provide a rescue, or does it exacerbate the child's problems?

There is substantial debate on the self-esteem of minority children who perform poorly in schools (e.g., Banks, 1994; Grossman, 1995; Vasquez, 1994; Villegas, 1994). Some contend that these students' poor academic achievement contributes even more to the vicious cycle of defeat started by the poverty many face even before birth. Self-worth begins a downward spiral as the child experiences failure in his attempts to read, understand math concepts, and maintain an expected standard of behavior. Others consider such thinking as racially grounded in a white middle-class perspective and far from the real perceptions of those children. The argument is based on the notion that minority children with poor academic progress show evidence of maintaining a "foundation of intrinsic self-esteem" while being members of a stigmatized group (Vasquez, 1994). Thus, it may be possible for children to separate their personal worth from their school performance. Indeed, if a student perceived schoolwork as associated with standards and values of European American teachers whose values she intentionally rejects, her self-worth would be quite distinct from school performance, perhaps even negatively correlated to it. Poor performance in school, then, can be attributed to membership in a group, as self-as-person is distinguished from self-as-student (Vasquez, 1994). Erickson (1994) describes the dilemma these students must face: "Learning what is deliberately taught can be seen as a form of political assent. Not learning can be seen as a form of political resistance" (p. 383). The assent to authority requires the acceptance of the legitimacy of that authority as well as its good intentions. The assumption that one's best interests will result from the acquiesce to authority leads one to comply. If this assumption is proven wrong or is never even adopted, there is little to make one choose to submit. Doing well in school for some is attributed to "acting white." Erickson (1994) notes that the peers of high-achieving students have powerful social tools available "to enforce a stringent cultural standard that symbolizes group membership" (p. 389).

To what extent does race relegate one to a poverty class? Or does poverty confound the opportunities of any child, regardless of race? Poverty takes on a social and psychological meaning for a disproportionate number of ethnic and cultural minorities, inevitably linking it to racism. Brookins (1993), in describing poverty, refers to it as "an insidious form of violence that wreaks havoc on the lives of children" (p. 1058). There are disproportionate numbers of poor ethnic and cultural minorities. Approximately 44% of African American children and over 36% of Hispanic children are living in poverty. The 15% figure for European American children is less than half of the Hispanic amount and closer to one-third of the African American percentage (Brookins, 1993). Brookins notes that the meaning of poverty for parents trying to nurture and raise their children is grim. The children are less likely to have effective and responsive medical care and preventive care, and are likely to be exposed to diseases and conditions such as polio, hepatitis, abscessed gums, measles, and whooping cough.

The risks of suffering permanent damage are far greater for children living in poverty than for others. Poverty impedes children from receiving innumerable givens for other children, including proper nutrition, adequate housing, good education, and access to appropriate and effective health care. Brookins (1993) reminds us that "These societal deficits serve to produce individuals ill-equipped to meet the challenging imperatives of the broader society. Poor children are unprepared for the demands of school, even starting with kindergarten and first grade" (p. 1058).

Disproportionate Representation: Discrimination or Reality?

The fact that minorities are served in special education programs at a far greater frequency than European American children does not automatically lead to the conclusion that discriminatory practices are responsible for the discrepancy. Reschly (1988) noted two court cases more recent than *Diana* and *Larry P.* which support the notion that overrepresentation, in and of itself, is not discriminatory. As long as the schools could document that no child had been improperly classified and that the process used during placement had conformed to accepted professional standards and guidelines, no discrimination was found. However, in the previous cases it was these very professional standards and practices that had been successfully contested. Accepted assessment practices were deemed to be unfair and biased. Assumptions of equity in assessment practices, categorical diagnoses, access to services, and quality of instruction are being questioned by advocates who puzzle over the percentages of minorities both in and out of special education.

In some instances, minority children have been denied access to special education in spite of their low achievement because of an inability to display a wide discrepancy between ability and achievement (Rueda, 1989). When achievement is compared to a student's performance on IQ tests that are English-only and predicated on mainstream middle-class culture and values, the likelihood of finding a sufficient discrepancy between low achievement and measured potential is small for such students. Although the student might have an IQ low enough to justify a diagnosis of mental retardation, he or she clearly does not qualify for services on the basis of a learning disability.

Other targeted groups appear to be underserved rather than overserved. Indeed, figures now indicate that limited-English-proficient students are underrepresented in programs for students with behavior disorders, emotional problems, learning disabilities, and mild developmental disabilities (Grossman, 1995). Some speculate that the explanation of such apparent underrepresentations is associated with the inability and/or reluctance of school systems to deliver linguistically and culturally appropriate special education programs (Grossman, 1995). Once a child is referred and deemed eligible, the schools are obligated to deliver a program that meets the child's needs. Some contend that the schools resist allowing such referrals to occur when delivery of an appropriate program would be difficult. Do all the disproportionate statistics reveal an intolerable pattern of prejudice and bias in our schools today, or are they merely reflective of the disparities in society, well beyond the scope of special education to resolve?

Decision Point 2.1: Placing Minority and Limited-English-Proficient Children in Special Education

Arguments for Proposition One The resolution of misrepresentation of non-European American students in special education does not rest in the hands of special educators but rather in models of prevention and compensation, bilingual programs, and broad efforts to improve the socioeconomic status of families. The fact that students from non-European cultural groups are substantially misrepresented in special education is more reflective of their overrepresentation in lower socioeconomic groups than because special education placements are inherently culturally biased. The risk factors described earlier in the chapter are realities that directly contribute to a child's problems in school. General factors, such as poverty, contribute to poor nutrition and limited access to health care; transportation difficulties that increase absenteeism and other problems; quality of housing, which can influence health and safety; and so on. More specific factors are also directly linked to particular risks for certain groups of children. To argue that such risks create deficits for which the educational system must compensate is not denying the richness and variety of all cultures within our country. Instead, it is to accept the harsh realities of poverty, malnutrition, child abuse and neglect, and inadequate health care, along with their insidious effects on the young and growing.

Environmental risk factors do not fluctuate by racial identities, languages spoken in the home, cultural mores and values practiced, or genders of offspring. Their effects cross these lines in an unbiased yet unrelenting fashion. For example, prenatal exposure to cocaine results in increased risk of prematurity and its complications and other potential behavioral and cognitive difficulties for the infant, whether the mother is an upper-middle-class Caucasian or an impoverished Hispanic American. Children suffering the ill effects of such life influences deserve the benefits and best opportunities possible through the public education system, regardless of racial or ethnic identity. If greater proportions of non-European American children are placed at risk for disabilities as a result of their poverty, all should be served, not just a representative percentage of them. Special education should provide such children the safety net they need to succeed.

School Performance and Its Personal Meaning Children of poverty are at risk to have poor self-concepts and are, therefore, at risk to perform poorly in school and school-related assessments. These risks to the child's self-concept begin their

---

Proposition One

Once a child has reached school age and is struggling academically or behaviorally, the determination of eligibility for special education to assist that student to achieve his potential is essential, regardless of racial identity or cultural ethnicity. All who qualify have a right to the supports available through special education, regardless of their racial or ethnic identities.

---

work long before the children enter school and are not racially attached. A child for whom the basics, such as home, toys, food, and clothing, are inadequate due to the poverty of his family is not oblivious to these conditions. The words from the journal of a twelve-year-old boy whose family was homeless paint a bleak picture as he struggled against the attacks on his self-esteem:

> As I lay in bed crying myself to sleep in the Prince George Hotel, the largest hotel used to house homeless families in NYC, I could not bring myself to overcome the fear of what was happening to me. Over and over again I keep telling myself that I don't deserve this. I'm only 12 years old. I feel so alone. People in school call me a hotel kid....It seems like people are so afraid of ending up where I'm at that they want to punish me for reminding them that being homeless is possible. They have no right to punish me for something I have no control over. I'm just a little boy living in a hotel, petrified, wanting to know what's going to happen to me. (Ayers, 1989, p. 103)

Such relentless degradation coincides with the physical risks of poverty and weighs heavily on children as they enter the school system.

For some minority children, the schools might be perceived as dead ends regardless of their efforts. The value of an education may be questioned by multiple generations of their families who encountered racial discrimination and rejection when they sought employment. The schools expect all to acquiesce to a middle-class work ethic, but the prejudices, particularly historical, of the job market persuade some minority children in a different direction. The motivation to do well in school may simply not be present for these children. As a result, their poor performance in school will be of little concern to them, and the cumulative effects of their lack of interest can build to complete failure. Somewhere along the way, these children may be referred for special education. The system then has the opportunity to discover their hidden potential. The use of culturally sensitive assessments can avoid inappropriate labeling but should not become a means of eliminating children from eligibility. The first and foremost task that special educators face when working with such children is giving to them a personal meaning for their efforts in the classroom. It is appropriate that special educators, trained to personalize education and motivate frustrated students, take on this responsibility for the thousands of minority children tainted by years of racial prejudice of the larger society.

Disproportionate Representation: Discrimination or Reality? There is much rhetoric about the apparent overrepresentation of minorities in special education programs. There is a presumption that it implies racially discriminatory assessment practices, intentional tracking, and removal of minority students from educational opportunities. Before we accept such implications, it is appropriate to consider the facts from many angles. The data reflecting overrepresentation are aggregate national data based on thousands of individual school systems. Far different conclusions might be reached were we able to analyze the data on a local level. For example, the basic pattern of population concentrations might contribute to the distortion of the meaning of minority representation in special education. For a large metropolitan area in which minority groups have exceeded the Caucasian population in the schools, the rate of minority representation in special education should be substantially higher. Inner-city children face innumerable risk factors, such as poverty, violence in their communities, and single-parent homes that are less prevalent in suburban neighborhoods. When national figures are compiled from samples that might not account for such population clusters or that represent incomplete data, their accuracy and meaningfulness must be questioned (Reschly, 1988).

Even if the national statistics are reasonable estimates of actual overrepresentation, they might not represent blatant discrimination practices. The concept of expected prevalence is meaningless without consideration of risk factors. There may be issues associated with a particular group that would increase the likelihood of children being eligible for special education. For example, sickle cell anemia is a condition primarily affecting African Americans, Mediterraneans, Egyptians, and people from India. Similarly, neural tube defects are much more prevalent in individuals with a British or Irish heritage than in the population at large. An unfortunate positive correlation is seen in the incidence of Fetal Alcohol Syndrome and Native American populations. Prematurity occurs more often among users of cocaine than nonusers. The point is not a return to the Jensen-type argument that minorities are innately inferior to whites or that their culture is deficient. Rather, certain conditions cause specific subcultures to be more vulnerable to educational failure than others. A more telling statistic would factor out poverty, single-parent homes, and other high-risk indicators. Only then could racial overrepresentation be considered reflective of racial bias.

Children of the poor are at greater risk of biomedical problems associated with inadequate health care and nutrition. They are at greater risk of HIV and AIDS. Parental abuse of drugs, including alcohol, marijuana, cocaine, and other popular addictive drugs before, during, and after pregnancy, contributes to the increased incidence of disabilities among minority groups at a greater rate than among European Americans. Not only are infants born to women who have used drugs during pregnancy; these children may then be raised in homes characterized by chaos, in an environment of abuse and neglect (Rist, 1990). In one national study, cited by Grossman (1995), of the children who are reported to have AIDS, 53% were African American and 23% Hispanic American. Linguistic differences, modeled in the home and community, can also be a detriment to the student's ability to compete academically in mainstream schools with English as the language of instruction. Many students grow up facing educational disadvantages that affect cognitive skills, linguistic ability, self-concept, levels of educational aspiration, locus of control, and social behavior (Grossman, 1995). Such is the premise behind federally researched and supported compensatory programs such as Head Start.

Argument Summary   The implications of poverty for the education of high numbers of non-European American children go beyond their own personal limited resources. The schools themselves and the teachers staffing the schools have also been unfavorably compared to the schools and teachers serving children not already burdened with the disadvantages of poverty (e.g., Kozol, 1991). Special education should rise above the limitations of education in poverty schools to offer even the poorest child the best possible resources available. Special education programs should offer children with disabilities the same quality education, regardless of neighborhood resources. If a disproportionate number of minority and limited-English-proficient children are given the opportunity to benefit from these resources, it must be accepted as their right. Although special education does not have children of poverty or limited-English-proficient children as a primary target, it does have an obligation to serve all students to the extent that they experience educationally related disabilities. There can be no quota setting for access to the intended benefits of special education. If special education resources are, in fact, less than beneficial, distributed inequitably throughout a school district or state, or culturally insensitive to the needs of students so served, those issues must be addressed separately from the question of access. The contention that special education is not beneficial and, therefore, overrepresentation of minorities in its ranks is a discriminatory practice that should end is a serious indictment of special education, not a racial issue. White middle-class parents demand that their children with even slight learning problems have a right to special education, but entire school populations of inner-city children who suffer more significant academic difficulties may go unserved. Perhaps there should be even more minority enrollments in special education and fewer suburban children allowed to be labeled as learning disabled when they fall behind in school.

Arguments for Proposition Two   Grossman (1995) notes that special educators rely on assessment, instructional, and management techniques designed for students from middle-class, stable homes, with native-born, well-educated parents capable of understanding the system and with the time and resources to help their children. These children perceive that the schools are relevant to their lives. For most of them and their parents, there is an accepted positive correlation to hard work in school and opportunities for them as adults. These parents and children alike are willing to accept the authority of the schools, acceding to the

Proposition Two
The enrollment of minority students within the ranks of special education must be restricted to that portion of the population that has real disabilities, not cultural differences. Until special educators reject their racially and ethnically biased practices, general educators can avoid their responsibility to these highly vulnerable groups of students.

necessary standards of behavior and effort in class. When such children find themselves unable to achieve the expected standards in spite of their best efforts and
their parents' support, the special education system is available to them. However,
many children come from far different backgrounds and are far less likely to profit
much from their educational experiences. Their cynical attitudes, the inadequate
educational resources offered them by the system, and their limited personal resources all contribute to their school-related difficulties. The families of many
immigrants and most refugees must adjust to a new nation and culture in a state
of relative poverty. All the disadvantages and educational risks associated with
poverty confound the cultural and linguistic challenges faced by these children.
Native Americans grow up on reservations but may attend schools run by European American teachers and designed for European American students. Other
groups that experience similar risks are rural children who migrate to urban areas,
illegal/undocumented immigrants, and migrant students. Certainly, all these children face educational disadvantage and risk of failure, but they should not then
be blamed for their difficulties by placing a disability label on them.

The realities of inadequate schools for many non–European American children across this nation make the misuse of special education a tempting solution
to an overwhelming problem. Brookins (1993) describes the situation: "Good,
effective teachers are less likely to work in poorly resourced districts; those teachers in schools with high percentages of minority-status poor children often tend
to be less motivated to believe in and encourage their students to do their best"
(p. 1059). These are savage inequalities indeed (Kozol, 1991), but not cause for
labeling children.

School Performance and Its Personal Meaning Minority children do not inherently
have poor self-concepts. The logic that they do is based on the flawed presumption that these children hold a white perspective of themselves (Grossman, 1995).
Not only are they incapable of holding a white perspective of themselves, but also
they would reject it as absurd were it explained to them. The multi-generational
oppression of some minority groups that has been present in America cannot be
ignored as a contributing factor to the low school achievement of minority students (Erickson, 1994). Ogbu (1978) argues that these caste-like groups have taken
on a fatalistic perspective—employment opportunities will not be available to minority applicants, so there is no justification for putting forth an effort in school.
Such a negative view of one's opportunities in life need not have any influence
over one's self-esteem. The notion of self-worth might come from far different
sources than teachers or one's performance in academic arenas.

In some instances, the misuse of special education as a tracking system for
minority must be confronted. As Giroux (1994) notes, "At issue here is understanding that student experience has to be understood as part of an interlocking
web of power relations in which some groups of students are often privileged
over others" (p. 405). For example, there are people in power who might prefer
that the employment opportunities for female Hispanic Americans be domestic
work, child care, food preparation, and other low-end jobs. With such an agenda,
these powerful people will support a system that helps to achieve such ends.
Placement of the students in special education is a subtle means of restricting

their curricular opportunities, of lowering teacher expectations for them, and eventually of restricting their career paths. Rather than demanding that general education set in motion a means of working with the disenfranchised, the limited-English-proficient, and the other nonmainstream populations, special educators have allowed themselves to become enablers to the powerful. Special education is simply being used as a means by which these groups can remain oppressed. Unfortunately, most special educators are blind to such unspoken political manipulations, quietly assuming their responsibility for students who face educational disadvantage. The temptation to see others who are simply different as deficient is quickly endorsed when these children predictably perform poorly in white middle-class schools.

The role of language and communication is significant as members of minorities interact with school personnel who often have different patterns of communication. Erickson (1994) describes the relevance of personal speech networks when minority children enter school as young children and begin attempting to communicate with a number of adults who may have far different speech networks and styles of communicating. There is a high risk that the teacher will attribute any resulting communication difficulties to the child, missing the interactional nature of the miscommunication. The child and her family may be equally puzzled by the "poor" communication skills of the teacher but fail to hold the power to define the problem; thus, the child gets the label. Again, difference become deficiency.

Disproportionate Representation: Discrimination or Reality? If special education programs are a right designed to provide more appropriate educational experiences for students who are having difficulties in school, why is overrepresentation of minorities in these classes even an issue? Reschly (1988) posed this question and immediately honed in on issues of instructional effectiveness and the perceived benefits of special education.

We have allowed our practices of psychological assessment to legitimize the disabling of minority students by accepting that their academic problems come from within themselves (Cummins, 1989). As a result, we have avoided the critical scrutiny of our school programs as well as "the exclusionary orientation of teachers toward minority communities, and transmission models of teaching that suppress students' experience and inhibit them from active participation in learning" (Cummins, 1989, p. 116). The solution Cummins offers would dramatically shift the nature of assessment as well as the outcomes of assessment. The process would "involve locating the pathology within the societal power relations between dominant and dominated groups, in the reflection of these power relations between school and communities, and in the mental and cultural disabling of minority students that takes place in classrooms" (p. 116). He contends that these conditions are the more probable cause of the 300% overrepresentation of Hispanic students in programs for students with learning disabilities in Texas than "any intrinsic processing deficit unique to Hispanic children" (p. 116).

Educational placements and even the benefits and outcomes of special education differ by ethnic and socioeconomic class. Sigmon (1990) indicts our existing eligibility standards and characterizes special education in poor urban areas as "nothing more than holding tanks where hardly any learning takes place, and where expectations for achievement are virtually non-existent" (p. 187). In contrast, affluent school districts are able to offer high-demand remedial programs. The overrepresentation of minorities in special education is a problem that special educators have unwittingly contributed to in their quiet acceptance of children by the thousands. The disproportionate figures reported previously in the chapter are a clear indication of just how far out of hand this situation has become.

Argument Summary The continued abuse of the special education bureaucracy in fostering and encouraging a system of tracking that results in an inferior education for non-European American students must end. Alternative approaches to meeting the educational needs of all children, regardless of race, ethnicity, poverty level, linguistic preferences, can be offered without the necessity of labeling children as disabled merely because they are different. Simultaneously, diagnostic measures that are designed to eliminate the current biases inherent in psychological evaluations must be established so those children from minority backgrounds who do have disabilities can be properly identified and served.

HOMOGENEITY OF THE TEACHING FORCE

The behavioral and educational expectations for young minority children raised in poverty, upon entering school can be far different from anything they have experienced previously. This variance can partially be attributed to the "culturally different" teachers they will encounter (Williams, 1992). Schools comprise largely white faculties and are grounded in a white middle-class culture that holds no meaning for millions of minority and poor children. Williams also points out that the burden of responsibility then falls to the minority children to become bicultural. They must master all of the developmental demands of their own culture, while simultaneously learning the dominate culture's expectations as conveyed to them in school. The child is the one expected to carry the burden of responsibility to work out the cultural conflicts he might experience as he attempts to develop and live in two disparate worlds. The subtle and not so subtle messages to the child that the standards and expectations of his home are not just different but are considered inferior and even unsatisfactory can leave the child little room in which to maneuver. The words "You may be allowed to do/say/act like that in your home, but you are not going to get away with it in my classroom" set the tone of the school experience for these children as they attempt to establish their bicultural roots. As noted in the previous section, some will rebel against the very thought of developing such dual identities. The extent to which the racial makeup of the teaching force influences the development and academic success of African American and other non-European American students is at issue. Can non-European American teachers offer the children of their cultures something that European American teachers cannot? The logical implications of the contention that minority children require minority teachers can be highly segregating in nature.

Cultural Discrepancies

The percentage of children within our schools who are from minority cultures is substantially higher than is the number of teachers. Only 7% of schoolteachers are African American, a slight 3% come from other nonwhite heritages, and 90% are Caucasian (Williams, 1990). Although these figures represent a healthy increase from 1981 figures (U.S. Department of Education, 1994), projections to the year 2000 indicate that the percentage of educators from minority groups will drop to 6% but that minority enrollments in schools will continue to rise (King-Sears, Rosenberg, Ray, & Fagen, 1992). The vast majority (95%) of teacher education students are from rural and suburban areas and intend to return to these locales following the completion of their programs (Williams, 1990). The extent to which such uneven demographic patterns should be of concern is debatable. Related issues of additional concern are the appropriateness and effectiveness of white teachers with middle-class backgrounds teaching minority children and youth, the lack of role models for minority children in schools, differential learning styles of various cultural groups, and equity of access to a teaching career.

The extent to which children have motivational tendencies, gender-linked role identification, preferences between reflection and quick response to teacher questioning, and comfort with competition, cooperation, and individualism has been linked to cultural heritage (Grossman, 1995). These and other differences can influence the behaviors of a child in the classroom, teacher perceptions of the child, and reciprocal interactions between the teacher and the child. The argument that cultural sensitivity is essential for appropriate instruction can be persuasive, yet it carries with it several troublesome illogical conclusions. The potential use of these ideas to promote a resegregation of students and the teaching force could follow. Strange political bedfellows might unite with ultraliberal or ultraconservative agendas.

Teacher–Child Effects

Currently, the gap between the academic achievement of minority students in both elementary and secondary schools and white students is very large (U.S. Department of Education, 1994). The gap was reduced during the 1980s, particularly in mathematics and science, but 1992 data indicate that the gap may no longer be narrowing, with the lowest figures reported in 1987 (Grossman, 1995). As an example, the data for reading achievement indicate that previous gains made by minority groups relative to white students have been lost. The differential in minority/white achievement is attributed to the higher incidence of poverty in the minority families, the lower average educational levels of minority parents, a greater likelihood of the child living with only one parent, and community characteristics related to income-based residential segregation. In spite of the fact that the percentage of black children living in poverty is substantially higher than that of white children living with families whose income fell below the poverty line, evidence does exist confirming that excellent schools and teachers can and do make a difference in the achievement of minority children living in poverty (U.S. Department of Education, 1994). The role of teachers in these schools of excellence is most significant.

Decision Point 2.2: Expanding the
Diversity of the Teaching Force

Arguments for Proposition One   The academic performance of black students in reading, mathematics, and science as measured by the National Assessment of Educational Progress (NAEP) is lower than that of white students as early as nine years of age. Black children are reading on average two years behind their white peers by age thirteen. Although the black–white achievement gap has closed somewhat over time, it persists across ages, starting at age nine and remaining through age seventeen (U.S. Department of Education, 1994). Although there are many variables that appear to contribute to this consistent gap, stereotypic assumptions about minority families and minority children's academic abilities held by white teachers must be considered as possible contributing factors. To illustrate, the notion that minority parents have less interest in their children's education and offer less structure and guidance does not appear to be supported by data gathered through a survey of youth. Survey results have indicated that black children are equally likely to talk with their parents about their classes, have parents check their homework, and have limited television viewing time and time out with friends as are white children. In fact, black eighth-graders reported that their parents had spoken with a teacher or guidance counselor and visited their classes more often than had parents of white students (U.S. Department of Education, 1994).

There is a critical and growing underrepresentation of teachers from minority backgrounds in today's public schools, while the number of minority children unable to perform well in school multiplies. The absence of minority teachers in the schools directly contributes to the poor achievement records of the children. The urgency of this situation warrants immediate action on the part of schools and teacher education programs. Biased testing practices and economic roadblocks, such as college tuition, simply serve to cloak this discrepancy with a false appearance of fairness. The standards for admission to teacher education programs are predicated on a cultural superiority/cultural deficit model. For many potential candidates, the expectation is that they "overcome" their culture before admission can be considered. Minority candidates would become more acceptable to the teacher education establishment if a culturally different model were used in setting standards. Were current practices reversed and Caucasian applicants expected to demonstrate a knowledge of minority culture, communicate according to linguistic patterns unfamiliar to them, and prove that they hold no bias toward minority children, admission patterns would dramatically change. They would find themselves in remedial programs designed to catch them up due to their deficiencies, complete with a substantial cost for the service and no guarantees of success in the end.

Cultural Discrepancies   There are cultural biases in schools staffed by teachers who expect all students to have similar learning and behavioral styles, refusing to

---

Proposition One

The prejudicial teaching patterns of white teachers toward minority students and the lack of minority role models in today's public schools warrant the use of emergency measures to alleviate the shortage of minority teachers, even if that means altering or waiving some existing standards.

---

accommodate or honor the cultural differences present in both these areas of functioning. There is research evidence to support the contention that students from different cultural backgrounds differ in both these regards and that these differences play out in school to influence academic success (Grossman, 1995). Grossman (1995) makes the connection to special education by observing that cultural mismatches between teachers and students can lead to failure and referral to special education. Teachers', school psychologists', and school administrators' behaviors reveal their prejudices against poor and non-European American students. They hold beliefs, for example, that Standard English is superior to other forms of dialect rather than different from it.

The teacher education candidate pool does not offer any hope for increases in the numbers of minority teachers in the immediate future. In fact, there are forces in place that serve to reduce their numbers. Testing requirements recently imposed by state legislatures are ominous for African American potential teacher education students. The fear of completing all the university degree and licensure requirements but failing to achieve adequate scores on the licensure exams is very real for them (King, 1993). In her review of related research, King (1993) identified them as a deterrent in the recruitment process and "the most severe threat to the survival of African-American teachers" (p. 140). The vicious circle of poor quality education, lower academic achievement, poor performance on standardized tests, and limited career opportunities for minority students has to be broken by simultaneously creating change in K–12 and higher education. Capable minority students who have satisfactorily completed the required college courses and performed acceptably in practica and internships should not be barred from the profession because of their inability to achieve an arbitrary score on a standardized test with unproved connections to effective teaching.

Further discouragement of minorities entering the field of teaching is associated with the high cost of college tuition and the long-term nature of the training programs. Alternative teacher preparation models that allow minority teacher candidates to begin their training in the public schools, exploring their suitability for a teaching career without committing themselves to four or five years of participation in an expensive course of study, must be developed. Such programs would eliminate many issues for the minority population, including fear of the university culture and risk of failure concurrent with high financial cost. Instead, alternative teacher education models could be designed to put minority teacher candidates into the schools immediately as employees earning money concurrent with their participation in training and skill development. As their skills and self-confidence rise, these teachers in training could complete specially designed university courses to fulfill the requirements of a general degree, with their employers assisting with the costs of tuition as a part of their compensation for work. These new minority candidates could begin dramatically altering the racial composition of school faculties immediately.

Teacher–Child Effects Studies throughout the 1970s and 1980s indicate that teacher expectations are lower for minorities, with the exception of Asian American students, for whom expectations may be biased upward (Grossman, 1995). Curricular recommendations reveal a tendency toward tracking that maintains social class rather than being reflective of individual abilities. For example, Matute-Bianchi (1986) found teachers 3.5 times more likely to consider poor African American students as developmentally disabled than poor European American students. Troubling differential patterns associated with interactions along racial and ethnic lines are evident as well in the studies Grossman reviewed. European American students receive more praise and praise for more specific things than African American students, while the African American students receive more criticism. Hispanic American students, while preferring praise, are treated in much the same way as the African Americans. Although the research is sparse, there is some somewhat dated evidence that teachers speak to and attend to Native Americans less than they do European American students (Guilmet, 1979). African American female students are given attention for behavior and social behavior rather than academic performance, particularly by white teachers (Grant, 1984). Such uneven attention to social behaviors tends to diminish the females' motivation to excel in academics. These examples convey a pattern of less attending to and lowered expectations of minority children, as well as a gender bias compounding the racial bias.

Racial prejudice aside, the ability of teachers to be as effective teaching children whose life experiences are vastly different from their own is, at the very least, suspect. There is evidence that teachers of African American students do hold differentiated expectations for them (King, 1993). The fact is that white teachers have preconceived expectations that white students will achieve more than black children. Such biases inevitably come to be proven true by the ones who hold them. In general, African American teachers do not share these views. They are less prejudiced against African American students than are European American teachers (Simpson & Erickson, 1983). Even the percentage of non-European American teachers at a school has an effect on the discriminatory practices within that building (Meier, Stewart, & England, 1989). In one district, schools with a high percentage of African American teachers had less overrepresentation of African American students in special education programs serving students with developmental disabilities; less overrepresentation of African American students receiving corporal punishment, suspension, or expulsion; fewer African American students dropping out; fewer African American students being overlooked for gifted and talented programs; and more African American students graduating. It appears that minority children in schools with higher ratios of African American teachers are less likely to need special education due to disabilities and have less need to be punished.

Argument Summary Children from minority families typically experience a discrepancy between their culture and that of the homogeneous teaching staff found in most schools. American schools were founded in the culture of the white middle class, consistent with the values and expectations of a strong nuclear family; therefore, many minority and poor children who live in quite different circumstances do not naturally feel comfortable in school. The burden is then on the children to find their way in this unfamiliar culture and learn its standards and expectations simultaneously with the development of academic achievement and the developmental demands of their own culture (Fuchs & Fuchs, 1995). Radical efforts are needed to address the increasingly critical shortage of minority teachers who offer the most promise for future generations of non-European American students. The costs to schools and universities might seem high initially, but these costs are, in reality, investments that would cost less than the alternatives would ultimately cost our society.

Arguments for Proposition Two   Although the figures showing the homogeneity of the teacher workforce are accurate and a cause for real concern, they should not be used to justify quick fixes. The "crisis" nature of this issue may, indeed, be a social construction (Cizek, 1995). King's 1993 article addresses the "urgency" needed in alleviating the shortage of African American teachers in the field. The implied crisis then requires an emergency plan of action. There are plausible explanations for the diminishing numbers of minority teacher education applicants that are not associated with existing admission practices, costs of university training, or such racial issues as the cultural deficit/cultural differences debates. The fact is that a broader range of career choices is now open to African American adults, and educated females of all races are no longer limited to teaching and nursing as career choices. The limited numbers of African American teachers might actually reflect a significant improvement in social conditions and employment opportunities of some African Americans, which is well worth the cost of reduced numbers of teacher education candidates. As such, the shortage of minority teaching candidates could be viewed as a secondary problem that has resulted from positive social change, not a crisis, but certainly something worthy of the reasoned attention of the education community.

It could be argued that the trend of minority college students to abandon education as a major in favor of other options might offer minority children a wide diversity of role models. In 1977, black students were 42% more likely than white students to major in education, but by 1991, they were 33% less likely to choose education as a major. Rather, black students seeking a bachelor's degree were more likely than white students to major in business and management and in computer and information sciences (U.S. Department of Education, 1994). Such a shift might offer these students greater job opportunities, higher salaries, and

---

Proposition Two
Teacher educators and state education personnel need to collaborate in the development of long-term improvements in the ability of the teaching force to educate minority students successfully. Such a plan would include increasing the diversity of the teaching force over time, reducing teacher bias toward non-European American students, and improving the quality of K–12 education for minority children.

increased community acceptance, resulting in integrated housing and schooling opportunities for their children. Perhaps it is not really in the best interests of the minority community to expect most of the small percentage of college students from their group to major in education just for the sake of diversifying the teaching workforce.

Cultural Discrepancies The argument that the lower academic achievement of black children is partially caused by the homogeneous white teaching force certainly oversimplifies an issue with many confounding variables. For example, even with Head Start available, fewer African American children are enrolled in preschool programs than white children. In 1991, 40% of white three- and four-year-olds were in preschool programs, but only 31% of African American children and only 21% of Hispanic American children were enrolled. These differences may be due to the financial cost of preschool programs, which are not typically available in public schools. Preschool enrollment varies widely in relation to family income, with 1992 enrollment rates for high-income families at 52%, 30.5% for middle-income families, and 23.9% for low-income families.

In their school settings, black students are more likely to report disruptions by other students that interfere with their learning than white students (51% compared to 37%). In 1990, black sophomores were almost twice as likely to report that they did not feel safe at their school (13% to 7%). One in ten black students reported being injured with a weapon at school, whereas only one in nineteen white students reported such incidents. These conditions give cause to the students' poor performance but have no relation to the racial or cultural heritage of the teachers. In fact, there is some evidence to indicate that African American students are encouraged and advised to continue their education by the existing body of teachers (U.S. Department of Education, 1994). Fewer African American students were dropping out of high school in 1992 than in 1982; therefore, the number of African American students entering higher education should be expected to increase. Between 1981 and 1991, the percentage gains in bachelor's degrees made by Hispanic American, Asian American, and Native American men and women exceeded those made by Caucasians of the same sex. The number of bachelor's degrees earned by Hispanic American men and women has risen sharply since 1981, with a 50 and 86 percent increase, respectively. Such increases coupled with active recruitment of minorities by teacher education program faculty will increase the diversity of the teaching force without lowered or waived standards, which would only create divisiveness within the education ranks and perpetuate a two-tiered system of education.

Teacher–Child Effects King (1993) contends that research offers evidence that European American teachers hold qualitatively different expectations for minority students. But Ross and Jackson (1991) found differential expectations by race and gender across teachers with varying ethnicities. The teachers, regardless of their racial identity, had lower expectations for black males than for black females. There is no reason to assume that African American teachers alone have the ability to look beyond a child's racial identity and offer her proper instruction, and there is no evidence linking the shortage of African American teachers to the fact that minority students are subjected to differential teacher expectations. The suggestion that African American teachers are *de facto* better teachers of minority students on the basis of dated studies of interaction patterns, not even actual student achievement, is inaccurate (Cizek, 1995). Finding the skills that any teacher, regardless of race or ethnicity, needs to be effective is of far greater benefit than creating a pool of racially matched teachers.

The entire educational experience of poor minority children is at issue. If schools are relatively unstimulating, constraining, and monotonous places, as described by Boykin (1979), or more recently by Kozol (1991) as places of savage inequalities, "and if African-American children are disproportionately enrolled in the worst of these, then there exists a much more invidious systemic malignancy to be addressed than would be ameliorated by increasing the proportion of African-American teachers" (Cizek, 1995, p. 82). However, the call to eliminate standardized testing of basic skills in the admission and/or licensure process to address the non-European American teacher shortage could do more to hurt the African American and other minority communities than help them. The testing and standards bias claims seem to collapse in upon themselves. The tests generally comprise basic skills (mathematical computations, logical reasoning skills, and basic language skills) that classroom teachers should have achieved before they entered the classroom to teach. There is more reason to believe that the poor performance of African American teacher candidates on such tests is related to the limitations of their high school preparation than that the test items reflect racial bias (Cizek, 1995). The tests do discriminate between those who have a sound academic preparation and those who do not; unfortunately, the high school curriculum of African American students contains fewer courses in mathematics, social sciences, and the physical sciences than that of European American students (King, 1993). The allowance of African American teacher candidates, unable to meet standards expected for teaching, into the education community for the sole purpose of teaching African American children seems rather illogical. Cizek (1995) notes that increasing the number of African American teachers would not guarantee that they would end up teaching in predominantly African American schools and that, in fact, the best African American teachers would be recruited to teach in schools that had few, if any, African American students.

Argument Summary The shortage of minority teachers in relation to the growing number of minority students in public schools today is a concern, but it is not a crisis requiring emergency solutions, including lowered standards and shortened training periods for minority teacher education applicants. Such solutions would merely serve to continue a pattern of inferior education already in place at schools serving predominantly minority students. The emergency status implies the need for exigency plans, shortcuts, and lowered standards rather than long-term, well-constructed problem solving. Lasting improvements will require the latter. Breaking the cycle of failure and poverty would not be accomplished by allowing minority candidates to enter the teaching ranks and become teachers of minority children without passing standardized teacher tests or completing a university course of study. In fact, the lowering of such standards would eventually lead to a second-class category of teacher—one that would be unlikely to qualify for employment outside the poorest schools, perpetuating an uneven educational system, not alleviating it.

The critical issue for our teachers is their qualifications and ability to be effective in the classroom, not their ethnicity. Were one to argue that impoverished central-city children from nonwhite racial groups should be taught only by teachers representing their racial identity, the logic would quickly follow that white upper-middle-class children need teachers just like themselves as well. Diversity for all groups would be sacrificed for identity and role models, not necessarily quality or appropriateness of teaching. In fact, through the achievement of a goal focused on the improvement of K–12 educational experiences of non-European American children, the goal of increasing the diversity of the teaching force would be accomplished. There would likely be a natural increase in number of minority high school graduates entering college and, therefore, an increase in potential candidates for teacher education programs. Increasing the number of non-European American students attending college is the key to broadening the diversity of the teaching pool.

CLOSING THOUGHTS

The issues presented here are paralleled throughout U.S. society today. Debates over the need for or effectiveness of affirmative action programs are common in the political arena. The preferences of racial and ethnic groups to maintain a separateness and pride in their group identities balanced with the need for compatibility and cooperation across groups create a tension throughout the nation. The nation of immigrants has developed a heritage: social support systems funded by taxes, municipal ordinances controlling housing, and so forth. This evolution of the nation has brought with it numerous concerns that confound the attitudes all Americans have toward persons who are different from themselves. For Americans who have been unable to discover the American dream, there is a reciprocal distance growing from those who have. The welfare system, intended as a means of support and assistance, has become a financial trap for many, fostering social patterns that regenerate the need for assistance rather than independence. The welcome of refugees, immigrants, and other newcomers to the nation includes provision of an education to their children, employment opportunities for the adults, health care for all, and financial security for the elderly. Americans are finding themselves reluctant to take on the financial and social responsibilities associated with these new arrivals. To further exacerbate the situation, some individuals enter the country illegally and gain rights to programs and services funded by a tax base to which they have not contributed. The provision of an education to young children whose parents are refugees from war, migrant farm workers, welfare recipients with value systems derived from the welfare rules, residents of reservations (separate, yet a part of American society) occurs within a highly political context. The role that special education plays is a critical piece in this political puzzle. It can be used and manipulated to further the causes of innumerable political agendas, either liberal or conservative. We have the professional obligation to reflect on our own behaviors, understand our personal motives for action, and give critical thought to the motives and actions of others as policies and practices evolve within the nation.

REFERENCES

Ayers, W. (1989). *The good preschool teacher: Six teachers reflect on their lives*. New York: Teachers College Press.

Banks, J. A. (1994). Ethnicity, class, cognitive, and motivational styles: Research and teaching implications. In J. Kretovics & E. J. Nussel (Eds.), *Transforming Urban Education* (pp. 277–290). Boston: Allyn & Bacon.

Boykin, A. W. (1979). Psychological/behavioral verve: Some theoretical explorations and empirical manifestations. In A. W. Boykin, A. J. Franklin, & J. F. Yates (Eds.), *Research directions of black psychologists* (pp. 351–367). New York: Russell Sage Foundation.

Brookins, G. K. (1993). Culture, ethnicity, and bicultural competence: Implications for children with chronic illness and disability. *Pediatrics, 91,* 1056–1062.

Chamberlain, P., & Medinos-Landurand, P. (1991). Practical considerations for the assessment of LEP students with special needs. In E. V. Hamayan & J. S. Damico (Eds.), *Limiting bias in the assessment of bilingual students* (pp. 111–156). Austin: Pro-Ed.

Chinn, P. C., & Hughes, S. (1987). Representation of minority students in special education classes. *Remedial and Special Education, 8,* 4–46.

Cizek, G. J. (1995). On the limited presence of African-American teachers: An assessment of research synthesis, and policy implications. *Review of Educational Research, 65,* 78–92.

Cummins, J. (1989). A theoretical framework for bilingual special education. *Exceptional Children, 56,* 111–119.

Diana v. State Board of Education, No. C-70-37 (N.D. Calif. 1970).

Erickson, F. (1994). Transformation and school success: The politics and culture of educational achievement. In J. Kretovics & E. J. Nussel (Eds.), *Transforming Urban Education* (pp. 375–395). Boston: Allyn & Bacon.

Figueroa, R. A., & Ruiz, N. T. (1993). Bilingual pupils and special education: A reconceptualization. In R. C. Eaves & P. J. McLaughlin (Eds.), *Recent advances in special education and rehabilitation* (pp. 73–87). Boston: Andover Medical Publishers.

Feistritzer, C. E. (1987). Schools learn a lesson. *American Demographics, 9*(11), 42–43.

Fuchs, D., & Fuchs, L. S. (1995). What's "special" about special education? *Phi Delta Kappan, 76,* 522–530.

Giroux, H. A. (1994). Educational reform and the politics of teacher empowerment. In J. Kretovics & E. J. Nussel (Eds.), *Transforming Urban Education* (pp. 396–410). Boston: Allyn & Bacon.

Grant, L. (1984). Black females' "place" in desegregated classrooms. *Sociology of Education, 57,* 98–110.

Groce, N. E., & Zola, I. K. (1993). Multiculturalism, chronic illness, and disability. *Pediatrics, 91,* 1048–1055.

Grossman, H. (1995). *Special education in a diverse society*. Boston: Allyn & Bacon.

Guilmet, G. M. (1979). Instructor reaction to verbal and nonverbal styles: An example of Navajo and Caucasian children. *Anthropology and Education Quarterly, 10,* 254–266.

Harry, B. (1992). Making sense of disability: Low-income, Puerto Rican parents' theories of the problem. *Exceptional Children, 59*(1), 27–40.

King, S. H. (1993). The limited presence of African-American teachers. *Review of Educational Research, 63,* 115–150.

King-Sears, M. E., Rosenberg, M. S., Ray, R. M., & Fagen, S. A. (1992). A partnership to alleviate special education teacher shortages: University and public school collaboration. *Teacher Education and Special Education, 15,* 9–17.

Kozol, J. (1991). *Savage inequalities.* New York: Crown.

Larry P. v. Riles, 343 F. Supp. 1306 (N. D. Cal. 1972) (preliminary injunction). Aff'd 502 Γ. 2d 963 (9th Cir. 1974); 495 F. Supp. 926 (N. D. Cal. 1979) (decision on merits). Aff'd (9th Cir. No. 80-427 Jan. 23, 1984).

Matute-Bianchi, M. E. (1986). Ethnic identities and patterns of school success and failure among Mexican-descent and Japanese-American students in a California high school: An ethnographic analysis. *American Journal of Education, 95,* 233–255.

Meier, K. J., Stewart, J. Jr., & England, R. E. (1989). *Race, class, and education: The politics of second-generation discrimination.* Madison: University of Wisconsin Press.

Natriello, G., McDill, E. L., & Pallas, A. M. (1990). *Schooling disadvantaged children: Racing against catastrophe.* New York: Teachers College Press.

Ogbu, J. U. (1978). *Minority education and caste.* New York: Academic Press.

Orum, L. S. (1986). *The education of Hispanics: Status and implications.* Washington, DC: National Council of La Raza. (ERIC Document Reproduction Service No. ED 274 753).

Reschly, D. J. (1988). Minority MMR overrepresentation and special education reform. *Exceptional Children, 54,* 316–323.

Rist, M. C. (1990). The shadow children. *American School Board Journal, 177,* 19–24.

Ross, S. I., & Jackson, J. M. (1991). Teachers' expectations for black males' and black females' academic achievement. *Personality and Social Psychology Bulletin, 17,* 78–82.

Rueda, R. (1989). Defining mild disabilities with language-minority students. *Exceptional Children, 56,* 121–128.

Sigmon, S. B. (1990). Conclusion: A critique of special education's major problems with suggested solutions. In S. B. Sigmon (Ed.), *Critical voices on special education* (pp. 183–192). Albany: State University of New York Press.

Simpson, A. W., & Erickson, M. T. (1983). Teachers' verbal and nonverbal communication patterns as a function of teacher race, student gender, and student race. *American Educational Research Journal, 20,* 183–198.

Sontag, J. C., & Schacht, R. (1994). An ethnic comparison of parent participation and information needs in early intervention. *Exceptional Children, 60,* 422–433.

U. S. Department of Education, National Center for Educational Statistics. (1994). *The condition of education, 1994.* Washington, DC: Author.

Vasquez, J. A. (1994). Contexts of learning for minority students. In J. Kretovics & E. J. Nussel (Eds.), *Transforming Urban Education* (pp. 291–300). Boston: Allyn & Bacon.

Villegas, A. M. (1994). School failure and cultural mismatch: Another view. In J. Kretovics & E. J. Nussel (Eds.), *Transforming Urban Education* (pp. 347–359). Boston: Allyn & Bacon.

Williams, B. F. (1990). The challenge of education to social work: The case for minority children. *Social Work, 35,* 236–242.

Williams, B. F. (1992). Changing demographics: Challenges for educators. *Intervention in School and Clinic, 27,* 157–163.

3

Educational Placements and Administrative Systems

INTRODUCTION

Within the field of special education, there has been a series of changes to the delivery of services since the 1950s and 1960s. This evolution has included the expansion, the elimination, and the alteration of options for students with disabilities and their families. Segregated centers and categorical self-contained classes, which were commonly the only available choices in the 1950s and 1960s, are used far less often in the 1990s (Putnam, Spiegel, & Bruininks, 1995). Pull-out resource programs became common in the 1970s as enrollments mushroomed and self-contained classes could not accommodate the need. The proliferation of services through the 1970s occurred as special educators expanded their vision of who could benefit from their services and some general educators realized how they could remove poor learners and students with unruly behavior from their classes. MacMillan and Hendrick (1993) noted that "since the inception of special classes, teacher judgment has always preceded assessment, regardless of whether that assessment included mental tests" (p. 39). The stay-put resource model, consultant models, and inclusive placements for students with severe disabilities were added to the mix in the 1980s and 1990s.

Structural changes such as these occur as a result of both litigation and political persuasion. As delivery models fail to live up to the demands placed on them, the community becomes critical and seeks more appealing alternatives (Osborne & DiMattia, 1994). For example, the segregated special education day schools, often targets of due process hearings in the parents' pursuit of placements for their children in the least restrictive environment during the late 1980s, are no longer the prevalent, operating-at-capacity schools that they were in the late 1970s and early 1980s. For some special educators, the disfavor of these centers was puzzling, because they had often been strong advocates for students with disabilities when it seemed no one else cared. The greatest arguments in favor of the center-based approach included the notion that comprehensive services could be delivered efficiently to large numbers of students and that students could have a school in which they were the leaders, had their own athletic teams, attended the prom without ridicule, and so forth. For others, these schools were perceived as archaic facilities, used in a blatantly discriminatory and exclusionary fashion to keep students with disabilities out of neighborhood schools and away from "normal" children. For them, the contention that children with disabilities should be clustered together so they could be with others like themselves, happy in this protection from mainstream society and satisfied with the comprehensive nature of services provided, was an example of those with power attempting to convince those without power that center-based programs were in their best interests.

Calls for Reform

The current reformation of both special and general education services is resulting from two key movements—the regular education initiative and school restructuring. In spite of its name, the regular education initiative was begun and is best known in special education circles. On the other hand, awareness of and attention to school restructuring has been more prevalent in the general education arena and literature base. The regular education initiative has been closely linked to the concept of inclusion and, for some, the elimination of special education as a dual administrative structure within the educational environment. School restructuring relates back to the national cry for reform and improvements in public education and is closely linked to such concepts as outcomes-based education, accountability, school choice, and equity of opportunity. The government establishment of Goals 2000 and grant programs to reach these goals are examples of ongoing restructuring movement efforts.

School restructuring is typically traced back to the report *A Nation at Risk* (National Commission on Excellence in Education, 1983), which documented the plight of American education. Multiple reform calls were heard simultaneously and have resulted in the past several presidents (representing both major political parties) claiming the desire to be known as the "education president." The politicians, through appointments of various commissions and awarding of grants to conduct research on school reform, have joined with the education community in a partnership with business in the reform effort. All concur with the need for reform as works such as Kozol's (1991) *Savage Inequalities* decry the nation's educational inequities and newspapers consistently report about violence in the schools. However, financial pressures on state budgets have left little room to pump additional funds into an educational system that some would argue should be scrapped anyway. To continue funding the existing system is considered by some as pointless because the needed reform could be accomplished only by establishing a completely new system (Sarason, 1997).

As director of the Office of Special Education and Rehabilitation, Madeline Will (1986) spoke out in sharp criticism of the state of special education in her initial call for reform in *Educating Children with Learning Problems: A Shared Responsibility*. Will's monograph ushered in the move that came to be known as the regular education initiative (REI) and helped trigger a delivery system change that has taken on the name of inclusion. Exactly what inclusion incorporates that was not intended in the conception of mainstreaming is subject to one's vision of inclusion (McCoy, 1995). In Will's critique of the system, she made four critical points (Jenkins, Pious, & Jewell, 1990). The first issue had to do with the "hopelessly fragmented" categorical programs that were evident throughout the delivery system. The fragmentation was associated with both a loss of program effectiveness and an increased risk that children could fall through the cracks created by the categorical system. Second was the inefficiency of special and general education operating as dual systems. Special education programs for students with mild learning problems were largely pull-out models at the time, typically without adequate efforts being made to coordinate instruction with that of the classroom teacher. The delivery model itself served to undermine any sense of responsibility that general education teachers or administrators might have been willing to assume for the students with disabilities. The third point addressed the social segregation of students with disabilities and the resulting stigmatization and risk of related negative consequences, such as lowered self-esteem and the development of poor attitudes toward learning. Finally, the rigid eligibility requirements and placement options inevitably caused conflicts between parents and school personnel about placements and labels used to describe children. These issues took aim at the bureaucratic mire that Will felt was surrounding special education. Most in the field agreed that change was needed; however, not all have agreed on the direction that Will's initiatives have taken the field.

The established system of special education currently serves over 5.3 million children and follows a wide array of federal and state rules and regulations (U.S. Department of Education, 1995). As special education has grown, general educators have reacted with mixed feelings—grateful for the relief and help available, envious of the funds flowing into special education and the apparent small class sizes, confused when the system refuses to provide support for ineligible students whom they see as needing the help, and, in some instances, resentful of the demands the special education community places on them through mainstreaming and inclusion. Additionally, special educators have shifted from fighting to achieve the basic right to a free public education for students with disabilities to focusing on the quality and effectiveness of that now well-established right. Looking to the outcomes of our efforts, such as dropout rates, illiteracy rates of adults, and employment of special education graduates, special educators have had to acknowledge the critical need for improvement and revision of our efforts (U.S. Department of Education, 1995). Will (1986) noted in her original call for the regular education initiative that the system had created many unintended obstacles to learning. Thus, she was stating that in some respects the existence of special education was actually making things more difficult for some children and their teachers.

Special education programs today place substantial financial burdens on state and local school districts. The federal government has never exceeded contributing more than 12% of additional costs of the mandatory special education programs in spite of authorization to go as high as 40% of additional costs to implement them (U.S. Department of Education, 1995). However, definite economic incentives to place children in special classes existed in some states prior to the passage of the Individuals with Disabilities Education Act (IDEA). For example, MacMillan and Hendrick (1993) noted that during 1963–1964 California provided an extra $356.62 for each student with mild retardation and $637.16 for each student with severe retardation. In addition, although not mandatory, a program that provided excess costs to children identified as "educationally handicapped" was adopted by 77% of California school districts. By 1980, special education was well into its tremendous growth period. The relationship between this growth and the increased monetary allotment available per pupil is merely speculative but thought provoking, nonetheless.

Defining what the least restrictive environment (LRE) is or should be has produced an ongoing debate since the passage of IDEA. The critical concept that creates the debate is what is considered to be *appropriate* for a child or groups of children who share the same disability. Are students who are deaf or severely hearing impaired more or less restricted in a residential school? Can students with severe emotional disorders remain in mainstream settings, make any progress toward improving their mental health, and allow other pupils the opportunity to learn? What are the rights of students with disabilities in view of the disproportionate time and energy that one student may require from the teacher in contrast to the needs of other students? What is the impact of inclusion on the curriculum? Are general education teachers adequately trained and supported when assigned to teach students with a wide array of disabilities?

The standard for defining appropriateness of educational services has been addressed by the courts (Osborne, 1992), establishing that "appropriate" is not equivalent to "best" but is something more than just providing access. In fact, the first IDEA-related court case to make it all the way to the Supreme Court dealt with this very issue. The Supreme Court, in *Board of Education of Hendrick Hudson Central School District v. Rowley* (1982), did not support the claim that the child, who was deaf, was entitled to a free sign language interpreter. The basis for the decision was that the student, who was in a mainstreamed setting, was already performing above average and, therefore, was having her educational needs met. Disabilities advocates were disappointed with the outcome, but others pointed out that the Court had established the fact that children with disabilities were entitled to an educational program from which they are able to benefit, not just access to the educational system. Even states that require special education to achieve the "maximum potential" of students with disabilities are not expected to provide the "best" education possible (Osborne, 1992). This "benefit" concept has been further refined to "meaningful educational benefit," not simply trivial educational advancement (Osborne, 1992). Another case, *Board of Education of East Windsor Regional School District v. Diamond* (1986), involved a challenge to the trivial progress a student had made in contrast to his measured intelligence. The Third Circuit Court of Appeals ruled that an appropriate IEP must entail a plan that would likely provide educational benefit, not simply minimal progress.

There are differing concerns as the concepts of the REI are applied to students with mild disabilities in contrast to those with severe disabilities. Additionally, the REI movement has been occurring concurrently with increased separation of students who are considered gifted and talented into magnet schools and other alternative opportunities. Thus, the impact of the inclusion and other special education reform efforts linked to the REI on the general classroom teacher and the students in her classes can be understood only by considering many perspectives and influences on the educational system today. The heat of the debates regarding the best future directions for special education is intense. For example, at the 1994 Council for Exceptional Children (CEC) convention a small group of demonstrators, including persons with and without disabilities, picketed and protested CEC's adoption of a policy supporting a continuum of services instead of full inclusion (CEC Delegate Assembly, 1993). They proclaimed that anything less than full inclusion for all persons with disabilities was oppressive. The protesters even urged convention attendees to drop their CEC affiliation and join a different professional organization that was advocating full inclusion. However, many members of the deaf community stridently argue the importance of their culture and identity separate and apart from the hearing world and consider efforts to mainstream children with hearing impairments as oppressive. Published debates, such as those of Taylor (1995), Fuchs and Fuchs (1995a), or O'Neil (1995), reveal the strength of feelings associated with these issues. There are extreme sides to these debates; therefore, how clearly the views of either extreme can be articulated by the other must be questioned as we study the works of both camps as well as those claiming to hold a balanced view.

Purposes of Education

Placement decisions force our consideration of questions about the purposes of education. Our legislation addresses the right of every child to have the opportunity to achieve his potential. Over the years the courts and legislatures have consistently agreed to a broadened definition of *education* so as to include all children, regardless of the level of their abilities (e.g., *Pennsylvania Association for Retarded Citizens,* 1971). Yet issues remain regarding what least restrictive environment placements are, varying across disabilities and levels of functioning. Do we hope to bring children to their full potential academically, socially, physically, morally? When making placement decisions for children with disabilities, parents and professionals alike may find conflicts in these areas, forcing the diminishment of one for another. For example, what may be the placement of choice for social inclusion may, in fact, not be the most effective placement for content-related instruction (e.g., *Bonadonna v. Cooperman,* 1985). Inclusion might prove a worthy experience for a child with severe disabilities but offer little in the way of appropriate curriculum and development of life skills.

The commentary of Paul Greenberg (1990, April 22, as cited by Halpern, 1992) presents a scathing critique of educators' proclivity to fads and bandwagons that is particularly relevant to the integration of students of varying abilities into groups for instructional purposes:

> The latest fad in Educanto is to eliminate "tracking," the grouping of students by ability. Such an approach might make sense to simple laymen like you and me, but the educationists have just about decided that it's ineffective—not to say elitist, racist, fascist and possibly even old-fashioned. Can any more serious indictment be imagined?…The newest approach is to throw kids together regardless of ability or knowledge; it is assumed that the superior knowledge and skills of the sharpest will rub off on the rest. Uh-huh. This is the kind of assumption that would make Pollyanna look like a hard-bitten cynic. (p. 3C)

Greenberg's caustic editorial seems to come to life in Lovitt's (1993) call to return to something akin to the one-room schoolhouse as a progressive move. He argues that, given the many negative outcomes associated with grouping and tracking, it would be appropriate to end the pattern. Although acknowledging that there were "some grim tales about education in those austere situations" (p. 67), with some critical adjustments he considers the model to hold possibilities. Accordingly, he describes a plan based on the creation of many small elementary schools located near homes and/or parental workplaces. Classrooms of ten to fifteen heterogeneous children would be mixed across all ages and ability levels in his scenario. Are these plausible suggestions worthy of thought or another educator looking to solve the wrong problems in the wrong ways, further jeopardizing an already compromised school system?

With the authority of President Bush in 1990, a series of national educational goals known as Goals 2000 was established (National Educational Goals Panel, 1991). The goals have been expanded and edited since then. The current version of the goals reflects a commitment to have *all* children achieve standards and to increase graduation rates and group performance on achievement tests (National Educational Goals Panel, 1995).

There are now objectives and data collection procedures associated with each goal, with core indicators intended to document progress toward the goals. For example, the core indicators for the goal that all children will start school ready to learn are (a) reduction of the percentage of infants born with one or more health risks,[1] (b) increase in the percentage of two-year-olds who have been fully immunized against preventable childhood diseases, (c) increase in the percentage

---

1. Risks are late (in third trimester) or no prenatal care, low maternal weight gain (less than twenty-one pounds), mother smoked during pregnancy, or mother drank alcohol during pregnancy.

of parents of three- to five-year-olds who read to or tell their children stories regularly, and (d) reduction of the gap between preschool participation of high- and low-income families. These indicators are not unrelated to the goal, but they fall far short of providing a comprehensive means of measuring our achievement of the goal for "all" children.

The appropriateness of the inclusion of some of these goals that speak to the achievement of specific academic standards by *all* children must be questioned by special educators, parents of children with disabilities, and persons with disabilities themselves. The fact that there are goals which cannot be achieved by "all" students certainly forces the special educator to question exactly how much students with disabilities have even been thought of by the creators of the goals. Will students with disabilities be included when the test scores to determine progress toward these goals are compiled? Hocutt, Martin, and McKinney (1990) make the point clearly: "The silence about the needs of, or outcomes for, handicapped children in the current reform movement is deafening" (p. 24). Kauffman and Hallahan (1993) have also challenged the meaning of these goals for special education populations, noting that the use of "all" seems to indicate a lack of awareness of the full range of children's abilities, "with the implicit assumption that *all* means, in actuality, 'most' or 'a somewhat greater percentage'" (p. 76). The question of what content children are supposed to be ready to learn when starting school will vary for those with severe cognitive disabilities, children of average and above-average intelligence, and those with unusually high intellectual abilities. Without consideration of this and similar questions, Kauffman and Hallahan "see *all* in most of the goal statements of education reform as implicitly excluding many exceptional children" (p. 76).

Concurrent with the development of national educational goals, various professional organizations have been seeking to establish national subject matter standards. The National Council of Teachers of Mathematics (NCTM) has been at the forefront of this trend in the development of both process and content standards, including the following: "that students (1) learn to value mathematics; (2) become confident in their ability to do mathematics; (3) become mathematical problem solvers; (4) learn to communicate mathematically; and (5) learn to reason mathematically" (NCTM, as cited in Ysseldyke, Thurlow, & Shriner, 1992, p. 40).

Whether the intention is to exclude or include them from the target group expected to achieve the standards, the implications of such national standards for students with learning problems are disturbing (Hanley, 1994). If a structure is in place that is designed to recognize and possibly even provide financial rewards or other incentives to the schools, districts, or states making the most progress toward these goals, teachers and administrators will be motivated to exclude special education students either from their classrooms or from the outcomes-based measures of evaluation. If they have been included in general education through an inclusion model but are exempt from accountability standards, the teacher has a disincentive to spend her time working with these students. On the other hand, if the students are included in outcomes-based assessment, teachers, because their ability to teach will be evaluated based on the performance of their students and made public, may be much more reluctant to welcome them into mainstream settings. The fact that some of the students were placed there for inclusionary purposes and that it was never intended that they would follow the same curriculum may not be included in the test-score reports.

The quality of any and all reform and restructuring rests finally in the hands of the individuals at a building level who will actually implement policies. Building-level personnel need an understanding and commitment to outcomes-based models of education, inclusion, or any other reform effort coupled with appropriate training and technical support before such models can be adequately judged. Poor implementation of any model will not offer any meaningful critique, but will inevitably lead to its failure. For example, recycling a child through the same material repeatedly with no adjustments to the instructional style or content because an identified outcome has not yet been obtained is not outcomes-based education. A tolerance for variability in individual abilities and speed of mastery should benefit all children, not just those served through the special education conglomerate. The shift to outcomes-based education could allow for the "success for all," as we are freed from the bell curve, quotas, and nine-month blocks of time for all to learn the same material (Spady, 1992). However, the claim that something is going to work for "all" immediately raises the question as to who is really included in "all" or the extent to which it could possibly satisfy individual needs of children.

Special education is founded on the notion of individual needs, as stipulated in individualized educational plans. Yet even when special educators have joined the reform movement, there have been claims made that programs can address the needs of "all." Kauffman and Hallahan (1993) suggest that one education reform program put forth as an alternative to special education, Success for All, might better be titled "Higher Achievement for Most." The following passage from an article summarizing research associated with the Success for All program reveals the exclusion its authors did intend for the group of "every" child: "The Success for All program is built on the assumption that every child can read. We mean this not as wishful thinking or as a philosophical statement, but as a practical, attainable reality. In particular, every child without organic retardation can learn to read" (p. 43). Exactly who is excluded from the group "every child" by virtue of having "organic retardation"? Would other disabilities preclude membership as well? The choice of phrasing and use of the word *every* when a group of children with disabilities is indeed excluded seems to negate their existence. The special education program Adaptive Learning Environments Model (ALEM) is another program that Kauffman and Hallahan (1993) cite as claiming to be suitable for all types of students when, they contend, such has not been demonstrated. The use of the word *all* throughout the reform literature may hold a worse implication than would be the case if standards and goals were described as specifically written for children functioning within some minimum range. At least such language would indicate that the authors know other children existed for whom balancing a checkbook or walking a balance beam would never be a necessity or a reality.

Focus of Discussion

The remainder of the chapter sharpens the debates about inclusion and the proposed elimination of special education as a separate administrative structure. To debate this as an all-or-none issue would be considered appropriate by those who have gone beyond "full inclusion" and are now calling for "uncompromised inclusion." Others would see such a starting point for discussion as having already abandoned neutrality (see Fuchs & Fuchs, 1994). It is far beyond the scope of this chapter to thoroughly investigate all the nuances of inclusion, but attempts to offer some reasonable coverage of the key points of contention are made. No single group's platform (e.g., the Deaf culture) is fully defined, but an attempt has been made to cite the primary perspectives throughout. The second issue discussed in the chapter is the elimination of the perceived dual educational systems. Whether dual systems even exist and, if so, whether that process should occur as an equal merger, a takeover (hostile or friendly), or in some other fashion is in debate.

INCLUSION AND SPECIAL EDUCATION

The research documenting the poor progress of students served by segregated pull-out programs has been coupled with the socially and politically correct stance in support of inclusion of all. The belief held by the group now referred to in the field as "full inclusionists," or "radical inclusionists" by some, and uncompromising inclusionists by themselves (Fuchs & Fuchs, 1995b) is that the lack of success for students served through pull-out programs is directly related to placement, not just curriculum or quality and quantity of instruction issues. Jenkins et al. (1994) describe this "values-based" argument for inclusion as one not dependent on empirical data, but one that contends that any kind of separate education is inherently unequal. Fuchs & Fuchs (1995b) note that some have even stated that segregated special education is "the moral equivalent of apartheid and even slavery" (p. 523).

The first point to clarify in a discussion of inclusion is who is to be included. In the introductory section of this chapter, the misuses of the words *all* and *every* were discussed, particularly when it was obvious that at least some groups of children with disabilities were not meant to be included or their existence was simply forgotten when authors used these terms. Thus, to argue that inclusion is and must be for "all" would seem dangerous from the outset. Although it might be sociologically appealing as an inducement to reduce the seeming invisibleness of students with disabilities, it would inevitably start requiring exceptions. For some children, their disabilities put them at high risk for illness or involve serious medical conditions, requiring restrictions of movement. It should be noted that children who are too ill to attend school, whether or not they have disabilities, temporarily refrain from attending class until it is appropriate and safe to return. We all must follow public health regulations and show consideration of others as medical conditions necessitate our temporary separation from the group. Illness does not take from the child her belonging to the group of "all" but may temporarily (or in some cases, such as terminal cancer, permanently) require her to avoid the group for her own sake or for the sake of others. Parents of children whose lives are complicated by illness or medical conditions associated with disabilities may choose to remove their children from mainstream settings accordingly. Such educational placement decisions, whether temporary or permanent, need not be based on a child's disability but rather on medical concerns and public health standards in combination with the personal preferences of the persons involved. The notion that virtually all but the most fragile children belong in the general educational system, regardless of the severity of their disabilities, is a fairly radical stance, but it is one that is advocated quite persistently by some disabilities activists and professional groups (Lipsky & Gartner, 1989, 1990; Stainback & Stainback, 1992).

The appropriateness and wisdom of including children who have chronic significant behavioral difficulties in the inclusion movement has been questioned (Kauffman, Lloyd, Baker, & Riedel, 1995); even its suitability has been questioned for children with mild learning disabilities (Gerber, 1995; Learning Disabilities Association, 1993; Martin, 1995; National Joint Committee on Learning Disabilities, 1993), children with hearing impairments (Commission on the Education of the Deaf, 1988), and for other constituency groups. For the group calling for uncompromised inclusion, such chipping away of the population of "all" may be troubling, but it is a stance with which other more moderate supporters of inclusion are more comfortable (Fuchs & Fuchs, 1994). Since the following discussion is intended to cover the issues of the debate without preferential treatment of any position, no group or category of disability will be arbitrarily dismissed from the discussion. Throughout the remainder of this section, *all* will be used as associated with referenced material, or as the absolute maximum group of students for whom it would be *feasible,* giving consideration to medical and behavioral conditions that might preclude participation in general educational settings. The issue as to for whom inclusion is *appropriate* and to what extent other alternative services should even be available is the heart of the controversy, and the arbitrary elimination of any other groups (regardless of that group's preferences) would prematurely end the debate. The nuances of defining for whom it is feasible (e.g., dying AIDS patients, teens convicted of violent crimes) are acknowledged and accepted as necessary subjective limitations to the clarity of the discussion.

The goal of inclusion is to establish an educational community that allows children to come together in a mutually supportive environment to share in their work and learning experiences. The goal is not the negation and elimination of individual differences (Stainback, Stainback, East, & Sapon-Shevin, 1994) or the restriction of opportunity for students with high cognitive abilities. Stainback, Stainback, East, & Sapon-Shevin describe the intent of inclusion as creating "a world in which all people are knowledgeable about and supportive of all other people" (p. 487). Such a goal is not reached, they remind us, through the creation of a false image of homogeneity. The use of the word *all* by these authors excludes none but does not mean that all are expected to become alike. Zigmond and Baker (1995) offer a comparable goal of inclusion "to provide an accommodating, personalized education for *all* students, including those with LD, within the context of a general education classroom" (p. 110). However, the question remains of the extent to which "all" students' needs can most suitably be addressed in general education classes.

Substantial theoretical and political material has been published, but the research on inclusion models for students with mild disabilities is just emerging and is highly dependent on the nature of the inclusion programs in use within the research settings (e.g., Zigmond, 1995). Anecdotal reports, narratives, and case studies are the prevalent style to date, as opposed to the empirical studies popular in the earlier efficacy studies. Some appear to confirm the fears that children with severe disabilities in regular classes will demand time that diminishes the instructional opportunities for others in the class, and that students with mild learning problems will have very poor academic achievement because of the inadequate supports available (Baines, Baines, & Masterson, 1994). On the other hand, Barry (1994) writes of very positive outcomes through inclusionary models of collaborative teaching, and others have documented successful experiences as well (Logan et al., 1994). The following sections focus separately on the inclusion issues for students with mild disabilities and those who have severe disabilities. There are both supporters and resisters in each group, but the curricular and instructional needs of these two groups vary substantially, necessitating separate discussions.

Mild Disabilities

Inclusion for students who have mild learning disabilities or physical and sensory impairments that do not effect cognitive abilities is partially grounded on the assumption that their curriculum will be similar to that of the other students. Instructional approaches, speed of work, types of assessment, and possibly expected levels of performance might need to be altered, but the basic content would not require significant adjustments. At the secondary level, in particular, students who receive credits for classes are expected to have learned the content of those classes, not just to have been present during instruction. The idea that students with mild disabilities should remain in the general educational program, with appropriate support services, is consistent with the principle of least restrictive environment and, theoretically, can be accomplished at less cost than segregated programs. However, the nature of appropriate support services is not something on which there is universal agreement. Proponents of self-contained classes, pull-out resource programs, stay-put resource programs, consultant models, and collaborative teaching approaches all claim to have desirable models. But advocacy for one model is sometimes coupled with the rejection of others. For example, in the case of full inclusionists, the only suitable placement for students with disabilities is the regular class (Lipsky & Gartner, 1989). Others contend that the instructional needs of children with learning disabilities may be incompatible with general education classroom environments (Fuchs & Fuchs, 1994).

Research is available investigating the ecological patterns of the varying delivery systems for children with learning disabilities (e.g., Carlberg & Kavale, 1980; Madden & Slavin, 1983; Zigmond, 1995). Often the critical variable in this research, *engaged time,* has proven to be a highly consistent variable in effective teaching and student learning in general education (Brophy & Good, 1986; Wittrock, 1986). Every day, teachers must decide how much attention to give to each child and how much instructional time to allot to components of the curriculum. These decisions ultimately result in the determination of the amount of engaged time for students in the class and relate not only to the amount of time on task but also to allocated time and instructional appropriateness for the individual child. If it were found, for instance, that engaged time for students with learning disabilities were higher in one setting over another, we could predict associated higher academic gains. Additionally, if there were evidence that the inclusion of students with disabilities reduced the engaged time of nondisabled students in the classroom, such findings would be problematic. In summarizing a series of research studies on classroom environments, Bulgren and Carta (1993) note that while there are some differences in classroom structure between special education and general education settings, differences in time allotments for subjects and instructional tasks are very few across the two settings.

Additional research that Bulgren and Carta (1993) reviewed focused on the quality of interactions between teachers and students with learning disabilities. Consistent qualitative differences were revealed in teacher interactions between students with learning disabilities and their peers, characterized by fewer academic interactions and a greater frequency of interactions related to behaviors. Alves and Gottlieb (1986) speculated that one possible explanation of the lack of academic interaction could be that the teachers' understanding of the primary purpose of the child's placement was related to socialization and emotional adjustment; therefore, the teacher felt less responsibility toward the teaching of content to these children than to their classmates. The teachers' behavior might also be explained by the possibility that they held beliefs that the children with learning disabilities had inherent limitations of ability, diminishing their expectations. In reference to a series of studies by Slate and Saudargas, Bulgren and Carta (1993) point out that the behavior in which students who have disabilities are engaged triggers differential responses from the teachers, revealing a pattern of leaving the students alone when they were working on schoolwork but interacting with them when they became engaged in other types of behavior. The greatest likelihood of teacher interaction came when the students with learning disabilities were off task, either out of their seats or interacting with other children.

The research findings related to delivery systems for students with mild disabilities have offered a rich variety of contradictions for many years. Carlberg and Kavale (1980) conducted a meta-analysis of the research on the effectiveness of various delivery systems and found that special class placement was significantly inferior to regular class placement for students with below-average IQs, but special classes were significantly superior to regular classes for children with behavioral disorders, emotional disturbance, and learning disabilities. Rich and Ross (1989) reported that children spent greater amounts of engaged time in resource rooms than in regular classes, special classes, or special schools. The research on inclusion will necessarily have to take on new designs, for program models differ, teacher roles and selection processes vary, and limited or comprehensive inclusion may be occurring within a building or school system. As Baker and Zigmond (1995) note in a summary of five case studies, special education no longer has the same meanings, such as a unique curriculum, careful monitoring of student progress, data-based instruction, or individual advocacy. The changes might offer the field the opportunity to move forward with a redefined mission and structure (McLaughlin, 1995), present the fertile ground for visionary transitions of teacher education (Sindelar, 1995), or verify that the needs of children with learning disabilities cannot be met if the distinct roles of special education specialists fade into general teaching and remediation (Gerber, 1995; Martin, 1995).

Severe Disabilities

Students who have severe disabilities may in some ways find the road to inclusion and peer interaction smoother than those with mild learning and motor problems. Students who clearly have an alternative curriculum and set of educational outcomes, whose performance the teacher will not be held accountable for on academic achievement tests, might be accepted by the teacher and peers more readily than those children who are expected to follow the basic academic curriculum and behavioral standards. The aims of inclusion for students with severe disabilities are to achieve peer interactions, improve socialization and behavior of the student, offer the maximum possible stimulation and motivation, and give the age peers an opportunity to interact with and be comfortable around persons with disabilities. The focus is not on striving for the student to compete at age or grade level academically, as may be the case for students with milder learning problems.

Inclusion of children with severe disabilities has been primarily a philosophical debate, with one of the issues being the rights and protections of other children in the classroom. Speculation as to the possible humanitarian benefits and/or academic harms that might come to the nondisabled peers has been a part of the discussion. Hollowood, Salisbury, Rainforth, and Palombaro (1994) decided to shift from the speculative debates and gather data regarding the instructional time in classrooms that include students with severe disabilities in comparison to those that do not include any such children. The amounts of allocated time, used and engaged time, and lost time were monitored for three groups of children (those with severe disabilities, nondisabled peers in classes with children with severe disabilities, and nondisabled peers in classes without children with severe disabilities). Allocated time was comparable for the two nondisabled groups, but was approximately 10% greater for the group with disabilities. Engaged time percentages of all three groups were comparable, with the greatest differential being only 3%. Incidents of lost time were recorded and classified by cause of the disruption to determine the effects of the presence of students with severe disabilities. Hollowood et al. found no differences in the sources or duration of lost time between the two settings. The greatest causes of lost time were administrative interferences, transitions, and disruptions from other students. The authors noted that classmates typically continued with their work when students with severe

Proper equipment and assistance helps this boy tackle his assignment in the regular classroom.

disabilities would vocalize loudly or behave in other potentially distracting ways. Cole and Meyer (1991) have also produced comparative research that indicates that inclusive settings better produce both social and learning outcomes for students with severe disabilities. Baines et al. (1994), however, found that the inclusion of students with severe disabilities detracted from the age peers' opportunities to learn; left less time for instructional supports for students with milder disabilities; and, in spite of efforts on the part of the school staff, left parents dissatisfied and continuing to pursue legal remedies. There are obvious contradictions within our professional literature base as we begin the shift from philosophical and political debates to research and practical experience with the inclusion models.

Decision Point 3.1: Inclusionary
Practices for Students with Disabilities

Arguments for Proposition One Students with disabilities have difficulties in regular educational settings and need the benefit of teachers with specialized skills, educational environments free from distractions, and maximum opportunities for individualized attention. The full inclusion proponent who shifts the burden of responsibility to general classroom teachers to take any and all students regardless of their school coping skills or level of academic knowledge has little concern for these needs. Likewise, the administrator who makes a building- or system-level decision to serve all students with mild disabilities through full inclusion would have no need for an individualized decision-making approach that takes into consideration individual environmental needs. Economics can be persuasive when administrators have to find the cheapest approach to the implementation of underfunded federally mandated educational programs, yet the heart of special education is found in individualization.

Proposition One

A continuum of services must be offered to every child with an aim toward maximum desirable inclusion in general education programs. This continuum must include the entire array of placement options, from residential facilities to indirect consulting services.

There are three lines of reasoning popular with full inclusionists that fail to stand up to the most basic analysis (Smelter, Rasch, & Yudewitz, 1994). First is the notion that all children learn best in the regular classroom. Were this the case, the need to remove children from regular classroom settings would never have materialized. The second line of reasoning is that the goal of social equity should take precedence over how much children learn. The slippery slope of this belief would lead us to the understanding that lower achievement standards for students with learning disabilities are acceptable as long as these students are making friends and are accepted by their peers. The final argument is that pull-out programs are a violation of civil rights for students who must have access to the least restrictive environment. This final argument politicizes the issue rather than allowing it to remain a sound, individual educational decision. The move has created a curious mismatch of ultraconservatives and ultraliberals in the same camp, with conservatives resenting the special privileges of a few and the liberals demanding that the children needing special education be returned to regular classes in which all of their special education needs be met through accommodation and weakening of the curriculum.

One of the biggest issues of concern to the individual children who make up the rank and file of special education rosters is the selection of an educational placement suited particularly for them. When wholesale decisions are made that limit options for all students, the rights of the remainder are restricted. Placement decisions cannot be made individually, thoughtfully, and with consideration to family concerns and priorities if every placement is identical. Kauffman and Hallahan (1993) stress the importance of maintaining choices. Limiting placement choices to the mainstream is just as restrictive as limiting special education services to segregated settings was. The overenthusiasm with which some are pushing full or uncompromised inclusion may prove as destructive as the overenthusiasm for the institution seen earlier in this century. The conceptualization of inclusion must take on a broader vision than simply that "all individuals occupy a common space, regardless of whether that space has the features appropriate for their needs" (Kauffman et al., 1995, p. 545). A more suitable definition would allow for a variety of placements to match everyone's needs. As Gerber (1995) notes, "Special education was the beginning of inclusion, not exclusion, and it has always had the same goal" (p. 184).

Mild Disabilities The ability of mainstream classroom teachers to address the many demands on them and offer the most appropriate instructional interventions for students with learning disabilities is questionable. The Learning Disabilities Association, based on the experiences of its membership, has expressed concerns, and does not accept "the assumption that regular education teachers in traditionally-organized schools can improve overall class performance while at the same time meeting the special needs of students with learning problems" (Gallagher, 1993, p. 24). The political and philosophical zeal is being challenged by the initial research reports, since there are indicators that for the student with mild disabilities, inclusion is proving to be the disaster many feared it would be (Martin, 1995). In a series of case studies on inclusion conducted by Zigmond and Baker, the special education provided was "bland, and uninspired, relying on a weak form of team teaching and without regard to any long-term goal of correction or compensation for learning deficiencies" (Gerber, 1995, p. 182). The participating teachers had experience and excellent teaching records as special educators, yet they could not put in place their specialized skills within the context of inclusion.

Every classroom teacher must achieve a balance between the stressors placed on available resources (e.g., parental expectations, administrator priorities and policies, curricular requirements, learner outcomes assessments) to deliver a suitable instructional program. One critical variable is classroom tolerance, which is the informal, unspoken establishment of a modal group of students who are expected to perform within a normative range and for whom instructional arrangements are primarily designed (Gerber, 1995). Teachers define this range from their cumulative observations of students in a variety of instructional arrangements.

If teachers are to accommodate students who are not within their tolerance range, they must have access to additional instructional resources or are likely to develop other, less desirable coping strategies (e.g., removing involved children from the class, excusing students from particular instructional assignments). However, the inclusion model is so overtaxing the existing special education resources that the regular classroom teachers seeking help for students outside of the tolerance range are no longer finding the instructional resources that have previously enabled them to maintain children with learning disabilities in their classes. Baker and Zigmond (1995) describe the problem as evidenced by the changing role of the special educators in their case studies. They found a concern shifting away from the individual toward the smooth progression of the mainstream class, including "the progress of the reading group, the organization and management of cooperative learning groups or peer tutoring" (p. 171).

General education teachers have been persuaded over the past twenty-five years that they lack the specialized training necessary to be effective with students who have disabilities. The special education field has based its practice on the contention that it offers a qualitatively different educational experience characterized by intense, highly individualized, data-based prescriptive instruction. However, in an inclusive educational model, the special educator must assume many other roles besides that of specialized instructional interventionist for individual children. She may have to take on the role of providing instruction to large groups of primarily nondisabled students, avoid specialized instruction that would single out a particular child, and act as a "guest" in another teacher's room, subordinate to the teacher, becoming merely another pair of hands similar to a paraprofessional rather than a decision-making teacher (Baker & Zigmond, 1995). When special educators did suggest instructional adaptations in the case studies, they seemed to do so in a stereotypic manner rather than on an individual basis. The entire class would get an instructional approach that might be considered generally helpful to many students with learning disabilities rather than individual children receiving interventions specifically designed for them. The specialized, unique contribution of special educators appears to be at risk of getting lost as their efforts diminish over time while the inclusion movement robs them of their role.

The argument that inclusion is more economical is particularly disturbing. Baker and Zigmond (1995) describe what they found in their case studies: "To economize, schools used peers, paras, and parents in instructional roles, the *least well trained* individuals to teach the *most difficult to teach*" (p. 177). If the supports needed by children with learning disabilities in the regular classroom can be provided by far cheaper persons than special educators, then logic tells us that the perceived need to continue hiring qualified special educators in the same numbers will lessen. The trend seems already apparent in the 31% drop in the numbers of universities having doctoral programs in special education between 1987 and 1992 (Fuchs & Fuchs, 1995b).

Classroom teachers show differential interaction patterns with students with learning disabilities—having lower academic standards for them, showing less tolerance for their misbehavior, and shifting their goals for mainstreamed students from academic to primarily social, based on their misunderstanding of the goals of a child's placement (Bulgren & Carta, 1993). The mainstream classroom has not been a placement in which these children thrived, or they never would have been identified in the first place. The logic of returning them to the scene of their troubles, taking their specialized teachers and making those teachers become more like the general educators who have been unable to find success for these children, is untenable.

The very fact that a child has been referred to special education is an indicator that the course of study and instructional approaches being used were not working. Special educators do not arbitrarily remove students from supportive "communities of learners" in which they have been progressing nicely to offer them isolated splinter skills and social confusion. Rather, for whatever reasons, these children have been unable to succeed in the regular curriculum, resulting in teachers seeking support and help. So traditional reasoning follows that after the whole curriculum, offered in large doses, has led to child failure, then streamlining, reducing, simplifying, and pruning out all but the essentials enables the child and his teachers to focus on a limited content, thereby raising the possibility of success. Evidence indicates that such modifications for students with disabilities are not routinely implemented in regular classroom settings (McIntosh, Vaughn, Schumm, Haagen, & Lee, 1993; Zigmond & Baker, 1994).

In a system that includes a continuum of services, students who need an outlet have the opportunity to escape the pressures and failures represented by the mainstream classroom setting. The resource room can serve as a haven for students who, by virtue of the fact that they have been placed in special education, have already "failed" or, at least, had serious difficulties in the regular educational program. The sociometric patterns of classrooms, even with an inclusion model that eliminates the labeling of children, still reflect the poor status of children with learning disabilities (Sale & Carey, 1996). For children with mild educational disabilities, the provision of adequate support services in a private, personal fashion, wherever is most suitable for the *individual* child, offers the best hope for success.

Severe Disabilities The largest group of students considered to have severe to profound disabilities is those with mental retardation. The cause of the retardation may range from genetic conditions to brain injury, and at this level the retardation is often accompanied by multiple disabilities. Children within our educational system who may be considered to have severe to profound disabilities include those who are medically fragile, some even attending school with Do Not Resuscitate instructions in their medical files, and those who are in comas resulting from brain injury. The demand for full or uncompromised inclusion of students with severe disabilities reflects an unwillingness on the part of their advocates to accept them as people with disabilities—different, and perhaps not finding the best possible educational opportunities in general classroom settings. Kauffman and Hallahan (1993) describe it as "a demeaning attitude toward those with disabilities" (p. 81). They further argue that the advocates of total integration have distorted in rationale and intent the normalization principle, upon which the inclusion movement is based. Used as the basis for wholesale mainstreaming and deinstitutionalization, the significance of the principle is diminishing, for it has been codified into a single rule that *requires* all students with disabilities to be educated in mainstream classrooms. It is unreasonable as well as unsafe to expect general educational programs to serve as the primary educational placement for all students with severe disabilities, some of whom are medically fragile and need a multitude of related services throughout the day. Classroom teachers cannot be responsible for the life-sustaining needs of some students, nor should they be expected to attend to their personal needs at the cost of instructional time for the class (Baines et al., 1994).

Students with severe behavioral disorders can be so disruptive and/or dangerous that no students would be safe or able to learn if they were present in a mainstream class. One student does not have the right to jeopardize the education of many others. General education teachers have not chosen to work with these students and may have extreme fears about and resistance to working with students with such severe disabilities. They need not be judged as immoral, uncaring, insensitive teachers who need to be sent away from the classroom because of their attitudes toward working with such students. Neither the curriculum nor the environment matches these students' cognitive or emotional functioning; therefore, the students require an unreasonable amount of planning and/or cause disruption to the classroom routine.

Since there are many educators today who advocate placement of all students, regardless of severity of disability, into regular education classes, curriculum and time allotments are relevant issues. These students will not find a basic life skills curriculum offered in the general education classroom, yet they are not expected

> **Proposition Two**
> All students (for whom it is medically and behaviorally feasible), regardless of the nature or severity of their disabilities, should be educated in general education classes located within neighborhood, age-appropriate schools. Necessary support services should be provided within the same settings.

to learn the curriculum that is offered to the rest of the class. In a series of interviews seeking advice regarding effective integration of students with moderate and severe disabilities, Janney, Snell, Beers, and Raynes (1995) found some strong resistance to curricular guides and other mandates. One teacher even said, "Tell them to get rid of the curriculums and let us teach what we want so we can include everybody in it" (p. 431). Inclusion has been debated largely in regard to the rights of all students to a place in the educational system that is not deemed exclusionary or isolating rather than on the appropriateness of curriculum and methods present in the mainstream class.

Argument Summary As we broaden the options for students with disabilities to contain inclusion-based stay-put resource programs and consultant support system models, we must avoid the pitfalls of wholesale change. A school system cannot adopt a systemwide mandate for inclusion of all and maintain the integrity of a truly individualized system of special education. Inclusion must not be allowed to force the elimination of choices on the continuum of delivery options.

Within the traditional structure of thirty students per teacher in a closed setting, with a teacher untrained in the qualitatively different approaches to instruction used in special education, the expectations of uncompromised inclusion are not reasonable. Who is responsible for the child who has been identified as qualifying for one of our "labels" and whom we have set apart from the others as needing something not available in the regular program? If we expect children to participate in the regular classroom and succeed there, appropriate support services must accompany that placement decision, even if those services must be provided outside the mainstream, for long or short periods of time. The special education field cannot risk the educational lives of a generation of students with learning problems to a failed experiment that took a wrong turn for all the wrong reasons.

Arguments for Proposition Two Students with disabilities are members of the general education community and, as such, should find their educational homes in their neighborhood schools alongside their neighbors. The creation of educational communities in which variability of ability levels is not seen as a problem but merely part of the characteristic of the setting can make possible the appropriate inclusion of students with disabilities. Stainback and Stainback (1991, 1992), Lipsky and Gartner (1989, 1990, 1992), and others have advocated for a full inclusion model, with the elimination of a continuum of placements. Now research is proving the model to be not only philosophically correct, but also beneficial to students both with and without disabilities. There is evidence of improving academic, behavioral, and social outcomes for both groups (Lipsky & Gartner, 1995).

With the tensions created by a call for increased standards coming simultaneously with the inclusion movement, the opportunity for real educational change has emerged. The required restructuring that allows schools to employ creative strategies to serve all students is now evolving throughout the country as lockstep, grade-based classes of thirty students each, and segregated special education services are being replaced by multi-age groupings designed to be heterogeneous in nature rather than as homogeneous as possible. Success has required visionary leadership, collaboration, refocused use of assessment, supports for staff and students, funding that is sufficient and "follows the student," and effective parent and family involvement (Lipsky & Gartner, 1995). In spite of the temptation of some to accept a compromising continuum of placements, thus avoiding the tension needed to produce real change, others have been willing to experiment with and find approaches to the education of all children, including those with mild learning disabilities and profound physical and mental impairments.

Mild Disabilities Far too many students have been channeled into special education the minute they ran into difficulty in school. For years, general education teachers were told that they did not possess the skills needed to work with any but the average child and that all others required the expertise of specialists. The proper solution for a child experiencing difficulties was referral to special education, not the pursuit of accommodating instructional strategies. The pattern became so well established that the expectation that teachers at least attempt some interventions before referral had to be legislated through the support team process. The dramatic increase in the number of students with learning disabilities followed the availability of financial incentives to local schools. For many students, these circumstances resulted in their removal from the general classes, where they really did belong, as evidenced by the inflated number of students diagnosed with learning disabilities as compared with initial projections (U.S. Department of Education, 1995). It is apparent that we need to reestablish the fact that variability within the general education classroom is natural, desirable, and can be accommodated. The tolerance level of which Gerber (1995) spoke appears to have been shrinking as special education has become a readily available escape valve for general education teachers.

Further, the contention that special educators have the ability to design unique programs individually based on assessed deficits of each child has not been supported by research (Bulgren & Carta, 1993). Instructional techniques effective for students with learning disabilities are not unsuitable or ineffective with other children. Individualization has been used to justify the fragmentation of the curriculum and separation of students from the mainstream, yet the actual instruction that occurs in special education might not be so different anyway (McLaughlin, 1995). As cited in Zigmond (1995), Bereiter, Brophy, and Madden and Slavin all argue that good teaching, not qualitatively different instruction, is the key to helping students with mild learning difficulties achieve success.

Students have the legal right to be educated in the least restrictive environment that is appropriate for them. For students with mild disabilities, the educational system should be able to make accommodations that not only allow them to be present in general education classes but also to make meaningful educational progress in the mainstream curriculum. Marston and Heistad (1994) compared the impact of a collaborative inclusion model with a traditional pull-out resource model in a study involving 670 students with disabilities in 26 different schools. Student growth was similar in both models, and both general and special education teachers considered that the quality of services had improved in the collaborative model. There was also a reduction in the rates of referral to special education associated with the collaborative model, possibly indicative of its preventive benefits for other unidentified pupils.

Inclusion is not simply a debate over where education is delivered (McLaughlin, 1995). As research on the differential treatment students with disabilities have received from general classroom teachers indicates (Bulgren & Carta, 1993), children may be physically present in classes without truly being included. The goal of inclusion for students with mild disabilities is to put meaning behind their educational placement in general education classes. Special education should offer remediation to these students in connection with the mainstream curriculum, not invent its own curriculum as segregated programs tend to do. Unfortunately, both special education and other compensatory pull-out programs such as Chapter One have been characterized by a lack of continuity and curricular integration with the general curriculum (Pugach & Warger, 1993). The problem is exacerbated if children go in and out of general education classes, dropping in as their schedules permit rather than through careful scheduling of the curriculum. Allington and McGill-Franzen (1989) have also noted the curricular fragmentation that can occur in special education resource programs and Chapter One reading. They found that students in the pull-out programs had to deal with unrelated reading activities while in the mainstream and were assigned additional unrelated activities and tasks in the support setting. The pull-out programs were not offering supports for the child in the mainstream curriculum but were, instead, presenting them with a competing set of assignments. The curricular materials in use even included an assortment of approaches to reading instruction developed from "competing theories of reading development, varying levels of difficulty in curriculum materials, and differing task emphases" (p. 85). The conclusion that the authors felt compelled to draw was that "The extraordinary fragmentation of instruction experiences of these children simply undermined the good efforts we often saw—good efforts from both learners and teachers" (p. 85). The curricular fragmentation and contextualization of special education have combined to disenfranchise students with disabilities from the full range of educational opportunities accessible to others (Pugach & Warger, 1993). The structure of segregated and pull-out special education serves to restrict the opportunities for students with disabilities to become fully participating members of unified learning communities. McLaughlin (1995) has also stressed the importance of allowing students access to the broad curriculum and the importance of educators holding accountability for all students achieving outcomes of similar value.

Since the general education teacher cannot rationally be expected to progress at a reasonable pace, adequately cover basic curriculum, and stop to make all the individual adjustments needed by every member of a full class of children, the special educator is intended to be her collaborator. However, the context of the special educator's work has been the student's IEP, not the regular classroom curriculum. The special educator's charge has been to identify student needs and address them, not necessarily in the context of the student's educational placement. However, these students typically have poor organizational skills, poor time management abilities, and need their educational content redundant and focused rather than fragmented and scattered.

It is true that research does indicate that the resource room model is superior to the regular classroom in terms of engaged time for students with mild disabilities. However, retention of the pull-out resource model is not the only conclusion that can be drawn from these findings. The argument can be made that the instructional practices which increase engagement in the resource room should be brought to the mainstream classroom rather than assuming that the resource model is the best approach based on this single instructional variable. Although engaged time might be higher for students while they are in the resource room, the transition times and the hours spent less engaged in the regular classroom are realities of the noninclusion model. Allowing the child to remain in the regular class would eliminate the transition times altogether and, if done properly, could provide the child with the ability to become engaged at higher rates all day, while in his general education classes. These possibilities offer far broader solutions than do linear interpretations of the research.

Severe Disabilities There are students whose cognitive capacities are severely to profoundly impaired. There are many others who have sensory impairments, multiple physical disabilities, and serious conditions related to their physical or mental health, who are also considered severely disabled, but they, nonetheless, may have cognitive abilities at a higher level. For some persons with severe physical limitations, possibly including an inability to produce speech, their true cognitive capabilities can remain unknown unless particular efforts are made to uncover their potential. Our history of segregating such people from us under the guise of wanting what is best for them can no longer be sustained.

There are three critical benefits of inclusion of students with severe disabilities that have proven to have reasonably consistent research-based support (Snell, 1990). First is the idea that through inclusion the students have an opportunity to develop social skills across all age groups. These skills are of vital importance when these children enter their adult lives and need to be accepted in the mainstream community. For them to get and keep a job, be accepted in a neighborhood as a welcome resident, be gladly received at restaurants, pubs, and recreational facilities within the community, and so forth, social skills are essential. Normalization as a principle is based on the reciprocal adjustment of both the community and persons with disabilities. The community has been expected to reduce its discrimination practices while the education of persons with disabilities has shifted to a focus on life skills and successful community integration.

The school setting is the ideal location in which to begin this training. Anything less than inclusion is actually counterproductive for these students because their educational goals include becoming accepted members of the community. Without a normal environment in which to learn and practice social skills, the child's education is without context.

The second major benefit of the integration of students with severe disabilities is the improvement in the attitudes of nondisabled peers toward students with disabilities. For our society to attain the goals of normalization, such attitude changes are imperative. Rather than fearing the unknown, children can become comfortable around individuals with severe cognitive limitations and find that they can even help their own parents have a more accepting perspective toward adults with disabilities in the community. Those who fear a loss of instructional time for the nondisabled students resulting from inclusion may wish to reconsider the overall goals of education. Academic achievement is not the sole purpose of education. The development of humanity—consideration and appreciation of others who may be different, acceptance and understanding of persons less capable than oneself, the willingness to assist others with a spirit of patience and empathy—is included in the goals of education. There can be no greater means of offering the nondisabled students opportunities to develop in this area than through the inclusion of students with severe disabilities in their community of learners. For parents who equally value the development of their children's humanity with their academic progress, the presence of children with severe disabilities could be considered a highly desirable feature of an educational environment rather than a drawback that one must reluctantly accept.

The third benefit of integration, which Snell (1990) mentions, is the development of positive relationships and friendships. Segregated services, outside of neighborhood schools, compound the isolation these children and their parents might have already experienced as a result of the disability. For a young child with severe disabilities, the recognition of another child from his school on the neighborhood playground and a chance to smile and wave at this acquaintance was not possible under the segregated structure. Now these children attend school with the same group with whom their families live and shop from preschool through high school graduation. At the secondary level, these students will have a curriculum to follow and goals to achieve just like every other student in the building and can join their peers in homeroom meetings, assemblies, activities periods, after-school athletic events, and so forth. They can become a real part of the community of learners to which they belong.

Students have a legal right to access to equal educational opportunities and need the best possible peer role models to encourage the highest possible achievement. Although the legal rationale for inclusion is the least preferable of all the arguments in its favor, it is nevertheless a valid one. Some might contend that general education teachers have not elected to work with this population of students and that it should not be forced on them. As a result, some models of inclusion are contingent upon teacher volunteers who accept the call to duty. The premise is absurd. Teachers are not free to accept or reject the pupils of their liking (Sindelar, 1995). Teachers should not be given assignments without adequate training and preparation, coupled with a full complement of necessary support services. However, it would be a disservice to both the teachers and the students involved to require schools to implement full inclusion without the proper transitions and respect for parents of students with disabilities who might be uncertain about the program changes.

Argument Summary As long as special education represents removing a child from the general classroom setting, the inducement to abuse it as a dumping ground to improve the quality of pupils remaining in the general setting is a reality. On the other hand, inclusion must not be considered a politically correct means of reducing special education costs by dumping students off on unwilling, untrained general educators. It requires comprehensive change in our attitudes, a sense of responsibility for children's education, and suitable educational structures. The reconceptualization of special education as an inclusionary program must be accompanied by a restructuring of the mainstream to create collaborative work structures that will enrich the educational opportunities of nondisabled students as well as those with disabilities. Inclusion models that avoid the stigma of labeling and social devaluing that can occur when students are required to participate in pull-out programs also offer nondisabled students a chance to gain understanding of and positive attitudes toward people with disabilities. Full inclusion is the only road to achieving the principles of normalization.

ADMINISTRATIVE STRUCTURES

Regardless of the stance one takes regarding a continuum of services or the use of full inclusion, it is generally acknowledged that the nature of the relationship between general and special education is changing. As inclusion (whether full or partial) advances, even greater changes will be required for the field to remain (or become) effective. The boundaries between special education, Chapter 1, migrant education, bilingual education, and general education are blurring as children in the schools present educators with more and more diversity of heritage and abilities (Schrag, 1993). The resulting changes necessitate new working relationships between general and special education teachers. The two education communities have the opportunity to become cooperative and leave behind their previous rather tangential relationship (Janney et al., 1995).

   The ability of general and special educators to solve problems collaboratively requires that both assume new roles and responsibilities. Phillips and McCullough (1990) have identified five central tenets of a collaborative ethic for teachers seeking to assume these new roles. The first is the assumption of joint responsibility and concern for all students. The separation of "your" students and "my" students between educators would disappear as everyone assumed responsibility for all students. The second related tenet is that teachers must hold joint accountability and credit for problem resolution. For example, a scheduling conflict would be resolved through collaboration, not a unilateral decision on the part of one teacher, in which she disregards the preferences of the other. The third tenet is that pooling of talents and resources is mutually advantageous to both teachers and all the students. The fourth tenet holds to the belief that the time, energy, and resources spent on the resolution of teacher or student problems have been well spent. The final tenet is that the conditions necessary to successful collaboration, such as group morale and cohesion, and acceptance of alternative classroom interventions, are important and desirable. These tenets reflect a change in current relationships and lines of responsibility between many general and special educators. Can or should they be used to foster the complete integration of special education as a unified component within the structure of general education or to serve as worthy guidelines for working relationships within the existing dual structures?

Political and Economic Influences

Operating parallel to the general education structure, a second education system currently exists in funding, administration and supervision, teacher training and licensure, curriculum development, accountability, student progression and exit criteria, discipline options, and so forth. This dual system grew out of the efforts of advocates of students with disabilities to develop educational opportunities for them. Students with disabilities had been legally and intentionally excluded from educational opportunities and were in need of strong advocates who would continue to watch out for their interests after the court battles and legislative struggles were over. Historical compulsory attendance laws, through their exclusion clauses for those who were morally, physically or mentally unfit, document the reality of this rejection. The litigation and legislation of the 1970s and 1980s have eliminated these discriminatory exclusions, but have we eliminated the need for separate administrative structures? The resulting special education empire, as we know it today, was not even a vision (or nightmare, as the case might be) at the outset.

Even while leaders in the field have been attempting to protect and ensure the rights of students with disabilities, this expansion of special education as a secondary system has created problems. In her call for reform in 1986, Will (1986) pointed out some of the various unintended disadvantages of the dual system. She noted the lack of coordination between all the federal programs that were offering special programs for students facing certain disadvantages. The resulting confusion has caused concern about the leadership of the programs while it obfuscated the lines of responsibility and accountability. The majority of general education school administrators believed that students with learning problems belong to special education or other special programs whose administrators have generally been members of the central administrative staff, not building level personnel. Since the programs are actually delivered at the building level, principals have been unable to develop a sense of ownership or authority over the programs. The programs may be housed within neighborhood schools, but they have largely been administered through a central office. This model has disenfranchised the programs within their own buildings. The result is a diminished impact of the programs, since "principals may not be able to use their influence to set the high expectations and standards for students with learning problems nor encourage teachers to 'go the extra mile' for these children" (Will, 1986, p. 8).

In the past classroom arrangements and teaching strategies left little room for individualization or diverse methodologies.

Paradigm Shift or Evolution

Included in the CEC policy statement regarding inclusive schools and community setting is acknowledgment of the complications of the dual system for building-level administrators of inclusive programs (CEC, 1993). The policy statement recommends that building-level administrators, assisted by special education administrators, hold primary responsibility for students with disabilities. In the process of giving programmatic and personnel authority to building principals, it is seen as critical to provide them with the necessary support and technical assistance just as it is necessary to prepare teachers for their new inclusionary roles. With the added authority and autonomy comes greater accountability for the establishment and achievement of high standards for the students with disabilities served by the school. However, the lack of special education administrators available to offer assistance and guidance to the building-level principals remains in the picture. The adjustments and collaboration needed to improve the system do not require the elimination of special education.

Some states have already made a clear decision regarding the elimination of a dual structure. For example, the Kentucky Education Reform Act (KERA) of 1990 mandates the transformation of education into a single system (Kentucky Department of Education, 1992). Other states are also experimenting with unification systems or other collaborative efforts between general and special education (Schrag, 1993). However, there remain many questions about the logic and motivations behind the call to restructure (dismantle) special education as a unified component of general education. Attempts to sort out what is best or right for the future of students with and without disabilities require consideration of ideologies, review of conceptual frameworks of education, and analysis of historical, existing, and future social and political climates.

Proposition One

Special education should be united with general education into a single system, eliminating the current dual structure. A duplicative system is not needed and is causing significant interference with program delivery as well as producing extreme and unnecessary financial expenditures in redundant or even competitive administrative structures.

Decision Point 3.2: Administrative Structures for General and Special Education

Arguments for Proposition One   The argument that special education needs to retain its power and, therefore, its segregated position in education is grounded on the faulty assumption that an outsider power base is more significant than a power base from within the ranks of general education. The opportunities to bring about change within the ranks of general education can be far greater for special educators who enter the system and become members of it than for those who chose to remain apart from it, always criticizing from the outside. To illustrate, general and special education teacher educators have squabbled for years over the need for general educators to have more special education training, with little change occurring in the curriculum other than what was legislatively mandated. Today, unified programs that reflect real changes in preparation models are emerging as segregated departmental structures are being diminished and teacher educators are clustering themselves around theoretical commonalities instead of the issue of whether the children being educated happen to have disabilities (e.g., Feden & Clabaugh, 1986; Kemple, Hartle, Correa, & Fox, 1994).

As noted earlier, the issues of inclusion and unification of general and special education create some unusual political partners who have come to the same conclusion through far different reasoning. This is most evident here as persons who see special education as a failed experiment (e.g., Lipsky & Gartner, 1990) and others who consider it to have produced many quality programs and services (e.g., Schrag, 1993) concur that it is time to bring general and special education into a unified system. The rationales of both camps will be used here in defense of the unification proposition.

Political and Economic Influences   Special education is an evolving, developing field. Through federal mandates and political action, more and more services have been made available for students with disabilities. Congress has improved and expanded the legislation over the years, adding assistive technology as a related field, putting greater emphasis on the transition to adulthood and employment, clarifying the importance of unbiased policies and procedures, and seeking other reforms as needed. However, one unintended outcome has been the growth of special education into a separate system that has been poorly coordinated with other support programs and general education. In an effort to remedy this problem and to reduce the conception among many general educators that special education is a "place" rather than curricular and instructional supports, "a more coordinated

Today's classroom can offer a variety of techniques, active learning, and many opportunities for individualization.

and interfaced educational system that focuses on the 'whole child' and curricular and instructional improvements is needed to assure better outcomes for our students with disabilities and their families" (Schrag, 1993, p. 205). The data regarding school outcomes for students in special education (e.g., dropout rates, involvement in the criminal justice system, poor employment records) all further point to the need to create a more integrated and coordinated system of education.

The changes that are occurring today are intended to produce long-term systemic change, not quick fixes. Programs such as Goals 2000 are designed to achieve broad underlying changes in our educational system through the support of locally conceived and developed projects. The integration of special education into the general education program is a critical piece of this systemic change, with mutually beneficial outcomes for both special and general educators. The power base of the special education empire has been far removed from the local building where the children and teachers try to survive each day. Decisions and mandates outside of local arenas can destroy the worthy progress that individual teachers and administrators would like to make on behalf of students with disabilities. The reality is that government can mandate neither peer acceptance of students with learning disabilities nor positive community attitudes toward adults with disabilities. These critical issues for anyone seeking to advocate for students with disabilities require personal grass-roots efforts that involve general educators even more than their special education colleagues. The empowerment of general educators in this endeavor is vital to the reformation of special education. Unity of administrative structures is the first step in this empowerment process.

Paradigm Shift or Evolution   The fact that some programs within the special education umbrella might have proven effective with some children is not really sufficient to contend that special education has accomplished its intended goals. There is a need for change because, overall, the system has failed to serve the students well (Lipsky & Gartner, 1990). Because it is impossible to "fix" special education without altering the context within which it operates, it is time to achieve educational reforms that encompass the entire educational system. Johnson (1990), in reference to the deinstitutionalization of persons in the mental health system, noted that "Our mistake was in thinking that to initiate the process was to complete it" (p. 255). The entire movement toward inclusion is in jeopardy if inclusion becomes the goal. Rather, it is one means to the achievement of far more significant goals related to development of knowledge and skills and the normalization of life for students with disabilities.

The process of reform now necessitates a radical paradigm shift. Students with disabilities must not be viewed as the responsibility of special educators. They are the responsibility of general educators who will need appropriate support services to fulfill their responsibilities to these children. Just as educators use guidance counselors, nurses, social workers, ophthalmologists, and other appropriate professionals to support their educational programs, they can also find guidance and support from special educators for students with disabilities. The semantic shift from "handicapped children" to "students with disabilities" was partially based on the notion that children requiring special education are first and primarily children. However, the continued reliance on administrative structures, professional organizations, and funding systems that define themselves as exclusively serving students with disabilities contradicts the heart of the meaning intended in these semantic changes.

Argument Summary The building up and protecting of an empire just for the sake of feeling some sense of power is not the way to achieve the best educational opportunities for students with disabilities. Certainly, there are risks involved in changing the nature of the relationship between general and special education. However, taking those risks is a necessary component of the establishment of collaborative partnerships among the different splinter groups. Certainly, not all general educators are eager to assume a sense of responsibility for students whom they have been able to dismiss as second-class students, nor can they all be trusted to seek the best for students with disabilities. Some might even be eager for unification, hoping to diminish the power and influence of special education in the process. However, there are far greater risks in remaining segregated from the mainstream, while concurrently attempting to dictate practices to the educators in it. For inclusion to succeed, even as an option along a continuum of services, its influence must be felt throughout the field—in classrooms, school district central administrations, state education departments, federal agencies, teacher education programs, professional organizations, and ad hoc groups aiming at the improvement of education. Unification of general and special education is the means by which students with disabilities and their teachers can move from second-class citizenship to first-class citizenship within the education ranks. They would no longer be an appendage to the mainstream of education but an integral part of it. Building-level resources, the full curriculum, field trips, guest speakers—everything would belong equally to all members of the community of learners to be distributed equitably for all.

Proposition Two

Although collaboration and partnerships between general and special education are needed, special education must remain a distinct administrative unit within the education system. Regardless of the educational placements of students with disabilities, the oversight of special education and related support services requires knowledgeable administrators qualified to pursue the best possible educational outcomes for students with disabilities.

Arguments for Proposition Two   The jargon issued by educational reformers who recommend the unification of general and special education is a series of contradictions of terms—that *all* education will be special, that an elite education should be provided for everyone, that the practice of identifying learning problems as residing within the child must stop. Concurrently, we are shifting to an educational environment in which children are responsible for their own learning or failure to learn (Kauffman & Hallahan, 1993). As Keogh (1988) notes, "It is a strange logic that calls for the regular system to take over responsibility for pupils it has already demonstrated it has failed" (p. 20). The logic used by some to suggest the radical restructuring of special and general education is predicated on an assumption of a similarity between disability and ethnicity. They follow the logic to the conclusion that separate services or administrative structures on the basis of the child's disabilities are inherently discriminatory. The line of reasoning is flawed in that it treats the segregation of students by the "instructionally irrelevant variable of skin color" as equivalent to the maintenance of programs and services for students specifically because they need instructional differentiation. Kauffman and Hallahan (1993) remind us that the basic concepts supporting special education are equal protection of law and equal educational opportunity—exactly the same principles supporting the integration of all ethnic groups in public schools. However, these authors point out difficulties in continuing the comparisons to argue that separate is unequal. For example, debates can rage over the appropriateness of segregated schools for children with sensory impairments, but the supporters of these schools have far different motivations than those who resisted racial integration in the fifties. The merits of the separateness of special education must not be politicized into a discrimination issue when it is a legitimate professional debate.

Special education has been described as a failure by its critics (e.g., Lipsky & Gartner, 1990), a series of second-class programs that are based on serving children primarily defined and sorted from others simply by virtue of a disability. However, these critics also point to the techniques and principles embedded in special education as models for general education to emulate (Kauffman & Hallahan, 1993). The call for reform is predicated on the illogic that the merger of general and special education, both of which are considered by these critics to be failing, will somehow be transformed into a successful unified system. Kauffman and Hallahan (1993) point out that for students with disabilities, the stigma and separation can sometimes be more painful in the mainstream than in alternative settings. The reality of that social stigma is heard in the voices of students with learning disabilities (Guterman, 1996) as well as the sociometric realities of inclusive settings (Sale & Carey, 1996). The wishful thinking of adults cannot make schools any less painful for students struggling to balance their academic achievements, social status, and self-concepts. The most helpful programs are based on realistic acknowledgment of the social pressures faced by students with disabilities, not naive assumptions that removal of special education structures can take away the social problems these children may encounter.

Political and Economic Influences The regular education initiative was and remains a part of a political agenda to diminish social services funded by the federal government (Anderegg & Vergason, 1993). When the financial burden of social service programs, which had been started as a part of the Great Society, was considered too great by Washington politicians, the funds were reduced and merged into block grants. These block grants were accompanied by a shift from Washington-based decisions to local decision making on how best to allocate the limited funds. Those opposed to the role of government in social services used the increasing numbers of qualifying recipients as evidence of the programs' failures. The Reagan administration sought to diminish the government role in social welfare by diffusing and diminishing the programs. Special education advocates fought successfully to retain separate funding, enabling dedicated funding for special education to increase while funds for other social programs were lessened. However, with the cutback of other social welfare programs came increased needs for special education (Kauffman, 1990). As had been the case with the other programs, the expansion of special education rolls commanded the attention of politicians concerned about the increasing flow of resources into special education. Kauffman noted that education was "the last program of government to become the target for restructuring based on politically conservative notions of social management" (p. 61). The regular education initiative and all the surrounding calls for reform were designed to rein in special education (Anderegg & Vergason, 1993; Kauffman & Hallahan, 1990, 1993). It became a part of the "trickle-down" theory, popular with the Reagan administration, applied to education, and it has never represented the best interests of students with disabilities. Creation of an image of reform was important for the conservative politicians and their appointees, but the real aim was reduction of the fiscal resources channeled into the education of the poor and low achievers.

The calls heard today for the integration of general and special education, elimination of special education departments in higher education, and the merger of professional organizations follow this same political agenda. Many involved in this reform movement would reject the reality of the situation; nevertheless, it is a reality. Special educators can get a sense of the future by looking at the current direction of reforms in general education, which focus on raising standards, increasing achievement, and improving standardized test scores in global competition. Concerns for enhancing the learning opportunities of students with disabilities or for sensitizing nondisabled peers to students with disabilities are not consistently heard from the general education community. Rather, the authority to discipline and remove students with disabilities appears to be of far greater interest to them than unification for the purpose of creating positive learning environments for all students. It would not seem wise at this time to relinquish any power to this group for the sake of collaboration.

Paradigm Shift or Evolution Full inclusionists claim that special education is immoral, intellectually bankrupt, and fiscally irresponsible. Special education is certainly visible and vulnerable. When these harsh criticisms are made, they contribute to the demoralization of the field rather than providing a healthy stimulus for ongoing development and improvement. In claiming that special education is more harmful than helpful, they have created dissension, not reasonable calls for reform (Fuchs & Fuchs, 1995b). The ongoing claim that special education has not worked, that it is a failure for students with disabilities, diminishing and segregating these students, ignores research and the testimony of many. Efficacy studies and meta-analyses do reveal that special education can be effective as well as ineffective. The task is to sort out the factors that contribute to effectiveness and develop them, not eliminate special education because some programs have proven ineffective. After all, some general education teachers and schools are ineffective as well. Shall we abolish general education as the solution to its failures? The call for the establishment of a unitary deregulated educational system is a naive stance that neglects both a historical and empirical perspective toward the future and the inevitable neglect of students with disabilities that would result (Fuchs & Fuchs, 1990).

However, greater collaboration and greater cohesiveness within administrative structures are essential elements for the future of both general and special education. Kauffman and Hallahan (1993) offer a framework for establishing special education as a unit within a comprehensive educational system that is predicated on the assumption that special education, while imperfect in its delivery, is based on sound principles. They have identified eight basic postulates and numerous related corollaries to achieve this end. The beliefs included in these postulates include several critical ideas that refer directly to the need to retain a distinct special education administrative structure while creating greater unity among the two fields of education. A comprehensive public education system that addresses the educational needs of all children will necessarily include permanent explicit structures intended to ensure the accommodation of students with disabilities. The differentiated structures must include special teachers, administrators, funding mechanisms, and procedures to define alternative goals and programs for students. Special educators would all begin their training in general education, develop successful teaching skills over a period of time, and then receive intensive specialized training in special education and collaboration techniques. The final point is that the transformation of special education into a marginalized structure through its assimilation into general education must not be allowed.

Argument Summary The motives of general educators seeking unification must be considered suspect. The motives of special educators seeking unification must be considered naive. Whereas ideally a total unification between general and special education could be the most suitable for all, in reality, it is unwise to seek it. The leverage and power present in special education are needed in the current political climate as much as ever. Collaboration and partnership offer effective means to reform, not the collapse of our current structures.

CLOSING THOUGHTS

What will special education services look like twenty years from now? Special educators have a tradition of making programmatic change on a wholesale basis rather than adhering to our principle of *individualized* education programs. For example, the logistics of mandated education for all and the call for placements in the least restrictive environment contributed to the need for delivery systems to change. In contrast to self-contained classes, resource room models increased the number of students served by one teacher, reduced resources needed to support the programs, and served greater numbers of students with fewer teachers. We started putting an end to the practice of lumping students together regardless of age or educational needs based solely on a categorical diagnosis. Teenagers who were moderately retarded were no longer expected to remain in the elementary school because their mental age remained at that level. Students with mild disabilities could retain their connection with the mainstream while receiving the specialized educational support available through resource programs.

However, the special education mandates meant that many more special education teachers and related support services staff were needed. The field has continued its growth cycle and is now under the gun to find more creative ways of serving the vast numbers of students identified as needing services. Inclusion is the new reform cry. It is an even bigger change than was necessary in the shift from self-contained classes to pull-out resource room models.

Change is inevitable. Whether a continuum of options remain, or full inclusion is the future, many students are already being served through inclusion models—creating the need for new staffing patterns in special education, expanded collaboration skills for both regular and special educators, and a better understanding of special education by the school community, including parents of students without disabilities. A resource teacher serving students in a pull-out program can serve numerous students from several classrooms simultaneously. A consulting teacher working cooperatively with a regular classroom teacher in an inclusion model can be in only one classroom at a time. Special education aides do not hold teaching credentials, and they cannot collaborate as equal partners with regular classroom teachers. Special educators have not traditionally been trained to supervise a staff, manage large groups of children, or take on other new roles associated with inclusion models but rather have skills in direct instruction techniques appropriate for individual students with special needs. General education teachers have not been taught about co-teaching and partnerships, sharing their authority and leadership within the classroom, or coordinating the work of multiple adults present in the room at one time. Building-level principals have difficulty with the presence of programs within their buildings over which they have no authority or control. They cannot take ownership and pride in the successful programs, nor can they contribute to their improvement if problems arise in these separately administered units. The need for adjustments in the educational administrative structure between general and special education and the expansion of inclusion-based educational placement options for students with disabilities is creating the tension essential for change. The question is just how radical the reactions to that tension should be.

REFERENCES

Allington, R., & McGill-Franzen, A. (1989). Different programs, indifferent instruction. In D. K. Lipsky & A. Gartner (Eds.), *Beyond separate education: Quality education for all* (pp. 75–98). Baltimore: Paul H. Brookes.

Alves, A. J., & Gottlieb, J. (1986). Teacher interactions with mainstreamed handicapped students and their nonhandicapped peers. *Learning Disability Quarterly, 8,* 77–83.

Anderegg, M. L., & Vergason, G. A. (1993). Litigation, legislation, and politics of special education: Implications for the practitioner. In R. C. Eaves & P. J. McLaughlin (Eds.), *Recent advances in special education and rehabilitation* (pp. 167–177). Boston: Andover Medical Publishers.

Baines, L., Baines, C., & Masterson, C. (1994). Mainstreaming: One school's reality. *Phi Delta Kappan, 76,* 39–40, 57–64.

Baker, J. M., & Zigmond, N. (1995). The meaning and practice of inclusion for students with learning disabilities: Themes and implications from the five cases. *Journal of Special Education, 29,* 163–180.

Barry, A. L. (1994). Easing into inclusion classrooms. *Educational Leadership, 52,* 4–6.

Board of Education of East Windsor Regional School District v. Diamond, 808 F.2d 987, 36 Ed. Law Rep. 1136 (3d Cir. 1986).

Board of Education of Hendrick Hudson Central School District v. Rowley, 458, US 176, 102 S.Ct. 3034, 73 L.Ed.2d 690, 5 Ed. Law Rep. 34 (1982).

Bonadonna v. Cooperman, 619 F. Supp. 401, 28 Ed. Law Rep. 430 (D.N.J. 1985).

Brophy, J., & Good, T. (1986). Teacher effects. In M. C. Wittock (Ed.), *Handbook of research on teaching* (3rd ed., pp. 328–375). New York: Macmillan.

Bulgren, J. A., & Carta, J. J. (1993). Examining the instructional contexts of students with learning disabilities. *Exceptional Children, 59,* 182–191.

Carlberg, C., & Kavale, K. (1980). The efficacy of special versus regular class placement for exceptional children: A meta-analysis, *Journal of Special Education, 14,* 295–309.

Cole, D. A., & Meyer, L. H. (1991). Social integration and severe disabilities: A longitudinal analysis of child outcomes. *Journal of Special Education, 25,* 340–351.

Commission on the Education of the Deaf. (1988, February). *Toward equality: Education of the deaf.* Washington, CD: U. S. Government Printing Office. (ERIC Document Reproduction Service No. ED 303 932).

Council for Exceptional Children Delegate Assembly. (1993). CEC policy on inclusive schools and community settings. *Teaching Exceptional Children, 25,* supplement.

Feden, P. D., & Clabaugh, G. K. (1986). The "new breed" educator: A rationale and program for combining elementary and special education teacher preparation. *Teacher Education and Special Education, 9,* 180–189.

Fuchs, D., & Fuchs, L. S. (1990). Framing the REI debate: Abolitionists versus conservationists. In J. W. Lloyd, A. C. Repp, & N. N. Singh (Eds.), *The regular education initiative: Alternative perspectives on concepts, issues, and models* (pp. 241–255). Sycamore, IL: Sycamore.

Fuchs, D., & Fuchs, L. S. (1994). Inclusive schools movement and the radicalization of special education reform. *Exceptional Children, 60,* 294–309.

Fuchs, D., & Fuchs, L. S. (1995a). Counterpoint: Special education—Ineffective? Immoral? *Exceptional Children, 61,* 303–306.

Fuchs, D., & Fuchs, L. S. (1995b). What's "special" about special education? *Phi Delta Kappan, 76,* 522–530.

Gallagher, L. N. S. (1993). Integrating students with special needs in the regular education classroom. In National Education Association (Ed.), *Integrating students with special needs: Policies and practices that work* (pp. 23–27). Washington, DC: NEA.

Gerber, M. M. (1995). Inclusion at the high-water mark? Some thoughts on Zigmond and Baker's case studies of inclusive education programs. *Journal of Special Education, 29,* 181–191.

George, N. L., & Lewis, T. J. (1991). EASE: Exit assistance for special educators—Helping students make the transition. *Teaching Exceptional Children, 23,* 34–39.

Guterman, B. R. (1996). The validity of categorical learning disabilities services: The consumer's view. *Exceptional Children, 62,* 111–124.

Halpern, A. S. (1992). Transition: Old wine in new bottles. *Exceptional Children, 58,* 202–211.

Hanley, T. V. (1994). The need for technological advances in assessment related to national educational reform. *Exceptional Children, 61,* 222–229.

Hocutt, A. M., Martin, E. W., & McKinney, J. D. (1990). Historical and legal context of mainstreaming. In J. W. Lloyd, A. C. Repp, & N. N. Singh (Eds.), *The regular education initiative: Alternative perspectives on concepts, issues, and models* (pp. 17–28). Sycamore, IL: Sycamore.

Hollowood, T. M., Salisbury, C. L., Rainforth, B., & Palombaro, M. M. (1994). Use of instructional time in classrooms serving students with and without severe disabilities. *Exceptional Children, 61,* 242–253.

Hunt, P., Farron-Davis, F., Beckstead, S., Curtis, D., & Goetz, L. (1994). Evaluating the effects of placement of students with severe disabilities in general education versus special classes. *Journal of the Association for Persons with Severe Handicaps, 19,* 200–214.

Janney, R. E., Snell, M. E., Beers, M. K., & Raynes, M. (1995). Integrating students with moderate and severe disabilities into general education classes. *Exceptional Children, 61,* 425–439.

Jenkins, J. R., Jewell, M., Leicester, N., O'Connor, R. E., Jenkins, L. M., & Troutner, N. M. (1994). Accommodations for individual differences without classroom ability groups: An experiment in school restructuring. *Exceptional Children, 60,* 344–358.

Jenkins, J. R., Pious, C. G., & Jewell, M. (1990). Special education and the regular education initiative: Basic assumptions. *Exceptional Children, 56,* 479–492.

Johnson, A. B. (1990). *Out of bedlam.* New York: Basic Books.

Kauffman, J. M. (1990). Restructuring in sociopolitical context: Reservations about the effects of current reform proposals on students with disabilities. In J. W. Lloyd, A. C. Repp, & N. N. Singh (Eds.), *The regular education initiative: Alternative perspectives on concepts, issues, and models* (pp. 57–66). Sycamore, IL: Sycamore.

Kauffman, J. M., & Hallahan, D. P. (1990). What we want for children: A rejoinder to REI proponents. *Journal of Special Education, 24,* 340–345.

Kauffman, J. M., & Hallahan, D. P. (1993). Toward a comprehensive delivery system for special education. In J. I. Goodlad & T. C. Lovitt (Eds.), *Integrating general and special education* (pp. 73–102). New York: Macmillan.

Kauffman, J. M., Lloyd, J. W., Baker, J., & Riedel, T. M. (1995). Inclusion of all students with emotional or behavioral disorders? Let's think again. *Phi Delta Kappan, 76,* 542–546.

Kemple, K. M., Hartle, L. C., Correa, V. I., & Fox, L. (1994). Preparing teachers for inclusive education: The development of a unified teacher education program in early childhood and early childhood special education. *Teacher Education and Special Education, 17,* 38–51.

Kentucky Department of Education. (1992). *Procedures for inclusion of students in KIRIS.* (Program Advisory No. 92-OAAS-004). Frankfort, KY: Author.

Keogh, B. (1988). Improving services for problem learners: Rethinking and re-structuring, *Journal of Learning Disabilities, 21,* 20.

Kozol, J. (1991). *Savage inequalities.* New York: Crown.

Learning Disabilities Association. (1993, January). *Position paper on full inclusion of all students with learning disabilities in the regular education classroom.* Pittsburgh, PA: Author.

Lipsky, D. K., & Gartner, A. (1989). *Beyond separate education: Quality education for all.* Baltimore: Paul Brookes.

Lipsky, D. K., & Gartner, A. (1990). Re-structuring for quality. In J. W. Lloyd, A. C. Repp, & N. N. Singh (Eds.), *The regular education initiative: Alternative perspectives on concepts, issues, and models* (pp. 43–56). Sycamore, IL: Sycamore.

Lipsky, D. K., & Gartner, A. (1992). Achieving full inclusion: Placing the student at the center of educational reform. In W. Stainback & S. Stainback (Eds.), *Controversial issues confronting special education: Divergent perspectives* (pp. 3–12). Boston: Allyn & Bacon.

Lipsky, D. K., & Gartner, A. (1995). The evaluation of inclusive education pro-grams. *NCERI Bulletin, 2.*

Logan, K. R., Diaz, E., Piperno, M., Rankin, D., MacFarland, A. D., & Bargamian, K. (1994). How inclusion built a community of learners. *Educational Leadership, 52,* 42–45.

Lovitt, T. C. (1993). Recurring issues in special and general education. In J. I. Goodlad & T. C. Lovitt (Eds.), *Integrating general and special education* (pp. 49–71). New York: Macmillan.

MacMillan, D. L., & Hendrick, I. G. (1993). Evolution and legacies. In J. I. Goodlad & T. C. Lovitt (Eds.), *Integrating general and special education* (pp. 23–48). New York: Macmillan.

Madden, N. A., & Slavin, R. E. (1983). Mainstreaming students with mild handicaps: Academic and social out-comes. *Review of Educational Research, 53,* 519–569.

Marston, D., & Heistad, D. (1994). Assess-ing collaborative inclusion as an effec-tive model for the delivery of special education services. *Diagnostique, 19,* 51–67.

Martin, E. W. (1995). Case studies on inclusion: Worst fears realized. *Journal of Special Education, 29,* 192–199.

McCoy, K. M. (1995). *Teaching special learners in the general education classroom.* Denver: Love.

McIntosh, R., Vaughn, S., Schumm, J. S., Haagen, D., & Lee, O. (1993). Obser-vations of students with learning disabil-ities in general education classrooms. *Exceptional Children, 60,* 249–261.

McLaughlin, M. J. (1995). Defining special education: A response to Zigmond and Baker. *Journal of Special Education, 29,* 200–208.

National Commission on Excellence in Education. (1983). *A nation at risk.* Washington, DC: U.S. Government Printing Office.

National Educational Goals Panel. (1991). *The national education goals report: Build-ing a nation of learners.* Washington, DC: U.S. Government Printing Office.

National Educational Goals Panel. (1995). *The national education goals report: Build-ing a nation of learners.* Washington, DC: U.S. Government Printing Office.

National Joint Committee on Learning Disabilities. (1993, January). *A reaction to "Full Inclusion": A reaffirmation of the right of students with learning disabilities to a continuum of services.* Author.

O'Neil, J. (1995). Can inclusion work? A conversation with Jim Kauffman and Mara Sapon-Shevin. *Educational Leadership, 52,* 7–11.

Osborne, A. G. (1992). Legal standards for an appropriate education in the post-Rowley era. *Exceptional Children, 58,* 488–493.

Osborne, A. G., & DiMattia, P. (1994). The IDEA's least restrictive environment: Legal implications. *Exceptional Children, 61,* 6–14.

Pennsylvania Association for Retarded Citizens (PARC) v. Commonwealth of Pennsylvania, 334 F. Supp. 1257, 343 F. Supp. 279 (E. D. Pa. 1971, 1972).

Phillips, V., & McCullough, L. (1990). Consultation-based programming: Instituting the collaborative ethic in schools. *Exceptional Children, 56,* 291–304.

Pugach, M. C., & Warger, C. L. (1993). Curriculum considerations. In J. I. Goodlad & T. C. Lovitt (Eds.), *Integrating general and special education* (pp. 125–148). New York: Macmillan.

Putnam, J. W., Spiegel, A. N., & Bruininks, R. H. (1995). Future directions in education and inclusion of students with disabilities: A Delphi investigation. *Exceptional Children, 61,* 553–576.

Rich, H. L., & Ross, S. M. (1989). Students' time on learning tasks in special education. *Exceptional Children, 55,* 508–515.

Sale, P., & Carey, D. M. (1996). The sociometric status of students with disabilities in a full-inclusion school. *Exceptional Children, 62,* 6–19.

Sarason, S. B. (1997). *How schools might be governed and why.* New York: Teachers College Press.

Schrag, J. A. (1993). Restructuring schools for better alignment of general and special education. In J. I. Goodlad & T. C. Lovitt (Eds.), *Integrating general and special education* (pp. 203–228). New York: Macmillan.

Sindelar, P. T. (1995). Full inclusion of students with learning disabilities and its implications for teacher education. *Journal of Special Education, 29,* 234–244.

Smelter, R. W., Rasch, B. W., & Yudewitz, G. J. (1994). Thinking of inclusion for all special needs students? Better think again. *Phi Delta Kappan, 76,* 35–38.

Snell, M. E. (1990). Schools are for all kids: The importance of integration for students with severe disabilities and their peers. In J. W. Lloyd, A. C. Repp, & N. N. Singh (Eds.), *The regular education initiative: Alternative perspectives on concepts, issues, and models* (pp.133–148). Sycamore, IL: Sycamore.

Spady, W. G. (1992). It's time to take a close look at outcome-based education. *Communique, 20,* 16–18.

Stainback, S., & Stainback, W. (1992). Schools as inclusive communities. In W. Stainback & S. Stainback (Eds.), *Controversial issues confronting special education: Divergent perspectives* (pp. 29–44). Boston: Allyn & Bacon.

Stainback, S., Stainback, W., East, K., & Sapon-Shevin, M. (1994). A commentary on inclusion and the development of a positive self-identity by people with disabilities. *Exceptional Children, 60,* 486–490.

Taylor, S. J. (1995). Point/Counterpoint. On rhetoric: A response to Fuchs and Fuchs. *Exceptional Children, 61,* 301–302.

U.S. Department of Education. (1988). *Tenth annual report to Congress on the implementation of the Education of the Handicapped Act.* Washington, DC: Author.

U.S. Department of Education. (1995). *Seventeenth annual report to Congress on the implementation of the Individuals with Disabilities Education Act.* Washington, DC: Office of Special Education Programs.

Wiggins, G. (1989). A true test: Toward more authentic and equitable assessment. *Phi Delta Kappan, 70,* 703–713.

Will, M. (1986). *Educating children with learning problems: A shared responsibility.* Washington, DC: Office of Special Education and Rehabilitative Services, U.S. Department of Education.

Wittrock, M. C. (Ed.). (1986). *Handbook of research on teaching* (3rd ed.). New York: Macmillan.

Ysseldyke, J. E., Thurlow, M. L., & Shriner, J. G. (1992). Outcomes are for special educators too. *Teaching Exceptional Children, 25,* 36–50.

Zigmond, N. (1995). An exploration of the meaning and practice of special education in the context of full inclusion of students with learning disabilities. *Journal of Special Education, 29,* 109–115.

Zigmond, N., & Baker, J. M. (1994). Is the mainstream a more appropriate educational setting for Randy? A case study of one student with learning disabilities. *Learning Disabilities Research and Practice, 9,* 108–117.

Zigmond, N., & Baker, J. M. (1995). Concluding comments: Current and future practices in inclusive schooling. *Journal of Special Education, 29,* 245–250.

4

Curricular Enrichment
in a Democracy

AUTHORS: LAURENCE J. COLEMAN
AND MARIE E. PEINE

INTRODUCTION

Children with special intellectual abilities and unusual talent can be found in every school district in America. They come in many forms. These children are everywhere, but they are not always readily recognized or given opportunities to maximize their abilities. Some of our brightest children may go undiscovered; therefore, their educational needs may be unmet as well. Ignorance about the signs of giftedness, lack of opportunity, and social forces such as racism, sexism, and classism can all contribute to this educational system problem. The loss of potential from these talented individuals is tragic for the individual person and for society.

Ability and the right to have opportunities to capitalize on it are neither the prerogatives of any one class or ethnic group nor simply a consequence of inheritance. Outstanding abilities and talents develop in enriched environments but rarely in impoverished ones. The implication is that education and experience are necessary pre-conditions for the emergence and development of talents. Consequently, an appropriate education for children with enhanced abilities is critical. Without such an education, most of these children will likely not realize their potential.

Schools play an important role in the development of talents because of the pivotal place they occupy in children's lives. Children who possess intellectual gifts and/or unique talents present problems for school administrators because they are typically out of step with the standard school program. The educational

Bill Gates connects with up and coming students from the Young Achievers Science and Math Program in Boston.

issues that arise are a part of the general problem of how an institution deals with the general education of children in a supposedly egalitarian society. What is the "norm," and how far can one deviate from it and still be a part of the group? Does a teacher have only a responsibility to raise the class average, or must she attend to individual progress, regardless of how far above the average a particular child might be?

Historical Perspectives

Special education for gifted and talented children in public education goes back to the turn of this century. At that time, pioneers in the field such as Lewis Terman and Leta Hollingworth demonstrated that gifted and talented children exhibited traits and behaviors that make them distinguishable from other children. These differences, which today we say are found in 3% to 5% of the school-aged population, were assumed to be the means by which we could identify them. The intelligence test, which was emerging during that period, became one of the methods by which children who had advanced abilities were identified. As the century progressed, other indicators, such as achievement, creativity, leadership, and talent in the arts and music, were used. It was assumed that children with advanced abilities would best be served in programs offering a differentiated educational program that would prepare them to be contributing members of society.

Three broad options of educational programming (e.g., grouping, acceleration, and enrichment) have been implemented to serve these children (Coleman, 1985). Grouping brings children with like abilities together into instructional groups, acceleration provides opportunities for children to move at a faster pace through the curriculum, and enrichment exposes students to a wide variety of

Sometimes giftedness can be recognized more easily on a global level than in our local schools.

supplementary experiences to broaden and deepen their learning. Schools at all levels often have programs that use one or a combination of these programming options. Most programs use enrichment as their guiding principle. Relatively few programs use acceleration. Renzulli has proposed the Schoolwide Enrichment Model (Renzulli & Reis, 1985). Although not all programs follow his recommendations, his notion of having three types of enrichment activities (general exploratory, group training, and independent and small group investigations of real problems) is widely accepted (Maker & Nielson, 1995). Examples of activities falling in each category, in order, are making a field trip to a zoo, learning how to use the library, and studying the habits of local wild animals.

Acceleration permits children to move faster through the curriculum so that they are learning material typically reserved for older learners. Grade skipping, early entrance, and single-subject acceleration are common variants of acceleration. In the field, fast-paced instruction in subject matter for children who want it is sound educational policy (Howley, Howley, & Pendarvis, 1995; Stanley, 1979). Critics maintain that there is nothing special about acceleration because children simply move quickly through the standard curriculum (Coleman, 1985).

Controversy and Ambivalence

Special educational provisions for students considered to be gifted and talented have been a source of controversy in the United States. Throughout the history of educational programming for children with advanced abilities, recurrent questions of equity and excellence have emerged (Howley et al., 1995). The 1990s are no different. Interest in programs for these children apparently goes in cycles. When the country is in a period of crisis and uncertainty, such as in the 1960s after Sputnik, calls for programs for gifted children have been popular. At other times, when socioeconomic conditions seem more stable and prosperous, programs for gifted children tend to diminish. Although such fluctuation occurs, children who are well advanced beyond the normal curriculum are always present in classrooms. Their presence and the persistent debate over issues of equity and excellence form the backdrop to the issues presented in this chapter.

How to handle the presence of variations in human characteristics in the school is a major subtheme in the debate over special programs and inclusion. Should all children receive the same treatment or type of teaching? Much of the debate on gender issues and multicultural education is on that very question; that is, what are the best practices for meeting varied needs while accounting for and appreciating the range of individual differences (Oakes & Lipton, 1990)? Should differences be pointed out, simply acknowledged, or ignored? What is the effect on the development of children of accepting one of these three possibilities? No simple answers to such questions exist.

Focus of Discussion

Persons react to the idea that there are children who are gifted and talented in positive and negative ways. Few stay neutral for long. Because most persons have observed or have had experience with persons who have this label, discussion tends to become heated and grounded in personal experience. While reading the issues presented here, you are likely to identify with points in the discussion that correspond with your own experience. The fact that the concept—gifted and talented—is a fuzzy one with imprecise boundaries further contributes to the emotional context of the discussion. Additionally, because the presence of advanced abilities in some, but not all, bothers Americans' egalitarian sentiments, the matter is not easily resolved.

As with all areas of special education, in gifted education there is much to debate. Many of the issues discussed throughout this text have parallel arguments in the community of gifted educators. At the same time, there is general agreement in the field that giftedness is not a single phenomenon such that one program can be appropriate for all gifted children, and that special attention needs to be devoted to identifying and nurturing minority youth. In this chapter, two issues are presented that illustrate the nature of the debate among those concerned with the education of children who are gifted and talented. They were picked because they are "hot" issues. Each topic has its own particular and arcane points, and each issue contains echoes of debates across the entire field of special education. The first topic focuses on whether programs for gifted and talented students solve or cause educational problems. The second issue debates the use of cooperative learning with high-ability learners. For each issue, we present background or introductory information followed by arguments for two opposing positions.

SOLVING OR CREATING EDUCATIONAL PROBLEMS THROUGH GIFTED EDUCATION

A fundamental contradiction exists in American culture between individualism and conformity. In essence, the contradiction is how to nurture giftedness in some individuals and concurrently develop a sense of common values and purpose among all individuals. This contradiction provides the context for the political and social conflict that surrounds gifted education today and in past decades (Coleman, 1985). Special programs for children who are gifted and talented generate criticisms about definition, identification, and programming of children. A major part of the critique has much in common with the general argument for more inclusive schools (Skrtic, 1991). The analysis by critics (e.g., Margolin, 1994; Sapon-Shevin, 1994a, 1994b) leads them to question the enterprise of "gifted education" and to recommend that it be returned to the general education classroom. In some instances, critics would like programs for the gifted to be abandoned altogether.

Inclusionists argue that the best educational placement maximizes diversity in all classroom situations (see Chapter 3 for further discussion of inclusion). Proponents of special programs interpret the world in a much different fashion than the critics of such programs (Callahan, 1996). It seems as if each side lives on a different planet.

Defining *Giftedness*

Determining who is gifted is a complex matter, for it is not always obvious who fits whose criteria. Education for the gifted is grounded in the belief that there is a group of persons who have unmet needs. The characteristics of these needy persons can be specified and used to identify them. The fact that workable identification systems can be devised is accepted. Implicit in those systems is the assumption that the proportion of children who are gifted and talented is evenly distributed across our society (Borland, 1996). Once an identification system is implemented, it becomes obvious that disproportionate numbers of children are included or excluded. This pattern is most apparent among groups of minority, economically disadvantaged, and disabled youth (Coleman, 1985). This fact raises questions not only about our imperfect identification system but also about who are the gifted. It is the latter question that sparks the debate that is raging at present. On one side are those who accept the utility of the notion of giftedness, and on the other are those who question the meaningfulness of the category.

Homogeneity, Heterogeneity, and the Curriculum

Following from the idea that there is a definable group of gifted children is the belief that a special program can be designed and executed that will meet their needs and that their development will be enhanced beyond that which would have happened in the general program. It is the responsibility of advocates to marshal evidence supporting the effectiveness of the special programs (Coleman,

Gifted students can put leadership skills to work in peer groups.

1995). The possibility of gathering meaningful information on effectiveness is hampered by the variety of program arrangements and lack of agreement on what are appropriate outcomes for those programs. Are there some program arrangements that might be better than others? Do special programs have unwelcome side effects that abrogate beneficial effects? (Borland, 1966). The ambiguous results of that research open the door to the questions about which special arrangements are most effective and whether special programs are necessary.

In the 1990s, professionals and parents involved in special education are deliberating the idea of inclusion. Inclusion has been put forward by some as the most appropriate way to program for gifted children. Much of the debate about inclusion for gifted children centers on how classroom groups should be formed (Howley et al., 1995). Since chronological age is the traditional basis by which schools are organized, in most cases the argument for organizing classroom groups refers to variations in ability. Should grouping be done in a manner that minimizes or maximizes the range of ability in a room? Narrowing the range of differences on the basis of some single characteristic, such as membership in the gifted and talented group, is one option (homogeneous grouping). Leaving the range to include children of all ability levels is another (heterogeneous grouping). Evidence on the effectiveness of either grouping option in schools is generally mixed (Callahan, 1996).

Decision Point 4.1: Inclusion or
Separation of Gifted and Talented Students

Arguments for Proposition One This proposition is based on the question of whether a category of children who are gifted and talented even exists. Sapon-Shevin (1994a) asks this question: "Does it make sense to call any children gifted?" (p. 8). Certainly, all children are different and have gifts and talents that can be developed (Margolin, 1996). Since all have gifts and all children should be

---

Proposition One

Children who may be gifted and talented are best served by being instructed in the inclusive, general education classroom, where children of diverse abilities learn together. Special programs that separate children attack imaginary problems that do not need to be fixed.

---

appreciated for their own particular talents, the need for a separate category of exceptionality and, therefore, programs for them is simply not present.

Defining Giftedness   Does giftedness exist in the real and natural world? The creation of a category of children considered to require unique education because of the presence of special intellectual gifts and/or other talents is not based on the reality of the category (Treffinger & Feldhusen, 1996). Giftedness is merely a "socially constructed" classification (Howley et al., 1995; Margolin, 1994), which some have used as a means to foster an elite education for a few at public expense. Briefly, "socially constructed" refers to the fact that social groups, using some unknown process, create categories and labels in order to understand the complexity of people and of social events in their lives. Without a socially invented label, this and other categories, such as learning disabilities (see Chapter 1), would not exist. The category of giftedness is one that people have created. The notion of "gifted" has no reality, which becomes evident through examination of how the label emerged, who controlled that process, and who gets rewarded by the use of the label (Margolin, 1994).

The presence of the label gives rise to varying interpretations of human differences, to the development of social services that correspond to the perceived needs of those in that category, and to the maintenance of social advantage for some groups and not for others (Margolin, 1994; Pendarvis & Howley, 1996). If one deletes a category, there is no need for programs. By redefining a category, the kinds of services needed change also: "Recognizing giftedness as a social construct means acknowledging that without school rules and policies, legal and educational practices designed to provide services to gifted students...would not exist" (Sapon-Shevin, 1994b, p. 17). The existence of significant differences among children in terms of ability, temperament, etc., is not denied; rather, the argument is that such differences are arbitrary and insignificant, and attention is not warranted by the evidence. Because there is no need to give special attention to one set of children's characteristics over another set, there is no need to have the category at all (Margolin, 1996).

Homogeneity, Heterogeneity, and the Curriculum   Correlated with the artificial nature of this category is the contention that a separate curriculum is warranted for gifted and talented students. Programs developed in response to differences among children do not deserve to be called special educational provisions for the gifted if (a) all children could benefit from such a curriculum and (b) the curriculum is not significantly different from the standard (Borland, 1996; Pendarvis & Howley, 1996).

© Michael Siluk.

Student boredom in school can cause the loss of time as well as opportunity.

By examining the goals and objectives of gifted education, one can get a strong sense of the curriculum. A reading of the textbooks in gifted education published over the past fifty years (Margolin, 1996) shows the similarity of the goals and the persistence of the same goals since the 1950s. In essence, these goals indicate that programs are striving to promote a sense of competence, independence, love of learning, commitment to democratic principles, higher level thinking, and social responsibility. Are these goals different than those we would wish for all children? Since the goals sound strikingly similar to those of "regular" education, they cannot provide sufficient justification for having a special program.

An additional curriculum argument against gifted education looks at the content of typical talented and gifted programs. Most programs use enriched content, and few use advanced content (Daniel & Cox, 1988; Howley et al., 1995). Enriched content, by definition, extends the general curriculum into challenging and creative activities. What sense does it make to reserve these activities only for gifted children? Do so-called gifted children warrant less tedium and boredom in school and more projects of interest than do others? The connection between the special characteristics of so-called gifted and talented children and the content of enrichment programs is tenuous at best. Indeed, the inability of teachers to develop programs that are uniquely suitable for one group and of no value to others adds additional evidence of the unreality of the category itself. Furthermore, this practice effectively excludes some children from these more interesting kinds of activities (Pendarvis & Howley, 1996).

Advocates for the special education of students labeled as gifted need to supply evidence showing that the programs produce benefits that would not occur without the programs. This position is the efficacy argument. Studies of the effectiveness of separate programs as well as studies of enrichment, acceleration, and grouping practices are central to this part of the debate. Studies unequivocally documenting the effectiveness of any educational practice are difficult to find, and it is particularly hard for advocates of special programs for the gifted to find such evidence (Borland, 1996). Evidence on the value of separate, homogeneous, self-contained programs is enlightening but not very comparable to what goes on in most school situations. George (1992) notes that gifted programs are effective because they take the best students, they give them the best resources, and they get the best results. Why should we be surprised by this situation? It is clearly the plentiful resources and strong learning environment, not grouping, that delivers the benefits.

Not only is there little evidence to suggest that gifted children benefit from such programs, but there is also evidence to suggest that the presence of special programs negatively affects the entire school and harms children (Pendarvis & Howley, 1996). In essence, the concept of gifted education has negative utility. One consequence of the gifted category is that it fosters the notion that some children have no talents or gifts and, as such, are unworthy. Such notions defy common sense because children are valuable as persons, not because they have special gifts. Programs promote, whether intentionally or not, this nonsensical viewpoint (Sapon-Shevin, 1994a; Treffinger & Feldhusen, 1996).

Linked to the idea of a special group are questions of how children came to be gifted. A conventional presumption is that such children are born that way. Because a smaller proportion of persons of color and of low socioeconomic circumstances are sorted into the gifted category in most schools, the process of identification feeds implicit notions of classism and racism that are present in our society (Margolin, 1994). In other words, those others who are not gifted and talented are that way because it is the natural order of things. The result is that all involved, the gifted and the nongifted, think the designation is deserved. Those who are not considered gifted define themselves as less worthy and believe they cannot really achieve or accomplish in an outstanding manner. Those who are gifted feel that they deserve to be picked and that those who are not picked do not have the ability to be gifted (Pendarvis & Howley, 1996). In this situation, the meaning and value of differences become apparent, and notions of giftedness become bound to notions of goodness and virtue. The claim is made that persons who are gifted deserve to be that way because they are inherently more worthy and moral. Persons who are not chosen for this special status are equally deserving. The gifted category is a means by which the advantaged in society promote their own values and devalue those of others. This view is based on the answer to the question "Who benefits from this belief [that giftedness exists]?" (Margolin, 1994, p. xiii). In this situation, it is the middle and upper middle classes that benefit, and it is minorities and the poor who lose. The proportionately lower number of students identified as gifted from the latter two groups is evidence of who is advantaged in this situation. Sapon-Shevin (1994b) has stated the following: "As opposed to other educational programs designed to address a specific educational need, programs…for the gifted target children of privilege and appeal to a clearly meritocratic mind set" (p. 182). This means that advantaged children continue to get more benefits that further their advantage and that the disadvantaged do not get opportunities to develop their talents and potentially change their place in society (Howley et al., 1995). The program for gifted and talented children is a form of meritocracy, an anathema in a democratic, pluralistic society.

Another consequence, and maybe a more dangerous one, is that the removal of children from general education classes perpetuates the poor educational conditions in most schools. In fact, it may make the situation worse because the middle-class and upper-middle-class parents who tend to be vocal critics of the school are removed from the debate. The effect is to split our attention and our limited resources between general education and special programs, hiding the fact that general education is in need of serious reform. Put in other terms, the gifted program allows the rigid, unbending general education curriculum to continue. If this general education curriculum were adapted appropriately for all children, the need for a special program would be prevented (Sapon-Shevin, 1994b). Acceleration has the effect of permitting some children to jump over the regular lockstep curriculum; enrichment has the effect of putting interesting material into the classroom so that gifted children do not have to bear the boring regular curriculum to which other children are subjected (Pendarvis & Howley, 1996). Thus, two of the three programming options for children who are gifted and talented actually exempt them from participating in parts of the regular program, drain resources away from the typical program, and camouflage the deficiencies of the regular program.

Argument Summary Gifted education perpetuates an effective system of instruction that enables some children to escape for a time but, in the end, keeps everything the same. The result is that our democratic system is undercut. Tracking (homogeneous ability grouping) disadvantages most children, and it is not essential to provide educational benefits for the gifted children in the highest tracks (Oakes & Lipton, 1990). At the same time, the system of special programming unintentionally undermines the professionalism of teachers (Pugach, 1988). Teaching is taken away from teachers, so they come to believe they do not possess the special skills needed to teach the gifted, and they accept that they have little responsibility for educating gifted children (Sapon-Shevin, 1990). When this effect is combined with the inattention to the ineffectiveness of the regular program, the entire educational system is in a serious crisis of denial of the basic problem.

If we wish to achieve a society in which all people are valued for their contributions, then the nature of schooling must reflect that goal. When time and resources are allocated for the achievement of a select few, those who remain are made to feel less worthy and valuable. Special programs should be abandoned, and gifted children should receive instruction in the regular class. The inclusive school can be the model for a society that recognizes the worth of each individual, regardless of his or her difference.

Arguments for Proposition Two *Inclusion* as defined by full inclusionists is an inappropriate way to understand the issues pertaining to gifted education because it selectively ignores the legitimacy of decades of evidence supporting the effectiveness of special programs (Gallagher, 1996). While the information on the effectiveness of homogeneous grouping is inconclusive for the general school

---

Proposition Two
Children who are gifted and talented should receive instruction in programs that are attuned to their special abilities. Gifted students are a diverse group and need an array of services ranging from placement in general education classes to placement in special schools. Ignoring their educational needs is a serious ethical problem.

---

population (Kulik & Kulik, 1991), the information for gifted children is so favorable to the practice of grouping being used along with other programming options, such as enrichment and acceleration, that Rogers (1993) believes the evidence clearly suggests that gifted and talented youngsters should spend the majority of their school time with others of similar ability and interests. In other words, differences exist among children that are markers of giftedness, and attention to those differences leads to appropriate education.

Defining Giftedness Implicit in the debate over the meaning of differences is the position that maintains that by arbitrarily selecting some characteristics and affixing the label "gifted and talented" we risk undermining the school and destroying a feeling of community (Sapon-Shevin, 1996). This position is based on denial of the fact that some children, by virtue of their rapid learning, their advanced knowledge, and their seriousness about learning, experience schooling differently from those who do not exhibit such characteristics. This difference deserves to be acknowledged, and programs to deal with it need to be developed (Borland, 1996; Coleman, 1995).

The arguments for and against inclusion as it applies to children who are gifted and talented take several forms. One gambit in the inclusion debate is to argue against the presence of qualitative differences between gifted and nongifted learners. Evidence for the presence of quantitative differences in terms of learning and development is obvious. For example, some children are bigger, more verbal, or more creative than their chronological peers. Evidence on the presence of qualitative differences is more subtle and inferential. Quantitative variances can be so extreme between a youngster and her classmates that the differences warrant being defined as qualitative because the discrepancy has direct, practical instructional implications and real personal significance for a child (Robinson, 1995). For example, a child who is in the second grade and reading on the sixth-grade level in a typical mixed-ability class is so far ahead of his peers as to make the educational experience for that child qualitatively different.

Avoiding the issue of differences is a mistake. Averting our eyes from human variations does not make them go away. Ignorance is the perfect breeding ground for incorrect and dangerous notions of the meaning of variations. Once one examines the idea, ignoring differences among children because some have more or less of some ability or talent is ridiculous (Gallagher, 1996). Would one eliminate the basketball program because some children are taller, more agile, and good at ball handling? Does it make sense to limit the kinds of opportunities the top players have so that you could improve the shot-making skills of the other students in the school? Inclusion does not mean ignoring differences; rather, it should mean honoring differences and making meaningful adjustments for persons who need them. As Subotnik (1995) has remarked, "Talents and achievement occur among all ethnic groups and social classes and must be identified and nurtured in all domains of the schooling experience. The best form of inclusion is the vigorous search for talent among all segments of society" (p. 458). Proponents such as Subotnik believe the searching for talent should be a continuous effort. Careful identification is needed so that we can pick out the children with high potential in minority and economically disadvantaged areas. This need becomes more critical, since the numbers of such children are increasing. A host of techniques is available, and if used properly, these techniques can help identify these children (Callahan, Tomlinson, & Pizzat, 1993; Richert, 1985). Not to look actively for such children does a disservice to them and their families.

Homogeneity, Heterogeneity, and the Curriculum   Identification is not enough. Special programs are needed so that talents can flourish. The lack of a correspondence between high ability and outstanding accomplishment is a powerful indication that special programs must be provided to nurture special talent (Sears, 1979; Terman & Oden, 1947). Without such programs, the development of special abilities is left to chance, and talent is typically not realized. The conventional notion that "cream rises to the top" so that special programs are not necessary is not supported by the evidence. Stories of children with learning and physical disabilities (e.g., Thomas Edison and Albert Einstein) who were not identified in the school and were somehow successful is not evidence that talent emerges (Shore, Cornell, Robinson, & Ward, 1991).

If we want to maximize the development of high abilities in children, then selection and placement in rigorous programs are mandatory. Numerous studies of eminent persons in fields ranging from athletics to music to natural science provide evidence that outstanding accomplishment in a field is associated with and supported by instruction from special teachers and placement in special programs (Bloom, 1985; Csikzentmihalyi, Rathunde, & Whelan, 1993). The lives and achievements of these successful individuals are the strongest evidence that we have for the powerful effects of education.

All advocates of inclusion assert that children need to be together in heterogeneous groups (Skrtic, 1991). Some accept the least restrictive environment philosophy; others believe that mixing of children of diverse abilities and backgrounds in all situations is the best way to organize schools. Full inclusionists believe that mixing is always the best alternative and that the end of programs for the gifted and talented is warranted. Persons who support special programs and inclusion for children who are gifted and talented maintain that the instructional situation and student needs should determine the decision about placement (Coleman & Gallagher, 1995).

Interestingly, critics of gifted education typically recognize and salute the acceptability of grouping children on the basis of some characteristics for special opportunities. For example, we commonly select children for programs such as drama, basketball, debate, math club, and band on the basis of ability and interest. Some might argue that these are really extracurricular activities and as such are not the major business of the school. The contention is weak because the school typically provides time for pep rallies, play rehearsals, and service organization meetings during the regular school day. Outstanding students in those areas receive much praise and popular acclaim. Are not those exceptions to the schedule a clear message that some abilities and interests are more worthy than others? Why is it that academic abilities are more likely to disrupt the school community and engender feelings of worthlessness among students than those other abilities? (Gallagher, 1996).

Most persons have been in situations where they had to wait because they knew about something or how to do something and those around them did not. Those experiences link them to gifted children. But in the case of the gifted child, large amounts of time, frequently 50% of their time in classrooms, are spent waiting for others to catch up. This "quiet crisis" (Ross, 1993) is largely invisible unless children become disruptive. Should children simply wait when that time could be used more profitably to further their learning? An educational system that does not recognize this reality is not appropriate for any children. Programs for children who are gifted and talented are needed.

Advocates of programs for gifted and talented children support innovations such as inclusion that promote the development of individual differences because programs for the gifted are only one among an array of options needed for acknowledging and supporting differences. One standard program is not the best for all gifted children because gifted children form the most heterogeneous group in the school. However, they share three characteristics: (a) rapid rate of learning and development in some domain, (b) advanced knowledge in various subject areas, and (c) a seriousness about learning. A program of education that does not address these educationally relevant characteristics in a practical and meaningful way is inappropriate for gifted and talented children (Subotnik & Coleman, 1996). In a time of scare resources, we must continue to argue for the maximum amount of attention to all children on the basis of each child's needs.

Although some evidence exists that indicates that homogenous grouping has been used to perpetuate inequitable treatment of minority and economically disadvantaged youth, that is not the fault of special programs. Rather, it is a problem that is linked to larger societal forces (Gallagher, 1996). It defies common sense to eliminate special programs for children who need them in order to have retribution for the mistakes and biases of their elders (Pendarvis & Howley, 1996).

Another argument for disbanding programs for gifted children is that children who are developmentally delayed or learning disabled are more deserving of the limited resources available to schools. Some persons see some intuitive appeal in this point, but in actuality, it is indefensible, unethical, and impractical (Newland, 1976; Sapon-Shevin, 1996). Once one maintains that a single group, gifted children or children belonging to one among many kinds of disabilities, is more deserving, one enters an absurd world filled with philosophical debates about the value of various human differences and arguments about measuring those differences. Arguing that one group is more deserving than another drags everyone into an inescapable quagmire. The debate inexorably degenerates into one about the worth of one group over another. The only valid position is one that asserts that every child deserves to be instructed in ways that address that child's needs, and the school has the responsibility for delivering such instruction at that child's level.

Argument Summary Conventional wisdom is incorrect; the gifted will not "do OK" if they are not challenged. Outstanding talent does not develop unless it is encouraged (Feldman, 1980). The common denominator of special programs is the gathering of persons of high ability along with expert teachers in resource-rich, nurturing environments. By identifying persons of high ability and placing them in appropriate programs, we can encourage the development of their special strengths and talents and magnify their accomplishments (Coleman, 1995).

Leaving gifted and talented youngsters alone without any special programming is equivalent to neglecting children. The school careers of gifted children are not filled with good moments. Frequently, the school is experienced as a highly frustrating place that is not conducive to the development of their high cognitive ability. The school is typically unresponsive to children's advanced abilities (Bloom, 1985; Csikzentmihalyi et al., 1993) and treats the gifted child as though something were wrong with him or her (Coleman & Cross, 1988; Robinson, 1996). The child becomes handicapped by a lack of expectation and absence of differentiation that would provide an appropriate learning experience. In this instance, the problem is clearly the school's, but school personnel regard the child's natural need to learn and grow as antagonistic and problematic to the smooth functioning of the school. Many parents of gifted children report such interactions with their local schools (Robinson, 1996).

All children should have different learning experiences because they have different needs. The statement that all children can learn does not mean that all children learn at the same time, learn at the same rate, and achieve the same outcomes. Evidence on the development of talents other than academic (e.g., sports, theater) supports the importance of specialized instruction for children (Bloom, 1985). Where mixed-ability grouping is the only option, the persons who get stimulated the most are the teachers, not the students. It is as inappropriate to put children in situations where they face a chronic lack of challenge as it is inappropriate to put children in situations where they face persistent failure. Learning to work together and helping others is a worthwhile goal, but it is inappropriate when a child is rarely challenged academically and intellectually. In order to meet the goals of excellence and equity, more, not less, attention to individual differences is needed.

COOPERATIVE LEARNING
AND GIFTED CHILDREN

The school restructuring movement has provided many opportunities for a reexamination of traditional educational practices. If schools are to be responsive to diversity, what is the best way to proceed? However, current thought proposes that differences should be addressed in a more inclusive atmosphere. Among the many models of appropriate practice that are being implemented, cooperative learning (CL) is one instructional strategy that is being widely used to meet the goals of restructured schools. Cooperative learning is being touted as an inclusive strategy, but it can also be used in conventionally organized schools. Many papers have appeared proclaiming CL as an important instructional tool in many different learning environments (Anderson, Reder, & Simon, 1996). Cooperative learning involves a set of instructional strategies that uses small groups of students working together to facilitate the learning of all children in the group. CL theorists recommend that the majority of the school day be spent in cooperative learning groups (Slavin, 1988).

The three most widely recognized models for cooperative learning are those proposed by Robert Slavin (1988), Spenser Kagan (1990), and David and Roger Johnson (1990). Slavin describes CL as "classroom techniques in which students work on learning activities in small groups and receive rewards or recognition based on their group's performance" (Robinson, 1990, p. 10). Johnson and Johnson describe cooperative learning as "the instructional use of small groups so that students work together to maximize their own learning and other's learning" (Nelson, Gallagher, & Coleman, 1993, p. 117). CL differs from earlier "small group" teaching strategies "by emphasizing: (a) positive interdependence, (b) individual accountability, (c) group processing, (d) the development of social skills, and (e) face-to-face interaction of students" (Coleman & Gallagher, 1995, pp. 365–366).

The three models are also slightly different. Slavin's model (1988) is directed most specifically at two content areas, mathematics and reading/language arts. The math program, Team Assisted Individualization (TAI), forms learning teams of four to five students of high, average, and low abilities. The Cooperative Integrated Reading and Composition model (CIRC) matches pairs of students from one reading group with pairs of students reading at different levels.

The Johnson and Johnson (1990) CL model uses cooperative groups of two to six members from high-, average-, and low-ability groups. Group members are given assigned role(s) in the group to ensure their active participation. This model can be adapted to any curriculum area (Ellett, 1993).

Kagan's (1990) model uses a number of "structures" that are taught to students to aid in the completion of tasks. Two of the structures used are "Think-Pair-Share" (students think to themselves, discuss with a partner, share with the group) and "Jigsaw" (each student becomes an expert on a topic by working with members from other teams, then returns to the home team to share information).

Generally, the models share four practices in addition to those listed above: teacher introduction of new material, team practice, team recognition, and team rewards. Since the focus of CL is the group investigation and mastery of the material, traditional teaching is limited to introducing new material. Lecture or other systematic teaching procedures are used in a lesson. The instruction and materials are usually at the basic skill level, with students proceeding through the material at the same general pace.

Cooperative learning is assumed to occur in heterogeneously grouped classrooms so that CL groups are composed of students of similar ages and high, average, and low abilities. Thus, age-peer groups are formed rather than intellectual-peer groups. Group members practice what they learn from one another. Because all students have opportunities to achieve, the motivational problems of many low-achieving students are relieved. Individual recognition is done through work sheets, quizzes, or essays completed without the help of other group members. Team recognition may be in the form of group certificates. The CL groups are organized so that rewards for achievement go to the entire group. Rewards are directed toward learning information as well as using group processes. Even though these materials and skills are at the basic level, students are learning material that is new to all of them (Slavin, 1991). In the initial phases of a unit, student work is usually based in common materials such as basal readers (CIRC) or standard content-area texts. With TAI, a week-long, group-paced instructional period is sequenced after three weeks of individualized work in basic mathematics operations. In most models, students are placed in heterogeneous teams; they receive a teacher-directed lesson, and then they help one another master the material.

Effectiveness of Cooperative Learning

Cooperative learning has proponents and critics. CL can be used both in heterogeneous (mixed) settings and in homogeneous settings. Whereas some research studies have reported substantial gains in learning for mixed groups of children and others report no differences (Anderson et al., 1996), the impact of CL on the achievement of gifted students has not been studied. The limited research base plus the widespread increase in the use of cooperative learning for all students without substantial evidence supporting it is vexing to supporters of education of the gifted. The situation is especially bothersome because in some districts CL is being used to replace programs for the gifted as schools implement their restructured organizational plans (Gallagher, 1996).

In school systems where CL is being used, a consultant with expertise in gifted education assists the classroom teacher in selecting content, in planning, and in teaching lessons. This consultant can provide a valuable service by identifying materials and techniques that foster more appropriate learning for high-ability group members (Coleman & Gallagher, 1995). At the same time, the consultant with gifted expertise can provide specific examples of content and practice that provide to entire classes these formerly exclusive opportunities (Sapon-Shevin, 1996).

Interpersonal and Leadership Issues

Cooperative learning is believed to have academic and social benefits. Among the nonacademic outcomes, interpersonal and leadership skills are mentioned in the debate over the use of CL with children who are gifted and talented. Some believe that gifted and talented children have serious interpersonal problems that cooperative learning can fix. Others see the gifted as being potential leaders who need opportunities to develop those skills not generally available in homogeneous classrooms. As schools move forward to implement cooperative learning models, questions arise about CL's effect on the learning and social development of all children (Anderson et al., 1996). Does cooperative learning bring differential benefits to the gifted and their nongifted peers? The differences articulated between the opposing positions is based on philosophical differences about schooling and about interpretations of the research literature. The propositions present divergent views of cooperative learning.

Decision Point 4.2: Including Gifted Children in Cooperative Learning Groups

Arguments for Proposition One   Schools are filled with children of diverse abilities, interests, and backgrounds. Because cooperative learning promotes learning and builds important social skills, it is an effective way to meet the needs of all students, including those who are gifted and talented (Sapon-Shevin, 1996). Heterogeneous cooperative learning groups benefit all students and hurt none. Students of diverse abilities working and learning alongside one another in the same group gain experiences unavailable in segregated educational settings. High-ability students are good learning models for average- and low-ability students. In turn, high-ability students have the opportunity to prove to themselves that they really understand concepts by explaining those concepts to the other group members. Slavin (1990) argues that the act of teaching content to others in mixed groups improves gifted students' understanding and retention of the material.

Effectiveness of Cooperative Learning   Slavin (1990) has shown that high achievers gain as much from cooperative learning (compared with high achievers in traditional classes) as do average and low achievers. Although he concedes that not all cooperative learning methods are effective, those that have the most consistent record of enhancing students' achievement include as components group goals and individual accountability. High achievers also gain from the routine opportunities to explain to groupmates the concepts of a particular series of lessons.

Cooperative learning groups work best when high-ability children are present. Some research supports the idea that CL groups are less effective when they do not have a high-ability student who masters the material quickly and is available to help others in the group (Robinson, 1991). Furthermore, high-achieving students in CL groups do more critical thinking and analysis than when they are engaged in more typical competitive or individual learning situations (Ellett, 1993). Given the fact that cooperative learning engenders more learning and produces none of the negative effects of homogeneous grouping, gifted children should be instructed in mixed CL grouping.

Interpersonal and Leadership Issues   High-ability students are frequently thought to be deficient in social skills. "Many educators feel that it is *particularly important* to

---

Proposition One
Cooperative learning is an effective educational strategy with gifted and talented children. Not only does it promote academic achievement, but it also advances important social skills and attitudes.

give high achievers cooperative learning experience to help them learn to accept and get along with others" (Slavin, 1990, p. 6: italics added). By being placed in cooperative learning groups, gifted students will have more contact with others and become friends with a wide range of children. Gifted learners will learn to share opinions, respect others, and be tactful as a result of CL. Without the opportunities inherent in cooperative learning groups, gifted children are less likely to develop these skills.

A positive feature of cooperative learning groups for gifted learners is the possibility that they will learn leadership and interpersonal skills. Cooperative learning helps to break down the traditional school values of "do your own work," and "don't let anyone else see your paper," which are antithetical to the future expectations for cooperation in the adult work world (Gallagher, 1991).

From the team's progress toward an assigned goal, group processing skills are learned and group effort is seen to result. These groups reflect the diverse nature of the adult world. The workplace is filled with persons of diverse abilities and backgrounds, so it is good for children to develop and practice strategies for dealing with all types of people. Important discoveries today are very seldom the product of the brooding genius working in isolation. Children who are gifted and talented need these experiences.

In the team-practice component of cooperative learning, the model of the effective, efficient learner—the high-ability student—serves a positive function for the other members of the group. Studies of heterogeneous cooperative learning groups indicate that the process of group practice is effective in improving achievement and social-skill development. Team practice allows all students, but especially gifted students, to gain experiences in leadership skills. The idea is that the more advanced students will develop abilities in decision making and transforming the goals of the group, thereby increasing the growth and commitment of group members by raising their expectations for achievement. At the same time, learners who are gifted learn that others make worthwhile contributions to group goals (Ross & Smyth, 1995).

Argument Summary In general, the ideal of cooperative learning offers hope in the midst of current inequities of educational opportunities and declining resources. As the financial resources that support education become scarcer, the heterogeneous classroom has a fiscal appeal and provides unexpected social benefits. Fiscally, it is possible to have fewer specialists and special programs so that money is saved; socially, students learn to work and collaborate in pluralistic settings. The idea of developing a cooperative peer atmosphere and group rewards goes a long way toward building "community" because it makes the point that all children, in fact, do need and deserve richly stimulating, nurturing, and heterogeneous classrooms (Sapon-Shevin, 1994).

Arguments for Proposition Two Cooperative learning is not the panacea claimed by its proponents (Anderson et al., 1996). In actuality, cooperative learning has something to offer students who are gifted and talented, but in its typical form, CL enacts a toll on students who are gifted and talented. It also may not be

Proposition Two	However, cooperative learning does not have
Cooperative learning exploits gifted children in	these shortcomings when used in homogenous
the service of a simplistic notion of school reform.	settings.

the best learning situation for other children. Proponents of heterogeneous CL who maintain that there is "no discernible damage to the high achiever" with cooperative learning groups are evading the issue. The ways in which heterogeneous cooperative learning lessons are introduced, implemented, and taught hurt gifted and talented learners (Robinson, 1990).

Effectiveness of Cooperative Learning Cooperative learning models stress that the same materials be used for all students. It is assumed that the information is new to the students. No differentiation of content is made for students who are ready for advanced content. If "between 39–49% of the curriculum in mathematics and 36–54% of the curriculum in language arts" (Robinson, 1991, p. 6) at the elementary level has been mastered by gifted students prior to instruction, how can schools justify presenting the same material to all students? The pace of instruction in CL is fixed for the entire group. Children who learn rapidly are limited by the rate of instruction because they must wait until new material is offered to them: "*In the classroom, time is a fixed resource.* If children are organized in cooperative learning groups studying grade level material for the majority of their school day, they will have time to do little else. They will not have time to learn anything *new* to *them*" (Robinson, 1990, p. 19). By being asked to relearn the already known content, their advanced learning is inhibited. Why it is that low-achieving students have the right to be challenged by the curriculum, but not gifted students? (Pendarvis & Howley, 1996).

Since studies report that the achievement levels of all students improve with CL, these gains may be not as great for gifted students as they would have been with another form of instruction. In fact, the sensibility of comparing children who enter the instructional situation knowing 50% or more of the material to those children who are learning most of the material for the first time must be questioned. None of the research studies that cite achievement gains in cooperative learning groups focuses specifically on the gifted population; rather, they look at the whole group and compare CL classes to classes where teaching is done in the traditional manner (Robinson, 1990). Until that kind of research is reported, it is unwarranted to claim that gifted children are achieving at levels at which they are capable. Logically, the lack of opportunity to learn new material and/or pursue one's interests will inevitably depress achievement levels.

In cooperative learning there are few opportunities for learners to self-select topics for study or for subject-matter acceleration. These teaching strategies have been demonstrated to promote the learning of children who are gifted and talented (Coleman, 1985). The content of lessons must be at the appropriate level for gifted students in order for CL to be considered an appropriate educational strategy. For heterogeneous groups, appropriate content must be mixed-level content, not the same content for all. The type of material used in mixed-ability groups is in many cases simply not appropriate for gifted students.

The fact that the whole group gets a unified grade is a source of concern for gifted students. Unified grades are thought to encourage cooperation and group responsibility for the outcome of the assignment. Many able students are highly motivated to achieve good grades. In CL groups, if members are not willing to do their fair share, the more able students think that they are being penalized for something that is beyond their control. Gifted students voice resentment at having to do most of the work of the group, having to teach other students, and receiving lower marks when their performance is averaged with that of other group members (Ross & Smyth, 1995). In actuality, heterogeneous CL groups may depress an individual's confidence and motivation if the members are not of similar ability (Ellett, 1993).

Interpersonal and Leadership Issues   Children who are gifted and talented are used in the CL group process. In some cooperative learning models, specific roles, such as recorder, explainer, and motivator, are assigned to group members, and the team members practice what they are learning. Frequently, the role of explainer is assigned to the high-ability, above-average student because advocates of cooperative learning maintain that above-average learners must be part of the learning group (Ellett, 1993). Team practice of the assigned material assumes that the gifted student will have the skills and knowledge to be the explainer of the concepts that are to be learned and that such a responsibility would be wanted by the gifted child.

The procedures of assigning roles and team practice create problems for some gifted students. High-ability students get stuck pulling the group along. They are not asked; rather, it is expected of them because they are gifted. This role belongs by definition to the classroom teacher, not gifted students. Motivation should be inherent in the challenge of the material presented in the class, not in the composition of learning groups (Robinson, 1990). The group task often gets accomplished, but at the expense of the gifted learner who becomes identified with having the answers and insisting that the group do high-quality, original work. It is a fiction that the gifted and talented serve as learning models for average and below-average learners. These qualities, such as being a know-it-all or being a perfectionist, play into stereotypic notions of giftedness. In other words, the role gifted students are assigned forces them into situations that work against their identification as individuals instead of stereotypes.

High-ability students also report becoming frustrated when the rest of the group does not understand the more sophisticated concepts that they think the group should present. A CL group working on the idea of ancient Egyptian culture may not appreciate the input of an able student who wants to demonstrate the relationship between the hierarchy of Egyptian religion and that of the beliefs of Greeks and Romans who have been studied earlier. What is a young learner, or explainer, to do in this kind of situation? Often, the gifted children in a group have not developed the skills or the intellectual strength to persevere in the face of knowledge challenges from other group members. Young children who are incorrect, but certain of their knowledge, are able to persuade students who are correct, but uncertain. Many times, social reasons interfere with the purpose of the explainer. For example, a gifted child who knows the correct answer may yield to another child because she fears being rejected by the group (Ross & Smyth, 1995).

The message to bright students is that the group will do as well as its members. For quality production, they may feel that they need to be in charge. Unfortunately, we expect them to lead in socially acceptable, unobtrusive ways. They have no models for that type of leadership. Classroom teachers most often model didactic methods of instruction. Is it fair for us to expect gifted students to meet our hidden expectations of "teacher" while they still labor under the required role of student? Robinson (1990) claims that the emphasis on talented students as tutors encourages educators to take a utilitarian view of these learners and exploit them only for their achievements and their usefulness to others: "Talented children should be held no more nor no less accountable than others" (p. 21).

The notion that children who are gifted and talented have a greater need for developing social skills is unfounded. It is false that "gifted children need socialization skills as they tend to be intolerant, competitive, creative, independent, and individualistic" (Nelson et al., 1993). From the earliest studies of gifted children conducted by Terman and Hollingworth, we have known that these stereotypes are inaccurate and lead to negative conclusions about the needs of these learners: "These stereotypes are fodder for the cooperative cannon" (Robinson, 1990, p. 20). In the most extreme cases, the argument is used to justify overzealous implementation of cooperative learning with gifted students—for example, "Gifted and average students will become friends if they are assigned to the same learning groups and stay there until they learn to like one another" (Robinson, 1990, p. 20).

Argument Summary In order for CL to be effective with any student, it has to be used correctly. Teachers who incorporate CL into their classes may not have the necessary depth of training to implement the model effectively. Successful implementation depends on appropriate preparation of teachers. Slavin (1990) reports that thousands of teachers have been trained with one-day workshops and a teacher's manual; other teachers have merely used the manual. Johnson and Johnson (1990) maintain that implementation of cooperative learning involves six-day training modules and a districtwide program that takes three to five years to complete. Through the Gifted Education Policy Studies Program, it was reported that classroom teachers receive training but that "they do not receive the coaching and assistance for successful implementation" of cooperative learning (Nelson et al., 1993, p. 119). In essence, teachers are inadequately trained and supported to implement CL in their specific classroom situations.

While it may be generalized that cooperative learning is an appropriate strategy to use to accomplish certain classroom and student goals, a lack of appropriate training for teachers and static grouping arrangements can cause more harm than good. If teachers are to use cooperative learning to the advantage of all students, then the teachers must have the appropriate skills, materials, and time for program design. A boring, biased, or inconsequential lesson, even if done using CL, is not appropriate: "Cooperative learning is a deceptively simple strategy that requires more training and forethought than many teachers misusing cooperative learning have" (Nelson et al., 1993, p. 119).

Given all these arguments, one should not conclude that advocates for programs for children who are gifted and talented reject cooperative learning as a useful teaching strategy. Although gifted students have a lower preference for cooperative learning than they have for individualistic or competitive structures, they do like it in some instances. Furthermore, CL settings can lead to important learning related to group functioning and leadership skills (Ross & Smyth, 1995). The preferred mode of educators of the gifted is for cooperative learning in homogeneous groups with students of similar ability levels. Gifted children favor it as well (Coleman & Gallagher, 1995). Because in the postmodern world problem solving and creativity frequently occur in groups and not solitary settings, cooperative learning is favored by proponents of special programs. Therefore, cooperative learning can be implemented in a manner that circumvents many of the criticisms associated with mixed-ability grouping.

CLOSING THOUGHTS

The chapter has presented two current, important issues in the education of gifted and talented children. There are no facile assumptions in an examination of gifted education in the context of our society. The issue of which differences are worthy of educational support cannot be dismissed. Nor can we allow the devaluation of the personal worth of some by providing benefits for selected others.

In this time of changing national priorities, shrinking fiscal resources, and growing social conservatism, the fate of programs for gifted and talented children is unknown. As special education in general undergoes changes, so will education of the gifted. The inherent controversies in this topic of education for the gifted and talented have many stakeholders (e.g., children, teachers, administrators). Although these issues appear to be primarily educational issues, they are also political, social, and moral concerns. Decisions at the national and local level will be made as a consequence of these forces. Among all those involved, children who are gifted and talented are the stakeholders with the least say in what happens. The fact that critics and proponents of the various positions interpret the world of schooling differently has significant and unsettling implications for building a consensus on education for the gifted and talented. It is by a cooperative examination and discussion of the spectrum and effects of gifted/inclusive education that we will generate the most workable and advantageous solutions for all.

Clear resolution is unlikely, yet several possibilities are more likely than others. The notion of giftedness will become fragmented, and more attention will be given to the idea of individual talents. IQ will continue to decline as a sign of giftedness, to be replaced by indicators of advanced abilities in talent areas. This will create a new set of controversies on which talents are most valuable and what are signs of those talents. The inclusion issue will become muted, but it will never disappear. Schools will continue to struggle with the best way to deal with individual differences in a diverse society. Issues of excellence and equity will be raised. The wealth of school districts will have an effect on the availability of special programs. If past is prologue, gifted programs will decrease in availability and interest until the nation perceives a national emergency. At that time, someone will remind us of the untapped talent in our society, and programs will again begin to flourish.

REFERENCES

Anderson, J. R., Reder, L. M., & Simon, H. A. (1996). Situated learning and education. *Educational Researcher, 25,* 5–11.

Bloom, B. S. (1985). *Developing talent in young people.* New York: Ballantine.

Borland, J. (1996). Gifted education and the threat of irrelevance. *Journal for the Education of the Gifted, 19,* 129–147.

Callahan, C. M. (1996). A critical self-study of gifted education: Healthy practice, necessary evil, or sedition? *Journal for the Education of the Gifted, 19,* 148–163.

Callahan, C. M., Tomlinson, C. A., & Pizzat, P. M. (Eds.). (1993). *Contexts for promise: Noteworthy practices and innovations in the identification of gifted students.* Charlottesville: National Research Center on the Gifted and Talented, University of Virginia.

Coleman, L. J. (1985). *Schooling the gifted.* Palo Alto, CA: Addison-Wesley.

Coleman, L. J. (1995). The power of specialized environments in the development of giftedness: The need for research on social context. *Gifted Child Quarterly, 39,* 171–176.

Coleman, L. J., & Cross, T. L. (1988). Is being gifted a social handicap? *Journal for the Education of the Gifted, 11,* 41–56.

Coleman, M. R., & Gallagher, J. J. (1995). The successful blending of gifted education with middle schools and cooperative learning: Two studies. *Journal for the Education of the Gifted, 18,* 362–384.

Csikzentmihalyi, M., Rathunde, K., & Whelan, S. (1993). *Talented teenagers: The roots of success and failure.* Cambridge, UK: Cambridge University Press.

Daniel, N., & Cox, J. (1988). *Flexible pacing for able learners.* Reston, VA: Council for Exceptional Children.

Ellett, P. (1993). Cooperative learning and gifted education. *Roeper Review, 16,* 114–116.

Feldman, D. (1980). *Beyond universals in cognitive development.* Norwood, NJ: Ablex.

Gallagher, J. J. (1991). Educational reform, values, and gifted students. *Gifted Child Quarterly, 35,* 12–19.

Gallagher, J. J. (1996). A critique of critiques of gifted education. *Journal for the Education of the Gifted, 19,* 234–249.

George, P. (1992). *How to untrack your school.* Alexandria, VA: Association for Supervision and Curriculum Development.

Howley, C. B., Howley, A., & Pendarvis, E. D. (1995). *Out of our minds: Anti-intellectualism and talent development in American schooling.* New York: Teachers College Press.

Johnson, D., & Johnson, R. (1990). Social skills for successful group work. *Educational Leadership, 47,* 29–32.

Kagan, S. (1990). The structural approach to cooperative learning. *Educational Leadership, 47,* 12–15.

Kulik, J. A., & Kulik, C. L. (1991). Ability grouping and gifted children. In N. Colangelo & G. A. Davis (Eds.), *Handbook of gifted education* (pp. 178–196). Boston: Allyn & Bacon.

Maker, J., & Nielson, A. (1995). *Teaching models in education of the gifted* (2nd ed.). Austin: Pro-Ed.

Margolin, L. (1994). *Goodness personified: The emergence of gifted children.* New York: Aldine De Gruyter.

Margolin, L. (1996). A pedagogy of privilege. *Journal for the Education of the Gifted, 19,* 164–180.

Nelson, S. M., Gallagher, J. J., & Coleman, M. R. (1993). Cooperative learning from two different perspectives. *Roeper Review, 16,* 117–121.

Newland, T. E. (1976). *The gifted in socio-educational perspective.* Englewood Cliffs, NJ: Prentice-Hall.

Oakes, J., & Lipton, M. (1990). *Making the best of schools: A handbook for parents, teachers and policy makers.* New Haven: Yale University Press.

Pendarvis, E., & Howley, A. (1996). Playing fair: The possibilities of gifted education. *Journal for the Education of the Gifted, 19,* 215–233.

Pugach, M. C. (1988). Special education as a constraint on teacher education reform. *Journal of Teacher Education, 59,* 52–59.

Renzulli, J., & Reis, S. (1985). *The school-wide enrichment model: A comprehensive plan for educational excellence.* Mansfield, CT: Creative Learning Press.

Richert, S. (1985). Identification of gifted children in the United States: The need for pluralistic assessment. *Roeper Review, 8,* 68–72.

Robinson, A. (1990). Cooperation or exploitation? The argument against cooperative learning for talented students. *Journal for the Education of the Gifted, 14,* 9–27.

Robinson, A. (1991). *Cooperative learning and the academically talented student.* National Research Center on the Gifted and Talented, No. 9105.

Robinson, N. (1995). Rescuing the baby: A commentary on *The Bell Curve. Gifted Child Quarterly, 39,* 180–182.

Robinson, N. (1996). Counseling agenda for gifted young people: A commentary. *Journal for the Education of the Gifted, 20,* 128–137.

Rogers, K. (1993). Grouping the gifted and talented: Questions and answers. *Roeper Review, 16,* 8–12.

Ross, J. A., & Smyth, E. (1995). Differentiating cooperative learning to meet the needs of gifted learners: A case for transformational leadership. *Journal for the Education of the Gifted, 19,* 63–72.

Ross, P. (1993). *National excellence: A case for developing America's talent.* Washington, DC: U.S. Department of Education.

Sapon-Shevin, M. (1990). Gifted education and the deskilling of classroom teachers. *Journal of Teacher Education, 41,* 39–48.

Sapon-Shevin, M. (1994a). Playing favorites: Gifted education and the disruption of community. *Rethinking Schools, 9,* 8–9.

Sapon-Shevin, M. (1994b). *Playing favorites: Gifted education and the disruption of community.* Albany: State University of New York Press.

Sapon-Shevin, M. (1996). Beyond gifted education: Building a shared agenda. *Journal for the Education of the Gifted, 19,* 194–214.

Sears, P. S. (1979). The Terman genetic studies of genius. 1922–1972. In A. H. Passow (Ed.), *The gifted and the talented: Their education and development* (pp. 75–96). Chicago: University of Chicago Press.

Shore, B. M., Cornell, D. G., Robinson, A., & Ward, V. S. (1991). *Recommended practices in gifted education: A critical analysis.* New York: Teachers College Press.

Skrtic, T. (1991). *Behind special education.* Denver: Love.

Slavin, R. (1988). *Student team learning: An overview and practical guide.* Washington, DC: National Educational Association.

Slavin, R. E. (1991). Point–counterpoint: Ability grouping, cooperative learning and the gifted. *Journal for the Education of the Gifted, 14,* 3–8.

Stanley, J. (1979). The study and facilitation of talent for mathematics. In A. H. Passow (Ed.), *The gifted and talented: Their education and development.* Chicago: University of Chicago Press.

Subotnik, R. (1995). Talent developed: Conversations with masters in arts and sciences: A formative synthesis. *Journal for the Education of the Gifted, 18,* 440–466.

Subotnik, R., & Coleman, L. J. (1996). Establishing the foundations for a talent development school: Applying principles to creating an ideal. *Journal for the Education of the Gifted, 20,* 175–189.

Terman, L., & Oden, M. (1947). *Genetic studies of genius: The gifted child grows up* (Vol. 4). Stanford, CA: Stanford University Press.

Treffinger, D., & Feldhusen, J. (1996). Talent recognition and talent development: Successor to gifted education. *Journal for the Education of the Gifted, 19,* 181–193.

PART II

Assessment, Instruction, and Professional Practices in Special Education

The chapters included in this section represent the day-to-day workings of special education. Assessment practices, curricular options, instructional approaches, and transition plans for those ready to exit secondary schools, along with the qualifications of the teachers who deliver special education, have a substantial ongoing impact on the education of students served through special education. Throughout these chapters the themes of categorical and noncategorical approaches to service delivery, inclusion, and multicultural concerns remain.

The issues tackled in the assessment chapter focus on determining eligibility and diagnosis via norm-referenced intelligence and achievement testing, as contrasted to alternatives such as teacher referral and behavioral observations. The chapter also covers assessment practices associated with accountability and the implications such testing holds for special education. Chapter 6 directly addresses the curricular and methodological tensions evident between general and special education but avoids narrowing the debate to reductionism versus constructivism. Rather, the discussion centers on the process of introducing new ideas into the educational system. In Chapter 7 the focus turns to the successful transition of secondary students to employment, postsecondary education, and independent living. The final chapter in Part Two directs attention to higher education, the design of teacher preparation programs, and alternative licensure practices.

Several topics explored within these chapters, although not exclusive to special education (e.g., progression and graduation assessments, alternative licensure), have particular relevance for the field. The discussion of these issues from a special education perspective should encourage our field to take an active role in all education-related issues, for they do, indeed, affect special educators as well as students with disabilities.

5

Assessment Practices

INTRODUCTION

Special education is heavily influenced by the assessment system associated
with it. Eligibility, placement decisions, curricular programming, educational goals, and instructional approaches all ride on the outcomes of assessments. The ability to avoid being labeled, or the opportunity for a child to receive
special education supports, rests on the results of assessments. The most critical
assessment associated with eligibility typically involves the calculation of a child's
intelligence or "potential." Performance on this test is then compared with performance on norm-referenced achievement tests and used for diagnosis. With
the exception of students with speech and language delays, most children take
intelligence tests to determine their potential for academic learning and/or predict their functional abilities (Reschly & Wilson, 1990; Reschly, 1992).

The number of students needing to be tested puts a heavy demand on school
psychologists to produce quantities of assessments, sometimes at the expense of
quality. They conduct approximately seventeen intellectual assessments per
month, about one per working day, as the "refer-test-place" sequence has become the prevalent routine (Reschly & Wilson, 1990). The immediate need to
serve students in a timely fashion leaves school personnel with little time to consider changing assessment practices in accordance with evolving theoretical perspectives. Nevertheless, developers of numerous alternative assessment techniques
claim to have procedures superior to traditional intelligence testing, with popular
theoretical foundations of cognitive processing and potential (e.g., Haywood,

Brown, & Wingenfeld, 1990; Laughon, 1990; Naglieri, Das, & Jarman, 1990; Reschly & Wilson, 1990). Some perceive these newer assessments as merely variations of the currently used tests and would prefer to see the adoption of functional assessments (Reschly & Wilson, 1990).

Adelman and Taylor (1993) describe both psychology and education as "dominated by relatively weak theories and methods for measuring causes and correcting problems" (p. 80) associated with learning disabilities. Biased research designs, selective literature reviews, and the identification of conflicting solutions to the same problems are all evident. To illustrate, most professionals today agree that the research on aptitude–treatment interaction fails to support its value (Fuchs & Fuchs, 1986), yet conclusions from that research vary from recommendations for the abandonment of mild disabilities categories to greater precision being applied in the diagnostic process. How these assessment issues within special education, and accountability issues within all of education, are or should be changing the practices within the field are explored in this chapter.

Theoretical Influences on Assessment Practices

The notion that intelligence is a stable, unchangeable general characteristic, with the exception of its deterioration through environmental deprivation or neurological damage, is a standard assumption in the field of psychological testing (Salvia & Ysseldyke, 1995). The psychometric properties of intelligence tests serve to confirm and verify this belief. The intelligence test that produces the most consistent scores receives high marks in the marketplace competition for tests with strong psychometric properties. The possibility that a child's cognitive traits could change due to shifting circumstances is not negated by the belief that intelligence is stable and that scores represent a meaningful summarization of generalized, interdependent cognitive traits. However, in the absence of significant environmental changes, a child's measured intelligence at age eight is expected to be the same at age twelve, fifteen, and into adulthood.

Debates over intelligence tests include if they should be given, and, if so, how they should be given, and the meaning and accuracy of the results. Frisby and Braden (1992) have noted that some consider standardized intelligence testing to be "an indispensable, nonbiased tool in the diagnosis of learning problems" whereas others condemn the practice "as a vicious social evil that has been misused and has done children more harm than good" (p. 282). Numerous alternative approaches have evolved as differing theoretical perspectives regarding the nature of intelligence and how it develops in children have challenged the concept of a primarily innate general factor intelligence. Critics contend that the adoption of such views of intelligence place an undue value on intelligence testing and associated theoretical assumptions, limiting the structure and content of the curriculum in schools, particularly special education programs (e.g., Sabatino & Vance, 1993). According to this perspective, there is a resulting failure of educators to strive toward improving students' problem-solving skills, because the teacher accepts the intelligence test as a reasonable measure of a student's potential and focuses her energies on enabling the child to achieve as close to that mark as possible.

Since the introduction of intelligence testing, our understanding of the concept of intelligence has been evolving to acknowledge the interactive nature of our problem-solving ability and cognitive processes. Gardner (1993), in the preface to his tenth anniversary edition of *Frames of Mind,* refers to the importance of both contextualization and distribution in discussing intelligence as a concept. In regard to contextualization, Gardner points out that intelligence is not viewed as something independent of the culture and times in which an individual exists, and thus it has been contextualized. He contends that "many scientists now see intelligence as an interaction between, on the one hand, certain proclivities and potentials and, on the other, the opportunities and constraints that characterize a particular cultural setting" (p. xiii). Beyond the broad culture and value system of a society, individuals find themselves in very specific environments that directly contribute to the development of their intellectual capacities. Indeed, even the ability to take advantage of the resources available within one's environment can expand a person's intelligence beyond just that which sits within the skill. As Gardner (1993) writes,

> My intelligence does not stop at my skin; rather, it encompasses my tools (paper, pencil, computer), my notational memory (contained in files, notebooks, journals), and my network of associates (office mates, professional colleagues, others whom I can phone or to whom I can dispatch electronic messages). (p. xiii)

With this view toward intelligence, having access to and knowing how to use the library would expand a child's access to usable knowledge and therefore her intelligence, not something measured on traditional intelligence tests.

Rather than a single general intelligence, which has been the most frequent theoretical framework associated with the intelligence testing field, Gardner (1983) has conceived of multiple intelligences, including linguistic, musical, logical–mathematical, spatial, bodily–kinesthetic, and the personal intelligences (both knowledge of self and one's awareness of others). Even within each of these intelligences, Gardner presents a multifaceted construct. For example, linguistic intelligence covers such far-ranging abilities as the composing of poetry, verbal memory for long strings of numbers, and the effective use of speech in the art of political persuasion. Supporters of a general or global intelligence might view more than one of Gardner's intelligences as skills or talents that some possess in greater quantities than others, but not factorially distinct from one's general intelligence. Although Gardner discusses the importance of the interdependence and relationship across these intellectual potentials, each, he argues, is also unique and separated from the others.

Scheffler (1985) has spoken to what he considers to be the myths that educators associate with the concept of potential, addressing the inconsistencies and flaws of popular reasoning. The first myth he identifies is the notion that we each possess some fixed potential that we must strive to achieve. When a student's assessed potentials are locked in as fixed and durable traits in a teacher's mind, then they become so. However, Scheffler notes the irony of this notion. Without the opportunity to achieve today's potential, the child's potential for the next day is at risk and thus is an ever-changing variable contingent on both the past and the future. Sabatino and Vance (1993) likewise contend that teachers ought to direct some of their energies toward teaching children to think, expanding their memories, heightening their abstract reasoning abilities, and developing their spatial-relations skills. The failure to teach such cognitive skills has resulted, according to them, in the devaluing of problem-solving skills, with a corresponding increased emphasis strictly on academic achievement. Consequently, the argument follows, programs designed to teach cognitive skills ought to become a part of the curriculum, particularly for children who have experienced environmental disadvantages.

Educators then must attempt to determine how best to enable children to realize their full potential(s), avoiding the undesirable effect of wasted opportunities. The associated assessment process involves an attempt to get a fix on a student's potential. Scheffler (1985) brings us back to the difficulty of such attempts by pointing out the myth of harmonious potentials. The notion that an individual may have various potentials that are not jointly realizable conflicts with the assumption that the educator's job "is simply to identify the potentials that are there, and then to promote the realization of all in the most efficient manner" (p. 14). The achievement of some potentials will necessarily come at the expense of others. Similarly, the realities of shrinkage of potential, either through the passage of critical periods without learning opportunities, or negative experiences early in life, must also be acknowledged: "The flexibility of mind, adventure-someness and confidence required for exploring the novel are precious and fragile learning instruments that lose their edge with disuse or abuse" (p. 13). It becomes the educator's job to advance the development of potentials not yet apparent as well as to pursue to the fullest possible extent the potentials that are apparent but may soon disappear. His job necessitates simultaneously looking at the past, present, and future of children.

The third myth of potentials that Scheffler addresses is uniformly valuable potentials. Although educators have not generally attended to the notion that people have negative potential as well as positive potential, Scheffler considers it a reality of life. The desirability of shrinking one's potential for evil is as important as the move to strengthen desirable potentials. Does a child have the potential to hurt others physically or achieve great success in athletic pursuits? Does the possession of potential leadership skills create in a child the opportunity to develop expertise in the manipulation and deceit of friends to achieve power and control over them, or does this potential enable the child to become an effective leader in the pursuit of improvements in group circumstances? The records of political leaders in this country certainly reveal these two sides of leadership potential. If our goal in education is simply to enable children to achieve their greatest potential, Scheffler cautions us against assuming that potential is only for good. Potential must be equated with the capacity for the acquisition of outcomes, both positive and negative.

We strive to eliminate or reduce barriers that would interfere with positive outcomes in the future. The concept of potential incorporates conditions exterior to an individual that might block learning, prevent development, and lead to failure. If such circumstances can be avoided, potential is different than if damaging circumstances are inescapable. The prevention of malnutrition during infancy, reduction of the risk of brain injury for children who ride bicycles or ride in automobiles with basic safety precautions, in utero surgery—all are intended to maintain the opportunity for individuals to achieve their potential. Along with these biological and physical factors, cultural factors, such as particular belief systems, institutions, and policies, can influence the achievement of potentials. The goodness or badness of this influence can be considered only from within a culturally biased belief system. Thus, cultural mores that most in the mainstream of America would consider interfering with the achievement of one's potential may be viewed positively within a particular subculture. For example, a child with exemplary but unknown musical potential born into a culture that prohibits music, devalues it, sets gender restrictions on participation in it, or restricts it to one style, would likely not have the opportunity to develop her musical potential or would do so at the expense of cultural rejection. Does the child's failure to achieve her musical potential represent a terrible waste or a culturally valid adherence to a more significant belief system? More relevant to special educators might be the issue of whether children who are deaf should work on their speaking abilities, or whether children with physical disabilities should expend their energies on the development of walking skills instead of the efficient use of a wheelchair. These questions cannot be answered apart from one's cultural belief system.

Potential can be reduced or even eliminated by policy, as evidenced in the prevention of disease through immunizations. In fact, biological factors associated with enhancing or limiting potential may be more easily addressed than purely cultural ones. Scheffler (1985) contends that "cultural factors may be recalcitrant, deeply ingrained attitudes proving impervious to policy initiatives" (p. 51). Stereotypic assumptions about the potential of children based on their personal characteristics, such as gender or race, do accurately predict potential because they change adult behaviors toward children. Such can be seen as well when considering the likely "potential" of children with disabilities. Sometimes decisions regarding the worthiness of a child's receiving interventions are based on predictions of potential. Personal beliefs that certain goals are unobtainable for the individual may, in turn, cause themselves to become accurate predictions. The beliefs may have served to limit the individual's achieved potential, not what could have been the achievable potential. Accordingly, complete assessment of an individual's potentials would need to include the personal belief system of the person being assessed and of those who will be assigned to teach the child. In some instances, individuals are able to achieve potentials that they doubted they had. The teacher can enable a child to contradict himself if she considers the child capable of more than the child considers himself capable. Initially, children entering school have no valid means of assessing themselves, but soon they "learn what they can do by absorbing the beliefs of their elders as to what they can do" (Scheffler, 1985, p. 66). Children find that a teacher's confidence in their potential, which they do not believe that they have, enables them to achieve mastery of new skills.

Feuerstein is another who has explored the concept of potential, particularly the measurement of a child's potential for learning. His efforts, along with others (e.g., Budoff, 1969; Campione & Brown, 1987), have led to the development of dynamic models of assessment using a test-teach-test sequence (Haywood, Brown, & Wingenfeld, 1990). The dynamic assessment model is based primarily on the theoretical perspectives of Vygotsky, particularly his concept of the zone of proximal development. The goals of dynamic assessment are to assess the modifiability of basic cognitive structures, the extent of modification needed for a particular child, the generalization of modifications achieved in one area of functioning, and the amount of teaching needed to stimulate the desired degree of cognitive functioning. Accordingly, the developers of dynamic assessment seek to put an emphasis on assessment of processes of perception, thinking, learning, and problem solving instead of products based on past learning. The Feuerstein approach to dynamic assessment is considered by many of its North American advocates (e.g., Hausman, 1988; Haywood, 1988) as a means to "reduce educational inequalities by providing what is perceived to be a more compassionate, fair, and equitable means for assessing students' cognitive capabilities" (Frisby & Braden, 1992, p. 283). However, others do not see it in such a positive light. Frisby and Braden consider Feuerstein's approach to be "little more than an ideological philosophy in search of empirical support" (p. 283). When changes in test performance are witnessed on Feuerstein's Learning Potential Assessment Device, he claims that those score changes are attributable to cognitive structural changes within the individual, equivalent to the structural changes described by Piaget as children mature from sensorimotor processes into abstractly thinking adults. However, there are many other possible explanations for test performance changes than the claim of such dramatic cognitive structural changes occurring within the child.

Frisby and Braden (1992) assert that the extent to which intelligence is modifiable requires exploration of three interrelated concepts: biological intelligence, psychometric intelligence, and social intelligence. Biological intelligence "refers to individual differences in the structure, physiology, and biochemistry of the human brain that are determined by one's genetic code (genotype)" (p. 284). Brain damage, chromosomal aberrations, malnutrition, drug-induced effects, or normal maturation can trigger changes in biological intelligence. Psychometric intelligence is the general intellectual functioning measured on objective, standardized intelligence tests, which is not a measure of biological intelligence. Social intelligence is the capacity to adapt and function as a member of a society within the accepted standards of one's culture, a concept that is "highly subjective and situation specific" (Frisby & Braden, 1992, p. 287). The definition varies depending on the theoretical perspective taken and the context of behavior. Whoever makes the judgments as to what constitutes social intelligence and the context of those judgments has an influence on perceptions of a child's intelligence. Agreements on what constitutes the nature of intelligence and/or potential(s), the usefulness of measuring them, and the best approaches to measure them are unlikely. However, criticism of current practices is clearly coming from many directions.

Accountability, Performance
Standards, and Special Education

The testing industry has been quick to respond to demand for comparative reports of school performance based on student achievement by creating comprehensive, highly efficient standardized instruments. The demand for information combined with the available efficiency of optical-scan scoring methods and the absence of any competing approaches to assessment, choice-based achievement tests became "one of the most visible and influential manifestations of scientific technology at work in education" (Eisner, 1993, p. 221). The decreases in American performance in international comparisons and diminishing performance averages have triggered numerous blistering critiques of education. One of the most significant responses by the education community has been the development of increased progression and graduation standards for students.

Simultaneously, however, there has been an emerging dissatisfaction with traditional choice-based assessments and a cry for outcomes-based education coupled with authentic assessment. Authentic assessments are characterized as being "contextualized, complex intellectual challenges, not fragmented and static bits or tasks" (Wiggins, 1989, p. 711). Student performance in real-life situations replaces traditional tests. The outcomes-oriented model of education involves a shift from evaluating programs through group achievement test scores, average daily attendance, number of pages in texts that were covered during the year, and so forth to evaluations based on students' abilities to apply knowledge during authentic assessments. A variety of outcomes-based education models have been developed, including the Outcomes Driven Developmental Model (ODDM) (Champlin, 1991) and the High Success Network Strategic Design Model (Spady, 1992). These both rely on the assumption that instructional planning must follow and be directly tied to the development of outcomes.

Closely linked to the outcomes-based education movement has been the establishment of standards of performance and a rewards/sanctions structure of accountability. Ysseldyke, Thurlow, and Shriner (1992) have delineated the movement at the national, state, district, and building/classroom level. Student performance on assessments documenting student achievement of the standards is becoming a means of teacher evaluation and, in some instances, even being used to determine pay raises. Following an industry model, education is seeking to improve its product and have fewer defects or recall notices. Consequences follow outcomes-based assessments of the performance of an individual, a teacher's class, a grade, a building, a school district, or even a state. Just how direct those consequences should be and who should be held accountable for each student are questions with no simple answers. Sanctions associated with accountability are based on the assumption that school personnel have the knowledge and ability to enable students to achieve positive outcomes but have previously had no motivation for doing so.

In some instances the consequences or threat of consequences in high-stakes assessments may have some unintended effects. For example, the linkage of student performance to teacher wages has led to numerous negative consequences for students with disabilities (Ysseldyke, Thurlow, & Geenen, 1994). Such systems have increased referrals to special education, resulted in theft of test answers by teachers, and direct encouragement of truancy for low-performing students on testing days by teachers and administrators. For students with disabilities who spend most of their day in direct contact with general educators and very little time with a special educator, who holds accountability is particularly subject to discussion.

Ysseldyke, Thurlow, & Geenen (1994) point out that even high-stakes accountability does not mean that educators will have the remedies for poor educational outcomes for some students. They argue that the accountability system itself should be designed to provide guidance in the improvement of student performance, not merely record student outcomes. However, as Eisner (1993) points out, assessments for different purposes require fundamentally different approaches. The move toward an accountability system based on student outcomes that would also provide formative feedback to teachers and administrators will most likely be multifaceted. The use of authentic assessments that are based on open, constructed responses in which multiple answers may be credited will not readily or easily replace the optical scanner for large-scale state-of-the-schools assessments, but Eisner (1993) would contend that curiosity regarding an individual student's problem-solving skills, ability to work as a member of a group, to plan ahead, and so forth can be tapped in no other meaningful way.

The popularity of policies through which students individually receive sanctions for failing to achieve stipulated standards, such as withholding of diplomas and/or graduation, varies. Some contend that such sanctions serve as a motivation for learning, but others consider that they discourage students with disabilities and those from disadvantaged homes (Ysseldyke, Thurlow, & Geenen, 1994). The penalties for students who are working their best but are unable to meet arbitrary cutoff scores or demonstrate proficiency in performance-based assessments seem unduly harsh in the eyes of some. Special educators have been writing individual goals and objectives based on criterion-referenced assessments and are familiar with outcomes-based assessments, particularly for students with moderate to severe disabilities. However, accountability for the teachers and the students based on student achievement is something to which special education teachers have neither been accustomed (Thurlow, 1994) nor automatically feel to be equitable. Most often, if students with disabilities are required (or allowed) to participate in the examinations, their scores are deleted prior to any analyses (U.S. Department of Education, 1995).

Many states already have in place student assessment systems that contain associated procedures regarding the inclusion or exclusion of students with disabilities in the process (Ysseldyke, Thurlow, & Shriner, 1992). Some permit a variety of adapted testing procedures, and others exclude special education students from the data analysis even though they might have participated in the assessments (U.S. Department of Education, 1995). For example, Maryland allows exclusions due to student disability but is attempting to avoid excessive exclusions by establishing specific exclusion criteria and assigning any students who were inappropriately excluded zeros to be averaged in with that school's scores (Ysseldyke,

Thurlow, & Geenen, 1994). Variability is increased even more because such state policies may be implemented at the local level without consistency. The students with disabilities most likely to participate in the general education assessments are those with mild disabilities; however, the actual extent to which they do so is uncertain. Kentucky recently restructured its entire educational system and has included a performance-based assessment component intended to be adaptable to all children, indicating an acknowledgment that all children may not find the same standards appropriate but should not be unilaterally excluded from this latest approach to accountability (Kentucky Department of Education, 1992). The reform law states that "schools shall expect a high level of achievement of all students," which speaks to the need for high expectations without mandating that they all be the same. The *all* in this statement can actually apply to all. However, with authority from a medical doctor indicating that participating in the assessment process could prove harmful to a child's health, children can still be exempted. Whether children participate through performance-based assessment or an alternate portfolio assessment, no child is automatically excluded from this system of accountability by the school system.

Historically, volumes of data have been collected on students with disabilities, but the contents have been primarily placement and program data, with little or no student outcomes information (Ysseldyke, Thurlow, & Shriner, 1992). Very little data have been available regarding the nature of former special education students' lives as adults. We could document how many days students attended school, how many hours a day they spent in the general education program, and what their achievement test scores were, but we have been unable to determine who was employed, who was living independently, who was pursuing higher education or vocational training, who could balance a checkbook, who could drive a car or use available public transportation without assistance, or who had friends and satisfying personal relationships upon completion of their special education programs. Over 50% of the states are now gathering some data on graduates of special education programs, and the federal Office of Special Education Programs has begun supporting projects related to the transition from special education to postsecondary training and/or employment (Ysseldyke, Thurlow, & Shriner, 1992). Reports that contain information on these functional outcomes might have far greater value to special educators seeking formative evaluation of their programs than do standardized test scores.

The appeal of outcomes-based assessment and other alternative forms of assessment has been apparent in general education as well. Alternative assessment involves any methods of finding out what a student knows that is not standardized or traditional. The knowledge is considered authentic if it faithfully reflects the knowledge and process that the subject matter requires and the conditions under which the achievement normally takes place (Hughes, 1993). To illustrate, store clerks relying on a cash register to calculate change, then counting that change back for the customer, need not recall addition and subtraction math facts, but are required to punch the correct register buttons and count change back to the customer. Tests with addition and subtraction problems that include dollar signs and decimal points have little if any correlation to the skills required for the job.

Focus of Discussion

The majority of special education-related assessments are conducted in connection with either eligibility and diagnosis or curricular and instructional planning and the monitoring of student progress for additional planning or program graduation. Recently, there has been criticism of diagnostic tests due to their inability to offer information of a prescriptive nature. Resulting debates on the value of diagnostic tests as they stand point to the need to consider radical reformation of assessment practices. In the next section of this chapter, the practice of determining eligibility and diagnosis via norm-referenced intelligence and achievement testing is debated. Included in this discussion is the concept of potential and our ability to measure and foster the achievement of it, the relevance of intelligence testing to diagnostic discrimination of disabilities, and the prescriptive value of intelligence testing. The next section addresses the new wave of assessment practices in general education associated with accountability, such as national performance standards and authentic assessment, and their implications for students with disabilities.

ASSESSMENT FOR DIAGNOSIS, ELIGIBILITY, AND PLACEMENT

There is a pervasive demand that available assessment instruments offer sound psychometric properties, broad-based representative norm groups, unbiased test items, and ease of administration. Intelligence tests, although used extensively, rarely stand alone in the diagnostic process and have become one of a variety of assessment tools used to determine a child's eligibility for special education. Today, intelligence test scores are compared to student performance on achievement tests, accompanied by home and/or classroom observations, interviews with caregivers and teachers, the completion of behavioral checklists, and other measures of student performance. However, intelligence tests continue to serve as the common base of the assessment process, typically wielding heavy weight in final eligibility and diagnostic decisions. Yet these tests are the focus of much criticism, including complaints about their cultural bias, inconsistency between theory and test construction (Hughes, 1993), and exclusion of special populations from their norm groups (Fuchs & Fuchs, 1986). For some critics, the concepts of cognitive development and intelligence are insufficiently differentiated on traditional intelligence tests (e.g., Haywood, Brown, & Wingenfeld, 1990; Naglieri, Das, & Jarman, 1990). The critics contend that what is missing is the opportunity to explore how children are thinking, and what their cognitive processes are apart from their previously learned knowledge, as is assessment of their thoughtful problem-solving abilities. Intelligence tests developers would counter that such skills are indeed embedded into their tests (Sattler, 1992). Sabatino and Vance (1993) describe the relationship between educators and intelligence tests as one of love–hate, with research indicating that special education administrators view intellectual assessment and testing as an important and necessary evil.

Individual intelligence tests could be considered special education entrance exams.

Michael Siluk.

The correlation of school-induced learning difficulties and a child's performance on an intelligence test is subject to debate. Those arguing that intelligence testing is linked to opportunities and exposure to content represented on the tests would consider it unfair to define a student's ability or potential as a direct product of his learning opportunities (Haywood, Brown, Wingenfeld, 1990). Others contend that intelligence testing as it is practiced in eligibility assessments today reflects primarily innate cognitive abilities of children not significantly correlated to their life circumstances or academic opportunities prior to the point of testing. The issues hover around the meanings attached to intelligence test scores, the usefulness of intelligence tests in the diagnostic process of discriminating disabilities, and the value of intelligence testing for planning interventions.

Discriminating Among Diagnoses of Disabilities

Distinctions are made during the diagnostic process between learning disabilities, mental retardation, emotional disturbance, language disorders, and each of the other disabilities. The extent to which these distinctions are valid or necessary, and can be accurately determined through current assessment practices, is contested by many but unquestioned by others. What should be appropriately involved in the diagnostic process is subject to interpretations of the disability definitions. The disability definitions and even state-level eligibility criteria contain abstract elements that must be translated into concrete empirical indicators (Kavale & Mundschenk, 1991). Although each of the categorical disabilities has unique diagnostic issues associated with it, the category of learning disabilities has been selected to illustrate the dilemmas and debates associated with eligibility assessments. The learning disabilities category was selected because it is currently the most common diagnosis and because it offers some of the strongest points of disagreement associated with diagnostic procedures. Some even take the view that the condition is a social construction (e.g., Lipsky & Gartner, 1989; Sleeter, 1990); therefore, efforts to develop accurate diagnostic criteria are irrelevant as well as a poor use of time and resources. Persons who argue this point challenge the numerous professional organizations, parent groups, authors and editors of professional journals, federally funded research institutes, and teacher-training programs based on the concept of learning disabilities.

On the horizon of assessment of children for the learning disability diagnosis are two disparate trends. First is the move toward elimination of the expensive psychoeducational battery of tests in pursuit of the critical discrepancy, replaced by the adoption of teacher referral based on student performance (Gerber & Semmel, 1984). Second is a move, in the opposite direction, to eliminate from the ranks of the population of children certified as learning disabled all but those who exhibit abnormal neurobehavioral indicators (Adelman & Taylor, 1993). The diagnostic process for learning disabilities currently relies on the translation into test performance of concepts such as perception, intelligence, potential, and discrepancy. However, these abstract concepts do not translate directly and can be measured in several different ways, including achievement, memory indicators, social indicators, perceptual indicators, and motoric indicators. The significance of each of these and/or the degree to which a deficit must be displayed and how many indicators must register deficits for a child to be considered deficient as well as disputes over how best to measure them contribute to inconsistency in diagnostic policies throughout the country. Because of the "inherent complexity and vagueness of the concept of learning disabilities" (Kavale & Mundschenk, 1991, p. 109), measurement practices are highly variable, leaving the concept of learning disabilities open and somewhat uncertain.

Some who continue to value the discrimination of disabilities as a part of the diagnostic process have noted deficiencies in tests such as the Wechsler Intelligence Scale for Children—III (Wechsler, 1991) or the Binet-IV (Thorndike, Hagen, & Sattler, 1985), particularly for the diagnosis of learning disabilities (Naglieri, Das, & Jarman, 1990). According to the critics, the ineffectiveness of intelligence tests in differential diagnosis is directly linked to the manner in which they have developed. The major emphasis in their development has been on criterion-related validity with a reduced emphasis on discriminant validity. The tests have taken too narrow a concept of intelligence, predominantly measuring verbal ability achievement, nonverbal functioning, sequencing, memory functioning, and quantitative abilities, but neglecting cognitive processes. The Kaufman Assessment Battery for Children (K-ABC, Kaufman & Kaufman, 1983) shifted from content assessment to process-based assessment, but Naglieri, Das, and Jarman (1990) contend that this series did not really extend the processes measured on intelligence tests. They suggest that current standardized tests have outward differences but are really all the same, citing the high criterion validity between the tests as a good indicator of this similarity.

To resolve this deficiency, Naglieri, Das, and Jarman have developed the Planning Attention, Simultaneous, Successive Model (PASS) for discriminatory assessment and intervention planning. The model is derived from neuropsychological work of Luria, who considered human cognitive processing to involve three functional systems defined as a constellation of brain areas or units that function together to produce a class of behavior. These three constellations are (1) regulation of cortical tone and maintenance of attention, (2) receipt of processes and storage of information using simultaneous and successive information coding, and (3) programs regulation and direction of mental activity. The PASS model incorporates a series of questions in the analysis of a child's planning processes during the act of problem solving. Does the child conceive of the need to create a plan, or is the problem simple enough to be resolved without one? Is it a problem that requires a plan already within the child's knowledge, or must a new plan be developed? Once a plan has been developed, is it a reasonable plan, or should it be improved or changed? Can the child actually execute and monitor the plan, altering it as needed? Can the child continue on with a plan to successful completion of the task? Naglieri, Das, and Jarman (1990) cite research confirming that simultaneous, successive, and planning processes are related to achievement, including measures of reading comprehension, reading decoding, performance in college-level English courses, and mathematics. Planning and achievement also correlate, including mathematics computations, written composition, reading decoding, and reading comprehension. The PASS tasks have discriminated between students who are progressing normally in school and those who have a variety of disabilities that interfere with school performance (reading disabled, attention deficit/hyperactivity disorder, and delinquents). A new system will be of value only "if it has the essential characteristics of validity, diagnostic utility, and standardizability" (p. 437) present in the existing tests. The developers of the PASS model claim it offers each of these by maximizing the benefits of traditional assessment with a reliable norm-based general index of cognitive functioning. Developers also claim that it diminishes culture-loaded items based on past learning and increases the assessment of psychological processes. By focusing on problem-solving approaches and including multiple tests to assess processes so often problematic for the child with learning disabilities, the developers argue that it can identify children with learning disabilities.

Systematic data gathering within natural environments of the child's life could offer a more meaningful (although less precise and standardized) assessment than that of formal intelligence testing as practiced today. Gerber and Semmel (1984) have proposed that teacher referrals themselves be treated as "evaluative conclusions." Their arguments include four basic points. First is the possibility that such a policy would result in a dramatic reduction of costs. Second is the notion that placement teams already rely heavily on classroom teacher information, so their input actually serves as a system of child find. The third point Gerber and Semmel address is the multitude of observational opportunities that teachers have. They have a rich database from which to determine who should be referred into the special education system. The fourth argument relates to the teacher's ability to correlate student behaviors with likelihood of success in his classes, given self-knowledge about tolerance and ability to make adjustments required to meet a particular student's needs.

In 1987 Shinn, Tindal, and Spira reported the results of an extensive study of the accuracy and biases found in the teacher referral process. They established local norms on curriculum-based measurements related to reading skills and monitored the performance of children who were referred and were not referred to special education. Additionally, they checked for increased referrals related to gender and ethnicity. In general, the data support the contention that teachers are a reliable referral source for students with reading difficulties. However, there was an interesting overlap in performance between those children who were referred and those who were not, with not all poorly performing students being referred. Gender and ethnicity factors did, in fact, increase the likelihood that a child would be referred, although the referrals were consistently for students who were achieving at very low levels. That is, the referrals were not inappropriate based on student performance, but the performance standard did not appear to be the sole criterion in the referral decision. Males and black students were more likely to be referred than females or white students with similarly poor reading skills. Speculation regarding the interpretation of these findings can range from the benign notion that the teachers might operate on the assumption that a referral is a kind action, seeking to increase a student's resources and hopes for success, to the more cynical idea that teachers seek to remove from their classrooms those students with whom they prefer not to work. Nevertheless, the idea that teacher referral could be increased in value as a part of the eligibility standard for special education appears to be viable in theory.

Current diagnostic practices related to learning disabilities rely heavily on traditional norm-referenced intelligence testing. Examiners look for patterns of scatter on the various subtests within intelligence tests as well as discrepancies between predicted potential based on performance on an intelligence test and the actual achievement of a student. The size of the discrepancy required for a child to qualify for the diagnosis varies across the country (Adelman & Taylor, 1993). Originally, the predicted number of students who would be served through IDEA as learning disabled was relatively small. Today, it is the largest and fastest growing category (U.S. Department of Education, 1995). Administrators struggle to meet the financial obligations of serving the unanticipated large numbers of students qualifying for services as learning disabled. Psychologists fight to keep evaluation deadlines to remain in compliance with regulations. Teachers are now well acquainted with the referral process and know they can insist on help from special education quarters when children appear unable to achieve up to their potential. Parents have expectations that their struggling children will be better off educationally once a diagnosis of learning disability has been confirmed through proper assessment techniques. Some special educators contend that the category was never meant to be used for such a broadly encompassed group as has come to be the case today (e.g., Adelman & Taylor, 1993). Others would posit that a failure to succeed in the classroom is the critical behavioral variable (assuming that other plausible causes such as vision problems and personal crises have been explored and ruled out), and the need to distinguish between students with learning disabilities and other mild high-incidence conditions is unnecessary (e.g., Reschly, 1992).

Adelman and Taylor (1993) distinguish among learning problems caused by external factors, interactions between a child and his environment, and those considered to be learning disabilities, based on minor central nervous system dysfunction. However, such distinctions are typically not evidenced in the diagnostic process for learning disabilities, if the primary focus becomes documenting a discrepancy between potential and achievement, not the reasons for the discrepancy. Potential is equated with IQ, and achievement is generally measured with norm-referenced standardized tests. Adelman and Taylor attribute the current confusion and controversy on who belongs in the category to the failure of current diagnostic practices to differentiate learning disability from other learning problems. They contend that the resulting misdiagnoses cause many students to be inappropriately "treated as if the cause of their problems was some form of personal pathology" (p. 15). Accordingly, these children then receive prescriptions and unneeded treatments for their nonexistent internal dysfunctions, which offer them no help for their other learning problems. Adelman and Taylor further argue that such misdiagnoses then contribute to the confusion regarding the effectiveness of various treatments that may inaccurately appear to be ineffective because much of the population receiving the treatment does not have the condition for which it was intended. Since performance on intelligence tests and school achievement has a high correlation, Naglieri and Braden (1992) contend that it is inconsistent to use a discrepancy formula for diagnosis. After all, the discrepancy can appear only when the instrument measuring intelligence has failed to detect the cognitive deficiency that is causing the academic deficiency. The discrepancy formula itself is based on the failure of current instrumentation.

The misclassification problem associated with learning disabilities further exacerbates the problems of eligibility testing, with over half of the students with that diagnosis inaccurately diagnosed (Adelman & Taylor, 1993). Shepard (1991) acknowledges that many of the current students certified as learning disabled would be "more aptly described as slow learners, linguistically different children, misbehaving boys, children who are absent or whose families move too frequently, or as average learners in above-average contexts" (p. 23). The idea that learning disabilities have come to encompass such a broad spectrum of children is inconsistent with the original intended target population. Obrzut and Boliek (1991) recommend that neuropsychological assessment procedures be used in the diagnostic process. Yet such assessments also have limitations. When the emphasis is placed back on pathology within the child, the nature of the diagnostic process changes. Neurobehavioral markers, evidence of neurochemical imbalance, genetic factors, and difficulties in cognitive integration overshadow achievement testing and teacher referrals.

Since learning problems do not constitute a category within special education, the removal of children with learning problems from the learning disabilities category (assuming they did not qualify for one of the other disability categories) would make them ineligible for special education services. Thus, with a restriction of the category of learning disabilities to just those students exhibiting some neurological dysfunction would come the elimination of many children from eligibility who are failing to achieve up to their "potential" as currently diagnosed through discrepancy formulas. Following the logic used to consider exclusion of these children from the learning disabilities category, several confounding issues materialize.

Assessment practices for determining who qualifies for the learning disabilities category would have to be altered to focus on deficits of cognitive processing disorders, not the presumptive symptom of a discrepancy between potential and achievement. However, this solution to the diagnosis issue is based on the assumption that learning disabilities are indeed a real disability distinguishable from other mild learning problems and that specialized treatments for learning disabilities are significantly different from those needed by other children. This solution is focused on improving our ability to discriminate among different types of educational disabilities as the appropriate goal to strive for in the pursuit of best practices. Others who do not accept the assumption of learning disabilities as a real, significantly differentiated disability, and those who find the assessment of abstract concepts such as intelligence or potential too flawed to continue their use, would prefer to put an end to such assessments rather than improve them (e.g., Reschly, 1992). Assessments would shift from what they consider to be futile attempts at discriminating among conditions that cannot be validly distinguished to functional assessments. Reschly (1992) defines *functional assessment* as the use of information-gathering procedures "that have direct applicability to the definition of problem behaviors, determination of current levels of problem behavior, the development and design of interventions, the monitoring of intervention implementation, and the evaluation of intervention outcomes" (p. 127). Such assessments involve direct measurement of socially valid observable behaviors in natural settings following repeatable procedures. The mystery and shroud of secrecy surrounding intelligence testing and the calculation of discrepancy formulas between the abstract concepts of potential and achievement would disappear, not be strengthened and fine-tuned.

Haywood, Brown, and Wingenfeld (1990) point out that regardless of the success of group prediction and classification associated with normative test results, these assessments produce many suspected or actually confirmed cases of misclassification that are unevenly distributed over population subgroups. The extent to which current assessment instruments should be held accountable for these misclassification problems is another point of contention. The misclassification errors may be more caused by the misuse of the tests than by the tests themselves. Testing practices that contribute to test error, overreliance on IQ scores in the diagnostic process, and failure to consider environmental influences on child performance should not be equated with faults in the tests themselves. The test results can be no better than the persons conducting and interpreting the results, regardless of their normative nature.

Prescriptive Intervention Planning

Although developers of traditional intelligence tests did not intend that the tests become the basis for planning interventions, attempts have been made to identify patterns of performance on tests such as the Wechsler intelligence scales for use in instructional planning (e.g., Witt & Gresham, 1985). However, links from intelligence test results to instructional practices have not been empirically supported. In sum, these remediation efforts have been characterized as dismal failures (Laughon, 1990) and generally fall outside the stated purposes of the tests anyway. Content of the tests is criticized as too abstract, atheoretical, and unrelated to school tasks for instructional planning. Critics contend that the overemphasis on product over process offers virtually no remediation guidance to those wanting to know how quickly the child learns new concepts, his motivation for learning, his approach to problem solving, and so forth. The categorical diagnosis and delivery of services has been based on the assumption that the educational needs of children vary according to their disabilities. Diagnosis has carried with it implications for program planning. For example, today there are many instructional materials and methods texts targeted to the learning disabled population, again indicating an implied value of the diagnosis for instructional planning.

Some argue that the overreliance on discrepancy formulas without pursuit of additional evidence of neurobehavioral indicators of central processing disorders in the diagnostic process has opened the flood gates of children qualifying for services as learning disabled. In response to the need for assessments that could be helpful in the discrimination of disabilities and offer insights into intervention planning, a variety of measures designed to assess cognitive processing have come on the market. These include instruments such as the mainstream product K–ABC, as well as those popular in the dynamic assessment movement and other tools emerging into the market (e.g., PASS, described elsewhere in this chapter). Some consider that the greatest potential for dynamic assessment to make a contribution to assessment practices will be in providing remedial information for instructional planning (Laughon, 1990).

The issue at hand is not the nature of intelligence but the assessment practices embedded in the delivery of special education. However, assuming that the notion of multiple intelligences and historical views counter to the general factor intelligence theories, such as factor analytic theories of intelligence (e.g., Thorndike, 1927), and views of intelligence that emphasize fluid concepts, such as learning potential (e.g., Feuerstein, 1979; Campione & Brown, 1987), are worthy of serious consideration, there are significant implications for our established system of measuring that characteristic of children. Is there then a need to create new, psychometrically sound instruments that accommodate a view toward multiple intelligences or adopt some of the testing paradigms that have developed in association with other alternative views? Can we possess a numerical representation of children for each of their intelligences according to Gardner's theories, or would we even want to do so? Do the existing tests, with their solid psychometric properties, actually offer the best approach to intelligence testing within special education? Can or should we increase the value of diagnostic assessments for planning interventions?

Decision Point 5.1: Assessing
Eligibility for Special Education

The decision point below actually represents multiple divergent perspectives integrated into two positions, creating a somewhat false dichotomy for the sake of discussion. The first proposition continues to value traditional testing but recommends that it be supplemented with dynamic assessments designed to measure cognitive processing. The combination of these two approaches into a single position is based on the attempts of both types of assessment to adhere to psychometric standards of reliability and validity, and the contention that the discrimination of disabilities is a worthy endeavor. In those regards, both traditional intelligence testing and cognitive processes assessment have more in common with each other (Naglieri & Braden, 1992) than either have with the second proposition, which is based on the application of nonstandardized functional assessments. The cognitive processing tests (both traditional formats and test-teach-test models) have been created to offer the field greater variety and to fill a perceived unmet assessment need because the developers consider the traditional tests not to be bad, merely insufficient. After all, in their pursuit of psychometric validity, test developers continue to strive to achieve the highest possible correlations with existing traditional instruments but also hope to offer greater insights into how children think, how to expand their thinking skills, and what the nature of their educational programs should be.

In the contrasting proposed model of functional assessment, psychometric issues are replaced with a concern for ecological validity, and the discrimination of disabilities is eliminated as a goal of assessment in favor of assessment for program planning. Strong advocates for the exclusive use of traditional testing, cognitive processing assessment, or dynamic assessment (all of which are incorporated into the first proposition) who dispute their merger into a single position should reconceive the battle lines according to the criteria that they consider more relevant than the value of psychometric test features and the significance of discriminating among disabilities. Since the proposition is based on the complementary rather than competitive nature of these testing approaches, attempts are made within the first argument to differentiate between them, particularly their usefulness regarding the ability to discriminate disabilities and value for prescriptive program planning.

Arguments for Proposition One Traditional standardized intelligence testing is reliable. After decades of effort by developers to improve the tests' representativeness and psychometric features, we now have available extremely effective assessment tools. Critics who too quickly belittle the value of the consistency and accuracy of these tests may find that they are unable to achieve comparable standards for their own instruments. Indeed, developers of some alternative assessment approaches have yet to establish this credibility and accuracy, which years of development have provided for the traditional assessments. To illustrate, Haywood, Brown, and Wingenfeld (1990) acknowledged that even "world class experts" were unable to derive consistent judgments interpreting children's performance on the Learning Potential Accomplishment Device (LPAD), the dynamic assessment tool developed by Feuerstein, Rand, and Hoffman (1979). The current tests have extremely high examiner agreement, producing highly consistent, stable scores over time—features not easily available in observational, qualitative, or curriculum-based assessments (Reschly, 1992).

Intelligence testing that is used to determine a student's eligibility for special education represents the best of an imperfect world. The instruments and examiners administering the tests are far from perfect, but there is consistent evidence

---

Proposition One

Intelligence tests are useful tools in the process of diagnosing educational disabilities and planning educational interventions for students with disabilities. The introduction of additional means of assessing intelligence that use dynamic assessment and focus on processing skills offers a needed complement to the assessment field, holding particular value for students with moderate to severe disabilities.

---

in support of their ability to predict success in school. The traditional standardized intelligence tests have shown a strong relationship with achievement, offering consistently accurate predictions of school performance (Salvia & Ysseldyke, 1995). Even lengthy observations and analyses of parent–child interactions have proven no better at predicting school difficulties of minority preschoolers than administration of the short form of the Wechsler Primary and Preschool Intelligence Scale (Pianta, Erickson, Wagner, Kruetzer, & Egeland, 1990). What better tool could be devised to ascertain who would benefit from receiving specialized instruction designed to circumvent learning difficulties? The testing is done on an individual basis and requires lengthy personal examination periods for each child. Continued pursuit of improvements in standardized testing (e.g., ensuring better representation of minorities in norm groups, eliminating timed performance items that are inherently unfair to students with physical disabilities) are certainly important for available instruments to be used for their intended purpose: the discrimination among individuals according to intellectual abilities. Such discrimination is not always popular, but the tests do, in fact, offer a highly consistent approach.

Professional standards for appropriate test administration and interpretation for all who are licensed to give the tests are designed to protect students from inequitable uses of these tests. They are designed to be free from the influence of irrelevant personal characteristics, such as gender or physical appearance, which would be at issue if teacher referrals or other nonstandardized qualitative approaches to eligibility classifications were used. Although some have criticized the standardized instruments as being culturally biased, in the hands of a competent psychologist, this bias need not be a factor. Today, the popular intelligence tests can be used to assess intelligence accurately in both majority and minority populations (Reschly, 1992).

Hoy and Gregg (1994), while acknowledging significant limitations of intelligence tests for children with severe cognitive disabilities, physical disabilities, and multiple disabilities, proclaim the usefulness of IQ tests in special education. The accuracy of these tests in predicting long-range academic achievement offers both parents and teachers help in anticipating and planning for the child's progress (Sattler, 1992). This predictive accuracy can become a negative if allowed to set limits on a child rather than provide a general guide of expected performance. The tests should not be condemned if they are misused by psychologists or teachers any more than behavior management principles should be universally condemned because they are misapplied in some settings. If problems reside within special education regarding the practices of interpreting and using testing results, reform need not require the abandonment of the tools, rather their improved use. To illustrate, because someone with poor eye–hand coordination might cause injury to his body when attempting to use a hammer, should we conclude that hammers are dangerous and that no one, including skilled carpenters, should be given access to them? Test users are simply too quick to accept on faith the exaggerated claims of test authors and publishers (Buros, 1974).

Standardization of instruments designed to measure intelligence with consistency and accuracy is intended to produce a fair and equal opportunity for all children. The tests are specifically designed to minimize examiner bias, present identical opportunities for success to each child taking the test, and avoid ambiguity and personal opinion. The deviation from such a system that seeks unbiased perspectives as a goal could be viewed as contrary to the many protections necessitated by past practices. The replacement of our psychometrically solid intelligence tests with laborious month-long observational systems and teacher referrals would increase the subjectivity of the process and could be seriously challenged as racially biased if overrepresentation of minorities continued. The distance between the abstract concepts found in our definitions of disability and our empirical indicators would only become greater in such a radical shift of assessment practices.

Discriminating Among Diagnoses of Disabilities The distinction between different disabilities, while probably not as clear as the diagnostic process implies, is nevertheless real. Children with learning disabilities have different characteristics and learning needs from those with mild retardation, school failure due primarily to emotional problems, or disabilities limited to language disorders. The planning of proper educational interventions necessitates the distinctions. Certainly, many effective instructional techniques can be applied to numerous disability groups and children without disabilities, but that does not negate the importance and value of proper diagnosis. The ability of parents and teachers to engage in long-range planning, curriculum selection, and educational outcomes is associated with and guided by diagnostic information. Noncategorical service delivery, inclusion, and the arbitrariness and limitations of numerical and formula-driven standards do not negate the need for these distinctions. Exclusive reliance on functional assessment techniques recommended to replace intelligence tests could eliminate the ability to discriminate among disability types, because the students often have similar achievement records and/or behavioral patterns. Surely there is value and significance in differentiating children who are experiencing delays in educational achievement due to hearing impairments from those with mental retardation (Reschly, 1992).

When a child exhibits a discrepancy between standardized test scores and actual classroom functioning in favor of the testing situation, appropriate diagnostic practices should include an analysis of the environment to determine what adjustments could be made to improve student performance in the classroom before labeling the child. Comparisons of the child's performance in his natural setting for diagnostic purposes can and should include interventions, such as increasing classroom structure to be more like the testing conditions. Sorting out the "why" of a discrepancy is as important as discovering that there is a discrepancy (Hoy & Gregg, 1994). When diagnosticians fail to live up to such practices, making a learning disabilities diagnosis as soon as a discrepancy is found, the issue is again not with the diagnostic principles or the quality of the testing instruments, but in their implementation. Additionally, the comparison of test scores for discrepancies in the process of diagnosis is intended to involve sound professional judgment, not strictly numerical calculations. Psychologists should neither be allowed to hide behind their numerical calculations in defending their diagnostic procedures nor prohibited from making sound clinical judgments contrary to formula-driven findings. Careful analysis of psychometric properties of assessment instruments, with particular emphasis on standard errors of measurement, is critical to the process. The fact that some psychologists might fail to use sound professional judgment, either adhering strictly to a formula diagnosis or noting discrepancies across tests that do not warrant such comparisons, does not indicate problems with the process any more than poor teaching implies that the instructional materials in use are faulty or successful malpractice suits indicate surgery is universally an unwise choice.

Prescriptive Intervention Planning The traditional tests do an excellent job of what they were designed to do—predict school achievement and classify children, but the field now has different needs. Most standardized tests used for classification are not prescriptive. Since the best predictor of any criterion performance is a sample of that criterion performance, the most useful tools for prescriptive programming would not be the same as those used to assess intelligence in the traditional manner. The traditional tests answer questions such as how much the child has learned and what things he does well. Other questions also need to be asked: How does this person define, analyze, and solve problems? How much effort is required by the examiner to get an acceptable response from the child? Does the child show the ability to apply general knowledge? Intervention planning demands assessments either in addition to or other than intelligence testing. The PASS (Naglieri & Braden, 1992) offers more to generate recommendations for the remedial process than traditional techniques do. Although acknowledging that dynamic assessment is lengthy and therefore costly, Haywood, Brown, and Wingenfeld (1990) believe that "if an examiner is trying to determine the types of cognitive intervention that would be most helpful to an individual student, dynamic assessment may be critical, regardless of the costs" (p. 417). Tzuriel (1992) asks this question: "When IQ predicts low achievement, what is necessary to defeat that prediction?" (p. 319). The logical answer for Tzuriel is the improvement of how one learns to learn. Whether one's IQ score increases is not so much of a concern as is the notion that children be given a chance to improve their ability to think without set restrictions of an IQ score or curriculum-bound material. Intervention planning cannot be conducted outside of the context in which the child exists. The diagnostic information is a part of that context regardless of its direct value in the program planning process. Awareness that a child's IQ—and therefore expected rate of learning—is low is viewed from this perspective as a characteristic subject to change and improvement. Exploration of the nature of a child's thinking behavior during an examination that includes teaching on novel, content-free items can be coupled with intelligence test scores to offer a broader, fairer base of knowledge of the child than IQ tests alone, or reliance on strictly achievement-oriented assessments that focus on previous learning.

Those who would propose the elimination of intelligence tests and tests designed to evaluate cognitive processing for the sake of better program planning information are ignoring the dangers involved in the loss of testing standards and the absence of rigorous test instruments. Making major decisions based on unreliable data, chance observations, and other random data gathering is not in any child's best interests regardless of any perceived or real historical abuses of intelligence tests. The tests need not be condemned because the information derived from them might be misappropriated by users or because users have evaluated them on criteria for which the tests were not designed. The use of behavior models to replace formal diagnostic assessment is insufficient in a number of ways, including the problem of cultural tyranny. As Naglieri and Braden (1992) point out, "Although legal and political realities call for greater acceptance of and accommodation to diversity, the measurement of children against the arbitrary, highly culture-loaded standard of the curriculum defines success as conformity to a single standard" (p. 121). The arbitrariness of the curriculum certainly exceeds that of intelligence testing and cognitive processing assessments.

Argument Summary The need for well-designed assessments to assist teachers and parents in setting curricular goals and planning instructional strategies is real. The fact that current tests designed for diagnostic purposes do not provide such information does not mean that they are of no value. The continued use of these tests for diagnosis in concert with other, newer instruments that offer more information regarding the cognitive processing of children and their potential for learning new material offers a well-conceived complement of testing alternatives. As these instruments appear in the market, they will be in need of refinement and improvements, similar to the evolving improvements witnessed in intelligence testing. The extent to which the existing instruments claiming to measure cognitive processing or learning potential fill the void for intervention planning may be questioned. However, their need for improvements should not become the rationale for rejecting the well-established value of formal standardized psychoeducational testing. Throwing out existing assessment practices in favor of the practical yet unsophisticated, psychometrically weak practice of relying solely on behavioral and functional assessments would be very short-sighted.

Current tests are reliable, show a strong relationship to achievement, are non-biased when used appropriately, and are relatively practical (Naglieri & Braden, 1992). Critics of existing tests must offer alternatives that are at least as good as what they are proposing to replace before we accept any radical calls for reform. Intelligence tests are less sensitive to color, culture, and gender bias than teacher ratings and many other proposed alternatives. Furthermore, the behavioral approach offers no theoretically based explanations of child failure. The behavioral model will select students on the basis of their failure to respond to educational interventions, a diagnosis of exclusion that presumes all other plausible explanations have been explored and rejected, which is unlikely without thorough diagnostic examinations.

Arguments for Proposition Two Our theoretical understanding of intelligence far exceeds the notion of a general (measurable) intelligence that is the framework for the major individual intelligence tests in use today. The attempt to take an individual's many abilities and disabilities, thoughts and ideas, skills and deficiencies and summarize them into one single number is not consistent with this broader perspective. An individual's abilities, her resourcefulness in using the world around her to gather information that she need not retain, and her understanding and processing of information across various disciplines and domains will not be equal and, therefore, could never be gathered together into a single score that would have any true meaning. The determination of a need (rather than eligibility) for specialized instruction through adjustments in the environment, the curriculum, or teaching methods can best be established through careful observation and analysis of the student's performance across a variety of educational settings, using a functional approach to assessment (Reschly, 1992). A formal IQ score as we know it today, in fact, can cause more harm to children than educational benefit, and the practice needs to be dramatically curtailed, if not eliminated.

Potential is comparative and relative. One child might be considered to have greater potential than another child, assuming an equal level of effort or instruction. Potential is relative to the conditions. Conditions develop into chains of sequential conditions, each influenced by the preceding ones. The interactive nature of these sequential stages of conditions does not permit predictions of final outcomes based on initial conditions. Even the representation of a child's potential in a score can and does influence its own outcome. When we seek to measure potential, we do so assuming that permissive circumstances will be available to enable the individual to achieve that potential. What does this mean for the infant born to a poor, single fifteen-year-old with virtually no understanding of child development or infant nutrition and no job skills or means of support? Can we predict the life outcomes of that infant without knowledge of how her conditions might change over the next two years? What of the child who is unable to achieve control over voluntary muscles for intentional movement, eating, and communication? Can we reasonably separate these children from their immediate and future circumstances to ascertain their potential? How much effort

---

Proposition Two
Intelligence testing should be eliminated as a part of the initial special education assessments and replaced with functional performance-based assessments useful for planning educational interventions as well as determining the need for special education free from the necessity of quantifying a child's potential.

should go into the pursuit of which "potentials" for individual children requires independent value assumptions and contextualization of the potential. To illustrate, employment opportunities might set the direction and context for the achievement of a person's primary potential, whereas other interests are reduced to the levels of hobbies or outside interests. After all, how many special educators initially entered the field because opportunities for employment exceeded those of general education? Had the job market not affected their choice of training, their potential to work effectively with students with disabilities might never have been realized.

Currently, school psychologists devote 65% of their time to determining and maintaining special education eligibility rather than assisting in the analysis of effective intervention strategies (Reschly, Genshaft, & Binder, 1987). The benefits of these eligibility assessments are far from sufficient to justify the costs in terms of dollars or personnel time. The tests determine eligibility, but offer little for intervention planning, and are used again in reevaluations, but are not linked to the curriculum and cannot be used to determine program effectiveness or appropriateness.

An alternative approach that offers greater value than norm-referenced standardized tests for diagnostic utility, intervention implications, and treatment validity is a functional/behavioral assessment approach (Reschly, 1992). Functional assessment involves information-gathering procedures with direct applicability to defining problem behaviors, determining current levels of problem behavior, developing and designing interventions, and monitoring and evaluating intervention outcomes. Functional measures that have diagnostic utility include consideration of a child's resistance to interventions (i.e., the ease with which problems can be resolved within the general educational setting using techniques familiar to the teachers in those settings), his performance in relation to the school curriculum, and basic social competencies. The pursuit of internal deficits of children in order for them to receive special education services is replaced by a focus on environmental conditions contributing to or associated with poor student performance (Reschly, 1992).

Accepting the general premise that children could and should be sorted out by deficits, test developers primarily began seeking reliability and validity, not theoretical critique. The most stable scores, which are the summary scores, took precedence over the less stable but perhaps more interesting individual trait measures. Accordingly, "Cognitive traits were summarized as intelligence, which become synonymous with IQ, a global summation, that became an American twentieth-century trademark" (Sabatino & Vance, 1993, p. 32). Sabatino and Vance (1993) take a highly critical view of the ways in which testing practices have come "to cheapen the process of diagnosing how learning occurs in various children who evidence academic and social problems" (p. 34). They note that some states even require descriptions of the cognitive strengths and weaknesses of children receiving special education services. The absurdity of the expectation is that these cognitive descriptions be obtained from intelligence tests. With disappointment, Sabatino and Vance conclude that what examiners label as cognitive traits of children and treat as though they were of use are merely their subtest scores on a Wechsler or Kaufman test.

As early as 1975, there was already the sentiment that assessment needed to be of benefit to our work with children, not merely a necessary prelude to it (Reynolds, 1975). Through effective educational interventions, we hope to improve the ability of a student to learn and to reduce the discrepancy between his potential and his actual achievement. By so doing, we can no longer consider the child as learning disabled, because the discrepancy has diminished. So was the label necessary or even accurate in the first place? If a learning disability, like an ear infection diagnosis that leads directly to the correct intervention and a rapid cure, can so easily be diagnosed and treated, why are certification and placement in special education really necessary? Some consider that failing to offer educational variation and adjustments prior to certification and placement in special education inevitably results in the presence of students who would meet our established criteria (Gelzheiser, 1990).

Discriminating Among Diagnoses of Disabilities The primary justification for the use of expensive intelligence testing in special education has been the necessity of obtaining accurate diagnoses. However, the logic is based on the presumption that such diagnoses are meaningful and accurate, and both conclusions have been questioned. The use of traditional intelligence testing for diagnosis and eligibility determination for students with moderate to severe disabilities is even more troublesome than for the students with mild disabilities. Diagnostic assessment practices used with these children are of no benefit to the children and can cause great harm. What parent or educator profits from being told that a child is untestable, is too impaired to perform on the test, has earned a score too low to have any meaning, or has an IQ of 40? Such practices provide no benefit to the child whatsoever and are unnecessary in the diagnostic process. Clearly, children experiencing disabilities at this level qualify for services. The need to categorize and label those children is a very poor justification for the expenditure and pain caused by the diagnostic intelligence testing process.

The tests are used to distinguish among children based upon changing categorical definitions that are subjective, socially constructed concepts treated as clinically diagnosable as if they were high blood pressure. Although highly reliable as individual instruments, the tests do not render consistent diagnostic outcomes. The reasons for this inconsistency range from differing state definitions and criteria to personal interpretations of test results by examiners. The inability of the traditional intelligence tests and even the newer cognitive processing instruments to be used consistently and accurately to distinguish students with learning disabilities, mild mental retardation, behavior disorders, and those who would be considered slow learners or educationally disadvantaged from one another makes them poor tools for eligibility determinations.

Even if one were to accept the value of distinguishing children with mild disabilities from one another, current practices are inconsistent with definitional constructs. The case of learning disabilities again offers the best example. The premise that various standardized, norm-referenced tests can be used document a discrepancy in potential and actual achievement and therefore be the basis for a learning disability diagnosis is not credible. The central notion related to the concept of learning disability, the presence of basic psychological processing deficits, is in no meaningful way represented by the discrepancy model. Diagnosis of learning disabilities should require confirmation of cognitive dysfunction, not merely the identification of academic underachievement. The diagnostic model used in the determination of the presence of a learning disability must focus on the interactive cognitive traits of a child rather than disparate test scores. Observations, informal teacher reports, in-depth caregiver interviews, neuropsychological assessments, and functional approaches to assessment culminating in professional judgments would be far superior to the formula-driven discrepancy models based on static test administrations in use today.

The aftermath of current testing practices is appalling. For example, children are classified as learning disabled on the basis of an arbitrary statistical relationship between two test scores. Diagnoses are treated as though they offer guidance for instructional and behavioral interventions, treating eligibility and placement as if they were intervention planning. If the only decision to be made is to determine if a special educational program is needed, then children should be placed based on functional assessments and teacher recommendation, eliminating diagnosis as a prerequisite to intervention (Sabatino & Vance, 1993). Shepard (1991) points out that for children with mild disabilities, "costs of assessment and staffing procedures use up half of the extra per-pupil resources available without any evidence that pro forma administration of tests adds to the scientific integrity of placement decisions" (p. 23). Shepard also notes that initial teacher referrals are far less costly and show a very high correspondence to final placement decisions based on testing. The entire diagnostic process practiced today is unnecessary and of virtually no value in program planning. Since children currently diagnosed with learning disabilities are not a distinct group with educational needs clearly different from all other children, the diagnostic process attempting to sort them out from others is destined to fail as well as be irrelevant, particularly given the associated costs. The translation of the abstract concepts found in the disability definitions into empirical indicators is so flawed that any attempts to do so have been of no great value for the student. Analysis of functional patterns of behavior can offer a far superior insight into the nature of a child's learning difficulties and provide teachers and parents with information useful in planning educational interventions.

Intelligence tests offer nothing to assist persons seeking to evaluate attention patterns of children with ADHD, or deficient strategic behavior patterns and the disorganization of students with learning disabilities (Naglieri & Braden, 1992). To compensate for the lack of material addressing these domains, some propose overanalysis of the limited samples of behavior witnessed during intelligence testing. An unfamiliar examiner in an unfamiliar setting, with unfamiliar materials in a testing atmosphere, can hardly presume to get a typical or average display of behaviors or problem-solving strategies.

Consistent with his notion of multiple intelligences, Gardner (1983) offers some thoughts on the assessment of intelligence predicated on the acknowledgment that the best opportunities to assess intellectual potential differ with the age, sophistication, and cultural background of the individual. For example, to assess performance in the spatial realm, "one might hide an object from the one-year-old, pose a jigsaw puzzle to the six-year-old, or provide the pre-adolescent with a Rubik's cube" (p. 387). He provides a very different notion of assessing intelligence from any of the testing procedures designed to produce scores by carefully observing children over approximately one month while they participate in regular classroom activities. Five to ten hours of such observation "should indicate which lines are already launched in an individual, which lines show a decided potential for development, which are more modestly endowed or entail some genuine obstacles (such as tone-deafness, meager visual imagery, or clumsiness)" (p. 388). The development of a profile of performance and depth of understanding of the child's abilities via such observations offers far greater insights into the nature of the child and her cognitive processes than do single-sitting tests, whether they be product or process oriented.

Prescriptive Intervention Planning An expanding awareness of and acceptance of the interactive nature of a student's difficulties in school and the environments of her home and school is eroding confidence in standardized assessments of intelligence. The field is shifting away from the understanding of the nature of learning difficulties popular over the past twenty years (Hegarty, 1994). The perception that children are defective, unable to learn in normal ways, and need "special teaching quite different from the teaching required by other children" (Hegary, 1994, p. 126) is certainly not applicable to many students served by special educators today. The historical logic that because of these differences defective children need separate educational programs led to development of the massive sophisticated system of diagnostic assessments used in special education today. It is time to shift assessment resources to determining effective intervention strategies instead of labels.

The contention that intelligence and/or cognitive processing assessments are needed for diagnostic purposes has to be questioned in light of the findings regarding the relationship between diagnostic categories for which they are used and interventions. Reschly (1992) notes that "recent evidence further suggests that effective instructional programming or psychological treatment utilizes the same principles and very often the same procedures regardless of whether the student is classified as LD, MMR, ED, slow learner, or educationally disadvantaged" (pp. 129–130).

Treatment implications of traditional achievement, cognitive processing, ability measures, and functional/behavioral assessments do differ. However, these differences seem unable to prove their value. Deficit training has not proven capable of improving student performance in the school curriculum but merely improves performance on the measures of cognitive processing. The cognitive processing assessment raises another issue for program planning that has already proven controversial within the special education ranks (Reschly & Wilson, 1990). Once the identification of processing deficits has been completed, then does the goal become to remediate the weak ones or teach to the strong ones? Further, there is an absence of evidence supporting aptitude-treatment-interactions (Fuchs & Fuchs, 1986) or the efficacy of modality testing and teaching (Kavale & Forness, 1987). Once an effort to ascertain an individual's potential is made via intelligence testing or newer tests of cognitive processing, then there are no ready prescriptive treatments for the child (Reschly, 1992).

Laughon (1990) declares that if dynamic assessment is to make a contribution to the field, it will be in providing remedial information for program planning. In critiquing the available literature on the matter, Laughon notes that the Bud-off material (e.g., Budoff, 1969) does not include a remediation component, the Feuerstein material (e.g., Feuerstein, Rand, & Hoffman, 1979) is intentionally unrelated to school curriculum, and no substantive data were available referencing Campione and Brown. The instrumental enrichment training associated with Feuerstein does not include transfer to novel or school-based tasks, and research that focuses on its link to school performance reveals little to no effect (Savell, Twohig, & Rachford, 1986). Thus, the associated intervention materials developed to modify children's cognitive processes seem unrelated to improving a child's performance in school. The lack of generalization is reminiscent of the perceptual–motor activities popular in the 1970s that also proved to have no carryover into academic improvements. It appears that the value of these dynamic assessment approaches for academic and behavioral program planning is suspect. There is no need for the field to add to or replace existing assessment practices with others that are more expensive, are time consuming, and offer no additional useful information for program planning.

Functional assessments offer a direct correlation between assessment efforts and research regarding effective schools in numerous specific ways. They facilitate the teacher's ability to provide instruction directly at the student's level. The absence of such information in traditional testing has long been a frustration of both special and general educators. The specific knowledge of how a child is currently functioning allows teachers and parents to establish clear objectives and high expectations, without the burden of focusing on the child's limits set by an IQ score or even an estimate of learning potential. The assessment process includes the gathering of information about what skills need to be developed for effective instruction to occur (e.g., working independently, question asking skills, control of impulsive behaviors, conversational skills). The instruction provided to students following functional assessments can be systematic and intentional, with the natural inclusion of continual monitoring of student progress. When student progress toward goals is insufficient, program intensity can be adjusted, or when students have achieved their stated goals, additional goals can be stipulated. Taylor's (1988) illustrative case study documenting the intervention benefits of a functional assessment focused on behavior in the classroom clearly documents the benefits of such an approach. At the point of initiation of the assessment, the child in the case study was characterized as exhibiting uncontrollable disruptive behaviors that had led the majority of the school staff to label him as emotionally disturbed and give up hope for improving his behavior. Following a highly structured behavioral intervention and continual observations of on-task behaviors, teachers no longer felt the need to request a change of placement, the need for standardized testing was eliminated, and everyone was pleased with the student's improved behavior.

Argument Summary Reschly and Wilson (1990) caution that both traditional intelligence testing and new tests of cognitive processing "are quite useless and potentially harmful to children if the context for their use does not emphasize interventions and if the results are not closely related to significant decisions about students" (p. 444). As states move away from classification systems based on internal child-based deficits and concentrate more on skill deficiencies and the needed interventions, there should be diminished use of intellectual measures. The need for IQ tests in special education would be greatly diminished if it were not necessary to distinguish among children who were mildly mentally retarded, those who were learning disabled, and those with behavioral difficulties. The testing should come only after well-designed interventions are offered to help the child overcome academic or social difficulties, not before. A functional assessment and teacher referral system can find the same students with far less cost and consumption of time while offering information directly relevant to intervention in basic academic and social domains.

The IQ test score that a child receives can take on meanings and interpretations far exceeding its qualifications to do so. Efficiency and accuracy have taken precedence over the exploration of meaningful information about cognitive traits. The tests have been designed for the demands of the market, which is under pressure to meet deadlines for psychological evaluations with far less demand for thoughtful interpretation of results within a child's contextual circumstances. Perhaps a future without the need to discriminate among disabilities will allow for the elimination of traditional IQ testing and cognitive processing tests in favor of curriculum-based, adaptive behavior and social skills measures that could actually be helpful in designing, monitoring, and evaluating interventions. The discrepancy formulas are typically based on the grade placement in school, not a child's chronological age. Had a child delayed a year in starting school, it would take longer to document a discrepancy sufficient to warrant labeling. Further, the child who is retained might be delayed in being diagnosed, because the expected level of progress (i.e., potential) was adjusted when the retention occurred. The discrepancy formula model is based on the assumptions that agreed-upon curricular standards by grade level are stable and have real meaning, grade placement is an accurate prediction of potential for a child who has a normal or above IQ, and measurement of potential and achievement can accurately and consistently reveal child-based problems that warrant diagnosis of the condition. Just as we "cured" 13.4% of the population of mental retardation in the early 1970s, we can increase or decrease the number of children diagnosed as learning disabled by adjusting age of school entry, placement of curricula on achievement tests, and/or expansion/reduction of the discrepancy required to be documented.

HIGH-STAKES ACCOUNTABILITY
AND STUDENTS WITH DISABILITIES

Historically, the separation of general and special education has included their accountability systems. Test performance has typically been used in general education whereas compliance monitoring was treated as the accountability system for special education (Ysseldyke, Thurlow, & Geenen, 1994). If every child had an IEP with all the proper assessment information and signatures, that was presumed to be sufficient evidence that the schools were offering children an appropriate program. With the massive restructuring and the movement toward inclusion, occurring simultaneously with reforms in accountability for general education, students with disabilities and their teachers will be facing new dilemmas. Is accountability based on student performance something that special educators want to embrace in their demands for inclusion or something from which they would prefer their students be waived? If outcomes-based accountability is to apply to *all* students, what suitable adaptations and alternatives can make the system equitable and to whom should they apply, and who would get to decide for whom the adaptations and alternatives are appropriate?

The Council for Exceptional Children, in testimony before the House Subcommittee on Elementary, Secondary, and Vocational Education, expressed concerns regarding the move to national standards (CEC, 1992, as cited in Ysseldyke, Thurow, & Shriner, 1992). The issues of concern included the arbitrariness of the standards, with no empirical evidence on the whats and whens of educational outcomes. As professional organizations proceed with the identification of their standards, the absence of policies regarding the consideration of students with diverse needs implies either a blatant lack of concern for or an unawareness of their presence in schools. With the trend to set standards in core subject areas only, some areas of and approaches to the curriculum will be penalized and probably dropped for the sake of meeting standards in the core subjects. Both gifted and disabled children are likely to feel the brunt of such narrowing of the curriculum more than others. The final point made by CEC personnel was that any proposed national assessment system must address a means by which all students be included, not ignored through exemptions or other means of removing them from the benefits of accountability intended by the system.

Accountability Through Standards or Choice

The accountability reform movement has two disparate paths as well as some compromise proposals (Sizer, McDonald, & Rogers, 1992–93). In concern for the standing of U.S. children in global rankings, reformers have proposed "ratcheting up the standards to improve the educational outcomes for all kids" (p. 2). These new standards are also characterized as shifting from those of norms to value-based standards, which some consider to involve unexamined contradictions and conceivably "deeply undemocratic consequences" (p. 2). However, the move to establish standards is not the only idea afoot to increase accountability and performance of U.S. schools. Sizer, McDonald, and Rogers refer to the move to advance rigorous standards as a neoliberal strategy and that of allowing accountability to be achieved through a choice system, in which parents and students would be free to choose the schools that satisfied them and free to abandon the schools that were inadequate, as neoconservative. Both groups find dissatisfaction with traditional means of holding schools accountable, with the emphasis on resources provided (e.g., student–teacher ratios, access to computers, library holdings) and norm-referenced multiple-choice assessments. Although special education is not an element of consideration in the political rhetoric surrounding these contrasting approaches to accountability, the path taken will certainly influence the educational opportunities and expectations we hold for students with disabilities.

Neoliberals contend that textbook publishers and the testing industry have already created an undesirable national curriculum and national assessment system. We would be well served by overthrowing this curriculum in favor of one developed in conjunction with the standards thoughtfully derived by professional educators (e.g., National Council of Teachers of Mathematics). Embedded within the standards movement are discussions of what the nature of the associated assessments should be like. The adoption of performance-based approaches (both simulated and authentic) is clearly prevalent in the standards movement. To illustrate the nature of performance-based assessments, Sizer, McDonald, and Rogers (1992–93) describe a required senior presentation at one high school in Providence, Rhode Island, as the culmination of the year's interdisciplinary study for *all* students. Parenthetically, either the school has no students in its student body for whom this task is unobtainable or *all* excludes such children (e.g., those with severe disabilities) from consideration.

The group Sizer, McDonald, and Rogers refer to as neoconservatives are ready to let the freedom of choice in schools lead to the natural selection process—the closing of schools proven unsatisfactory. For supporters of the free choice concept of accountability there are fears that the democratic school governance system engenders bureaucracy and instability, rendering school choice incapacitated even before initiated (Chubb & Moe, 1992). A choice system that proved to offer only partial choice—with limited slots in schools considered acceptable, no access to transportation for some who lived distant from the best schools, or even no access to comprehensible comparative information regarding schools—could create greater inequities than present zoning policies do with an appearance of just the opposite. The use of choice as a means of accountability is far less visible than the move toward standards is, yet such a highly limited choice system is already in place. Some may move to a public school district/zone of their choice, whereas others abandon the public schools in favor of home schooling or private and church-affiliated schools. Reasons for making such choices include safety, curriculum, and rejection of the currently popular values-based outcomes and standards spreading throughout the public schools. However, not everyone can meet the criteria for home schooling or the financial obligations associated with the other "choices." Thus, just as those supporting standards contend that textbook publishers and the testing industry have set our current curriculum, those favoring choice can argue that choice for some is already available, indicating a far less desirable circumstance than choice for all would create.

Standards and Diagnosis

The adoption of standards and performance-based outcomes will come to set the achievement expectations used in the diagnostic process. The content of the material expected of students at each grade level must coincide with the goals and objectives that will be measured for accountability. As noted previously,

Sleeter (1990) postulates that learning disability is a social construction, evolving in concert with social and political events within this country. The logic of this position is based on a contextual analysis of the increases and decreases in categorical disabilities. When reading and other achievement standards were raised in the late 1950s and 1960s in response to Sputnik, a group of white middle-class children struggled to keep the pace, but could not. They did not belong in any of the existing special education categories, but parents would not allow their children to simply flounder and fail in school, hence the establishment of a newly identified condition, learning disabilities. However, social change and economic conditions concurrently led to a reduction of the category of mental retardation, through a changed definition, and diagnostic controversy surrounding minimal brain dysfunction led to its demise. Those changes resulted in the increased use of the learning disability category for many different students.

Sleeter notes that today's educational reform climate is once again focusing on the issue of raising standards. She argues that focusing on the issue of which label to place on the child is putting the emphasis in the wrong corner, contending that "Schools need to focus much greater attention on how to teach children rather than on how to categorize those who do not learn well when offered 'business-as-usual'" (Sleeter, 1990, p. 33). As we move toward increased standards, the implications for the diagnostic procedures used to label are clearly affected. The level at which we expect a child to have the ability to master material is the essential ingredient in the currently prevalent discrepancy model of diagnosis for learning disabilities. If material that a child can accomplish is considered to be on a second-grade level but the child is in the third grade and has a "normal" IQ, we note a slight discrepancy—typically not sufficient for diagnosing the child as learning disabled. However, if that material were redefined as something that should have been mastered at the first grade, we now find a discrepancy sufficient to warrant certifying the child as learning disabled. The setting of performance standards and expectations for students with disabilities to achieve them and/or the exclusion of students with disabilities from those expectations raises dilemmas for diagnosticians.

Decision Point 5.2: Outcome-Based
Accountability for Special Education

Arguments for Proposition One The goal for special education teachers is to achieve the best possible outcomes for every student for whom they have instructional responsibility. They have accepted the assignment of working with students with mild disabilities who have been facing frustration and failure with the general education curriculum or students with moderate/severe disabilities who appropriately pursue an alternate curriculum. Exactly what or how much any one of these children is most likely to achieve during an academic school year is originally better known in terms of what they have failed to accomplish in the past than in what progress they might make in the future. Variables that remain influential, but speculative when IEPs are written, include the child's remaining motivation and enthusiasm for learning, the benefits of providing

---

Proposition One

Accountability for students with disabilities must center on access to educational opportunity and the efforts made to achieve the outcomes stipu-

lated by IEPs rather than student performance on achievement tests and/or performance-based assessments.

---

external structures for controlling internal impulses, the influence of neurological impairments requiring pharmaceutical interventions, and the developmental spurts or plateaus that a child might experience. The use of traditional benchmarks and fixed standards for students already experiencing risk of educational failure might serve the final discouraging blow to these children. Surely they must be held accountable for their own learning just as their teachers and school administrators must equally be held accountable for making the greatest possible efforts to enable the students to achieve high expectations based on *individual* standards for each student.

Accountability Through Standards or Choice Inclusion of students with disabilities in the main system of accountability would undermine much of the progress to date in having such children become a vital, welcome part of general education. Teachers will fear the inclusion of any student less than average in their classes who may jeopardize their professional standing by corrupting their test results They may attempt to eliminate from their classes children likely to perform poorly on any measures of achievement or resist acceptance of such an accountability system. In order for students with disabilities to retain their hard-fought places within general education, separate accountability systems are essential. This policy applies equally to students across all levels of disability. For those with moderate to severe disabilities who are now spending time in general education settings, no one is likely to propose that they be held accountable for the National Council of Teachers of Mathematics standards. Yet those diagnosed with mild disabilities are at risk of being expected to achieve such standards in order to progress in school or even retain their seats in mainstream classes.

The claim that testing accommodations are appropriate and equitable for students with disabilities is simply inaccurate. The modification of testing procedures is unfair to the mainstream student body who get no such accommodations, the testing industry whose tests are misappropriated, the teachers who are accountable for the performance of the students on the tests, and the students with disabilities who have traditionally been excluded from norm groups during test development. Does a student with a learning disabilities in mathematics get modifications only on mathematics portions of the test, possibly necessitating his movement back to a large group under timed conditions for other portions of tests, or do allowed modifications apply to the entire test? The use of modifications in standardized assessments jeopardizes the tests' reliability and validity and inevitably risks exposing students with disabilities to inequitable testing conditions. A traditional choice-based test that is standardized under timed conditions in group settings is not equivalent to one given untimed in a room with no other test takers present. Such accommodations might appear to favor the student with disabilities, but there is no consistent, reliable means of eliminating the impact of a disability during testing, nor should there be if the integrity of the test would be threatened. For example, a test designed to measure a student's ability to quickly scan reading material and retain accurate information from that reading could not be altered to eliminate the effects of a reading disability. The test is specifically designed to discriminate on the basis of reading skills.

Rather than creating altered testing conditions for students with mild disabilities to take tests from whose norming groups they have been excluded, IEP outcome statements must provide the context of accountability for those students, just as they can for students with moderate to severe disabilities. Student IEPs based on accurate, individualized assessment of current performance offer far greater opportunity for meaningful accountability for students with disabilities than forced attempts to make group assessments work for these children. However, the accountability for both teachers and students must lie in the efforts put forth toward the achievement of these outcomes, not their actual achievement. Were accountability to be based on actual outcome achievement, the temptation to write self-limiting outcome statements would be real, whereas accountability based on efforts towards achievement and documentation of progress actually encourages the setting of high expectations with no reprisals. Throughout the year, as IEP outcomes are achieved, parents, teachers, and students can set higher goals without any anxiety that they will be held accountable for failing to achieve these new aspirations.

Standards and Diagnosis Americans want students who can compete in a global market in mathematics, science, technology, and every other field. Such a goal need not be achieved by the raising of standards for every single child in America. Indeed, such an outcome might be better reached through the pursuit of special educational opportunities for students displaying an unusual interest and ability in various subjects rather than a wholesale raising of standards. Children who are unable to achieve the high standards that are appropriate for some need not be denied their high school diplomas or placed in special education programs. We must resist allowing raised standards and greater accountability to increase the number of referrals into special education. Simultaneously, we must ensure that those students with legitimate disabilities affecting their ability to perform in school are not suffering either through their mandatory inclusion or exclusion from standards and accountability systems. Teachers must not be penalized for having students with disabilities in their classes, and students must not be subjected to unrealistic standards in order to progress with their classmates.

Argument Summary Education requires accountability, but that accountability must be fair and accurate for all. The forced inclusion of students with disabilities in an accountability system that measures them against a fixed standard is destined to be biased. It seems rather absurd to diagnose a child as having a disability that will impede his performance in educational settings to the extent that special education services are required, provide that child with an IEP stipulating personal outcomes that a multidisciplinary team anticipates that he can reasonably achieve, and then hold him to the fixed standards set for children without disabilities. The child with a mild disability, discovered only after he performs poorly in school, is expected to make up the deficits and progress at regular speed from here on out—such indicates a lack of belief in the presence of a disability. Indeed, reliance on accurately developed IEPs to determine student and educator accountability is individualized, which is at the heart of special education efficacy.

Arguments for Proposition Two The field of special education has long held to the notion that the identical treatment of students with disabilities breeds inequities. Yet professionals in the field have also come to critique society's fostering learned helplessness and dependence through the sheltering of such students from opportunities that might prove painful or require hard work. The loss of potential caused by someone's kind-hearted protectionism can cause far greater loss than the exposure of students to possible failure. An accountability system based on dual standards of achievement of outcomes for students without disabilities, and access to education for students with disabilities, would come to undermine all of special education. Priority and urgency for those whose accountability is based on their actual test scores or demonstrated abilities would inevitably overshadow those for whom access to learning opportunities is the only measure of accountability.

Accountability Through Standards or Choice Inclusion of students with disabilities in a single system of accountability is absolutely essential to the long-term achievements of students with disabilities. Suitable modifications adhering to the standardization principles of any assessment system, whether it involves traditional choice-based responding or performance-based constructed responding, can be specified for the vast majority of students with disabilities. This is evidenced by the fact that only 1%–2% of students in Kentucky needed to be placed in their alternative portfolio assessment system (Ysseldyke, Thurlow, & Geenen, 1994). Suitable accommodations have become well established in the testing industry as greater numbers of students with disabilities are remaining in general education settings and come to key points in their education where such tests are mandatory. Currently, the testing performance of these students is not always included in data banks or easily available. However, it has been only relatively recently that such students have begun participating in accountability measures. Clearly, greater consistency in policy statements regarding test reporting and improved testing standardizations that include psychometric analyses of testing under modification

---

Proposition Two
Students with disabilities must be fully included in the general education accountability system, with the provision of appropriate testing accommodations and/or alternative assessment procedures for students pursuing special curricula (e.g., life skills curriculum for a special education diploma).

conditions and/or suitable modification standards for performance-based assessments (if necessary) are needed. However, the need for such improvements, refinements, and adjustments should be expected as states face the responsibility of developing a suitable accountability system that meets the needs of both general and special education students and faculty.

Standards and Diagnosis Fixed standards offer a clear benchmark for all to track their educational progress. In the same manner that we chart a child's height and weight by fixed measurement standards, so we can monitor a child's achievements. Such fixed standards can be used for comparisons between the individual and the group *and* between the individual and his own progress, just as the child's growth charts allow for the plotting of her height and weight in a manner that shows comparisons to averages as well as individual progress. Both comparisons offer essential information needed to plan for a child's future. The comparison to group performance allows teachers and parents to have a warning system to alert them to delays that need watching. The rate of delay/progress evidenced in comparing a child's performance to group norms can continue to provide useful, albeit painful, information for those concerned about the child's educational progress. Just as the infant who shows abnormal patterns on the growth charts needs the group comparisons for meaningful interpretation of her own data, we must use fixed benchmarks of normal academic progress to interpret accurately the progress of students who may have disabilities. However, a consistent, unified accountability system does not require that all children be held to the same standards based exclusively on chronological age. Indeed, the documentation of progress, not merely grade-level functioning of all students, should be a component of any comprehensively designed accountability system. Reward and sanction programs can be based on advancement of student performance (e.g., value-added formulas), not single test administrations. The issue of discrepancy formulas and the diagnosis of learning disabilities based on the placement of curriculum are quite unrelated to the issue at hand—the means of establishing accountability systems for schools and teachers that include students with disabilities in an equitable fashion. Standards and test scores are set by the performance of thousands of students, not arbitrary grade-level assignments. Obviously, manipulation of discrepancy formulas is possible through artificial means, such as promotion or retention decisions. It is the responsibility of diagnosticians to use the system of diagnosis in accordance with their best clinical judgment, based on multiple sources of assessment data, including observations of the child in various settings and parent and teacher reports. The implementation of standards of progression should in no way negatively alter or affect diagnostic policies or outcomes.

Argument Summary The strong link between teachers' high expectations and student performance must be a central tenet in the design of any accountability system. McLaughlin and Warren (1994) observed that "Fixed standards promote high expectations for all students and set criteria that can be used consistently across scoring rubrics" (p. 10). The establishment of universal benchmarks for each type of diploma, whether it be high honors, college prep, vocational, or special education, clarifies the meaning and value of the diploma for all others. The students who receive each diploma have achieved a minimum standard associated with it and can present themselves for employment with clearly delineated outcomes.

CLOSING THOUGHTS

Our current system of determining eligibility for special education rests on both the determination of the lack of potential as well as the identification of under-achieved potential. We presume to obtain a measure of student potential and so design instructional programs that will enable children to become the best they have the ability to become. Commercially available curricular materials have variability in terms of readability and grade placement of content, yet the assessments used to diagnose a learning disability based on a discrepancy formula are common throughout the country. Although student exposure to information and expectations for learning vary, the approach used in the diagnosis of a condition considered to lie within the child (i.e., the condition should not be considered to be associated with environmental factors or poor teaching) assumes that we all agree on the appropriate grade levels for curricular materials and that these agreed-upon grade levels are not subject to change. The child's chronological age must also be factored in, not just grade placement. The use of standardized tests in the assessment process is expensive, is time consuming, and can be incompatible with other services such as prereferral interventions (Reschly, 1992). Costs associated with eligibility assessments were approximately $1,200 per student in the early 1980s (Shepard & Smith, 1983) and are likely significantly higher now. The questions about what we are getting for our money are appropriate to consider. The supporters and beneficiaries of existing practices must be held accountable to the critics, and the critics must offer acceptable alternatives. So what becomes of the student struggling but unsuccessful in her schoolwork? If the only way to get this child the supports that she needs is the diagnostic process resulting in certification as learning disabled, we will do so, even if she does not really exhibit any symptoms associated with cerebral dysfunction.

REFERENCES

Adelman, H. S., & Taylor, L. (1993). *Learning problems and learning disabilities: Moving forward*. Pacific Grove, CA: Brooks/Cole.

Budoff, M. (1969). Learning potential: A supplementary procedure for assessing the ability to reason. *Seminars in Psychiatry, 1*, 293–309.

Buros, O. K. (Ed.). (1974). *Tests in print II*. Highland Park, NJ: Gryphon.

Campione, J. C., & Brown, A. L. (1987). Linking dynamic assessment with school achievement. In C. S. Lidz (Ed.), *Dynamic assessment: An interactional approach to evaluating learning potential* (pp. 82–115). New York: Guilford.

Champlin, J. R. (1991). Taking stock and moving on. *Journal of the National Center for Outcome Based Education, 1,* 5–8.

Chubb, J. E., & Moe, T. M. (1992). *A lesson in school reform from Great Britain.* Washington, DC: Brookings Institution.

Eisner, E. W. (1993). Reshaping assessment in education: Some criteria in search of practice. *Journal of Curriculum Studies, 25,* 219–233.

Feuerstein, R. (1979). *Dynamic assessment of retarded performers.* Baltimore: University Park Press.

Feuerstein, R., Rand, Y., & Hoffman, M. B. (1979). *Learning potential assessment device, theory, instruments, and techniques.* Baltimore: University Park Press.

Frisby, C. L., & Braden, J. P. (1992). Feuerstein's dynamic assessment approach: A semantic, logical, and empirical critique. *Journal of Special Education, 26,* 281–301.

Fuchs, L. S., & Fuchs, D. (1986). Effects of systematic formative evaluation: A meta-analysis. *Exceptional Children, 53,* 199–208.

Gardner, H. (1983). *Frames of mind.* New York: Basic Books.

Gardner, H. (1993). Introduction to *Frames of mind* (10th anniversary edition). New York: Basic Books.

Gelzheiser, L. M. (1987). Reducing the number of students identified as learning disabled: A question of practice, philosophy or policy? In S. B. Sigmon (Ed.), *Critical voices on special education: Problems and progress concerning the mildly handicapped* (pp. 43–50). Albany NY: State University of New York Press.

Gerber, M., & Semmel, M. (1984). Teacher as imperfect test: Reconceptualizing the referral process. *Educational Psychologist, 19,* 137–148.

Hausman, R. M. (1988). The use of Budoff's learning potential assessment techniques with a Mexican-American, moderately handicapped student. In R. L. Jones (Ed.), *Psychoeducational assessment of minority group children: A casebook* (pp. 65–75). Berkeley, CA: Cobb & Henry.

Haywood, H. C. (1988). Dynamic assessment: The Learning Potential Assessment Device. In R. L. Jones (Ed.), *Psychoeducational assessment of minority group children: A casebook* (pp. 39–64). Berkeley, CA: Cobb & Henry.

Haywood, H. C., Brown, A. L., & Wingenfeld, S. (1990). Dynamic approaches to psychoeducational assessment. *School Psychology Review 19,* 411–422.

Hegarty, S. (1994). Integration and the teacher. In C. J. W. Meijer, S. J. Pijl, & S. Hegarty (Eds.), *New perspectives in special education* (pp. 125–131). New York: Routledge.

Hoy, C., & Gregg, N. (1994). *Assessment: The special educator's role.* Pacific Grove, CA: Brooks/Cole.

Hughes, S. (1993). What is alternative assessment and how does it impact special education? *Educational Horizons, 72,* 28–35.

Kaufman, A., & Kaufman, N. (1983). *Kaufman Assessment Battery for Children.* Circle Pines, MN: American Guidance Service.

Kavale, K. A., & Forness, S. R. (1987). Substance over style: Assessing the efficacy of modality testing and teaching. *Exceptional Children, 54,* 228–239.

Kavale, K. A., & Mundschenk, N. A. (1991). A critique of assessment methodology. In H. L. Swanson (Ed.), *Handbook on the assessment of learning disabilities* (pp. 407–432). Austin: Pro-Ed.

Kentucky Department of Education. (1992). *Procedures for inclusion of students in KIRIS.* (Program Advisory No. 92-OAAS-004). Frankfort, KY: Author.

Laughon, P. (1990). The dynamic assessment of intelligence: A review of three approaches. *School Psychology Review 19,* 459–470.

Lipsky, D. K., & Gartner, A. (1989). *Beyond separate education: Quality education for all.* Baltimore: Paul Brookes.

McLaughlin, M. J., & Warren, S. H. (1994). *Performance assessment and students with disabilities: Usage in outcomes-based accountability systems.* Reston, VA: Council for Exceptional Children.

Naglieri, J. A., & Braden, J. P. (1992). Norm-referenced intelligence tests: What we have and what we need. In W. Stainback & S. Stainback (Eds.), *Controversial issues confronting special education: Divergent perspectives* (pp. 111–126). Boston: Allyn & Bacon.

Naglieri, J. A., Das, J. P., & Jarman, R. F. (1990). Planning, attention, simultaneous, and successive cognitive processes as a model for assessment. *School Psychology Review 19,* 423–442.

Obrzut, J. E., & Boliek, C. A. (1991). Neuropsychological assessment of childhood learning disabilities. In H. L. Swanson (Ed.), *Handbook on the assessment of learning disabilities* (pp. 121–146). Austin: Pro-Ed.

Pianta, R. D., Erickson, M. F., Wagner, N., Kruetzer, T., & Egeland, B. (1990). Early predictors of referral for special services. Child-based measures versus mother–child interactions. *School Psychology Review, 19,* 240–250.

Reschly, D. J. (1992). Special education decision making and functional/behavioral assessment. In W. Stainback & S. Stainback (Eds.), *Controversial issues confronting special education: Divergent perspectives* (pp. 127–138). Boston: Allyn & Bacon.

Reschly, D. J., Genshaft, J., & Binder, M. S. (1987). *The 1986 NASP survey: Comparison of practitioners, NASP leadership, and university faculty on key issues.* Washington, DC: National Association of School Psychologists. (ERIC Document Reproduction No. ED 300 733).

Reschly, D. J., & Wilson, M. S. (1990). Cognitive processing v. traditional intelligence: Diagnostic utility, intervention implications and treatment validity. *School Psychology Review 19,* 443–458.

Reynolds, M. C. (1975). Trends in special education: Implications for measurement. In M. C. Reynolds & W. Hivehy (Eds.), *Domain-referenced testing in special education* (pp. 15–28). Minneapolis: University of Minnesota Press.

Sabatino, D. A., & Vance, H. B. (1993). Describing the cognitive aspects of intelligence. In R. C. Eaves & P. J. McLaughlin (Eds.), *Recent advances in special education and rehabilitation* (pp. 30–48). Boston: Andover Medical Publishers.

Salvia, J., & Ysseldyke, J. E. (1995). *Assessment.* Boston: Houghton Mifflin.

Sattler, J. M. (1992). *Assessment of children's intelligence* (3rd ed.). San Diego: Author.

Savell, J., Twohig, P., & Rachford, D. (1986). Empirical status of Feuerstein's "instrumental enrichment" techniques as a method of teaching thinking skills. *Review of Educational Research, 56,* 381–409.

Scheffler, I. (1985). *Of human potential.* Boston: Routledge & Kegan Paul.

Shepard, L. A. (1991). Interview on assessment issues with Lorrie Shepard. *Educational Researcher, 20,* 21–23, 27.

Shepard, L. A., & Smith, M. L. (1983). An evaluation of the identification of learning disabled students in Colorado. *Learning Disability Quarterly, 6,* 115–127.

Shinn, M. R., Tindal, G. A., & Spira, D. A. (1987). Special education referrals as an index of teacher tolerance: Are teachers imperfect tests? *Exceptional Children, 54,* 32–40.

Sizer, T., McDonald, J. P., & Rogers, B. (1992–93). Standards and school reform: Asking the essential questions. *The Stanford Law and Policy Review, 4,* 2–7.

Sleeter, C. E. (1990). Learning disabilities: The social construction of a special education category. In S. B. Sigmon (Ed.), *Critical voices on special education: Problems and progress concerning the mildly handicapped* (pp. 21–34). Albany, NY: State University of New York Press.

Spady, W. G. (1992). It's time to take a close look at outcome-based education. *Communique, 20,* 16–18.

Taylor, J. M. (1988). Behavioral assessment and special education evaluation: A successful and necessary marriage. In R. L. Jones (Ed.), *Psychoeducational* assessment of minority group children: A casebook (pp. 225–235). Berkeley, CA: Cobb & Henry.

Thorndike, E. L. (1927). *The measurement of intelligence.* New York: Bureau of Publications, Teachers College, Columbia University.

Thorndike, R. L., Hagen, E. P., & Sattler, J. M. (1985). *Stanford-Binet intelligence scale: Fourth edition.* Chicago: Riverside.

Thurlow, M. L. (1994). *National and state perspectives on performance assessment and students with disabilities.* Reston, VA: Council for Exceptional Children.

Tucker, J. A. (1980). Ethnic proportions in classes for the learning disabled: Issues in nonbiased assessment. *Journal of Special Education, 14,* 93–105.

Tzuriel, D. (1992). The dynamic assessment approach: A reply to Frisby and Braden. *Journal of Special Education, 26,* 302–324.

U.S. Department of Education. (1995). *Seventeenth annual report to Congress on the implementation of the Individuals with Disabilities Education Act.* Washington, DC: Office of Special Education Programs.

Weschler, D. (1991). *Wechsler intelligence scale for children—III.* San Antonio: Psychological Corporation.

Wiggins, G. (1989). A true test: Toward more authentic and equitable assessment. *Phi Delta Kappan, 70,* 703–713.

Witt, J. S., & Gresham, F. M. (1985). Review of the Wechsler intelligence scale for children—revised. In J. Mitchell (Ed.), *Ninth Mental Measurements Yearbook* (pp. 1716–1719). Lincoln, NE: Buros Institute.

Ysseldyke, J. E., Thurlow, M. L., & Geenen, K. (1994). *Implementation of alternative methods for making educational accountability decisions for students with disabilities. Synthesis report 12.* Minneapolis, MN: National Center on Educational Outcomes.

Ysseldyke, J. E., Thurlow, M. L., & Shriner, J. G. (1992). Outcomes are for special educators too. *Teaching Exceptional Children, 25,* 36–50.

6

Curriculum Development and Instructional Approaches

INTRODUCTION

After the referrals, the assessments, and the placement decisions, what remains for students with disabilities and their parents and teachers is the determination of specifically what will be taught and how it will be taught. Placement decisions may partially set the curriculum available to a child, but program content must be more specifically addressed in the development of individual educational outcomes as stipulated on the IEP. Eligibility, categorical definitions, cultural bias, inclusion models, and other issues all fade into the background when the focus becomes the quality and effectiveness of the instruction that goes on in the classroom. Indeed, Kauffman (1993) has noted the potential insignificance of the many structural reforms currently popular because they are not even aimed toward improving the "teacher–student interactions that constitute academic instruction and behavior management" (p. 7). Curriculum and pedagogy define the goals of education and set the means of achieving those goals. As Gerber (1994) has noted, "Because curriculum is infused with beliefs about learning and learners, it is never neutral or innocuous with respect to the quality of learning opportunities provided for students with disabilities" (p. 372). Teacher attention and instructional efforts are allocated according to the curriculum and its implicit priorities.

In general education, the process of curriculum development typically originates with establishment of basic requirements by state departments of education. This curricular development involves outlining specific topics to be afforded at least a minimum amount of instructional time per week for elementary schools and curricular graduation standards for secondary schools. Within the state parameters, school districts add further specification to the curricular decisions, usually controlling textbook adoption decisions and other general policies related to curricular issues, such as field trips and use of community resources. Further refinements occur at the building level. For example, the decision to implement an integrated curriculum at an elementary school would need to have the support and enthusiasm of the faculty to have any chance for success. At the secondary level, specialty subjects depend on teacher availability.

The precise control of curriculum varies throughout the nation but generally reflects the needs of society, the contribution that curricular areas make to education, and the needs of the students (Pugach & Warger, 1993). However, decisions regarding what teachers should teach and what students should bother learning are becoming ever greater challenges as the world continues to discover new information and experiences an evolving society. Even for the students who have not been identified as having special needs, the curricular issues strike intense debate—should we produce problem solvers who know how to retrieve facts; should we produce citizens well-grounded in a culturally rich education, with the acquisition of job skills following; or should the emphasis be placed on job skills and providing students with those skills essential to achieving economic independence? Should the answers to these questions differ for students with disabilities? To date, many contend that although the academic content is often dull, it controls education (Pugach & Warger, 1993). Pedagogical decisions, although linked to curriculum, are more typically made by the child's teachers over the course of a school year, with far less group discussion.

The appropriateness of the general education curriculum and popular pedagogical approaches for students with disabilities who are being placed in mainstream settings have received far less attention than has the right of a student to be placed in the least restrictive environment (Fuchs & Fuchs, 1994). Stainback and Stainback (1992) have recommended that the standard curriculum be replaced with a constructivist approach in which children can enjoy purposeful projects and activities. They recommend that textbook-set curricula that hold little or no meaning for most students be dropped in favor of approaches to curricular development that allow for a diversity of interests and abilities. When special educators and parents call for students with disabilities to be included in mainstream education, is it for curricular inclusion or a physical and social presence that does not necessarily involve the curriculum? If, through inclusion, students with disabilities encounter an inappropriate curriculum, should the student receive a modified program, or should the curriculum be altered? After all, the curriculum of an individual child receiving special education is spelled out in her IEP, whereas the regular education classroom teacher uses a far different point of reference when developing curriculum. Can or should the IEP remain as it has been, a highly behavioral instrument (Mahoney & Wheatley, 1994) that sets an individual course of study, or should it be transformed into a document more compatible with the general education curriculum and/or currently popular constructivist principles?

Decisions regarding methods of instruction are typically made at the system, building, and classroom teacher level, but do not have the legal status of curriculum. Obviously, however, textbook adoptions, particularly in curricular areas such as reading and mathematics, carry with them pedagogical intentions. There have even been attempts recently to legislate methods, such as the use of phonics in reading instruction, in a few states. The threat of legislated pedagogy seems to be a political reaction to constructivist ideas currently popular in general education coupled with a concern for falling achievement test scores. To date, however, within the parameters set by system and building level policies, public classroom teachers continue to design their own instructional programs, choosing when to use individual instruction, small groups, large groups, deductive or inductive approaches, and so forth.

Special education programs, which vary widely in their pedagogical relationship to general education, have been heavily influenced by behaviorism in both instructional approaches and classroom management techniques. Some, which focus on the goal of maintaining students in the regular program or returning them to it as quickly as possible, use identical materials, varying the level and/or speed of the instruction while complementing the material with additional supports. Other programs, which focus on a tradition of diagnosis and prescription, are predicated on the notion that materials and methods of instruction need to be highly structured, based specifically on an individual student's profile of strengths and weaknesses. These programs are far less concerned with matching instruction to the general education curriculum than with identifying a curriculum perceived to be suitable for each individual student. In other cases, a supervisor's discovery of an effective instructional program for students with disabilities may result in its adoption systemwide. Thus, the freedom allotted to special education teachers to select their pedagogical style is influenced by system- and building-level policies as well as the stipulations noted on IEPs.

Constructivism and Special Education

Until recently, special education methodology has been dominated by approaches that are reductionist in nature, characterized by task analysis, applied behavior analysis, and diagnostic/prescriptive instructional analyses (Poplin & Stone, 1992). These and other popular special education approaches (e.g., direct instruction), although grounded in behavioral theory and research on effective teaching, place a premium on student achievement of specific goals and objectives. This pattern is consistent with Mallory and New's (1994) observation regarding early childhood special education that "the *theoretical* bases of research, programs, and practices are often neglected in favor of an emphasis on intervention outcomes and efficient service delivery" (p. 323). Whether such an emphasis is appropriate or less than ideal is subject to debate. The rationale for the emphasis on pragmatic concerns is the assumption that no time can be wasted on theoretical reflections when dealing with highly vulnerable children with disabilities. However, Mallory and New contend that interventions that appeared to create positive benefits have proven to have had little lasting benefit or generalization effect and even caused harm in some instances, when teachers neglect to consider theoretical issues, the "ecological contexts of children's lives or the multiple, transactional causes of disability" (p. 323). Concurrent with the dissatisfaction some within the special education ranks have felt toward the pedagogical domination of behaviorism has been the move toward inclusion. Meanwhile, general education has been heavily influenced by constructivist theories of learning, with resulting pedagogical changes. Constructivism is based on a rejection of the notion that children passively respond to their environments and that learning takes place through the internalization of knowledge presented by others. Instead, constructivists see children as actively building their own developmentally appropriate knowledge while interacting with the perceived world. All mental activity is set within a social context that defines its meaning.

The integration of young children into mainstream early childhood programs based on developmentally appropriate practices (DAP—Bredekamp & Copple, 1997) created a dilemma for special educators. The construction of knowledge as a program foundation and teacher-directed instruction focused on the efficient achievement of goals and objectives, as is the tradition in special education, have not naturally blended, yet inclusion has been retained as a highly valued objective. Many special educators wanted young children placed in mainstream settings, but they also wanted to change the nature of both the curriculum and instructional approaches within these settings. The early childhood educators were not so anxious to abandon their own beliefs. Similar dilemmas have emerged in K–12 programming with widespread adoption of whole language and experiential-based science and mathematics occurring simultaneously with inclusion becoming more prevalent. The pedagogical implications of constructivism, forced on special educators through their own calls for inclusion and pedagogical reform, have created a chasm within the field. Not everyone enthusiastically accepts the benefits of constructivism, even when they acknowledge the need for reform in special education. The notion that constructivism offers "necessary scope and intensity of learning opportunities for 'all' children" (Gerber, 1994, p. 376) is clearly antithetical to special education principles. Gerber argues that reformers focused on the theoretical notion of the construction of knowledge miss the critical social value attached to the actual knowledge that develops over years in school. He further contends that the trade-off necessarily puts at least some children at certain risk for failure.

Somewhat parallel debates regarding the appropriateness of qualitative research paradigms for special education have also been apparent, with qualitative approaches popular among the constructivists, and reductionists preferring the established empirical research base (Scruggs & Mastropieri, 1994–95). Kirk and Kutchins (1992) note that virtually every listing of author publication guidelines in major peer-reviewed journals publishing research on developmental disabilities stipulate that the experiment is *the* scientifically valid method acceptable for publication, and that case studies or qualitative reports should be submitted to lower-status practitioner journals. Anderson and Barrera (1995), in reference to the research paradigms debate, comment that special education finds itself at "a stage at which apparently contradictory opinions are strongly debated with little recognition that it is the nature of reality itself that is being debated" (p. 146). Although this observation seems equally relevant to the debates regarding extreme

Instructional activities that actively engage students in learning appeal to many children.

reductionist and constructivist instructional methodologies, there are instructional approaches falling within the constructivist paradigm that incorporate the blending of both direct teaching and discovery learning. Harris and Graham (1994), referencing the work of Moshman, cite distinctions between endogenous, exogenous, and dialectical constructivism, allowing for some differentiation in pedagogical style. Whereas endogenous constructivism is based on the notion that the child constructs new knowledge internally and develops best in an atmosphere of child-directed exploration and guided discovery, exogenous constructivism accepts the child as an active learner who has a reciprocal interactive relationship with the environment. The latter can be compatible with behavioral approaches to the extent that students are viewed as learners (not just constructors of new knowledge) who belong in natural environments using approaches such as reciprocal teaching or peer tutoring (Kimball & Heron, 1988). Dialectical constructivism is grounded in contextualism, with an emphasis on dynamic interactionism. Harris and Graham (1994) cite scaffolded instruction (e.g., reciprocal teaching, strategies training), teacher-guided or prompted discovery, and instruction intentionally arranged for students to encounter principles related to their misconceptions or incompletely formed conceptions as illustrative teaching approaches consistent with this paradigm, all of which combine direct teaching and discovery elements. Thus, the dichotomy between reductionism and constructivism shifts from black and white to shades of gray, with pedagogical approaches designed to tap into both perspectives.

Today, within the ranks of constructivists in early childhood education there is ongoing debate on the value and appropriateness of even attempting the delineation of universal developmentally appropriate practices as prescribed by

NAEYC. Mallory and New (1994) contend that it is "neither feasible nor appropriate to establish a set of universal practices that can apply across diverse settings with diverse populations" (p. 329) because each setting and social group requires uniquely constructed strategies. The attempted application of DAP with disadvantaged African American children has been particularly contested (Lubeck, 1994; Mallory, & New, 1994). In lieu of DAP, Mallory and New (1994) have proposed four guiding principles to provide criteria for classroom practice. These include the notion that inclusive classrooms function as communities of learners in which young children with disabilities belong as equally as any other child, even if they require direct instruction or behavioral approaches on occasion or the elimination or alteration of sacred rituals and routines (e.g., story time) that prove to be exclusionary in nature. This perspective is far different from the more prevalent practice of seeking theoretically acceptable (e.g., consistent with developmentally appropriate practices) interventions that enable a child with disabilities to function within an existing community of learners, and unless such interventions are successful the child does not belong and can be removed from the community of learners. Another of the principles stipulates that content and context are linked through inclusive curriculum and instruction. Direct instruction can be transformed from the transmission of boring, repetitive, teacher-selected skills to a form of guided participation in which the child selects a task and the nature of the activity gradually shifts from other-regulated to self-regulated.

Some advocates of applied behavioral analysis and direct instruction and some who are supporters of models of instruction based on constructionism are ardent in their rejection of the other (e.g., Tarver, 1992; Bredekamp & Copple, 1997), whereas others are ready to adopt a multiparadigm approach (Poplin & Stone, 1992). Indeed, some writers specifically criticize the tendency to create debates regarding the good or bad of direct or discovery teaching, individual or social grouping, competitive or cooperative instructional designs, as extreme dichotomies (Alexander, Murphy, & Woods, 1996). The push for inclusion and dissatisfaction with reductionist approaches to education have served as motivation for many to persevere in their pursuit of resolutions to the dilemmas caused by these conflicting perspectives. Constructivist approaches are emerging specifically intended for use with special education populations (e.g., Graham & Harris, 1994; Scruggs & Mastropieri, 1994), triggering debates between advocates of traditional skill development and holistic learning.

Disability Variables Interacting with
Curricular and Pedagogical Decisions

Curricular and pedagogical issues do differ for children according to the nature and severity of disability. There is near-universal agreement within the field on the life skills approach to curriculum development for individuals with severe to profound cognitive disabilities (Hazel, Barber, Roberts, Behr, Helmstetter, & Guess, 1988). The only other voice heard related to this population would recommend custodial care be provided outside the educational system, with essentially no curriculum offered. The popular notion of a life skills curriculum or the politically incorrect (yet very real) undercurrent that these children need not continue to be placed within the educational system is not really a curricular debate, but rather one much broader in context. It cuts to the basic premise of IDEA, that the educational system operate with a zero-reject policy.

For children with sensory impairments, placement decisions regarding residential schools or mainstream locales hold significant curricular implications. Students whose severe disabilities are primarily physical or visual might follow a mainstream curriculum with only minor adjustments, with the heart of changes being seen in the methods of instruction, student production of work, and disability-specific content. For example, a student with visual impairments might need large-print resources and instruction in the use of low vision aids, but can learn mathematics with the same basic strategies used with children of normal sight. However, students with severe hearing impairments present a unique group for which curricular issues are inextricably linked with and sometimes overshadowed by the debate regarding methods of communication.

Students do not always present themselves with clearly defined functioning levels implied by our classification systems. Issues are raised particularly for those students hovering between a classification of moderate to mild disability and often facing two very divergent curricular options. Yet children present an ongoing continuum of abilities, not lockstep rigid increments of ability. Additionally, most would acknowledge that assessment techniques offer less than flawless diagnoses.

Students with mild cognitive disabilities constitute the largest group for which the curricular debate is significant. Students with mild disabilities who retain their places in general education are typically expected to follow the standard curriculum (Pugach & Warger, 1993). There may be negotiations for modifications of instructional and evaluative approaches used by classroom teachers and exemptions or modifications in standardized testing, but the basic curriculum is most often unchanged. However, curricular considerations need to be approached differently from the past, when curricular accountability in special education was given far less consideration (Sheehan & Keogh, 1984). Before, we assumed that separation and alternative curriculum and methods were the solutions for these students. Such segregated programs tended to focus on IEP goals and objectives as isolated skills, with less consideration given to comprehensive curriculum (Sands, Adams, & Stout, 1995). Such an emphasis is consistent with legally defined "appropriate education" and has been held as good practice within the field. The IEP replaced state curricular standards for students served through special education. Today, the benefits of such an approach are being challenged, with its accompanying emphasis on the individual and his or her immediate needs outside of the context of the general education curriculum and long-term planning.

Focus of Discussion

Although much has been written about the dichotomy between reductionism and constructivism, current trends appear to indicate that these debates will result in greater variability and eclectic teaching styles rather than the exclusive adoption of one without the other. What appear to be more viable debates for today are the value and role of IEPs in the curricular planning of students with disabilities and the processes that we use to allow new pedagogical ideas to enter the classroom. In the first issue, the questions surrounding curricular development in special education are addressed. In the second debate, rather than targeting specific instructional approaches that some currently consider to be on the cutting edge and others view as charlatan, the discussion centers on the process of introducing and incorporating of new ideas into the educational system. How much caution must we take, and should teachers be free to explore and experiment with previously untested ideas or different theories of learning and development? What accountability do we have to use only those approaches known to be effective, and whose research is or is not credible?

CURRICULAR DEVELOPMENT AND IEPS

The diagnostic/prescriptive intention of IEPs spells out an individual child's present level of functioning, followed by the specification of appropriate goals and objectives intended to be carefully matched to that functioning. Concurrently, empirical research has dominated our efforts to corroborate programming effectiveness. Recently, however, a tension has developed between those who would continue in this vein and others who are espousing the application of a constructivist model of both research (e.g., Anderson & Barrera, 1995) and instructional models for students with disabilities (e.g., Tarver, 1992; Poplin & Stone, 1992). Special educators who challenge the reductionist tradition have been accused of abandoning the critical essence of special education.

Most often, the principal rationale for the referral and placement of students into special education is their inability to succeed in the standard academic curriculum (Pugach & Warger, 1993). Once students are placed there, their teachers consider the curricula to be that stipulated on IEPs (Sands, Adams, & Stout, 1995). However, using an IEP format to determine student curriculum has been criticized as resulting in a fragmented, skill-oriented course of study (Pugach & Warger, 1993). As educational programs continue to advance toward greater inclusion and educators struggle with the development of appropriate student outcomes, the curricular variability evidenced today will certainly be scrutinized carefully. The interplay between pedagogy and curriculum is particularly relevant for students with disabilities.

Gerber (1994) argues that special educators are and will remain in a reactive posture if they attempt to develop prescriptive programs based on constructivist ideas now prevalent in general education settings without first critically analyzing the school curriculum. Gerber describes curricula as "social constructs, consensual theories of learning and learner, that impinge upon and constrain all students' opportunities to construct their own knowledge" (p. 372). It is the teacher's responsibility to promote learning, regardless of constructivist/reductionist debates, not merely wait for students to emerge as having achieved developmental readiness. Teachers must promote learning by mediating between "students' lives and the content of the curriculum" (Jackson, Reid, & Bunsen, 1993).

Individualization of the Curriculum

Pugach & Warger (1993) have characterized the general education approach to curriculum development as lacking individualism. On the other hand, they describe special education curriculum as watered down at best. With the current emphasis on inclusive education, much more than the physical location of the child is at stake in curriculum planning. Yet, to date, far less attention has been directed toward curricular development than any other aspect of inclusion (Fuchs & Fuchs, 1994). The inclusion issue should indeed be considered as equity in access to knowledge rather than simply where a child sits while he is doing his drill work (Goodlad, 1993).

The power and control of the curriculum are embedded within the IEP process for special education students. The IEP is a higher authority for the individual child served through special education than state requirements, but its completion does not guarantee that child will earn a regular diploma. Some would argue that the IEP has become merely a document for compliance, verifying stipulated services and placements with no real information to guide instruction or evaluation (McLaughlin & Warren, 1994). Thus, the content of appropriate curricular components and requirements for students served through special education remains uncertain.

For some children, the determination of appropriate life goals and, therefore, curriculum seems basic and straightforward. For others, whose future is represented in the curricular decisions being made, there may be varying opinions about realistic life outcomes and aspirations. The issue can differ across severity of disability as well as the categorical nature of disabilities. In some instances, there may be a conflict between what parents see as the best outcomes for their child with disabilities and what the teachers and/or other parents consider to be reasonable future expectations. Further, the value of exposing a child to standards of behavior and curricular opportunities in inclusionary settings can appear to be in conflict with making the most efficient use of available instructional time for very different educational goals for students who are not following the general education curriculum. The pursuit of an appropriate balance between these conflicting goals comes to define the curriculum for each child served through special education.

Standards and the Curriculum

Progression standards, graduation requirements, and state testing mandates all help define the general education curriculum. Testing policies can set in motion changes in district or school practices and teacher behavior much faster than do proposed alterations to curricular frameworks (Gerber, 1994). Standards, once set in place, become the benchmark of success for schools as well as individual students. Teachers, whether held individually accountable or not, have a sense of responsibility and pride in having their students perform well on required examinations. Community newspapers, reporting comparisons of student performance across schools and districts, stir great interest as parents and teachers seek to be in those schools with the best performance data. When policy-related decisions are made for states, school districts, or teachers and students directly linked to the performance of students on standards testing, such testing involves high stakes (Gerber, 1994). Resource allocations are controlled by the outcomes of student testing, leading educators and their pupils to a significant crossroads. If school personnel notice a slip in average math scores on such tests, remediation plans are set in place immediately. If a slippage is seen in reading scores, attention goes in that direction. The standards by which a school and its pupils are publicly judged will weigh heavily in the development of that school's curriculum.

With state imposition of testing mandates, the basic curriculum is set for every child seeking a regular diploma. To the extent that a testing program reflects the desired competencies appropriate for students with disabilities, there is no conflict in the curriculum. Although students with moderate to severe disabilities are generally not addressed in this particular debate, students with mild disabilities often do get caught in the standards question. Some might argue that a functional, outcomes-based program would bring many such students greater likelihood of possessing job skills and achieving success following their secondary education. Yet the issuance of a high school diploma conveys with it that certain curricular standards as well as basic skills have been achieved that may be very difficult, if not impossible, for some students. The relevance of some of these standards to the successful transition to adulthood for individual children is debated. A team responsible for writing a secondary student's IEP must conclude that what they consider to be meaningful curriculum is, in fact, more meaningful than the earning of a diploma when choosing to deviate from the general education requirements. Since the diploma holds the symbolic as well as the actual key to progression in education and training or employment, this conclusion is not simple. What constitutes the most useful knowledge and skills for students with disabilities might be argued between those favoring academics and those preferring functional skills, whereas the symbolic value of a diploma is not questioned. Special educators are left with a basic dilemma: How influenced should a student's curriculum be by progression and graduation standards set for students in general education when those appear to conflict with needed functional skills?

Decision Point 6.1: Developing
Curriculum for Students with Disabilities

Arguments for Proposition One   The purpose of education is not simply the acquisition of certain knowledge and the development of a series of skills, but involves the transformation of an individual through development of a personal connection to knowledge. Within the educational system there is room for all, regardless of functioning level, to achieve such a personal connection. One need not have acquired a set of prerequisite functional skills to participate. However, there must be planned direction and purpose in the course of a child's education, not random component parts set in place without comprehensive planning. The use of IEPs for curriculum planning for students with disabilities presents a scheme that fails to provide students with disabilities this comprehensive planning. IEPs are written annually without even the benefit of the same school personnel remaining involved with a child from one year to the next, much less throughout twelve years of schooling. Although IEPs do contain the means by which to evaluate whether a child has achieved specific program objectives, the appropriateness of the objectives themselves and how they might or might not fit into a comprehensive curriculum are not monitored. Since there are no clear standards as to what belongs on the IEP or how the student and teachers are held accountable, the opportunity for that program to be characterized by randomness and arbitrariness is real. The child's curriculum then is at risk to be inordinately influenced by the whims of the teachers for the year, not merely personalized by a teacher's style and experiences.

Individualization of the Curriculum The use of IEPs in curricular development for students with disabilities is justified on the basis of individualization. In reality, IEPs offer far less assurance of individuality and clearly jeopardize the integrity of the curriculum for students with disabilities. To illustrate, schedules of teachers and itinerant therapists and their preferred instructional routines probably influence the parts of the general education curriculum to which an elementary school-age child is exposed more than systematic goal-setting does. The "appropriateness" assumed to be stipulated on the IEP is arbitrarily defined by those who contributed to its development, without the benefit of a rigorous public system of accountability for the stipulated curriculum. Teacher familiarity and comfort with instructional materials or beliefs in theoretical models can even preclude instructional content being presented to individual students. For example, in some cognitive-mediation or strategy-learning programs the strategy becomes the curriculum (Pugach & Warger, 1993). A teacher, convinced of the importance of strategies training, persuades the parents of students with disabilities to let it form the basis of the program stipulated on the IEPs. It becomes so far removed from traditional academic content that there is no academic progress even when students are doing well in the program. Pugach and Warger (1993) argue that "Strategies themselves, taught in isolation and devoid of linkages to academic content, do not constitute a curriculum" (p. 134). Yet, once set on IEPs as an appropriate course of study, no further curricular accountability is in place.

There are clearly established standards and criteria of performance set for general education, whereas special education has been far looser in the design of

---

Proposition One
Students with disabilities need programs adhering to curriculum standards of equivalent value as those in general education. For students with mild disabilities, these standards should be based on general education requirements, monitored in the same manner as for students without disabilities. Students with moderate to severe disabilities should have an equally comprehensive and monitored functional life-skills curriculum, with equivalent public accountability of these programs.

programs and the achievement of outcomes. Educators do not leave curricular decisions to the whims of individual teachers, parents, and students, yet they manage to provide students with sufficient curricular exposure so as to enable students to pursue individual points of interest, whether those be in creative arts, hard sciences, literature, or any other field of interest. The reliance on an orderly, comprehensive curricular standard does not negate individual needs and interests, but allows them to be accommodated in a systematic fashion. Individualization and teacher preferences are best subjected to curricular standards rather than curricular standards being dominated by individualization and teacher preferences.

Standards and the Curriculum The power to allow a student to deviate from the standard curriculum implies a deviation from performance standards. If graduation rests on satisfactory performance on a state-approved assessment and a student with disabilities wants a regular diploma, the contents of the test must be included in the student's curriculum. The test represents accountability to a basic curriculum, equally applicable to all students capable of succeeding in the standard academic program. Although accommodations to offset educational handicaps caused by student disabilities (e.g., large print or Braille examinations for students with visual impairments) are essential, the basic content of performance standards examinations must apply equally to all students seeking the associated progressions. Without a comprehensive curricular framework and companion standards-based system of accountability, students with disabilities become second-tier students for whom standards (and therefore accountability) are waived. For example, if progression to the ninth grade requires that students demonstrate the ability to read and perform mathematical calculations at a set level, students with disabilities will find it necessary to achieve these skills as well, or be exempt from the examinations. Exemptions, although initially appearing to be kind, can lead to false hopes raised through progression without achievement, lowered student motivation to continue working at points of frustration, or embarrassment.

IEP goals that relate to socialization opportunities (e.g., percent of time spent in mainstream settings), behavioral goals (e.g., increasing time on task), or the use of specialized nonacademic content (e.g., strategies training) may appear to be highly suitable and closely matched to a student's current levels of performance, yet fail to provide the comprehensive guidance needed to set a curriculum. The eighth-grader who as a second-grader managed to increase time on task from 20% to 80% but is still unable to meet the progression standards for ninth grade needed his parents and teachers to understand the context of his program and its long-term implications, not merely set up a program that seemed good at the time. The comprehensiveness of a K–12 curricular framework set by state and local standards is not replaced by the production of yearly IEPs that fail to ensure continuity or comprehensiveness throughout a child's schooling.

Argument Summary The lack of ensured continuity and long-range planning associated with IEP development put students with disabilities at risk for disjointed programs that can jeopardize their ability to achieve broad academic goals. Spe-

Reading groups are a traditional part of school instruction.

cial education must switch to allow students with disabilities to receive a broad and balanced curriculum as opposed to the exclusive reliance on individualized educational outcomes (McLaughlin & Warren, 1994). Students with disabilities must be given the opportunity to pursue the highly socially valued educational outcomes of general education accompanied by a measure of high-stakes accountability associated with their progress. The argument that IEPs are needed to ensure that students with disabilities receive individually appropriate programs is really irrelevant to the curriculum debate. Indeed, students could continue to have IEPs of a different nature if they were assigned to follow one of a number of possible curricular options. The emphasis could shift to adaptive instructional approaches, alternative means of assessments, and other useful guidelines for general education teachers. We undermine our own intentions by presenting students with mild disabilities a competing curriculum, thus drawing them away from the community of learners into which inclusion is intended to draw them.

Arguments for Proposition Two Criticisms of IEPs as creating fragmentation of the curriculum because of too great of a focus on specific skills must be viewed within the historical context that led to IEPs. Some children with disabilities were not even allowed in educational settings before their exclusion became illegal. Others, unable to make satisfactory progress in the mainstream, were set aside in special education classes or neglected until they disappeared. Teachers did not assume responsibility for accommodating their curriculum or methodology to failing students. There was typically one curriculum, one behavioral standard, and one instructional methodology to which students were expected to adjust. In the absence of any accommodations, many students, particularly those with mild disabilities, were unable to remain in general education settings. The IEP has provided a legal tool through which needed accommodations can be clearly stipulated in curriculum, methodology, and evaluation. Students with disabilities

Proposition Two
Special education, by definition, is for those students who have a wide diversity of needs and interests. IEPs offer the best curricular guide for each individual student receiving special education services.

can be protected from the single-minded approach to education. Historical neglect and the failure of students with disabilities without individualized programs need not be repeated in our haste to improve IEPs or curricular programming for students with disabilities.

The move toward inclusion does not set curriculum but is predicated on the assumption that a wide diversity of needs can be met within classrooms. If inclusion comes to mean that students with disabilities lose the personalization of curriculum and methodology presently ensured through the IEP, it is doomed to failure. To illustrate, Billingsley (1993) points to the risk that inclusion of students with severe disabilities is facing due to the lack of coordination between the individual needs of students and the constructivist teaching popular in some general education classrooms. These students, left to learn only when they show signs that they are "ready," may never receive any education at all. In his nightmare version of the future, Billingsley fears that when the progress these children had been making in segregated settings fades and they are making no progress in inclusive settings, people will suggest that they would be better served in segregated settings. In this nightmare vision of colliding inclusion and constructivism, both appear to be abysmal failures when measured by the outcomes for students with severe disabilities. Rather, inclusion can be held separate from curriculum, since IEPs continue to offer individually appropriate curricular guides within diverse settings. The success of heterogeneity of the classroom, a valued commodity, is possible through the retention of IEPs.

Individualization of the Curriculum   General education curriculum and performance standards must not dictate individual needs. Rather, individual needs must be given primary consideration when curricular options and performance standards are selected. Developers of IEPs are always free to designate any portion of the general education program as suitable. For some, academic curricula is relevant and appropriate for their development. For others, such might prove to be a frustrating waste of time. Personal choices of parents, life goals for the student involved, and the uncertainties of our profession require maintaining as much individuality and flexibility as possible. The ability we have to customize the curriculum for each child is an essential component of effective special education.

Special educators have been criticized for selecting instructional programs because they offer efficient or "technological" approaches to education and/or rely on a heavy dose of behavior management. These instructional programs, it is argued, are highly focused on specific educational outcomes rather than being built upon broad curricular designs. However, one could argue that the need to offer a curriculum of basic skills led teachers to select their instructional programs. A broad curriculum has proven the downfall of many students with disabilities, who are far better served by these highly focused materials designed to give them basic skills. There is ample support for this view in the special education literature. Adaptive instruction is tied back to curriculum through an ongoing circle of instruction based on the careful assessment of student performance (Wang, 1989). The highly individualized notion espoused in special education is based on an ongoing diagnostic/prescriptive cycle of assessment-instruction-assessment-adjustment-instruction-assessment-adjustment-instruction pattern, grounded in criterion-referenced assessment.

However, as currently conceived, the general education curriculum is not developed in a similar fashion. In elementary grades, the curriculum is individualized to the extent that each student might be allowed to select from an approved list a book for an assigned book report or pick the topic of a social studies project. In high school, students do have the opportunity to choose some electives, but the content and methodology within these classes are usually predetermined. The prescribed curriculum takes over the needs and interests of the individual student in general education. In contrast, the conception of working with students as individuals in the determination of their programs has been perceived both as a real strength of special education and its weakness. The ability to individualize is worth the risk of curricular fragmentation.

Standards and the Curriculum The ability of a student to perform at a certain level on an assessment should not take precedence over planning a pertinent course of study. For some students, the performance standards may reflect a suitable curriculum and educational goals. For others, exemption from the standards will actually produce a more satisfactory outcome. Many students with mild disabilities have their educational programs dictated by performance standards, not their educational needs. For example, the ability to identify which part of a sentence contains a grammatical error is a skill many such students may never need other than to pass the test required to earn a diploma. Such content can be traded for functional life skills and vocational preparation that will better prepare students for the transition to employment and independent living. The diploma is of little value to the graduate who has none of the skills needed to set up his own household, get and keep a job, or perform successfully in additional training or education.

The notion of a universal curriculum for which students with moderate to severe disabilities and their teachers would be accountable is in direct conflict with the very spirit of special education. These children develop at highly individual rates, have varying physical needs (e.g., surgeries, adjustments of medications) that may interfere with educational progress for extended periods of time, and need educational programming specific to their individual circumstances. For example, in some communities, public transportation is a readily accessible means of transportation, but it is not available in other locations. The health and current functioning of the children, the concerns and priorities of parents, the nature of communities, and the housing and employment options for persons with moderate to severe disabilities all must be given consideration. The greatest likelihood of successful transition from school to adulthood and community living requires the best possible match between individual needs and educational programming.

Neither curriculum nor accountability can be mass produced for students with disabilities. School personnel are morally obligated to offer as rigorous a program as possible for every pupil. However, accountability must be set in terms other than student performance for those working with students with moderate to severe disabilities. Variability of performance and uncertainty of potential are realities for teachers working with this population. A child experiences a prolonged seizure, and the progress she made over the past year disappears. An adolescent moves into a group home and makes tremendous strides in independent living skills in a three-week period. Surgery requires that a child be out of school for six weeks, followed by an extensive rehabilitation program. The individual circumstances of this nature are infinite. Accountability is to the individual student and her parents, that they be offered a quality program according to the circumstances of the moment, not documented progress on a standard curriculum.

Argument Summary Since the ultimate goal for children with mild disabilities is often to maintain them in or return them to the regular curriculum, sustaining at least some contact with it could be justification for "fragmentation" associated with IEPs. Breaking down generalized components of curriculum into meaningful parts is one of the real strengths of special education. Materials adopted for use in general education are not designed to be consistent with each individual student's instructional needs. Students who are unable to maintain the pace and reap benefits, such as incidental learning, from general education settings depend on educators to isolate tasks and information into obtainable parts. Students do have the right to be different and to expect tolerance of diversity from educators (Gelzheiser, 1990). Uniformity in pace and manner of instruction for the majority leaves some punished for their differences. Educators have the responsibility to help students with disabilities integrate their learning into a meaningful relationship with other material through generalization. The need for enhancement of the existing IEP process and the need for improved integration of generalization into many special education programs do not necessitate abandonment of the IEP system.

SELECTING PHILOSOPHICAL AND INSTRUCTIONAL APPROACHES

Appropriate instructional approaches are debated as well as suitable curriculum. Some perceive cooperative learning as an effective technique to use to include students with disabilities (e.g., Pomplun, 1996) whereas others question its value (e.g., Tateyama-Sniezek, 1990). The assumption has been that, since the majority of children are reasonably successful, general educational programs are basically effective and that unsuccessful students are deficient in some way. However, the recent shifts in theoretical views of intelligence should force educators to give this assumption careful scrutiny. The notion of multiple intelligences, in contrast to the traditional notion of general intelligence, must inevitably influence the meaning of school readiness, curricular expectations, the adoption of instructional methods, and classroom organization patterns. Such a reformed understanding of cognitive development could be of particular benefit to students who find themselves experiencing mild learning difficulties in scattered patterns. Teacher sensitivity to the development of varying types of intelligence can change the nature of education for all their students, not just those experiencing educational difficulties (Goldman & Gardner, 1989).

Historical (Hysterical) Patterns

When new theories lead to new instructional approaches, they generally have an enthusiastic group of developers who are engaged in their own research to document effectiveness, early adopters, independent researchers who are cautious, and skeptics who warn the field and parents that there are no universal quick fixes. Alexander, Murphy, and Woods (1996) pose a question: "why do so many of the promising and highly touted innovations fade into obscurity or later face ridicule?" (p. 31). They speculate that one possible explanation is the lack of acknowledgment and linkage of ideas to their historical roots. The market seems to crave complete newness, so each time an idea emerges, its proponents attempt to separate it from anything that has come before, rather than building on the knowledge gained when related ideas were in vogue. To illustrate, Tarver (1992) begins a chapter defending Direct Instruction with this statement: "Direct Instruction originated in 1968 with the work of Siegfried Engelmann and his colleagues" (p. 141). Granted, she is referring specifically to a commercially available package of materials, but "originated" still seems to be a rather lofty claim considering that the nature of instruction in this country for many years could only be characterized as "direct instruction." Later in the article, Tarver even has a section titled "direct instruction is *not* 'Direct Instruction'" in which she argues diligently to separate the Engelmann approach from other generic direct instruction models. On the other hand, she critiques constructivist teaching as merely being "minor modifications" of old approaches with a few name changes, implying that any similarity to existing or previously discarded ideas is negative. Likewise, Alexander, Murphy, and Woods (1996) observe that "the culture of American education appears more invested in finding the next panacea than struggling with any long-term, multifaceted treatments that promise hard work and offer no guarantees" (p. 36).

The claim of effectiveness associated with the various treatments represents big business. Whatever the condition a child may have, parents and teachers alike are seeking the most effective interventions. The target audience may often have reached the point that they are willing to try anything, making the marketing of treatments a highly profitable business. Adelman and Taylor (1993) note the sizable market for tests, instructional materials, training programs, and other products claiming to be of benefit to students with learning disabilities, mentioning the irony of techniques becoming viewed as valid simply because of their wide adoptions. If an idea espoused by an "expert" has appeared in enough methods texts, is marketed by a respected publishing company, is endorsed by legislative bodies, and is purchased by consumers, the product can achieve "market" or "cash" validity regardless of its actual validity.

The issue of market validity applies across the board to all of special education, not just the learning disabilities arena. One of the most controversial treatments seen recently, intended to expand the communication abilities of students with autism, is Facilitated Communication (Biklen, 1990, 1993). This technique has been both widely acclaimed and harshly denigrated as a cruel hoax (Cummins & Prior, 1992). The debate on this technique continues, with much discussion on the need to validate interventions empirically prior to their marketing and adoption versus the urgency with which we must get treatment breakthroughs to the waiting public. Gerber (1994) describes the field as having a broad and deep philosophical chasm in both its scholarship and practice.

The points of disagreement do not reside merely within special education. Debates are prevalent both within general education and between general educators and special educators as to the merits of constructivist approaches to learning and the empirical techniques historically popular within special education. The extreme dichotomies between constructivism and alternative approaches have resulted from the association of constructivism with a narrow view of what precisely constitutes a whole language approach (Harris & Graham, 1994). The acceptance of whole language and other constructivist approaches to education as philosophical rather than singular in nature offers a far greater likelihood of their being considered as viable for use with students with disabilities. However, some advocates would contend that this represents an untenable compromise of the critical elements of constructivism in education, whereas opponents would deny its accuracy of description. For example, there are whole language proponents who perceive it as including virtually no direct instruction or practice in basic skills. There is dissension between these members of the whole language camp and those who are willing to accept the value of some contextually appropriate direct instruction of basic skills. Further debate ensues between the opponents who might perceive only one definition of whole language and target it for criticism while debating with proponents holding broader views of the approach. The backlash resulting from rigidity of interpretation of constructivist approaches in general education will likely be followed even more strongly in special education programs with a demand to return to basic skill instruction anytime constructivist teachers have failed to respond to student needs in a flexible manner (Harris & Graham, 1994). It would be tempting to lump constructivists in a group unwilling to meet the needs of individual students if those needs appear in conflict with their pedagogical preferences. However, such would not be accurate, nor would it bring any progression to the debates. Nevertheless, the rigidity with which some teachers adopt their own beliefs accelerates the problem.

Research Settings and Styles

Do our research techniques have the ability to provide answers on what constitutes effective instruction? Can the notion of effective instruction be answered collectively when we claim to individualize instruction within special education ranks and dispute among ourselves on what the goals of our instruction ought to be? Currently popular teaching strategies that might be weighed for their effectiveness include direct instruction, cooperative learning, prescriptive teaching, mediated learning, and cognitive strategy training. The issue is not so much whether any one of these approaches is effective, but if modifications to traditional teaching are needed, what should those changes be, when and where should they be used, and who should select and evaluate them? Just as doctors try to find the least intrusive and minimally disruptive yet effective treatments for their patients, educators might try to find the least different approaches to producing effective learning for each child. As a medicine's side effects might make it a last resort, educational approaches might also be placed hierarchically in descending order of preference—not good versus bad or right versus wrong or appropriate versus inappropriate, as we have tended to dichotomize techniques. Dixon and Carine (1994) argue that neither explicit or discovery instruction is virtuous or superior to the other in the abstract. Other factors, including the interactions among instructional practices and learner characteristics, must also be considered. Constructivism is not *an* instructional methodology per se, but it is actually a set of beliefs about how humans learn (Jackson, Reid, & Bunsen, 1993). These beliefs include the notion that the learner's goals and purposes are the primary force behind the selection and performance of complex behaviors and that only "active" learners can take in information from the environment. Can such notions be unilaterally dismissed as inappropriate for students with disabilities? The value and appropriateness of these ideas are embedded in the context in which they are applied, as well as the effectiveness with which they are applied.

The question of the usefulness of the research in education is frequently raised by practicing teachers. Fuchs and Fuchs (1990) argue that one of the difficulties with educational research is that it has been designed to formulate laws of universal applicability rather than to solve school-based problems. Others point to a distinction between research knowledge and practice knowledge. Malouf and Schiller (1995) describe the fallacy of a "linear model" which would follow the logic that classrooms should be "research-replication sites" for the implementation of research-proven principles and interventions. They argue that such a model contains an incorrect implicit assumption that the research available on student learning is easily converted to knowledge about teaching. Further implied in the model is the notion that we can eventually obtain all the information we need to be effective teachers. In contrast to the research knowledge base is that of practical knowledge which teachers learn through experience and from one another. This knowledge base grows from and can easily be used to respond to the complexities of educational settings. Yet it has also been described as being local, context bound, concrete, and with limited applicability across settings or individuals. The fact is that all instructional ideologies are based on the simple observation that learning occurs over time, whether it be behaviorists shaping behavior or constructivists witnessing the assimilation and accommodation of knowledge (Dixon & Carnine, 1994).

Decision Point 6.2: Introducing
New Techniques in Special Education

Arguments for Proposition One Special educators must move conservatively in their adoption of new instructional approaches and therapies. The medical credo "First do no harm" is certainly applicable to the field of education as well. Premature adoption of and enthusiasm for questionable techniques have all too often been the trademark of special educators. Caution and documented research represent a far more appropriate approach to introducing new therapies to the field than does freedom of experimentation. Whereas we have the Food and Drug Administration and the medical community protecting us from premature use of experimental medical interventions, educators seem to be free to go about trying any new thing regardless of its ineffectiveness or risks of harm.

The value of qualitative research methodology in the determination of treatment efficacy is subject to innumerable problems. Scruggs and Mastropieri (1994–95) argue that such research techniques do not offer any means of evaluating whether specific treatments directly cause desired outcomes or simply make one feel that a treatment has been effective. To illustrate, Scruggs and Mastropieri (1994–95) note that the use of qualitative research in the validation of facilitated communication has revealed the dangers of reliance on this research technique in documenting intervention effectiveness. Whereas Scruggs and Mastropieri (1994) have used qualitative methods of inquiry in their study of the efficacy of constructive educational approaches in teaching science to students with mild mental retardation, they argue that such methodology must be combined with quantitative approaches to gain sufficient information to evaluate interventions. They argue that had qualitative methods been used to validate past treatments, perceptual–motor training and other ineffective interventions would still be in use if we relied on rational argument and testimonials rather than experimental evidence. Today, the narrative case studies supporting the outcomes of facilitated communication appear to be in conflict with substantial experimental evidence disconfirming the validity of the technique. Do testimonials and narrative stories outweigh the empirical minutia that we have been prone to gather systematically in our efficacy research efforts? As Kirk and Kutchins (1992) point out, "Conceptualizing and documenting positive changes in intervention goals such as personal fulfillment, self-determination, happiness, friendships, and even contributions to the social good, will, no doubt, be difficult" (p. 227), but may be of greater value than highly discrete behaviors that have become the measure of success for intervention with persons with severe disabilities. We need outcomes that have consequence to our daily lifestyles, not behaviors so insignificant that they have to be graphed to be seen. The broadening of the research paradigm can increase our knowledge base without abandoning the expectation that

---

Proposition One

Innovations in therapies and instructional approaches that represent radical new approaches to intervention with children and/or their families must be developed through independent research that is designed to measure both the benefits and dangers of the proposed interventions before being introduced into any educational programs, especially those serving students with disabilities.

---

classroom instruction be grounded upon something more than trial and error and teacher whimsy.

Historical (Hysterical) Patterns The presence of fad treatments and the introduction of legitimate new experimental interventions all in the same marketplace quickly draw the emotions of teachers, parents, and materials producers. Teachers and parents do not enjoy looking foolish but have a sincere dedication to doing whatever it takes to find the best approaches, including suffering the ridicule of the community and bearing the financial costs of the program that a child needs. Most often within the field we debate the merits of a particular therapy or intervention technique. These techniques come and go and, on occasion, return with some new jargon and packaging. We voice opinions about the appropriateness of medicating children with hyperactivity and attention disorders; the merits of behavioral interventions, parent training programs, and reading methods; the most suitable curricular content; the best alternative means of communication for the nonspeaking child; the most effective location for instruction; the benefits of using process strategies as a prerequisite to academic instruction; and so forth. With the exception of the use of medications in the above list, educators and others in related fields are free to introduce to the market whatever appeals to them that they can persuade others to accept. Additionally, parents can push through the IEP process for the use of interventions that they wish to have for their children. Professional or parental knowledge of these interventions may come from personal beliefs, television programs, friends in distant cities, popular magazines, professional journals, educational research, a neighbor, or any other source. Within the field, there are both an eagerness to experiment and a lack of quality controls (Kavale, 1987).

Patterning, facilitated communication, strategy training, sensory integration therapy, brain compatible learning, aversion therapy, discrete trial training for children with autism, biofeedback, and diet therapies have all had effusive supporters and great cynics. Generally, the discussions regarding these and other approaches trigger biased emotional responses from both sides. Most have triggered bitter legal battles. There is clearly a need to have accountability and verification of intervention techniques, for the popularity of new approaches sometimes sweeps through the education community like wildfire. Money is spent on new materials and equipment, personnel is sent to training sessions, and instructional time is allocated to new techniques before their efficacy is well established. The means by which interventions can be evaluated for long-term benefits and effectiveness requires impartial experimental documentation.

Research Settings and Styles Wang (1989) reports that the efficacy research supporting adaptive instruction has produced results indicating student achievement scores are equal to or greater than those of students receiving teacher-directed, group-paced instruction. Additional positive benefits of adaptive instruction include (a) constructive student interactions with peers, (b) high levels of student self-responsibility, (c) ability to work independently, (d) close linking of diagnosis in the planning and implementation of instructional accommodations, (e) student cooperation and helping one another with learning tasks, and (f) student self-responsibility and self-directed and peer-assisted exploration. Wang contends that the combination and coordination of the many features of adaptive instruction, rather than any single element, produced these benefits. There are clearly means of documenting the effectiveness of education without relying on overly quantified data collection or mere acceptance of personal testimonials.

Qualitative researchers argue that their methods can and do produce different types of results, with an implication that their results are better in that they are contextual and meaningful. Such logic does little more than "sharpen the divisions between proponents of constructed versus instructed knowledge" (Scruggs & Mastropieri, 1994–95, p. 255). The documentation of efficacy of treatments must involve the integration of both quantitative and qualitative research designs. When findings between the two methodologies appear to be in conflict regarding the benefits of particular interventions, results from each methodology can be evaluated in light of the other. Blanket dismissal of the other research because it was the "wrong kind" is no better than refusing to investigate a treatment's efficacy at all.

Argument Summary The principles of democratic freedom do not warrant license to mislead, to foster false hopes in parents and teachers, or to profit through deception. Although the day-to-day decisions of the teacher or therapist must always be based on professional judgment of the moment and situation, the adoption of broad instructional principles and instructional approaches requires far greater system-level control and approval. New ideas and approaches need to be introduced into the educational market only after careful review and screening by individuals capable of making sound research-based judgments with no financial or professional conflicting interests. Little can be done to control the companies publishing the latest miracle cures or the individuals selling them on the open market, but the actual acceptance and use of new approaches within our educational institutions must be set to higher standards. Volatile statements such as that of Fuchs and Fuchs (1994), arguing that inclusion is a "radical constructivist blueprint unsubstantiated by research" (p. 304), will not draw the opposing sides any closer to the truth.

Arguments for Proposition Two Students who have faced failure and poor progress in mainstream educational programs and some who have never even been allowed to enter the mainstream come to special education seeking alternatives. Often, it is necessary for their teachers to pursue many approaches before finding the right match for an individual child. Through this trial-and-error process, failures will inevitably occur, and some interventions may actually prove detrimental. Such are the necessary risks for educators who must seek the new and different. Even in medicine, physicians are, at times, forced to place children at risk (e.g., vaccinations, surgical procedures, chemotherapy) in order to provide the best possible care. Through experimentation we find new approaches that are beneficial, and, on occasion, these approaches even come to be adopted by the mainstream.

An open marketplace is the only truly democratic forum for the review and evaluation of new ideas. Teachers and parents alike are capable of discerning judgment. Inevitably in our quest for more effective interventions, some efforts will prove to be failures and a few may even cause harm directly (e.g., needlessly separating children from their parents) or indirectly (e.g., delaying the use of a more effective intervention). The cost of progress and improvements in special education includes these false starts and sometimes the creation of false hopes. The consumer of ideas has to assume the responsibility to question and investigate the motives and value of the ideas just as he would a car or home or any other product available on the open market. Without open experimentation and exploration of new concepts within classroom settings, we could have very little likelihood of discovering any breakthroughs for any of the students we are concerned with in special education. Without the experimental nature of special education, we would quickly lose the ability to forge ahead (Algozzine, Maheady, Sacca, O'Shea, & O'Shea, 1990). The teacher's ability to explore and invent is tied directly to the notion of individualization and meeting a specific child's needs.

Historical (Hysterical) Patterns Visual-perceptual training, carefully analyzed psycholinguistic abilities matched to detailed prescriptive interventions, sight conservation for students with visual impairments, and innumerable other techniques have come in and out of vogue since the widespread growth of special education. Although these approaches have been unable to sustain their credibility within the field, they represented legitimate efforts of professionals to pursue the best-known interventions at the time. Without these pioneering efforts, we would not know of their inadequacies. Today, we hotly debate the degree to which our interventions should be based on ideological terms or concrete findings of effective practices. Often, the practices recommended by differing ideologists prove to be similar in intent as well as outcome. For example, the behaviorist recommendation that programming include generalization is hardly different from the cognitivist concept of transference and certainly quite consistent with the call for contextualized learning. The division of education into multiple ideational

---

Proposition Two
The field of special education is based on experimentation and innovation. Special educators are obligated to pursue experimentation and innovation by definition, having a responsibility and obligation to be on the cutting edge, always seeking more effective solutions to their students' learning difficulties.

factions creates conflicts even when commonalities exist (Dixon & Carnine, 1994). A further point that Dixon and Carnine make is that bad practices can be associated with any ideology, making those who espouse one particular perspective vulnerable to association with any other person claiming to represent a similar ideology. We may come to realize that educators hold more in common with those whose ideas have been associated with a different paradigm than those whose theoretical principles are similar, but whose practical application of those principles is far different. Efficiency of learning is not the highest aim that our educational enterprise need concern itself with anyway. Values, civil rights, and advocacy all make scientific knowledge less important than societal decisions about how people are treated (Meyer & Evans, 1993).

Research Settings and Styles Some would argue that through the use of research knowledge it is possible to determine what constitutes effective instruction for children with disabilities and "teacher-proof" the classroom, essentially ignoring the concept of practical knowledge and its value to the instructional setting. However, Shulman (1986) describes the teacher's case knowledge and strategic knowledge (professional judgment) as the only real basis in which research knowledge can have meaning. Research done in clinical settings is not likely to have a big impact on practices in the context of the typical classroom (Kirk & Kutchins, 1992). Since educational research often leaves us with inconsistent, oppositional findings of a rather abstract nature, the practicing teacher must have the discretion and freedom to find the appropriate applications of and adjustments to research findings. Alternative research-on-practice approaches may offer a solution. The acceptance and valuing of multiple research methodologies while simultaneously respecting the concept of practitioner knowledge can lead the field into a new era of tolerance for discovery.

Acknowledging that researchers focused on students with severe disabilities have gotten stuck in the behavioral paradigm, Kirk and Kutchins (1992) note the negative effects of their failure "to incorporate or even to recognize alternative approaches as they individually accumulate a knowledge base that references only self-generated information sources" (p. 226), allowing applied behavior analysis to be credited as having made the only significant contributions to our understanding of teaching and learning. Innovative instructional approaches other than behavioral interventions (e.g., cooperative learning, interdisciplinary teaching, and natural language instruction) that have been validated through sound educational research have been missing from this literature base.

Argument Summary Some interventions might prove highly effective but hold no social validity whatsoever (Kirk & Kutchins, 1992). For example, the use of aversive techniques on individuals with severe disabilities might be empirically valid but are simply unacceptable to the majority sense of what constitutes humane treatment. Children are far more complex in their makeup than we might assume them to be. Researchers in education offer efficacy studies that afford little or no consequence to the events in the children's lives throughout the study, or the nurturing and support available from other sources, or whether their focused interventions are even being conducted properly as a part of the research, offering results reported in means and statistical significance—not individually. We honor and accept the reports that support our credibility and refute those in conflict—gaining little in true knowledge. The temptation to draw up battle lines and pigeonhole approaches as good or evil misdirects our energy into fighting within educational ranks rather than having our collective energy moving toward improved outcomes. Dixon and Carnine (1994) offer this observation of our pursuit of unilateral answers to questions as complex as how best to educate children: "It is an insult to human intelligence to offer simple, global, unconditional solutions to complex cognitive problems. It is dogmatic" (p. 364). We must recognize that we are dealing with a human science and that human behavior simply does not follow the law-like relationships we attribute to the physical world (Kirk & Kutchins, 1992). When intervention decisions are made, they represent far more than mere technical problems requiring only the most effective path to achieve a desired end. The path taken in reaching toward a goal may be of greater educational significance than its achievement.

CLOSING THOUGHTS

Educational goals, placement issues, models of delivery, and instructional approaches all have a reciprocal relationship with the curriculum. The heavy emphasis on increased standards and outcomes-based education coupled with adoption of state competency testing for accountability eventually comes to bear on the classroom teacher. The sheer volume of students being referred for special education services and the growing ranks of students with attention disorders whose needs must be accommodated through the Individuals with Disabilities Education Act, Section 504 of the Rehabilitation Act, or the Americans with Disabilities Act will force efficacy issues to a head. More and more students continue to be funneled into a system that is currently hard pressed to document its differences or effectiveness. Accountability of the educational community is increasing through the use of student proficiency examinations, and soon greater scrutiny may be focused on special education students. As Malouf and Schiller (1995) note, special educators have an even greater responsibility for being accountable than those in general education.

The inclusion model of special education delivery has not resulted in lowering the class size by making more instructors available for an equal number of students, but it is accompanied by an expectation that the classroom teacher will, through her special education support system, use and become skilled in a wider assortment of "routines" and appropriate instructional strategies. If we fail to see dramatic results in student performance, the clinical researcher may have quite different interpretations than the "practical knowledge" derived from the teachers striving to find effective interventions. Reforms associated with inclusion have failed to take into consideration the powerful influence of teachers' fundamental educational beliefs, knowledge, and methods of instruction that inevitably affect the efficacy of this model of service delivery (Gerber, 1994).

Referencing the work of Fullan and Fleming, Malouf and Schiller (1995) note that the application of research in the educational setting is often flawed, such as adopting an accepted innovation that is wrong for the situation or over-adopting and implementing innovations that have potential but that are not fully developed and ready for use in real settings. As Shavelson (1988) has noted, educational settings are characterized by an indeterminate number of novel situations, inevitably requiring an "inferential leap" in the quest to teach according to sound, research-based principles. Drawing research knowledge and practical knowledge into an integrated model, in which innovations are developed and studied through research but not considered valid until applied across a range of settings, may offer a realistic option.

There are many characteristics of effective teachers that are far removed from pedagogical approaches, including passion toward children and teaching, warmth, enthusiasm, involvement, organization, planning, patience, knowledge, and providing meaningful feedback (Harris & Graham, 1994). Hoshmand and Polkinghorne (1992) conceptualize a new science–practice relationship that mutually emphasizes the critical contributions of both science and practice. Such seems the most restorative for the field, yet harder and harder to achieve as battle lines become entrenched along more ideological and methodological debates than we can follow.

REFERENCES

Adelman, H. S., & Taylor, L. (1993). *Learning problems and learning disabilities: Moving forward.* Pacific Grove, CA: Brooks/Cole.

Alexander, P. A., Murphy, P. K., & Woods, B. S. (1996). Of squalls and fathoms: Navigating the seas of educational innovation. *Educational Researcher, 25,* 31–36, 39.

Algozzine, B., Maheady, L., Sacca, K. C., O'Shea, L., & O'Shea, D. (1990). Sometimes patent medicine works: A reply to Braaten, Kauffman, Braaten, Polsgrove, and Nelson. *Exceptional Children, 56,* 552–557.

Anderson, G. L., & Barrera, I. (1995). Critical constructivist research and special education: Expanding our lens on social reality and exceptionality. *Remedial and Special Education, 16,* 142–149.

Biklen, D. (1990). Communication unbound: Autism and praxis. *Harvard Educational Review, 60,* 291–314.

Biklen, D. (1993). *Communication unbound.* New York: Teachers College Press.

Billingsley, F. F. (1993). In my dreams: A response to some current trends in education. *Journal of the Association for Persons with Severe Handicaps, 18,* 61–63.

Bredekamp, S. Copple, C. (Eds.). (1997). *Developmentally appropriate practice in early childhood programs:* Revised Edition. Washington, DC: National Association for the Education of Young Children.

Cummins, R. A., & Prior, M. P. (1992). Autism and assisted communication: A response to Biklen. *Harvard Educational Review, 62,* 228–241.

Dixon, R., & Carnine, D. (1994). Ideologies, practices, and their implications for special education. *Journal of Special Education, 28,* 356–367.

Epps, S., & Tindal, G. (1987). The effectiveness of differential programming in serving students with mild handicaps: Placement options and instructional programming. In M. C. Wang, M. C. Reynolds, & H. J. Walberg (Eds.),

Handbook of special education: Research and practice: Learner characteristics and adaptive education (Vol. 1, pp. 213–248). New York: Pergamon.

Feiler, A., & Thomas, G. (1988). Special needs: Past, present and future. In G. Thomas & A. Feiler (Eds.), *Planning for special needs: A whole school approach* (pp. 5–31). Oxford, England: Basil Blackwell.

Figueroa, R. A., & Ruiz, N. T. (1993) Bilingual pupils and special education: A reconceptualization. In R. C. Eaves & P. J. McLaughlin (Eds.), *Recent advances in special education and rehabilitation,* Boston: Andover Medical Publishers.

Fuchs, D., & Fuchs, L. S. (1990). Making educational research more important. *Exceptional Children, 57,* 102–107.

Fuchs, D., & Fuchs, L. S. (1994). Inclusive schools movement and the radicalization of special education reform. *Exceptional Children, 60,* 294–309.

Gelzheiser, L. M. (1987). Reducing the number of students identified as learning disabled: A question of practice, philosophy or policy? In S. B. Sigmon (Ed.), *Critical voices on special education: Problems and progress concerning the mildly handicapped* (pp. 43–50). Albany, NY: State University of New York Press.

Gerber, M. M. (1994). Postmodernism in special education. *Journal of Special Education, 28,* 368–378.

Goldman, J., & Gardner, H. (1989). Multiple paths to educational effectiveness. In D. K. Lipsky & A. Gartner (Eds.), *Beyond separate education: Quality education for all* (pp. 121–140). Baltimore: Paul H. Brookes.

Goodlad, J. I. (1993). Access to knowledge. In J. I. Goodlad & T. C. Lovitt (Eds.), *Integrating general and special education* (pp. 1–22). New York: Macmillan.

Graham, S., & Harris, K. R. (1994). Implications of constructivism for teaching writing to students with special needs. *Journal of Special Education, 28,* 275–289.

Harris, K. R., & Graham, S. (1994). Constructivism: Principles, paradigms, and integration. *Journal of Special Education, 28,* 233–247.

Hazel, R., Barber, P. A., Roberts, S., Behr, S. K., Helmstetter, E., & Guess, D. (1988). *A community approach to an integrated service system for children with special needs.* Baltimore: Paul H. Brookes.

Hoshmand, L. T., & Polkinghorne, D. E. (1992). Redefining the science–practice relationship and professional training. *American Psychologist, 47,* 55–66.

Jackson, L., Reid, D. K., & Bunsen, T. (1993). Alternative dreams: A response to Felix Billingsley. *Journal of the Association for Persons with Severe Handicaps, 18,* 292–295.

Kauffman, J. M. (1993). How we might achieve radical reform of special education. *Exceptional Children, 6,* 6–16.

Kavale, K. A. (1987). Introduction. In M. C. Wang, M. C. Reynolds, & H. J. Walberg (Eds.), *Handbook of special education: Research and practice: Learner characteristics and adaptive education* (Vol. 1, pp. 131–132). New York: Pergamon.

Kimball, W. H., & Heron, T. E. (1988). A behavioral commentary on Poplin's discussion of reductionistic fallacy and holistic/constructivist principles. *Journal of Learning Disabilities, 21,* 425–428.

Kirk, S. A., & Kutchins, H. (1992). *The selling of DSM: The rhetoric of science in psychiatry.* New York: Aldine De Gruyter.

Lubeck, S. (1994). The politics of developmentally appropriate practice: Exploring issues of culture, class, and curriculum. In B. L. Mallory & R. S. New (Eds.), *Diversity and developmentally appropriate practices: Challenges for early childhood education* (pp. 17–43). New York: Teachers College Press.

Mahoney, G., & Wheatley, A. P. (1994). Reconceptualizing the individual education program: A constructivist approach to educational practice for young children with disabilities. In P. L. Safford (Ed.), *Early childhood special education, Yearbook in early childhood education* (Vol. 5, pp. 118–141). New York: Teachers College Press.

Mallory, B. L., & New, R. S. (1994). Social constructivist theory and principles of inclusion: Challenges for early childhood special education. *Journal of Special Education, 28,* 322–337.

Malouf, D. B., & Schiller, E. P. (1995). Practice and research in special education. *Exceptional Children, 61,* 414–424.

McLaughlin, M., & Warren, S. H. (1994). *Performance assessment and students with disabilities: Usage in outcomes-based accountability systems.* Reston, VA: Council for Exceptional Children.

Meyer, L. H., & Evans, I. M. (1993). Science and practice in behavioral intervention: Meaningful outcomes, research validity, and usable knowledge. *Journal of the Association for Persons with Severe Handicaps, 18,* 224–234.

Pomplun, M. (1996). Cooperative groups: Alternative assessment for students with disabilities? *Journal of Special Education, 30,* 1–17.

Poplin, M. S., & Stone, S. (1992). Paradigm shifts in instructional strategies: From reductionism to holistic/constructivism. In W. Stainback & S. Stainback (Eds.), *Controversial issues confronting special education: Divergent perspectives* (pp. 153–180). Boston: Allyn & Bacon, 153–179.

Pugach, M. C., & Warger, C. L. (1993). Curriculum considerations. In J. I. Goodlad & T. C. Lovitt (Eds.), *Integrating general and special education* (pp. 125–148). New York: Macmillan.

Sands, D. J., Adams, L., & Stout, D. M. (1995). A statewide exploration of the nature and use of curriculum in special education. *Exceptional Children, 62,* 68–83.

Scruggs, T. E., & Mastropieri, M. A. (1994). The construction of scientific knowledge by students with mild disabilities. *Journal of Special Education, 28,* 307–321.

Scruggs, T. E., & Mastropieri, M. A. (1994–95). Reflections on "scientific reasoning of students with mild mental retardation": Investigating preconceptions and conceptual change. *Exceptionality, 5,* 249–257.

Shavelson, R. J. (1988). Contributions of educational research to policy and practice: Constructing, challenging, changing cognition. *Educational Researcher. 17,* 4–11, 22.

Sheehan, R., & Keogh, B. K. (1984). Approaches to evaluation in special education. In B. K. Keogh (Ed.), *Advances in special education* (Vol. 4, pp. 1–20). Greenwich, CT: JAI Press.

Shulman, L. (1986). Those who understand: Knowledge growth in teaching. *Educational Researcher, 15,* 4–14.

Stainback, S., & Stainback, W. (1992). *Curriculum considerations in inclusive classrooms: Facilitating learning for all students.* Baltimore: Paul H. Brookes.

Tarver, S. G. (1992). Direct instruction. In W. Stainback & S. Stainback (Eds.), *Controversial issues confronting special education: Divergent perspectives* (pp. 141–152). Boston: Allyn & Bacon.

Tateyama-Sniezek, K. M. (1990). Cooperative learning: Does it improve the academic achievement of students with handicaps? *Exceptional Children, 56,* 426–437.

Wang, M. C. (1989). Adaptive instruction: An alternative for accommodating student diversity through the curriculum. In D. K. Lipsky & A. Gartner (Eds.), *Beyond separate education: Quality education for all* (pp. 99–120). Baltimore: Paul H. Brookes.

Wang, M. C., & Lindvall, C. M. (1984). Individual differences and school learning environments. In E. W. Gordon (Ed.), *Review of research in education* (pp. 161–225). Washington, DC: American Educational Research Association.

7

Transition to Adulthood

INTRODUCTION

A merican society is predicated on the value of individual independence and the autonomy of adults. Our pride in freedom seems to be coupled with the expectation that we achieve this independence as quickly as possible upon entering adulthood. Dependence is considered far less desirable or appropriate, whether its nature be financial, physical, or emotional (outside the acceptable emotional bonds deemed suitable for marriage, family, and friendships). The goals of education, then, typically relate to the development of productive, well-informed citizens who are prepared to become independent contributors to society economically, morally, socially, and physically. The aim is for youth to achieve community adjustment in terms of employment, housing, and social and interpersonal networks as they exit secondary schools and begin their lives as adults (Halpern, 1985). Participation in postsecondary education does offer one acceptable alternative for adolescents seeking further education prior to establishing their autonomy.

The impact of transition issues varies for students with disabilities depending on the nature and extent of their disabilities. For some students served under the label of learning disabled, the biggest concern might center on the curriculum and projected postsecondary opportunities, such as college. For those with moderate to severe mental retardation, the issues focus more on when employment and living outside the home should begin and where their education/training should be provided between the ages of nineteen and twenty-two (McDonnell, Mathot-Buckner, & Ferguson, 1996).

Historically, parents and teachers alike have focused on immediate needs rather than considering the best curriculum to enable the individual to achieve independence and employability upon school exit. As a result, many former special education students have simply been unable to partake of the fruits of U.S. society (Edgar, 1987). The professional community discovered that many students served by special education, upon exit from their educational programs, "were entering segregated, dependent, non-productive lives" (Ward & Halloran, 1993, p. 4), certainly not what was intended by the many teachers and therapists who worked with these students over the years. Virtually all the relevant studies documenting transition from secondary schooling to adulthood have been consistent in their revelation of this unsatisfactory state of affairs (Wagner, 1991; Peraino, 1993). Adults who were considered learning disabled during their schooling experience both vocational and social difficulties evidenced by high unemployment and underemployment rates and a general lack of satisfaction with their personal and vocational lives. Only approximately 50% adults with learning disabilities are able to live independently, and the majority are not self-supporting (White, 1992). Students with more severe disabilities fare poorly as well (McDonnell, Wilcox, & Boles, 1986). Many such young adults found themselves placed in highly restrictive employment and residential programs, or simply left in their own homes with no community service options.

Beyond Secondary School
for Youth with Disabilities

For youth with disabilities, secondary schooling can end in one of three ways—graduation (with regular or special education diploma), dropping out, or aging out. Both dropping out and aging out are closely associated with poor transition outcomes (Blackorby & Wagner, 1996; Wagner & Blackorby, 1996). With an employment rate of 65%, high school graduates with disabilities have significantly better employment patterns three to five years after leaving secondary education than do either dropouts (47%) or ageouts (37%). Although dropouts initially gained greater residential independence, after three to five years secondary graduates held the highest rate of independent living, at 31%, compared to 20% for dropouts and 15% for ageouts. For students with moderate to severe disabilities, dropping out is less likely to occur because they choose to pursue alternative graduation criteria and/or remain in school until a job opportunity is available. For students with learning disabilities or other mild disabilities, dropping out is an unfortunately common means of exiting their secondary education. Numerous studies conducted during the 1980s specifically documented the dropout rates of students with learning disabilities, and the results were indicative of the unsuccessful manner in which many initially embark on adulthood. For example, Zigmond and Thornton (1985) reported a 54% dropout rate for students with learning disabilities, compared to 33% for a nonlearning-disabled population. In other studies, the dropout rate for students with learning disabilities was 26% (White, Schumaker, Warner, Alley, & Deshler, 1980), 36% (deBettencourt, Zigmond, & Thornton, 1989; Wagner, 1989), and 42% (Cobb & Crump, 1984).

These dropout rates were particularly disturbing because students with learning disabilities tend to manage better than other disability groups in their pursuit of employment (Blackorby & Wagner, 1996). Gajar, Goodman, and McAfee (1993) also note the fact that school dropouts with mild disabilities are more often males, are members of ethnic minorities, have a lower socioeconomic background, and have been labeled as having learning disabilities or emotional disturbance. The interactive nature of these multiple risk factors puts certain groups in far greater jeopardy of dropping out and suffering the consequential disadvantages than others.

High school graduation contributes to the likelihood of attending a postsecondary school, with about 37% of secondary school graduates with disabilities attending postsecondary schools as contrasted with only 11% of dropouts and 18% of those who aged out. Several patterns are apparent in the data available on dropout rates (U.S. Department of Education, 1995). For exiters between the ages of fourteen and twenty-one, the data indicate a general pattern of increases in the dropout rate with age.

According to reported figures, the dropout rate is variable by disability category, with far greater frequency of dropping out evidenced for students with speech/language impairments, learning disabilities, and emotional disturbance than for those considered to have mental retardation, traumatic brain injury, or hearing impairments. Other disability categories, such as multiple disabilities, autism, and orthopedic impairments, have relatively low percentages of dropouts—generally less than 3% across all ages. An exception to this pattern is deaf/blindness, with figures ranging from 3.33% to 17%.

The unemployment and dropout rates for students with disabilities noted during the 1980s (Edgar, 1987) awakened special educators, parents, and government funding agencies to the need to plan for the post-education lives of students with disabilities in a more systematic fashion (Browning, Dunn, & Brown, 1993; Halloran, 1993; Wehman, 1993), including the amendment of IDEA to require transition planning for secondary students (Gajar, Goodman, & McAfee, 1993). Today, within the ranks of special education there is greater concern for long-term outcomes and the ability of students to become productive members of the competitive workforce than previously (Reiff & deFur, 1992). However, the concern is accompanied by a call for the shifting emphasis toward employment and life goals and away from educational programming designed to follow a developmental progression of academic and adaptive skills (e.g., Boyer-Stephens & Kearns, 1988). The vocational emphasis on educational planning can cause conflict for those who are reluctant to abandon a general education for students with disabilities (Gajar, Goodman, & McAfee, 1993). The emphasis on preparing a student for employment will naturally produce other benefits since employment is generally a financial prerequisite to other aspects of independent living. However, the emphasis on employment, functional life outcomes, and vocational education can bring to the forefront issues pertaining to life expectations and realistic educational outcomes far sooner than a student or parents may be able to perceive them accurately or be emotionally prepared to consider them.

The transition to college is an exciting step toward independence and adulthood for many.

In addition, underlying cultural and racial issues must not be ignored. In 1987, Edgar projected the quandary that educators are now facing in their efforts to reform secondary special education programs. The path one prefers in the reformation process may carry with it some undesirable implications. The limiting nature of setting students with disabilities on a vocational track and the overwhelming failure of the current academic curriculum for these students leave few attractive options. As Edgar explains, there must be a shift away from the presently weak academic curriculum, resulting in a separate track that emphasizes functional vocational, independent living tasks—a track "populated, primarily, by poor, minority, male students. What a dilemma—two equally appalling alternatives; integrated mainstreaming in a nonfunctional curriculum which results in horrendous outcomes (few jobs, high dropout rate) or separate, segregated programs for an already devalued group, a repugnant thought in our democratic society" (p. 560).

The Process of Transition

Transition is a outcome-based process involving numerous complex decisions that must include the selection of a student's secondary curriculum. Transition planning is legislated to take place during the teen years, but Szmanski (1994) predicts that such efforts are unlikely to produce much better results than have been previously documented. She advocates that successful transitions require a broad lifespan focus, extending downward to preschool and far beyond the initial departure of young adults from secondary schooling, emphasizing that the ultimate goal of transition interventions is empowerment of the students, families, and the communities in which they reside.

For adults, work serves as the financial means to participate in the community and often serves as a source of friendships and other community connections. The likelihood that individuals with disabilities can achieve a satisfactory

level of community participation and interaction with their peers increases dramatically when they are able to get and keep jobs (Peraino, 1993; Wagner, 1991).
Yet many with disabilities begin their pursuit of adulthood ill-equipped to compete in the open job market. Gerber (1994) describes the current state of affairs
by acknowledging that "For children with disabilities, the adult world of competitive employment is a hard, irrevocable fact that must either discipline the organization of their education or be ignored in hopes that a better, more
compassionate world will emerge" (p. 376). Within the political context of welfare reform, income tax reform, and balanced budgets, the likelihood of a more
compassionate world emerging appears even more remote than it was in 1994.

Hasazi, Hock, and Cravedi-Cheng (1992) noted that only approximately 30%
of former special education students were working full time, with 25% in part-
time jobs and many unemployed or underemployed. Further contributing to
their poor circumstances, many students with disabilities are able to earn only a
low rate of pay. When they do acquire employment after secondary school, it is
often at minimum wage or lower. Fortunately, there is some evidence that wages
do increase three to five years after school exit (Blackorby & Wagner, 1996). Initially, only 9% of employed youth with disabilities earn more than $6 per hour,
but after three to five years the figure increases to nearly 40%. This pattern of increases is apparent for both white youth and Hispanics, but African American
youth do not show a similar increase in wages over time.

In terms of residential independence, youth with disabilities again have far
different patterns than those seen in the general population, one-third of whom
generally establish a form of independent living within the first two years upon
exiting from secondary schooling (Blackorby & Wagner, 1996). For youth with
disabilities, the figure is a mere 13%. After three to five years, more individuals
have established independent residences, moving the total for youth with disabilities up to 26% and that of the general population to 60%. The majority of disability categories have percentages between 38% and 46%, with a few notably
lower percentages evident. Deaf/blindness is the lowest at just under 6%, multiple disabilities sits at 13%, and other health impairments and mental retardation
figures hover around 25%. One significant ethnic pattern is apparent in the difference between the percentage of white youth with disabilities establishing residential independence after three to five years (42%) and that of African Americans
(26%).

There are many forms of schooling available after secondary schooling has
ended, including traditional community colleges and four-year colleges, vocational training, high school equivalency training, vocational rehabilitation training, job corps, and military training (Halpern, Yovanoff, Doren, & Benz, 1995).
Although the most prevalent notion of postsecondary schooling in the transition
literature refers to community college and four-year college programs, each of
the others in this list can reflect positive progress for an individual. For example,
a high school dropout who chooses to participate in and complete a GED program is increasing his employability as well as his knowledge and skills as contrasted with one who makes no such effort. Thus, one could argue that
enrollment in a GED program should hardly count as postsecondary training, yet

when contrasted to failure to enroll in a GED program, it would be considered a positive outcome.

Our assessments of transition efforts associated with IDEA depend to this point on evidence available within the first few years after students exit their secondary programs. Only a small number of students with disabilities enroll in postsecondary education shortly after high school exit (Hasazi, Hock, & Cravedi-Cheng, 1992). Using two data points of follow-up from the National Longitudinal Transition Study (NLTS), two years after secondary school exit and three to five years after secondary school exit, Blackorby and Wagner (1996) have further delineated this enrollment pattern. Up to two years after secondary school exit only 14% of youth with disabilities were attending some type of postsecondary school, compared to 53% of the general population. Over the next three years, an additional 13% of youth with disabilities attended a postsecondary school, as did an additional 15% of the general population. Thus, given more time following secondary school, more youth with disabilities enter postsecondary schools, but the total percentages continue to be dramatically lower than those of the general population. This pattern of difference remains even when data were matched for gender, ethnic background, and head of household's educational level. At the two-year level, postsecondary enrollment percentages range from 4% of youth with multiple disabilities to 30% of those with speech or sensory impairments. The largest increases after additional years occur for students with hearing impairments, of whom 32% enroll in postsecondary schooling. For youth classified with learning disabilities, serious emotional disturbance, mental retardation, or multiple disabilities, the percentage does not increase significantly with the passage of time. Three to five years following secondary school, the percentage of youth attending postsecondary schools ranges from lows of 9% for those with multiple disabilities and 12% for individuals with mental retardation to highs of 60% for those with hearing impairments or deafness. Other groups with rates approaching the 68% figure for the general population include youth with visual impairments at 57% and other health impaired at 56%. Approximately 31% of youth with learning disabilities attend postsecondary schools, a rate slightly less than half of that of the general population.

Individual characteristics of youth with disabilities that may contribute to their poor rates of enrollment in postsecondary schools include poor academic achievement, low self-concept, external locus of control, and inadequate social functioning (Fourqurean, Meisgeir, Swank, & Williams, 1991). Additionally, social bias or structural barriers can contribute to their absence from such programs (Rojewski, 1994). The aspirations that one holds for the future can play an indirect role in determining an individual's future attainments in that they are often based on past experiences and perceived barriers to future opportunities (Gottfredson & Becker, 1981). These aspirations do not determine the future, but they do reflect one's orientation toward it. It appears that youth with disabilities are particularly vulnerable and hold lowered aspirations for themselves than do youth without disabilities (e.g., Dowdy, Carter, & Smith, 1990). For students with learning disabilities, these lowered aspirations may result from their failures in school, past discriminations, social attitudes, cultural expectations, and either systemic or self-imposed limitations (Rojewski, 1996). Over 50% of high school seniors with learning disabilities hold educational aspirations of less than a four-year college, whereas two-thirds of youth without disabilities aspire to attain a baccalaureate or graduate degree. Are these differences evidence of healthy, reality-based perceptions of the future or of an inordinately negative perspective with which youth with learning disabilities tend to enter their adulthood?

Just as Brown and Gerber (1992) note that transition to employment is only the beginning of a continuum that goes from job entry to moving up in one's career, admission to and enrollment in a postsecondary program is not the point at which there is a guaranteed positive outcome. Does the student progress in his program of choice, whether that be taking real college courses toward a degree or completing a credible vocational training program that will enable her to obtain employment? The encouragement to apply and even the enrollment and participation of adolescents with disabilities in advanced college programs in no way ensure that they will be able to identify, maintain, or pursue high-prestige occupational aspirations as adults. Career guidance for such students must be conceived from the reality of educational requirements associated with occupations coupled with complete knowledge of support services available to help them in their endeavors (Rojewski, 1996). The aim is reconciliation of the disparate educational and occupational aspirations that one may hold or fail to hold in order to find the highest level of achievement for all.

Focus of Discussion

Accommodations are permitted for the competency testing required for graduation and college entrance, and many colleges offer developmental classes and specialized assistance for their students with disabilities (Gajar, Goodman, & McAfee, 1993). To what extent these accommodations build up unrealistic expectations, delaying the inevitable academic failure and redirection toward more appropriate educational outcomes or offering the critical bridge to successful adult outcomes, is an issue currently facing both educators and admissions officers in higher education. The anticipation of and planning by secondary students and their parents for the future constitute a very natural developmental sequence—options weighed, colleges visited, military recruiters contacted, and applications galore completed for postsecondary schooling, employment, and housing. Recommendation forms come due for the teachers and guidance counselors who were asked and agreed to write the needed documentation of applicant worthiness. For some, the process goes smoothly; their secondary schooling has adequately prepared them for the next phase of their lives. For others, most notably youth with disabilities, the process requires far greater systematic planning than was previously available. Still, the match between secondary programming and the transition to adulthood remains questioned. The first point of discussion and debate centers on the need for secondary programs to aim toward employment versus developmental education for students with disabilities. The second debate, somewhat removed from the traditional K–12 arguments, concerns the appropriateness of providing developmental and remedial courses at the college level.

SECONDARY PROGRAMMING
TO MAXIMIZE SUCCESS

Employers have been harsh critics of the public school system, stepping up their call for a rigorous academic curriculum in our secondary schools to stop the apparent descent of standardized test scores and the inadequacy of job applicants. They envision hiring workers who possess a comprehensive set of characteristics, such as good work habits, company loyalty, dependability, honesty, and teamwork, but complain that such workers are not available. Employers continue to demand greater academic rigor in our schools, hoping to improve their applicant pools (Goodlad, 1994). However, scores on the standardized tests designed to measure content knowledge have a low correlation with such worker traits. Yet when teachers set out to teach, they are impelled by neither remote notions of improving the nation's workforce and its economic competitiveness nor enhancing the school's test scores. Goodlad notes that "Instead, they are driven by a desire to teach satisfyingly, to have all their students excited about learning, to have their daily work square with their conception of what this work should be and do" (p. 203). At the secondary level, the aim of that work encompasses numerous worthy outcomes, such as giving all students a solid general education necessary for good citizenship, aiming some toward vocational opportunities, and preparing others for further study and scholarship. Secondary subject matter teachers take pride in the quality and depth of their classes, whether the content be academic or vocational. The notion of allowing students to earn good grades in their classes when traditional standards have been waived or significantly altered is not popular with these teachers or the students' future employers. Employers expect young adults to enter employment with a sense of responsibility and initiative, reflecting self-confidence as well as adequate grounding in basic skills.

However, the comprehensive mission of our secondary schools has not seemed to offer the most effective programming for youth with disabilities. Even with the focus placed on transition to adulthood for youth with disabilities, there continues to be a lack of clear guidance and direction in programming for these students (Fourqurean, Meisgeir, Swank, & Williams, 1991). The expectations and intended outcomes are obviously not the same for all students with disabilities, but their poor transitions to adulthood and the need for well-conceived transitions for all groups are apparent. The youth with severe disabilities and his family may be hoping for supported employment with a job coach and accompanying residential accommodations in a community-based group home, whereas the student with learning disabilities might set his sights on attending college. For both, the question remains when and how best to prepare for successful entry into adulthood. The debates regarding the best secondary preparation for adult-

hood, employment, independent living, and the establishment of satisfactory social relationships involve both the nature of and content of secondary programs.

Developing Autonomy

The years in secondary school generally afford youth opportunities to develop
decision-making skills and familiarity with community resources, which enable
them to begin gradually assuming an appropriate level of responsibility for their
own affairs. First, they may open their own savings account with money earned
in jobs around the neighborhood. Shortly thereafter, many are ready for their
first checking account, as the savings account proves too inaccessible. Even planning the high school prom requires teamwork—negotiation, resourcefulness,
and leadership—all skills that are needed for independent adult life. For students
who are college-bound, dorms offer the perfect transition (so to speak) from
dependent housing to independent housing. Eventually, the dependent teen is
expected to transform herself into an independent adult across all areas of life.

However, such a transformation may be delayed, incomplete, or unattainable
for youth with disabilities, regardless of the level of severity or physical impact of
their disability. In a ethnographic study of moderately to highly successful adults
with learning disabilities, Gerber, Ginsberg, and Reiff (1992) found many still
seeking to establish a comfortable level of autonomy. The prevailing theme in relation to success in their lives was that of gaining control of their lives, including
making internal decisions and demonstrating external manifestations of control.
Internal decisions involved orientation to goals, having the desire to succeed, and
positively reconceptualizing their learning disabilities. External manifestations
were associated with adaptability, including persistence, the use of coping mechanisms, matching one's abilities to the environment, and establishment of a pattern of personal support to foster success. Is the difficulty caused by deficits within
the individual with disabilities and/or their experiences (or lack thereof) while
K–12 students?

At a secondary level, teachers indicate that they are more controlling of students who are labeled as learning disabled than their nondisabled peers (Grolnick
& Ryan, 1990). Further, teachers rate students with learning disabilities as being
less competent and motivated, having more learning problems than other students matched for IQ, displaying lower self-esteem, and achieving at lower levels
when compared to a random selection of nondisabled peers. These findings offer
evidence that educators are failing to give students with mild disabilities such as
learning disabilities an opportunity to develop an internal locus of control, in
terms of both self-regulation and motivation to complete their work with high-
quality standards. Students are more self-regulating and autonomous when they
do not feel pressured or controlled by significant adults (Grolnick, Ryan, & Deci,
1991) and when they perceive themselves as understanding and possessing the
behaviors associated with success in school (Connell, 1985). Support services for
students with mild disabilities that foster dependence on external sources,
whether they be individuals or materials, could be challenged as taking students
away from rather than toward the behaviors associated with autonomy.

Mithaug, Martin, and Agran (1987) argue that the most typical instructional approach employed in special education "assumes a level of student dependency that reinforces behaviors incompatible with independence and student initiative" (p. 501). Teachers deliver instructional cues and consequences, set the schedule for task completion, provide immediate direct reinforcement of work, and so forth. In contrast, employers need workers who can work and problem solve independently, be able to critique their own work, identify the proper sequence for task completion, and complete work assignments within specified time limits. Deci, Hodges, Pierson, and Tomassone (1992) note the strong emphasis among special educators on controlling behavior through behavior modification programs. They posit that while such controlling contexts may reduce confusion and increase on-task behaviors within the classroom, the unintended costs could be "interfering with the students' developing greater self-regulation and leading to poorer achievement and adjustment in the classroom" (p. 470). Differentiation between providing structures as opposed to controls is the essence of their point. Whereas controls merely impose an external pressure on students to behave in specified ways, structures allow students to understand the relationship among behavior, outcomes, and personal performance. The authors argue that even subtle controls, such as tokens or gold stars, as well as other, more coercive ones, are a risk to development of self-regulation.

In describing the need for family involvement in the transition process, Nisbett, Covert, and Schuh (1992) criticize systems designed to serve individuals with disabilities as failing to recognize them as "whole" human beings, where "the individual is not included in making the decisions that affect the very quality and direction of his or her life" (p. 408). If secondary programming in regard to controls and structure is focused primarily on the current performance of the student, without consideration to the future, a student might be deemed unable to perform without controlling supports. Professionals may evaluate the student's current abilities as insufficient to allow him a voice in the decision-making process. By making that very decision, they undermine the student's ability to achieve decision-making skills by denying him the opportunity. The failure to drop the controls and allow more decision making and empowerment for the student does not seem likely to prepare him for postsecondary education, training, or employment (Szmanski, 1994).

If students plan to go to into unsupported work or postsecondary education, they need at least some ability to make decisions and operate in an environment devoid of cues, prompts, and reminders. Given the expectations of college students, it is important to arrive on campus prepared for a new life of responsibility and autonomy (Brinckerhoff, Shaw, & McGuire, 1992). Students in secondary special education programs may be even further disadvantaged in their transitions to such environments not because of their disabilities, but because the nature of the services they have received has been controlling. Using a self-report survey method, Mellard and Hazel (1992) investigated the differences on a variety of skills associated with social competence between community college students eligible for services for students with learning disabilities and those of the general campus population. They found significant differences in how these two student

Adulthood offers new freedom and new responsibilities.

groups responded on items associated with domains such as language, pragmatics, humor, personal/social involvement, peer relations, helping others, applied academics, money management, coping, time management, personal responsibility, and goal setting/organization. The special education programs that these students experienced in their elementary and secondary programs seem to have failed to foster in them these general coping and life adjustment skills that were evident in the other college students.

Today, there is a positive paradigm shift emerging in special education and other disability service professions, involving professionals changing their roles from helpers to enablers (Reiff & deFur, 1992). Rather than setting up transition services that are done to and for students with disabilities and their families, the students and their families collaboratively plan and implement the transition services that are needed. If the shift simply gives the control over to the parents, not the individual student, the student could still be left in a dependent role. The critical variables of control and self-determination must shift from the professional to the individual student, with parental support and involvement. Students who are allowed to influence the goals of their program have opportunities to gain control of their lives rather than being controlled externally while a teacher's goals are imposed on them.

Curricular Considerations and Work Experience

The most popular curriculum today for students with disabilities is that of a general education rather than vocational training, with only around one-third taking a vocational concentration (Blackorby & Wagner, 1996). Such is not surprising since most special education teachers serving students with mild disabilities typically have far less training in career or vocational areas than in academic areas. They have historically placed a higher value on academic achievement than vocational training and, therefore, offered primarily academic instruction and social skill training to their students. Most often, students with disabilities do leave secondary school without specific career or vocational training (Reiff & deFur, 1992). The little vocational training that students with disabilities do receive is primarily at the introductory level, insufficient to allow them to develop any real vocational skills (Wagner & Blackorby, 1996). In the recent past, students with moderate to severe disabilities were prospering no better, having been sequestered in programs based on traditional academic skill sequences along with task analysis and isolated "prerequisite" skill development rather than the actual accomplishment of activities (McDonnell, Mathot-Buckner, & Ferguson, 1996). Since these programs have proven to have little correlation to successful post-school adjustment, curricular models based on life activities (e.g., School and Community Integration Program) are gaining in popularity.

Other curricular areas, such as social skills, have also been suggested as needing to rise in importance in the secondary curriculum for the sake of improving the transition to adulthood for students with disabilities. Students are described in the literature as talking excessively, acting out without thinking, being unbearably shy, experiencing frustration in their attempts at dating, lacking self-confidence, and failing to control emotions appropriately for their age (White, 1992). White, citing Chelser's national study of over five hundred adults with learning disabilities, notes that the need most frequently named by participants in the study was assistance in social skill training and that the fourth most frequent was overcoming dependence, whereas academic areas (e.g., reading and spelling) fell toward the bottom of their top ten concerns. Social skills are needed for personal adjustment as well as for obtaining and keeping a job. Workplace skills certainly include responding to the undesirable behaviors of others, coping with stress situations, tolerating and working with ambiguity, interacting with others, and the sharing of responsibility. Specific communication skills needed in the workplace include perceiving and interpreting voice inflections, reading body language, adjusting to different personal communication styles, and resolving conflicts. The ability to use critical listening skills includes listening for content, listening to conversations, listening for long-term contexts, listening for emotional meaning, and listening to directions (White, 1992).

The best balance among vocational preparation, academic content, problem-solving skills, life activities with their "prerequisite skills," and social–emotional development for youth with disabilities is at issue. In the following debate the emphasis is placed on determining the most suitable educational goal for special education students, which, in turn, determines the nature and content of secondary and transition programs.

Decision Point 7.1: Improving Postsecondary Outcomes

Arguments for Proposition One Although there are many types of students with disabilities and the intention is that each one will receive an individually planned educational program suitable to his or her needs and aspirations, the reality is that a finite number of basic options are available that can be customized to some extent. Today, those basic options for students with mild disabilities are characterized by watered-down academics, introductory vocational courses, an

> **Proposition One**
> Secondary programs for youth with disabilities must be focused on realistic employment options, regardless of the level of functioning of the child.
>
> Delayed focus on vocational or other employment interests puts students at risk for dropping out, poor transition outcomes, and unemployment.

overabundance of structure and control, and no real target outcomes for the students. The progression of students through these academic programs inundated with exemptions and modifications has weakened educational standards, increased the dropout rate, and given parents and students a false sense of hope but no direction. Eventually, the individual who is unable to derive much meaning from his reading, calculate accurately, or write a coherent sentence will need to function in the real world without accommodations or lowered standards. Therefore, these students should begin following a course of study appropriate to realistic life goals during their secondary education rather than persisting in focusing on the academic progress that has eluded them. Realistic career counseling during the middle school years and curricular focus on functional life outcomes should help students with disabilities stay in school and achieve successful employment and personal adjustment following graduation. Whereas postsecondary training or even a four-year college program might be appropriate for some, it should not continue to be given an inappropriately high value for students unable to struggle through even the most basic academic skills. The goal of the educational program for these students must be centered on expanding realistic employment opportunities rather than abstract notions of achieving "maximum potential" or getting a better grade in social studies.

Adults with mild disabilities, including those who drop out as well as those who complete either academic or vocational programs, have often been unable to make a successful transition from secondary school into appropriate jobs. Patton and Polloway (1992) describe the situation: "The scenario for many young adults is characterized by unemployment and/or underemployment, low pay, part-time work, frequent job changes, nonengagement with the community, limitations in independent functioning, and limited social lives" (p. 413). The most common target of recommended reform is, indeed, the secondary school program and its need to shift to a focus on the future of these children and the prevention of adult failures (e.g., unemployment) rather than remediation of basic skill deficits left over from elementary school (Patton & Polloway, 1992). The need for such a shift is consistent with the fact that it has been estimated that approximately nine million individuals between sixteen and twenty-four will lack the necessary skills to meet the entry-level job requirements of employers as they enter the workforce (U.S. General Accounting Office, 1990).

In the current state of affairs in secondary programs serving students with mild disabilities, most students are faced with the choice of muddling through weak academic programs with the assistance of special educators serving as tutors and instructional and assessment modifiers, taking a modified vocational program with no real skill development, or placing themselves into a radically different nonacademic track used by those with moderate to severe disabilities, with far different educational outcomes. Given the changing nature of the job market today, one that requires greater competence at entry level than ever before, the "watered-down" curricula typical of these programs is unlikely to provide these students the needed preparation for employment (Reiff & deFur, 1992). They are equally inadequate for entry into many postsecondary schools or any other than entry-level low-wage positions.

Student perceptions seem to contribute to the poor match between employer needs and the competencies of job applicants. Students with learning disabilities, in particular, may set unrealistic goals and/or be totally unfamiliar with requirements for specific jobs (Blalock, 1982) when following a strictly academic curriculum.

In the *Sixteenth Annual Report to Congress on the Implementation of IDEA,* the authors summarized troubling results from the NLTS in regard to absenteeism and dropout rates that were higher for students with disabilities than for the general population of students, and disproportionately experienced in high-incidence categories such as learning disabilities. The "NLTS data suggest that regular education academic classes of the late 1980s were difficult environments for students with disabilities" (U.S. Department of Education, 1994, p. 104). Students enrolled in general education classes were significantly more likely to fail courses than other students, which resulted in these students falling behind in earning credits toward graduation. With the failures and loss of credits also comes the increased probability of students dropping out. On the other hand, students who enrolled in a vocational concentration or who even took survey courses in a variety of occupation areas were significantly less likely to drop out of school. The probability that students would have better attendance records, pass more courses, and graduate was increased more for those who participated in a work experience program as part of their vocational education. These findings explain the dissatisfaction some feel regarding the use of general education as a course of study for students with disabilities. There are higher student-to-teacher ratios in general education classrooms, resulting in a reduction of the opportunities for individualized attention. In these more crowded classes, the teachers still expect the vast majority (92%) of students with disabilities to keep up with other students (U.S. Department of Education, 1994). Findings also indicate that for mainstreamed students the most common accommodation in general education classrooms was monitoring of the student by a special education teacher without any direct support to the student.

A year later in the *Seventeenth Annual Report to Congress* (U.S. Department of Education, 1995), there was a somewhat different interpretation of the data offered. The authors placed emphasis on the fact that for those students who successfully remained in general education classes, there were better post-school outcomes. However, the caveat was also included that it is those who successfully participate in general education courses who are the most intellectually and socially competent of the group, indicating that ability rather than placement was the determining factor in successful outcomes. The failure rate for students with disabilities in general education classes, particularly in the ninth and tenth grades, is high and continues to serve as a predictor of dropping out.

During their secondary education, the average GPA for students with learning disabilities increases from a 1.7 in ninth grade to a 2.1 by the twelfth grade (U.S. Department of Education, 1995). Possible explanations include the fact that the poorer students drop out, that the harder required subjects are behind the older students and they are able to perform better in electives, and that teachers begin to show leniency in their grading closer to graduation. Of ninth-graders with learning disabilities, 44.6% failed a course, whereas the number failing a course in twelfth grade dropped to 24.1%. Participation in vocational education is associated with lower dropout rates for upperclassmen (U.S. Department of Education, 1994). Those who dropped out earlier most likely would have chosen a vocational education had they remained in school. Access to courses of interest to them and relevant to their post-school opportunities might have kept the ninth- or tenth-graders in school to completion.

Developing Autonomy Today, the immediate short-term goal of passing grades in content classes can inadvertently take precedence over the more significant long-term goals that students develop a positive self-image, feel competent about their abilities in school settings, and eventually graduate with social, vocational, and academic skills needed to be successful in their future pursuits. Okolo and Sitlington (1986) argue that typical content tutoring found in special education programs offers little to the students other than help in passing those classes and fitting into the system of which they are currently a part. Smooth transitions to other systems or problem-solving tactics needed for the next situation the students may encounter are not considered relevant. Ellis (1990), commenting on the tutorial approach, said that "many teachers appear to remediate, placate and suffocate students while intending to be supportive and empathetic" (p. 61). Reiff, Ginsberg, and Gerber (1995) conducted a survey of successful adults with learning disabilities and found that the variables that they attributed to their success were not their academic prowess but characteristics such as persistence, learning to overcome adversity, and gaining control over events in their lives.

The changing skill requirements and alterations in the nature of the workplace leave the adult with mild disabilities at potentially an even greater risk in the future than is currently the case. The already documented difficulties of many adults with mild disabilities coupled with the rapidly occurring changes in the job market make curricular reform even more pressing. Employer expectations include the use of an employee's basic skills for problem solving, communication and negotiation with others, and cooperative team membership (White, 1992). The high school curriculum for students with learning disabilities needs to include career education, social skills training, building interpersonal skills and knowledge (Reiff & deFur, 1992), compensation skills, and the ability to generalize knowledge to work situations (Rojewski, 1989). Even an academic curriculum that uses a functional framework and emphasizes basic skills falls short of what is needed.

Whether a student is moving straight into an entry-level job or plans to attend postsecondary education/training, she needs to be prepared to progress successfully, displaying responsibility and maturity on the job or in the classroom. Organization, time management, effective communication skills, and so forth are essential elements needed for one to succeed beyond the initial point of entry.

Some might argue that giving students supports, such as teacher-prepared out-lines and lecture notes, frees the student from the strain of getting all the right information down, enabling her to concentrate on the content of instruction. Having the student gain the narrow content of a course takes precedence over that student's developing independence and general problem-solving strategies or gaining practical skills, such as note taking.

In truth, teaching the student note-taking skills and other means of retaining information presented in class is a more significant life skill than simply providing the student with content to be memorized and learned for the next test. The ability to process and sort information into significant clusters and the process of attaching meaning to material presented orally is as at the very least as important as is the retention of content for anyone who will participate in future training or education, either on the job or in school. Note taking is an area that often is identified as one for which educational programs should make reasonable accommodations—find an alternative for students with disabilities so they do not have to attempt this arduous task and are free to concentrate on the content at hand. We use note takers, tape recorders, and access to instructor notes as means to eliminate the note-taking requirement in secondary and postsecondary programs, all in the name of supporting and helping the student. However, active note taking can be a vital part of retaining and understanding the information. Suritsky and Hughes (1991) have described the recording of lecture contents as a physical act involving four broad processes of listening, cognitive processing, recording content in written form, and reviewing noted information. Through active engagement in these processes, students learn to paraphrase information, discriminate between relevant and irrelevant information, predict future information, relate new content to previous knowledge, and revise content into a personally meaningful form. We seem to have become the providers of immediate short-term fixes rather than maintaining a focus on the skills needed of adults. Taking the time to develop students into note takers, problem solvers, and autonomous adults might be of far greater value.

Curricular Considerations and Work Experience The connection between the participation of students with disabilities in secondary vocational education and positive post-school outcomes is strong. For students who spent their most recent year of school in vocational education, there is a decreased likelihood of dropping out (Wagner, as cited by U.S. Department of Education, 1994). Additionally, there are significantly lower dropout rates for students with disabilities who take either survey or concentrated coursework in vocational education in high school when compared to those who take nonvocational (academic) or prevocational (e.g., career exploration, basic work skills) coursework. Although many students with disabilities do take some form of vocational education, in the NLTS findings only 34.4% actually enrolled in and completed a vocational education concentration. The students who took either survey courses or vocational concentrations, particularly those with learning disabilities, speech or language impairments, mild mental retardation, or emotional disturbance (not institutionalized), were more likely to be employed and have higher incomes than those who did not. Students who completed vocational survey courses had an income nearly $4,000 greater than that of students who did not. However, the most beneficial course of study for post-school employment was that of the vocational concentration, with students following such a program earning $6,247 more per year than those who had taken nonvocational or prevocational courses (U.S. Department of Education, 1995).

The indictment of current secondary programs for students with learning disabilities has been sounded by Mellard and Hazel (1992), who note that a rather dismal profile of the young adult with learning disabilities emerges from their review of several follow-up studies. They found that students confront obstacles to high school graduation and that completing high school offers little incentive for postsecondary education or training, which, in turn, contributes little to future employment. They make the painful observation that the poor results of secondary programs for students with learning disabilities are particularly difficult to accept, given the differential funding of which special education programs have been the beneficiaries. These findings lend support to the argument in favor of increased vocational education programs for students with learning disabilities.

The group that one is most likely to argue should retain an academic orientation is that of students classified as learning disabilities. Currently, the data indicate that the majority of students with learning disabilities are unable to function independently and contribute appropriately to the community. The data confirm that, as adults, these individuals have difficulties across a wide range of functional areas and settings, not just isolated academic settings. To continue offering them a traditional curriculum at the secondary level, with an emphasis on basic skills in reading and mathematics outside of an applied context, would seem to be unresponsive to the consistently negative findings of the available research (Mellard & Hazel, 1992). Rather, Mellard and Hazel argue that the answer lies in the area of vocational and technical education. By offering students with mild disabilities such programs, we could increase dramatically the numbers who complete high school, function independently, and are able to demonstrate social responsibility.

The pursuit of academic curricula over vocational training necessitates the progression from high school to postsecondary education or training of some sort before young adults can begin working in jobs paying anything above minimum wage, thereby lengthening the time they must remain out of the workforce. Yet many will be unable to be successful in competitive postsecondary training without extensive modifications and supports, further prolonging their entry into the workforce and adding additional risk of failure to their lives. Minskoff and DeMoss (1992) have developed a model program that provides vocational education offered with support services for work-related academic skills, such as reading an analog meter in electronics or reading texts and studying for vocational content tests. Such a program is evidence of the potential reform of the curriculum to a vocational emphasis without abandonment of academic content. The redirection of secondary curriculum for youth with disabilities away from remedial academics toward preparation for their vocational futures compels secondary special educators to expand their knowledge base to include vocational values and domains and technological skills (Repetto, 1995).

To prevent students from dropping out and to ease the transition from education to employment, work-study programs offer an excellent supplement to vocational programs. The students get to begin the transition to employment while still having a structured support system available. Issues of responsibility in attendance, preparation for work, and attitude as well as job skills can be addressed by the students' school support team. If the employer has concerns about the employee with disabilities, he has teachers to call upon to assist with his concerns, increasing the likelihood that the loss of the job can be avoided. Further, the student can directly experience the need for academic skills in his job placement, boosting his interest in these courses. Hasazi, Hock, and Cravedi-Cheng (1992) observed that students who had paid work experience during high school were more likely to be employed than those who had no work experience, and that those who had participated in vocational education were more likely to be working in higher paying jobs. Several reports indicate that students with actual work experience were more likely to find work after leaving school (U.S. Department of Education, 1994). Work experience increases student interest in education and reduces the chances of a student dropping out. The reports do not document any reduction in school performance during periods of student employment, with both absenteeism and course failures reduced for students in work-experience programs. It can be speculated that if students who dropped out early could have been kept in school long enough to move into vocational concentrations and work-experience programs, they might have remained in school until graduation.

Argument Summary Curriculum within our schools must remain comprehensive in nature, adequately addressing the many layers of job skills needed throughout society. Today, the politics of minimum wage, reform of the welfare system, the critical need for quality child care, and the abundance of unfilled low-skill jobs should not be divorced from the issues at hand. Our society needs workers at all levels who are responsible and willing to contribute to our democratic culture through good citizenship, regardless of their inability to achieve high SAT scores. The overemphasis on high standards for all and minimum competency testing actually devalues the critical role that workers at all levels play in the smooth running of our communities.

Although the analyses of the NLTS findings indicate that no single special education policy or strategy will universally provide the appropriate benefits to all students (U.S. Department of Education, 1995), the findings do affirm the failure of the prevalent basic skills remediation model for large numbers of students and the need to shift to an alternative. Rather than starting with a basic academic curriculum and modifying it to the extent needed to accommodate a student's deficits, secondary school programs must be based on the future lives and employment opportunities for youth with disabilities and build appropriate academic curricula around this future-oriented foundation.

Arguments for Proposition Two Post-school outcomes for youth with disabilities have been disappointing at best. Special educators have discovered that many students whom they served have been unable to progress into successful

> **Proposition Two**
> Secondary programs for youth with disabilities must be designed to offer the student the greatest possible success during the secondary program and flexibility for the future. Premature focus on adult life and "realistic" options can restrict the student's educational opportunities, aspirations, and interests.

productive adult lives. The quick fix is a call for radical curricular revision in our secondary schools rather than sharpening our focus on the individual student and his most suitable course of study. A blanket shift from academic courses to vocational programming for these students will eliminate neither their disabilities nor their need for support structures. Without suitable accommodations and adjustments, a student can fail in a vocational concentration just as easily as in a college preparation program. Prerequisite skills for successful participation in vocational concentrations include basic academic and social skills training anyway (Elrod, 1987). The student who has difficulty following more than one instruction in an academic class will have the same problem when confronted with multiple instructions in a vocational class. A student with poor concentration or listening skills can get lost regardless of the topic at hand. It is simply ungrounded to assume that disability-related problems can disappear by the reassignment of a student's classes from academic courses to an employment-oriented curriculum. *Wholesale* reprogramming of students in special education to vocational programs will narrow their life choices, further set them apart from their peers, and fail to use their last years in secondary school to improve their basic skills.

Shapiro and Lentz (1991) conducted a follow-up study of young adults who had followed a vocational program six, twelve, and twenty-four months after high school graduation and discovered that fewer than half remained in the jobs for which they had been trained. The participants in the study indicated that their greatest need was for additional academic skills rather than vocational skills. From the employers' side, these skills seemed critical as well. After contacting twenty-five companies in the greater Richmond area while involved in consulting and providing technical assistance on employability and employment issues for persons with learning disabilities, Gerber (1992) noted that business and industry were willing to hire people with learning disabilities. They did, however, expect them to have mastered basic skills as well as social skills and other general skills critical to the work environment. It is the responsibility of secondary schools to provide such basic skills and let postsecondary training facilities and employers deliver job-specific training.

Developing Autonomy The successful achievement of autonomy in adulthood is not predicated on the achievement of autonomy as early as possible. Indeed, children need the opportunity to grow and mature in a highly dependent state before they can successfully begin the achievement of independence. Teens, in particular, need the nurturing support of parents and teachers as they begin the independence process in earnest. Not all children develop preparedness for independence at the same rate, or accept the responsibilities associated with autonomy as easily as others. Some children may be concerned about their assignments and schoolwork from an early age, whereas others are unable to understand the long-term consequences associated with incomplete, late, or missing assignments that they find particularly difficult anyway. The freedom and pleasure of skipping the assignment take priority over a distant threat. When the distant threat arrives in the form of an angry teacher or parent and failing grades, the cycle of failure and another short-term decision to drop out become a common response. For youth with disabilities, the insertion of external short-term consequences and rewards, instructional supports, and modifications of curriculum, instruction, and evaluations into these failure cycles do not negate autonomy. Rather, they should provide the bridge between the independence and responsibility for which the student as an individual is being prepared.

A student's disability may contribute to the creation of discrepancies between expectations that teachers and parents hold for the student based on chronological age, the student's own assessment of her preparedness for autonomy, and the reality of her demonstrated behaviors. It is the responsibility of the special educator to work with the student individually to set just the right tension between support and autonomy, avoiding the failure cycle while encouraging the student to assume a reasonable level of independence. The criticism that secondary students with disabilities are overcontrolled by their teachers and the extensive support systems offered to them certainly demands consideration. Just as the beginning driver would not take his first lessons in Manhattan or on a Los Angeles freeway, youth with disabilities need not be left to make their way through high school without appropriate supports. Some students will find the need to create external mechanisms to compensate for the realities of their disabilities all of their lives. The acknowledgment and acceptance of limitations set by disabilities and reliance on external structures are preferable to attempting to deny their existence or the need for external supports. It is the pursuit of this balance that is the special educator's responsibility.

The illustrative argument regarding note taking and whether students should be taught note-taking skills or be provided supports and training in coping mechanisms offers an excellent case in point. Students with many different disabilities are hampered in their ability to take notes. Physical disabilities can interfere with note taking. Students who rely on lip reading and/or sign language need to keep their heads up and eyes focused on the speaker and/or interpreter. Students with learning disabilities tend to be inefficient and ineffective in their note-taking ability, lacking the organizational skills, auditory processing speed, and/or handwriting skills needed to get down successfully the significant content of a lecture. Hughes and Suritsky (1994) compared the note-taking skills of college students with and without learning disabilities and found that the students with learning disabilities had less information in their notes than did the others. Obviously, these students are at risk to perform poorly in class when forced to rely exclusively on their own note-taking abilities. However, there are also lecturer-controlled variables that influence the difficulty of note taking, such as rate of presentation, information density, lecture format, and use of cues. A ninth-grader with learning disabilities who is enrolled in world geography does not have the luxury of learning note-taking skills if he hopes to pass the course with his peers. Certainly, special education programming for this student over his entire secondary years must address his preparedness for the future, including the development of note-taking strategies (e.g., the use of a tape recorder, listening for teacher cues), as a complement to his basic academic or vocational program, not in lieu of it. Note taking need not be a prerequisite skill that further reduces the life opportunities of youth with disabilities.

Curriculum Considerations and Work Experience Secondary school programs and their mission have evolved over the years in concert with the changing nature of society and the job market. Increased job opportunities for college graduates and the expansion of college and university systems throughout the nation as well as the increasing skill levels required by many entry-level blue-collar jobs have influenced the secondary curriculum. Comprehensive high schools typically offer a standard academic track, a college preparation track, and numerous vocational concentrations. No single course of study is presumed to be suitable for all the students attending such a school. Rather, as individuals, students select the course of study suitable to their interests, abilities, and post-school aspirations. Some may find this a difficult task, having uncertainty as to their life interests or ambitions, and generally choose to follow a program that will keep as many doors open as possible. This decision point can be particularly difficult for youth with disabilities, who may be more uncertain than others what their abilities and limitations will be as adults. The standard recommendation for such students should be no different from that given to others—keep as many doors open for your future as possible.

Basic academic skills are not superfluous to successful adulthood for anyone. For those who pursue postsecondary education or training, they are minimal essentials. Since the most positive long-term outcomes come to those who enroll in postsecondary education, it would be unfair and discriminatory to presume that such skills were less relevant to students with disabilities than giving them vocational training. Halpern, Yovanoff, Doren, and Benz (1995) found that performance in five instructional domains, reading, writing, math, problem solving, and getting along with other people, are empirically effective predictors of participation in postsecondary education for youth with disabilities. These authors' conclusions are simple and easy to understand—if the goal is to increase participation in postsecondary education, we must address these domains at the secondary level.

Placement of high school students with mild disabilities in paid work experiences as a part of their high school curriculum further reduces the limited amount of time available for these students to achieve academic skills. These students have to work harder and devote more time to achieve basic skills. The replacement of instructional time with a part-time job will do little to improve the long-term educational goals for these students and may contribute to a dubious sense of freedom and autonomy. Students develop a false sense of wealth because they typically are still supported by parents and have no housing, medical, or food costs to cover with their low wages. Work experience reduces the available time for the student to study and do other schoolwork and creates a "premature prosperity" that increases the student's immediate interest in work, thereby reducing her interest in long-range planning and education. Ultimately, the young adult who makes the transition directly into low-paying jobs within the workforce will have very limited opportunities to expand her skills and will lack the ability to seek higher levels of employment.

On the practical level, the move toward community-based training and pre-exit placement programs for students with moderate to severe disabilities raises logistical staffing problems for schools—the coordinating teacher cannot be at school and multiple job sites simultaneously, nor can the schools afford to hire licensed teachers to accompany each individual student to a job site. No single teacher can be on the phone and in the community negotiating placements, in the classroom providing preplacement training for her students, and at multiple job sites serving as a job coach. Many unlicensed teaching assistants fall into the role of providing a substantial portion of the education of some special education students because the licensed teacher is off-site with a portion of the class. Work experience for this group of students must be set in a comprehensively designed program that taps new categories of personnel (e.g., job coaches) and models of instruction (e.g., community based).

There need be no rush to place young teens with moderate to severe disabilities into supported work settings. For many of these individuals, their years in school offer their best opportunities to become aware of community resources, develop social skills, gain functional basic skills, and identify accessible leisure and recreational activities of interest to them. They will have many years of adulthood in which to work and do not need to be precipitously pushed into the responsibility of daily work. The separation of students between the ages of nineteen and twenty-two for participation in work-experience programs would offer age-appropriate programming for these students, eliminate the need for licensed teachers of younger students to be in multiple locations simultaneously, and serve as an appropriate transition period.

Argument Summary Secondary schools are for teens who are far more than future adults. There is no need to rush them through their developmental stages into premature independence or force their selection of career goals before they are ready or able to make such decisions. The delay of an individual entering the workforce because vocational training is completed in a postsecondary program rather than during high school is not necessarily negative. If the student uses his time in secondary school to gain basic academic skills, develop social skills, and identify appropriate means of coping with his disability limitations, then it is time well spent. Secondary programs should offer students with disabilities the supports and dependence they need to gain confidence to launch out on their own instead of using a "sink or swim" approach. Clearly, we need improved transitions for these students, but we should not take a radical swing toward vocational programming as the primary course of study for all youth with disabilities. Particular caution is appropriate since most such recommendations are based on the findings of a study focused on students who left their secondary schooling in 1987. Programmatic shifts have already been initiated that address many of the concerns associated with post-school outcomes uncovered in the NLTS, and these must be further assessed before we have a clear understanding of the remaining problems and suitable future directions for change.

DEVELOPMENTAL INSTRUCTION IN COLLEGE

There is a significant positive relationship between participation in postsecondary education or training and successful transition to adult roles and responsibilities in the community (White, 1992). When including all who enrolled in postsecondary education up to three to five years following their exit from secondary schools, only approximately 27% of students with all types of disabilities attend postsecondary schools, compared with 68% of the general population (Blackorby & Wagner, 1996). For some disability groups (e.g., visually impaired, hearing impaired/deaf, and speech impaired), enrollment in postsecondary education does approximate that of the general population, reaching up to 60%. For those with learning disabilities, however, enrollment rates are clearly lower than that of the general population, with the majority not even entering postsecondary education or training programs. Wagner (1989) reported that only 16.7% of this population attend any postsecondary program as compared to 50% of the general population, with only 9% attending community or four-year colleges. These figures differ slightly from the 13.9% enrollment figure reported by Blackorby and Wagner (1996) for students with learning disabilities within the first two years following secondary school exit, which rises to 30.5% when a three-to-five-year period is used. Regardless of these varying reports, students with learning disabilities enroll in postsecondary education far less often than their peers from the general population. To the extent that a description of students with learning disabilities as capable students who possess average to above-average intelligence but are hampered somewhat in their academic achievement by isolated processing disorders is accurate, it would seem that far greater numbers of these students should be entering postsecondary programs.

The picture worsens when sustained progress in college is also considered. Enrollment is merely the first step and is of little value if not followed by attendance and program completion. In a survey of 911 students with learning disabilities one year after their high school graduation, Sitlington and Frank (1990) found that whereas 50% of their sample had begun postsecondary education, only 6.5% remained in those programs at the time of the survey. With evidence of a high correlation between adult success and participation in postsecondary education and training, a case for increasing the numbers of students with learning disabilities attending and remaining in such programs could certainly be argued. Such efforts would most likely require the increased availability of postsecondary-level support systems for these students. Both what the nature of these supports ought to be and the standards by which colleges (either two- or four-year schools) ought to admit and retain students with disabilities trigger further debate.

It is beyond the scope of this chapter to debate fully the merits of offering developmental courses on college campuses, but some consideration of their general effectiveness is appropriate because of their current prevalence and availability to students with disabilities. Many community colleges even require students to take a placement test, and students failing to achieve a minimum standard must take such courses (e.g., Laramie County Community College, 1995). The value and benefits of developmental classes have been studied on individual campuses based on measures of student retention, grade point averages, performance in subsequent college-level courses in the same subject matter, and program completion rates. For example, at Laramie County Community College (1995), a study of the effectiveness of the developmental program revealed that after two years, the 42% retention rate for the students who had taken developmental courses was higher than the 23% rate for nondevelopmental students. Initially, grade point averages were higher for students enrolled in developmental courses, but by the end of two years they became roughly equal. At Sinclair Community College (1994), the retention rate for students who took all recommended developmental courses was also higher than for those who took some or none of the recommended courses, as well as for those who did not need remediation. Additionally, they found that students who took developmental courses and enrolled in subsequent courses performed satisfactorily. Although such studies of single institutions have limited generalization value, when considered together they can reveal patterns and trends across institutions.

The Nature of Support Structures

A disability can be much more debilitating in a postsecondary educational or training setting than during high school because of the responsibilities demanded by the environment and the absence of supportive assistance (Mellard & Hazel, 1992). Responsibility for support services associated with secondary programs and decision making regarding them are held in large part by school personnel and parents, with little responsibility for their pursuit given to the student. At the postsecondary level, students do hold the responsibility for initiating and pursuing requests for services. However, once a college student initiates a request for services on the basis of a disability and has been deemed eligible, any institution receiving federal supports of any kind must provide suitable auxiliary aids and academic adjustments. Many of the students with disabilities on college campuses have needs specific to a physical or sensory disability. Students with visual impairments may need readers, note takers, access to technology, and so forth. The student who is deaf may require interpreters, and the student in a wheelchair may need classes offered in accessible locations. For students with learning disabilities, accommodations become a bit trickier. Not many of the college personnel who are responsible for providing support services to these students have had specialized training in the field (Bursuck & Rose, 1992). In an effort to improve the level of services given to these students, California has established a requirement that people working with students with learning disabilities at the college level receive training and a special certificate. Evaluators of the effectiveness of college level support systems must, therefore, avoid blaming internal flaws of the student for his difficulties without giving consideration to external factors (e.g., curriculum, poor teaching, overcrowding, limited instructional methods and materials used within educational programs) as a possible cause of failure.

Raskind and Scott (1993) have noted two basic approaches to addressing the difficulties of students with learning disabilities at the postsecondary level—remediation and compensation. Remediation is intended to improve the individual's skills in deficit areas whereas compensation is aimed toward the development of coping strategies to work around the deficit. Thus, the ongoing issue of providing the student with remediation or compensatory training (e.g., instruction in taking notes or a note taker and/or a tape recorder) continues into the postsecondary years. Although not common, in some instances it is possible to combine the two approaches. The use of a word processor as a compensatory aid to a student for essay writing might serve to improve her writing skills in general. Other troublesome policy decisions center around curricular requirements (e.g., waiving foreign language) and course load recommendations (reduced loads versus development of time-management skills). Brinckerhoff, Shaw, and McGuire (1992) pose a rhetorical question: "Is it [the goal of postsecondary services for students with learning disabilities] to prepare students for the challenge of adult life or to help them to function in school so they can eventually graduate?" (p. 425). They further wonder whether these differing goals are not mutually exclusive. In their own answer to these questions they assert that, after years of experience with secondary LD programs, the incompatibility is apparent to them.

Brinckerhoff, Shaw, and McGuire (1992) also note that strictly legal accommodations might prove to be insufficient for students with learning disabilities and that effective accommodations are very difficult to deliver without substantial attention to individual student needs. The needs are many, particularly for students with learning disabilities who may be facing college underprepared, with both skills deficits and curricular deficiencies from having taken noncollege-preparatory secondary programs. As more students with learning disabilities attempt postsecondary education and colleges and universities are offering far greater support services for them, the retention and completion rates are not encouraging (Durlak, Rose, & Bursuck, 1994). Task persistence and long-term goal setting are both needed for successful independent learning as are problem solving, time management, note taking, test taking, organization of written language, textbook reading, and monitoring strategy use (Bursuck & Jayanthi, 1993). Task persistence may be difficult for students with learning disabilities who have experienced repeated frustration and failure. Further, they may be disinclined to formulate long-term goals when simply getting through an immediate crisis is always more pressing. Both require "a long-term commitment that persists even in the presence of short-term failures; a commitment that...college students with LDs may lack due to a history of failure" (Bursuck & Jayanthi, 1993, p. 181).

Setting Standards

The variable performance of students with learning disabilities has been a source of concern for college administrators for many years. At Harvard, waivers for a select few students whose difficulties with foreign language could not be linked to a lack of motivation or overriding anxiety were made as early as the 1950s (Ganschow & Sparks, 1993). This curricular modification substantially predates even the defining of learning disabilities, much less the move to establish legal mandates for disability accommodations on college campuses. In terms of students with learning disabilities and foreign language requirements, choices on the college campus include various accommodations short of waivers, such as special sections offered at a slower pace, a shift in emphasis from oral language to written language, the provision of tutorial support, and enhanced instructional approaches. The student could also make choices that avoid the need for a waiver or accommodations, such as selecting a major that does not require foreign language. However, this option would be of no help to the secondary student who needs foreign language credits to receive the college-prep high school diploma necessary for admission to many colleges.

The variable nature of what constitutes a learning disability is certainly at play at the postsecondary level. Students might perceive themselves to be comfortably above average while attending a community college but appear to develop symptoms of learning disabilities when attempting to compete at an Ivy League university. Indeed, Brinckerhoff, Shaw, and McGuire (1992) note that Mellard recommended the adjustment of eligibility criteria for learning disabilities according to specific postsecondary settings. A student is normal at the state university, but becomes learning disabled upon matriculating at a more demanding institution. Eligibility criteria already vary from state to state, and even district to district at the elementary and secondary level. Perhaps such variability at the college level would only be a continuation of the state of affairs already practiced in public education today.

Decision Point 7.2: Accommodation of
Disabilities Through Developmental Courses

Arguments for Proposition One   Many students may find the need for a bridge between their secondary programs and the performance levels expected on a college campus. The reasons for this need include poor preparation during secondary school, student selection of a noncollege prep course of study in high school, student adjustments in moving to a college environment, and disability-specific academic difficulties. A student may be prepared for the college experience psychologically, socially, and academically with the exception of one area of deficiency. The availability of developmental courses on the college campus allows such students to progress in all other areas of development and education while simultaneously addressing deficit areas. It would be unreasonably punitive were such students required to remain in high school, complete adult education courses, or attend a preparatory program to clear such isolated skill deficits before being

---

Proposition One
Colleges should offer developmental courses and other remedial supports to enhance the educational opportunities of youth with disabilities and others whose secondary programs provided insufficient preparation for collegiate academic success.

---

admitted to college. Students with disabilities would be particularly vulnerable.

The opportunities associated with attendance at colleges and universities must be as open to students with disabilities as to those without disabilities. The college environment sets the stage for personal development and maturation well beyond the expansion of one's academic knowledge. Although some students may lack sufficient skills to succeed immediately in all college-level courses, they should not have their life opportunities reduced or removed because of relatively minor deficiencies. Since their secondary programs failed to bring them to a point at which they could perform successfully in college-level classes, they need the availability of developmental courses to ease their transition to postsecondary education. The availability of such courses can make a dramatic difference in the educational outcomes for these students. It affords them the college environment in which to explore their interests and discover their abilities, some of which may have previously been hidden by the biases held by teachers and peers who may have focused more on their disabilities than their strengths. The opportunities to learn cooperation and collegiality through dorm life, discover outside interests through special-interest clubs and cultural events, and develop greater coping skills for successful academic performance must be as available for students with disabilities as they are for the general population of youth. The inclusion of a few developmental courses in college offerings seems a minor effort toward increasing the chances of a successful postsecondary schooling outcome for students with disabilities.

The Nature of Support Structures   The support services that college students with disabilities require vary with the nature of the disability. For students with physical and sensory impairments, there are few, if any, arguments about the nature of these support structures. However, students with learning disabilities are equally deserving of accommodations on our college campuses. The offering of developmental courses and other remedial services (e.g., tutoring) enables such students to fill the gaps and continue the progression of their studies. Such an approach allows them to operate as autonomous students on campus, attending class and maintaining a schedule and assignments just like all other students, while simultaneously receiving remedial instruction. The remediation is embedded in the developmental courses and offered through tutoring services for any course required in the student's program.

Students enrolled in college-level courses who have exited their secondary programs unprepared for college-level work will get little more from available support personnel working with them in a compensatory manner than they did at the secondary level. The time pressures of college terms and the students' lack of prerequisite skills will doom them to an endless series of crises if compensatory techniques are the only available option. Compensatory programs without remediation create dependence patterns that do not further the students' autonomy, independence, or self-esteem, much less their progress toward graduation. Further, overdependence on accommodations made by professors or arranged by support personnel does not reflect the work world that follows college. The student who needs more time to take a test will not get paid to take longer to do the same work that others do quickly. Taking fewer courses each term, with program completion extending well beyond four years, might ease the student's load as a college student but does not give the person an opportunity to experience true time management with full-time commitments.

What job accommodations would it be reasonable to expect of employers hiring individuals with learning disabilities? Legally, an individual seeking employment must be qualified and able to perform the essential functions of a job. However, the employer must also provide reasonable accommodations to a qualified applicant who is disabled. Giving a student more time to take a test or read an assignment does not carry the equivalent implications for an employer who is asked to give an employee more time to complete projects. If accommodations would constitute an "undue hardship" on the employer or alter the basic nature of the job, they are not required. To illustrate, one would not be required to hire and provide a spell checker for an applicant for a proofreading job whose learning disabilities caused her to read slowly and be unable to detect spelling errors on her own. However, a schoolteacher unable to qualify for a bus driver's license might be accommodated by having driving duties shifted to another employee (Grossman, 1992). Self-accommodations that rely on the use of outside assistance from others might be challenged as well. If the employee is dependent on others to perform the essential functions of his job, the job has inadvertently been restructured; therefore, the person employed is not qualified for the job. Needing a ride to get to work or assistive technology to perform one's responsibilities is an appropriate accommodation for employers to make. Faculty and staff struggling with the appropriateness of accommodations and allowances at the postsecondary level can use the future work environment as a barometer for evaluating their own decisions.

Setting Standards The courts have consistently ruled that postsecondary institutions are not expected to lower standards or overlook significant physical qualifications needed to perform satisfactorily in their programs. The inclusion of developmental courses in college offerings is not intended to force a lowering of standards, but affords students the opportunity to boost isolated deficits up to the college level before they tackle college material related to that particular subject. Certainly, a student who needed developmental English need not be accepted as a journalism major, but should encounter far less difficulty if pursuing a program of study in which writing skills are less crucial. Likewise, a student deficient in mathematics could pursue many majors in which math is a minimal component of the course of study.

Some community colleges and junior colleges have open admission policies for all in-state high school graduates. Graduates who were served by special education are equally eligible, regardless of any diagnostic labels they might have. Some of this group are likely to need developmental English and mathematics courses in order to succeed. The open admission policy sets the moral expectation that those admitted have at least some minimal likelihood of succeeding. Developmental courses, then, appropriately complement open admission policies.

Argument Summary The provision of developmental courses and other remedial supports on college campuses does not necessitate the lowering of any existing standard for admission or retention. However, it does open the door for many otherwise qualified students with disabilities who have isolated basic skill deficits to matriculate and progress into college. These supports offer the ideal bridge to college-level material for students who need the benefit of a remedial course within a college setting. Students can become accustomed to the college environment and course structure while completing one or two courses with content that is familiar and not immediately overwhelming.

Arguments for Proposition Two To offer a series of remedial or developmental courses for students unable to succeed in the regular college curriculum is of no real benefit to the student and inherently unfair to those who may have been denied admission. The notion of admitting individuals to college who are not really equipped to engage in college-level work can actually cause harm by distracting college personnel from their responsibilities toward qualified students and depleting resources as well. Spending time in developmental courses on a college campus can undermine a student's self-concept and actually delay his pursuit of appropriate educational training or employment opportunities if college proves to be too difficult. For students who are interested in continuing an academic education but who lack the skills needed to enter college-level programs, careful career counseling combined with enrollment in community-based adult education courses (which are far cheaper than equivalent courses taken on a college campus) can provide them with continuing opportunities to achieve the skills needed for college entrance. The solutions to inadequate secondary preparation should not include this downward creeping of college missions to help compensate for resulting student deficiencies. Far more appropriate and individualized compensatory plans can meet the needs of students with disabilities.

The Nature of Support Structures The low rates of enrollment and high rates of attrition for college students with learning disabilities indicate that existing support

---

Proposition Two
Colleges should not offer developmental courses because they are not part of any course of study and lead to no degree, cost the same as courses taken for degree credit, and create for students a false sense of progress. Support services on a college campus should be compensatory in nature, not remedial.

services are inadequate. The argument in support of admitting students with known deficits to college and placing them in developmental courses on college campuses is oxymoronic. It is contradictory to argue that a student is qualified to attend college, but only if that college offers less than college-level material. Once a qualified student is admitted and enrolled in college-level courses, the provision of appropriate compensatory programs and support structures is not only appropriate, but also mandated by law.

The college support system must be clearly differentiated from the dependency models prevalent in secondary schools (Yost, Shaw, Cullen, & Bigaj, 1994). Yost, Shaw, Cullen, and Bigaj surveyed a variety of colleges regarding the types of services available and attitudes of college personnel toward the needs of adult learners. The results indicate that, in fact, a greater emphasis is placed on providing services that promote dependence than those that foster independence and self-determination, even at the college level. Many of the college support programs had no plans to reduce the students' reliance on the LD services or increase their self-advocacy skills. Raskind and Scott (1993) note that compensatory support services are preferable to remediation because most students with learning disabilities carry a negative attitude toward remedial services. Further, the remedial approach is one that takes much longer and might not be of much benefit for the student who eventually needs to register for college-level courses and learn the required material by the end of the term.

The design of programs aimed at greater self-determination could become a critical variable in the effort to increase the number of students with learning disabilities completing their studies. Self-determination is related to the assumption of personal responsibility for goals, accomplishments, and setbacks, and includes personal characteristics of assertiveness, self-advocacy, creativity, and independence (Durlak, Rose, & Bursuck, 1994). These powerful personal traits will have a substantial impact on a person's career choices, education, vocation, and life pursuits. The "teachability" of self-determination skills was the focus of an investigation by Durlak, Rose, and Bursuck (1994). Specifically, they considered four skills—stating the nature of one's disability and individual strengths and weaknesses, stating the impact of the disability on academic and social performance, identifying accommodations that might be of help, and identifying strategies for arranging accommodations within their regular classroom settings. Their findings support the notion that students can be taught these skills, although some of the students were unable to generalize the skills outside the training sessions. Durlak, Rose, and Bursuck speculate that parents and special educators may have encouraged an inappropriate dependency by protecting and advocating when the students should have been encouraged to do more self-advocating.

Setting Standards For faculty at the postsecondary level, the issue of reasonable accommodations arises well after the time of a student's admission to the institution. The admission decision should indicate that the student with disabilities has met the academic and technical standards for the program. Therefore, the provision of reasonable accommodations for such students is not an optional act of charity for their instructors but a legal obligation (Rose, 1993). However, the adjective *reasonable* is obviously subject to wide variance in interpretation. Rose draws a parallel between the need for extended time on a test and taking unfinished work home or staying at the office for extra hours when one has fallen behind at work. However, he also notes that in some instances the argument for extended time is inappropriate, as when a nursing student must demonstrate the ability to take fast, effective lifesaving measures. Real standards must retain their value equally for all, whereas standards that are arbitrarily biased on the basis of disability, race, or gender must be challenged.

Brinckerhoff, Shaw, and McGuire (1992) have attributed the lack of preparedness of college students with learning disabilities back to their following of noncollege preparatory courses of study while in high school. Their logic then followed that, because of this unpreparedness, developmental courses should be made available to these students. At the time the student was enrolled in secondary school, the curricular path was chosen by the student and a multidisciplinary team based on the academic abilities and aspirations of the student. A reasonable presumption is that the student found the college-prep program too difficult and opted for a standard program instead. Having avoided the college-prep program in secondary school, the student would naturally face difficulties when attempting to compete at the college level. The necessary prerequisite courses were open and available to the student while in high school and need not be offered again on a college campus. It is not the responsibility of college administrators to provide a curriculum to students that compensates for deficiencies in their self-selected secondary course of study.

Argument Summary Enrollment in college involves risk financially, emotionally, and psychologically. For the student with disabilities, admission to college that results in failure can do more harm than a denial that redirects the individual to another more appropriate postsecondary alternative. Students with disabilities who are prepared to succeed in college-level courses belong on college campuses. Those who need developmental courses should take advantage of adult education courses and/or attend additional preparatory classes rather than look to college programs to deliver remedial studies. It is critical that suitable compensatory support systems be made available to those who qualify and enroll in college-level courses and who choose to take advantage of such services.

CLOSING THOUGHTS

The best suggestions for reform take many different directions. Some cry for functional relevance and improved links between secondary schools and employment opportunities, whereas others believe that students with disabilities need opportunities to develop greater autonomy and independence in thinking. Autonomy and self-determination may be a far greater need than either watered-down academic curricula or singular and quickly outdated vocational training. The overwhelming tendency has been for weaknesses in schooling to become the targets of "systemic reform," which sounds impressive until translated into linear means–ends connections, a new curriculum, and test measures to determine effectiveness (Goodlad, 1994).

The improved efforts at planning for the transition from secondary programs into postsecondary training and/or employment do not preclude the adult from dropping out, or losing a job in the future. A disability may contribute to the circumstances associated with such a lack of success, as might be the case if a student were unable to perform well in college classes even with regular attendance and the use of other supports. On the other hand, circumstances could have nothing whatsoever to do with a disability, as would be the case of job layoffs due to plant closings. At these future points of transition, an adult might choose to ignore available support services, be unaware of their availability, or use such services. If an adult is functioning well in her employment and personal life adjustment, having no real need for support services beyond her normal personal resources, she may have no need to continue to carry the label of disabled. If, however, she continues to experience difficulties that can be attributed to a disability, further support services might be sporadically needed well beyond the transition from secondary education programs.

The precise numbers of people confronting significant problems as adults due to disabilities are rather illusive. Jacobs and Hendricks (1992) note that the estimates of adults with learning disabilities range from five million to eleven million, based on numbers of children served by school programs. Some who were so labeled during their years in school might blend into the adult population and lead successful productive lives, no longer needing or receiving any benefits from the label. Others might drop the label but continue to face frustrations and failures associated with their learning disabilities. Adults with moderate to severe cognitive impairments or sensory or physical impairments have no such option, but may or may not choose or need to tap into disability support services as adults.

Any conceived curricular reform should not just reflect previous follow-up studies that document the unemployment and dropout rates of students labeled as learning disabled in high school, but also must be in touch with the future of society. Entry-level jobs are abundant because there is a reduction of sixteen- to twenty-four-year olds entering the job market (a drop from 23% to 20% between 1972 and 1986, with projections for the percentage to drop to 16% by 2000). However, these jobs do not often pay sufficiently to allow one to live independently. The prevalence of jobs that provide a middle-class standard of living is shrinking, while low-paying service jobs are being added to the workforce. Further, low-skilled and semi-skilled jobs in the manufacturing sector will be decreasing. The greatest growth will be seen in high-technology fields and information management, which require skilled workers (White, 1992). The teacher's job is to design an instructional program that makes a direct link to the real tasks that students will be facing as working adults.

REFERENCES

Blackorby, J., & Wagner, M. (1996). Longitudinal postschool outcomes of youth with disabilities: Findings from the National Longitudinal Transition Study. *Exceptional Children, 62,* 399–414.

Blalock, J. W. (1982). Residual learning disabilities in young adults: Implications for rehabilitation. *Journal of Applied Rehabilitation Counseling, 13,* 9–13.

Boyer-Stephens, A., & Kearns, D. (1988). Functional curriculum for transition. *Journal for Vocational Special Needs Education, 11,* 13–18.

Brinckerhoff, L. C., Shaw, S. F., & McGuire, J. M. (1992). Promoting access, accommodations, and independence for college students with learning disabilities. *Journal of Learning Disabilities, 25,* 417–429.

Brown, D. S., & Gerber, P. J. (1992). Introduction: Special issue on employment. *Learning Disabilities Quarterly, 15,* 235–36.

Browning, P., Dunn, C., & Brown, C. (1993). School to community transition for youth with disabilities. In R. C. Eaves & P. J. McLaughlin (Eds.), *Recent advances in special education and rehabilitation* (pp. 193–209). Boston: Andover Medical Publishers.

Bursuck, W. D., & Jayanthi, M. (1993). Strategy instruction: Programming for independent study skill usage. In S. A. Vogel & P. B. Adelman (Eds.), *Success for college students with learning disabilities* (pp. 177–205). New York: Springer-Verlag.

Bursuck, W. D., & Rose, E. (1992). Community college options for students with mild disabilities. In F. R. Rusch, L. DeStefano, J. Chadsey-Rusch, L. A. Phelps, & E. Szymanski (Eds.), *Transition from school to adult life: Models, linkages, and policy* (pp. 71–92). Pacific Grove, CA: Brooks/Cole.

Cobb, R. M., & Crump, W. D. (1984). Post-school status of young adults identified as learning disabled while enrolled in public schools: A comparison of those enrolled and not enrolled in learning disabilities programs (Final Report). Washington, DC: Special Education Programs, Division of Educational Services.

Connell, J. P. (1985). A new multidimensional measure of children's perceptions of control. *Child Development, 56,* 1018–1041.

deBettencourt, L. U., Zigmond, N., & Thornton, H. S. (1989). Follow-up of post-secondary age rural learning disabled graduates and dropouts. *Exceptional Children, 56,* 40–49.

Deci, E. L., Hodges, M., Pierson, L., & Tomassone, J. (1992). Autonomy and competence as motivational factors in students with learning disabilities and emotional handicaps. *Journal of Learning Disabilities, 25,* 457–471.

DeStefano, L., & Wagner, M. (1993). Outcome assessment in special education: Implications for decision-making and long term planning in vocational rehabilitation. *Career Development for Exceptional Individuals, 16,* 147–158.

Dowdy, C. A., Carter, J. K., & Smith, T. E. C. (1990). Differences in transitional needs of high school students with and without learning disabilities. *Journal of Learning Disabilities, 2,* 343–348.

Durlak, C. M., Rose, E., & Bursuck, W. D. (1994). Preparing high school students with learning disabilities for the transition to postsecondary education: Teaching the skills of self-determination. *Journal of Learning Disabilities, 27,* 51–59.

Edgar, E. (1987). Secondary programs in special education: Are many of them justifiable? *Exceptional Children, 53,* 555–561.

Ellis, E. S. (1990). What's so strategic about teaching teachers to teach strategies. *Teacher Education and Special Education, 13,* 59–62.

Elrod, G. F. (1987). Academic and social skills pre-requisite to success in vocational training. *Journal for Vocational Special Needs Education, 10,* 17–21.

Fourqurean, J. M., Meisgeir, C., Swank, P. R., & Williams, R. E. (1991). Correlates of postsecondary employment outcomes for young adults with learning disabilities. *Journal of Learning Disabilities, 2,* 400–405.

Gajar, A., Goodman, L., & McAfee, J. (1993). *Secondary schools and beyond: Transition of individuals with mild disabilities.* New York: Merrill.

Ganschow, L., & Sparks, R. (1993). "Foreign" language learning disabilities: Issues, research, and teaching implications. In S. A. Vogel & P. B. Adelman (Eds.), *Success for college students with learning disabilities* (pp. 283–322). New York: Springer-Verlag.

Gerber, M. M. (1994). Postmodernism in special education. *Journal of Special Education, 28,* 368–378.

Gerber, P. J. (1992). Personal perspective—at first glance: Employment for people with learning disabilities at the beginning of the Americans-with-Disabilities-Act era. *Learning Disabilities Quarterly, 15,* 330–332.

Gerber, P. J., Ginsberg, R., & Reiff, H. B. (1992). Identifying alterable patterns in employment success for highly successful adults with learning disabilities. *Journal of Learning Disabilities, 25,* 475–487.

Goodlad, J. I. (1994). *Educational renewal: Better teachers, better schools.* San Francisco: Jossey-Bass.

Gottfredson, L. S., & Becker, H. J. (1981). A challenge to vocational psychology: How important are aspirations in determining male career development? *Journal of Vocational Behavior, 18,* 121–137.

Grolnick, W. S., & Ryan, R. M. (1990). Self-perceptions, motivation, and adjustment in children with learning disabilities: A multiple group comparison study. *Journal of Learning Disabilities, 23,* 177–184.

Grolnick, W. S., Ryan, R. M., & Deci, E. L. (1991). The inner resources for school achievement: Motivational mediators of children's perceptions of their parents. *Journal of Educational Psychology, 83,* 508–517.

Grossman, P. D. (1992). Employment discrimination law for the learning disabled community. *Learning Disabilities Quarterly, 15,* 287–329.

Halloran, W. D. (1993). Transition services requirement: Issues, implications, challenge. In R. C. Eaves & P. J. McLaughlin (Eds.), *Recent advances in special education and rehabilitation,* Boston: Andover Medical Publishers.

Halpern, A. S. (1985). Transition: A look at the foundations. *Exceptional Children, 51,* 479–486.

Halpern, A. S., Yovanoff, P., Doren, B., & Benz, M. R. (1995). Predicting participation in postsecondary education for school leavers with disabilities. *Exceptional Children, 62,* 151–164.

Hasazi, S. B., Hock, M. L., & Cravedi-Cheng, L. (1992). Vermont's post-school indicators: Using satisfaction and postschool outcome data for program improvement. In F. R. Rusch, L. DeStefano, J. Chadsey-Rusch, L. A. Phelps, & E. Szymanski (Eds.), *Transition from school to adult life: Models, linkages, and policy* (pp. 485–506). Pacific Grove, CA: Brooks/Cole Publishing Co.

Hughes, C. A., & Suritsky, S. K. (1994). Note-taking skills of university students with and without learning disabilities. *Journal of Learning Disabilities, 27,* 20–24.

Jacobs, A. E., & Hendricks, D. J. (1992). Job accommodations for adults with learning disabilities: Brilliantly disguised opportunities. *Learning Disabilities Quarterly, 15,* 274–286.

Laramie County Community College. (1995). *Academic progress of developmental students, Fall 1993–Spring 1995.* Cheyenne, WY: Author. (ERIC Document Reproduction No. ED 386 236).

McDonnell, J., Mathot-Buckner, C., & Ferguson, B. (1996). *Transition programs for students with moderate/severe disabilities.* Pacific Grove, CA: Brooks/Cole.

McDonnell, J., Wilcox, B., & Boles, S. M. (1986). Do we know enough to plan for transition? A national survey of state agencies responsible for service to persons with severe handicaps. *Journal of the Association for Persons with Severe Handicaps, 11,* 53–60.

Mellard, D. F., & Hazel, S. (1992). Social competencies as a pathway to successful life transitions. *Learning Disabilities Quarterly, 15,* 251–273.

Minskoff, E. H., & DeMoss, S. (1992). Facilitating successful transition: Using the TRAC model to assess and develop academic skills needed for vocational competence. *Learning Disabilities Quarterly, 16,* 161–170.

Mithaug, D. E., Martin, J. E., & Agran, M. (1987). Adaptability instruction: The goal of transitional programming. *Exceptional Children, 53,* 500–505.

Nisbett, J., Covert, S., & Schuh, M. (1992). Family involvement in the transition from school to adult life. In F. R. Rusch, L. DeStefano, J. Chadsey-Rusch, L. A. Phelps, & E. Szymanski (Eds.), *Transition from school to adult life: Models, linkages, and policy* (pp. 407–424). Pacific Grove, CA: Brooks/Cole.

Okolo, C. M., & Sitlington, P. L. (1986). The role of special education in LD adolescents' transition from school to work. *Learning Disabilities Quarterly, 9,* 141–155.

Patton, J. R., & Polloway, E. A. (1992). Learning disabilities: The challenges of adulthood. *Journal of Learning Disabilities, 25,* 410–416.

Peraino, J. M. (1993). Post-21 follow-up studies. How do special education graduates fare? In P. Wehman (Ed.), *Life beyond the classroom: Transition strategies for young people with disabilities* (pp. 21–70). Baltimore: Paul H. Brookes.

Raskind, M. H., & Scott, N. G. (1993). Technology for postsecondary students with learning disabilities. In S. A. Vogel & P. B. Adelman (Eds.), *Success for college students with learning disabilities* (pp. 240–280). New York: Springer-Verlag.

Reiff, H. B., & deFur, S. (1992). Transition for youths with learning disabilities: A focus on developing independence. *Learning Disabilities Quarterly, 15,* 237–250.

Reiff, H. B., Ginsberg, R., & Gerber, P. J. (1995). New perspectives on teaching from successful adults with learning disabilities. *Remedial and Special Education, 16,* 29–37.

Repetto, J. B. (1995). Curriculum beyond school walls: Implications of transition education. *Peabody Journal of Education, 70,* 125–140.

Rojewski, J. W. (1994). Applying theories of career behavior to special populations: Implications for secondary vocational transition programming. *Issues in Special Education and Rehabilitation, 9,* 7–26.

Rojewski, J. W. (1996). Educational and occupational aspirations of high school seniors with learning disabilities. *Exceptional Children, 62,* 463–476.

Rose, E. (1993). Faculty development: Changing attitudes and enhancing knowledge about learning disabilities. In S. A. Vogel & P. B. Adelman (Eds.), *Success for college students with learning disabilities* (pp. 131–150). New York: Springer-Verlag.

Shapiro, E. S., & Lentz, F. E. (1991). Vocational–technical programs: Follow-up of students with learning disabilities. *Exceptional Children, 58,* 47–59.

Sinclair Community College, Office of Institutional Planning and Research. (1994). *The impact of developmental education on student progress: A three year longitudinal analysis.* Dayton, OH: Author. (ERIC Document Reproduction No. ED 383 382).

Sitlington, P., & Frank, A. R. (1990). Are adolescents with learning disabilities successfully crossing the bridge into adult life? *Learning Disabilities Quarterly, 13,* 97–111.

Suritsky, S. K., & Hughes, C. A. (1991). Benefits of note-taking: Implications for secondary and post-secondary students with learning disabilities. *Learning Disabilities Quarterly, 14,* 7–18.

Szymanski, E. M. (1994). Transition: Life-span and life-space considerations for empowerment. *Exceptional Children, 60,* 402–410.

U.S. Department of Education. (1994). *Sixteenth annual report to Congress on the implementation of the Individuals with Disabilities Education Act.* Washington, DC: Author.

U.S. Department of Education. (1995). *Seventeenth annual report to Congress on the implementation of the Individuals with Disabilities Education Act.* Washington, DC: Author.

U.S. General Accounting Office. (1990, May). *Training strategies: Preparing noncollege youths for employment in the U.S. and foreign countries.* (GAO/HRD-90-98). Washington, DC: Author.

Wagner, M. (1989). *The transition experiences of youth with disabilities: A report from the national longitudinal transition study.* (USDOE, DSEP Contract #300-87-0054). Menlo Park, CA: SRI International.

Wagner, M. (1991). *Youth with disabilities: How are they doing?* Palo Alto, CA: SRI International.

Wagner, M., & Blackorby, J. (1996). Transition from high school to work or college: How special education students fare. *The Future of Children, 6,* 103–120.

Ward, M. J., & Halloran, W. D. (1993). Transition issues for the 1990s. *Office of Special Education and Rehabilitative Services News in Print, VI,* 4–5.

Wehman, P. (1993). Transition from school to adulthood for young people with disabilities: Critical issues and policies. In R. C. Eaves & P. J. McLaughlin (Eds.), *Recent advances in special education and rehabilitation* (pp. 178–192). Boston: Andover Medical Publishers.

White, W. J. (1992). The postschool adjustment of persons with learning disabilities: Current status and future projections. *Journal of Learning Disabilities, 25,* 448–456.

White, W. J., Schumaker, J. B., Warner, M. M., Alley, G., & Deshler, D. D. (1980). The current status of young adults identified as learning disabled during their school career (Tech Report No. 21). Lawrence, KS: University of Kansas, Institute for Research in Learning Disabilities.

Yost, D. S., Shaw, S. F., Cullen, J. P., & Bigaj, S. J. (1994). Practices and attitudes of postsecondary LD service providers in North America. *Journal of Learning Disabilities, 27,* 631–640.

Zigmond, N., & Miller, S. E. (1992). Improving high school programs for students with learning disabilities: A matter of substance as well as form. In F. R. Rusch, L. DeStefano, J. Chadsey-Rusch, L. A. Phelps, & E. Szymanski (Eds.), *Transition from school to adult life: Models, linkages, and policy* (pp. 17–32). Pacific Grove, CA: Brooks/Cole.

Zigmond, N., & Thornton, H. (1985). Follow-up study of postsecondary age learning disabled graduates and dropouts. *Learning Disabilities Research, 1,* 50–55.

8

Teacher Preparation
Practices and Licensure
Standards

INTRODUCTION

The preparation and licensure of special education teachers have become vital components of many teacher education programs throughout the United States. Typically, personnel from state departments of education work collaboratively with faculty at institutions of higher education to set licensure categories and standards and to establish a program approval process. State department personnel further assume the responsibility for developing comprehensive state plans for personnel development, which include strategies for reducing any special education shortages. Although particular locales may have sufficient teachers and positions for low-incidence disability groups (e.g., visual impairments, deaf/blind) may be limited, there is generally a shortage of special education teachers throughout the nation. This shortage is influenced by at least two significant factors: the ever increasing population of preschool and school-age students certified as requiring special education (Simpson, Whelan, & Zabel, 1993; U.S. Department of Education, 1995) and a high teacher attrition rate in special education (Fuchs & Fuchs, 1995). Nationwide, 7.3% (17,500) leave the profession annually, with rates estimated as high as 30% to 50% in some districts (Fuchs & Fuchs, 1995). In fact, approximately 50% of all new teachers leave the classroom by their fifth year of teaching (Smith-Davis, 1991). Brownell and Smith (1993) identified five variables contributing to the special education attrition rates, including historical influences (e.g., scope of preservice preparation; teacher characteristics such as age, race, gender, and academic ability), bureaucratic policies that formalize service delivery, external influences (e.g., life cycle and economic considerations), and environmental influences of the workplace. Each year that brings an increase in students needing teachers, increases in teacher resignations in special education, and reductions in the number of persons completing traditional special education licensure programs, school administrators are forced to hire more unprepared teachers for some of the most challenging teaching positions available.

Categorical and Noncategorical Licensure

One of the issues related to the availability of credentialed teachers is the number and categories of special education licensure. Teacher licensure generally follows state decisions regarding categorical/noncategorical delivery of services to PreK–12 students. Since each state is responsible for developing its own standards and requirements, the current teacher licensure requirements related to special education are fraught with confusion and inconsistency (Cranston-Gingras & Mauser, 1992). In fact, the problem is evident in all areas of education. For example, a 1987 national study identified 181 different titles for teaching positions and requirements for dual licensure for special education teachers in eighteen states (Fearn, 1987). Chapey, Pystowski, and Trimarco (1985) noted that twenty-five states were moving toward noncategorical special education licensure, while twenty-five plus the District of Columbia remained categorical.

The overwhelming influence that licensure policies exert over teacher education programs is perceived as virtually dictatorial in regard to categorical versus noncategorical teacher education programs by special education faculty (McLaughlin, Valdivieso, Spence & Fuller, 1988). In a national survey of licensure practices related to the areas of learning disabilities, mental retardation, and emotional disturbance, including all fifty states, Putnam and Habanek (1993) found confusion in licensure categories, grade combinations, requirements for general education licensure as a prerequisite for special education licensure, and terminology used. From the surveys, they were able to gather usable data on forty-eight states. Of those, 54% offer licensure in LD and MR, and 58% offer licensure in ED. However, some of these states also offer generic noncategorical or multicategorical licensure options, with a total of thirty-two (of the forty-eight) states offering generic licensure for mild to moderate disabilities. Fifteen of the forty-eight states (35%) expect special education teachers to hold a credential in regular education also. For the states that have a generic mild to moderate disabilities licensure area, there are further discrepancies in what is included or excluded. Some include LD, MR, and ED; some exclude ED but include the others; and other states seem to use the category exclusively for teachers whose students are certified as mentally retarded, having categorical licensure in the other areas. Between the Chapey et al. study in 1985 and the Putnam and Habanek findings from 1993, it appears that the number of states offering a generic/noncategorical licensure rose from twenty-five to thirty-two (of forty-eight). The trend is obviously in this direction but may be influenced by the continued categorical labeling of students required for IDEA funding. The categorical/noncategorical teacher licensure patterns remain a great source of frustration for special educators moving across state lines as well as developers of teacher examinations for use in multiple states.

Reform in Education

The education field in the 1990s is inundated with reform at all levels, including much attention directed toward the reformation of teacher education. While much of this reform emphasis has been on general teacher education, special education has begun commanding greater attention as its enrollments and funding allotments increase, inclusion becomes more common, and co-teaching models of service delivery are used more frequently. Reform debates have included the extent to which a liberal education is critical to educators, the types and timing of field experiences, and the role of school-based personnel in teacher preparation. Romanish (1993) bemoans the lack of teacher voice in the reform movement, noting that the bottom line for the efficacy of education reform efforts seems to be linked to children's test scores. Such a basis for reform creates a dangerous proposition for the special educator seeking effective inclusion and shared responsibility and partnership with the general education teachers in the school.

One of the reform issues has centered on the knowledge base appropriate for beginning teachers. The value of liberal arts courses, content specializations, and pedagogical content are debated. Questions are asked about what future teachers need to know and be able to do at the point of completion of an initial licensure program. Sorting out the volumes of knowledge from which we have to choose, deciding what gets covered and what is left for another day, and determining who has the authority and qualifications to make such determinations are at stake. Currently, these decisions are made by teacher educators who operate within the context of accrediting bodies and their myriad of standards, state licensure requirements, and the professional examinations that fall between graduation and licensure. In fact, Goodlad (1994) has noted the domination and control of curriculum by the systemics of schooling (e.g., texts, tests, Carnegie units, graduation requirements) and the mechanics of teaching to the detriment of the educational role of schools. However, politicians have challenged the qualifications and rights of teacher educators to determine the nature and scope of licensure requirements, enacting a wide variety of legislation allowing and supporting alternative routes to the teaching field. Pugach (1992) considers absence of programmatic coherence as a prevailing problem historically inherent in teacher education.

One of the most sweeping reforms emanating from the field of special education is the move toward inclusion. Although the concept of least restrictive environment has been a part of special education law since 1975, the shift from "mainstreaming" to "inclusion" represents more than another semantical evolution characteristic of special education and certainly has significant implications for teacher education programs. For the most part, however, the inclusion model of education has not been established in teacher education programs prior to its implementation in the field. Special educators, trained through recent preservice programs, inservice sessions, and their own experience, have sought to take the concepts of inclusion to the grass-roots level and make changes in their own practices and the practices of educators with whom they work. General educators with whom special educators seek to collaborate typically have very limited training in the field of special education and vary widely in their interest in and commitment to the education of students with special needs. Even today, at the preservice level, training in the consultant model is typically only given to the special educator, who then strikes out to "consult" with general educators who, whether they are veterans or first-year teachers, may be neither aware of nor trained in the consultant model.

Focus of Discussion

There are obviously many issues related to the preparation of both special and general educators. Some encompass all of education, such as the role of school-based personnel in teacher education, the move toward national professional licensure standards, and the homogeneity of the teaching force (discussed in Chapter 2). Others relate more specifically and directly to the field of special education. Two such topics are addressed in the remainder of this chapter. The first is the issue of reorganization in higher education settings to integrate special education and general education faculty and programs. Second is the appropriateness and value of alternative routes to teaching, with particular emphasis on special education. Although not unique to special education, this process is particularly relevant because of the chronic shortages of personnel in the field combined with the challenge of working with students who have been unable to succeed.

REORGANIZING TEACHER EDUCATION

Special education teacher preparation programs are most commonly found as separate from those of general education, whether they be located within the same department or in a distinct special education department (Heller, 1992). However, there is unquestionably a trend within higher education to reorganize special and general education faculty and programs into alternative configurations. Fuchs and Fuchs (1995) point to data from the Higher Education Consortium on Special Education (HECSE) that reflect this trend. Thirty-nine of the forty-five universities that grant doctoral degrees in special education and form the HECSE group responded to a survey regarding the placement of special education programs within their institutions. The number reporting the existence of separate special education departments dropped from thirty-six in 1987 to twenty-five in 1992, a 31% drop over that five-year period. Further evidence indicating that this trend is viewed favorably by a majority in the field and will most likely continue was apparent by the results of a survey conducted by Putnam, Spiegel, and Bruininks (1995). Although the disappearance of special education as a separate department within higher education might be the trend, and viewed as desirable by many special educators (e.g., Pugach, 1992), there are voices warning against the move (e.g., Fuchs & Fuchs, 1995; Heller, 1992). At issue are not only administrative structures, but also programmatic content and delivery. Although related, these separate issues can be used in favor of and/or against one another.

The Knowledge Base in Teacher Education

The Council for Exceptional Children (1995) has put forth a set of international standards for the preparation and certification of special education teachers, including both general and categorically specific standards. Other professional organizations have stipulated standards specific to their disciplines as well. Some categorical licensure areas within special education, particularly hearing impairments/deaf and visual impairments, require highly specialized knowledge and skills. In general education, similar specializations can also be found, including areas such as foreign languages and the sciences. However, in order for an institution to receive accreditation for its teacher education programs, those programs must be built upon a research-based common body of professional knowledge (National Council for Accreditation of Teacher Education, 1987). There is an expectation that teacher education programs offer the prospective teacher, regardless of licensure area, a succinct body of knowledge related to the act of teaching. The task of selecting a definitive knowledge base for teacher education programs generally triggers debate among faculty about preferred theoretical orientations, prioritization of content, and depth of coverage appropriate for particular topics. However, this generic body of knowledge generally covers basic information, such as the effects of teacher expectations on learners, characteristics of effective teachers and effective classrooms, classroom management strategies, and the effects of various teaching approaches, such as cooperative learning, on student learning. Clearly, the knowledge and skills that special educators need are not identical to those required of other teachers, yet there is much that all teachers have in common and need to understand about the act of teaching and working with children and youth and other teachers.

The extent to which faculty feel that the fields of special and general education share a professional knowledge base can influence the extent to which they are comfortable in reorganizing their programs and departmental structures. Beyond the negotiated knowledge base identified for all teacher educators, should special educators be expected to acquire further knowledge of general education and content-specific methods along with their special education training? Likewise, should general educators be expected to know their subject matter, expected to know methodologies pertinent to that subject matter, and be held accountable for knowing and implementing adaptive instructional techniques for students with differing disabilities?

Special education has developed, among other reasons, because students had educational needs that were not being met in general education classrooms. Special education instructional approaches and adjusted teacher–pupil ratios have proven to be effective for the students who need them (Wang, 1989). The basic foundation upon which these successes have been built is the concept of individualization. Special educators have been given freedom from responsibility for large groups of children in order to focus on the individual child, becoming intimately familiar with the individual's current abilities, interests, learning styles, motivations, and instructional needs. General education teachers find it not only impractical but also logistically impossible to focus on the individual needs of each child during every period of the day. Further, there are inevitably points at which the needs of the group will be in conflict with the needs of individuals within the group. Classroom teachers must attend to structures that ensure a smooth-running classroom characterized by orderliness and cooperation, the presence of stimulating activities, and a comfortable pace throughout the day. For a committed teacher, these operational priorities can produce effective learning for approximately 90% of their students (Fuchs & Fuchs, 1995). It is the remaining 10% for whom special educators strive to achieve better outcomes through instruction individually tailored to the student. Do the necessary differences in the approach to education preclude the integration of teacher preparation programs and/or their associated administrative structures for general and special education teachers or serve to complement and enhance one another?

Administrative Structures

Within the K–12 arena there has been intense debate on the benefits and limitations of dual administrative structures for general and special education. Some contend that the move to consolidate into a single system is a much needed paradigm shift (Schrag, 1993). However, Schrag warns that there is an implication embedded in this belief that one system has to be disposed of for another. She prefers that special education be viewed as an evolving and developing system, not one simply subsumed by general education. Schrag's comments, although focused on restructured schools, are equally applicable to the programs that prepare teachers to work in those schools. There appears to be agreement that change is needed in teacher preparation and that no one recommends the dissolution of special education into general education, but the extent to which that reformation should include a departure from existing departmental structures is hotly contested (Fuchs & Fuchs, 1995). Tradition has held that colleges, schools, departments, and programs throughout higher education be organized by ever increasing specialization. Academic departments are expected to have clearly defined goals, with affiliated faculty members feeling a sense of identification to a common departmental mission. With education in the midst of reform, it is appropriate for teacher education faculty to review and revise their own organizational mission and program goals and either affirm that their existing administrative structures are best suited for the current mission and program goals or begin the process of creating new ones.

Proposition One
Special education faculty must retain their identity and power of influence as a separate administrative unit with separate programs of study within teacher education as they pursue greater collaboration with general teacher educators.

Decision Point 8.1: Reforming Special Education Teacher Preparation in Higher Education

Arguments for Proposition One   The precipitous abandonment of special education departments in favor of collaborative programs puts special educators at far greater risk than it does the general educators with whom they are merging. To date, many of the "mergers" appear to be more like the absorption of special education into other existing units, reflecting a loss of power for special education and no real change for general education (Heller, 1992). Special educators are the ones giving up the departmental status for the sake of collaboration. Inclusion has become the basis for the dismantling of separate special education departments without the thoughtful consideration of the need to retain specialists who will work alongside the generalists in both special and general education (Fuchs & Fuchs, 1995).

Although there is a need to better integrate the preparation of general and special education teachers, there must remain an appropriate distinction between the goals of their teacher education programs. The special educator and general educator certainly need to be able to communicate and collaboratively plan interventions for children, but each must retain a unique perspective and set of skills as well.

The Knowledge Base in Teacher Education   Aside from the foundational knowledge base needed by all teachers regardless of teaching field, each discipline has its own knowledge base. Special educators have a role to play in education that is different from that of general educators, and this role requires specialized skills and training. Certainly, there are areas of overlap, and both groups of professionals must know and understand what the other does well enough to be able to collaborate, but neither is expected to know all that the other knows. Furthermore, they are expected to know far more than the other about their own field so that they may contribute their expertise to collaborative efforts. Making everyone know a little about everything and preparing no specialists, either content specialists or special educators, will reduce the quality of education and actually eliminate the need for collaboration. Everyone will know the same thing—but not very much of anything.

Collaboration in the delivery of services to children and youth served in PreK–12 programs is best achieved through the preparation of well-qualified specialists, not the creation of multiple generalists trained in merged programs. As the move toward inclusion puts more and more children and youth in mainstream classes, classroom teachers must have easy access to the nature of disabilities,

© Carolina Kroon, Impact Visuals.

University-based teacher education programs vary widely in instructional quality and rigor.

including educational, psychological, and physiological implications. It is the special educator who should provide such expertise to the classroom teacher, who is, in turn, expected to have a greater depth of knowledge regarding both content and methods associated with her teaching assignment. Preschool-level special educators need a depth of understanding regarding working with families, the causes of disabilities and their impact on child development, the debates between developmentally appropriate practices and behavioral approaches to early intervention, and so forth. Elementary-level special education teachers should have a specialized knowledge in areas such as individualized assessment, alternative instructional approaches, compensatory mechanisms, assistive technology, behavior management, and culturally diverse values and perceptions of disability. The content of a specialized knowledge base for which secondary special educators must assume responsibility includes vocational values and domains, technological skills, systems change, and developmental skills (Repetto, 1995).

Administrative Structures   The wave of inclusion enthusiasm has led many special educators, school administrators, politicians, and even members of the media to reach the conclusion that special education is actually more harmful than helpful (Fuchs & Fuchs, 1995). Special education faculty have even allowed the debates to be used as justification for seeking and/or accepting the diminishment of visibility and importance of their own academic programs, while increasing the controlling power and authority of general teacher education over the special education programs. Even the elimination of special education as both a department and a program has occurred in some instances. Collaboration and the development of improved teacher education programs do not necessitate the deletion of special education departments and might actually be harmed by such moves (Heller, 1992). Rather than collaboration occurring from a point of equal strength, elimination of departmental status immediately lessens the organizational influence that special educators can wield in further negotiations concerning program development.

It is not necessary or even desirable that special education faculty be in the same departments with other teacher educators to move toward improved preparation of all educators for heterogeneous classrooms. As Heller (1992) notes, "Departments are not mutually exclusive structures designed to keep colleagues out; instead they are structures designed to maximize the expertise and common interests of a particular group toward a particular problem, population, or goal" (p. 279). He further argues that departments do not operate in a vacuum, but necessarily assume an interdependent relationship with one another. There is no basis upon which to accept the assumption that placing faculty within a single administrative unit will automatically lead to better collaboration or smoother program integration. The achievement of departmental status does not come easily in higher education, and it will not easily be regained if faculty begin to have second thoughts. Special education departments should not be eliminated as the quick fix to the unquestioned need for greater integration of special education approaches and philosophy into the general education program to prepare teachers for inclusive classrooms.

Argument Summary Special education has only recently become a real part of the educational community within the United States. Historically, for general educators the field was often not much more than a tolerated afterthought. Only a little over one generation ago many of the children now served by special educators were excluded from public schools. The cliché "Those who do not study history are bound to repeat it" seems to be an appropriate warning in this situation. Special educators in higher education need to maintain a distinct identity, act as advocates for the groups they serve, and continue to serve as advocates for students with disabilities. Although collaboration and greater blending of teacher education programs are essential to the progression of teacher education and the success of PreK–12 reform efforts, sacrificing the existence of separate departments of special education is not the right approach. The loss of the political strength of a separate department is far greater than the benefits of potentially closer working relationships with other educators. The retention of separate departments and programs of study for general and special education groups can help each retain a clear vision of its unique contribution to the education community without negating the opportunity for collaboration. The pursuit of program content and administrative structures that produce the best specialists, not the friendliest generalists, is what is needed.

Arguments for Proposition Two   The reorganization of general and special teacher education must not merely be a merger of two former programs into a single administrative unit, but must entail a complete refashioning of both with a unique outcome (Pugach, 1992). Special educators in higher education have been educating their students to the need for collaboration and collegiality with their peers in general education. Remaining separate in their own efforts to

Proposition Two
Special and general educators must reorganize

higher education to create integrated faculty groupings and teacher education programs.

prepare teachers for inclusive schools is no longer desirable or realistic. Faculty from special education must expand their sense of responsibility toward the preparation of general educators. To ensure that the classrooms into which students with disabilities are being placed offer welcoming environments in which success is possible, it is time for special education faculty to become stakeholders in the preparation of general educators (Pugach, 1992). General educators must be trained alongside special educators in collaborative consultant models of service delivery for such instructional models to be as effective as possible. Concurrently, special education faculty must relinquish their exclusive control over the program design of special education teacher preparation, allowing general education colleagues to contribute as partners in their design and delivery.

The Knowledge Base in Teacher Education   Pugach (1992) notes that many components of the current research-based knowledge base are relevant to the achievement of equity in education for all students, particularly those with disabilities. Their relevance can be defined and understood in no better fashion than through an integrated program of general and special education. Pugach uses the powerful effects of teacher expectations on student learning and self-esteem and the cognitive–mediational perspective as two illustrative examples. The teacher expectation literature can be presented to prospective teachers concurrent with an awareness of their attitudes and sensitivities toward students with disabilities. The implications can take them to a new self-awareness that would not likely occur without the connection being directly addressed in this fashion. For a child who has unintelligible speech, uses a wheelchair for ambulation, is unable to see, or is missing an arm, what expectations do teachers hold? The collaborative ownership, planning, and delivery of joint programs for special and general educators offer far different opportunities than segregated programs or even those characterized by teamed delivery of content.

Traditional special education training has placed a heavy emphasis on individual differences, alternative means of instruction, and behavioral strategies, with far less attention directed toward content-specific methodology. Special educators will need to acknowledge this discrepancy and give greater consideration to subject-specific pedagogy to collaborate successfully with general education teacher educators. Equally, the general educators must value the material that special educators hold vital to their teacher preparation programs (Pugach, 1992). Whereas certain categorical distinctions and their implications for education are real (e.g., hearing impairment, autism, traumatic brain injury), too often the distinction between "normal learner" and "special learner" has been artificially created or enhanced (Jolly, 1990). There are now numerous subgroups of children (e.g., low-income, poor reader, at-risk, educationally disabled), each identified as having unique needs that require specialized teacher preparation. Both human and fiscal resources could be conserved were this practice of typing children abandoned in favor of a merged system of education and teacher preparation.

Administrative Structures In its infancy, special education had to establish itself as a legitimate discipline, and its leaders served a critical advocacy role. Now the field is maturing and is best served through the blending of general and special education faculty and teacher education programs. The fight for special education came on the heels of civil rights, with the cry that separate was not equal. The time has come to risk unification for the good of both. It would certainly be a contradiction to agree to honor a basic set of principles for reform predicated on no preexisting limitations in the process of redesigning teacher education, but begin with the assumption that special education must retain its separate departmental status. Such an attitude is protectionist and inherently undermines the process of collaboration (Pugach, 1992). Once the issue is free to be placed on the table, the merits and risks can be weighed and evaluated throughout the redesign process.

Collaboration between general and special educators in the redesign of teacher education is based on an assumption of equality. It is not appropriate for one group to give up its identity and status within the university and subsume itself within another existing department if the group hopes to retain its influence. Rather, the redesign process affords teacher educators the opportunity to create all-new administrative structures that will represent new coalitions, not annexes. For example, the reorganization of general and special education by age/grade levels might make more programmatic sense than the current discipline-related divisions. After all, do teachers working with elementary students with mild disabilities have more in common with elementary teachers or with secondary special educators in terms of curriculum and instructional resources, classroom management concerns, interactions with parents, and so forth? Coincidentally, such a move might bring to light the deficiencies of many special education departments in the preparation of secondary special educators. Such mergers by age have been described for early childhood educators (e.g., Kemple, Hartle, Correa, & Fox, 1994; Goodwin, Boone, & Wittmer, 1994). Such programmatic redesign efforts offer a clear response to the external forces exerting pressures on both early childhood education and early childhood special education to change (Goodwin, Boone, & Wittmer, 1994).

Tradition has held that departments are organized by specializations and common interests rather than diversity. A parallel could be drawn with doctors who generally set up practices with other physicians with like specialties. The arrangement of an internist, heart specialist, dermatologist, allergist, gynecologist, orthopedist, and so forth all within the same medical practice is not the custom but could potentially offer patients an efficient alternative structure to the prevalent one. The creation of new teams of faculty who share a common focus while holding different (perhaps conflicting) perspectives does not put special education interests at risk. Rather, such organization brings the special education voice into the mainstream to be heard continuously by other faculty. Perhaps such groupings will not be as comfortable for special educators, but they do more closely parallel the PreK–12 conditions that the majority of special educators routinely face.

Argument Summary For too long, our solution to heterogeneity and diversity within student groups has been classification and separation. With the move to celebrate diversity within the mainstream of education should come an end to the separatist camps for special educators within teacher education programs. Special educators do not hold a monopoly on caring for children who fall outside the small parameters of "normal." We have an opportunity to replace the separatist tradition that has served only to antagonize and alienate our colleagues with clear communication of the basic values that special educators hold (Pugach, 1992).

ALTERNATIVE ROUTES
TO TEACHING LICENSURE

Following publication of *A Nation at Risk,* states began enacting education reform legislation, including some that directly affected teacher education. The use of alternative licensure and shortcuts to careers in education was accepted by policy makers and school systems looking for teachers (Goodlad, 1994). In some instances the impact these reforms had on traditional teacher education was dramatic. For instance, in 1987 Texas limited teacher education programs to a maximum of eighteen hours of undergraduate degree credit, including student teaching (Warner, 1990). Other states have also imposed restrictions on the percentage of the undergraduate curriculum that can be professional education and/or have authorized alternative routes to teaching for persons already holding college degrees. Such politically authorized reforms concomitant with personnel shortages in special education make debates regarding alternative licensure options particularly relevant to teacher educators in the field of special education.

  Alternative licensure models involve school-based routes to teacher licensure in which persons have teaching responsibilities and are paid teachers of record as they simultaneously receive training and mentoring in education. These alternative credentialing routes generally entail one or more from a combination of three components: alternative means of meeting standards set for all teacher licensure candidates with no alterations to the standards themselves, alteration of the standards themselves, or alteration of state licensure requirements (Darling-Hammond, 1990). The model is predicated upon the availability of a cadre of carefully selected and trained teachers suitable for the mentoring role they play in the induction of teachers into their profession. Although the actual count seems to vary based on the precise definition of alternatives used, Wise, in 1994, noted that forty-two states had developed such alternative routes to licensure, but others have previously reported counts up to forty-eight (Sandlin, Young, & Karge,

1992–93). Regardless of the precise count, alternative routes to teacher licensure are clearly prevalent throughout the country.

Benefits/Costs of Alternative Licensure

For many states, alternative licensure was initially proposed as an answer to critical teacher shortages, particularly in math and sciences, in urban and rural locales, in special education, and in bilingual education (Hawley, 1990). The most common argument for their establishment was not that traditional teacher education was defective or undesirable but that alternative licensure would be superior to issuing large numbers of emergency credentials to persons with little or no training in education. However, Hawley notes that others have argued that alternative licensure is philosophically and qualitatively preferable to conventional teacher education programs. The sentiment that teaching is an art which cannot be taught, combined with the characterization of colleges of education as dull vacuums that actually interfere with the proper education of teacher candidates, has been expressed by advocates of alternative licensure (e.g., Dill & Stafford, 1994). A commingling of these somewhat conflicting philosophical views toward alternative licensure has occurred since they were first developed. For example, states that originally created alternative routes to teaching as an undesirable temporary solution to address teacher shortages have now expanded their models to include nonshortage areas of licensure (Hawley, 1990). The addition of nonshortage areas to the teaching licenses available via alternative programs is indicative of a shift in rationale for the programs and current valuing of university-based teacher education. Rather than serving as a temporary solution to a critical teacher shortage, alternative programs have become permanently accepted routes to careers in teaching.

Control of Teacher Education

Fenstermacher (1990) describes in political terms the tension between supporters of traditional preparation programs with their controlled forms of entry and those favoring alternative routes to teaching. He characterizes the two camps as seeking conflicting political aims—that of professionalization versus democratization of the field. Fenstermacher contends that educators interested in the professionalization of teacher education prefer that teacher education remain housed in institutions of higher education. Those holding this position argue that a unique professional body of knowledge is, in fact, an essential prerequisite to becoming a teacher. Some school-based personnel and policy makers have challenged this assumption, claiming that practicing educators serving as mentors to novice teachers and on-the-job training constitute a valid, even superior, means of inducting new teachers into the field. Although the majority of these arguments are occurring away from the field of special education, the impact of them on the field may be proportionally greater than that of general education, because teacher shortages are prevalent in special education and especially in central-city areas, where higher percentages of students are served by special education.

However, a word of caution as the debate between traditional teacher preparation models and alternative licensure programs ensues is appropriate. Lilly (1994) reminds us that little empirical information regarding the effectiveness of alternative routes to licensure is currently available. Until comprehensive evaluation data are available from the major alternative licensure programs, Lilly holds that the debates rest on emotion and logic more than the relative merits of the alternatives. Lilly further notes the lack of conclusive research regarding the effects of standard setting, program approval, and teacher licensing, which characterize higher-education-based teacher education programs, on the actual quality of teaching in public schools. Do the students assigned to teachers who completed teacher education programs certified by the National Council for Accreditation of Teacher Education (NCATE) perform better than others whose preparation did not include an NCATE-approved program? Rather than having state and national certification regulations grounded in the emerging knowledge base of education, Lilly argues, we actually have a system of teacher licensure and program approval that are more realistically socio-political events with heavy symbolic value. Although it is far beyond the scope of the present discussion to debate the merits of certifying teacher education programs, we must consider the merits of alternative licensure.

Decision Point 8.2: Evaluating
Alternative Routes to Teaching Licensure

Arguments for Proposition One   The arguments in support of alternative routes to teaching are sociological, economic, educational, and political. The themes that run throughout these arguments are related to the historically poor quality of education courses, the inability of teacher education programs to recruit and graduate diverse groups of teachers, the need for teachers combined with the suitability of well-educated college graduates to teach, and the claimed superiority of school-based mentoring programs to those of university-based preservice teacher education models. In reality, alternative licensure programs are too new for there to be much information about the effectiveness of teachers progressing through them over extended careers (Lilly, 1994), but then even traditional state licensure requirements have not really been examined in regard to their link to teacher effectiveness (Hawk, Coble, & Swanson, 1985; Lilly, 1994).

Benefits/Costs of Alternative Licensure   The needs for and benefits of alternative licensure are numerous (MacDonald, Manning, & Gable, 1994). They can reduce the number of emergency certificates issued; increase the teacher pool in high

---

Proposition One
Alternative routes to teacher licensure offer a valid means of expanding the number of quali-

fied teachers available to assume classroom teaching responsibilities in our schools.

Effective teachers can serve as models for teacher apprentices.

shortage areas, including special education; increase the number of teachers in rural and urban areas, both of which have high rates of students with disabilities; attract a more diverse population to teaching (minorities, males, second-career people—see Chapter 2 for further discussion of this concern); and allow bright college graduates to enter teaching without having to progress through extended teacher education programs.

Although alternative routes to teaching have been available only a relatively brief period of time and vary greatly in their nature and quality, there is a beginning body of research that documents the positive benefits relevant to the teacher applicant pool. In a review of the research, Hawley (1990) concludes that alternative licensure programs have, in fact, successfully recruited greater numbers of males, persons over twenty-five, minorities, and persons with college degrees in mathematics, sciences, and foreign languages than traditional programs have. Stoddart (1993) and Houston, Marshall, and McDavid (1993) offer additional evidence of the successful recruitment of diverse groups to teaching through alternative licensure programs. In general, the population of candidates attracted to these programs is favorable, including applicants with high grade point averages, previous teaching experience (e.g., Peace Corps), and nontraditional perspectives (MacDonald, Manning, & Gable, 1994). Further, attrition rates during the first one to two years of teaching are lower for those who followed an alternative route than they are for graduates of traditional programs (Hawley, 1990). These lower attrition rates are particularly significant in light of the fact that teacher shortages necessitated the development of many of these programs. They put teachers in classrooms faster, cost less for the teacher candidates, attract diverse candidates, and produce teachers who remain in the field.

Some misinformation about attrition rates used to argue against alternative programs is based on incomplete or ill-designed research. For example, Banks and Necco (1987) surveyed 203 special education teachers in West Virginia and concluded that teachers who completed a full training program stay in the field longer than those who completed alternative licensure programs. However, Lilly (1994) notes that the survey included only currently employed teachers and that no data of actual rates of leaving were presented in their study. Policy making on such misinformation would be inappropriate as well as inaccurate. In comparing beginning teachers who had completed a traditional university program with a highly structured alternative internship program that required a minimum of two years' previous paid work experience with children, Sandlin, Young, and Karge (1992–93) found that the interns in the alternative track actually began the year with more confidence than the traditional beginning teachers. At the completion of the first year of teaching, the trained observers detected no differences in classroom management or instructional skills between the two groups.

When the applicant pool for teaching positions is broadened beyond just those who completed a teacher education program through an institution of higher education, schools can afford to consider only those who meet the highest professional and academic standards. In Texas, where school-based teacher education programs have existed since 1985, the selection process for candidates for new teaching positions is very rigorous, with only about one in twenty candidates admitted (Dill & Stafford, 1994). Further school-based teacher education features a delivery system that is far more accessible to minority candidates. University-based programs have tended to screen out minorities with standardized test requirements. They offer little, if any, scheduling flexibility for students needing to work part time, creating high costs both in terms of time, tuition dollars, and lost income potential. In contrast, the school-based programs developed in Texas offer evening training sessions, convenient locations, and paid internships, making these programs more accessible to minorities and people with low incomes (Dill & Stafford, 1994). The figures support their claims of greater accessibility since over half the teachers trained in those programs have been minorities, compared to a figure of approximately 5% in traditional teacher education programs.

Rosenberg and Rock (1994) reported positive results from a collaborative alternative program specifically designed for special educators. When supervisors, principals, and mentors were asked to rate the alternative teacher candidates' performance in comparison to average beginning teachers, the ratings indicated that they were considered to be equal to the average beginning teacher in general during their first year. Second-year comparisons improved their ratings so that mean ratings of each of the three groups considered them to be performing ahead of the average beginning teacher. Although these ratings were subject to bias since the same individuals who rated them had contributed to their training, the principals did ask for more trainees when they next had vacancies, providing incidental evidence of the quality of the teachers in the program. Whether they were "better" than average beginning teachers is a subjective matter of less importance than the fact that the program was able to produce teachers whom professionals in the schools found to be worthy of becoming their colleagues.

In California, the demand for new teachers has far exceeded the number completing requirements for a teaching credential for well over a decade. In California between 1983–84 and 1988–89, there was a 139% increase in the number of teachers working in general education on the basis of an alternative permit (Simpson, Whelan, & Zabel, 1993). Whereas alternative routes to teaching might be developed because of their superiority to traditional teacher education programs, they also can be directly linked to areas of teacher shortage. Schools can operate alternative licensure programs on an as-needed basis rather than always seeking to maintain the credit hour production so necessary at university-based programs. The quantity of teaching candidates need only be sufficient for existing and anticipated shortages, with no graduates from unneeded areas.

Control of Teacher Education   Teacher education faculty within institutions of higher education operated for many years without fear of accountability to their students, the public schools, or the voting public. Their own graduates, who staff the faculties of our schools, decried the quality and relevance of their training. Arguing for school-based education, Dill and Stafford (1994) are quite direct in their criticism of university-based teacher education programs. However, many teacher education programs have been undergoing massive reform efforts. NCATE has strengthened its national accrediting standards, and most states have upgraded their standards and program approval process. However, Lilly (1994) notes that while a research-based claim can be made for the positive effects of teacher education, the relationship between those effects and adherence to any particular set of professional standards is not evident. It could well be argued that the component of teacher education programs that make them successful is that which is directly linked to school-based experiences, with little or no benefit deriving from the university connection or on-campus training.

Fenstermacher (1990) describes some political benefits of alternative licensure programs, including the reality that for politicians and policy makers it provides an opportunity to be identified with the school reform movement. As these public figures draw attention to teacher education programs, they expose the university-based programs to a new level of public scrutiny and a resulting accountability. The public can begin exerting a voice in teacher education as they become aware of the issues and existing practices and vote for Congressional representatives who support their preferences for the future of teacher preparation. Further, alternative licensure programs create a means by which other entities, such as foundations and corporations, can become directly involved in the formation of teaching policy and can end the monopoly that teacher education institutions have had on controlling entry into the teaching profession. Alternative licensure programs expand the routes available by which one can enter teaching as a career, consistent with a political ideology favoring choice and deregulation of government control.

One of the strongest arguments in favor of alternative routes to teaching is the fact that the school personnel who train the teacher candidates and document their worthiness as teachers must then become their colleagues and peers. School personnel have a much greater stake in restricting the field to competent teachers than do the faculty of institutions of higher education, who have only a limited number of years of contact with students in a student–professor relationship, never one of equality and shared labor. Universities are susceptible to being driven by incentives that can be unrelated to the quality of their graduates. The supervision of a preservice teacher is a time-consuming activity often removed from the standards set for tenure, promotion, or other rewards within the institution. For school-based personnel assigned to a mentoring role in an alternate licensure program, the teacher candidate is a top priority, directly related to the mentor's work standards and expectations for advancement.

Argument Summary The development of alternative routes to teaching has put pressure on traditional programs to improve themselves, draw a closer link to the field, and raise the quality and educational experience of their teacher candidates. Thus, the presence of real competition in the teacher education market place is both directly and indirectly serving the public schools well. The alternate programs have been the recipients of a diverse pool of competent teacher candidates, while traditional teacher education programs have awakened to the need to improve the quality, diversity, and efficiency of their programs. In the final analysis, alternate routes will be considered successful to the extent that they improve teacher preparation and actually increase the supply of qualified and committed teachers.

However, schools do not have the option of sending the children home due to the lack of teachers. Someone, qualified or not, must fill the vacancies. The development of quality alternative routes to teaching enable schools to staff their classes and expand their nontraditional teacher population. As long as such programs blend discussion of the professional knowledge base of teaching with practical skill development through mentoring and ongoing training for the participants, the field will be well served by these programs. Such programs actually strengthen the profession overall and encourage greater collaboration between the schools and higher education.

Arguments for Proposition Two The need for reformation in teacher education is not disputed. The need to fill teacher shortages, particularly in special education, is not disputed. The need for teacher educators to draw into a closer working relationship with school-based personnel is not disputed. But the need for alternative routes to careers in teaching to achieve these ends *is* disputed. Teaching is a profession, characterized by a unique knowledge base, standards of performance, and accountability. However, the status of teaching as a profession is clearly in jeopardy with the advent of school-based alternative licensure programs. The fact that such programs have documented the ability to produce "teachers" who can function satisfactorily in classrooms for a few years is not evidence that these individuals are teachers in the professional sense of the word. Many experienced teaching assistants could make it through a day, a week, or even longer managing a classroom in the absence of the teacher. Such ability does not indicate that they are teachers, capable of assuming full responsibility for a teaching assignment. So, too, a "teacher" entering the profession through an alternate route may be quite capable of setting up a classroom, planning and teaching lessons, conducting parent conferences, and so forth. However, the depth of her understanding regarding her own teaching decisions—as well as her preparedness when a child struggles to learn but is unable to do so, when a par-

Proposition Two
Alternative licensure programs undermine pro-   fessionalism in education and must be eliminated
                                                    as accepted means of teacher credentialing.

ent becomes angry and upset and will not be calmed down, when colleagues challenge her teaching methods, or when other incidents occur—will test her real level of professionalism. The depth of challenges that she is actually facing as a teacher may even go by unnoticed for many years as she goes about the routine surface-level tasks associated with teaching.

The belief that practical skill development is essential and of far greater value than a teacher's development of theoretical, philosophical, and historical understanding of education has not only led to the creation of alternative routes to teaching but has also been eroding traditional teacher education programs (Goodlad, 1994). Reflection in decision making, healthy professional discussion and debate between individuals with varying perspectives, scholarly review of research-based professional literature, and awareness and understanding of the historical evolution of teaching and the role of schools in American society are just some of the components of university-based teacher education programs that contribute to the making of a professional teacher. Such would likely be absent, if not specifically devalued as irrelevant to the act of teaching, in school-based alternate licensure programs.

Darling-Hammond's (1990) review of the research on the effectiveness of teachers prepared through alternative routes indicates that teachers qualified through comprehensive teacher education programs are, in fact, more effective. Quick-route teachers have difficulty with curriculum development and pedagogical content knowledge. They are less able to attend to students' different learning styles and levels, experience more difficulties with classroom management and student motivation, and are less sensitive to students. They have proven weak in planning and redirecting instruction to meet student needs or even to see the need to do so. They are less skilled in implementing instruction and less able to anticipate students' knowledge and potential difficulties while quicker to blame students if their own teaching is not successful. These last findings are of particular concern to persons concerned about the educational welfare of students with disabilities. Critics of traditional teacher education programs need to be cautioned that although teacher education may be in need of reform, the field has its share of poor models of teaching as well. The teacher candidate who is pursuing licensure through an alternative program has nowhere to turn, no other professor to seek out, if those surrounding him prove to be inadequate or incompetent themselves.

Benefits/Costs of Alternative Licensure   A critical shortage of teachers in special education does not justify the staffing of special education classrooms with untrained personnel on a permanent basis. Anyone would consider it ludicrous to allow an untrained "attorney" to represent defendants in court in spite of the backlog in many courts today, yet untrained personnel are used to fill teacher shortages while policy makers pronounce what a good thing they have done. The extent to which criticisms aimed at teacher education and the emotional calls for radical change have been politically motivated must be considered. Schnur and Golby (1995) challenge our readiness to accept, at face value, the "essentially unsubstantiated findings" of reports such as *A Nation at Risk*. These reports, which characterized education and teacher education as being in a state of disrepair, initiated movements that have heralded calls to radical reforms, including the virtual elimination of university-based teacher education programs. Regardless of the need for reform and improvement, the abandonment of traditional teacher education programs is not an appropriate solution.

In fact, teacher shortages could have finally provided the field with an opportunity to improve the status and pay of teachers and streamline and improve teacher education. Unfortunately, this opportunity was missed because access to quick cheap labor became possible through alternative licensure options (Darling-Hammond, 1990). The alternative routes to teaching have clearly undermined an opportunity to allow a natural economic balance for teachers that would have altered both the pay and the status of teachers. Simpson, Whelan, and Zabel (1993) even argue that financial incentives should be greater in a specialized area such as special education: "Rather than lowering (or eliminating) entry requirements, the marketplace must offer financial incentives to address the shortages. Since specialized preservice preparation requires study and practice beyond that of classroom teachers, salary incentives must be commensurate" (p. 10).

There is substantial variation in what constitutes alternative routes, ranging from Maryland, where applicants must complete a twelve-month preparation program before entering the market, to Tennessee, where progressing at the rate of six credits every five years is sufficient to keep a nonlicensed teacher in the classroom (Darling-Hammond, 1990). The alternate route programs in states with high standards (e.g., Maryland, Connecticut) tend to have higher selection standards and more rigorous preparation programs than states with low standards (e.g., New Jersey and Texas). One consequence of this variance in the quality of alternative routes to teaching has been the erosion of reciprocity, which, in turn, reduces teacher mobility and fuels the demand for alternative programs to fill teacher shortages.

Although the success of alternative programs in recruiting minority candidates is evident, it might prove to be shortsighted as well as short-lived. Selecting and giving minority teaching candidates teaching responsibilities for which they are insufficiently prepared will do little for the students who need to get the most possible from their education, the public acceptance of minority teachers, or the teaching candidates themselves, who are at risk to experience failure and return to the job market within a few years. Darling-Hammond (1990) specifically refers to alternative licensure as a strategy for an underinvestment in the preparation of minority candidates that may actually impair their prospects for retention and success in the profession. The ultimate result could be exacerbation of minority shortages through the premature employment of those attracted to the profession. Without adequate skills, they may be unsuccessful and leave the profession rather than becoming full-fledged professional teachers with sustained careers as educators. Rather than using alternative routes to teaching to attract diverse groups to teach at the lowest wages, funds could be directed toward scholarships and stipends to enable such candidates to pursue traditional entry into the field—without shortcuts and lowered standards. Darling-Hammond (1990) notes that such programs have proven successful in New York and in other states.

The dangers associated with alternative licensure programs hold even greater significance when their connection to the teaching areas where there are teacher shortages is considered. Teacher candidates with the least preparation are sent forth into the most challenging of classrooms. The morality of the practice of using alternative licensure candidates with little or no preparation to staff center-city schools seems to make the barbs thrown at teacher education and its needed reform rather blunt. Some states are using alternative routes to boost the supply and maintain a salary structure below market wages, filling classrooms with relatively low investments in teacher training. Other states, which have established competitive salary schedules and programs subsidizing the costs of teacher preparation, have proven that it is possible to develop better prepared teachers while increasing the supply of teachers.

The limited experience inherent in alternative licensure models of induction into teaching is another powerfully negative aspect of such programs. These models are predicated on the assumption that the quality of the teaching and mentoring available within school settings where there are shortages is worthy and reflective of the most current knowledge of effective teaching. Goodlad (1994) questions that assumption:

> It is a status quo approach at best and an immediately obsolete approach at worst....If future teachers are not to become robotic clones of present teachers, and if future schools are not to be mere replicas of present schools, teacher education must develop its own independence of thought and inquiry. (pp. 15–16)

Even if the mentoring teacher offers excellent qualifications for the role, she already has a full-time job. With obligations to her own class(es), where would she find the time or energy to take on the responsibility of preparing new teachers without diminishing the quality of education for her own students? Thus, the impact of hiring unprepared teachers to be mentored through their first year or two of teaching jeopardizes the education of students assigned to the novice teacher as well as those assigned to the mentoring teacher.

Costs of alternative routes to teacher licensure are greater for taxpayers because they must pay for teachers who have little or no training, whereas individual teacher education candidates incur greater personal costs in traditional programs (Hawley, 1990). The schools are paying for less than beginning teachers, while students in quality traditional programs are struggling to pay tuition for four or five years. Then, when seeking employment, teachers from traditional programs have no advantage over teachers in alternative programs—perhaps even a disadvantage because of the close connection between alternative programs and the schools. The cost factor alone would make the shortcut more attractive to persons interested in teaching. Thus, the applicant pool for traditional programs is at risk of being drained by the existence of the alternative routes, which offer employment and a paycheck concurrent with training.

Alternative licensure programs fill classrooms at a much lower cost than it would take to raise salaries and improve working conditions for the teaching profession to attract sufficient numbers of applicants (Hawley, 1990). Those supporting the alternative routes as good education policy fail to acknowledge that low entry costs may also contribute to increased attrition rates and that some consider alternative licensure as an opportunity to "serve" as a teacher for a few years, not to develop a lifelong career. Since beginner teachers (one to two years of experience) are known to be less effective than ones with more experience, the development of alternative routes to teaching, which inevitably increase attrition after the first few years of teaching, further erodes the quality of teaching available to children in public schools. Students and taxpayers bear the cost of training teachers who are likely to exit after a few years.

The perspectives and beliefs regarding special education and students with disabilities to which these alternate route teachers would be exposed, whether they be general or special education teachers, would likely be quite narrow. General education teachers who enter the field through alternative routes may be less able to respond to the needs of students with disabilities. They would likely encounter some students with learning difficulties during their training, but they may have received no additional information, resources, or adaptive instructional techniques regarding students with other types of disabilities beyond those whom they encountered during this initial period. Special education teachers from alternative programs would be equally at risk for having a knowledge base limited to students enrolled at a single school and attitudes reflective of their mentoring teacher.

Control of Teacher Education Licensure in other professions is not in the hands of employers, who have an immediate conflict of interest. Hospitals do not license doctors, nor do law firms license attorneys. Rather, professional standards and legal policies are set in place as a protection for the public. Only qualified individuals who have achieved these standards are legally permitted to hold these professional licenses. Such standards are not considered to be an impediment to worthy individuals who wish to practice other professions (e.g., nurses, clinical psychologists, architects, dentists, pharmacists), but rather provide a critical protection of the public against those who would practice in a chosen field unprepared. However, it appears that some consider such protections and standards unnecessary for the children in public schools today. The need for a classroom teacher to fill a vacancy seems to necessitate that a principal seek the cheapest, most expedient means of staffing the class, especially for the most challenging of cases. In no other field is its preparatory education viewed as an "obstacle and a monopoly."

For those who contend that colleges of education offer no substantive content and argue that subject matter knowledge is the only necessary ingredient in effective teaching, Hawley (1990) refutes the merits of their assumptions. These notions, popular with policy makers who are seeking to dismantle efforts of teacher educators to continue the professionalization of teaching, deny the existence of a unique body of knowledge essential as a prerequisite to teaching. Whereas basic subject matter knowledge is important, preparation in child development, curriculum development, and teaching methods has a stronger influence on teacher effectiveness than more subject matter preparation (Darling-Hammond, 1991). It is inconceivable that the shortage of doctors in rural communities in this country could or should be addressed by placing college graduates as apprentices under the supervision of licensed physicians and have them attend some intensive training sessions to practice medicine. Patients as well as the apprentice physicians would become victims of an ill-conceived underinvestment in the preparation of doctors. Yet that very model is in use to fill teacher shortages, often in the most challenging of classrooms.

The dichotomy between traditional teacher education and alternative routes to teaching is not, however, as simple as higher education programs versus school-based programs. A typical alternative route program is school-based, but has enlisted the assistance of neighboring teacher education programs to lend it credibility. The inconsistency of condemning as unnecessary and inadequate these teacher education programs, while relying on faculty from them to collaborate in the development of teacher candidates who are in alternative programs, seems lost on the advocates of alternative licensure. For many in teacher education, the opportunity to contribute to these programs and address the teacher shortage in this manner is acceptable. However, it could also be seen as another situation in which immediacy of needs, both teacher shortages and credit hour generation, have been allowed to take priority over professional standards for the field.

The reformation of teacher education could take on a far different slant than merely acquiescing to the pressures for democratization of the field, quick solutions to shortages, and abandonment of professional standards and control. Licensure is one of the major forms of quality assurance, yet education standards fall far short of the standards practiced in other professions, such as social work or psychology (Wise, 1994). The resulting confusion is characterized by inconsistency on the part of policy makers, teacher educators, state credentialing officers, and school-based personnel. Wise notes that state legislators who created the existing standards and credentials requirements are the same group who now view these requirements with disdain, describing the standards as both a hindrance to recruiting and maintaining a quality workforce. They have created an "end run" around the professional structure that has been developing for years.

Argument Summary The teacher education community has sold itself out very cheaply by endorsing alternative routes to teacher licensure. Politicians, government officials, and school administrators needing quick, cheap labor have convinced many educators that alternative routes offer a positive contribution to the field. Rather, educators should have demanded that the market react naturally to shortages. There does exist a unique body of knowledge that teachers should be introduced to well before assuming teaching duties. To give anyone who holds a college degree the responsibilities of a teacher with no prerequisite exposure to educational theory, philosophy, history, child development, or skill development is to consider teaching far less than it is.

Alternative programs work to suppress teacher salaries because candidates in such programs can be hired at lower wages than a fully credentialed teacher. Assuming that the traditional programs offer significantly more qualified candidates for long-term careers as professional educators, these financial effects of alternative routes, while subtle and indirect, weaken the applicant pool by offering quick access to a paycheck, with no tuition expenses. Therefore, they are more detrimental to traditional programs rather than sources of healthy competition for such programs.

CLOSING THOUGHTS

The recommendation that teacher education reform include at least some version of the professional development school (PDS) is pervasive throughout all the reform literature and one that many teacher educators have been enthusiastically endorsing (Harris & Harris, 1992–93). The PDS concept may offer the reasonable bridge between the two extreme positions of professionalization and democratization, as defined by Fenstermacher (1990). It would be illogical for faculty in teacher education to push for a professionalization of the field that did not honor and respect their own graduates as professionals who must contribute to the process of inducting new teachers into the profession. The PDS concept is built upon a mutual professional respect between teacher educators and practicing teachers, all of whom share an equal concern for the quality of education for children and youth and the nature of the training provided to prospective teachers.

In the act of redesigning a principal preparation program with particular focus on the changing environment of K–12 schools, participants produced six key principles for redesigning teacher education that are instructive to all reformers (Goodlad, 1994). Although not specifically addressing the special/regular education merger issue, these principles challenge anyone's temptation to accept the status quo. The first principle is that "business as usual" in teacher education is not sufficient. For special educators, this principle is readily apparent when faculty in segregated departments, teaching students in segregated programs, attempt to teach collaboration for inclusion. The general and special education teacher candidates, who need to be preparing to collaborate, are instead kept separate from one another. Once a commitment to the reform process is made, brainstorming sessions on administrative structures and collaborative programs are essential.

Ultimately, the debates must come down to whether integrated programs and administrative structures in higher education as well as alternative licensure programs improve conditions for students with and without disabilities, not the lives and careers of education faculty. One state has moved precisely in this direction (Schalock & Myton, 1988). In place of teacher education regulations, Oregon has tied teacher education programs directly to the achievement of children in K–12 classes, in which university graduates serve as teachers. In this state, teacher educators have been freed of the regulatory paperwork and given license to establish outcomes-based programs. The extent to which such deregulation might become one of the results of the current state of confusion and conflict between increased state regulation and control of licensure, juxtaposed with the acceptance and encouragement of alternative routes to teaching by the same policy makers who helped create the regulations, remains for the future.

REFERENCES

Banks, S. R., & Necco, E. (1987). Alternative certification, educational training and job longevity. *Action in Teacher Education, 9,* 67–73.

Brownell, M., & Smith, S. (1993). Attrition/retention of special education teachers: Critique of current research and recommendations for retention efforts. *Teacher Education and Special Education, 16,* 270–282.

Carnegie Forum on Education and the Economy. (1986). *A nation prepared: Teachers for the 21st century.* New York: Carnegie Corporation.

Chapey, G. D., Pystowski, I. S., & Trimarco, T. (1985). National trends for certification and training of special education teachers. *Teacher Education and Special Education, 8,* 203–208.

Council for Exceptional Children. (1995). What every special educator must know? The International Standards for the Preparation and Certification of Special Education Teachers. Reston, VA: Author. (ERIC Document Reproduction No. ED387 958).

Cranston-Gingras, A., & Mauser, A. J. (1992). Categorical and noncategorical teacher certification in special education: How wide is the gap? *Remedial and Special Education, 13,* 6–9.

Darling-Hammond, L. (1990). The alternative certification of teachers. *Peabody Journal of Education, 67,* 123–154.

Darling-Hammond, L. (1991). Are our teachers ready to teach? Teacher education results in better student learning. *Quality Teaching, the Newsletter of the National Council for Accreditation of Teacher Education, 1,* 6–7, 10.

Dill, V., & Stafford, D. (1994). School-based teacher education. *Phi Delta Kappan, 75,* 620–623.

Fearn, K. M. (1987). *Report on the status of certification of special educators in the United States and territories.* Reston, VA: Council for Exceptional Children.

Fenstermacher, G. D. (1990). The place of alternative certification in the education of teachers. *Peabody Journal of Education, 67,* 155–186.

Fuchs, D., & Fuchs, L. S. (1995). What's "special" about special education? *Phi Delta Kappan, 76,* 522–530.

Goodlad, J. I. (1994). *Educational renewal: Better teachers, better schools.* San Francisco: Jossey-Bass.

Goodwin, W. L., Boone, H. A., & Wittmer, D. S. (1994). The puzzle of redesigning a preparation program in an evolving, fast changing field. *Teacher Education and Special Education, 17,* 260–268.

Harris, G., & Bradford, J. (1987). Literacy. In J. Minahan et al. (Eds.), *Encyclopedia of social work* (18th ed., Vol. 2, pp. 50–58). Silver Spring, MD: National Association of Social Workers.

Harris, R. C., & Harris, M. F. (1992–1993). Partner schools: Places to solve teacher preparation problems. *Action in Teacher Education, 14,* 1–8.

Hawk, P. P., Coble, C. R., & Swanson, M. (1985). Certification: Does it matter? *Journal of Teacher Education, 36,* 13–15.

Hawley, W. D. (1990). The theory and practice of alternative certification: Implications for the improvement of teaching. *Peabody Journal of Education, 67,* 3–31.

Heller, H. W. (1992). A rationale for departmentalization of special education. In W. Stainback & S. Stainback (Eds.), *Controversial issues confronting special education: Divergent perspectives* (pp. 271–281). Boston: Allyn & Bacon.

Holmes Group. (1986). *Tomorrow's teachers: A report to the Holmes Group.* East Lansing, MI: Author.

Houston, W. R., Marshall, F. & Mc David, T. (1993). Problems of traditionally prepared and alternatively certified first-year teachers. *Education and Urban Society, 26,* 78–89.

Jolly, D. V. (1990). *Adjusting the system instead of the individual to meet student needs.* Tucson, AZ: Rural Education Symposium of the American Council on Rural Special Education and the National Rural and Small Schools Consortium.

Kemple, K. M., Hartle, L. C., Correa, V. I., & Fox, L. (1994). Preparing teachers for inclusive education: The development of a unified teacher education program in early childhood and early childhood special education, *Teacher Education and Special Education, 17,* 38–51.

Lilly, M. S. (1994). Research on teacher licensure and state approval of teacher education programs. *Teacher Education and Special Education, 15,* 148–160.

MacDonald, R. H., Manning, M. L., & Gable, R. A. (1994). An alternative certification program: Career transition. *Action in Teacher Education, 16,* 19–27.

McLaughlin, M. J., Valdivieso, C. H., Spence, K. L., & Fuller, B. C. (1988). Special education teacher preparation: A synthesis of four research studies. *Exceptional Children, 55,* 215–221.

National Council for Accreditation of Teacher Education. (1987, December). *Standards procedures and policies for the accreditation of professional education units.* Washington, DC: Author.

Pugach, M. C. (1992). Unifying the preservice preparation of teachers. In W. Stainback & S. Stainback (Eds.), *Controversial issues confronting special education: Divergent perspectives* (pp. 255–269). Boston: Allyn & Bacon.

Putnam, J. W., Spiegel, A. N., & Bruininks, R. H. (1995). Future directions in education and inclusion of students with disabilities: A Delphi investigation. *Exceptional Children, 61,* 553–576.

Putnam, M. L., & Habanek, D. V. (1993). A national survey of certification requirements for teachers of students with mild handicaps: States of confusion. *Teacher Education and Special Education, 16,* 155–160.

Repetto, J. B. (1995). Curriculum beyond school walls: Implications of transition education. *Peabody Journal of Education, 70,* 125–140.

Romanish, B. (1993). Teacher empowerment: The orphan of educational reform. *Action in Teacher Education, 15,* 1–8.

Rosenberg, M. S., & Rock, E. E. (1994). Alternative certification in special education: Efficacy of a collaborative, field-based teacher preparation program. *Teacher Education and Special Education, 17,* 141–153.

Sandlin, R. A., Young, B., & Karge, B. D. (1992–1993). Regularly and alternatively credentialed beginning teachers: Comparison and contrast of their development. *Action in Teacher Education, 14,* 16–23.

Schalock, H. D., & Myton, D. V. (1988). A new paradigm for teacher licensure: Oregon's demand for evidence of success in fostering student learning. *Journal of Teacher Education, 39,* 8–16.

Schnur, J. O., & Golby, M. J. (1995). Teacher education: A university mission. *Journal of Teacher Education, 46,* 11–18.

Schrag, J. A. (1993). Restructuring schools for better alignment of general and special education. In J. I. Goodlad & T. C. Lovitt (Eds.), *Integrating general and special education* (pp. 203–227). New York: Merrill.

Simpson, R. L., Whelan, R. J., & Zabel, R. H. (1993). Special education personnel preparation in the 21st century: Issues and strategies. *Remedial and Special Education, 14,* 7–22.

Smith-Davis, J. (1991). *Percentage change—Teachers by state to 1993*. SpecialNet, Supply Demand Bulletin Board ERIC Document Reproduction No. Msg: FGJB-4583-8108.

Stoddart, T. (1993). Who is prepared to teach in urban schools? *Education and Urban Society, 26,* 29–48.

U.S. Department of Education. (1995). *Seventeenth annual report to Congress on the implementation of the Individuals with Disabilities Education Act.* Washington, DC: Author.

Wang, M. C. (1989). Adaptive instruction: An alternative for accommodating student diversity through the curriculum. In D. K. Lipsky & A. Gartner (Eds.), *Beyond separate education: Quality education for all* (pp. 99–120). Baltimore: Paul H. Brookes.

Warner, A. R. (1990). Legislative limits on certification requirements: Lessons from the Texas experience. *Journal of Teacher Education, 41,* 26–33.

Wise, A. (1994). The coming revolution in teacher licensure: Redefining teacher preparation. *Action in Teacher Education, 16,* 1–13.

PART III

Social Change and Its Impact on Special Education Practices

In this final section of the book, we address the most challenging issues. The content covers deep moral concerns as well as the mundane matters of funding the services we consider to be needed by students with disabilities. For some, the issues may seem too far removed from the day-to-day issues of the field, of which there are an ample number. However, the intent of the book is to place the issues within the context of American society—its political, sociological, economic, moral, and religious realities. Although none of the topics can be explored at the depth an entire volume on each would entail, there is considerable intertwining of the topics throughout this section. Undeniably, money and/or the lack of it is far more pervasive than one might prefer. Other themes that are relevant throughout are equity in education, quality and value of life, the identification and pursuit of meaningful outcomes in life, and the meaning of power in our society.

Chapter 9 focuses on what might seem a rather straightforward topic—that of funding special education. Most funding is predicated on the notion of excess funding, which has proven far more difficult to define on ledgers than in the concept. The tenth chapter is focused on two challenging issues relevant to disability and technological advancements in our society: the allocation of resources and the meaning of disability. Within the eleventh chapter, the balance between the need to protect persons with disabilities and their rights is discussed, as is the role of educators in assisting graduates to begin their adult years with a satisfactory quality of life. The issues presented in Chapter 12 focus on a contrast between modern and postmodern theories and their meaning for special education. The evolution of our society away from modern values and lifestyles to those characterizing the postmodern world is creating a collision of thought and policy in schools and the education community. Politics, power, and the culture of disability within a postmodern context leave us pondering the benefits and unintended outcomes of special education.

9

Funding Special
Education and
Related Services

INTRODUCTION

Historically, special educators have tended to devote less of their energy and attention to monetary matters, focusing rather on sociopolitical issues, educational methodologies, and developmental theories (Lewis, Bruininks, & Thurlow, 1991). Economically related outcomes are rarely employed to evaluate the cost effectiveness of instructional programs. Rather, the focus is typically on progress of students, improving behavior, or successful transition outcomes. Special education and related services do trigger extra expenditures for school systems in numerous ways, regardless of the delivery model in place. Self-contained classes have low enrollments and are typically accompanied by a variety of related services. Other models of service delivery, such as consultant models and resource programs (both pull-out and stay-put models), and full inclusion necessitate hiring supplemental teachers and purchasing additional materials and supplies, providing additional classroom space, and so forth. Nevertheless, topics such as excess costs, funding formulas, marginal costs, cost ratios, and benefit-cost analyses are not routine matters of conversation among special educators.

However, school administrators, who hold responsibility for the fiscal soundness of their school districts and state education programs, are most concerned about such matters. Bringing the sociopolitical agenda of special education in concert with the fiscal restraints of well-run school systems has proven to be a difficult task. The entitlement nature of IDEA and relative underfunding at the federal level (U.S. Department of Education, 1995) have fostered financial battles at local levels. Some of these have resulted in due process hearings and represent some of the hardest fought cases. In some instances school administrators have even pursued the use of third-party billing to fund related services provided by the schools (Rogers, 1991). Administrators, striving to keep costs contained and maintain strong educational programs for everyone, fear the financial impact that a single case can have on an entire school district or beyond.

Federal and state mandates for special education and related services are implemented by local schools that are competing for a fair share of available revenues with transportation, health and human services, parks and recreation, law enforcement, libraries, waste management, and many other vital community services. The negotiating and bargaining continue within education as the disbursement of education dollars within each district stimulates more debates, requiring the prioritization of spending. Building projects, reductions of student-to-teacher ratios, investments in technology, increased availability of social workers and guidance personnel, the purchase of new textbooks, improvement of food services, provision of adequate transportation, funding raises, support of extracurricular activities, and many other important issues come to the front as school budgets are set.

Federal- and state-level funding contributions are intended to offer supplements to the districts rather than supplant their basic fiscal responsibility for the education of all of their children. These contributions have never even approached the allowable 40% allotments authorized in IDEA (U.S. Department of Education, 1995). Previously funds have been allocated to states based on a relative count of children with disabilities being served (Parrish, 1993). The 1997 reauthorization of IDEA includes a change to population and poverty-level funding after initial expenditures reach $4.9 billion. This change is similar to recommendations offered by the Council for Exceptional Children (1995). Infant and toddler programs, now referred to as Part C, continue to be allocated based on participating states' total child population birth through age two. Some states, including Massachusetts, Montana, Pennsylvania, and Vermont, have already moved their state-level Part B disbursements to a total 3–21 population formula, rather than disability counts (CEC, 1995).

The terms are often used interchangeably, but there is a distinction between special education costs and expenditures (Center for Special Education Finance, 1993). Costs involve consideration of both the benefits and resources used in the delivery of special education as well as the price of various services and resources in a locale. When finite resources are directed toward certain special education programs, they are necessarily directed away from other programs. This funneling of resources away from some programs to support others should be included in a cost analysis, whereas expenditures refer to the actual amounts spent on special education. However, the terminology used in the related literature and school policies does not consistently reflect this semantic distinction. For example, special education expenditures are often figured and reported in terms of total costs and excess costs. Total costs calculations are based on the sum of prorated expenditures for instruction and administration associated with special education, instruction and administration associated with general education, related services, and any required specialized equipment.

The calculation of both expenditures and resource costs is used in cost analyses and policy development. Expenditure models rely on school district budgets to determine per-pupil estimates of general and special education expenses. The fact that school districts do not maintain identical accounting systems and that some do not specify expenditures by program does put limitations on this approach (Raphel, Singer, & Walker, 1985). Other threats to the accuracy of this model result when previously purchased resources or those provided by another agency are not counted, pricing estimates of resources underestimate true costs, or costs of a specific intervention are imbedded in a comprehensive budget (Levin, 1983). The resource cost model, based on Levin's (1983) work, corrects for these limitations but requires extensive data collection and detailed accounting. The costs of all resources (both direct and indirect), such as salaries, equipment, facilities, are gathered and totaled. Per-pupil costs are then determined by dividing total program costs by the number of students in each program. We must retain some concerns regarding both the means of calculation and the accuracy of the data presented throughout the remainder of this chapter.

Escalating Costs of Special Education and Equity of Distribution

The federal presence in elementary and secondary education was minor prior to the 1960s. In 1966, Congressional hearings revealed that only about one-third of 5.5 million children and youth with disabilities were receiving appropriate special education services (U.S. Department of Education, 1995). Legislation that grew out of these hearings and concurrent litigation established a two-year grant project for states with funding based on the population of exceptional children age three through twenty-one. Federal legislation continued to evolve, and population-based grants were replaced by formula grants, so the maximum grant became equal to the actual number of children with disabilities age three through twenty-one receiving special education and related services multiplied by a percentage of national average per-pupil expenditures. Today, IDEA funds both formula grant programs and discretionary grant programs intended to stimulate improvements through recruitment and training of personnel, research and demonstration projects, development and dissemination of instructional materials and information, and some direct services to children. For states and local school districts striving to achieve compliance with IDEA, the availability of financial supports is a critical matter.

Demographic factors, such as economic status and cultural characteristics, are associated with need and demands for special education (Sage & Burrello, 1994). High-density urban and economically depressed rural areas have greater needs than do affluent and middle class urban/suburban areas. Although the wealthier systems with well-developed services do experience a magnet effect, systems with greater wealth can more easily provide a greater quality of services and

A teacher makes do with a hallway for instruction in an overcrowded school.

concurrently tend to have far fewer students with special education needs. If poorer districts offer something less, the parents may be less aware of their rights and/or lack the mobility to change school systems. Wealthy school districts have greater resources to offer quality programs, are pushed by aggressive parents to provide even more, and gain more state resources as they attract greater numbers of students to their district. The development of quality special education programs is irrefutably linked to the funding of these programs as well as the funding of all education.

Both costs and expenditures associated with special education and related services have increased as the number of students has increased. Nebraska offers an illustrative example, with dramatic increases in the number of students served by special education and the resulting impact on state budgets (Tappe, 1995). In 1994, $115 million was appropriated for special education, whereas the 1995 figure rose to $122 million—a $7 million increase in the span of one year. Likewise, Hartman (1993) reported dramatic increases in Pennsylvania between 1988–89 and 1991–92. In 1989, there was a $100 million shortfall in state special education funding, and an additional $148 million debt just two years later. The existing funding formula was targeted as a critical factor in the rapid increases in special education expenditures at the district level and was then altered.

The reasons for such expenditure increases appear to be many. Tappe (1995) noted that the increased costs in Nebraska have been associated with increased survival rates, deinstitutionalization of children with severe disabilities who need multiple services, extension of the school year and school day, inflation of equipment costs, increased costs associated with inclusion, facility improvements to increase accessibility, provision of services to students in private facilities, excessive paperwork, transportation costs, shifting financial responsibility between state agencies, and increased referrals from regular education. Additional factors affecting costs throughout the country include expansion of federal categories, broader interpretations of learning disabilities definitions with resulting increases in students so labeled, improved conditions in the intensive care nursery, and apparent increases in the use of alcohol and drugs during pregnancy.

Any one of these factors can place a heavy financial load on limited educational resources. It has been predicted that social problems such as drug usage and AIDS infection, combined with technological and medical advances, will more than double the number of children with severe disabilities in our schools (CSEF, 1993). Chaikind and Corman (1990) followed up a national sample of approximately 8,000 children ages six to fifteen and determined that children who weigh less than 2,500 grams at birth are almost 50% more likely to be enrolled in some type of special education than those of normal weight. At an average cost of $4,350 per student (based on 1989–1990 figures) for special education, they projected a resulting increase of $370.8 million per year due to low birth weight. Our responsibility and accountability for the education of these and other students who require educational resources beyond those provided to general education are real, but cannot be met without direct confrontation of the associated cost issues.

Cost Factors of Free
Appropriate Public Education

A cost analysis of public education formula was developed to determine the costs of elementary and secondary general education and special education across five components: comprehensive costs (including transportation and supplemental expenses), service costs (maintenance/operations and supplemental expenses), administrative costs (general, level-specific, and site-based costs), support costs (assessment, direct services, and related services), and instructional costs (special education, general education, and supplemental expenses) (Moche, 1995). When applied to the 1992–1993 cost data from three southwest Virginia school systems, the following results were obtained: special education annual per-pupil expenditures averaged 1.2 to 1.6 times the cost of general education; per-pupil costs of inclusive programming were almost twice as great as costs of traditional mainstreaming, but 30% to 60% less than segregated special education services; and per-pupil expenditures for special education were more costly at the secondary level than the elementary level. These findings are not necessarily what would be found in other areas, because no universally agreed-upon accounting principles or definitions of programming exist across states. As a result, inconsistency and confusion often characterize efforts to determine costs associated with service delivery models. For example, Picus and Miller (1995) described a California case study of San Mateo County between 1971 and 1986 in which segregated services cost $9,064 per pupil whereas educating a student in an integrated model cost $11,166. However, during this study the school district changed its policy for serving students with severe disabilities and transferred them from out of district placements back into new programs within their home district. The policy shift might offer an explanation of why these results were inconsistent with those of a previous study, in which costs for integrated students

Computer labs and other educational resources contribute to the costs of general education.

were found to be 9% less than for those in segregated classrooms. In interviews, eight directors of cooperative service centers said it was too soon to say what the cost effects were, four indicated increased costs, ten said there was a decrease, and three did not know. The confusion is apparent.

The states hold primary responsibility for providing special education services and currently fund 56% of the necessary financial support. Thirty-six percent comes from local sources and 8% from the federal government (Sage & Burrello, 1994; U.S. Department of Education, 1995). Both litigation and the philosophical beliefs of many in the field hold that cost of services must not dictate educational programming available for children with special needs (Bartlett, 1993). The justifications for these demands have been primarily political and moral, not economic, yet they have a substantial economic impact on local, state, and federal education budgets. A rural community with a limited tax base and few resources to spend on education might find the expense of educating a single child with a low incidence condition, such as deaf-blindness, a threat to their continued solvency. The extent to which that district can look to the state or federal government for relief may be critical. District personnel must either create a specialized program for the child, support an out-of-district placement, collaborate with neighboring districts in the creation of a cooperative venture, or rely on a state-supported school. Any of these choices is expensive, regardless of the rightness of providing the services for the child in the least restrictive environment. For a large metropolitan district, children with such a condition would likely have less of an impact on the school budget, simply because there may be a sufficient number of other children who share similar needs and the team of resource personnel who have the needed expertise would work with multiple students.

Special education financing has increased in importance as the number of students served has grown and the federal contribution to support IDEA has failed to accelerate. The Center for Special Education Finance within the Department of Education has been established to determine how to maximize the quality of educational services for students with special needs given limited resources (U.S. Department of Education, 1995). At the federal level, debates center on broad strokes, such as the use of population formulas versus disability head count formulas to disburse funds to the states (CEC, 1995). At the state level, the merits of numerous formulas are disputed, including various excess cost formulas and actual expenditure reimbursement patterns. Any suggestion that special education funds be combined with regular education dollars into a single budget is generally not popular with special educators, but might be considered more consistent with many of newer inclusionary programming options than are current policies.

Focus of Discussion

Funding formulas have proven to have implications never anticipated by their originators, and the current inclusive direction of special education could not have been predicted when many state legislatures were developing the first funding formulas. Advocates who once argued heavily in favor of one type of special education funding may now find themselves opposing those formulas. These issues are addressed in the following section. The second discussion included in this chapter is directed toward the notion of cost/benefit analyses and special education. Although great debates have focused on the use of least restrictive placements, less has been said directly about the identification of the most cost-effective means for delivering special education. In this period of corporate downsizing, increased government accountability for its use of tax dollars, and a move toward outcomes-based education, such considerations will become a reality for educators as well.

FUNDING FORMULAS

States disburse funds to local school districts for special education based on their own funding formulas, which are in turn based on one of several common types of funding formulas (U.S. Department of Education, 1995; CSEF, 1993). Each formula varies in its basis of allocation and the nature of its impact on policy. Placement, disabling condition, a combination of placement and condition, classroom unit, allowable costs, actual expenditures, number of special education staff, special education enrollments, and total district enrollment each take priority depending on the formula in place. Generally, the goal is to cover all or a portion of costs of special education deemed over and above those of general education. These formulas can directly or indirectly affect the number and types of children served, the type of programs offered, the duration of services, placement options, class size, and caseloads (O'Reilly, 1989). The formulas have been targeted as causing overidentification, underidentification, overreliance of restrictive placements, use of programs lacking the comprehensive support services needed by some students, and so forth (CSEF, 1993). Although there is little empirical evidence to support the implications attached to each of the formula types they are considered theoretical presumptions.

The extent of current or anticipated reform does suggest a widespread dissatisfaction with current funding patterns. Some states (e.g., California and Oregon) have capped the growth of special education aid by limiting the number of students eligible for reimbursement. Some states, such as Massachusetts, Montana, Pennsylvania, and Vermont, are trying to remove fiscal incentives for identifying special education students by decoupling funding from the special education student count. These states use a census-based funding system instead. Some states are moving away from traditional pupil-weighted formulas, and others are considering adopting them. In an attempt to develop a system that was easy to understand, placement neutral, and would reduce the need for documentation and paperwork, Oregon adopted a single funding weight system whereby the per-pupil special education allocation was made twice that of the per-pupil general education allocation (Sage & Burrello, 1994).

Excess Costs as a Concept

In 1975, the concept of excess costs was used as a principle for the disbursement of federal funds to support IDEA. Typically, excess costs have been defined as the difference between special education and general education costs on the basis of per-pupil costs. The concept appears simple at first, but the determination of precisely what to include in the calculation of each figure has proven troublesome for state and local school systems. State regulations generally identify allowable costs, typically including salaries for personnel working directly in special education programs (primarily teachers and teaching assistants, although special education supervisors and administrators may also be included); personnel benefits; and purchased services, supplies, books, and equipment. Some general education costs might also be allowed, such as prorated portions of professional and clerical salaries for guidance counseling, psychological testing, and school libraries; administrative and clerical salaries; and expenditures for the operation and maintenance of facilities. Allocation percentages of these items are then based on the percentage of students served by special education. Total instructional costs per pupil are finally determined by dividing the total costs by the number of students in special education on a full-time equivalent (FTE) basis. General education costs are determined in a similar fashion.

The concept of excess costs seems straightforward and equitable until the numerous incongruities become apparent. Some variables, such as drops or increases in enrollment, or general expenditures, influence excess cost calculations when no real cost differentials have occurred (Hartman, 1990). To illustrate, the purchase of new computers for a system would increase the costs of general education, raising per-pupil expenditures of general education, thereby creating a decrease in the excess cost figure for special education. Enrollment decreases in general education have a similar effect—as enrollments drop, costs per pupil rise. Further complications occur with student counts. The majority of special education students are served by resource or itinerant teachers and are in special education only a small portion of their school day. The most common solution to this problem is counting individual time spent in special education and determining full-time equivalency (FTE), which requires extensive record keeping. It seems to be neither an accurate economic system nor practical for program management. When calculations are based on actual attendance, there is a faulty assumption that the real cost of education is reduced when students are not present. The teacher is still there, the facilities and operations have not been reduced, but the allotted dollars have. When a student in a self-contained class spends part of the day in the general education program, excess costs tend to increase rather than decrease, because the special education count is lowered (and costs per pupil rise) and the general education count is only negligibly increased by the small increments of FTE represented by these students. Another difficulty is that not all students in special education require the same level of services. Speech therapy twice a week for thirty minutes does not cost the same as full-time placement in a special education classroom. Excess costs models have generally been based on average costs of these widely disparate services.

Achieving Program Goals Through Funding Patterns

Many states use the child-based formulas with pupil weights, involving the creation of two or more categories of student-based funding for special programs, often expressed as a multiple of general education costs. For example, for each student with mild disabilities served, a district might receive twice the amount needed per pupil for regular education and five times that of general education for students with severe disabilities. Child-based formulas may encourage overclassification but seem necessary in states that fund general education on pupil enrollment or attendance for funding pattern compatibility. If the formula is based on types of children, it necessarily depends heavily on labeling students. However, the use of unweighted formulas might increase a tendency to identify borderline children and underserve those with more extensive needs. Weighted formulas, on the other hand, might encourage overplacement of students in those programs that generate the most funds.

A simple financing system is the flat grant approach, based on a fixed funding amount per student. Funding is based on student counts, most often those with disabilities, but some states are now using total population counts. Since there are no allowances made for variability of the cost of resources or wealth of a district as a whole, the approach does not offer any compensatory benefit. Because of these nonequalizing characteristics, the approach is not in wide use today (Sage & Burrello, 1994). However, when balanced against complex funding formulas, which require extensive record keeping and paperwork, the approach appeals to a desire for simplicity and reduced government bureaucracy. A similar appeal to simplicity of reform is heard in political proposals today for a "flat tax" for personal income.

Others rely on resource-based formulas, with funding fixed on an allocation of specific education resources (e.g., classroom units). Classroom units are generally derived from prescribed staff/student ratios by disabling condition or type of placement. Resource-based formulas emphasize resources supplied, such as teachers or other personnel. The disbursement of funds can be a flat amount per teacher or based on actual costs, which makes it more equalizing for all school systems and does not necessarily require labeling of students. Such formulas are less likely to lead to overidentification because the link between child counts and dollars is indirect. The approach does require that states regulate the funding with policies on the proper quantity of units to authorize, class size standards, and accounting of other costs of the programs, which may discourage local creativity in educational programming (Sage & Burrello, 1994).

Another funding pattern is use of cost-based formulas, typically percent reimbursements, that entail funding based on a percentage of allowable or actual expenditures after they have been incurred. Cost-based formulas are theoretically fiscally neutral if excess costs are fully reimbursed, but an unlimited ceiling on expenditures in local or state budgets is not realistic. These systems minimize the labeling of children and allow the maximum in programming flexibility, but they do require complex cost accounting procedures. Precision in accountability regarding the percentages of time individual students spend in different programming options and strict adherence to policies of eligibility for services are necessary elements of this approach.

States are struggling to maintain special education programs while gaining some control over the associated escalating expenditures, so many of them are in the process of finance reform. In 1994, eighteen states had implemented some type of financial reform within the past five years, and twenty-eight (some of which were the same) were considering major fiscal policy changes (U.S. Department of Education, 1995). The consensus among those participating in a government survey regarding special education funding was that there are primarily two needed reforms: the provision of special education in more flexible ways and the elimination of incentives that lead to restrictive placements (U.S. Department of Education, 1995). Other responses indicated that goals pertaining to improving fiscal accountability, simplifying formulas, ensuring adequate service, establishing equity, controlling rising special education costs and enrollments, and influencing acceptance of more inclusive educational practices were also important.

Decision Point 9.1: Funding
Special Education for the Future

Arguments for Proposition One   Without the maintenance of separate special education funds with dedicated uses, local school administrators would be free to reallocate funds intended to support special education and related services to general education. The courts have already confirmed that resources are needed to provide an appropriate education for students with disabilities and that individuals with disabilities may necessitate sacrifices in services provided to the rest in order to achieve equity (Bartlett, 1993). The abandonment of funds dedicated to the exclusive use of educating students with disabilities would negate the battles and struggles of the past. These battles would need to be refought, ulti-

---

Proposition One

Accountability for the use of special education funds to achieve equity and high minimum standards for students with disabilities must be safe-guarded through the maintenance of a well-designed formula approach for funding the excess costs of special education.

---

mately costing schools more effort than any funding formula accounting procedures might require of them to maintain equitable programs for students with disabilities. Instead of investing our energies into designing the most productive educational services for all children, we would be back to a point of reestablishing the legal rights of some of those children to an equitable chance for an education.

Although none of the formulas in use today are completely free from drawbacks, there are viable compromises that can be considered during this period of massive finance reform. The goal of the states should be to develop formulas that are fiscally neutral from the perspective of the service recipients (students) and that of the resource providers (taxpayers) (Sage & Burrello, 1994). Unquestionably, the reform formulas can and must be set up to avoid the accounting complexities seen in the past. These principles are apparent in some states where reforms have begun. For example, the reformed New York system is designed to achieve both fiscal neutrality and simple accounting, by combining an approved excess-cost concept with a variable weighted pupil-attendance unit approach based on the intensity of services provided rather than disability classification. Reforms such as this one will serve to help all the states experiment with and identify suitable new formulas.

The concept of equality in education is generally defined as equal access to some minimum standard, such as class size, teacher qualifications, and curricular content. Sage and Burrello (1994) suggest that a more reasonable interpretation endorses the understanding that equal treatment necessitates the provision of unequal resources in order to compensate for the unequal needs of students. Such a principle is at the very foundation of both special education and compensatory education programs. Yet another interpretation of equality could involve the achievement of equal outcomes (Clune, 1994b).

Excess Costs as a Concept The specific formulas used vary, yet all are based on the notion that the provision of special education costs more than the provision of general education and, therefore, needs a broader base of funding than that of the local school district (Sage & Burrello, 1994). The rationale for this position is threefold. First, children with special needs are a small but significant minority group whose rights need special protections. Second, there is not an equal distribution of students with disabilities across all districts, nor is there an exact proportion of students with similar diagnoses present within each district. Third, the cost of educational services to meet special needs will be greater than the cost of educating students who do not require such services, and these costs will vary based on geographic locale, subcategory of special need, and the particular patterns of service delivery employed.

However, the concept of excess costs, as it has been defined and used, has been fraught with inconsistency and inappropriate fluctuations. Hartman (1990) has proposed that excess costs be redefined in terms of programs and services rather than emphasizing costs per pupil. Two basic categories of services would be identified: supplemental services and replacement services. Supplemental services would include all programs and services provided *in addition to* general education, and all costs would be considered excess costs. Replacement services would comprise those programs and services provided *instead of* a general education program. Replacement excess costs would be the difference between the special education costs and those of the replaced general education programs. *Supplemental* and *replacement* would be defined by a simplified time-in-program calculation based on the policy whereby less than 50% time would be considered supplemental. Special education programs in which students spent over 50% of their school time would be defined as replacement programs. Simple enrollment counts would replace the need for FTE calculations, so parallel calculations of both general and special education per-pupil costs could be maintained.

The model is designed to supply a financial incentive for integrating students with disabilities into general education classes while providing adequate funding of an entire continuum of program options. The most obvious possible abuse of this approach is the incentive to misplace students in special education to increase funding. If supplemental services are fully reimbursed and replacement programs are not, the potential for inappropriate placement is real and would need to be safeguarded against. The reality is that the potential for the misuse of any funding system, either consciously or unconsciously, is ever present (Hartman, 1990). Although Hartman, himself, points to flaws in his proposal, it offers real evidence of our ability to create new approaches to the calculation of excess costs that will diminish some of the current deficiencies and avoid the political drawbacks inherent in combining special education funds with general education funds.

Achieving Program Goals Through Funding Patterns State-level studies reveal that although funding systems are not perfect, the basic structures in place have been functional. Coleman et al. (1994) sought to determine whether, in New Jersey, special education funding influences the number or types of pupils referred to special education services, the designation of their disability, and the setting of services. The findings indicate that in special education decisions, costs incurred by local districts are more important than the amount of available state aid and that state aid for special education did not promote excessive identification of children with disabilities. In fact, requirements associated with special education actually inhibited identification, because additional costs were not fully covered and administrators preferred to keep special education rolls as low as possible. State aid did not promote the selection of classifications with higher reimbursements or additional cost factors, nor did it appear to be a primary factor in determining student placements. Instead, financial resources became an important factor in placement decisions. The claim that state funding formulas encourage local systems to abuse the system either by overidentifying students or placing them inappropriately in the most reimbursable placements was not apparent. Further evidence from Illinois also indicates that radical reform is not needed in the financing of special education, although the tax base for supporting it and all of education does need to be broadened beyond that of local property taxes (Arnold, Genge, & Anthony, 1994). Arnold, Genge, and Anthony examined the costs incurred by local education agencies for the delivery of special education and determined that although costs were high, they were consistent with other educational programs targeting individual needs. The importance of meeting the individual educational needs of children is certainly worth these extra costs.

Some argue that the restriction of special education dollars to serve only those children who meet eligibility criteria penalizes those who need support and specialized instruction but who fail to meet precise categorical criteria, and/or fosters an unnecessary reliance on labeling. Such logic is based on the assumption that schools are not free to spend all the rest of their funding as they see fit. In fact, schools are free to establish student-to-teacher ratios below a maximum level, have as many computers in classrooms as are wanted, support guidance counselors in elementary schools, offer supplemental instructional supports to all students based on educational need, and/or fund bands, art programs, and athletic activities at will. Obviously, the community or state must be willing to pay for these choices. In the absence of such willingness, it does not then become the obligation of special education funding to address every deficiency or gap in educational programming that the taxpayers and administrators have created. To do so would only exacerbate the problem of abdication of responsibility for this population of students by general educators.

There are guidelines that can be useful in the development of funding formulas that will foster progressive trends within the field. The U.S. Department of Education (1995) has developed specifications for fiscal policies that advance inclusion, such as removing fiscal incentives that favor restrictive and separate placements, focusing close scrutiny on all private placements while eliminating barriers to the creation of local services, allowing funds to follow students into less restrictive placements, and offering training in effective instruction for existing regular classroom personnel. Balancing these criteria to meet differing program objectives can be difficult, because putting a major focus on one objective often comes at the expense of others. Parrish (1995) notes that an effective formula should be understandable, equitable, adequate, predictable, flexible, neutral as regards specific disability identification, reasonable in reporting requirements, fiscally accountable, cost-based, neutral regarding type of educational placement, able to lead to stabilized costs, accountable for outcomes, connectable to general education funding, and politically acceptable. States must seek to achieve greater equity in funding systems without bankrupting the entire educational system.

Reforms in funding policies within several state—in addition to those of New York, mentioned previously—are indicative of the continued validity of this approach to special education funding. Oregon restructured its special education funding system in 1991, providing local systems with grants that are twice the regular per-student allocation for every identified special education student up to

11% of the total school population (Montgomery, 1995a). This formula is neutral as to disabling condition and placement, eliminates the need for additional paperwork, does not restrict funds for use with special education students but sets a funding cap to protect the interests of those with disabilities, and includes a weighting to adjust for district wealth. Vermont restructured special education funding in 1990 to increase equity, predictability, and flexibility in program design and to ensure placement neutrality (Montgomery, 1995b). Specific objectives of the new formulas were to increase prereferral services and inclusion, incorporating three components—a mainstream block grant to school districts based on total student enrollment; an extraordinary service reimbursement, providing compensation to districts for unusually high-cost individual cases; and an intensive services reimbursement to help with all allowable special education costs not otherwise covered. These examples lend further support to the idea that funding formulas can be revised to reduce the negative impact that previous funding patterns have had on special education services. Funding formulas must be designed to be consistent with the programmatic goals of special education, not punish school districts for using inclusive settings.

Argument Summary Paperwork and documentation of enrollments have long been considered major drawbacks associated with special education. Some might jump at a chance to drop the record keeping currently associated with many formula funding approaches. However, the dramatic escalation of technology and networking combined with simplified formulas will continue to reduce the weight of this problem. When funding matches as closely as possible with actual expenditures and there are a sufficient number of levels of support, formula-related problems can be minimized (Sage & Burrello, 1994). The argument is not that all states universally adopt one single best definition of excess costs or funding formula, because educational funding patterns, tax base differentials, wealth, and resources are real variables affecting each state differently. However, principles to which funding patterns should adhere are essential. Formula funding simply represents an opportunity for school districts to obtain a bonus when they fulfill their constitutional obligation to provide education for all students within their area. Special education is a system based on individual needs, whereas general educational fiscal policy is designed around average group needs and is not sufficient to satisfy the needs of individual students.

Arguments for Proposition Two As long as there is a separate fund of dollars for special education, the provision of such services will be viewed by local administrators as an underfunded burden, not a basic right of the students so served. Funding formulas represent an outdated approach to special education financing and now actually interfere with the development of improved programming models. For example, funds are available to help those who meet eligibility criteria, but these funds often cannot be used to help school personnel seeking to implement prevention models for students who must fail for several years before finally achieving eligibility. We have integrated our students and are striving to collapse the barriers and walls between general and special education, but we continue to

---

Proposition Two
The merger of all educational resources into a single comprehensive fund would enable schools to provide a seamless system of services to meet the wide array of educational needs of children without wasted hours of documentation, accounting, and complying with innumerable government regulations.

---

hang on to the dollars as though special education were continuing to be a segregated affair. The time is right to integrate funding as well as students.

The least local flexibility is available in those states reliant on allocations directly linked to placement, whereas allocations based on total district enrollment or other similar broad criteria have allowed more freedom for local special educators to identify unique methods of serving all students, not just those eligible for special education (U.S. Department of Education, 1995).

Excess Costs as a Concept Limitations put on the uses of the dollars distributed for special education can directly influence the nature of programs offered. Currently, thirty-three of the states have already dropped the requirement that all special education funds be spent exclusively on special education services (U.S. Department of Education, 1995). Such states can more easily implement inclusionary programs and focus on meeting the educational needs of all children, rather than wasting substantial sums of money assessing children and arguing about their compliance with eligibility criteria. Separate formula funding only makes the process of collaborative education more difficult because it implies a lack of equal ownership and responsibility on the part of the education establishment for all students. Would we line up all of our potential first-graders and put one hundred on a waiting list because the money ran out? Those children would then have to go uneducated unless the federal or state government gave the system extra funds to support the *excess costs* they represent over and beyond what the local school district was willing to spend on first-grade education. Give those children a disability, and suddenly what seemed ludicrous has been a prevailing attitude. Even before IDEA was enacted, in the *Mills v. Board of Education* case "insufficient funds" was ruled an unconstitutional excuse for failing to provide children with an education (Bartlett, 1993), and it can no longer be used as an excuse to avoid the responsibility of local school districts to all their students.

In some states, the restriction of special education dollars appears to force the increased identification of students with disabilities, because it is perceived as the only means by which help can be obtained for these children. Sage and Burrello (1994) cite a statement of the National Association of State Boards of Education that recommends severing any link between funding and programming, and the labeling of children. The underlying basis for our programming and placement decisions must not be funding issues. Similar sentiments were incorporated in a recommendation from the Council of Administrators of Special Education to support a unified system of shared funding without prejudice or labeling of children. In considering possible solutions to the escalating costs of special education in Nebraska, Tappe (1995) notes that placing a cap on special education spending is not the answer and recommends that some costs become the responsibility of general education, the Department of Public Institutions, and the Department of Social Services. Such an interagency collaborative approach cannot be achieved when special educators approach the negotiating table demanding the continuation of protected dollars and arbitrary definitions of excess costs, expecting all other special interest groups to pool their resources.

Achieving Program Goals Through Funding Patterns For the most part, results analyzing costs of various service delivery models are restricted state reports with limited generality to other states. This limitation is partially a result of the variability seen in data keeping and definitions used by the states (CSEF, 1993). Nevertheless, individual state reports can be compared to reveal certain patterns that result from funding formulas. Dempsey and Fuchs (1992) analyzed Tennessee data from 1979–80 to 1987–88, comparing two formulas for funding disbursement: flat grants that provided a fixed amount per child, teacher, or classroom unit, and weighted calculations based on types of children with specific disabilities multiplied by an average per-pupil cost weighted to the type of service or degree of disability. Their findings were indicative of the problems inherent in many funding formula systems, with the weighted formula being associated with a statistically significant decrease in less restrictive placements and a reliable increase in more restrictive placements. A follow-up survey of ninety district special education directors indicated that they believed that the change was really due to service needs, not monetary incentives for the district. The statistical differential was real, but the administrators involved were apparently not prepared to entertain any possible link or subtle influences of funding patterns on their programming decisions. Such findings are not unlike the self-fulfilling prophecy patterns of teacher behavior consistently witnessed in classrooms throughout the nation. The benefits of freedom from such formulas could be tremendous.

The Department of Education-funded CSEF wants some specific issues addressed when states consider retention or adoption of pupil weight formulas. First, they recommend that attention be given to whether funding amounts ought to vary by type of placement or type of disabling condition, or be based on a single weight for all. CSEF holds that weights based on placement have the advantage in being closer to actual program costs, but may create incentives for more costly and more restrictive placements. Formula weights based on disability type have the advantage of being placement neutral but are generally not closely related to actual costs. Any pupil weight system creates an incentive to identify students as needing special education services. Some say that this is good because it strengthens the link between state aid and district costs, but others argue that any fiscal incentive for identifying students as needing special education should be eliminated and replaced with census-based funding systems. This apparent confusion and inconsistency in expectations of funding formulas that ought to be compatible with best practices are further evidence of the need to drop them altogether.

Special education costs and funding have grown, with a resulting shrinking pool of funds available for general education. Current funding patterns have forced the fields into a competitive relationship rather than a collaborative one, characterized by separateness of employees, materials and supplies, and instructional ideas. Since IDEA was enacted in the mid-1970s, general educators' dependence on special education to address the needs of students beyond either their real or perceived skills has interfered with improvements in instruction for all children in regular classes (Case, 1992). In some instances, funding for single children or very small groups of children has competed with general education for tens of thousands of dollars (Bartlett, 1993). Unification eliminates the competitive atmosphere prevalent today and enables everyone to direct attention to cost-manageable solutions for all.

Argument Summary As the need for special educators has risen, so has the demand for multiple associated personnel, including teaching assistants, psychologists, supervisors, and directors. The numbers and costs continue multiplying as the general educator has fewer resources available to her, is facing higher student/teacher ratios, has an increasing need to refer more children to special education as her only source of support, and is concurrently expected to reintegrate students with disabilities into her classroom. As long as the financial patterns remain competitive, there is no end to the cyclical nature of this problem. We can expect children's problems to continue rising; therefore, it is pointless to expect that special education costs can be successfully reduced or even contained in the long run. For too long, special education has followed the old medical model with an emphasis on treatment rather than prevention, and it needs to update just as medicine has done by supplementing (and on occasion avoiding) prescriptive medicine with diet and exercise treatment plans. It is time for the transition into a collaborative prevention/services model, in which funding supports all efforts rather than special interests at the expense of the common good.

COST EFFECTIVENESS
AND PROGRAM ADEQUACY

The right to a free appropriate education designed to offer equitable access to educational opportunity is clearly established for all students. The extent to which educational programming for a student in special education is directly linked to her IEP determines its legal appropriateness but does not necessarily offer the most cost-effective approach to the stated educational outcomes. In fact, any attempts to link teacher evaluation or accountability of the schools with effectiveness or efficiency generally ignites professional resistance (Sage & Burrello, 1994). If school personnel are offering what appears to be a reasonable program in the least restrictive environment and are making a good-faith effort to enable a student to achieve the stated outcomes, nothing else is expected. The belief that cost must not be a primary consideration for educational placement further seems to deter special educators from much pursuit of cost-effective means of delivery. Yet the cost of special education as well as all of education has accelerated over the past twenty years (Barnett, 1994), courts have required

The poverty that children face in their homes can be seen in their educational opportunities as well.

schools to provide expensive services for single children (Bartlett, 1993), and accountability for the actual achievement of outcomes remains tenuous (Hilliard, 1992).

There is debate and some confusion not only about the role that cost should play in the determination of appropriate special education, but also regarding whether accountability should be focused on inputs to educational programs or on their achieved outcomes. Should our goal be to deliver education to students with disabilities that offers equality in access to education resources, or should it be to offer programs that are adequate to enable students to achieve high minimum standards? Some even point to the futility of attempting to define suitable measures when the effort reveals only the extent of our value conflicts regarding the basic purposes of education (Sage & Burrello, 1994). However, methods of evaluating educational programs for cost effectiveness have been presented in both the education and economic literature (e.g., Akin, 1970; Levin, 1983; Lewis, 1993; Lewis et al., 1991). Some methods are based on experimental designs that might be deemed unsuitable for use in conjunction with programs serving students with disabilities, but others focus on inputs and outputs as a measurement (CSEF, 1993). For example, integrated and segregated services in Madison, Wisconsin, for students with severe disabilities were compared using a benefits–cost analysis based on factors such as the cost of schools, costs of adult vocational services needed, and the financial benefits of post-school programs for recipients, taxpayers, and society (Piuma, cited in CSEF, 1993). Resources spent on the education of students were the inputs, and graduate participation in one of three types of employment was identified as outputs. Results of the analysis consistently indicated that there were long-term financial benefits associated with the integration model. The issue at hand is not the merits of integration versus segregation, but the feasibility of conducting cost-analysis studies with the intention of increasing the cost effectiveness of special education. The task requires maintaining a balance between philosophical and ethical principles and reasonable concern for the costs of special education. Can we attempt to address the cost effectiveness of our educational systems, particularly that of special education, without defensive, reactionary responses or fear of misplaced priorities? Cost data separated from meaningful data regarding the outcomes for program participants hold very limited utility, if any at all (CSEF, 1993).

Economic efficiency requires that the most productivity be achieved for the least investment. However, efficiency must be balanced with oftentimes conflicting notions of adequacy, such as is evident in student-to-teacher ratios. Economic efficiency is achieved by placing more students in each classroom, yet the adequacy of education offered is diminished in overcrowded classrooms (not to mention teacher replacement costs when working conditions become unbearable). Special education is caught in this adequacy and efficiency paradox. It is characterized by high cost factors such as low teacher ratios and provision of many supplemental services rather than basic services, and it is predicated on attention to the individual rather than groups. It presents the greatest financial burden to districts with the highest numbers of students with disabilities, which tend to be the poorest and least able to afford associated costs. Does the outside funding brought in through state and federal aid improve conditions, or do the demands to provide special education actually hamper the ability of such schools to offer comprehensive adequate educational programs?

The Economics of Special Education

Estimated average total per-pupil special education costs were $7,800 in 1989–1990 dollars, about 2.3 times the cost of educating a child in general education (Chaikind, Danielson, & Brauen, 1993). This figure is based on an average of a wide range of annual per-pupil costs, spanning from a low of approximately $1,000 for those with speech/language impairments to over $30,000 for students with deaf-blindness. The more prevalent conditions, such as learning disabilities, have far lower average costs than do low-incidence conditions, which require extensive specialized services. Types of services also influence costs, with resource rooms having the lowest average costs, whereas self-contained classrooms and residential schools are relatively high in cost. Chaikind et al. (1993) note that other factors influencing special education costs include eligibility and placement criteria set at district and state levels as well as the budgetary environment within the community and state. The entitlement nature of IDEA and the associated reimbursement formulas, Congressional annual appropriations, state funding formulas, and programmatic goals of each state (e.g., objectives of equity, local control of special education programs, and efficiency of service delivery) also affect overall costs.

Marginal cost is a concept that has emerged from the field of economics and refers to the cost of the next single unit of something, such as providing special education services for the next eligible child (Chaikind et al., 1993). This cost obviously depends on the extent of disability, district placement policies, location

Children from affluent neighborhoods feel the benefits of their socioeconomic status at school.

and size of the district, and numerous other variables. In special education, marginal cost is generally used to refer to the average cost of the next group of placements, rather than actual next placement costs, which remain unknown until a specific child is identified for services and an IEP is developed. In 1985–1986, the states reported special education expenditures of $16 billion in excess of the general education costs, which averaged an additional $3,696 per pupil served (Chaikind et al., 1993). Some argue that such expenditures create extraordinary financial burdens for local school districts, especially when the next child added figure might be $100,000 if it is a child with multiple disabilities (Bartlett, 1993; Chaikind et al., 1993). However, it is also possible that the next child with multiple disabilities could fit nicely into an existing program, actually lowering the average costs per pupil, because costs already in place (e.g., personnel, building maintenance) would be divided by one additional pupil. Cost efficiency would be gained with each addition to the program until finally an additional student would necessitate the infusion of substantial additional resources, such as personnel or transportation.

Cost ratio is the ratio of the average total per-pupil cost for special education to the average total per-pupil cost for general education, exclusive of costs for any special programs, including special education, Chapter One, and bilingual programs. It appears to have been relatively stable over the last thirty years, calculated at 1.92 from 1968–1969 data, 2.17 from 1977–1978 data, and 2.28 from 1985–1986 data (Chaikind et al., 1993). The upward trend may simply be an insignificant accident of the quality of the data, or it might be real, indicative of slightly proportional increases in the cost of providing special education services due to increases in mandated services, changing delivery models, more experienced teachers drawing higher salaries, or the need for specialized facilities for increasing populations of students with disabilities.

Related services costs are also considered a part of the financial obligation of the schools in conjunction with special education. The figures associated with the cost of related services are somewhat tenuous because there are rather large discrepancies between the two primary sources of data—the expenditures study of Moore, Strang, Schwartz, and Braddock (1988) and data reported by the states to the federal government (Chaikind et al., 1993). The expenditures study findings included per-pupil expenditures for supplemental services, which were defined as services in addition to primary instruction—assessments, transportation, adaptive physical education, occupational therapy, psychological services, social work, and school health services. Resource room supplemental services were 22% of the total per-pupil costs and 46% of average special education expenditures. For self-contained rooms, the figures were 19% of total per-pupil costs and 24% of average special education expenditures. Costs in 1985–1986 ranged from transportation at $1,583 per pupil to $1,206 for assessment services for the 6% of students who received assessments during the one-year period. Other average per-pupil expenditures involved special vocational services at $1,444, related services at $595, and adaptive physical education at $615. State-reported data indicated that a total of $3 billion was spent on related services in 1985–1986, which was 19% of the special education expenditures documented in these reports. The difference, particularly between the 46% from the expenditure study and this 19% figure, may be indicative of the variation in interpretation of categories of expenditure, state funding formulas (e.g., how excess costs are calculated), and inconsistencies in accounting procedures across states.

Cost Efficiency and Standards of Placement

Courts have been partially inconsistent in their consideration of cost as a relevant factor in the provision of special education services for individual children (Bartlett, 1993). This lack of consistency has the potential to undermine the very framework of public education; however, cases since 1982 have been more consistent than those before that time. Bartlett (1993) noted that cases related to cost considerations tend to fall into one of three groups: those in which cost was not considered relevant, those in which cost could be considered, and those in which cost was a relevant factor between appropriate and best programs. Confusion was apparent in a single case when a federal district judge in Florida refused to approve a settlement that involved the annual payment of $100,000 for the educational placement of a child with multiple disabilities on the grounds that it was excessive and, while perhaps in the best interests of the child, definitely not in the best interests of Florida taxpayers. However, the Eleventh Circuit Court overruled his opinion and accepted the settlement with apparently no consideration whatsoever of the cost of the educational program.

The inconsistency is also apparent in a number of different cases. Bartlett (1993) notes that in *Springdale School District #50 v. Grace* the school district had no program for a prelingual deaf child and developed an IEP to send her to a state school. The school district argued that it should not bear the cost of establishing a program for one student that would be of lower quality than the one already available through the state. The court ruled that the school district had ignored the least restrictive environment concept and that the child need not be given the "best" program, but must be given that which was in the least restrictive environment. In *A. W. v. Northwest R-I School District,* similar facts resulted in a different conclusion, where cost of special education placement could be considered in determining mainstreaming appropriateness. In a Nebraska case, excessive costs involved with mainstreaming were allowed as a factor having a negative impact on scarce revenues without significant benefit to the child. A mainstream environment was going to require $67,000, whereas a more restrictive program costing $4,000 was available and appropriate. Various other court opinions have included sentiments positing that cost is certainly a factor in the determination of appropriate education for students without disabilities; that educational funding is not without limits, because the funding of a single child at an exorbitant rate comes at the expense of other students with disabilities; and that school systems do have a responsibility to maintain up-to-date special education programs even when expense is involved.

Many claim to know the nature of cost factors linked to various instructional models, but all do not share common opinions. Inclusion is a favorite target for such assertions (Mawdsley, 1995; McCormick & First, 1994; McLaughlin & Warren, 1994), with some contending that it costs more than traditional special education models, others arguing that costs will be less, and finally some debating that inclusion must not become a justified means of reducing special education costs for local school districts. Other debates are heard regarding whether prevention models produce cost savings in the long run or whether centralized services offer a cost-efficient means of using related service personnel. For example, in a case where a program was available twenty-five miles away from a child's home, but not in the neighborhood school, the court noted that state resources were relevant (Bartlett, 1993). Other rulings have supported the idea that a concentration of resources at satellite schools is efficient and legal as long as such programs are within mainstream buildings. If exceptions were made for one child, the school would then be obligated to provide each similar student with individualized accommodations and efficiency would be lost. The efficiency argument has been persuasive to the courts *if* a standard of least restrictive environment has been addressed.

The issue of what constitutes an adequate educational program is a highly subjective, imprecise dynamic standard. The failure to provide any education at all is clearly inadequate and has been established as unconstitutional. Other general agreements on what constitutes adequacy do exist as well. The customs of our country have evolved to establish consensus agreements about the appropriate length of the school day and the school year. However, proponents of year-round schooling, particularly for students with disabilities, ask that even these well-entrenched understandings of adequacy be reevaluated. In a Mississippi case, for example, the court specifically ruled that lack of funds was no excuse for failing to provide more than 180 days of schooling when such was appropriate and needed for a student with disabilities (Bartlett, 1993). The court ruled that students who are educationally disadvantaged by a disability are entitled to a greater share of educational resources to enable them to have equitable access to educational opportunity.

Other target groups besides students with disabilities have also been the recipients of funds intended to help them compensate for some particular disadvantage and bring greater equity to their educational experience. However, Clune (1994b) has argued that the pursuit of equity through compensatory programs is the wrong goal. He proposes that the goal shift from equity to adequacy to achieve high minimum standards for all, including the most disadvantaged children. He has even proposed that cost figures such as $10,000 per child to enable children to achieve this end would not only be appropriate but also very similar to private school tuition payments. He defends the notion of funneling this much money into the education of disadvantaged children by asserting that such costs are justified because of the outcomes. Many more graduates of public school who had faced harsh disadvantages would be able to progress on to successful adulthoods, ending the destructive cycles set by poverty. Clune (1994a) defined *program adequacy* as (a) the cost of raising educational outcomes of poor children to the level of full functioning in society and (b) the systems of finance, governance, organization, implementation, and educational practice needed to guarantee these high minimum outcomes.

Since low-income school districts have high numbers of children labeled and served by special education, Clune's proposal raises several issues for the field. In fact, ideas about the most appropriate sources for funding a paradigm shift from equity models to ones based on adequacy make the connection quite clear. Levin (1994) contends that a major share of the costs associated with the shift to an adequacy model could be paid largely through the reallocation of resources currently used to fund special education. He argues that the creation of early academic success and greater inclusion of all students in rich instruction would substantially reduce the need for referrals to special education and virtually eliminate grade retentions. The proposal to fund low-income school districts on a level at which all children can achieve high minimum standards would ultimately require a reconfiguration of current special education funding and eligibility practices. Levin suggests that the shift from equity of inputs to the achievement of adequacy could be viewed as an expansion of the definition of special-needs students who are entitled to extra funding.

Although Clune contends that special education is already more directed toward adequacy of outcomes, many in the field might disagree. He argues that special education is already an adequacy model because of the process of identifying individual outcomes on the IEP. However, compliance monitoring has focused primarily on the input of resources and instructional efforts by the schools, with little consideration of the efficacy or efficiency of programs (Hilliard, 1992). The consistently poor outcomes for youth with disabilities following secondary schooling has only recently stimulated special educators to give greater consideration to the notion of adequate post-school outcomes for program participants.

Three types of measures have been used over time in education to control spending: (a) statutory caps on per-pupil revenues or expenditures, (b) tax-rate limits, and (c) annual budget negotiations (Sage & Burrello, 1994). These controls do hold costs down but do not necessarily lead to cost efficiency, nor do they in any way address the effectiveness of educational programs. We have cost figures and efficacy research on instructional techniques, but we have not connected the two. Research regarding the costs of special education consistently indicate that a minimal figure twice that of general education has been needed, with some estimates as much as five and even seven times as great when serving students with severe disabilities (Picus & Miller, 1995). It is appropriate to consider how accountable special educators must be for their expenditures to their students as well as to the taxpayers and in what manner that accountability should be measured.

Decision Point 9.2: Seeking Educational
Equity or Adequacy in Special Education

Arguments for Proposition One   Special education is predicated on the constitutional right of all children to equal access to education. The cost of an equal education for students with disabilities may necessarily exceed that of nondisabled students. The definition of *equality* has been the subject of numerous court cases, as has the extent to which cost is an acceptable factor to consider in the provision of special education (Bartlett, 1993). The notion that expenditure for one limits opportunity for all is often used as an explanation for why a particular service cannot be provided. For example, some have argued that the provision of clean intermittent catheterization for a child to be maintained in the regular program would divert limited funds from other special education students, but the courts found such an intervention to be a cost-effective means of placing the student in a mainstream setting (Bartlett, 1993). This and similar debates run throughout special education as well as education in general. Equity in the access to educational opportunities must remain a means of holding school personnel accountable to all students with disabilities and their families.

Responsible decisions and fiscally sound management of special education funds are important, but shifting accountability from equity of access to the cost-efficient achievement of outcomes is not appropriate. Education is a social science and, as such, is influenced by countless variables, only some of which can or should be controlled by teachers or school administrators. Whether students succeed or fail, teachers and support personnel put forth equal effort and should be held accountable only for that effort, not a student's performance. In fact, the failing student might have received more energy and focused attention from the teacher and other support personnel than the one who succeeds. In such a case, accountability for achieved student outcomes would not offer the teacher or support personnel equitable evaluations or reveal any useful information to inform future funding decisions or the efficacy of integrated placements.

The Economics of Special Education   Some school administrators hold perceptions that inclusion models are more costly than previously used service delivery mod-

Proposition One

Special education programs should be designed to be as cost effective and efficient as possible while maintaining the primary goal of achieving equity in services for students with disabilities.

els and continue to question the responsibility of their schools to provide free appropriate education in the least restrictive environment. Vergun and Chambers (1995) summarized the findings from a series of interviews of special education directors and principals from ten schools in nine Oregon school districts, exploring their perceptions of associated costs (e.g., one-time start-up costs and ongoing costs), with a focus on the relationship between cost and benefits of supported inclusionary educational practices. The results were indicative of their primary concern for costs, with particular attention given to concerns about the need to increase the staff size of special educators, modify buses, and offer professional development to staff. Such financial concerns must not take precedence over programming decisions. Of even greater concern are the sentiments expressed by McCormick and First (1994) when they indicated that the lifelong benefits to persons with disabilities were financially *punishing* public schools. Whether or not inclusion models do actually cost more, if they are considered appropriate and other choices for the individual students involved are deemed inappropriate, such models must be used. Just as we would not accept fifty children in an elementary class with one teacher on the argument that it is more cost efficient than having a mere twenty-five pupils per class, we must not allow the cries for cost efficiency to jeopardize the quality of special education services. Outcomes are not automatically better measures of our investments than the careful monitoring of our inputs.

Cost Efficiency and Standards of Placement Litigation outcomes specifically related to use of cost to avoid school district obligations to provide education have been consistent even prior to the implementation of IDEA (Bartlett, 1993). Cost is no excuse for failing to offer an appropriate education to all children. Both *Mills v. Board of Education* and *Pennsylvania Association for Retarded Citizens v. the Commonwealth of Pennsylvania* were landmarks in this regard and helped lead the way to the passage of IDEA in 1975. Since then, there has continued a stream of children and their families whose battles have helped to solidify the establishment of this policy. *Board of Education v. Rowely,* heard by the Supreme Court, resulted in a decision that did not require schools to provide the best possible education or maximize a child's educational potential, but they were expected to offer a personalized program from which the child could benefit. This ruling "indirectly removed any express or implicit consideration of cost as a factor in determining appropriateness" (Bartlett, 1993, p. 36). The ruling in *Irving Independent School District v. Tatro* stipulated that clean intermittent catheterization must be provided by the schools but that medical treatments provided by physicians were not required. The Court intended to spare schools from an obligation to provide medical services that might prove too expensive or beyond their range of competence.

Indeed, physician services as a related service were particularly excluded from the responsibilities of school systems in IDEA, so the point of the case was that the particular procedure under discussion represented far less cost to society than would the loss of rights to an appropriate education in the least restrictive environment for the children involved and those who will follow. The issue must be the child's educational benefit and rights, not cost or even the child's success in the programs provided.

The *Clevenger v. Oak Ridge School Board* case ended with the strongest and clearest court ruling involving cost factors to date (Bartlett, 1993). Cost was determined to be a legitimate consideration only when selecting between several appropriate placements that would meet the special needs of the individual student. "Cost is not relevant" rulings have been issued from the Third Circuit and North Carolina Federal District Courts regarding expensive residential placements. The placements were supported because the schools were obligated to accommodate a child's educational needs regardless of the financial or administrative burdens of these accommodations (Bartlett, 1993). Still another example involved a Texas case in which a child who had a medical need for air conditioning was offered a mainstream placement and the air-conditioning of a small cubicle, with the reasoning that air-conditioning the entire classroom would be too expensive. The court ruled that such cost should be weighed against the need to place the child in the least restrictive environment and that the entire classroom should be air-conditioned to achieve this goal (Bartlett, 1993). In this case, his assigned classmates and teacher were most likely quite eager to implement full inclusion for him anyway! Lack of funding or high cost factors could and would be used to eliminate any program not considered worthy or of lower priority than other special interests by a select group of school administrators and/or school board representatives. Unfortunately, it would be inappropriate to place such trust with these groups.

Clune (1994a, 1994b) has argued that compensatory education and the aim to achieve equity of educational opportunity for children of low-income families ought to be shifted to the provision of an adequate education designed to enable low-income children to achieve a high minimum standard. This shift would come largely on the financial backs of current compensatory and special education funding (Barnett, 1994; Clune, 1994b; Levin, 1994). This type of proposal seems to focus on the shifting of funds from one pot to another—from one priority to another—rather than addressing the obligation to consider the individual needs of particular children in an appropriate manner. The notion that government funding at the rate of $10,000 per child would enable children from low-income districts to achieve high minimum standards is really not much of a claim. Given that level of funding, current efforts to achieve equity of resources for the education of students with special needs or those from low-income homes would likely be more successful as well. However, the connection of this adequate education to concurrent adequate housing, successful family relationships, removal of drugs, avoiding violence, and removing the influence of gangs from communities remains illusive. The call to focus on offering an education adequate to enable children to achieve high minimum standards is appealing but seems lost in an

unrealistic vision of high standards in education, unlimited funds, and the ability
to isolate children from their context.

Argument Summary A reasonable expectation we can hold for our schools is that
they use the resources available to them to provide equitable programs for all students within their district. The extent to which those students then take full advantage of the education offered to them is well beyond the appropriate scope of
responsibility of the schools. As Sage and Burrello (1994) note, federal controls
are already disproportionate to the federal government's financial contribution to
special education and related services. Schools ought to seek the most appropriate program for every child and do so within fiscal constraints. However, the
quality of such programs must not be equated with their cheapness or with student achievement. An emphasis on the achievement of educational outcomes is
popular throughout much of education today. The influence of the time of day,
the subject matter at hand, the number of children present, access to instructional materials and resources, and so forth can all be controlled and are within
the jurisdiction of the schools and teachers. However, whether a child has adequate nutrition, has a warm coat to wear in the winter, returns in the afternoon
to a safe, nurturing home, and so forth are variables out of the control of the educators, but nevertheless influence the performance of the child in the classroom.

For some students with special needs, the per-pupil allotment used to fund
general education will fall far short of what they need to receive an appropriate
education. In light of this fact, the federal government offers supplemental funds
to help offset some of the additional costs of providing every child an appropriate
education. The task of the local district is to offer an appropriate education for
every child following the principles of least restrictive environment, not on the
basis of cheapness or convenience. Accountability and decision making in education must never become equated directly or exclusively with student performance or cost savings. For some children and their families, far greater intangible
benefits may be achieved than could ever be determined by documented progress
alone or financial ledgers.

Arguments for Proposition Two Cost alone cannot be used as a defense for
modifying or denying special education services. This reality has contributed to
educational spending, whereas special education funding has not kept up with
expenditures, forcing administrators to encroach on general education revenues
to fund special education. For example, over a quarter of special education program expenditures in California, on average, are paid by general education funds

---

Proposition Two
Program accountability must shift from a focus
on inputs to that of student achievement of high
minimum standards, which should be both individualized, linked back to student IEPs as developed by parents and professionals, and based on
universal standards of achievement.

(Beales, 1993). Because many students spend most of the day in general educa-tion classes, costs are actually greater than these program costs alone imply. Spe-cial education programs should no longer be funded simply because they appear to have face value or make people feel good. There must be evidence of their ef-fectiveness to warrant the continued expenditures.

To date, the actual effectiveness of instruction and student achievement of outcomes in special education remain largely unexplored in terms of a cost/benefits analysis. Equity in access to educational resources does not ensure that students with disabilities receive an adequate education. Special educators must move beyond moral debate for their work and be held accountable for the cost effectiveness of their practices as well as the abilities of their program graduates.

The Economics of Special Education Studies of school administrator behavior and economic theories of bureaucratic organizations make it highly unlikely that schools are cost minimizers, but rather revenue maximizers, maximizing quality as defined by inputs (Barnett, 1994). As educators seek solutions to student fail-ure, the focus is generally on the need for greater resources and more money to support these resources. Public elementary and secondary education costs have grown over 3% per year since 1960, with real spending per pupil nearly tripling (Barnett, 1994). In the past decade, real expenditures per student rose one-third, with a total expenditure around $250 billion, or 5% of the gross national prod-uct. These increases have come during a period of slowdown in growth of earn-ings and income. For example, real per-capita income grew 15% in the last decade, far less than the one-third figure earmarked for educational funding. In light of these disproportionate increases, the feasibility of increasing education dollars even further is far less likely to occur than is the redistribution of educa-tion dollars. These redistributions must be based on explicit concern for the ben-efits to students, taxpayers, and society at large, not fluctuating political favorites.

Special education has contributed greatly to the increase in educational spending over the years, with the swelling of the number of students receiving services and expansion of the age range served beyond typical school age atten-dance (3–21). Massachusetts has the highest proportion of students in special ed-ucation, serving 20% to 25% of its children at some point during their school years (Barnett, 1994). These figures are indicative of the uncontrollable snow-balling effect special education is having on funding within education. Barnett (1994) notes that "it is ludicrous to maintain that 1 in 5 children in Massachusetts has a disability and requires special education" (p. 440). There are no *real* com-mon standards for decisions about who receives special education or what depth of services must be provided. Special education has become an entitlement with-out any real evidence that it is more effective than general education. In fact, the challenges to the effectiveness of special education have been around for two decades, but have not slowed its growth. Barnett (1994) goes so far as to suggest that some children are actually harmed by special education, positing that "sub-stantive increases in educational outcomes might be achieved simply by eliminat-ing special education for many low-income children" (p. 443). Current special education funding could be redistributed to offer additional resources for all students who are achieving less than a state standard, regardless of income, socio-economic status, or other individual eligibility characteristics (e.g., physical disabilities and low scores on an intelligence test).

Cost Efficiency and Standards of Placement   A California case study mentioned earlier (Picus & Miller, 1995) offers the perfect illustration of how cost efficiency must become a more significant element of special education planning. Local districts reclaimed students from cooperatives that had been serving students with severe disabilities in centralized locations. Each district that elected to return students to its own jurisdiction was faced with a less-than-efficient number of children to serve in a new program, but the cost of providing services to students who remained at the centralized locations increased because all established services had to remain in place to serve a smaller number of students. At the time of the study, 5.8% of the school districts took back responsibility for some or all of the programs for students with severe disabilities. However, in several cases no physical relocations were involved, just program administration. The same people in the same buildings with the same curriculum continued to work with the same students, but now it was costing more than it had previously. Apparently, the local school districts were taking the programs back to profit from the higher support service ratio of the county-operated program, not to redesign their instructional programs to achieve a preferred standard of services. The authors reason that their study indicates that the program changes were allowed to occur with no real improvement or change in the nature of the program for the students, but with increased costs, reduced efficiency, and most likely further drain on the general education funds.

Although a lack of funds should never be allowed to excuse biased or prejudicial treatment of any child, the need to acknowledge the fact that there is a real limit to educational funds and that the good of a large number of students must sometimes prevail over the good of a single child is apparent. Some of the court rulings regarding cost considerations and special education programming seem to have lost any sense of reasonableness and point to the need to direct attention to cost effectiveness in concert with appropriateness. In some instances the courts are honoring this line of reasoning, particularly expressing sensitivity to the burdens associated with extremely high-cost private school placements. In one case involving a unilateral private school placement case, the court noted that "the funding of one student's program at a high cost could act as a detriment to many other students, both handicapped and nonhandicapped" (Bartlett, 1993, p. 39). Similar court rulings do cite cost as a proper factor to consider since excess costs spent on one child can deprive others of funds needed for their education. However, cost is not a defense for failing to offer a proper continuum of alternatives, especially one emphasizing inclusion options.

To achieve the adequate program that Clune (1994b) envisions, current federal aid to education would need to be consolidated under a single schoolwide improvement model, regulatory models would need to be scrapped, and a new system of technical assistance and professional development would need to be established. In the field of special education, Sage and Burrello (1994) have also sounded a voice to shift our accountability from inputs to outputs. We must look at student progress toward the outcomes spelled out on the IEP, not just the hours in special education or the process by which students are taught. Advocacy begins with the outcomes data. Student progress toward outcomes stipulated on an IEP is what teachers and schools should be accountable for. When students fail to make progress toward these outcomes, parents and the special education professionals together must advocate for changes in the nature of services provided or reexamine the appropriateness of the outcomes and timetables for achieving them.

The call to unite educational funds into a master program can free administrators and teachers alike to spend their efforts on student achievement rather than worrying over money and competing with one another. A small district in New York has proven that it is possible to cut costs and improve services for special education students (Casey & Dozier, 1994). The reform involved a complete overhaul of special education policies, procedures, and practices. Federal reimbursement in 1994 for New York was $300 per student, whereas the actual cost for the district was $1,400 per student. All students who were being served out of district came back into the system, the district hired needed teachers and related services staff, and coincidentally the district attracted other nearby districts to send tuition-paying special education students. The total savings created in the first year was $2,309,193. This savings in special education funds was used to support preventive programs—speech improvement, short-term psychological services, counseling, parent groups, remedial reading and math labs, and social work services. Such investments in prevention will continue to save the district money in the long term, with fewer students requiring assessments and special education services. Its spending patterns reveal a district's philosophy toward students with special needs that is moral and humane while also cost efficient.

Argument Summary Lewis et al. (1991) compared graduates of two special schools in terms of adaptive behavior, frequency of integration in the adult community, and average monthly earnings, and the costs of both programs were then used to produce cost-effectiveness ratios. Comparisons at both schools of students labeled as having severe retardation and those considered moderately retarded indicate that one of the schools exceeded the other in cost effectiveness on all measures and even produced higher ratios in two of the three measures for its students who were considered severely retarded than did the other school for the students labeled moderately retarded. The use of cost-benefit techniques involved in this study included consideration of employment earnings and taxes, housing costs, use of Social Security Insurance (SSI), disability payments, and other sources of government support. For example, if a person is able to move out of a subsidized residential home into private housing, the cost to society disappears. Housing continues to be a real need for the individual, but he and/or his family will pick up the expense as the rest of society is expected to do. Such research should become common practice as educators seek not only to offer appropriate programs but to do so in a manner that ensures progress toward stated outcomes in the most cost-effective manner possible. We are accountable for not only the provision of philosophically sound programs, but also ones that reflect the best possible stewardship of our tax dollars and the lives of students with disabilities.

CLOSING THOUGHTS

Funding sets the limits on or opens the doors for educational opportunity. When IDEA was enacted, it was not expected that local schools would have to provide an education to this new population of students without substantial federal support. Although the federal support has never been substantial, a responsibility for all students in a school district, regardless of disability, has become a reality. Costs and numbers served by special education are both up, and funding patterns are in need of reform. The promise of substantial federal funding must be reevaluated and either abandoned as a goal or endorsed as a viable means to funding reform. The recommendations for future funding of special education could focus on full federal funding of IDEA at 40%, which is highly unlikely in the political climate of the 1990s, continued use of formula funding with improvements to address current deficiencies, or elimination of segregated funding and the merger of educational dollars into educational programs inclusive of all children. The political reality is that any proposed change will produce financial winners and losers and will trigger powerful debates.

There are several key considerations in formulating financial policy that should be followed regardless of the direction ultimately taken in continued funding of special education (Hartman, 1992). There must be equity for the student as well as the taxpayer, accommodating both student needs and community wealth. Only educational programming that is appropriate can be accepted, with funding designed to discourage restrictive placements and improper classification or labeling. There must be a sense of rationality and simplicity so that all stakeholders understand the funding policies and their meanings. Funding must allow for a comprehensiveness of services and programming as needed without restricting approved services to any single model. The overall system must have the flexibility and responsiveness to adjust to local circumstances while also providing stability so that predictions of future spending can be reasonably accurate. There must be some element of accountability and cost effectiveness to follow both state and local expenditures and encourage cost containment, characterized by efficiency in the management of the system. Finally, in some manner, adequate funding levels must be provided so that appropriate programs can be offered.

Students at all income levels have disabilities and deserve individualized attention. The reasons for combining special education funds with general education dollars must not be predicated on the rationale that another special interest group needs the funds more for its cause. Nor should the maintenance of segregated funding be based upon past injustices. When the provision of a cost-effective appropriate education for all children is the shared goal of all, the competition for funding can become a collaborative endeavor. It would be unrealistic to assume that special interests will ever disappear or that education budgets will be overflowing. Priorities will always need to be set and adjusted as finances ebb and flow, but the right of all children to an equitable (if financially uneven) and adequate education remains a reality of the nineties. The needs of children and our ability to deliver the most effective programs must remain the focal point throughout consideration of these ideas, rather than merely what is in the best interests of bureaucratic organizations managing special education or compensatory education.

Beales (1993) suggests that reductions in costs could come about by implementing a reasonableness standard to protect schools from excessive costs, neutralizing adverse financial incentives, allowing more private sector participation, funding special education with block grants, and relaxing staffing requirements. The time is right to allow far greater experimentation and creativity in the movement toward positive educational solutions for all students.

REFERENCES

Akin, M. C. (1970). Evaluating the cost effectiveness of instructional programs. In M. C. Wittrock & D. E. Wiley (Eds.), *The evaluation of instruction: Issues and problems* (pp. 221–237). New York: Holt, Rinehart, & Winston.

Arnold, R., Genge, F., & Anthony, G. (1994). *Special education expenditure analysis.* Illinois State Univ., Normal. Center for the Study of Educational Finance. (ERIC Document Reproduction No. ED 378 677).

Barnett, W. S. (1994). Obstacles and opportunities: Some simple economics of school finance reform. *Educational Policy, 8,* 436–452.

Bartlett, L. (1993). Economic cost factors in providing a free appropriate public education for handicapped children: The legal perspective. *Journal of Law and Education, 22,* 27–60.

Beales, J. R. (1993). *Special education: Expenditures and obligations. Policy study no. 161.* Reason Foundation, Los Angeles. (ERIC Document Reproduction No. ED 359 735).

Case, A. D. (1992). The special education rescue: A case for systems thinking. *Educational Leadership, 50,* 32–34.

Casey, C. M., & Dozier, P. (1994). Cutting costs in special education. *American School Board Journal, 181*(10), 27–30.

Center for Special Education Finance. (1993). *Narrative review of literature.* (ERIC Document Reproduction No. ED 372 516).

Chaikind, S., & Corman, H. (1990). The special education costs of low birthweight. *NBER Working Paper Series.* National Bureau of Economic Research, Cambridge, MA. (ERIC Document Reproduction No. ED 350 730).

Chaikind, S., Danielson, L. C., & Brauen, M. L. (1993). What do we know about the costs of special education? A selected review. *Journal of Special Education, 26,* 344–370.

Clune, W. H. (1994a). The cost and management of program adequacy: An emerging issue in educational policy and finance. *Educational Policy, 8,* 365–375.

Clune, W. H. (1994b). The shift from equity to adequacy in school finance. *Educational Policy, 8,* 376–394.

Coleman, H. A., Burch, P. H., Ponessa, J. M., Reock, E., Storem, S. D., & Occhetti, C. (1994). Linkages in the delivery and financing of special education services in New Jersey, Project final report. Public Affairs Research Institute of New Jersey, Inc.; Rutgers, The State Univ., New Brunswick, NJ. Center for Government Services. (ERIC Document Reproduction No. ED 379 815).

Council for Exceptional Children (CEC). (1995). Change in special education funding proposed. *CEC Today, 1,* 1, 7, 9.

Dempsey, S., & Fuchs, D. (1992). "Flat" versus "weighted" reimbursement formulas: A longitudinal analysis of state-wide special education funding practices. Paper presented at the Annual Meeting of the American Educational Research Association (San Francisco, April 20–24, 1992). (ERIC Document Reproduction No. ED 349 720).

Department of Public Policy. (1994). Federal outlook for exceptional children: Budget considerations and CEC recommendations. Reston, VA: The Council for Exceptional Children.

Hartman, W. T. (1990). Supplemental/replacement: An alternative approach to excess costs. *Exceptional Children, 56,* 450–459.

Hartman, W. T. (1992). State funding models for special education. *Remedial and Special Education, 13,* 47–58.

Hartman, W. T. (1993). Changes in special education funding for Pennsylvania. *Educational Considerations, 21,* 12–16.

Hilliard, A. G. (1992). The pitfalls and promises of special education practice. *Exceptional Children, 59,* 168–172.

Levin, H. M. (1983). *Cost-effectiveness: A primer.* Beverly Hills, CA: Sage.

Levin, H. M. (1994). Little things mean a lot. *Educational Policy, 8,* 396–403.

Lewis, D. R. (1993). Economic evaluation of special education: A review of approaches and applications. *Educational Considerations, 21,* 58–64.

Lewis, D. R., Bruininks, R. H., & Thurlow, M. (1991). Efficiency considerations in delivering special education services to persons with severe mental retardation. *Mental Retardation, 29,* 129–137.

Mawdsley, R. D. (1995). Does inclusion cost more? The cost of special education. *School Business Affairs, 61,* 27–31.

McCormick, C., & First, P. F. (1994). The cost of inclusion: Educating students with special needs. *School Business Affairs, 62,* 30–36.

McLaughlin, M. J., & Warren, S. H. (1994). The costs of inclusion: Reallocating financial and human resources to include students with disabilities. *The School Administrator, 51,* 8–12, 16–19.

Moche, J. S. (1995). Moche CAPE formula: Cost analysis of public education. Paper presented at the Annual International Convention of the CEC, 73rd, Indianapolis, April 5–9, 1995. (ERIC Document Reproduction No. ED 384 419).

Montgomery, D. L. (1995a). A profile of special education finance reform in Oregon. State analysis series. Palo Alto, CA: American Institutes for Research in the Behavioral Sciences, Center for Special Education Finance. (ERIC Document Reproduction No. EC 303 876).

Montgomery, D. L. (1995b). A profile of special education finance reform in Vermont. State analysis series. Palo Alto, CA: American Institutes for Research in the Behavioral Sciences, Center for Special Education Finance. (ERIC Document Reproduction No. EC 303 875).

Moore, M. T., Strang, E. W., Schwartz, M., & Braddock, M. (1988, December). *Patterns in special education service delivery and cost.* Washington, DC: Decision Resources Corp. (ERIC Document Reproduction Service No. ED 303 027).

O'Reilly, F. (1989). *State special education finance systems, 1988–93.* Washington, DC: National Association of State Directors of Special Education.

Parrish, T. B. (1993). Federal policy options for funding special education. *CSEF brief,* No. 1, pp. 1–4. (ERIC Document Reproduction No. ED 370 286).

Parrish, T. B. (1995). Criteria for effective special education funding formulas. Policy abstract. Palo Alto, CA: American Institutes for Research in the Behavioral Sciences, Center for Special Education Finance. (ERIC Document Reproduction No. ED 381 934).

Picus, L. O., & Miller, C. J. (1995). Cost and service delivery trade-offs in providing educational services for students with severe disabilities. *Educational Administration Quarterly, 31,* 268–293.

Raphel, E. S., Singer, J. D., & Walker, D. K. (1985). Per pupil expenditures on special education in three metropolitan school districts. *Journal of Educational Finance, 11,* 69–88.

Rogers, J. J. (1991). Third party billing to finance special education: A case analysis. *Planning and Changing, 22,* 68–78.

Sage, D. D., & Burrello, L. C. (1994). *Leadership in educational reform: An administrator's guide to changes in special education.* Baltimore: Paul H. Brookes.

Strathie, J., & Anthony, P. (1993). Measuring the effectiveness of integrating students with disabilities into the regular classroom: A cost/benefit model. *Educational Considerations, 21,* 65–69.

Tappe, D. R. (1995). Nineteen reasons why special education should cost more than regular education. In *Reaching to the future: Boldly facing challenges in rural communities.* Conference Proceedings of the American Council on Rural Special Education, Las Vegas, March 15–18, 1995. (ERIC Document Reproduction No. ED 381 297).

U.S. Department of Education. (1995). *To assure the free appropriate public education of all children with disabilities: Seventeenth annual report to Congress on the implementation of the Individuals with Disabilities Education Act.* Washington, DC: Office of Special Education Programs.

Vergun, P. B., & Chambers, J. G. (1995). *A case study of "supported education" in Oregon: Resource implications of inclusion.* State analysis series. Palo Alto, CA: American Institutes for Research in the Behavioral Sciences, Center for Special Education Finance. (ERIC Document Reproduction No. ED 381 972).

10

Technology and Disability

INTRODUCTION

We are experiencing rapid changes in our everyday lives as a result of technology. Many of us have our paychecks delivered straight to the bank for direct deposit, pay for groceries with debit cards, insert credit cards into gas pumps, get cash via bank cards twenty-four hours per day, conduct searches of international lists of libraries from our own homes, enjoy computer games in our leisure time, shop and make travel plans via the Internet, write with word processors that offer spelling and grammar checkers, communicate with our government representatives electronically, possess and casually use cellular phones, have reluctantly become accustomed to electronic voice systems, are expected to own and use answering machines in our homes, and on and on. The microwave is now a standard feature of most kitchens, along with food processors, bread machines, and many other modern technological advances. What seemed like unbelievable science fiction a few years ago has quickly become today's out-of-date technology.

Families can now provide much of the needed care for children with special health needs in their homes, in part because of the growth of technologies, the miniaturization of equipment, and cost-containment efforts within medical rehabilitation (Perrin, Guyer, & Lawrence, 1992). Concurrently with our new technologies, businesses are restructuring and downsizing as a result of computerization, leaving many without jobs or in constant fear of being the next to be let go. Our relationships are moving away from the personal toward the electronic. Nichols (1992) even bemoans the fact that some supporters of technology speculate how technology will allow humans to communicate less, as though this condition would be positive. The technological advances that bring us improvements certainly pose new challenges as well.

Technology and Opportunity

Shapiro (1993) describes technology a the "great liberator" by virtue of its ability to diminish both physical and mental limitations: "The right 'assistive device' can turn passive patients into independent consumers who are able to go to school, work, rear families, and live on their own" (p. 219). However, Shapiro also points out that reliance on technology is not without risk: "Machines can close off worlds to disabled people just as quickly as they can open them. Not until nearly one hundred years after the telephone's invention for example, would deaf people begin to overcome the technology gap it created" (p. 226).

Educators have greeted technological advances with mixed reactions. Technology can be seen as the great equalizer: shrinking the world, increasing access to ideas and information for everyone, offering instructional approaches that are both stimulating and rewarding to learners at all levels. It can be seen in a different light as well. It is serving to increase the chasm between the haves and the have nots (both in terms of individuals and communities, and internationally between developed and developing countries).

Computers in the classroom are touted by some as a simple answer to the poor teaching evident in some classes (Callister & Dunne, 1992). Indeed, new inventions have historically been perceived as a tool to diminish the effects of ineffective teachers. However, Callister and Dunne (1992) remind us that virtually all such efforts have uniformly failed. In the classroom, technology can exacerbate bad teaching or provide rich and new dimensions to creative teachers (Solomon, 1992). The technology itself cannot cause good teaching to occur, nor can it transform boring teaching techniques into exciting learning opportunities. Callister and Dunne (1992) point out that in some instances, drill and practice software has tempted teachers who would not ordinarily be prone to use such methods simply because they are technology-based. The tools are only as effective and beneficial as those using them can make them be (Solomon, 1992).

Within the field of special education there is further debate over the provision of assistive technology. It is now designated as a required related service, but people continue to argue over exactly how inclusive the term *assistive technology* is, precisely for what the educational system is obligated to pay, the proper role of parents and students in the decision-making process, and how best to distribute limited resources (Holder-Brown & Parette, 1992). When education dollars are used to purchase highly individualized, expensive technological equipment, the items belong to the school but may never be needed again for any other child. On the other hand, families may be unable to afford experimentation with various pieces of expensive equipment before the best match for their child is found. In response to this particular problem, regional access centers are now available that can provide some relief to both the schools and the families as they explore technology-related options.

Undoubtedly, technology has made dramatic improvements in the lives of persons with disabilities. Persons with visual impairments or physical disabilities have computers to which they can now talk and listen, augmentative and alternative communication systems give people who are nonverbal a new outlet for universal expressive communication, and touch screens, joy sticks, and customized switches give people with physical limitations control over their environments as never before conceived. For many, these advances have not only enabled them to make fuller use of their capacities but have also opened up employment opportunities and new relationships with their family and friends. Although the initial development of some of these products was specifically for the disabled population, producers are finding many creative uses for them in a general market. Preschool children can have a great time with a touch screen as they interact with their favorite books via a computer, voice recognition devices represent the latest in security systems, computerized readers are being advertised on the radio to a general market, and so forth. As the applications of such technology continue to expand, persons with disabilities will gain more freedom and control over their lives. However, other arenas of technological research present real challenges to this same population.

Transdisciplinary Technology

For some children with multiple disabilities, technology was responsible for saving their lives at birth and continues to play a vital role in their lives as they move from hospital to home care. Once survival is reasonably ensured, parents and teachers can begin focusing on the child's development across cognitive, motor, and emotional domains. Technology can help compensate for the child's physical limitations. The early interventionist, physical therapist, parent, and technology expert can work together to design suitable technological toys to normalize the child's interactions with her environment. Technology matched to the child's developmental levels and physical abilities can ensure cognitive stimulation opportunities (e.g., toys controlled by simple switches to give the child a sense of cause and effect). Speech and language therapists can work with occupational therapists, parents, and technology experts in the development of functional communication alternatives for the child unable to speak.

The multitude of persons working in technological fields, medicine, rehabilitation, special education, genetics, engineering, and other emerging fields such as robotics and bionics are collectively creating fascinating new strategies to assist persons with disabilities or health impairments in living more productive lives. It has been predicted that nanotechnology, which involves the development of microscopic machines, will lead to the production of machines the size of viruses that will seek and destroy cancer cells in the body (Lewis, 1993). Other predictions in the field of genetic engineering focus on our eventual ability to detect and treat genetic disorders in utero. However, one need not look to future

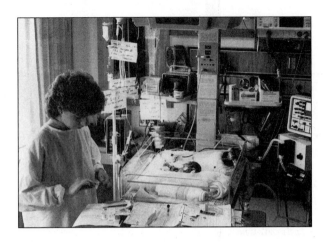

Technology gives
this infant the chance
to survive.

© David Witbeck,
The Picture Cube, Inc.

predictions to get a sense of the progression occurring with the exponential explosion of knowledge across disciplines.

This technological revolution, of which we are in the midst, will ultimately
result in changes to our society as radical as those following the Industrial Revolution. Biological manipulations possible through emerging technologies will
impose even more complex ethical challenges than we have already faced with
the atomic bomb, the computer, and the television. Because we have the technological ability to do something, does that mean that we should do it? Who has
been and should be setting the funding priorities for research and invention? To
whom are the benefits of technology available, and for whom are they inaccessible? On a more mundane level, when a school system provides a piece of equipment to a child, where should that equipment be when school is not in session?

Focus of Discussion

This chapter is focused on powerful issues that represent two of the most exciting, yet ethically challenging, arenas of technological advancement today. Both
directly and indirectly affect the lives of persons with disabilities and the field of
special education. They center on the critical issues of allocation of limited
resources within our society and the meaning of disability to our society. The
first topic is tied to the advances in medical technology associated with prenatal,
perinatal, and neonatal care. Genetic research as related to fertility and the mark-
ing of the human genome offers the second area for discussion. Special educators
are not the immediate decision makers in these medical domains, yet they must
think through their values and beliefs as responsible citizens of the education
community and be prepared to clarify those beliefs as the impact of these issues is
felt within the education community and among persons with and without disabilities. As Bowe (1995) has noted, special educators are already often asked to
provide informed opinions about difficult ethical questions and, therefore, have a
responsibility to be as informed in these matters as possible. To illustrate the

Technology gives adults the opportunities to participate in business meetings.

point, Bowe wonders whether we can "maintain the 'cognitive dissonance' of at one and the same time saying that the likelihood of disability is justifiable basis for abortion and that people with disabilities who live among us are just as human and entitled to as much respect and as many civil rights as others" (p. 33).

MEDICAL TECHNOLOGY AND PRENATAL, PERINATAL, AND NEONATAL SERVICES

The field of medicine, as most others, has been dramatically changed over the years through technological progress. The extent to which this progress has resulted in saved and/or improved lives, reduced pain and suffering, and eradication or elimination of disease is immeasurable. However, some would argue that the technology has advanced faster than has the consideration of many ethical issues surrounding these advances (Solomon, 1995). For example, new techniques and procedures are costly and, therefore, may be provided on an ability-to-pay basis rather than on an as-needed basis.

When the distribution of medical research funds and patient care costs is made, difficult priorities must be set that have many ramifications. Funding for the research to develop new technologies will necessarily take away from more routine care, such as prenatal and other preventive medicine programs. As of 1987, health care expenditures for children in the first year of life totaled $12.6 billion ($3,271 per infant). Of that figure, 18% was spent on normal newborn hospital stays, 72% went to initial hospitalizations and inpatient care of newborns with complications of birth or rehospitalizations during the first year of life, and 10% ($312) was directed to health care not requiring hospitalization, including well-child and preventive care (Lewit & Monheit, 1992). These distribution

Genetic research is producing new findings almost daily.

figures occur in spite of the fact that 80% to 85% of all newborns are discharged with the mother within a few days of birth. The vast majority of infants have no need for sophisticated technological equipment and incur no expenses beyond basic obstetrical and pediatric care. The few who do require technological assistance generally run up exorbitant bills.

Infant Mortality and Survival

Medical technology has led to the survival of smaller and smaller infants (Friedman & Sigman, 1992). But the survival of these very tiny babies comes with great risk. First, heroic efforts and substantial expenditures will still result in death a high percentage of the time, with the viability risks increasing as the weight of the infant decreases. Second, those who survive stand a substantial risk of facing significant disabilities throughout the remainder of their lives. Bowe (1995) cites a Johns Hopkins study indicating that infants born at twenty-five weeks of gestation have a good prognosis for survival without major problems, infants less than twenty-two weeks of gestation rarely survive, and those born between twenty-two and twenty-four weeks likely survive but have significant health problems.

These outcomes are quite different from the outcome Solomon (1995) reported for a twenty-eight-week-old infant whom a medical intern wanted to save in 1969, but whose inevitable death he finally had to accept because the technology required to save her simply did not exist. Today, the dilemma this intern faced is still present in neonatal care, but the infants who pose it are several weeks younger. The matter is even further confused by the fact that in 1973 the Supreme Court decision in *Roe v. Wade* allowed legal abortions up to twenty-eight weeks of gestation. There is now, depending on the circumstances, actually an overlap of several weeks during which time a fetus can be aborted or premature labor can trigger aggressive treatment to save a premature infant.

Opportunities to participate in the mainstream were limited for persons with disabilities in the past.

AP Newsfeatures Photo 1965

Drops in infant mortality rates reflect the dramatic improvement in medical care and advances in medical technology. The rate of infants dying during the first year of life per 1,000 in 1915 was 100, but only 9.1 in 1990 (Racine, Joyce, & Grossman, 1992; Perrin, Guyer, & Lawrence, 1992), and a rate as low as 8.5 was reported for 1992 (Solomon, 1995). This drop has been attributed to improved living conditions, pasteurized milk, clean water, adequate housing, sewage disposal, the introduction of anti-microbial drugs between 1935 and 1950, and advances in neonatology begun in the late 1960s. The 1990 figure reflected a 6% drop from 1989, perhaps due to introduction of treatment with artificial surfactant, which helps prevent deaths of premature infants from respiratory distress syndrome, and expansions of Medicaid coverage for prenatal care.

Currently, patterns of disparate rates of infant mortality across racial groups are of great concern. In fact, both the low birth-weight rate and the infant mortality rate for the black population in the United States is twice that of the white population. Black women's risk of having very low birth-weight infants is nearly three to one over others (Kleinman, 1992). Rates of low birth-weight infants are also higher than that of the white population for Puerto Rican women, whereas other groups (Cubans, Mexicans, Native Americans, and Asians) tend to have rates similar to that of the white population (Kleinman, 1992). Since the U.S. infant mortality rate is higher than other developed countries, even when just using figures based on the white population (Racine, Joyce, & Grossman, 1992; Perrin, Guyer, & Lawrence, 1992; McCormick, 1992), there are much discussion and debate on the best strategies to lower it. The 1988 infant mortality rate for the black population was 17.6 per 1000, far short of the projected goal. Although the low birth-weight rate for the black population was at an all-time low of 12.36% in 1984, in 1989 the figure rose again two years later (Public Health Service, 1986).

Today persons with disabilities find many ways to contribute in the mainstream of our society.

© James L. Shaffer

Technology and Child Care

The average cost of care of all babies, including premature infants, was $2,695 in 1990 dollars, while the average cost of care for preterm babies with birth weights between 500 and 749 grams, born between 24 and 27 weeks, was $119,339 each (Solomon, 1995). Changes in obstetrical and neonatal care have been accelerating since the mid-1960s to the present, with advances in technology continuing to direct the future. For example, in 1965, one in twenty deliveries was by cesarean section, while the 1989 rate was one in four. This rise is attributed to the increase in fetal monitoring (both positively and negatively), changes in the legal atmosphere surrounding obstetrical care, and the cumulative effect of previous C-section deliveries (Racine, Joyce, & Grossman, 1992; Perrin, 1992). Fetal heart monitoring practices are indicative of how we become reliant on technologies even when the evidence fails to support their continued use and unintended undesirable effects may be produced. Fetal heart monitoring in the delivery process is considered a vital data source for safe deliveries, but some argue that the process leads to an unjustified increase in cesarean sections and gives the doctor a record of the child's condition throughout the delivery if such is needed later in a legal battle (Neilson, 1994; Flamm, 1994; Albers, 1994).

During this same period, neonatal intensive care units (NICUs) were developing. Comprehensive guidelines for their establishment and management were in place by the early 1970s, including the definition of three levels of infant care. Estimates from the Office of Technology Assessment are that between 150,000 and 200,000 admissions to NICUs occurred annually in the mid-1980s. Anecdotal evidence indicates that the greatest proportion of NICU admissions have been infants weighing less than 1,500 grams and patients with extremely low birth weights (under 751 grams), which are increasing (Racine, Joyce, & Grossman, 1992; Perrin, Guyer, & Lawrence, 1992). The question that society must address is whether the net costs are worth the undertaking in view of the benefits produced by the program or whether alternative, less-costly strategies exist that can achieve different, yet worthy, health outcomes. Posing the question does not imply an answer but merely accentuates the fact that to date, the technology has, in fact, progressed largely unchallenged by these concerns (Solomon, 1995).

Decision Point 10.1: Prioritizing
Resources and Access to Technology

Arguments for Proposition One The policy prevalent in U.S. hospitals today that all infants, regardless of how small or damaged, should be aggressively treated seems shortsighted and based more on legal fears or the research interests of the medical community than on the best interests of individual families or society as a whole. The economic and emotional costs of "rescue treatment" as well as the physical cost to the infant herself combined with these costs for society need to become a central consideration in the decision process. At far less financial cost, less glamorous programs, such as access to high-quality prenatal care for high-risk groups, can offer a better prognosis for far greater numbers than the dramatic rescue of single children after they are born in highly vulnerable conditions.

Today, technology is being used to prolong the dying process of premature newborns at great expense and suffering of the child (Solomon, 1995), for advances within the NICU have been dramatic over the past thirty years. In 1973, only about 10% of the babies born at twenty-eight weeks with a weight of 1,000 grams survived. Today, only 10% of these children die, and even half of the infants born at twenty-four weeks survive (Solomon, 1995). But the use of technology to continue pushing the age and weight at which survival is possible is futile at best. Death rates have unquestionably dropped, and these drops are largely attributable to advances in drugs and technology for premature infants and the opening of hundreds of NICUs. However, these rates mask the other side—the number of survivors with problems, many of whom have very severe lifetime problems. Paris (1990) points out the illogic of the paths we have taken: "It is the elevation of technology to the ultimate value that has created the problems we see today and that has distanced us so far from the kind of wisdom every caring grandmother in this country would know how to apply to these questions" (p. 155).

Infant Mortality and Survival Approximately 300,000 babies are treated each year in NICUs in some 600 U.S. hospitals, of whom most are preterm (Solomon, 1995). During the 1980s there seemed to be a consensus within U.S. hospitals to

Proposition One
Preventive treatment programs aimed at reducing the number of infants born facing high risks for disabilities or premature death offer a more viable means of effective intervention than does the continued pursuit of expensive technological after-damage treatments.

treat all preterm infants aggressively, but this policy eroded. The costs of our heroic efforts to save the lives of all infants regardless of the damage they had suffered have been felt not only in the wallets and lives of those involved, but also in our society. When limited medical resources are directed toward the survival of a single infant who will likely have profound disabilities throughout his life, there remain fewer resources for programs aimed at reducing the factors that made that child and many others vulnerable in the first place. Even the child abuse amendments that were intended to protect infants with disabilities from discrimination in newborn nurseries allowed for no treatment when efforts would be "futile" or "inhumane." Doctors are now allowed some discretion on when to end their efforts to save the lives of some of the most vulnerable infants. The moral obligation is that medical personnel pursue a course of action that they deem to be in the best interests of the child.

Some argue that continued life is literally always in the best interests of the infant, regardless of the quality of that life. This position elevates the sanctity of life but neglects the suffering endured by very sick babies, which is made worse by invasive procedures required for treatment. Some doctors then operate with a technological imperative, with any technologically feasible intervention being offered, regardless of the child's prognosis. Such a black-and-white policy might seem morally solid, but its oversimplification ignores the sociological context of the problem. How did the baby come to be at risk in the first place? Had an effective prevention program been available, could the risk have been avoided and the child survive with no disabilities? What are the thoughts and considerations of the family? Could the survival of one child so drain the emotional and financial resources of the parents that all remaining siblings will suffer neglect? At current and future technological levels, our society may no longer be able to afford a policy based solely on the sanctity of all life.

Another policy option is to allow parents to take responsibility for determining the child's best interests. Unfortunately, such a policy also sets up numerous dangers and ignores context as well. Reliance exclusively on parents to make a decision about the aggressiveness of treatment gives them enormous power and responsibility at a point of extreme stress, particularly if they choose to end the infant's life. Parents also might continue demanding aggressive treatment even when the prognosis is extremely bleak. Doctors may feel that the child is suffering so severely that it would be in the infant's best interest to be allowed to die. And while parents are slowly accepting the doctor's recommendation that efforts to prolong the life should cease, the bills are mounting. The expenditure of $250,000 for a baby to live six weeks (Solomon, 1995), while parents gradually reach the decision to let their baby die, is simply not a viable reality for the future. While it might seem a humane practice, the drain of resources when multiplied by thousands brings to question the ethics of accepting universally aggressive medical interventions for vulnerable infants, whether based on physician judgment, a belief in the sanctity of all life, or parental authority positions.

As the country faces the growing need to define appropriate limits on access to medical resources, our priorities and the most effective uses of our resources must be clarified. It is not always the dramatic, high-cost programs that can do the greatest good for the largest number of people. The Center for the Future of Children has developed ten recommendations in reaction to the inadequacies of the health care system for children and pregnant women, including the replacement of "incentives for technology-intensive, high-cost care with incentives to identify high-risk children and pregnant women and to provide risk-reducing interventions for them" (Center for the Future of Children staff, 1992b, p. 6). They argue that the existing "wasteful, duplicative, and ineffective health services" could far better be rechanneled to provide quality care for underserved populations. Through the provision of such care the need for the dramatic high-cost interventions would diminish and the life outcomes of would-be patients could improve.

In 1990, one in four American infants was born to a mother who had not received early prenatal care (Center for the Future of Children staff, 1992a). Since the mid-1980s, the proportion of expectant mothers who receive early prenatal care has actually declined rather than increased. The women facing the greatest risk of giving birth to low birth-weight and premature infants are indigent, unmarried teenagers. As a result of the lack of prenatal care for these women, many children are born with unnecessary disabilities. For example, a child whose mother had received no prenatal care was born suffering from cataracts as well as liver and heart problems caused by the mother's undetected syphilis, easily treatable with a $20 shot of penicillin. This child survived for one month at a cost of over $70,000 (Nazario as cited by Mathieu, 1992).

Simply providing prenatal care to indigent teens will not solve the problems we are now facing. It would be shortsighted to ignore the myriad of social, physical, and psychological issues surrounding the patterns of infant mortality seen in America today. Lack of transportation, fear of the medical establishment, and lack of understanding of the need for prenatal care are just a brief sampling of the concerns that must be comprehensively addressed. Getting expectant mothers to accept prenatal care offers the means of breaking a cycle of risk and vulnerability that will never be resolved when disproportionate funds and resources remain targeted toward our belated rescue efforts. Efforts to achieve successful prenatal prevention programs will have to include extensive outreach and case management efforts, elimination of financial barriers, relocating facilities into underserved areas, and providing child care for women using these services (Racine, Joyce, & Grossman, 1992, Perrin, 1992).

Racine, Joyce, and Grossman (1992) noted that Joyce, Corman, and Grossman found in 1984 that expansion of prenatal care is a more cost-effective method of saving additional infant lives than the expansion of neonatal care. The average cost of saving an additional life through prenatal care for white women is $31, while the use of NICUs for their infants is $2,834; for black women the comparable figures are $39 and $2,150. Were we to focus on the provision and effective delivery of prenatal care for high-risk mothers, premature births would drop and the demand for high-cost technology would go down, as would the number of children facing their lives with disabilities resulting from their preterm birth. Prenatal care includes specialized tests (amniocentesis and ultrasound imaging to screen the genetic and structural development of the fetus), blood pressure and blood sugar monitoring, blood tests to detect exposure to certain viruses and to verify the mother's blood type, and sometimes special tests to evaluate fetal well-being. We can push the need for good prenatal care even further back to include strategies aimed at reducing the use of tobacco and illicit substances, and other environmental hazards (e.g., poor nutrition).

Technology and Child Care   There are estimates today that four million children die each year of vaccine-preventable diseases and that another four million become permanently disabled through a lack of medical intervention (Linder, & Ohel, 1994). There is a discrepancy between our level of knowledge and practices applied that seems largely attributable to our division of resources. The vaccination of pregnant women provides the mother with antibodies that may be transferred across placenta and provide her neonate with high antibody titers, diminishing the need for childhood immunizations. The provision of such vaccinations is beneficial and cost effective but is not happening, as our delivery model fails to offer such preventive medicine while working heroically to save lives that have been damaged. A group of visiting Chinese physicians found in an American pediatric intensive care unit a deaf and blind three-year-old who was ventilator-dependent and would always be so, with a life expectancy of less than one year. The child's bill up to that point was a half-million dollars. One of the visitors noted that he could immunize one million children for the same cost (Jonsen, 1992).

Cullen (1992) has noted that the U.S. health care system is driven by technological rather than social responsibilities. He argues that our medical culture "is more concerned with high-cost, life saving technologies than with care that is life enhancing. The imperative of high technology is to rescue endangered life" (p. 93). Intensive care units and major organ transplantation programs offer the most striking examples of his point. On an individual basis, the costs of our rescue efforts of low birth-weight babies are quite similar to other medical interventions. For example, the estimate for an artificial heart transplant is $150,000, including the cost of the device and follow-up care; liver transplants are about $200,000; bone marrow transplants run $150,000; care of a burn patient is in the same approximate range; and the cost of treating a psychiatrically disturbed adolescent may range even higher. Of course, we must also multiply these figures by the incidence to determine the overall cost. For example, heart transplants are needed by 17,000 to 35,000 people annually at a cost of $150,000, which puts costs in the $2.5 billion to $5 billion range per year. Another example is seen in the unique status held by end-state renal disease under Medicaid guides, which specifically provide coverage for this condition. The two billion Medicaid dollars spent on it mean that approximately 5% of the total Medicaid budget is serving less than one-half of one percent of recipients of Medicaid funds. Although the costs of care for a single premature baby are in the same range as other high-tech treatments, the cost benefit of providing aggressive intervention for all conditions for a society struggling with an increasing underclass must be questioned.

The high cost of such medical interventions for the limited good of a small number of people has already resulted in the first attempts to limit the use of medical resources for high-priced rescues. In 1989, Oregon enacted legislation no longer permitting payment for organ transplants, electing to spend the anticipated $1 million per year savings (the state was previously providing ten to twelve transplants per year) on prenatal care serving approximately 5,000 pregnant women. However, implementation of this life-enhancing ethic over the more popular lifesaving or rescue ethic has created a problem for the bordering states. Oregonians whose loved ones need a transplant are crossing the borders of their state to seek help elsewhere (Jonsen, 1992). These states have put no similar restrictions into place, but are reluctant to pick up the cost of another state's transplant needs. Massachusetts has put some limitations on transplantation surgery as well (Cullen, 1992). The financial realities of limited resources combined with our expanding technological expertise will likely trigger more and more states to follow suit. White (1993) has speculated that there will be more rationing of health care in the near future.

Very low birth-weight survivors average forty-five to fifty days in the hospital before coming home, with an average cost of $27,000 to $60,000 (McCormick, 1992). These average figures mask the costs of the smallest infants, who may spend up to ninety days in the hospital, running up bills of $150,000 before being discharged. The cost of much of this care falls to the hospital (self-pay becomes bad debt) or to the public through Medicaid. One-third to one-half of NICU graduates will be rehospitalized over the first three years of life and will incur average monthly costs for direct medical care during the first three years of life of $60 to $1,200 compared to $22 to $26 for others. These figures do not include transportation, special child care, equipment rental, and other related expenses (McCormick, 1992).

The competitive nature of medicine and hospitals is evident in NICUs as physicians and administrators succumb to temptations in conflict with best patient care. A technological advance showing up in many NICUs is the extracorporeal membrane oxygenation (ECMO) procedure, which should be reserved primarily for term infants, because the use of it risks intraventricular hemorrhage for premature infants (Southgate, Howell, & Kanto, 1990). However, since it is more sophisticated technology and is becoming available in more and more NICUs, cheaper, more appropriate therapies are being skipped in favor of this newer, more expensive approach. Treatment of premature infants suffering from respiratory distress syndrome (RDS) with artificial surfactant is usually appropriate and cheaper, but physicians tempted to gain experience with the ECMO procedure or anxious to defend their need to have the newest equipment in their NICU overuse the procedure with the wrong patients (Southgate, Howell, & Kanto, 1990).

Argument Summary Preventive care is far less dramatic but offers far more hope for greater good than does the expenditure of extreme sums in heroic measures and/or futuristic technological research and experimentation. Prenatal care offered to women at risk to deliver low birth-weight and/or preterm infants takes on a life-enhancing perspective rather than the rescue mentality displayed in the act of saving such infants after they are born and their tiny bodies have suffered irreparable damage. Prenatal care takes on the role of enhancing the lives of the children yet to be born by offering their mothers the needed care before children are born prematurely, experience multiple complications, and develop significant deficiencies with which they must deal throughout life (Jonsen, 1992).

Although the shifting of funds from big projects to more mundane programs may not be very feasible politically (e.g., shifting resources from heart transplants and work on artificial hearts to programs aimed at reducing smoking), it would make better use of our country's resources by enhancing the lives of far more than the small number whose lives we rescue today. The issues of sharing resources with other special interests within our society (e.g., the elderly) have not even been raised within this discussion, but offer even further evidence of the need for us to discuss and articulate how best this country can prepare for the future.

Arguments for Proposition Two   Medical advances over the years have consistently improved our longevity and the chances of survival for the at-risk infant, and have led to effective therapeutic treatments of conditions for which there has been no hope. There have also been unquestionably very challenging moral and ethical dilemmas accompanying these advances, yet such concerns do not warrant the halt of the advance of new knowledge and capabilities in this arena. The citations regarding exorbitant costs associated with cutting-edge interventions for newborns must be placed in perspective. The pioneering work in medicine necessarily requires the development of prototype equipment, experimentation and risk, uncertainty regarding life outcomes, and many other elements that raise both the financial and emotional costs to the families and the professionals working in the field. Often, costs of survival drop as specialized equipment becomes more accessible, expertise is shared among attending physicians, and treatment risks are reduced.

Technology in the NICU includes sophisticated technical equipment such as ventilators and monitors as well as medications, and relatively mundane items, such as proper infant formula or tubes the correct size for tiny airways and blood vessels, support services (blood banks, nutrition services, and laboratories), and organizational and financial arrangements (McCormick, 1992). Specific technology for the low birth-weight group includes ventilators for respiratory distress syndrome (RDS) and monitoring, noninvasive diagnostic tests such as ultrasound and echocardiography, and less invasive management such as bilirubin lights for jaundice. Such a specialized medical arena for neonates did not even exist in the early 1960s.

As the technology is emerging, physicians are pleased to offer a level of care to vulnerable infants that has previously been unavailable, but they inevitably encounter some whom our knowledge is insufficient to save. Throughout most of the 1990s a middle ground in regard to the level of aggressiveness in intervention has been taken, with decisions being made case by case (Solomon, 1995). However, such individualization of policy making inevitably results in inconsistencies

> **Proposition Two**
> The work today in medical technology is espe-
> cially critical, as seen in reproductive medicine,
> prenatal care, and the neonatal intensive care
> unit, all of which offer even greater promise for
> the future.

in care. It can mean that two babies with the same condition born in different hospitals with different doctors may not be treated with equal aggressiveness. The goal in each instance is to determine what is in the best interests of the child. However, conflict about the best interests of the child is likely. Furthermore, any-one who might contribute to the decision-making process could potentially have conscious or unconscious interests conflicting with those of the child. We need a consistent ethical standard that encourages the continued pursuit of the survival of vulnerable children.

Infant Mortality and Survival A careful analysis of the factors contributing to the current infant mortality rate reveals the critical role that technology must con-tinue to play in further reducing this figure. The majority of infant deaths are as-sociated with inadequate fetal growth, and the role of technology in improving outcomes is clear, as it has been in the past. Today, there is a well-networked group of NICUs strategically placed throughout the nation that has made sub-stantial strides in reducing the rates of infant mortality and infant morbidity since its beginnings.

In the second half of the twentieth century, infant mortality dropped from the 1950 figure of 29.2 per 1,000 live births to 11.0 in 1980, and was at 10.4 in the early 1990s (Racine, Joyce, & Grossman, 1992). Explanations of this pattern are partially found in the availability of reliable contraception and access to thera-peutic abortions, which have reduced infant mortality by lowering the number of high-risk pregnancies coming to term. Additionally, there are improved med-ical services for persons living in poverty, including prenatal care and general im-provements in perinatal and neonatal care. However, the evidence gives the most support to the improved survival of low birth-weight infants through NICU treatment, which can be credited with bringing down the infant mortality rate. Research techniques used to determine the effectiveness of NICUs include com-parison studies of infants treated at the same institutions at different times, the re-sults of which indicate that the NICU does improve the survival rate of all but the very smallest babies. Other studies use cross-sectional comparisons that have also produced results from which it can be inferred that appropriate application of assisted mechanical ventilation in NICUs can significantly reduce infant mor-bidity and mortality (Racine, Joyce, & Grossman, 1992). Thus, the ability of NICUs to improve survival rates and reduce risks to low birth-weight infants is consistently supported through the research.

Although the ability to save lives in NICUs is unquestioned, some argue that cost must come under consideration, just as it should for the implementation of any medical service. However, cost-effectiveness research and its interpretations are not clear-cut (McCormick, 1992). Since hospital accounting practices may cloud the actual expenditures associated with NICUs and the costs of long-term care of NICU survivors with severe disabilities are not easily determined, attempts to ascertain their cost effectiveness are inaccurate at best. Further, the technology in place can change so rapidly that the costs and outcomes are in constant flux, making the practice of policy decision making based on cost effectiveness figures inevitably out-of-date. There is no doubt that NICU services are extremely expense, but educational and life opportunities for persons with disabilities have greatly improved. Any attempts to project the institutional care costs for this population would be significantly out-of-date and overestimated simply because there are so many more available options today.

Technology and Child Care Recent innovations in the treatment of Hyaline Membrane Disease (HMD) combined with RDS, which is a major cause of infant mortality, are indicative of the many advances yet to be made (McCormick, 1992). In some instances, practitioners and hospitals must carefully monitor their decisions and the temptations associated with the availability of cutting-edge technology. As noted in the first argument, the introduction of new technologies into a medical arena may be accompanied by some undesirable side effects, such as duplication of equipment rather than collaborative sharing within communities, and overuse and inappropriate use of new equipment with little regard to patient costs. Such a situation does not imply that technology in the NICU should be halted but rather that it must be well organized and structured through continued establishment of the network of providers specializing in this area, and monitored by ethical review boards. The risks of human temptation to obtain and use the newest equipment in patient care regardless of its appropriateness are neither unique to this situation nor directly attributable to the availability of technology.

Current limits on the effects of neonatal technology are evident in our lack of anatomic information about the ability of the fetal lung to sustain respiration, the lack of improvement of survival rates below a certain gestational age/birth weight in the very recent past, and the futility of certain intense procedures for some very immature infants (McCormick, 1992). Continued work in these areas and others is critical. As we push the edge of the frontier of knowledge, we must proceed with thoughtful consideration for the families and infants whose lives are worth our efforts. Concurrently needed are efforts to improve the developmental outcomes of the NICU graduates through increasing the capacity of parents to provide needed supports and engaging in research on the most effective therapies and interventions for these children.

There are many technological improvements already designed to better the lives of these and other health-impaired children after their departure from the hospital. Some children need surgical techniques for heart disease, treatment for leukemia and other cancers, or therapies to reduce the symptoms of cystic fibrosis. The availability of home health services for children facing ventilator dependence and/or long-term intravenous feedings is another growing technological need. The Office of Technology estimates that 20,000 to 30,000 U.S. children require home care with significant technology dependence, at costs of care for some well over $100,000 per year, with costs shifting from hospitals and insurers to parents (Perrin, Guyer, & Lawrence, 1992). Such costs are far less than they would be were the technology to enable children to remain at home not available.

Argument Summary Advancing technology cannot be done cheaply, but the long-term, multigenerational benefits to society must become a part of any cost-effectiveness analysis of new treatments. Medical technologies are expensive and cannot produce risk-free outcomes, but are essential to our continued pursuit of improved treatment for high-risk infants. It was only through previous experimental efforts with smaller and smaller infants in the past that the medical community developed the ability to care for many premature infants.

Unquestionably, prevention efforts are needed to address the disturbing sociological patterns evident in the infant mortality figures. However, the concerns regarding vulnerable infants from at-risk populations far exceed a debate between the merits of preventive medicine and the continued advancement of technological breakthroughs. Prenatal care cannot be isolated as a single entity unrelated to issues of housing, education, employment, personal hope and aspirations for the future, and violence in inner-city communities. The medical community must be free to explore, discover, and treat patients with the best means available while our democratic society seeks answers to the problems of poverty, racial prejudice, and the dwindling of jobs with adequate pay for persons with limited skills.

GENETICS AND DISABILITY

There is exponentially increasing information in the field of human genetics today emerging from the existing network of genetics centers throughout the country and the more recent advent of the Human Genome Project. Therapies available in terms of both the prevention and treatment of genetic disorders are expanding. Today, we have both the ability to predict, even before conception, the risk of conceiving a fetus with many given genetic disorders and to identify a fetus with specific genetic disorders early in pregnancy (Perrin, Guyer, & Lawrence, 1992). Our knowledge and medical practices in genetics, prenatal diagnosis, and associated interventions have undergone radical changes in the second half of the twentieth century. Laws and social and cultural values have changed as well. We no longer routinely sterilize institutionalized females who are mentally retarded or legally restrict the marriage of two consenting adults who have been identified as retarded. The eugenics movement evident in the first half of the century no longer exists. Concurrently, we have made great strides in our knowledge of genetics, including the development of successful interventions for some genetic causes of retardation (e.g., PKU). For others, recommended interventions include therapeutic abortions and other means of preventing the birth of a child known to be carrying a genetic disorder, with the ultimate aim of eliminating genetic disorders as a cause of disability. Such options are far different from those in the past.

Advances in the discovery of genetic markers for specific disorders and even predispositions to conditions (e.g., obesity or cancer) are coming at a rapid rate through the work of the Human Genome Project. The project grew out of research by the Department of Energy aimed at the investigation of possible human mutations resulting from the nuclear explosions at Hiroshima and Nagasaki. The goals are to develop detailed maps of the human genome (genetic makeup) and to determine the order (sequence of the individual nucleotides in the DNA of these genomes) (Rossiter & Caskey, 1993). For now, however, the goal of complete sequencing of the human genome in fifteen years, which would cost an estimated $3 billion, has been postponed. The more realistic goal of establishing links between genes and the functions they influence is currently the focus of the project (Davis, 1993). Annas (1993) has noted that "congressional support of the project is based primarily on the hope that mapping the genome can help the United States maintain its lead in the biotechnology industry" (p. 36).

Mapping and sequencing the human genome could eventually result in screening on an almost unimaginable scale—not only for certain diseases and traits but also for tendencies toward diseases, such as cancer or manic-depression. When all genetic traits can actually be deciphered in the genetic code, we will take a qualitative leap in our understanding of inborn defects and tendencies toward diseases. Annas (1993) points out that "Exactly what the consequences of such a step will be are not entirely foreseeable" (p. 36). The ability to treat or even prevent conditions for which there is little or no hope today seems miraculous, but there will be many sensitive issues to be handled. Information control and privacy for employers, insurance companies, the military, the government— all with possible conflicting interests—are just a sample of the issues that face us in the 1990s. Already the issue of privacy rights and required DNA testing has been a problem for the military.

Prenatal Diagnosis and Intervention

Only one generation ago, amniocentesis was considered novel and strictly a research tool that would never have widespread use. At the time, abortions were both illegal and socially unacceptable. In 1973, abortion became legal, and shortly thereafter amniocentesis was commonplace. Today, 300,000 American women undergo the procedure each year (Bishop, 1993). In the mid-1950s, three technical advances led the way to the development of amniocentesis as used today. First, the ability to culture human cells in vitro was established. Second, techniques of cytogenetic analysis improved. Third, a safe and practical method of sampling amniotic fluid was developed. When amniocentesis came into wide use in the 1970s, many professionals anticipated that it would result in the prevention of Down syndrome and other chromosomal and genetic disorders through the termination of such pregnancies (Pueschel, 1991). Prevention has not occurred for two reasons. Some women, knowing their child will have Down syndrome, do choose to complete the pregnancy, and others who were not in a high-risk category and, therefore, never tested do give birth to children with this condition. Nevertheless, amniocentesis is in wide use today, and women now have the option to terminate an unwanted pregnancy or carry the fetus to term. Prenatal diagnosis can provide the parents who do not elect to terminate the pregnancy more time to prepare for the special needs of the infant. Possible adjustments can be anticipated and planned as needed, including a change in the timing or type of delivery or the provision of prenatal treatment, such as intrauterine surgery, transfusions, and delivery of medications that, in turn, increase fetal survival rates and enhance peri- and postnatal development.

Today, over two hundred disabling conditions can be detected through fetal tests conducted early in a pregnancy (Bowe, 1995). Although cost remains a significant issue for many such tests, a view into the future offered by Nobel laureate Walter Gilbert of Harvard University forecasts that by the year 2000, genetic testing for any of fifty or so genetic diseases will be as cheap as $300 to $500 and will drop rapidly in succeeding years: "By 2020 or 2030, gene testing will be so cheap that a customer could give a few drops of blood to his neighborhood pharmacy and receive his complete genome encoded on a compact disc, Gilbert ventures" (Bishop, 1993, p. 28).

Reproductive Technology

Transplants and other genetic advances are also influencing the lives of children with serious health conditions. In 1990, the seventeen-year-old daughter of Abe and Mary Ayalas was suffering from chronic myelogenous leukemia and needed a bone marrow transplant (Bishop, 1993). Since no match could be found, the parents hoped that by having a second child they could create an acceptable donor for her. For molecular geneticists throughout the country, the case was indicative of possible new uses of preimplantation embryo genetic testing (that is, genetic testing of an embryo before it becomes implanted in the womb to produce a pregnancy). If the second child were too genetically different, the transplant would certainly fail. Although it was not used in this case, test-tube conception followed with preimplantation diagnosis could have increased the probability of a good genetic match. The molecular geneticists knew that they could dramatically increase the odds of the match by simultaneously fertilizing six to eight ova and identifying an embryo whose genes most closely matched those of the intended recipient. That embryo would then become the one selected for producing a pregnancy, and the others would be discarded. The child who was born, conceived without test tubes, was a good match for her older sister. In 1991, at fourteen months of age, this child provided her sibling with new bone marrow. Both are healthy, leading normal lives today. The case sparked substantial controversy at the time regarding the ethics of producing a child to treat another one, but raised far greater issues than were evident in the particulars of the case.

Preimplantation technology was actually used as early as 1989 to help a woman avoid an inherited defect in her offspring (Bishop, 1993). Scientists were able to distinguish before fertilization which of several ova had inherited the defect and eliminate them from the fertilization process. In fact, the first test-tube baby, born in 1992, had been examined for cystic fibrosis as an eight-cell embryo two days after conception. A Virginia fertility clinic has already been offering preimplantation diagnosis for cystic fibrosis, and about one hundred couples had inquired as of Bishop's writing, although none had chosen to pay the $12,000 price of the testing (most of which was actually associated with the fertilization process rather than the genetic diagnosis) (Bishop, 1993). The potential to preselect genetic traits of a child even before a pregnancy occurs certainly sets the stage for much debate. The implications include the possibility that society will wish to determine which human genetic traits are desirable and even permissible, not simply use the procedures to aid in the treatment of a cancer patient needing a bone marrow transplant.

Advances in fertilization techniques, which are developing concurrently with the genetic coding research, interact to produce even more possibilities and pose more dilemmas. Fertilization procedures used today include in vitro fertilization, cryopreservation (freezing embryos, estimated as potentially viable for 600 years and perhaps up to 10,000 years), artificial insemination and sperm banks, ovum transfer, surrogacy, and artificial insemination. Cloning and ectogenesis (development of embryo without a host) are future possibilities in this arena. Many of these technologies are advancing far faster than the general public realizes.

By the mid-1980s, more than five hundred babies had been born to surrogate mothers. Although the initial cases made the headlines and occasionally a legal argument does ensue that brings a case to our attention, the public is unaware of such events. For those who are uncomfortable with the surrogate concept, ectogenesis has been proposed as a viable alternative for the future (Edwards, 1991). Edwards (1991) notes that the process has even been suggested as a means of supplying spare body parts to those in need of transplants. Abortions could be redefined as early births to offer the availability of fetal tissues needed to provide medical treatments to living children.

The first in vitro fertilization in the United States was in 1981 (the first in the world was in 1978 in England). By 1986, there had been more than 5,000 such fertilizations worldwide, with the number continuing to increase—approximately doubling each year. Today, over 170,000 women each year in the United States use artificial insemination as a means of fertilization. A conservative estimate indicates that over 350,000 women have conceived in this manner since its inception. Moreover, genetic engineering involving gene insertion has already been successful with both pigs and mice: "Nothing would prevent even embryos conceived in the 'old-fashioned way' from being flushed from the womb, genetically screened, having the 'necessary corrections' made, and then being reimplanted for gestation" (Edwards, 1991, p. 351).

Is this good news of medical breakthrough or the signal of the end of humanity? The issues surrounding advances in this field will have a significant impact on persons with disabilities as well as society in general. Whereas the issue of abortion is undeniably a pivotal point for some, it is not intended to be the primary differentiation in the arguments presented below. The intended focus is rather on the social meaning of the goal of eradicating genetic disorders.

Decision Point 10.2: Making
Decisions with Genetic Information

Arguments for Proposition One   Medical advances in genetics may carry with them serious implications that could lead society to repeat some of its most shameful policies. The legal precedent for mandatory screening of newborns for genetic disorders is already in place in most states, with required screening for PKU. Obviously, the ability to prevent severe mental retardation and behavior disorders resulting from a normal diet makes the early detection of PKU critical. The screening offers an excellent means of preventing a normal child who has a genetic code error from becoming severely impaired. However, such a screening practice does carry with it additional implications. Likewise, voluntary prenatal screenings are now commonplace. Both prenatal and infant screening practices will likely expand with the increasing knowledge of genetic markers. Eventually, the genetic screening of human embryos (already technically feasible) will not need to be mandated, because people can be made to want it, even insist on it, as their right.

From such practices we can become tempted to adopt eugenic motives, improving the species by weeding out genetic undesirables or increasing the number of desirable traits in offspring through genetic control (Annas, 1993). Annas (1993) compares the statements used by the Supreme Court in 1927 to justify sterilization of adults with mental retardation with remarks made by staff of the Office of Technology Assessment in 1988 regarding the Human Genome Project. The similarities are all too evident:

> It is better for all the world, if instead of waiting to execute degenerate off-spring for crime, or to let them starve for their imbecility, society can prevent those who are manifestly unfit from continuing their kind. (U.S. Supreme Court in 1927)
>
> Human mating that proceeds without the use of genetic data about the risks of transmitting diseases will produce greater mortality and medical costs than if carriers of potentially deleterious genes are alerted to their status and encouraged to mate with noncarriers or to use artificial insemination or other reproductive strategies. (U.S. Congress Office of Technology Assessment in 1988)

The moral risks that this line of "intervention" presents are of far greater concern than any sociological ones imposed by the presence of individuals in our population who have genetic disorders.

Proposition One
The goal of eliminating genetic disorders must not be held as superior to the goal of providing the best possible means of intervention for all human beings. Genetic diagnosis can assist families in understanding the nature of a child's disability and, as such, has the potential to offer useful information, but must not become the means for our second eugenics movement.

Prenatal Diagnosis and Intervention One of the most apparent concerns for special educators in regard to advances in genetics is the common practice of prenatal diagnosis of Down syndrome. Pueschel (1991), in debating this matter, asks us to consider who can assume that the birth of a child with Down syndrome will be absent of joy and rewards. What right do parents have to reject a child simply because it was not up to their standards? Human wisdom and integrity are not great enough to hold power over who should have life or threaten the most basic human right, that of life. Some in the medical field adhere to the use of selective abortions of all fetuses diagnosed with Down syndrome, with the aim of eradicating the disability. This social judgment on the part of the doctors is not equivalent to the eradication of polio. In the one instance, a type of person is targeted for elimination, whereas in the second, it is a virus that must be destroyed. Is the value of lives to be measured by scores on intelligence tests? Economic arguments that claim the costs to society for the care and treatment of persons with Down syndrome are too great miss the greater moral cost we face.

Probably the most disturbing point is the fact that the practice of aborting fetuses with this or other conditions has serious implications for persons with such conditions, their worthiness as human beings, and their right to resources within society. A news story regarding a transplant operation performed on an individual with Down syndrome brings home the point (Associated Press, 1996). Sandra Jensen, a thirty-five-year-old female with Down syndrome, is believed to be the first person with significant retardation in the United States to receive a major transplant, but it did not occur without a fight. She had a heart-lung transplant on January 23, 1996. Initially, doctors at both Stanford and the University of California at San Diego denied her request on the grounds that she would be unable to comply with the complicated post-operative regime. Stanford documents indicate that doctors originally viewed the surgery as not "appropriate" for a person with Down syndrome, but relented after an offer by California's Medicaid program to pay for a full-time caretaker to ensure that post-operative routines would be adhered to by Jensen. She is a high school graduate who has lived on her own several years. However, her worthiness for receipt of these transplants had to be questioned, as is the diagnosed fetus's worthiness for life.

Reproductive Technology The growth of prenatal testing, such as amniocentesis, is indicative that couples are willing today to take advantage of available technology to reduce or eliminate the risk of bearing a child with a genetic disorder. Access to preimplantation diagnosis will likely appeal to many couples but may result in the redefinition of certain traits as "disorders" (Bishop, 1993). Short height offers a perfect example of a trait that is generally viewed as normal but somewhat unfortunate, particularly for males. Were it possible to avoid the genes that would cause a child to be short as a part of the preimplantation selection, couples would likely consider this a socially acceptable opportunity to give their child the best possible start in life (Bishop, 1993). The technology for adding genes to a test-tube embryo is already possible in lab mice and is being extended to larger mammals. The only reason that it is not currently being done with humans is that there is general agreement that it would be unethical: "There is not much difference between selecting an embryo to avoid having a short child and inserting a gene into the embryo to make sure the child will be of normal height" (Bishop, 1993, p. 29).

Taken to their natural conclusion, the implications have us pricing all human characteristics (such as height, intelligence, race, eye color) while degrading children to commodities, having "no rights or interests of their own but that exist to further the interests of parents and future societies" (Annas, 1993, p. 37). The definition of what constitutes a "normal" gene complement and society's willingness to allow deviation at its expense may face an ever-shrinking definition. Competition among clinics will materialize, and whereas some might wish to restrict their business to the identification of genetic disorders, the competition will be in offering testing for nondisease traits. It will be cost effective for medical plans to pay for this testing to avoid letting a couple bear a child with a genetic disease who would need expensive medical care for years. Employers may find themselves determining which tests they are willing to pay for, and the government would begin making such decisions for the impoverished. If patients themselves must pay the costs of these services, then they will be available only to those who can afford them—middle and upper income—and denied to the poor. Humans are acquiring the ability to select the genetic traits of their own species, i.e., choosing to adopt unnatural selection (Bishop, 1993).

Some might argue that this discussion is unrealistic and reactionary, but Edwards noted in 1991 that there were already over five hundred clinics in Bombay, India, offering sexual selection services. Such moves to control the gene pool in the United States would be certain to have repercussions that we cannot begin to conceive. To whom shall we give the authority to define *abnormal, deviant,* or *diseased*—the Office of Technology Assessment?

> The Nazi atrocities grew out of the combination of a public health ethic that saw the abnormal as disposable and a tyrannical dictatorship that was able to give the physicians and public health authorities unlimited authority to put their program into bestial practice. (Annas, 1993, p. 37)

Annas (1993) argues for our need to move with caution by citing another statement from the Office of Technology Assessment: "New technologies for identifying traits and altering genes make it possible for eugenic goals to be achieved through technological as opposed to social control" (p. 37). Statements such as this, coming from members of our representative government who exert power and control over the distribution of our research dollars, are cause for alarm.

As the ability to screen embryos is combined with other genetic advances, such as preimplantation diagnosis, we could see "the creation of a market in 'high-grade embryos' that could be bought and sold; gestated by contract or surrogate mothers" (Annas, 1993, p. 37). Bishop (1993) has noted that each of the following can already be detected through preimplantation diagnosis: cystic fibrosis, muscular dystrophy, Huntington's disease, fragile X syndrome, some types of blindness, and some inheritable nerve and heart disorders. Additional genes that render individuals susceptible to cancer of the breast, colon, ovaries, and possibly other organs and genes for abnormally high cholesterol levels or tendencies to obesity have recently been discovered or are on the immediate horizon. Besides the genes for such physical characteristics as sex, height, and eye and hair color, the Human Genome Project will reveal the genes that protect against future illness and that contribute to longevity. The genes for musical, artistic, and athletic ability will become known, as will the complex of genes for the traits and abilities that make up intelligence (Bishop, 1993).

The overarching importance of the many biological innovations for the family has been largely ignored by sociologists (Edwards, 1991). Technology opens the door to the selection of the sex of offspring and the manipulation of appearance and perhaps intellectual capacity of offspring, allows gays and lesbians to have means of forming a family, and permits heterosexual couples to delay childbearing past normal years. When pregnancy is inconvenient for a woman's career or is considered to have undesirable cosmetic effects, women can opt for surrogacy. Such a remedy seems acceptable for a woman unable to bear her own children, but the use of it for lesser purposes is irresponsible at best.

The most frightening of the evolving technologies is that of ectogenesis, yet its difference from transplantation is not so remote as to dismiss it as a ridiculous notion of science fiction. The balance between the right-to-life values and concern for the quality of life currently makes ectogenesis an unacceptable reproductive procedure, but demand for a supply of spare body organs may change our attitudes toward the use of the technique. Longevity is increasing, and the use of fetal tissue in the treatment of a wide range of diseases, including epilepsy, diabetes, and nearly a dozen neurological ailments ranging from Alzheimer's disease to spinal cord injuries, adds further legitimacy to this notion (Edwards, 1991). Edwards cautions us that "in theory the new reproductive technologies signal the obsolescence of marriage and the family" (p. 355), because they open the door to reproduction without the traditional consanguineal bond as a necessity.

Argument Summary The inadequacies in health and nutrition of children alive today offer many worthy challenges for our medical community, which need not introduce into our society the means to engage in genetic engineering, selective breeding, and other practices of questionable moral value. The inevitable aim of seeking the prevention of physical, mental, or moral defects via genetic engineering, therapeutic abortions, and restraint from producing offspring for those at risk of producing genetically inferior offspring is dangerous in its very intentions. Furthermore, there is no means to stop these natural conclusions of genetic engineering once we are convinced that it is in our best interests to do so. Indeed, we are more likely to argue that we, as individuals, have a right to use all the latest innovations regardless of their impact and meaning for society.

Arguments for Proposition Two Advances in the field of genetics have introduced the world to new possibilities in medical treatment and benefits never imagined only a short while ago. Although these advances carry with them many challenging ethical dilemmas, they offer hope where only hopelessness has been. Gene therapy provides a perfect illustration of such an advance. In 1990, Ashanti

DeSilva, a chronically ill four-year-old, received the first gene therapy (Anderson, 1995). Since then, several hundred successful instances of gene therapy have occurred. During the next century the procedure will become commonplace. The work in this area constitutes a revolution of the magnitude of only three previous medical breakthroughs—the transition to public sanitation, surgery with anesthetic, and the introduction of vaccines and antibiotics (Anderson, 1995).

More than four thousand conditions can be traced to inborn damage to a single gene, and many other conditions also have a genetic link. The ultimate power of gene therapy to provide a cure for thousands of conditions is real. Already, many diseases are being treated through gene therapy, including cancer, severe combined immunodeficiency (SCID), cystic fibrosis, hemophilia, Hunter's syndrome, and AIDS. Whereas gene therapy is still experimental and, therefore, quite costly, it will become simpler and less costly in the future. One of the most amazing types of work in this research is associated with germ line gene therapy, which involves the alteration of germ cells such that there is a resulting permanent genetic change for the whole organism and subsequent generations (Rossiter & Caskey, 1993). For parents anticipating the birth of a child with a known genetic defect, the opportunity to free the child from the disabling and often life-threatening effects of that defect through such a procedure offers nothing short of a miracle. Somatic cell gene therapy, another gene replacement option, is analogous to an organ transplant, but only genes need be transplanted rather than a whole organ (Rossiter & Caskey, 1993).

Prenatal Diagnosis and Intervention The dramatic reductions in infant mortality over this century have been tremendous, yet infant mortality due to genetic factors remains unchanged over the years at 5 per 1,000 (White, 1993). However, as fewer babies die, the percentage of deaths attributed to genetic disorders has become greater and greater. In 1900, genetic factors equaled 3% of infant deaths, whereas today the percentage has increased to 33% (White, 1993). As we seek to lower our national rate of infant mortality, the reduction of genetic defects must take on greater priority. Today, congenital abnormalities are a leading cause of neonatal mortality, with about 25% of birth defects having a genetic basis (Racine, Joyce, & Grossman, 1992). The prenatal detection of conditions likely to result in the birth of a child too severely disabled to sustain life would enable women to avoid the unnecessary completion of such pregnancies that are destined to result in infant death anyway. Future genetic research offers the key to any progress on alternative treatments made in this area, whether it be through

---

Proposition Two
As in the past, genetic research and knowledge of the future will offer immeasurable benefits to individuals with disabilities and their families, while simultaneously leading the way in the reduction of genetic disorders as a cause of disability.

increased ability to make prenatal diagnosis, preimplantation diagnosis, gene therapy, or other techniques as yet undeveloped and unimagined.

There are now several procedures used for prenatal screening (Blasco, Blasco, & Zirpoli, 1994). Ultrasound, used to detect structural abnormalities, presents no risks and has a 90% detection rate for open neural tube defects. Chorionic villus biopsy (CVS) is done between nine and eleven weeks with less than 1% risk of miscarriage, whereas amniocentesis is performed later, at fourteen to eighteen weeks, with a .5% risk of miscarriage and very rare instances of fetal damage, leakage of amniotic fluid, maternal infection, and premature labor. It can be used to detect more than 250 genetic disorders, but some of the tests are time consuming and costly. It is now routine to refer women over thirty-five for amniocentesis and follow-up lab tests to determine the presence of Down syndrome in the fetus. As a result, the demographics of mothers giving birth to infants with the condition have shifted. Today, 80% are younger than thirty-five and, therefore, would not have routinely been tested unless the condition were known to be present in the family. Maternal serum alphafetoprotein (AFP) is done at sixteen to eighteen weeks with no risks and is used for detection of neural tube defects, some abdominal wall defects, the possibility of Down syndrome, and Trisomy 18. Deoxyribonucleic acid (DNA) analysis is the follow up procedure used after suspicious CVS or amniocentesis results, and it poses no risks. Samples of women who have used these procedures indicate that were they to become pregnant again they would use them again (Spencer & Cox, as cited by Blasco, Blasco, & Zirpoli, 1994). These procedures will continue to be improved upon and superceded as work in the field continues. Growing out of the work on gene mapping and gene cloning has been the detection of single gene defects—for example, sickle cell anemia, cystic fibrosis, Duchenne and Becker muscular dystrophy, growth hormone deficiency, Huntington's disease, phenylketonuria (PKU), and Tay-Sachs disease (Blasco, Blasco, & Zirpoli, 1994). Techniques to separate fetal cells from maternal cells will eventually eliminate the need for such invasive techniques as CVS and amniocentesis and simplify the prenatal diagnostic procedure.

As a result of the prenatal diagnostic techniques available today, 95% of expecting parents can be relatively assured that their child will be free from specific mental or physical disabilities within the first five months of pregnancy (Blasco, Blasko, & Zirpoli, 1994). Doctors have little choice but to use these prenatal diagnostic tests, because there is already an established pattern of lawsuits in which patients claim negligence if the doctor failed to recommend the test and the couple had a child with a diagnosable genetic disorder (Pueschel, 1991). These suits pursue the idea that the doctor permitted a "wrongful birth." Expectant parents who are told that their fetus has a disabling condition can be given information on the projected quality of life for that child and then make difficult, yet informed, decisions regarding abortion or other therapeutic options, including intrauterine surgery.

Fetal surgery offers early correction of a defect that would cause irreversible damage over time, with reduced chances of rejection of early allogenic grafts by the immature immune system and quicker postoperative healing (Blasco, Blasco,

& Zirpoli, 1994). Procedures currently in use for life-threatening problems include fetal blood sampling and transfusion, intrauterine shunting for hydrocephalus, repair of lung and diaphragm anomalies, and correction of urinary tract obstructions. However, the current success rates for these procedures (e.g., intrauterine shunting) are disappointing. There is a poor prognosis for most patients regardless of treatment of the shunt, in part due to the fact that the hydrocephalus may be just one of numerous associated anomalies. Continued work in this area should lead medical personnel to achieve better outcomes. Although open fetal surgery is still experimental and available only at a few research centers, an excellent outcome has been reported following open surgery of a congenital diaphragmatic hernia (Blasco, Blasco, & Zirpoli, 1994).

Abortion, which is inherently associated with prenatal diagnosis, is a topic that has produced strong views, regardless of disability. Although no one would argue that abortion is a positive experience or a healthy means of birth control, many do argue that there are rights and benefits to individual women and society at large that necessitate the availability of the procedure (Pueschel, 1994). A fetus has a right to be born healthy and protected from genetic defects. When a fetus known to have a genetic disorder is terminated, the family has made a decision with their own circumstances and beliefs balanced with the information available regarding the condition of the fetus.

Fletcher, as cited by Pueschel (1994), holds that a fetus with a severe defect has a lesser moral claim on the mother than a "normal" child because he is less likely to respond to the promise of becoming a person in the community of persons. Prevention of mental retardation is a worthy and appropriate public health goal, and abortion is one valid approach to that end. It is more just and less cruel to a suffering fetus to abort it than prolong the misery that the infant may suffer after birth, possibly requiring surgeries and prolonged hospital stays necessary for survival. The fact is that 70% to 80% of fetuses with Down syndrome spontaneously abort (Pueschel, 1994). The arguments do not relate to the worthiness of one's life once a person is born. The value and worthiness of life for all children and adults, regardless of disability, gender, race, and socioeconomic status, must be considered equal.

Financial considerations hold far less credence than do moral issues, but must be included in a comprehensive discussion of these matters. For example, the monetary costs of screening pregnant women and terminating the pregnancy for those who choose it are far less than those incurred by educating and supervising people with Down syndrome for a lifetime (Pueschel, 1994). The provision of such programs to individuals with Down syndrome was estimated at about $3,621,000,000 in 1985, contrasted with prevention via amniocentesis, chromosome analysis, counseling, and abortion at approximately $33,000,000. Some even argue that prenatal screening to locate as many defects as possible should be mandatory and is no more invasive than contact tracing of venereal disease patients. Society would benefit from the termination of unwanted pregnancies in that the procedure would reduce the financial and emotional burdens society must assume for the care and treatment of unwanted infants with genetic disorders. The need for beds in institutions and nursing homes that house many victims of severe genetic disorders today would be reduced as the number of individuals unable to sustain a minimally acceptable quality of life dropped.

Reproductive Technology The Human Genome Project has the potential for the rapid discovery of the estimated 4,000 disease genes residing in the human genome (Rossiter & Caskey, 1993). This discovery will be followed with a far better understanding of genetic-based diseases and possible treatments of such conditions. The work of the project should produce improved medical strategies, such as gene therapy involving the delivery of a functional gene to appropriate tissue in order to correct an inherited or acquired defect, and increased development of more effective drugs for the treatment of many conditions. Project personnel have recognized the critical role of ethics in their work and have, therefore, incorporated ethical considerations as one of their specifically funded lines of inquiry. Questions about the proper nature of genetic screening and counseling for people considering having children, whether to provide a genetic diagnosis of adult-onset conditions prior to the appearance of any symptoms, and whether insurance companies would be allowed to consider a presymptomatic diagnosis as a prior existing condition are illustrative of some of the concerns being addressed in this area (Rossiter & Caskey, 1993).

New reproductive technologies make pregnancy possible for many with a history of genetic disease, endometriosis, hyperthyroid conditions, and miscarriage (Edwards, 1991). These technologies offer a chance for a family to many who otherwise have no hope. They do not represent the demise of the nuclear family, as previously claimed. Although the family structure may indeed be threatened in our society today, one can hardly point to fertility clinics as the cause. Some concern has even been expressed that through our ability to prevent damage associated with some genetic disorders and/or expand those capable of producing offspring, increasing numbers of adults with genetic disorders will be included in the gene pool. The situation could reach a crisis level as our technological ability to enable more and more persons with genetic disorders to survive and reproduce increases, an ironic outcome for those so concerned about the morality of genetic advances. Selective abortions of affected fetuses may prove to be the best preventive step that medicine can offer to offset this danger.

Argument Summary The ongoing work in the field of genetics will enable couples to have clearer expectations about their future offspring and the ability to make better informed decisions about them. The seemingly remote goal of the elimination of genetic disorders and/or their harmful effects edges closer to reality through ongoing work. Our attempts to support children with disabilities to overcome those disabilities, achieve their greatest potential, and find independent fruitful lives run in parallel lines with the doctors and scientists seeking to find improved medical interventions for them and their families through genetics. Rather than pointlessly calling for a halt to medical progress, we must face the even greater challenge of seeking and finding moral guidelines while progressing in this most exciting arena.

Some argue that it is the nature of humanity to pursue control over the world and, therefore, we are obligated to seek and know as much about the realities of the world as possible. Pursuit of that knowledge in the hands of persons with the noble aims of reducing human pain and suffering is far superior to the placement of such knowledge in the hands of those seeking to gain power and control over others, or to find a profitable market for genetic engineering. The knowledge itself is neither evil nor to be avoided. Rather, knowledge must be sought and embraced as a means of defining the nature of genetic disorders and the most effective means of treating them.

CLOSING THOUGHTS

The issues raised here do not restrict themselves to reproduction and prenatal, perinatal, and neonatal care. At least 90% of children with very severe long-term illnesses survive to young adulthood, a dramatic change over the past twenty-five years (Perrin, Guyer, & Lawrence, 1992). On the other hand, by 1988 AIDS, which is highly concentrated in poor and minority families, had become the leading cause of death among Hispanic children ages one to four in New York and the second leading cause for African Americans in the same group. Since the main means of transmission for these children is through the mother, a reasonable conclusion is that their mothers are probably also ill and will be unable to care for these children as they mature. By late 1991, 10% of pediatric hospital beds were occupied by children with AIDS, and the percentage will likely continue to increase as treatments improve and survival rates rise. Technology continues to be the source of great hope and advance, while opening a Pandora's box of problems.

Nichols (1992) argues that the power of technology results in the subordination of the individual to machines over which we have less and less control. Decisions may not be made by rational, caring human beings, but rather by technology, legal systems, and fiscal policies. Because we face these moral dangers and because the technological revolution is unstoppable, it is most appropriate that we strive to develop guides for the moral use of technology rather than pretending that any other options remain. Nichols (1991) recommends that we acknowledge that educational biotechnology is indeed dangerous and "that many people with the desire and the ability to do so will use drugs, neural surgery, psychological training, and genetic manipulation to improve memories, thinking skills, and learning attitudes of their children" (p. 565).

The standards we create must offer us more than a collective consensus of opinion, for such might merely be those in control convincing everyone else of what seems to be in their best interests. Nichols (1991) makes his point with a rather dramatic yet believable scenario:

> I don't want us giving fetal brain tissue from deceased babies to pre-schoolers who are otherwise perfectly ready for learning, even if an entire community,

city, or state have agreed to do so…we need guiding over-riding moral principles because not everything nations and states agree on is moral. (p. 574)

As postmodernists question even the existence of concepts such as universal truth and morality, technology is defining our new world. Callister and Dunne (1992) articulate the problem: "Our society tends to imbue computers with technological and scientific truth and power. Instead of perceiving them as rather stupid machines that do onerous tasks very very quickly, we tend to view them as intelligent devices with 'judgment' and power" (p. 325). We will do well to consider the issues surrounding limiting access to medical resources and failing to limit access to medical resources as we advance or regress into the twenty-first century. The careful consideration of a proper balance and established hierarchy in the relationship among morality, legality, and the scientific pursuit of knowledge seems to be missing. The thought of allowing such an imbalance is disconcerting, yet the individualism of morality in our democratic society does not offer reassurance that a reversal of order would be preferable. The moral obligation of society is to encourage the pursuit of a course of action that offers the greatest benefit to the widest possible group, without regard to their ability to pay or to their racial or ethnic background, gender, or disability.

REFERENCES

Albers, L. (1994). Clinical issues in electronic fetal monitoring. *Birth: Issues in Perinatal Care, 21,* 108–110.

Anderson, W. F. (1995). Gene therapy. *Scientific American, 273,* 124–128.

Annas, G. J. (1993). Who's afraid of the human genome? *National Forum: Phi Kappa Phi Journal, 73,* 35–37.

Associated Press. (1996). Retarded woman receives heart-lung transplant. *Knoxville News-Sentinel,* A7. (Wednesday, January 24, 1996).

Bishop, J. E. (1993). Unnatural selection. *National Forum: Phi Kappa Phi Journal, 73,* 27–29.

Blasco, P. M., Blasco, P. A., & Zirpoli, T. J. (1994). Prenatal diagnosis: Current procedures and implications for early interventionists working with families. *Infants and Young Children, 7,* 33–42.

Bowe, F. G. (1995). Ethics in early childhood special education. *Infants and Young Children, 7,* 28–37.

Callister, T., & Dunne, F. (1992). The computer as a doorstop: Technology as disempowerment. *Phi Delta Kappan, 74,* 324–326.

Center for the Future of Children Staff. (1992a). Analysis. *The Future of Children, 2,* 7–24.

Center for the Future of Children Staff. (1992b). Recommendations. *The Future of Children, 2,* 6–7.

Cullen, T. A. (1992). When enough is enough—How to say no to technology. In M. Waterstone (Ed.), *Risk and society: The interaction of science, technology and public policy* (pp. 92–96). Boston: Kluwer.

Davis, B. D. (1993). Sequencing the human genome: A faded goal. *National Forum: Phi Kappa Phi Journal, 73,* 4–8.

Edwards, J. (1991). New conceptions: Biosocial innovations and the family. *Journal of Marriage and the Family, 53,* 349–360.

Flamm, B. L. (1994). Electronic fetal monitoring in the United States. *Birth: Issues in Perinatal Care, 21,* 105–106.

Friedman, S. L., & Sigman, M. D. (1992). Past, present, and future directions in research on the development of low-birthweight children. In S. L. Friedman & M. D. Sigman (Eds.), *The psychological development of low-birthweight children. Annual advances in applied developmental psychology* (Vol. 6, pp. 7–22). Norwood, NJ: Ablex.

Holder-Brown, L., & Parette, H. P. (1992). Children with disabilities who use assistive technology: Ethical considerations. *Young Children, 47,* 73–77.

Jonsen, A. R. (1992). Modern medicine as a risk to society. In M. Waterstone (Ed.), *Risk and society: The interaction of science, technology and public policy* (pp. 63–74). Boston: Kluwer.

Kleinman, J. C. (1992). The epidemiology of low birthweight. In S. L. Friedman & M. D. Sigman (Eds.), *The psychological development of low-birthweight children. Annual advances in applied developmental psychology* (Vol. 6, pp. 25–35). Norwood, NJ: Ablex.

Lewis, R. B. (1993). *Special education technology: Classroom applications.* Pacific Grove, CA: Brooks/Cole.

Lewit, E. M., & Monheit, A. C. (1992). Expenditures on health care for children and pregnant women. *The Future of Children, 2,* 95–114.

Linder, N., & Ohel, G. (1994). In utero vaccination. *Clinical Perinatology, 21,* 663–674.

Mathieu, D. (1992). Hazards of the American health care system: No treatment, under-treatment, and over-treatment. In M. Waterstone (Ed.), *Risk and society: The interaction of science, technology and public policy* (pp. 75–89). Boston: Kluwer.

McCormick, M. C. (1992). Advances in neonatal intensive care technology and their possible impact on the development of low-birthweight infants. In S. L. Friedman & M. D. Sigman (Eds.), *The psychological development of low-birthweight children. Annual advances in applied developmental psychology* (Vol. 6, pp. 36–60). Norwood, NJ: Ablex.

Neilson, J. P. (1994). Fetal heart rate monitoring during labor: Information from randomized trials. *Birth: Issues in Perinatal Care, 21,* 101–104.

Nichols, R. G. (1991). Toward a conscience: Negative aspects of educational technology. In D. Hlynka & J. Belland (Eds.), *Paradigms regained: Uses of illuminative, semiotic and post structural criticism as a mode of inquiry in educational technology* (pp. 121–137). Englewood Cliffs, NJ: Educational Technology Publications.

Nichols, R. G. (1992). Educational biotechnology and a search for moral opposition to it. In: *Proceedings of selected research and development presentations at the convention of the Association for Educational Communications and Technology and sponsored by the Research and Theory Division,* 563–580. (ERIC Document Reproduction No. ED 348 013).

Paris, J. J. (1990). Terminating treatment for newborns: A theological perspective. In J. J. Walter & T. A. Shannon (Eds.), *Quality of life* (pp. 151–160). Mahwah, NJ: Paulist Press.

Perrin, J., Guyer, B., & Lawrence, J. M. (1992). Health care services for children and adolescents. *The Future of Children, 2,* 58–77.

Public Health Service, U.S. Department of Health and Human Services. (1986). *The 1990 health objectives for the nation: A midcourse review.* Washington, DC: Office of Disease Prevention and Health Promotion.

Pueschel, S. M. (1991). Ethical considerations relating to prenatal diagnosis of fetuses with Down syndrome. *Mental Retardation, 29,* 185–190.

Racine, A. D., Joyce, T. J., & Grossman, M. (1992). Effectiveness of health care services for pregnant women and infants. *The Future of Children, 2,* 40–57.

Rossiter, B. J. F., & Caskey, C. T. (1993). Medical consequences of the Human Genome Project. *National Forum: Phi Kappa Phi Journal, 73,* 12–14.

Shapiro, J. P. (1993). *No pity: People with disabilities forging a new civil rights movement*. New York: Random House.

Solomon, G. (1992). The computer as electronic doorway: Technology and the promise of empowerment. *Phi Delta Kappan, 74,* 327–329.

Solomon, S. D. (1995). Suffer the little children. *Technology Review, 98,* 42–51.

Southgate, W. M., Howell, C. G., & Kanto, W. P. (1990). Need for and impact on neonatal mortality of extracorporeal membrane oxygenation in infants greater than 2,5000-gram birth weight. *Pediatrics, 86,* 71–74.

White, S. W. (1993). Health care: Multiplying paradigms. *National Forum: Phi Kappa Phi Journal, 73,* 2–3.

11

Quality of Life
and Disability

INTRODUCTION

Quality is a comparative notion. It runs along a continuum, with high and low extremes as well as a large middle ground. The nature of our homes and communities, the friends we have and the depth of our relationships with them, our family relationships, our use of recreational time, our freedom to make choices in our lives, our opportunities for employment, and many other variables all contribute to our quality of life. It is unique to the individual and changes over the life span, affected by a personal valuation of what is important and an accounting of how we expend our energy (Weisgerber, 1991). We hold differing opinions on what constitutes a satisfactory quality of life and may be tempted to impose our standards on others. City dwellers wonder how people in rural America stand the quiet, whereas those in suburbia question the sanity of anyone still living within a major metropolitan area. Proximity to museums and live theater is considered critical for some and takes a far lower priority for those who prefer proximity to nature and solitude. However, most seem to agree that a healthy balance between independence and social connectedness is desirable and needed to experience some level of satisfaction with life. Thus, there are elements within the total framework of quality of life that we will forever disagree on and other general principles with which the majority of Americans concur are relevant to quality of life. For the concert pianist, the loss of a single finger may represent a substantial blow to her quality of life; whereas it might be of far less consequence beyond cosmetic concern to those of us who have pursued other interests. Regardless of one's preferences, there is sufficient evidence "that functional or rewarding and enriching life experiences are necessary for an individual to report a high level of perceived life satisfaction or subjective well-being" (Herr, 1992, p. 254).

Who are the keepers of quality of life? Within America, white middle-class culture tends to dominate perceptions of what constitutes a high quality of life, whereas persons from other cultures might hold alternative priorities and standards. Native American, African Americans, Latinos, and Asian Americans, women and men, children and adults, rural and urban, rich and poor, blue-collar and executives—all experience life and culture differently, and do not universally favor middle-class values and lifestyles (Edgerton, 1990). America is grounded in "radical individualism," with a deemphasis on social interdependence (Dennis, Williams, Giangreco, & Cloninger, 1993). For example, career opportunities for young professionals may take higher value than do opportunities to remain within proximity to extended family. The national reliance on the automobile and the absence of comprehensive mass transit outside major metropolitan areas further illustrate our cultural mores of independence and self-reliance.

Special educators and other professionals often set as the primary goal, the greatest possible achievement for young adults with significant disabilities, to be living and/or working independently in a competitive job market. Such a goal is based on a presumption that it represents the greatest possible quality of life for the individual. Independence and "normalization" tend to take precedence over many other aspects of life. A similar emphasis is placed on independent walking following a spinal cord injury as opposed to focusing on the functional skills involved in the management of a wheelchair (Heller & Alberto, 1996). However, an acceptable quality of life requires social relationships and levels of interdependence, including reliance on basic community services (e.g., mass transportation, police, fire) and social service agencies (e.g., housing, income support, medical support, legal aid, and guidance in activities of daily living) for all of us (Dennis, Williams, Giangreco, & Cloninger, 1993).

The Culture of Disability

Access to individual rights is considered an essential aspect of quality of life in America. For persons with disabilities, these rights have historically been usurped, with the justifying logic ranging from their need for protection from society to society's right to be protected from them. For example, our society generally accepts the notion that preventing homelessness for persons who are emotionally disturbed is worth any sacrifice of their personal freedom that the provision of housing may entail. Furthermore, society considers the removal of such people from the streets highly desirable for the sake of the community. Regardless of the motives, the loss of rights for persons with disabilities has had a significant impact on the quality of life that has been available for many from this minority group.

Today, however, the role and behavior of persons with disabilities are shifting (Parmenter, 1992). In reaction to their lack of rights, persons with disabilities and their advocates have become politically active, seeking to establish basic rights to transportation, education, employment opportunities, building access, and independence and social freedom—all so easily assumed by people without disabilities. Persons with disabilities are taking a more active role in expressing their views and what they want out of life, moving from silence to assertion. Forty-three million Americans with disabilities and their families and friends have become an effective constituency, as seen with the 1990 passage of the Americans with Disabilities Act (Herr, 1992). Concurrent changing service models are following these shifts, with funds going to supports for individuals instead of programs, to persons rather than places, to identify person–environment matches, to provide services in natural environments, and to encourage consumer empowerment through the provision of real homes and real jobs for persons with disabilities.

The interaction between the concept of quality of life and the presence of disabilities in one's life is particularly emphasized for those endorsing a symbolic–interactionist view of quality of life (Parmenter, 1992). The basic principles of this theoretical perspective are that experiences are mediated by interpretation and that the "self" arises and is maintained in a symbolic and interactive context. Parmenter (1992) argues that "*Disability* is not a symbol for a condition that is already there in advance. Paradoxically, disability is part of the mechanism whereby the condition is created" (p. 265). For people with a disability, there is often an incongruence between the desired personal identity and their assigned social identity, because our stereotypes of persons with disabilities focus on generalities. Persons with disabilities may then have little choice but to fulfill the roles assigned to them. Under such conditions, their potential for achieving a highly satisfactory quality of life is jeopardized.

Although people with disabilities consider access to technology now a right, not a luxury, even advances in technology can further divide them from the nondisabled, accentuating differing values and attitudes regarding disability. For a typical nondisabled individual, the opportunity for a cure would seem to be the greatest event in a disabled person's life. Two recent inventions and the public reactions to them make the point dramatically (Shapiro, 1993). The cochlear implant seems to be a way to restore hearing to appropriate candidates who are deaf, a welcome advance in overcoming deafness. To many who are deaf, however, this is an instrument of cultural murder that is based on the premise that deafness is pathological, something to be corrected or eliminated, rather than an identity to be adopted with pride. The actual implant has proven to be of less benefit than hoped. It costs between $20,000 and $40,000, and it produces a sound that is weak and scratchy. Fewer than 1% of the 22 million Americans with hearing impairments could profit from it anyway. However, the question remains of whether we should continue refining and improving cochlear implants so that they will eventually be affordable and produce a higher quality sound so as to relieve some of the "burden" of deafness, restoring "normalcy" for some, or invest our efforts in learning sign language so that we might all better communicate with citizens who are deaf.

A similar dilemma is ongoing in association with the Functional Electronic Stimulator (FES), seemingly offering great promise to those unable to walk. Society's view is that a wheelchair is confining and to be "condemned" to live one's life dependent on such a device for mobility is sad indeed. However, such a view happens to be inconsistent with the views held by many who are so "confined." The wheelchair offers great freedom and mobility to someone whose body is unable to offer agility and motion. Placing an emphasis on movement by one's own leg muscles and implying that such movement, regardless of how faulty, tiring, or dysfunctional, is superior to and preferred over reliance on a wheelchair offer evidence of society's prejudice against persons with any level of dependence. Can such a society even attempt to define the best quality of life for persons with disabilities? The inclusion of people with disabilities and familiar others in assessing their needs and evaluating effects of services, the articulation of discipline-free goals, and the use of ecological discrepancy analysis to identify needed services and supports to maximize meaningful participation in the community are the direction for the future (Edgerton, 1990).

Defining Quality of Life

Used in various contexts, *quality of life* has different meanings, ranging from the medical arena, in which life-and-death judgments are made, to our social circles, in which engagement in conspicuous consumption to amass the greatest possible supply of material goods and comforts is often what it means. Medical decisions regarding the worthiness of a life are based on anticipated pain and suffering, dependence on technology for survival, awareness level of the individual, and so forth. These decisions most frequently involve neonates or the elderly. Elderly patients, family members, or parents of a newborn must contribute to the decision, determining at what point, if any, the conditions are too burdensome to continue efforts to maintain a life. For each of us, such decisions are highly personal matters. Other, less dramatic uses of quality of life are also prevalent, including self-fulfillment, pursuit of happiness, satisfaction in life, the richness of resources within a community or country, and the possessions of an individual.

In public health, the conceptualization of quality of life includes cost utility analysis, which is used by health economists to quantify relative benefits of medical procedures (Parmenter, 1992). In this approach, medical outputs are equated with the number of lives or life years saved so that there can be a redistribution of funds to projects with a low cost per life to the total number of life years created (Drummond, Torrance, & Mason, 1993). However, such an approach neglects the less tangible aspects of quality of life and treats all life years as of equal value. Being alive is equal regardless of pain, presence of mind, or any other circumstance.

Reaction to the perceived weakness of this cost-effective analysis has led to the concept of quality of life adjusted years (QALYs). QALY assumes that one healthy year equals one and regards a year of unhealthy life as less than a one. The criticisms of QALY are that it oversimplifies complex choices, values time lived instead of individual lives, takes a narrow conception of what quality of life might be, and is inherently unjust. Although QALY is in the field of health, not developmental disabilities or special education, Parmenter (1992) speculates that "it possibly has a pervasive effect on the way decisions are made regarding resource allocation to devalued groups in society" (p. 249).

Even the very meaning of *humanness*, as a moral rather than biological concept, interfaces with the concept of quality of life. Fletcher (1990) notes that four different traits have emerged in an ongoing pursuit of a definition of *humanness*: neocortical function, self-consciousness, relational ability, and happiness. Although these factors are not mutually exclusive, their relative importance is argued. Fletcher contends that the most basic one is neocortical function, whereas others posit that self-awareness or ability to have human relationships takes precedence. Still others plead against the creation of any such list of moral or psychological traits, but acknowledge that a biological definition might be of use. They contend that quality of life must not be used as an excuse to destroy another's life (New Jersey Catholic Conference, 1990).

American society has recently shown a trend toward valuing the lives of historically devalued persons, as evidenced in the Baby Doe case, which ultimately led to the Child Abuse Amendments of 1984 (Herr, 1992). In 1982, the parents of a baby boy born with Down syndrome, a tracheoesophageal fistula, and possibly other anomalies, declined to authorize surgery to treat the blockage to his digestive tract. At six days of age the infant died, much to the discomfort of attending nurses. The resulting legislation, although allowing for legal remedies for incidences of withholding medically indicated treatment on the basis of a disability, does include an exclusionary clause. Thus, the determination remains subjective and somewhat contradictory. In the Supreme Court case of *Cruzan v. Director, Missouri Dept. of Health* in 1990, a woman who became incompetent by an accident could not have lifesaving hydration and nutrition withheld, but the decision was based on a five to four margin. This case opinion "rejects so-called quality of life judgments as a basis for rationing medical treatment, upholding a state's right to 'properly decline to make judgments about the "quality" of life that a particular individual may enjoy, and simply assert an unqualified interest in the preservation of human life to be weighed against the constitutionally protected interests of the individual'" (Herr, 1992, p. 291).

Focus of Discussion

Quality of life is a topic relevant to every one of us. Does residence in a group home for persons with disabilities offer persons with disabilities a greater quality of life than does living in a large institution? Most would agree that the smaller group home is preferable for those with disabilities, but the selection of a neighborhood in which to locate the group home shifts the discussion over to quality of life within the community. Can both the person with a disability and the community have their "best interests" met as these decisions are hammered out? Is independence really the means to achieving the highest possible quality of life? Should the goals of education be to enable graduates to be independent or to achieve the highest possible quality of life? Specifically, within this chapter the first debate focuses on the need to protect persons with disabilities versus the need to honor their rights even when doing so appears to diminish their quality of life. The second issue discussed is the role of educators in assisting graduates to begin their adult years with a satisfactory quality of life as opposed to a life of independence.

INDEPENDENCE VERSUS
PROTECTION FROM HARM

For years, persons with disabilities have been perceived as needing protection and as dependent on the nondisabled population to look out for their best interests, even if their personal freedom and fundamental rights were sacrificed. Society assumed a responsibility to care for and protect those too disabled to fend for themselves. The number of persons with disabilities was relatively small, and they were considered appropriate recipients of society's pity and charity (Herr, 1992). However, circumstances have changed over the course of the century. Medicine, instead of achieving an implied promise of eliminating disability through the discovery of cures, has actually created an explosion of the number of people with disabilities who are alive today because of medical advances (Shapiro, 1993). Dramatic contrasts in the numbers of permanently disabled soldiers who survived their injuries after World War I and World War II reflect this changing nature of medical knowledge. Only 400 American soldiers who fought in World War I survived as paraplegics, and only 10% of them lived to make it home. In World War II, however, there were 2,000 such survivors, and over 85% of them were still alive in the late 1960s. A field doctor would have been unable to evaluate accurately the significance of such injuries for these men and their families. He might have allowed the injured men to die simply because the existing resources and supports for adult males with paraplegia were minimal in the 1940s. The irony was that the resources and supports would inevitably expand because of this same group's survival.

Shapiro (1993) notes that even in the 1950s a spinal cord injury was most likely going to end in death, resulting from respiratory, bladder, and other complications. Today, those problems can be treated effectively, and both paraplegics and quadriplegics live long, healthy lives. In the mid-1970s, 90% of people with severe head injuries died; today, 90% live, and traumatic brain injury has become a designated category of disability within IDEA. In 1991, the Institute of Medicine estimated that one in seven Americans had a disability interfering with daily activities such as work or keeping a household (Shapiro, 1993). Thus, the interaction between the concept of quality of life and the presence of disabilities in one's life is likely to affect most Americans at some point, either directly in their own lives or indirectly through the lives of their family and friends.

Evolving Concepts of Quality of Life

Initially, quality of life for children with disabilities was not a prevalent concern in the emerging field of special education. Physicians had used the concept to make medical decisions, but educators were primarily focused on improving the academic skills of children with disabilities, training those with moderate disabilities, and maintaining general education classrooms free of students unable to learn or behave as deemed appropriate. Those with more severe disabilities or multiple disabilities were not typically included in publicly supported educational programs; therefore, their quality of life was not a target of concern for most special educators.

Theoretical models of quality of life in the area of developmental disability began appearing as a part of the deinstitutionalization movement, which has been evolving since the mid-1960s (Borthwick-Duffy, 1992). Between 1968 and 1989, the number of individuals labeled as mentally retarded living in public institutions for the developmentally delayed dropped from approximately 195,000 to 87,000. The number of residents of psychiatric facilities diagnosed as mentally retarded went from approximately 37,000 to 2,000 (Stark & Faulkner, 1996). The first phase of this movement was the era of institutional reform (1965–1975), when litigation was used to establish standards to protect individuals from harm. Residents of institutions were deemed to have a right to a life free of physical abuse and harm—a rather low standard by which to measure one's quality of life. The second phase (1976–1986) began with the movement of institutional residents into community-based facilities. This deinstitutionalization was accompanied by an emphasis placed on defining the characteristics of quality programs. Some working in the field saw monitoring quality of life as the means of ensuring improvements in the living conditions of those with developmental disabilities. Living virtually anywhere outside the institution was assumed to be preferable to institutional existence. The current phase is the era of community membership, with concentration on community integration, quality of life, and development of individualized support systems for persons with developmental delays who reside in communities throughout the country.

The success of deinstitutionalization was originally monitored and evaluated using simple transition outcomes, such as whether individuals who had been removed from institutions stayed in their new arrangements or returned to institutions. Length of stay in new placement became a measure of success. The concept of placement success broadened in the 1970s to include the actual degree of community involvement, friendship patterns, and degree of normalization in the home of the persons involved. In the 1980s, a more holistic approach began, with the multidimensional nature of success being acknowledged. This approach incorporates a conception of quality of life that refers to an overall evaluation of an individual's life circumstances, preferably from his or her point of view (Borthwick-Duffy, 1992).

Freedom, Rights, and Best Interests

As individuals with disabilities moved from institutions to communities, new challenges arose. No longer were only young children still in the care of their families, or elderly persons the only people with disabilities living in communities. As the number of adults with disabilities living in communities increased, the need to improve their quality of life became apparent. Three types of policy initiatives to assist adults with disabilities emerged: rehabilitative services, income supports, and civil rights protections (Percy, 1989). Costs/benefits comparisons of these initiatives arose as implementations began (e.g., kneeling buses that were mechanically unreliable coupled with low ridership by wheelchair riders). How far society should go in making accommodations was and is still debated in the context of cost and benefits. For example, we have had to consider whether communities where no person who would benefit resides must take on the expense of renovating all public buildings to accommodate persons with disabilities. Other questions are also problematic. For example, who should be included in the disabilities rights laws—the unborn, persons with AIDS, the adult suffering from alcoholism? In the early decades of the twentieth century the federal government implemented programs to help persons with disabilities overcome their disabilities in order to join or return to the workforce, and provided other programs of temporary or permanent financial assistance for persons unable to return to work. Ongoing federal legislation has addressed the rights of persons with disabilities to education, public transportation, facility access, and employment. Over time, some of the legislation has evolved into entitlements, similar to a welfare system. Today, we must consider whether our federal and state programs protect and support persons with disabilities as they live out their lives, or suffocate them in a series of dependency traps.

Persons unable to live and work independently do need varying degrees of support, nurturing, and supervision. How much and under whose control these supports should be placed are questions no longer left unasked. The institutionalization, sterilization, and abrogation of the rights of persons with disabilities in the first half of the twentieth century coupled with the increases in the numbers of persons with disabilities have triggered a radical reaction. The importance of the rights of persons with disabilities—to them, as well as to the rest of society and culture—is evident. Today, a radical view represented by groups such as the Disabled in Action and publications such as *The Disability Rag* (Percy, 1989) is juxtaposed against a more moderate stance that some level of protection is really in the best interests of persons with disabilities, not just a means of society controlling the powerless with unspoken eugenic motives at heart. Does society have a responsibility to protect persons with disabilities from dangerous lifestyles, poor life choices, and bad influences, or do their rights as individuals to freedom and choice supersede their need for protection? Even more troubling is the question of whether society has a responsibility to determine that the quality of life for some will be so poor that they should be spared from having such lives at all.

Most who prefer to give as much freedom as possible back to persons with disabilities do acknowledge that society cannot abdicate all responsibility for setting limits on an individual's freedom of choice (Edgerton, 1990). Are there "universal needs" that a person is entitled to even if he does not realize it (e.g., food, clothing, housing)? If a person is unable to understand the dangers of AIDS, should he be allowed to expose himself to the risk of it or be protected by society? Edgerton (1990) points out the inevitable link between these questions and government policy. Where should the balance of power lie? The points of discussion in this chapter, although not restricted to persons with severe disabilities, become particularly troubling as we consider the lives of individuals with increasing levels of disabilities.

For these protestors from Not Dead Yet quality of life is not for one to decide for another.

Decision Point 11.1: Honoring the
Individual Rights of Persons with Disabilities

Arguments for Proposition One Although the historical picture in this country includes a very real eugenics movement and horrible tales of institutions and institutionalization under inhumane conditions (e.g., Blatt & Kaplan, 1974), this does not negate the fact that many persons with disabilities still need to receive protections and supports. Parents are morally obligated to offer their children guidance and protection, establishing a balance of age- and condition-appropriate restrictions with independence. Similarly, family members, educators, and other social services workers must work with persons who have disabilities to achieve a reasonable balance of power and control in their lives in accordance with their best interests.

Much of the historical abuse of persons with disabilities and usurpation of their rights was not even intended to be in their best interests, but was pursued in the best interests of society. Nevertheless, historical precedent should not be used to justify the neglect of our social responsibility today. For example, the mass sterilizations were not performed to help out the victims, but were intended to purify the gene pool and avoid allowing the person from bearing a child who would become a burden on society or his family. Even as recently as 1971, some

---

Proposition One
Persons with disabilities, especially those with severe disabilities, may lack the ability to make wise choices about their safety and health; there- fore, they must have a safety net of social supports to protect them, even at the expense of the loss of some personal freedom.

states had laws authorizing the sterilization of persons with epilepsy for this very purpose (Heller & Alberto, 1996). Today, an enlightened public that realizes the extreme dangers of such purification aims will not allow blatant abuses of power and so little regard for the rights of individuals. IQ score is no longer revered as the most significant determinant of a person's worth.

Evolving Concepts of Quality of Life Drawing on an extensive review of the literature and focus groups involving persons with developmental disabilities, Goode (1990) identified several principles regarding quality of life for persons with disabilities, including the notion that the same factors that influence the quality of life for persons without disabilities are at issue for persons with disabilities. An acceptable quality of life means that a person's basic needs are met and that she has the opportunity to pursue and achieve goals in major life settings. Goode (1990) further notes that the meaning of quality of life can be consensually validated by persons with different viewpoints, such as the person herself, family members, professionals, service providers, and advocates. The nature of one's quality of life is intrinsically related to the quality of life of others in her environment and will reflect the cultural heritage of the person and those around her. Efforts to improve it should be achieved by placing an emphasis on the strengths and capabilities of the person, not her deficits.

These principles offer a balanced guide for professionals and family members trying to define and maintain the best possible quality of life for persons with disabilities, helping them meet their basic needs, and understanding that men and women with disabilities have the same basic concerns as themselves. For example, the provision of housing, even if the individual has little say about others who share the house with him or the neighborhood in which the house is located or even the freedom to keep his room messy, certainly appears to offer a better quality of life than were he on the streets without basic needs being met and little opportunity to achieve any life goals. Although persons with disabilities who are not happy in their housing arrangements may not agree, family members and professionals likely do have their best interests in mind because they more fully understand the alternatives. The decision is not unlike that made by children to place a parent suffering from Alzheimer's disease in a secure setting.

Freedom, Rights, and Best Interests Extremists who are ready to proclaim the establishment of rights and freedoms for persons with disabilities have been quick to make assumptions that placements (employment, housing, and so forth) must be as close to the mainstream as possible. Radicals who insist that they are striving to reclaim the lost freedom and rights of persons with disabilities to be in the mainstream by moving them from sheltered workshops to supported employment settings take away the employee's freedom to stay in the sheltered workshop by implying that it is inferior and socially unacceptable. Edgerton (1990) notes that, following the transition from sheltered employment to competitive employment, some workers may actually experience a reduction in quality of life because their lives have become lonely and less personally satisfying in spite of the move to the mainstream.

It seems that persons with disabilities even need protection from their self-proclaimed advocates, who expect them to become "normal" in their preferences as well as their abilities. These linear thinkers assume that because a sheltered workshop does not appeal to them as a work site, it is undesirable for all. In actuality, such attitudes place the expectation and demand on persons with disabilities that they function as much as possible as though they had no disability and implies a lack of acceptance of the person as one who does, in fact, have limited capacities. Adults with disabilities might actually have a preference to be around persons with whom they can have real relationships instead of "normals" with whom they have to try to "pass." Bogdan and Taylor (1994) recount their friend Ed's miserable marriage which informs us of the danger in believing that marrying is a part of "normal" mainstream life and, therefore, always a worthy thing for which to strive.

The most extreme and controversial protection that society imposes is on fetuses diagnosed with disabilities, newborns with disabilities, and others who might have experienced trauma or illness that caused permanent severe disabilities. Although it is never an easy decision, life cannot be considered mere biological survival. The dignity of humanity and the essence of being a person are at issue. As Paris (1990) reminds us, "What we are to be valued for is our personhood, and if the treatment cannot offer substantial benefit to the person, not just to his or her chemistries, it is extraordinary and need not be applied" (p. 156). Quality of life is indeed a factor to be considered in determining what is best for the individual. The American Medical Association Council on Ethical and Judicial Affairs (1990) noted the fact that disabilities need not negate the value of life but that there are instances when a person's condition is too persistent, too painful, or too harsh to maintain life. Life should be cherished despite disabilities and handicaps, except when the prolongation would be inhumane and unconscionable. Under these circumstances, withholding or removing life-supporting means is ethical provided that the normal care given the individual is not discontinued. Writers for the Hastings Center (1990) further defend this stance by noting that "what kind of life is possible given the person's condition, and whether that condition will allow the individual to have a life that he or she views as worth living" (p. 325) is the essence of the concept. The life's worth is evaluated by the individual, not society.

However, the individual's view may sometimes be impossible to determine, particularly in the case of a fetus, an infant, or a child suffering trauma. In some medical intervention cases, a substitute judgment test must be based on the known interests and preferences of the patient, rather than his best interests. In one instance, doctors decided that withholding chemotherapy from a sixty-seven-year-old man who was profoundly retarded was in his best interests because the projected life extension was insufficient to make the man experience the frightening side effects of the treatment that could not be adequately explained to him (Herr, 1992). In such instances, others must act as surrogates, looking exclusively at the best interests or preferences of the individual. McCormick (1990) points out that the ambiguity of the term *hopelessly ill* represents the dilemma. Does it refer just to those "lives that cannot be saved, that are irretrievably in the dying process" (p. 27), or also those lives that can be saved and sustained, "but in a wretched, painful or deformed condition" (p. 27)? He offers as a guideline the potential for human relationships associated with an infant's condition. However, allowing some to die does not imply their lack of value.

More than half of the cases of severe to profound mental retardation are caused by genetically determined disorders. Advances in the identification of DNA markers "provide an almost awesome potential for the prevention of severe mental retardation" (Moser, 1992, p. 140). Technical advances will continue to reduce the costs of the "unit of detection," making the identification of these conditions affordable and efficient. Down syndrome accounts for 30% of severe mental retardation, fragile-X syndrome about 15%. Combined, that is 45% of severe mental retardation. Others with abnormalities in structure of the chromosome (1%–4%), and inborn errors of metabolism (5%–7%) may also be detected. These advances offer both fear and hope—hope in that the ability to predict a parent's risk or absence of risk will become precise and can help in reproductive choices, and that understanding the exact nature of the genetic abnormality may lead to effective treatment. Fears become more complicated in that the ability to detect disorders may become financially feasible, but the costs of large-scale applications of complex therapies might far exceed our current health expenditures, triggering the need for analysis of cost-benefit ratios, and priority setting. The balance between patient perspective and society perspective is real.

The sustainability of biological life is not the greatest value to be achieved. Although no life should ever be devalued because the individual involved has a disability, it is much too simplistic to argue that living is always in a person's best interests. We must seek the individual's perceptions or those who can speak on the person's behalf, and never resort to a single universal answer to this most challenging dilemma, which will continue to accelerate as medical technology continues its growth.

Argument Summary Exposure to the HIV virus through illicit sex, choosing to live in high crime areas, and failure to save money to pay for basic services (e.g., heating, telephone) throughout the month are examples of poor choices that can be avoided. Although freedom of choice is a high priority for all, for some the inability to make wise decisions can limit freedom rather than increase it. When no money has been saved to pay the rent and the individual who was given the freedom to spend his own money becomes homeless, the freedom to choose one's own housing is inconsequential. There must be levels of protection for persons with disabilities in their best interests, even at the seeming cost of the loss of their rights as individuals.

Responsibility toward our fellow citizen is certainly as critical as our right to freedom and independence. Were I to notice a young child set to dart out in front of oncoming traffic, I would not hesitate to physically restrain that child in order to save his life. Whereas he might be initially furiously his anger would likely shift to understanding when a car came whizzing by. Neglecting our responsibility toward persons with disabilities because of the logic that they too deserve the freedom to make bad choices equivalent to running out in the street is unjustified. We must certainly proceed with caution when we restrict any citizen's freedom and choices, but we must not abrogate our responsibility under the guise of civil rights.

Arguments for Proposition Two The prevalent view that disability is a tragedy and that persons with disabilities are to be pitied and protected is the greatest deterrent to the achievement and success of persons with disabilities. Advances in technology, a generation of persons with disabilities who received the benefits of an education, and new civil rights protections for numerous undervalued groups have all contributed to a consciousness raising. This increased awareness has been accompanied by the formation of politically active groups of persons with disabilities who are seeking jobs and greater daily participation in this nation's society (Shapiro, 1993). The need to use the courts and legislatures arose because "appeals to humanity and fellow feeling have failed in the past to remedy gross indignities against persons with mental retardation" (Herr, 1992, p. 280). Deinstitutionalization became a reality through the court system, not because people wanted to give it a try. Rights now established include broadly defined habilitation, medical care, freedom from coerced nonemergency treatments, and individual dignity.

Sources of negative and inaccurate public perceptions of persons with disabilities come from literary and media characterizations, social customs and norms, child-rearing practices, psychological fears and anxieties, and fears of vulnerability (Percy, 1989). In a survey of persons with disabilities conducted by Louis Harris and Associates in 1985, over half the respondents indicated that their disabilities prevented them from achieving full potential in life, and 56% said that their disabilities prevented movement in the community, attendance at cultural and sports events, and socializing with friends outside the home. Reasons cited as impediments to participating in mainstream society included fear that their disability would cause them to get hurt, sick, or victimized by crime, and physical obstacles to mobility—49% were unable to gain access to specialized transportation services, and 40% commented on inaccessible buildings or unequipped restrooms. Forty-seven percent of working-age persons with disabilities indicated that employers would not recognize that they were capable of working full-time jobs. Persons with disabilities and their advocates are now pushing for an attitude change so that they can be seen as individuals with a wide array of abilities, talents, and skills, not just as persons with physical or mental impairments, requiring supervision and protection.

Proposition Two
The assumption by society that it must remove freedom from some of its citizens because the decisions those citizens are likely to make might not be wise or proper in the eyes of the majority opens the door to the loss of freedom for all. Freedom of choice is the pivotal principle to which all other quality-of-life issues must be deferred.

Evolving Concepts of Quality of Life Progress has been made over the years through deinstitutionalization. In 1967, a record 194,650 were living in public institutions, but only 80,269 remained in such facilities by 1991. New Hampshire and Vermont no longer even operate public institutions, and several other states are in the process of phasing them out. Whereas large institutions and their dehumanizing effects and abuse are the extreme and are dying out, institutional practices by professionals are not. Bogdan and Taylor (1994) remind us that "Far too many people labeled mentally retarded live a controlled existence and remain cut off from the life of the community" (p. 230).

People with disabilities face discrimination based on paternalistic assumptions that they are not entitled to make their own decisions and lead their own lives. For example, a young woman with cerebral palsy unsuccessfully fought the California welfare system in 1988 for the custody of her two young sons. Officials claimed that she was too physically disabled to care for them, so the state would pay to place them in foster homes but refused to pay for in-home child care to assist her in raising her own children (Shapiro, 1993).

There is a presumption on the part of professionals that their perceptions and beliefs are accurate and real. They hold the "official" view about the world. The assumption is that mental retardation and our conception of it are accurate and true; therefore, people with the condition would have little to say about the condition. Bogdan and Taylor make the harsh statement that "To be considered retarded in this society is to be not taken seriously" (p. 231).

Although their meanings have evolved significantly over the years, the arbitrariness of intelligence tests has been ignored or denied. Mental retardation as a definitive characteristic must no longer be accepted without acknowledgment of other perspectives. We must now treat all views of reality as equally valid, rather than accepting some as true and others as false. For example, the same institution might be described as a "model facility" and as a "snakepit" (Bogdan & Taylor, 1994). Which opinion is closer to the truth—that of the objective professional or the resident who is labeled retarded? Mental retardation is merely a social construction, in spite of the fact that many professionals consider themselves to hold the true meaning of the concept. Mercer's idea in the 1970s was that the label did serve as a protective shield for persons with severe to profound retardation but was a burden and stigma for those considered mildly retarded. Bogdan and Taylor challenge the usefulness of the concept for anyone, regardless of the nature of his condition.

Gross, Cox, Tatyrek, Pollay, and Barnes (1983) attempted to define *quality of life* to assist in determining intervention for infants with myelomeningocele, even deriving a formula for the process ((QOL = NE (H + S), with natural endowment represented as NE and sum of contributions of home and society represented as H + S. Fortunately, this approach triggered strong debate (Miller, 1984; Orelove & Sobsey, 1991; Powell & Hecimovic, 1985) and has not been accepted by the U.S. medical community. Coulter's (1990) comments about the formula note just some of its inherent weaknesses: "Even if this formula were conceptually sound, there is no evidence that we have methodologically valid means for measuring its components" (p. 62). The power to determine whose life is deemed to have the potential for sufficient quality of life for existence was not meant to be a human choice.

Freedom, Rights, and Best Interests The low expectations that society holds for persons with disabilities, coupled with a history of a welfare and social service system that fostered helplessness and dependency while penalizing efforts one might have made to become independent, present roadblocks and frustrations for persons with disabilities. In turn, their dependent state is then used by society to justify and confirm the idea that they need protection and are unworthy of basic rights and responsibilities. Disabled citizens no longer accept their exclusion from the benefits and opportunities available in our country and are starting to make inroads in the establishment of their rights (e.g., the parking space). Even now, much of mainstream America is unaware of or unable to comprehend the revolution taking place in the community of persons with disabilities and their rejection of sympathy and pity (e.g., the resistance to the Jerry Lewis telethon by persons with muscular dystrophy). The new thinking by many persons with disabilities today is "that there is no pity or tragedy in disability, and that it is society's myths, fears, and stereotypes that most make being disabled difficult" (Shapiro, 1993, p. 5).

Self-advocacy is a growing movement within groups of adults with disabilities, including those with mental retardation (Shapiro, 1993; Ward & Keith, 1996). The foundational issue related to self-advocacy and the traditional roles of persons with mental retardation in conjunction with the professionals who work with them and provide them services is a matter of protection—how much protection do they need, and how much must they accept against their will? Protection is not necessarily good, compassionate, or progressive. Historical treatment of this powerless group offers ample evidence of just how demeaning it can be. The courts have consistently found that the institutions intended to protect and nurture persons with mental retardation were unfit for human habitation and did more to strip these individuals of their personhood and dignity than any damage caused by their disability. The paternalistic attitude that has prevailed up to this point has exacerbated dependency, hindering persons with disabilities from learning to care for themselves, extending the burden to society, and, in turn, leaving society expecting gratitude where bitterness and anger are now emerging. As Shapiro (1993) sadly notes, "There is a delicate blend of success and failure in any person's life, but people with retardation are rarely trusted to handle either" (p. 191).

Persons with disabilities do not deny their need for assistance; however, they argue fiercely about what the nature of such assistance should be. The demand for personal assistance services is a current issue in the disability rights movement. The Americans with Disabilities Act guarantees that stores and restaurants will not discriminate and that employers cannot refuse to hire on the basis of disability, but these rights are of little value for someone who cannot get the necessary help in activities of daily living and is forced to live in a nursing home. Today, 7.7 million Americans need some type of personal assistance, but only 860,000 (11%) receive it, and 77% of them are over sixty years of age (Shapiro, 1993). The provision of personal assistance services in a person's home is cheaper than nursing home care, but keepers of the budgets fear that the demand for it would be so great were it to be covered that the total costs would far exceed current expenditures for nursing home care. The rationale for such fears is that of the 7 million individuals currently needing long-term care, only 1.5 million are in nursing homes, with the remainder receiving needed assistance through family members or other means at no cost to the government, ignoring the potential gains such as tax dollars through incomes were family members free to enter the workforce.

Arizona has implemented a program that does allow for support of in-home care and is discovering that the program is paying for itself (Shapiro, 1993). Estimates of expenses related to the provision of home-based personal assistance services range from $500 million a year to serve 50,000 working-age people to $10 billion to assist 9 million disabled men and women of all ages, income, work status, and severity and type of disability. The concept that such service models reflect a higher valuing of the lives of persons with disabilities, give them greater opportunities to live and work independently, and are preferred by the people most directly affected by them seems lost in the fear that affording them this right might be more than we can afford.

Other prevalent attitudes and standards offer reminders to the disabled community that society does not view their lives with great meaning or as having equal value. Larry McAfee became quadriplegic from a motorcycle accident, was dependent on a respirator, and expressed a desire to end his life. The court agreed to allow his plan to be implemented, even praising him for his good sense and bravery. Had he been an able-bodied individual threatening suicide, those around him would have arranged for suicide counseling, not concurred with his threats and supported his decision:

> Instead of getting help to live on his own, McAfee was sentenced to indifferent nursing homes and hospitals and stripped of basic decision making about his life. . . . Over $1.5 million in private insurance, state Medicaid, federal Medicare, and Social Security payments was spent on McAfee in the four and a half years between his accident and the final court decision.
>
> But the generosity was often misspent and misplaced. For example, state Medicaid would pay every penny of McAfee's expenses in a nursing home. Yet it would not pay one cent for what he needed to live at home so that he could go back to work and be a taxpayer instead of simply taking welfare. (Shapiro, 1993, pp. 260–261)

Argument Summary In our society we honor the basic freedoms outlined in the Constitution and must do so for all our citizens. Although persons with disabilities do present some unique issues in this regard, the costs of inhibiting freedoms far outweigh the dangers of allowing individuals to make mistakes in their lives. The historical denial of the rights of persons with disabilities under the guise of protectionism has resulted in innumerable wasted lives and necessitated litigation to establish what is already provided for in the Constitution. Just as persons without disabilities are free to make bad choices, learn from their failures, and have fulfilling as well as painful personal relationships, so must the rights of persons with disabilities to have these experiences be cherished by all.

EDUCATIONAL GOALS
AND QUALITY OF LIFE

The limited opportunities for special education graduates, especially those with severe disabilities, to achieve successful life outcomes have drawn attention to curricular and transition planning for these students. School personnel are expected to work in collaboration with vocational rehabilitation counselors to set the stage for a smooth transition from school to work. Some have denounced this focus because it neglects the concept of quality of life, which is considered by them to offer a much more comprehensive view of life than employment alone (Halpern, 1993). Thus, although the importance of carefully planned transitions is not disputed, the wisdom of restricting their focus to employment/ training versus their expansion to address all aspects of quality of life is questioned (Taylor & Bogdan, 1996). These outcomes may not always coincide, particularly if individuals are permitted to operate with their own definitions of quality of life.

Individuality and Quality of Life

With this attention to the concept of quality of life, numerous definitions and scales of measurement are appearing in the literature, with no single definition or descriptors accepted by all (Hughes & Hwang, 1996). For example, Taylor and Bogdan (1990) focus on the subjectivity of quality of life. They argue that individuals experience similar circumstances from their own unique perspectives, and that what is an enhancement of life for some may well be considered a detraction for others. Satisfaction with one's lot in life and a sense of contentment are emphasized in their definition, not the accumulation of wealth and material goods. Brown, Bayer, and MacFarlane (1988) also accentuate the individual nature of the concept, defining it "as the discrepancy between a person's achieved and their unmet needs and desires" (p. 111), and the extent to which a person has control of his environment. Likewise, Parmenter (1988) focuses on individuality, emphasizing the importance of individuals being able to met their own needs and to create their own meanings in order to establish and sustain a viable self in the social world. Goode (1990) adds to the notion of an individual being able to meet her important needs in major life settings, the achievement of normative expectations that others hold for the person. Others offer definitions emphasizing personal satisfaction, with varying degrees of importance placed on contentment, happiness, success, fulfillment, and the pursuit of a "meaningful" life (Coulter, 1990; Stark & Goldsbury, 1990; Karen, Lambour, & Greenspan, 1990). Blatt (1987) emphasizes its temporal, relative, and individual nature: "There will be necessarily empty places, as it is equally certain that there will be times when there seems to be too much....The brimming cup has little to do with the size of the cup or the temporary nature of its contents....It is all in the mind and, for sure in the soul" (p. 358).

Most might agree to the inclusion of satisfaction in personal relationships as an outcome relevant to one's quality of life. However, that satisfaction might be achieved in innumerable ways. Marriage and companionship might appeal to one person whereas solitude is preferable for others. Contact with others through recreation and work may offer the latter group sufficient socialization. The interactive nature of multiple environmental and personal factors makes any individual's quality of life subject to fluctuation over time (Hughes & Hwang, 1996). Cultural variables (e.g., the importance of individual employment or family patterns) further influence the priorities that one may place on various dimensions of quality of life (Keith, 1996).

Measuring Quality of Life

The subjectivity and individuality of the concept are prevalent in most definitions used in the context of persons with disabilities, but the extent to which such is then measurable in their lives or is within the purview of education is less settled. The assumption of standards to define an acceptable quality of life may be difficult to achieve, and without this can any meaning be placed on measures of a person's quality of life? Today, those in the field who are working to develop theoretical models and putting greater emphasis on quality-of-life concepts debate among themselves the wisdom of creating scales to measure one's quality of life. A quality-of-life model should reflect values, aspirations, and self-perceptions of an individual, while concurrently incorporating societal variables. Today, person–environment fit, similar to the ecological perspective that is reshaping many current disability and special education policies, is advancing as best practice in the measurement of quality of life as well (Parmenter, 1992). The feasibility and wisdom of quantifying such individualistic matters are questioned. However, the absence of such measures leaves the concept as an abstract notion, dependent on the subjectivity of individual program administrators or program monitors.

Although the pervasive debates between qualitative and quantitative approaches are evident in this arena (Edgerton, 1996), as they are in many others, the notion that quality of life is a useful concept is now the view held by many in the field. Flece and Perry (1996) note the ambiguity of the concept and "Whether it refers to the life conditions and life-style of an individual or that person's subjective appraisal of their conditions and way of life" (p. 63). Measurement approaches vary on several dimensions—objective–subjective, absolute–relative, self–others reporting, authored by professional–developed by subjects—and must not become restricted to a single procedure or quantified into a number, as has happened to the concept of intelligence.

Since quality of life is becoming an accepted measure of the effectiveness of services, interventions are considered socially valid when outcomes affect quality of life. There is a shift to evaluating programs by the outcomes of services rather than merely the nature of the delivery. Such authentic outcome-based evaluation of service models offers a radical change from traditional input measures (e.g., ratio of professionals to service recipients, hours of service). The ability to form and maintain relationships and the accessibility to others who are willing to involve themselves in relationships appear even more crucial to quality of life than do social demographics such as socioeconomic status, race, ethnicity, gender, marital status, age, and education (Able-Boone & Stevens, 1993). In some instances, however, what might be seen by program staff or society as a positive intervention could be negative for the individual involved (Kozleski & Sands, 1992). For example, the forced acceptance of a supported employment position after failure to obtain or keep a competitive employment position offers just such a conflict for the person eager to obtain a mainstream job. Yet that same supported employment position might result in greater social opportunities, personal relationships, and recreation/leisure activities for the individual than would remaining unemployed and inactive. Any useful measurement system needs to accommodate such variability.

Decision Point 11.2: Educational Goals and Quality of Life

Arguments for Proposition One The transition of persons with disabilities from schools to communities must focus on the development of employment opportunities for them and achievement of skills that will increase their employability. Costs of their education are predicated on the assumption that through education and eventual employment of some type, graduates can increase their ability to contribute as citizens, thereby reducing their dependence on welfare and entitlement systems. There must be some reasonable limits put on the overburdened school system regarding what we expect it to do for our children. Making all children happy and satisfied as adults is well beyond the responsibility of the schools. However, offering programs that lead to employment will, in turn, provide a generalized benefit of strengthening individual economic resources and self-esteem, which should, in turn, contribute to a positive quality of life.

Parmenter (1992) warns us of the inherent danger of accepting too quickly the move toward quality of life as a viable concept. Politicians will pick up on quality-of-life rhetoric and then look to researchers to evaluate and quantify the ideas, which will ultimately take a far different turn. Since such is likely to occur "without first making a detailed examination of the premises on which the philosophies are grounded, researchers may find themselves trapped into a process that aids and abets the aims of the various pressure groups that abound in the welfare field" (Parmenter, 1992, p. 248).

Proposition One

All of us hope to achieve the highest quality of life possible, but this is a highly subjective concept and is not the responsibility of the school system. The outcomes of special education are best measured in terms of the basic demographics of program graduates, such as participation in higher education, employment, and independent living.

Parmenter (1992), citing Goode, wonders if we are not replacing the tyranny of normal with the tyranny of quality. Quality of life is quite personal but has become one of the catchwords in the field of disability. It is being bureaucratized to the extent that it may lose the richness of its meaning, and the result may be the increased isolation of persons with developmental disabilities who need to become full members of communities, not just located in them.

Individuality and Quality of Life The provision of education for students with disabilities is predicated on their right to a free appropriate public education equivalent to that provided for all U.S. children. They are not entitled to something more, nor should they accept anything less. However, to argue that their education should include efforts to ensure that they will be able to achieve an acceptable quality of life necessarily implies that they should get far more than is in the scope of general education today. The education community is not responsible for all of a child's life and development. In fact, some domains are specifically inappropriate for public schools to address, such as spiritual development and religious beliefs. Yet such personal beliefs can play a significant role in determining one's satisfaction and happiness in life. These factors most certainly influence quality of life but are not the responsibility of the public schools. Were the education community to assume accountability for making everyone achieve the greatest possible quality of life, educators would have to accept the duty to help families with their housing problems, personal relations, access to satisfactory leisure activities for all, protection from violence in their neighborhoods, and so forth. The intrusion into personal preferences, cultural differences, and regional variances would soon create a strong backlash from parents and children.

Definitions of quality of life all imply value judgments about how people should live their lives. These notions must vary over time and circumstances. There are simply no definitive indicators of the concept. The term should be abandoned because the practice of defining and measuring what it is can actually be dangerous (Luckasson, 1990). Measures of quality of life, regardless of the developer's attempts to make them sensitive to the perceptions of persons with disabilities and to enhance their dignity and worth, are inevitably scientific and most likely will be used as justification for the denial of rights to people with disabilities.

Measuring Quality of Life Edgerton (1990) argues the futility of attempting to quantify quality of life because it is an ongoing, changing phenomenon that must involve long-term involvement with the individual to ascertain. Quality of life for people with disabilities is not dependent on the extent to which an individual avails himself of certain programs and services, but in making life choices to find satisfaction that, at times, will inevitably be deemed as unrealistic by family members and service providers. Society's responsibility is the provision of options without the imposition of standards for a quality life. Whereas service providers must avoid dictating to others what constitutes a good quality of life, they must strive to offer the best in housing, health care, recreation, and employment opportunities (Edgerton, 1990).

Quality of life is both individually unique and subjective, defying objective measurement (Edgerton, 1990). The validity of psychological indicators may be questioned since one's answers to surveys either vary over time or are biased and sometimes may be more based on perceived preferred responses of the interviewer rather than the true feelings of the person being interviewed. Further, the interpretation of results involve subjective opinions of subjective factors. Self-report is problematic for people with cognitive impairments who lack a range of life experiences with which to compare their own. The use of objective measures of adaptive functioning to offset self-report is based on the assumption that higher functioning allows for greater integration into community and greater personal competence and, therefore, a better quality of life. However, there is no empirical evidence to support this assumption, and Blatt's (1987) notion that the size of the cup is of less importance than its fullness offers astute insight.

Our inability to measure such a subjective notion further contributes to our need to avoid setting it down as a standard part of the curriculum with a scope and sequence. Edgerton's (1990) illustrative story of a night manager of a laundromat with an IQ measured at 54, friends and sexual partners who included the homeless and prostitutes, and an apartment located in a crime-ridden part of Los Angeles gives evidence of the danger of attempting to measure the concept and intervene in persons' lives to help them achieve it: "He lives in a network of friends and acquaintances who value his friendship and help, and who do not know or care that he can neither read nor write. To many people, he is loved and respected. He is as satisfied with the quality of life as anyone I know" (p. 151). The use of an objective scale with items such as "safety" and "healthy intimate relationships" might produce a very poor quality-of-life "score" for this man, who would personally disagree. Likewise, he would most likely resent the intrusion of any well-meaning professional seeking to improve his life for him.

Argument Summary Educators should focus on reasonable student outcomes and be held accountable for the extent to which they keep their students actively engaged in tasks related to those outcomes. Teachers have a further responsibility to maintain an atmosphere within all instructional settings that contributes to a positive quality of life for the students in that setting (e.g., fostering positive social relationships and enabling students to experience a sense of achievement through successful experiences). It is in this manner that teachers and schools should contribute to quality of life rather than assuming additional responsibility for the quality of life their students will have as adults.

Quality of life, although important to us all, is not a concept that can be taught, measured, and evaluated as a meaningful universal, and it does not fit within the context of education or transition planning. The presumption that educators and other professionals can and should intrude themselves into influencing the quality of life for students with disabilities is paternalistic at best, manipulative and controlling at worst.

Arguments for Proposition Two Whether adults with disabilities are employed, isolated from society, leading lives devoid of friends and satisfying relationships, or displaying tendencies toward criminal activity has not been educators' concern as a new crop of younger students demanded our attention and we sent graduates out the door to find their lives. Although recent efforts to

Quality of life + Sp Ed

Proposition Two

Quality of life as a concept can be defined, improved, and measured directly in spite of its subjective nature, and we must be held accountable for addressing it in our educational programming and transition planning.

---

plan transitions to the adult world have begun to address this responsibility, much more is needed. Why offer an educational program for many years simply to send students on their way unprepared to maintain an acceptable quality of life? Our responsibility to this group is to help them strive toward a sense of personal achievement and satisfaction, not just place them in a low-paying job or sheltered workshop, house them in nursing homes, and move on to the next case. Job training and placement must be accompanied by attention to personal identity and the development of satisfactory personal relationships and other more elusive aspects of quality of life.

The 1984 Office of Special Education and Rehabilitation Services transition initiative focused all efforts on employment, based partially on the assumption that success in that domain would "spill over" into success in other areas (Halpern, 1993). However, there is evidence to the contrary. Successes in the three objective dimensions—residential environment, occupation, and social support/safety—do not appear correlated with one another (Halpern, 1993). Being employed was not found to be correlated with adequate housing, meaningful personal relationships, or satisfaction in life. Therefore, our transition programs must directly address these other arenas and drop the illusion that automatic generalization will spontaneously occur. Such thinking has plagued special education methodology in previous years and has proven to be a great disappointment.

Individuality and Quality of Life Quality of life offers a conceptual framework to evaluate transition outcomes. It incorporates numerous dichotomies that can be helpful when planning transitions and attempting to ascertain an individual's current quality of life and how it might be improved (Halpern, 1993). The first dichotomy is that of subjective versus objective perspectives, with *subjective* referring to an individual's point of view and *objective* referring to a societal point of view. For example, an outdoor job involving labor might appeal to some but would be viewed as highly undesirable by others—a subjective matter. However, objectively this job constitutes employment—the earning of money, which helps give a person a sense of self-worth as he contributes to his household and would typically be considered as making a positive contribution to his quality of life. The subjective dimensions of quality of life are idiosyncratic whereas the objective dimensions are normative.

The second dichotomy is that of personal choice versus universal entitlements. Should activities that are enjoyed by the participants be considered inferior simply because they are contradictory to a social principle such as normalization (e.g., Special Olympics)? Professionals must resist the notion that they have the responsibility to set a standard of behavior for persons with disabilities, because their choices might not actually reflect those persons' needs. The right of persons with retardation to marry need not make us put this expectation before them as a necessary condition for their ultimate happiness, nor should we assume that bearing children would automatically enhance the quality of their lives if they would be unduly challenged in their attempts to raise the child and face great emotional turmoil in the process.

A third dichotomy is personal needs versus social expectations. Participation in activities of personal preference—the nature of the foods we choose to eat, the clothes we wear, the frequency and thoroughness with which we clean our homes—is illustrative of what is at stake here. If a twenty-five-year-old male chooses to carry his personal items around in a Hercules backpack, he will trigger a reaction. Although doing so may be his personal preference and, thus, the opportunity to do so may make him happy, the behavior is so contradictory to social expectations that professionals would be sorely tempted to dissuade him from this choice, if not completely deny him the choice. It does not meet *our* standard of age-appropriateness.

The final dichotomy is that of personal intervention versus social policy development. The uses of quality-of-life information include helping individuals articulate and develop their own transition goals as part of the transition planning process and helping agencies and organizations develop programs and policies that address the perceived transition needs of the people whom they serve or should be serving. In the first instance, information is presented to a single individual to help that person make important transition decisions, whereas in the second case, information about many individuals is presented to help program and policy developers make decisions that will enhance the overall capacity of a community, state, or nation to provide good transition programs and services.

A positive approach to the development of a strategy for the integration of these divergent concepts is that personal choice is the underlying principle (Halpern, 1993). If a person selects an outcome (e.g., employment) as important, then it is relevant and can be evaluated both objectively (is the person employed?) and subjectively (is the person satisfied with the employment?). From a societal perspective, norms offer the most meaningful frame of reference. For example, adults are expected to contribute to their households either through outside employment or assumption of duties within the household. A person who prefers not to work but has no other means to provide for himself might find that social expectations have to take precedence over personal choice. We must identify socially desirable goals for groups of people as a whole, bearing in mind that conformity to these goals might not be appropriate or desirable for all members of the group. At times, the needs of the group will be in conflict with the preferences of an individual and must be negotiated within the parameters of democracy.

Measuring Quality of Life There are numerous techniques that can be used in the measurement of quality of life. A common approach involves the use of scales that consider many factors. Illustrative specific content domains include (a) physical and material well-being, (b) performance of a variety of adult roles, and (c) a sense of personal fulfillment (Dennis, Williams, Giangreco, & Cloninger, 1993). Stark and Goldsbury (1990) have conceived a model that, while acknowledging the significance of individual characteristics, is based on seven objective factors: health, living environment, family, social/emotional relationships, education, work, and leisure. Dennis, Williams, Giangreco, and Cloninger (1993) have identified several quantitative approaches used in the measurement of quality of life, including (a) the study of social indicators (e.g., the quality of community living for groups or populations), (b) the study of psychological indicators (e.g., an individual's subjective reactions to the presence or absence of certain life experiences, psychological well-being, and personal satisfaction), and (c) an ecological analysis/goodness of fit model (e.g., the match between the environment and an individual's resources or stressors).

Others prefer more qualitative approaches, relying on self-reports, reports by familiar others, and interviews as the most appropriate way to determine quality of life (Parmenter, 1992). From the symbolic–interactionist perspective, there is a need to include three components in a quality-of-life model: (a) the individual's perception of self, (b) the individual's behavior in response to ecological domains that might affect him, and (c) responses the settings might make to the individual. Interactions between these three components must be acknowledged as well. Schalock (as cited by Parmenter, 1992) perceives quality of life as coming from three aspects of life experiences—personal characteristics, objective life conditions, and perceptions of significant persons about individuals with disabilities. These are reflected in measures of independence: productivity, community integration, and satisfaction. The variables are entangled with a number of cultural factors, including values, legal foundations, and a paradigm shift regarding how society views problems and issues associated with persons with disabilities. A questionnaire is used to guide an interview that includes four factors: (a) independence (opportunities to exert control over one's environment and to make choices), (b) productivity (positive work outcomes, such as income or work contributing to household or community), (c) community integration (participation in the same patterns of life as nondisabled people, including social and interpersonal contacts), and (d) satisfaction (fulfillment of needs or wants and the happiness that goes with that fulfillment). Combining such approaches with ethnographic data gathering offers the most comprehensive means of evaluating quality of life (Schalock, 1996).

Goode (1990) has suggested that seven major categories (social–community and individual, life domains, life events, psychological/psychosocial, overall quality of life, and outcome behaviors) be used in quality-of-life evaluations. The model is described as a nonlinear process model that is client-centered, depicting interaction between objective and subjective variables, based on the premise that quality of life is specific to environments. Quality of life is the product of the relationships between people in each life setting and is influenced by the quality of life of people with whom one interacts. Subjective elements of the model emphasize relationships among perceived needs, capabilities, demands, and resources. A conflict between environmental demands and personal capabilities and perceptions of personal needs and environmental and social resources lowers one's quality of life. Goode's approach is in the tradition of ethomethodological perspective. He sees dangers inherent in quantifying the quality of life, noting the tyranny of quality when numbers become the standard of evaluation for programs. Rather, he suggests that we should keep the emphasis on the deeply personal nature of the construct and use observational methods (Parmenter, 1992).

Social indicators used as objective measures are supported on the basis that they offer scientific and systematic approaches, and provide a set of indicators that can be applied to community settings. Evaluators must bear in mind that some indicators (income, marital status, race, and sex) show low to moderate relationships with self-assessment of well-being, life satisfaction, and life quality. The consideration of psychological indicators should distinguish between happiness (a temporary emotional state) and satisfaction (a long-term contentment).

Argument Summary Quality of life is of critical importance to persons with disabilities. Educational programs and transition plans that ignore it are of limited value. Although we must carefully resist attempts to crystallize and overquantify the concept, it can be both measured and documented. Imperfections and limitations of measurements do not constitute justification for abandoning satisfactory quality of life as a desired program outcome. For persons with the most severe disabilities, it can become the most important target of our educational programs. Instruments and methodological techniques can be designed that honor individual preferences yet target basic parameters for the concept of quality of life.

CLOSING THOUGHTS

Adherence to democratic principles requires that those persons affected by decisions take a genuine part in debating the issues and making those decisions. Professionalism, on the other hand, is based on the premise that professionals have specialized expertise and are in the best position to make decisions (Parmenter, 1992). The tension between these two perspectives must be acknowledged, without negating the importance of either. The most basic legal protection is to ensure the physical and psychological integrity of every person from abuse, neglect, or degrading treatment. How free citizens are to make their own decisions, even against the advice and recommendations of trained professionals, defines the level of democracy of our society. The wisdom of singling out particular groups for less democracy than the rest of us becomes the issue. Certainly, we do not give children the rights and privileges afforded to adults, nor are persons deemed mentally incompetent allowed to control their own affairs. The loss of freedom and some rights is the cost of criminal activity. Where persons with disabilities fit in this picture certainly varies, as does the extent and nature of their disabilities. To what extent actual limitations of disabilities or society's reaction to persons with disabilities is actually the factor influencing restrictions of their rights and freedoms is unascertainable.

Our society has moved from neglect to protection of persons with disabilities (Herr, 1992). In some instances the protection means protection of rights, and in other instances it means the loss of rights. Sterilization laws have been replaced with legal protections of the rights of persons with disabilities to reproductive choices (even against the wishes of the parents or professionals who perceive themselves to have the best interests of their children in mind). Routine denials of lifesaving medical treatment and the inability of doctors to override parental decisions against treatment have been replaced with a focus on the physical health and well-being of children with disabilities. The institutionalization of persons suspected of mental retardation has been replaced with greater freedom and choice in housing for people with disabilities.

We argue that persons with mental retardation should not be tried with the same standards as others, particularly when capital punishment is an issue. Georgia and Maryland have statutes barring the death penalty for persons with mental retardation, as do Kentucky and Tennessee (Herr, 1992). With increasing social supports, advocacy services, and helping arrangements, the need for guardians is diminishing. Herr (1992) views the future optimistically as we move toward individually tailored supports.

For a newborn, the question is not merely a matter of the quality of housing, clothing, foods, and so forth, but one of life itself. The recommended treatment judgment standards range from the notion that all life is sacred to the formula-based evaluation of infants' projected quality of life (Mellien, 1992). Although the defining notion of this standard remains unsettled, it seems to be centering on the potential for human relationships. Economic considerations are real as well. Medical and social costs after pediatric intensive care unit (PICU) discharge are extensive, especially for long-term care of children left disabled by critical illness. Patients whose acute illnesses requires PICU care may account for over 20% of all profoundly retarded individuals (Pollack, 1994).

Common to most definitions of quality of life is the idea that individual characteristics and natural endowment should be included in the evaluation. But the role of disability in quality of life seems two-sided. Do factors such as opportunities offered, physical comforts, and control over one's life define quality of life, or rather do they influence it? Disability can be seen as a tragedy that diminishes one's life and, therefore, inevitably reduces its quality, or simply a characteristic present more or less in all people—in some instances actually enhancing quality of life. For example, a disability might afford opportunities to experience life at greater emotional depths when physical opportunities are limited—not a cause for sadness, but one of rejoicing for the person whose life is involved.

Whereas the advance of quality of life as a buzz word in the social services world is very evident, numerous fears about the eventual abuse and misuse of the concept are voiced by many. Borthwick-Duffy (1992) emphasizes the importance of including multiple subjective and objective measures across multiple settings, the individuality of persons with disabilities, and the instability of subjective measures. The ultimate use of data gathered regarding quality of life to defend the reestablishment of large institutions would be a worst-case scenario. To date, quality of life has been used to justify euthanasia and to determine personhood or humanness. Luckasson (1990) urges the disability community to reject the phrase because "the potential denial of human rights on the basis of 'pseudo-scientific predictions' of an individual's quality of life outweigh its usefulness" (p. 60). Taylor and Bogdan (1990) also wonder if it further singles out persons with mental retardation because we do not routinely measure it for people without disabilities. Some draw a parallel with the misuses and misinterpretations of IQ in special education, which are only now being seriously questioned in the field.

From another perspective, social scientists are seeking to find indicators of social well-being just as economists have created economic indices (Aiken, 1990). The term includes both eudaemonistic meanings—pursuit of happiness or fulfill-ment—and equalitarian meanings—minimal standards of comfort and posses-sions. But these may come in conflict. As Aiken (1990) wonders, "Should the attainment of the 'good life' by some take precedence over the attainment of a minimal human quality of life by all?" (p. 19). It can be argued that equalitarian quality of life is needed first. That is, the satisfaction of the needs of others to honor and ensure their existence as moral beings is a necessary condition of my own eudaemonia. The concept is used to offer a criterion by which to exclude some from the equalitarian standard and thereby exempt society from affording them the normal standards of moral treatment. Some are excluded from the nor-mal standards of moral treatment because it has been determined that they lack the specific goods needed to live a life with minimal human quality. It is the ex-treme costs (financial, resource allocational, and emotional) that cause the issue to be raised. The justification is utilitarian, involving the need to distribute scarce resources equitably. The further implication is that the person deemed possessing a life unworthy of living is not a valid member of the moral community and has no rights—a dangerous notion at best. Aiken questions whether it would not be better to continue to see these people as members of the moral community whom we choose to sacrifice for the sake of others, but at least not deny their personhood.

The value given to property rights and the individual's right to exclusive pos-session of goods is in conflict with the equalitarian value of providing a minimal level of material goods to all in order to achieve a moral community:

> But in order to protect my quality of life I am justified in ignoring the claims made by others on "my" goods—my means to happiness—even though others may need these goods to obtain a minimally human level of quality of life. Any redistribution will be seen to diminish my quality of life (my afflu-ence). So I am justified in protecting my "quality of life" against the claims of others. (Aiken, 1990, p. 23)

The illogic in this position is that equalitarian quality of life is necessarily a pre-requisite for achieving eudaemonian quality of life. The contradictions within our democratic society create a tension that offers us the opportunity to move toward or away from the ideal moral community. Responsibility, charity, free-dom, respect for others—all draw us as individuals and as members of social groups.

REFERENCES

Able-Boone, H., & Stevens, E. A. (1993). Towards an enhanced family and child quality of life. In M. Krajicek & R. Tompkins (Eds.), *The medically fragile infant* (pp. 119–134). Austin: Pro-Ed.

Aiken, W. (1990). The quality of life. In J. J. Walter & T. A. Shannon (Eds.), *Quality of life* (pp. 17–25). Mahwah, NJ: Paulist Press.

American Medical Association Council on Ethical and Judicial Affairs (1990). Quality of life and the withholding or withdrawing of life-prolonging medical treatment. In J. J. Walter & T. A. Shannon (Eds.), *Quality of life* (pp. 299–300). Mahwah, NJ: Paulist Press.

Blatt, B. (1987). *The conquest of mental retardation*. Austin: Pro-Ed.

Blatt, B., & Kaplan, F. (1974). *Christmas in purgatory*. Syracuse, NY: Human Policy Press.

Bogdan, R., & Taylor, S. J. (1994). *The social meaning of mental retardation: Two life stories*. New York: Teachers College Press.

Borthwick-Duffy, S. A. (1992). Quality of life and quality of care in mental retardation. In L. Rowitz (Ed.), *Mental retardation in the year 2000* (pp. 52–66). New York: Springer-Verlag.

Brown, R., Bayer, M., & MacFarlane, C. (1988). Quality of life amongst handicapped adults. In R. Brown (Ed.), *Quality of life for handicapped people: A series in rehabilitation education* (pp. 107–123). London: Croom Helm.

Coulter, D. (1990). Home is the place: Quality of life for young children with developmental disabilities. In R. Schalock (Ed.), *Quality of life: Perspectives and issues* (pp. 61–70). Washington, DC: American Association on Mental Retardation.

Dennis, R. E., Williams, W., Giangreco, M. F., & Cloninger, C. J. (1993). Quality of life as a context for planning and evaluation of services for people with disabilities. *Exceptional Children, 59*, 499–512.

Drummond, M., Torrance, G., & Mason, J. (1993). Cost-effectiveness league tables: More harm than good? *Social Science and Medicine, 37*, 33–40.

Edgerton, R. B. (1990). Quality of life from a longitudinal research perspective. In R. Schalock (Ed.), *Quality of life: Perspectives and issues* (pp. 149–160). Washington, DC: American Association on Mental Retardation.

Edgerton, R. B. (1996). A longitudinal–ethnographic research perspective on quality of life. In R. L. Schalock & G. N. Siperstein (Eds.), *Quality of life volume I: Conceptualization and measurement* (pp. 83–90). Washington, DC: American Association on Mental Retardation.

Flece, D., & Perry, J. (1996). Assessment of quality of life. In R. L. Schalock & G. N. Siperstein (Eds.), *Quality of life volume I: Conceptualization and measurement* (pp. 63–72). Washington, DC: American Association on Mental Retardation.

Fletcher, J. F. (1990). Four indicators of humanhood—The enquiry matures. In J. J. Walter & T. A. Shannon (Eds.), *Quality of life* (pp. 11–16). Mahwah, NJ: Paulist Press.

Goode, D. (1990). Thinking about and discussing quality of life. In R. Schalock (Ed.), *Quality of life: Perspectives and issues* (pp. 41–58). Washington, DC: American Association on Mental Retardation.

Gross, R., Cox, A., Tatyrek, R., Pollay, M., & Barnes, W. (1983). Early management and decision-making for the treatment of myelominingocele. *Pediatrics, 72*, 450–458.

Halpern, A. S. (1993). Quality of life as a conceptual framework for evaluating transition outcomes. *Exceptional Children, 59*, 486–498.

Hastings Center. (1990). Quality of life. In J. J. Walter & T. A. Shannon (Eds.), *Quality of life* (pp. 325–326). Mahwah, NJ: Paulist Press.

Heller, K.W., & Alberto, P. A. (1996). *Understanding physical, sensory, and health impairments.* Pacific Grove, CA: Brooks/Cole.

Herr, S. S. (1992). Beyond benevolence: Legal protection for persons with special needs. In L. Rowitz (Ed.), *Mental retardation in the year 2000* (pp. 279–298). New York: Springer-Verlag.

Hughes, C., & Hwang, B. (1996). Attempts to conceptualize and measure quality of life. In R. L. Schalock & G. N. Siperstein (Eds.), *Quality of life volume I: Conceptualization and measurement* (pp. 51–62). Washington, DC: American Association on Mental Retardation.

Karen, O., Lambour, G., & Greenspan, S. (1990). Persons in transition. In R. Schalock (Ed.), *Quality of life: Perspectives and issues* (pp. 85–92). Washington, DC: American Association on Mental Retardation.

Keith, K. D. (1996). Measuring quality of life across cultures: Issues and challenges. In R. L. Schalock & G. N. Siperstein (Eds.), *Quality of life volume I: Conceptualization and measurement* (pp. 73–82). Washington, DC: American Association on Mental Retardation.

Kozleski, E. B., & Sands, D. J. (1992). The yardstick of social validity: Evaluating quality of life as perceived by adults without disabilities. *Education and Training in Mental Retardation and Developmental Disabilities, 27,* 119–131.

Luckasson, R. (1990). A lawyer's perspective on quality of life. In R. Schalock (Ed.), *Quality of life: Perspectives and issues* (pp. 85–92). Washington, DC: American Association on Mental Retardation.

McCormick, R. A. (1990). To save or let die. In J. J. Walter & T. A. Shannon (Eds.), *Quality of life* (pp. 26–34). Mahwah, NJ: Paulist Press.

Mellien, A. C. (1992). Ethical dilemmas in the care of premature infants. *The Clinical Nurse Specialist, 6,* 130–134.

Miller, P. (1984). Quality of life and services for people with disabilities. *Bulletin of the British Psychological Society, 37,* 218–225.

Moser, H. W. (1992). Prevention of mental retardation (genetics). In L. Rowitz (Ed.), *Mental retardation in the year 2000* (pp. 140–148). New York: Springer-Verlag.

New Jersey Catholic Conference. (1990). Providing food and fluids to severely brain damaged patients. In J. J. Walter & T. A. Shannon (Eds.), *Quality of life* (pp. 343–348). Mahwah, NJ: Paulist Press.

Orelove, F., & Sobsey, D. (1991). *Educating children with multiple disabilities.* Baltimore: Paul H. Brookes.

Paris, J. J. (1990). Terminating treatment for newborns: A theological perspective. In J. J. Walter & T. A. Shannon (Eds.), *Quality of life* (pp. 151–160). Mahwah, NJ: Paulist Press.

Parmenter, T. R. (1988). An analysis of the dimensions of quality of life for people with physical disabilities. In R. I. Brown (Ed.), *Quality of life for handicapped people* (pp. 48–61). London: Croom Helm.

Parmenter, T. R. (1992). Quality of life of people with developmental disabilities. In N. Bray (Ed.), *International review of research in mental retardation: Vol. 18* (pp. 247–287). New York: Academic Press.

Percy, S. L. (1989). *Disability, civil rights, and public policy.* Tuscaloosa, AL: University of Alabama Press.

Pollack, M. M. (1994). Cost containment: The pediatric perspective. *New Horizons, 2,* 305–311.

Powell, T. H., & Hecimovic, A. (1985). Baby Doe and the search for a quality life. *Exceptional Children, 51,* 315–323.

Schalock, R. L. (1996). Reconsidering the conceptualization and measurement of quality of life. In R. L. Schalock & G. N. Siperstein (Eds.), *Quality of life volume I: Conceptualization and measurement* (pp. 123–139). Washington, DC: American Association on Mental Retardation.

Shapiro, J. P. (1993). *No pity: People with disabilities forging a new civil rights movement.* New York: Random House.

Stark, J., & Faulkner, E. (1996). Quality of life across the life span. In R. L. Schalock & G. N. Siperstein (Eds.), *Quality of life volume I: Conceptualization and measurement* (pp. 23–32). Washington, DC: American Association on Mental Retardation.

Stark, J., & Goldsbury, T. (1990). Quality of life from childhood to adulthood. In R. Schalock (Ed.), *Quality of life: Perspectives and issues* (pp. 71–84). Washington, DC: American Association on Mental Retardation.

Taylor, S., & Bogdan, R. (1990). Quality of life and the individual's perspective. In R. Schalock (Ed.), *Quality of life: Perspectives and issues* (pp. 27–40). Washington, DC: American Association on Mental Retardation.

Taylor, S. J., & Bogdan, R. (1996). Quality of life and the individual's perspective. In R. L. Schalock & G. N. Siperstein (Eds.), *Quality of life volume I: Conceptualization and measurement* (pp. 11–22). Washington, DC: American Association on Mental Retardation.

Ward, N. A., & Keith, K. D. (1996). Self-advocacy: Foundation for quality of life. In R. L. Schalock & G. N. Siperstein (Eds.), *Quality of life volume I: Conceptualization and measurement* (pp. 5–10). Washington, DC: American Association on Mental Retardation.

Weisgerber, R. A. (1991). *Quality of life for persons with disabilities: Skill development and transitions across life stages.* Gaithersburg, MD: Aspen Publishers.

12

The Challenges of
Postmodern Thought

INTRODUCTION

S ince the end of the Middle Ages, economic, political, social, and cultural
transformations developed in Europe and throughout the world, creating
the modern era. The primary characteristic of this period has been the belief in scientific knowledge and our ability to discover truth. Today, a majority of
Americans appear to continue to accept modern perspectives, including the importance of striving for progress in all arenas of life, the continual discovery of
greater understanding of the world about us through research and study, and an
acceptance of basic truths as foundations of the universe. However, this devotion
to progress, discovery of truth, and acceptance of the basic rationality of the world
is being challenged by an ever-increasing number of people. Such thought is apparent when postmodern theorists raise questions about the most basic tenets accepted by modern thinkers. These questions challenge the very existence of
universal truths that modern theorists purport can be revealed through ongoing
scientific inquiry. The standards of our social systems, government structures, religious beliefs, and educational curricula and methodology are all being questioned and subtly influenced by such postmodern thought. To illustrate, the basic
tenet that "all men are created equal" is no longer a simple straightforward statement with a universally understood meaning. A brief historical review of American culture or current affairs reveals the confusion and difficulty in interpretation
of a statement so basic to American standards and beliefs. Gender, race, disability,
wealth, heritage, and location of birth all contribute to the perplexity of the

problem. Special educators would be among the first to acknowledge that all are not created with equal abilities, but have based their profession on the premise that all are of equal value as human beings and, therefore, are deserving of access to equal opportunities even when such opportunities necessitate unequal resources. However, postmodernists might contend that the reality of American life over the past two hundred years is that powerful Americans do not believe the tenet but convince both themselves and those whom they see as unequal that they do accept and honor it. The special education machine in place today is not exempt from this deconstruction.

Concurrent with the emergence of postmodern thought, demographic patterns within the country have been shifting, affecting the nature of children attending school and the communities that schools serve, as well as the nature of teaching. American schools of the 1990s and onward will be characterized by tremendous ethnic and cultural diversity simply not evident a few decades ago. During the 1980s, nine million immigrants arrived in the United States—a number larger than ever before recorded in a single decade (Wang, Reynolds, & Walberg, 1995). With this immigration wave came two million students who began attending public schools in the United States. Minority populations also continue to increase as a percentage of the native population. In fact, in many large cities the "minorities" have become the majority (Hodgkinson, 1993). Educational opportunities and positive outcomes are not always possible for these students. For example, in Chicago and other major cities an increasing number of students never reach the ninth grade, and of those who do, nearly 30% drop out before graduation. The rates are even higher when figures for just Hispanic and African American students are considered (Lawson, 1994). Many of these children pass through special education or other compensatory programs along their educational paths prior to dropping out. The benefits of such opportunities do not seem to include reductions in the dropout rate for these populations.

Lifestyles are changing as the demographic patterns shift and postmodern beliefs evolve into new standards of behavior. The meaning and significance of these changes vary widely, as do recommendations for future directions. The roles of women and men in society are no longer defined as they were in the 1950s. Some argue such change represents the beginning of the end for the American family and cry for the return to well-demarcated gender roles. Others see the removal of gender bias and restriction as a positive that can allow the concept of family to evolve and expand as needed to adapt to a postmodern world. Sexual orientation and its significance for teachers who are influential figures in the lives of their students offer additional points of confusion for the modern thinker experiencing the transition to postmodern roles and values. In the past, standards were clear—persons with openly homosexual lifestyles were considered unfit role models for children and, therefore, not suitable for service in American classrooms. However, any individual who could appear to live a normal lifestyle would be accepted. Today, the value of such stated or unstated policies is widely debated and offers a classic example of the tensions between modern and postmodern thought. For the postmodernist, there is no "right" or better sexual orientation, so there would be no debate on the appropriateness of anyone who is an effective teacher serving in the classroom. Gender roles and sexual orientation are just two of the innumerable such dilemmas emerging as postmodern critical theorists deconstruct modern American society. The issues of changing demographics and patterns of poverty in our nation, evolution in the nature and causes of disability, and influences of postmodern thought provide the context for the decision points in this chapter.

Patterns of Poverty in U.S. Society

The statistics used to document many troubling aspects of our society are extensive, and somewhat overwhelming regarding children. The largest and fastest growing segment of the population living in poverty is children, and the younger the child, the greater are his chances of being poor. Although poverty rates are highest in inner-city areas, the largest number of poor people live in rural areas, small towns, and small metropolitan areas (Davis & McCaul, 1991). Children living outside metropolitan areas are actually more likely to be living in poverty than those living in metropolitan areas (Irwin, Brindis, Brodt, Bennett, & Rodriguez, 1991). Teenage mothers are giving birth to 500,000 children annually, with approximately 3.3 million children under the care and supervision of these teen mothers (Lawson, 1994). Young teenagers (under fifteen years of age) receive the least adequate prenatal care and have the greatest chance of having a low birth-weight infant. These babies also have the highest infant mortality rates. Traditional two-parent families are far less common than in the past, with one of every five children being raised by a single parent, and the number of children living in poverty is now estimated at twelve million (Irwin et al., 1991). The estimated percentage of children living below the poverty line today is 23% (Hodgkinson, 1993). The figure climbs to 39% for Hispanic children and 46% for African Americans (U.S. Department of Education, 1994).

Such global statistics are accurate, but they do not reveal the concentrations of poverty in rural areas or our central cities. Some schools may have no families within their entire community who have incomes below the poverty line, whereas other schools might have a significant majority, if not 100%, of their families living in poverty. Kozol (1995) tells of a school in the South Bronx where there are only two children out of an entire student body who do not qualify for free or reduced lunch. This concentration pattern is also apparent along racial lines. In 1992, African American children represented only 7% of all students in private schools but constituted 33% of the student body in central-city public schools. Four percent of children in public schools in nonmetropolitan areas are Hispanic, whereas they make up 21% of the central-city public school population (U.S. Department of Education, 1994). Although racial diversity may not be apparent in individual schools, there is clear evidence that within the K–12 population at large, racial variety is continuing to expand. However, evidence of comparable variety is missing in our higher educational programs. Figures from 1990 indicate that of K–12 public schoolchildren, 16% were African American,

12% were Hispanic, 3% were Asian, and 1% were Native American, whereas in higher education the figures were nearly half those for African Americans and Hispanics. Nine percent of students enrolled in higher education were African American, 6% were Hispanic, 4% were Asian, and 1% were Native American (U.S. Department of Education, 1994). These children, frequently faced with poverty, are struggling and often failing in their schools and are unable to advance on to higher education in representative proportions.

School failure can take on a variety of aspects. It might mean placement in special education for some, whereas others might make reference to report cards and Carnegie units. Students with aspirations in the South Bronx, Kozol (1995) reports, hope for jobs as sanitation workers—a far different expectation from the children attending school in Westchester County, a few miles away. The dropout rate is a common factor considered by politicians and educators alike as a barometer of the success of schools and the individuals in those schools. The assumption is that maintaining a child's presence in school is to the child's benefit. The use of suspension or expulsion is considered by administrators as the worst possible punishment a student can receive. Although limited information is available on the nature of who receives suspensions and expulsions, there is some evidence to indicate that higher percentages of minority students and/or special education students receive such punishments during their years in school (Wang, Reynolds, & Walberg, 1995). There is a greater likelihood of a student who has been suspended or expelled becoming a dropout than one not so punished, as is the case with students who have been retained. When problems and causes of school failure become too narrowly defined (e.g., the dropout rate), the immediate recommendations may not offer much meaningful help since the real problems are more likely a collection of innumerable factors (e.g., poverty, poor schools, inappropriate instruction, lack of parenting, drugs). Yet the problems become overwhelming if not analyzed and defined with specificity.

Education may not be the highest priority for children or families faced with the living conditions associated with extreme poverty, regardless of the fact that they are living within a society that is based on individual achievement and independence. Basic matters of survival overshadow and sometimes undermine the importance that education should have. For example, housing would be a more critical concern than education for some families. Adequate space and quality of housing (plumbing, heating, working appliances in the kitchen), although vital for healthy living, for some families take an even lower priority than finding *any* housing. Thousands of homeless children and their families know this firsthand. Homelessness for school age children is a harsh reality, with current estimates of homeless children at 322,000 (Davis & McCaul, 1991).

Health care presents another area of disturbing reality of greater consequence than education for those who have limited access. In urban communities with predominantly African American residents, the infant mortality rate is nearly twice that for Caucasians who have similar socioeconomic characteristics (Davis & McCaul, 1991). It seems that the ability to pay is not the only variable affecting health care outcomes. Nevertheless, the price of health care for the nation has increased, with costs in 1992 exceeding $800 billion (Davis & McCaul, 1991). The escalation of the cost of subsidized health care has contributed to a national budget dilemma—increased funding seems to have no end, but providing no health care for those unable to secure private insurance costs even more in terms of diminished lives and high-cost care provided through emergency rooms.

The total price of these existing school, family, and health problems associated with poverty include moral, social, and economic costs as well. A child is born into the world surrounded by adults using drugs, violence, the hopelessness of extreme poverty, and inadequate nutrition and housing. He may never have a real opportunity to grow and mature into a healthy, contributing member of society. The connection for such children to special education is fairly direct. Families who are in poverty are most likely to live in proximity to others with similar financial limitations and have their children in schools together. Although the numbers of children from such schools served by special education may be relatively high, it will include only those within the group who display the most substantial difficulties. Children with milder learning difficulties, who might receive services were they in a different peer group, are excluded. Does their lack of access to special education help them remain in the mainstream and succeed, or serve to increase their frustration and failure?

The appropriateness of our maintenance of such inconsistent standards within the field of special education is parallel to the larger dilemmas challenging our society in general. The living conditions that some children face challenge directly our democratic principles, the rights and responsibilities of parents, and our foundational beliefs in individualism and personal rights. American citizens living under the conditions of extreme poverty, violence, and fear suffer the greatest burdens, but unquestionably their condition takes a vicious toll on the entire nation in lost lives and productivity as well as lost freedoms. Fear of and protection from this group play an increasing role in our culture. The social costs similarly cut to the very core of our participatory government, which is based on an educated and informed public selecting individuals to represent their views and interests in the development of our laws. Lawson (1994) has noted that when the educational and health care systems, in concert with families, fail to serve everyone, we negate the concept of community and place at risk the ability of some to be productive citizens. In turn, the entire social system is at risk, not just the individuals facing a life of poverty, violence, poor health, or ignorance.

The loss of productive contributions to the economy associated with these personal conditions include direct, indirect, short- and long-term costs. They include factors such as the loss of the productivity of those persons who fail to acquire adequate education and motivation to seek and maintain employment, as well as the cost of providing social services, health care, and educational programs to them. The costs of the judicial system used to police gangs, drug trafficking, and violence in these communities must also be weighed into the costs. There are estimates that the provision of human services for children and youth alone cost $278.4 billion in 1989 (Lawson, 1994). Some argue that the inefficiency and duplication of many such services further exacerbate the costs. For example, Oregon (which is not alone in this pattern) was reported to have 238 different programs controlled by 37 different state agencies to provide services for their children and families. It is possible that each of these was a distinct entity with no overlap or conflict with the remaining 237, but such is unlikely.

Today, there are approximately 25 million adults who are labeled functionally illiterate but who are expected to live in a highly technological world—a world built on individual initiative and resourcefulness (Hodgkinson, 1993). Why they are illiterate and what, if anything, can or should be done to improve their lot in life is another of the many concerns facing educators today.

Although the prevention of school failure might be deemed a worthy notion by most persons, the directions that various reformers or theorists would have the schools take involve diverse and often contradictory paths. The reform cries heard today include many dichotomies. There are calls for the restoration of order and standards of behavior versus achievement of a deeper understanding of and sensitivity to the violent lives many children face from birth, new attention to developing life skills such as cooperation and moral judgment through projects and activities requiring research and analysis versus an emphasis on facts and knowledge as measured by standardized tests, and the total elimination of special education versus the strengthening and enhancement of special education. The influences of both modern and postmodern thought are heard as educators and policy makers define the problems differently and offer such conflicting solutions. The evolving nature of disability in our society must also be considered in these debates.

The Evolving Nature and Causes of Disability

The changing nature of society is precipitating an evolution in the causes of disability. Over the last twenty years, the numbers of babies prenatally exposed to drugs and alcohol, HIV-infected babies, and low birth-weight babies have multiplied. In major urban areas, it is estimated that one child out of fifteen faces risk of impaired behavior and/or learning due to a problem occurring during the prenatal period or associated with the child's birth (Crosby, 1993). The leading known cause of mental retardation in the United States is fetal alcohol syndrome, surpassing even the most common genetic disorders (Streissguth et al., 1991), and HIV is the leading infectious cause of pediatric mental retardation (Davis & McCaul, 1991). Such rankings are likely influenced by the increased awareness and diagnosis of fetal alcohol syndrome and the presence of prenatal testing and legal abortion options for pregnant women. It is reasonable to assume that children facing poverty and homelessness are at some risk for school failure and joining the ranks of special education at some point before they exit the school system (if they ever even enter it).

The role that education, and particularly special education, plays in the evolving nature and cause of disability must be considered. Does the education system, as presently designed with special and compensatory educational programs, offer solutions to the problems faced by the American society of the 1990s? Five key indicators known to be associated with poor educational performance are (a) living in a poverty household, (b) having a minority/racial group identity, (c) living in a single-parent family, (d) having a poorly educated mother, and (e) having a non-English language background (Pallas, Natriello, & McDill, 1989). Students affected by any of these variables are known to face educational disadvantage. Is this situation simply an unfortunate but inevitable fact of life, or is it a matter of those in power intentionally allowing the system to remain dysfunctional for this "disadvantaged" group?

A confounding influence that can heighten the effects of poverty is the spoken language in the home. In particular, Hispanic and Asian children typically speak a language other than English in their homes. The percentage of children aged five to seventeen who speak a language other than English in their homes and who report having difficulty speaking English continues to increase (Davis & McCaul, 1991). In today's political arena, such statistics have moved some to urge the legal identity of English as this country's official spoken language. The implications of such a move for the education of the children who do not have an adequate command of English to learn new concepts are substantial. (See Chapter 2 for further discussion of this issue.)

The relationship between parent and child and the incidence of child abuse must also be considered as contributing to the evolution in causes of disabilities. There is evidence to support the notion that certain behavioral and developmental characteristics, including developmental disabilities, medical fragility, temperament traits, prematurity, and low birth weight, may predispose children to maltreatment (Janko, 1994). The children who may present the greatest stress to the family are most frequently born into families with the most limited social and financial resources and lack of support structures. Janko notes with frustration a typical pattern when young mothers who give birth to a premature, low birth-weight, and drug-affected infant later return to the child protection system as reported child abusers. They have shifted from individuals needing support and training to criminals who must be prosecuted. The child in need of special education has grown up to become the cause of her offspring needing special education.

Economic and family structure factors present their own obstacles to educational achievement and other positive life outcomes. Lower socioeconomic status contributes to the likelihood of teens dropping out of school, becoming involved with the criminal justice system, and doing poorly in the competitive job market (Schrag, 1993). All the while, those in the mainstream of American society appear deeply troubled by the fate of those in poverty and perpetually speak of the need for change, reform, and the creation of programs that will really make a difference in their lives. There appears to be a sincere desire to give such impoverished persons an opportunity to experience and accept the values and life of the mainstream. The concerns and need for reform range from individual appearance and choice of attire to sexual mores to personal standards and work ethic. Postmodern thought is emerging in the context of these confusing concerns and struggles.

Modern and Postmodern Paradigms of Thought

Although there is great divergence of thinking within the parameters of modern thought, the belief in universal foundational knowledge is a common theme. Skrtic (1995c) has identified four paradigms of modern scientific thought,[1] all of which accept the existence of an underlying truth and consider its pursuit feasible. They do differ on how important time and circumstances are to the discovery of this truth and how it is perceived subjectively by individuals. Whether the nature of society is best characterized as one of order and regulation or conflict and change is another significant point of disagreement among the paradigms.

The most prevalent modern paradigm is that of *functionalism,* which is grounded in regulation and order and the assumption that there are objective rational explanations of social actions which can be used to predict children's behavior and achieve control over it in time. Educators strive to understand and apply the work of psychologists every day in their classrooms by implementing "proven" classroom management techniques. Sociologists also rely on their work to assist city planners and others to predict group behavior and maintain crowd control. Extreme functionalists believe that all existing components of society are essential to the overall system, so the structures that exist today should endure into the future. Thus, the argument would follow that special education has arisen within the educational system because a need for it arose, so it is now a vital part of our educational system and must not be targeted for destruction.

Skrtic (1995b) has identified four assumptions associated with functionalism that guide education, educational administration, and special education practices. The first is that school failure is a pathological condition that some students have regardless of circumstances. Second is the assumption that differential diagnosis for classification by ability or need is objective and offers a benefit to the students, teachers, and parents. The third assumption is that various forms of special programming, such as ability grouping, curricular tracking, and segregated in-class and pull-out special needs programs, are rationally conceived and offer benefits to diagnosed students. That progress and improvements in education come about gradually through incremental improvements of conventional diagnostic and instructional practices is the fourth assumption. Many special educators would probably identify with the functionalist paradigm and accept its assumptions, objectivity, and recognition of social order.

Radical structuralism is also based on an objective perspective but challenges the notions of regulation, order, solidarity, and maintenance of the status quo. Theorists espousing this paradigm characterize contemporary society in terms of power, domination, and exploitation. From such a view, special education was created to help normal children and schoolteachers be rid of the undesirables, not as a means of achieving greater educational benefits for those with disabilities. They contend that conflict between the needs of different social groups has historically been settled by those in power and control, who then convince oth-

---

1. The names used to describe theoretical perspectives similar to these paradigms vary from author to author, but those chosen by Skrtic have been selected for use here.

ers that what was happening was indeed in their best interests. For example, those in power convinced those concerned about the welfare of Native Americans that they would be better off on protected reservations. Another outdated example was the belief that women were too delicate for the full-court game and should play basketball with half-court rules. In special education, we might view the widely held notion that students with disabilities are best served through a separate educational system that could be designed to take into consideration their individual needs as a relevant example. Most special educators or parents of children with disabilities would probably not be comfortable with this perspective. Those who are, ironically, would have to become voices for the dismantlement of their own specialization or services that most within the field are convinced do offer benefits to the children so served.

The remaining two modern paradigms categorized by Skrtic advocate a subjective view that knowledge and truth may differ according to time and circumstances. The changing nature of accepted causes of disabling conditions, such as seizures or autism, offer examples to illustrate the meaning of this subjectivity. In the case of seizures, demonic possession was at one time a prevailing belief predating the scientific understanding of central nervous system functioning and its connection to seizures. Some prefer to accept this view even today and base their beliefs on personal, subjective life experiences and interpretations of biblical passages. For them, and for members of their families or communities, truth dictates that seizure disorders receive a far different intervention than that prescribed by a neurologist. Adhering to the modern premise that there is an actual universal truth to the cause of seizures, there are at least two camps claiming to hold that truth. For most of us, the scientific medical explanation is accepted as the "truth" as we sadly shake our heads at the ignorance of those who hold to old ideas that have been "proven" false. For the individual suffering from seizures who lives within a community adhering to other beliefs, the truth is that seizures are related to demonic possession and are accordingly so treated. The community beliefs make it a reality in the lives of those so afflicted. In the case of autism, the leading researchers in the field at one time offered the "theory as truth" that cold, ambitious mothers caused this complicated condition to overtake their children, sometimes even while the infants remained in the womb. Today, researchers exploring the causes of autism consider the cold mother theory as absurd as most consider demonic possession the real cause of seizures. Yet the theory was in psychology texts well into the 1970s and was accepted in clinical practice as well. What "truths" of the 1990s will be perceived in such radically different fashion twenty years hence we can not predict. However, acknowledgment that our understanding of the universe is time and place bound is a part of modern subjective thought.

Skrtic labeled the two subjective modern paradigms as *interpretivism* and *radical humanism*. Interpretivism he associates with four themes: (a) reality is constructed and intentional, (b) splitting subject and object is impossible, (c) splitting fact and value is impossible, and (d) the goal of research is understanding (Skrtic, 1995b). Although the proponents of this perspective might take issue with many of the analytical and behavioral techniques and approaches used in special education, they would not likely challenge its very existence or question its overall contribution to the improvement of education for children with disabilities. Radical humanists take a much more extreme position, holding to the notion that society is antihuman, inhibiting human development, fulfillment, and freedom. Such theorists contend that traditional schools prepare students to take orders, teach them to view their peers' thoughts and ideas as of little value, and strive to create the false impression that schools have a monopoly on learning. For humanists, the goal of education is not only the mastery of facts and the disciplining of bodies but also the development of ethical processes—reflection, discourse, and participatory action. The right answer is of less importance than the cultivation of ethical abilities. For the radical humanist, the failure of a student to meet the organizational demands of education suggests that the failure is located in the organization, not in the student. From such a perspective, special education has taken on the responsibilities of a bureaucratized educational system (Kiel, 1995) that has proven inadequate to provide a meaningful education to children who do not fit a precise mold. Special education serves as a means of blaming the student for the educational difficulties she is encountering rather than focusing on the deficiencies of the system or the inappropriate goals of the system. To the extent that popular texts, prevalent journal articles, and curricular materials accurately reflect the beliefs of special educators, the majority opinion overwhelmingly appears to support the emphasis on the presence of some condition within the child to which poor educational performance can be attributed and the need to address this condition with specialized interventions. The radical humanists and their dislike of the effects of society on the developing person appear to have had little impact on special education practices to date.

There is no means for debating the merits of each of these modern paradigms without adopting the assumptions of one of them, making it impossible to bring them to a point of resolution. The inability of theorists to determine the superiority of one paradigm over another has fostered a move toward *antifoundationalism* concurrent with the emergence of postmodern thought. It is easier to describe what antifoundationalism is against than what it is. The basic notion behind it is the absence of underlying truth in the universe. It challenges the foundational belief of all the modern paradigms that there is basic scientific knowledge and that we possess the ability to discover the final truth. However, the adoption of that idea then becomes contradictory with itself because it requires the acceptance of one universal truth. The one truth is that there are no truths.

Skrtic (1995c) notes the presence of two types of postmodern thought predicated on antifoundationalism. The *Continental perspective*, represented by writers such as Foucault and Lyotard, rejects all forms of modern social knowledge outright, and the *progressive liberal* version of postmodernism, represented by Bernstein and Rorty, offers a reconstruction of American pragmatism and the antifoundationalism of John Dewey, William James, and others. According to Skrtic, the key difference between the two versions of postmodernism is the value each places on modern social knowledge and democratic values, such as liberty, equality, community, and social justice. Radicals reject modern social knowledge (e.g., definitions of family, superiority of the modern nuclear family, gender-based roles in society) as oppressive and deconstruct all modern knowledge, rejecting democratic values in the process. Progressive liberals want to accept modern knowledge conditionally, as a starting point for developing new forms of emancipatory social knowledge. The Continental postmodern theorists would likely deny the progressive liberals the status of being postmodern because of their acceptance of these basic social values, yet Skrtic has so categorized them. They would prefer to challenge basic American truths, such as the assumptions that democracy is an imperfect yet superior form of government over all others, that capitalism offers the best incentives for personal achievement, that intact nuclear families offer the healthiest environment in which to live and raise children, and that all people are created equal. These postmodern theorists argue that modern paradigms are historically situated constructions of the social world, serving as outdated oppressive controls aimed at preserving their own status as the "truth" regardless of reality. The modernists, then, are not seen as seeking a real truth, but in maintaining a status quo consistent with their own limited beliefs. Progressive liberals remain committed to modern democratic values but seek to reappropriate, refine, and reground them. They accept or reject all forms of knowledge based on their "contribution to the realization of democratic social ideals rather than whether they are true in the foundational sense" (Skrtic, 1995c, p. 37).

For special educators seeking a direction for the twenty-first century, the shifting demographics, standards of behavior within American society, and deconstruction of their foundational beliefs are creating great turmoil. The challenges posed by both radical modern theorists and postmodern theorists alike should serve as catalysts for deep reflection rather than knee-jerk defensiveness on the part of special educators. If the result is the destruction of the discipline and advancement toward the realization of democratic social ideals for those with disabilities (who might come to be perceived merely as people), then we must champion the opportunity to move forward. If, on the other hand, the advocacy role that special educators perceive themselves to have played on behalf of children with disabilities is needed more than ever to advance us toward the realization of democratic social ideals for all, then let the field circle the wagons and defend itself indefinitely.

Focus of Discussion

The issues presented in this chapter are focused on a contrast between modern and postmodern theories on educational reform efforts. The shifting demographics of minority to majority status in numerous inner-city school districts, the socioeconomic patterns evident within society, and the ingredients necessary to improve school performance of all children are considered in the debates. The evolution of American society and families away from their modern values and lifestyles to those characterizing the postmodern world inevitably have a substantial impact on schools and the education community. The challenge of the postmodern idea that there are no foundational truths is in clear conflict with the popular educational principles through which we are constantly seeking and endorsing the most effective teaching practices and conveying our knowledge of the world. The remainder of the chapter is organized around two issues: the validity of the education knowledge base and its usefulness in educational reform efforts, and the validity of special education as a socially and democratically desirable presence within the educational structure. In each section, arguments that reflect modern ideas are posited against those more consistent with post-modern thought.

IMPROVING EDUCATIONAL PRACTICE
THROUGH ITS KNOWLEDGE BASE

From a modern view, scientific knowledge can be pursued and truth discovered through careful empirical study, proving (or sometimes disproving) hypotheses about the world. Although two of the modern paradigms described earlier do accept subjectivity of perspective, research based on personal perspectives and beliefs has been generally considered inferior and of limited value. The modern researcher strives specifically to remove bias and opinion from her methodology. Blind trials, equal groups, and so forth are critical to the value of the research—its generalization and the application of unbiased findings to broader groups, across time and space. Such objective research designs are in stark contrast to those being embraced by qualitative researchers of education, some of whom intentionally seek the personal construction of meaning. There is ongoing competition and conflict between the traditional modern scientific approach to the pursuit of knowledge and an interpretivist contextualized understanding of knowledge in use by postmodern researchers and others who regard themselves as modern, yet seek to expand the accepted research designs. However, the historical modern stance has been dominated by the importance of objectivity throughout the research process. Sarup (1993) describes a classic modern view:

> Narratives are classified by the scientist as belonging to a different mentality: savage, primitive, underdeveloped, backward, alienated, composed of opinions, customs, authority, prejudice, ignorance, ideology. Narratives are fables, myths, legends fit only for women and children. (p. 136)

The irony, Sarup notes, is that scientific knowledge has always been dependent on narrative knowledge to espouse and verify that it is the true knowledge. Once the quantifying and hypothesis testing are complete, the only avenue of communicating that results in meaning is narrative. What the empirical findings hold for us must come down to the personal conclusions and implications of the "facts" as told by the researcher.

Modern scientists have assumed that they could seek out and find universal truths, whereas the postmodern perspective is that no such universal truths hold. As Sarup (1993) argues, "The two myths which have acted as justifications for institutional scientific research—that of the liberation of humanity and that of the speculative unity of all knowledge—are also national myths" (p. 137). Even some qualitative research designs continue to be dominated by the "empiricist" standards of quantitative approaches (Hatch & Wisniewski, 1995). Educators, as researchers, have generally preferred using precise clinical trials and quantification of student progress in schools to determine effective teaching strategies. These scientifically verified strategies could then be translated into lists and rules for teachers to implement wherever they might find themselves with whomever they might be teaching. Such research practices have been particularly abundant in special education. Teacher stories and intuition have been put aside as unscientific and, therefore, unworthy of investigation and analysis. If "best practices" proved ineffectual, the teacher obviously failed to implement the techniques correctly, because the methods have been proven to be effective. On occasion, an explanation might also make reference to deficiencies within the target pupils as a possible clarification of a technique's failure. The approach was perhaps suitable for normal children, but not those experiencing learning disabilities or emotional difficulties. Thus, the problem lies within the pupil rather than the worthy technique, and scientific knowledge is preserved. Contextualized research that would seek out and include participant interpretations of the apparent findings holds no place in the pursuit of universal truths for the objective modern thinker.

Education has certainly not been the only social science affected by this devaluing of the narrative in favor of empirical knowledge: "There has been an unrelenting expansion of rationalized systems of administration and social control" (Sarup, 1993, p. 72). Postmodern acknowledgment of the embeddedness of knowledge in a particular framework rather than a universal framework does give the teacher another out. Perhaps those practices that were effective in clinical trials cannot really work in a busy classroom setting. Children who are hungry need to be fed before the teacher introduces a reading lesson to them. Developmentally appropriate practices as first defined by the National Association for the Education of Young Children (Bredekamp, 1987) may be inappropriate for children who have had no structure or security in their first three years of life. A revised version of these recommended practices reflects at least some acknowledgment of such contextual issues (Bredekamp & Copple, 1997). Although Dewey's pragmatism involves a relativism in application, only recently has acceptance of the contextualism in research methods been evident. The gradual emergence of qualitative research in educational research and journals is indicative of its infiltration into the arena of accepted practices. In special education literature, it has been somewhat slower to appear or to be valued by a field so predominantly objectivist in nature.

Since 1867, the federal government has deemed it the responsibility of the government to "collect, collate, and from time to time, report full and complete statistics on the condition of education in the United States" (U.S. Department of Education, 1994, p. iii). Such a directive is consistent with modern or structural theory characterized by scientific inquiry and the pursuit of understanding through statistical data gathering and research. Postmodern theorists, on the other hand, might find the detailed quantification available about education and such assurances of our "knowledge" of the condition of education today unworthy of the time and effort given, especially when done under the auspices of a federally funded agency committed to educational research and improvement as universal constructs. The multiplicity of modern paradigms coupled with the emergence of numerous postmodern theories offers many choices for future direction setting and the most beneficial approaches to take in pursuit of improving education or planning for the future. The following decision point represents an amalgam of these various perspectives as related to modern theory juxtaposed against postmodern thought. While considering these positions, readers are encouraged to alter and personalize the positions so that they are consistent with their own perspectives.

Decision Point 12.1: Improvement of
Education Through a Knowledge Base

Arguments for Proposition One The conclusion that education in the United States was being "eroded by a rising tide of mediocrity that threatens our very future as a Nation and a people" (National Commission on Excellence in Education, 1983, p. 5) has resulted in substantive recommendations and changes in American education. High school students are taking more academic courses, such as algebra, geometry, trigonometry, calculus, advanced science, and foreign languages, than did their counterparts a decade ago. The number of students taking advanced placement examinations has more than doubled, and the performance of high achieving students on standardized science tests has increased. Whereas drops in scores had been previously reported as a cause for alarm, the actual number of students taking the Scholastic Aptitude Test has increased, with a concurrent increase in the percentage of students scoring above 600 on the mathematics subsection and stable scoring for the verbal portion. Likewise, the scores of the lowest performing groups on standardized proficiency exams have shown increases, and dropout rates for students between tenth grade and twelfth grade are diminishing (U.S. Department of Education, 1994). Although continued reform and improvements in the educational system are needed, criteria such as these serve as time-honored measures of progress toward increasing school effectiveness. Through extension, refinement, and application of our knowledge base in both special and general education we can continue our march toward improving education, using refined instructional approaches and increased accountability. Additionally, our understanding of what constitutes effective schools must include a greater appreciation and awareness of the communities served by schools. The combined application of our professional knowledge base and adjustments based on community profiles will lead us toward more effective schools for the future.

The Special Education Knowledge Base The research base in special education is well grounded in the quality and effectiveness of practical instructional techniques (Reynolds, Wang, & Walberg, 1992). The analysis and documentation of student progress built into instructional approaches used by special education teachers across various delivery systems linked with the concept of individualized educational plans for every student with disabilities offer the potential for special

Proposition One

The knowledge base for educators has become well established. We know what works and what is inappropriate for children. Refinement of our understanding of the world must certainly continue, while we attempt to apply our existing knowledge base as effectively as possible in the present. Student progress and achievement can serve as a guide to monitor effectiveness along with measurement of a sense of satisfaction with the school climate and understanding of community profiles. The adoption of proven models of effective teaching and principles of effective schools will ultimately benefit all students.

educators to have available the data necessary to deliver effective programs. The quality of programs within the field certainly varies, but ongoing research efforts continue to provide greater insights and improvements in our understanding and delivery of special education and related services. When proven techniques fail to work, there are many possible causes that must be considered, ranging from poor or inappropriate application of the technique by poorly trained teachers to a child's mismatch with a particular technique. Nevertheless, both instructional techniques and structured lesson plan formats are available that can increase a teacher's chances for success. In some instances, instructional materials are developed that are intended to be "teacher proof" and have proven to be effective with a broad spectrum of students.

The program Success for All (Slavin, Madden, Dolan, Wasik, Ross, Smith, & Dianda, 1996) offers an example that combines elements of general and special education reading programs to ensure student success in reading. The standards and teacher training are very specific and direct. Detailed teacher's manuals and intensive in-service training address general teaching strategies and provide specific lessons for staff at replication sites. Slavin et al. note that while there is no way to guarantee charismatic principals or teachers for all pupils, it is still possible to ensure that all children have opportunities to succeed in school. The widespread successful replication of their model across widely differing sites is evidence of the feasibility of such an approach. They do not claim to have the only effective replicable model, as numerous other programs such as Reading Recovery (Pinnell, 1989) and the School Development Program (Comer, 1988) have also documented efficacy. A wide array of empirically proven models of effective instruction for both regular and special needs populations is well documented in innumerable methods texts, commercially available instructional materials, and scholarly summations of research findings in the field. The point is not that one single approach must prove itself to be superior to all others, but that appropriate implementation of numerous successful models of effective educational programming offers our greatest hope of witnessing student success in schools.

Unquestionably, improvements and advancements in our instructional approaches and teacher qualifications must continue and will emerge through ongoing research and development of precise instructional techniques. However, the works available to us on teacher effectiveness (e.g., Brophy, 1987; Brophy & Good, 1986) reveal much that can improve our performance in the classroom. Through the combination of such knowledge with that available in psychology,

sociology, and related fields, an even greater good can be achieved. Effective social interventions are real and can be used to offset the cruel beginnings that some
children do face (Schorr, 1989). Knowledge of what is needed is available to us.
Health programs, family support systems, child care, and early educational intervention that make a significant difference in people's lives can allow the transition
from childhood into adulthood to be successful rather than dismal. As Schorr
(1989) writes, "Unshackled from the myth that nothing works, we can assure
that children without hope today will have a real chance to become the contributing citizens of tomorrow" (p. 294). Although we may often lack the resources (personal and emotional as well as financial) to offer the programs that
can make a difference, we do not lack basic knowledge of what is needed to provide children with decent lives and all students effective instructional programs.

Broadening Conceptions of Effectiveness Measurement of educational effectiveness
by test scores and student progress, while important, is not sufficient to serve as
evidence of effective schooling. The existence of extreme social problems,
poverty, multi-generation welfare recipients, violence, gangs, drug trafficking,
and a weak tax base for funding is the real context of some schools, crippling
their students' ability to achieve academic excellence. Educators must acknowledge the powerful connections between student success and these variables external to the education system. The level of schooling of one's parents is, in fact,
the best predictor of success in school and scores on academic tests (Goodlad,
1994). When a child with well-educated, successful parents displays school difficulties, the possible causes are not the same as when students from impoverished
backgrounds fail. The determination of how best to achieve effective schools for
all groups must account for such variables rather than ignore their influence on
educational outcomes. Whether the students are upper-middle-class students
showing signs of learning disabilities or those who are suffering from the effects
of extreme poverty does make a difference. The act of evaluating schools serving
students from wealthy communities in a similar manner as those whose communities are characterized by poverty and transience is shortsighted. Treating the
children as though they began on an even playing field fails to acknowledge the
existence of these very powerful factors that are outside the control of educators.
To presume that all children hold the same innate proclivity to learning and
should be held equally accountable for their achievement negates the very notions of individuality of performance. Goodlad (1994) notes that what is missing
in our extensive data bank is how well groups of schools are working with the
conditions *under their control*. The ability of schools serving children from wealthy
backgrounds and highly educated parents to produce a majority of graduates who
make top scores on standardized tests and graduate from the most prestigious
universities is well established, but does not necessarily mean that these are good
places or are making the most of the potential of their students:

> Indeed, some are rather vicious places for boys and girls to be....Surely our
> best schools should be those most committed to and productive of human
> goodness....[I]n a democratic society, we *must* question a standard that in-

equitably distributes awards so that inherited attributes count for more than do diligence and effort. (p. 208)

The traditional standards of excellence in schooling must be broadened and reconsidered. High test scores might be more appropriately given less status whereas the development of alternative characteristics, such as high personal standards of integrity, cooperation, leadership, and personal achievement, might be given greater value. Goodlad suggests that we consider a standard of satisfaction in evaluating schools. Noting that we rely on a measure of satisfaction for many areas of our lives, such as choosing a mate, a car, a house, or a vacation spot, he argues that it need not be considered soft or vague. He contends that qualitative investigation of school climate, class climate, principal–teacher relationships, curricula, teaching, teacher–teacher relationships, school–community relationships, parent–teacher relationships, and so forth can be used to produce a quantitative index measuring the satisfaction of schools. As such, our knowledge base can be extended beyond simply what gets results to what gets the best results with the greatest possible satisfaction for students, teachers, parents, and administrators.

In spite of the numerous criticisms of schools in the 1980s and 1990s, they can be viewed as working better than many other parts of the community, especially in consideration of the many additional roles that schools have had to assume outside of education (Goodlad, 1994). Some might even argue that the education crisis so vividly described in *A Nation at Risk* and other similar publications never was a reality, but simply the presentation of images to the public to create the perception of a crisis. For example, the claim that SAT scores were dropping is quite misleading when taken at face value. Test takers at the SAT's inception were white males, the majority of whom had attended exclusive New England preparatory schools. By 1990, the demographics of the test takers had changed radically, with 50% of all test takers having family incomes under $30,000 and nearly 30% coming from a minority group (Ruenzel, 1995). Thus, any decline in SAT scores cannot be construed as evidence of the deterioration of America's public schools, but is more accurately a reflection of the expanding composition of the test-taking population. Over the past two decades, both SAT and Iowa Achievement Test scores have held steady, with some meaningful gains made by minorities (Ruenzel, 1995). In international comparisons, American students are holding their own in most subjects, with reading performance ahead of all other countries with the exception of Finland. Further, American schools have assumed the responsibility for educating a population of students of ever-increasing diversity. Our public schools are now far more democratically inclusive than they were historically, with close to 85% of all Americans, from all racial and socioeconomic groups, graduating from high school, as compared with 10% in 1910 and only 45% as recently as 1940 (Ruenzel, 1995).

Argument Summary The professional knowledge base now available in education on effective teaching and effective schools is well established and continues to be tested and refined. Through continuing reform and improvements in teacher education as well as in K–12 instruction, the education community is well grounded in both theoretical and applied knowledge. Experiments with innovations such as providing direct incentives (e.g., pay bonuses) for those teachers who prove to be the most effective in the classroom as evidenced by student performance or other measurable outcomes, adoption of outcomes-based education, use of cooperative learning in the classroom, and so forth will continue to expand our understanding of the best educational practices. Professionals do have access to unique knowledge that is needed by society to solve its problems as well as the ability to apply this knowledge in the interests of their students and the common good.

Arguments for Proposition Two   Within the education community there are high-caliber programs that enable many children with a wide variety of abilities to achieve, but the extent to which education and its formula-driven practices have accomplished these successes alone must be questioned. If we were to select the U.S. schools whose students have the highest standardized test scores and place children who are statistically at the greatest risk to face school failure in them, would these children likely be able to achieve success? The multitude of systemic influences upon a child and his success in school cannot be simplified into cookbook lists of effective teaching practices or guides for the development of effective schools. They must be explored on quite different levels. The intention behind special education programs is to make a difference for individuals, not groups. However, the commercialization and marketing of instructional techniques, textbook presentations of instructional strategies, and the federal endorsement of "effective" models and instructional packages all work to undermine the very essence of special education—individual, contextual appropriateness. The institution of special education has failed to resist universals and canned answers when individual progress and adjustment have been the real ends we should have been seeking. Meaningful change will more likely result from cultural change than top-down mandates from school administrators or politically driven school board members (Gitlin, 1990) who demand the adoption of delivery systems and methods consistent with their beliefs on what constitutes the right way to teach and run schools. Any contextualized use of the overly touted educational knowledge base in conjunction with localized pursuit of effective schools offers greater direction for the future than does the dissemination of and training in our "proven" models.

The Special Education Knowledge Base   Improvements in education must be localized, particular, diffused, and strategic. The worst error is to believe that personal successes should be brought together, networked, replicated as models, and adopted as possessing a set of universal principles to guide us to a better world together. Research is intended as the production of proof. Authors use the existing knowledge base presented in our popular texts to make universal claims about methodological efficacy and application. To illustrate, in McCoy (1995), after a listing of three general techniques associated with teaching reading, the following claim is made: "All children, with or without disabilities, progress when they are

---

Proposition Two

The notion that well-designed education is achievable through the scientific study of conditions that produce educational success is antiquated at best. The successful achievement of some groups of students and the failure of others cannot be understood through the quantification of facts and figures about student performance or even through volumes of quantitative data from successful schools. Teachers and administrators who perceive the multiple worlds within our society and the highly individualized character of success will soar beyond those stridently seeking to adhere to the "best practices" of the field. Best practices simply do not exist outside of context.

---

taught by a teacher who applies these techniques" (p. 259), with a citation to the work of Bos and Vaughn. For the teacher who faithfully adheres to these techniques but finds her students failing to progress, what are the conclusions she must draw, and what choices are left to her in seeking solutions to her problems? Educators have been compelled to adhere to the claims of educational research in applied settings and must find rational answers when results are disappointing.

Some would claim that special education represents a real advance in the educational opportunities available to all children, has proven to be effective, and honors the best interests of students with disabilities. However, from a postmodern perspective there may be a problem not just with our conclusions but even with the "objective" scientific method used to support the importance of special education and its textbook methods. A teacher struggling to find the reason why her "proven" methods are failing, the administrator unable to find a means of controlling disruptive students, and the school board grappling with policy decisions when standardized test results reveal that inner-city schools are failing to maintain standards set by them must all seek solutions to their concerns. What those solutions should be, however, are not the precise factual objective truths some hope the world will continue accepting. Sarup (1993) reminds us of the inability of "scientific" facts to be separated from individual perceptions, power, and wealth. Sailor and Skrtic (1995), citing Derrida, also argue that the laws describing order in a rational universe are not really laws at all but rather are political constructions, subject to reformulation with the changing ethos of social organizations.

The nature of educational research that will support the transformation of educational opportunities away from efficient consumption of facts into an evolving exploration of the meanings in the world is far different from the objective, quantitative approach entrenched over the past decades. Test scores may reveal the greatest consumption of facts and afford the greatest opportunities for a successful educational future, but need not be assumed to represent the greatest learning that has taken place. A constructivist approach, grounded in qualitative or interpretivist technique that contextualizes all meaning, should instead become the standard of practice. The contexualization of meaning is well illustrated in the notion of reward within the educational environment. What the teacher intends as a reward to the student might be viewed by the student, in fact, as a punishment. Even the presumption that high marks on a report card are valued rewards that all children desire is erroneous. Is free time a real reward to a student whose life goals reflect a high standard of achievement and success or to one who is a social isolate and will feel this isolation greater during free time than any other point in the school day? Reward becomes punishment, and punishment becomes reward. How can research on the effects of reward systems hold meaning for us when the premise upon which the research is based—rewards are seen as positive benefits by the students involved—is so flawed? And so it is with all of our decontextualized educational research findings.

Broadening Conceptions of Effectiveness General educators, special educators, publishers, lawyers, professional organizational staff, and others in whose best interests it is to maintain the special education bureaucracy hold the power and ability to persuade the public that it is the right model. The goal of research and work in the field has become increasingly efficient performance of the system, augmentation of its power and influence, and the diversion of more and more educational resources to special education in order to prove our morality and rightness. Sarup (1993) argues the connection between power and discovery of truth: "Since performativity increases the ability to produce proof, it also increases the ability to be right; the technical criterion cannot fail to influence the truth criterion" (p. 138). The challenges implied in these words apply as well to the needs of schools and educational programs, including those serving children who are at known risk for educational failure. Today's accepted solutions to the problems faced by these schools have centered on raised standards, input criteria to be met, test scores to be improved—functionality and performance, not ideals and values. These solutions have been presented by those in power and accepted as truth, progress, and movement from the dark to the light when, in fact, their truth must not be accepted. Chubb (1990) argues that what is needed for the improvement of inner-city schools and others that may have poor performance records is certainly not more bureaucratic constraints or even money but their own power and autonomy. The external creation of higher standards merely necessitates that larger numbers of students will need special support programs (Skrtic, 1991), not that poorly performing schools will improve.

Our schools are what we want them to be. Ruenzel (1995) noted that Richard Gibboney has asked the question of how schools can be better than the society of which they are a part. They can't, and we keep forgetting that. Gibboney contends that the reformers should address mass TV, urban sprawl, and the big money that buys elections rather than schools themselves. Although these sentiments are valid, they are predicated on an assumption that the reformers are actually seeking truth, not power, that the subtle maintenance of inferior schools while creating the appearance (even for oneself) of doing all one can to improve the plight of the unfortunate is not a reality greater than the reform efforts. Another reality must be considered. Ruenzel (1995) paints the picture:

> Schools scorn the cultivation of intelligence and the cultivation of the democratic spirit. What happens in our schools is that information is shredded into

a thousand pieces, and then students are tested on it. And then when the kids from the affluent schools knock the top off the SAT, everyone says, "See, Lower Merion is such a good school." But I'm sorry, no. (p. 33)

As we move into a postmodern world, knowledge has been replaced with contextualized knowing and is no longer a thing, but rather a fluid process. Danforth, Rhodes, & Smith (1995) point out that "It can no longer be given, hoarded, withheld, ultimate or privileged" (p. 220). Modernism over the years has been used by those in control to substitute classic Western thought for reality and knowledge, politicize knowledge to a single world view, and institutionalize educational structures based on this single notion of reality. There must be a shift from seeking to fill students with a preconceived body of knowledge to creating and developing problem solvers, seekers, and explorers within the world. The truth plays second fiddle to the critical discovery of knowledge that actually leads our communities closer to the ideals that we claim to honor—liberty, equality, social justice, and community.

Argument Summary We must resist the temptation to seek universals, to simplify a many-sided schemata into a commercial product through which we hope to achieve financial benefit and professional recognition. We must stop the pooling of ideas into teacher-proof structures, as well as the disbursement of federal funding of grants for pursuit and dissemination of universal models. The replication becomes our failure. Our pursuit of universal solutions to individual problems, opportunities for financial gains from "worthy" ideas, and professional prestige and fame resulting from the revelation of claimed universals all contribute to the wrong end. We must ask what is helpful for the children at one school, not all schools. Since educational institutions represent the very heart of our claim to the pursuit of equality and democratic ideals for all, they have the most insidious power to maintain the status quo while appearing to be striving toward greater equality and opportunity for all.

SPECIAL EDUCATION IN A POSTMODERN WORLD

Postmodernism is not just a belief system that one can consider the merits of and reject or accept as a useful view of the world. It embodies characterizations of the changing nature of our society and the patterns of our lives, since transitions from modern values and beliefs to those more compatible with postmodern thought are undeniably evident. The extent to which society, including professional educators, has awareness of these shifts and an understanding of their implications for us is somewhat unknown. Whereas some large research organizations, such as the American Education Research Association, do have a contingent of somewhat esoteric scholars pursuing postmodern dialogue among themselves, many of its members as well as members of other professional organizations seem unaware of the advance of the postmodern era into the modern classroom and home. For special educators, accustomed to the role of critic in regard to general educational practices, challenges resulting from postmodern thought may catch them unprepared. Danforth, Rhodes, and Smith (1995) note that "Modern constructs use language to describe and encode 'knowledge,' whereas postmodern constructs use language in dialogue to negotiate meaning" (p. 219). No longer can the arguments that the educational system needs special education and that particular children need special education be foisted on the American public as a given. There are today tension points that reveal the clash between modern and postmodern thought and lifestyles. Elkind (1994) has described these clashes in three themes of modernity and their counter-themes evident in postmodernity that influence our lives and the nature of our families. These same themes are influencing our educational structures, particularly special education, and provide a useful means of organizing the discussion of these differences. They are (a) progression of society, (b) universality versus particularity of truth, and (c) regularity and predictability of the world.

Progression of Society

The first modern concept that Elkind defines is the belief in *progress*—that society and individuals are gradually improving as contrasted with the postmodern notion that the world is *different* but cannot be assumed to be improving or progressing. To illustrate, from a modern vantage point the nuclear family is considered a superior familial structure to those that preceded it and is, in fact, the *right* way to live and raise children. From such a perspective, current divorce patterns and custody arrangements represent the disintegration of the family, as opposed to a liberating transition when new attitudes and laws regarding divorce and custody are taken from the postmodern perspective. Society's moving into a postmodern world has allowed substantial change in the family structure to become socially acceptable both legally and morally (e.g., divorce and remarriages, single-parent homes, single-sex couples). Accordingly, such redefinition of *family* is different, but need not be evaluated as evidence of society's progress or its deterioration.

For special educators, the distinction is made in the rightness and progressive nature of special education as an institutional structure within education. For the modernist, the coming of special education is heralded as the greatest advancement for students with disabilities, and its enemies who wish to undermine or diminish its power are to be fiercely resisted. Yet a postmodern perspective calls for the deconstruction of special education. It may not be the great salvation that its advocates purport it to be. Rather, it might even be serving the purposes of those who wish to maintain an inferior status for such "unworthy" pupils as those served by special education. Although similar thoughts are shared by the radical structuralists, these ideas certainly do not represent the dominant modern perspective. Are times really better for the child who is now defined by society as having a disability than before such "opportunities" were so widely available, and is our educational structure stronger and better serving our country and the development of all its citizens through the two-pronged system now in place?

The members of this family knew their roles and society's standards for acceptable behavior.

© FPG International 1996

Universality Versus Particularity of Truth

The second modern concept that Elkind addresses is that of *universality* of truth as juxtaposed against the *particularity* of truth for postmodernists. Such a generalization is most relevant to the predominant objectivist paradigms as categorized by Skrtic, but might be challenged by those holding to the modern subjectivist paradigms. To illustrate the point, for the modern family there were clear roles for each of the family members (e.g., fathers were breadwinners; mothers kept the home and cared for the children). In contrast, the postmodern family is experiencing a de-differentiation of role, with dual-career homes, husbands who serve as the primary caregivers to the children, and nonfamily members providing much of the nurturance and care to infants and toddlers. The proper education of children in postmodern society is expected to be free of gender bias, offer a multicultural perspective, and allow all children to see themselves in any role. For the family adhering to traditional modern values, such educational programming is further evidence of the deterioration of our society and offers cause to remove their children from public schools conveying such messages, thus avoiding the paradigm conflict in raising their children. Were these children to remain in the system, it would force a confrontation of these concurrently existing paradigms. In their absence, the changes are free to occur without the benefit of trial by challenges to their appropriateness or value. However, the prevailing attitude within the educational community is probably not regret that an opportunity for confrontation and conflict was missed, even if such an opportunity would have brought greater clarity to the mission and purposes of their schools. Most would more likely view the dissenters' departure with relief, since they can proceed unimpeded with their own agendas.

Similarly, some would argue that special education has been used all along as a means by which the educational bureaucracy has avoided its own deficiencies and need for reformation. Taken from a postmodern angle, when students prove

© 1994 Carolina Kroon, Impact Visuals.

This gay couple challenges modern standards and values and the definition of family.

difficult to handle in the classroom for whatever reason, special education has become the way that educators avoid confronting the limitations and fallacies of current systems. The pursuit of truth or reality for the nation's educational system has been cut short by the use of such escape routes. The postmodernist might further argue that the pursuit of such truth was never really as important to the modern parent or educator as personal benefit, thus revealing the lack of values and integrity by the very persons who have defended their personal choices by their claimed loyalty to them. What seems to be is not.

Regularity and Predictability of the World

The third modern concept is the belief in *regularity* and predictability of the world superseded by the acceptance of *irregularity* by the postmodernist. Modern families have lived in a world with a clear unilateral line of authority originating from the father, whereas the postmodern family is characterized by mutual authority, including not just both parents but the children as well. Even who the decision makers are will vary as the nature of the issues and circumstances change. Postmodern children are expected to develop a competence in coping with the irregularities of life far sooner than responsibility was expected from the modern child. These expectations of competence are evident in the classroom as well as the home. For example, even young children must know the dangers of drugs or exposure to HIV. It had been the responsibility of modern parents to shield their children from the realities of the world as long as possible rather than to prepare them to face such issues as soon as possible. Our clever public service announcements depicting a young child dialing 911 when her mother collapsed would never have appeared on television in the 1960s, nor would have advertisements for products providing sexual protection, not to mention the content of our popular television programs.

Special educators adhering to modern perspectives seek predictability in and understanding of child performance and behavior. With predictability comes the ability to plan interventions, develop contingency plans, and be prepared for your next moves. The postmodernist accepts irregularity and does not waste time with predictions, focusing instead on the moment and what it needs. No child's future will be limited by a postmodern teacher's expectation that he will fail or by the school system's rejection of that child due to his seeming unworthiness. Some argue that the segregated special education programs that were prevalent until recently were actually more effective than the inclusion models popular today will prove to be. Others contend that such models were never worth the detrimental effects of removing the child from the mainstream and that the schools must no longer take their challenging students away from the mainstream. Some would take this argument to the point of complete elimination of special education as a separate educational structure. Is the elimination or substantial reduction of special education needed, or is the maintenance of a powerful special education structure essential for the postmodern future into which we appear to be headed?

Decision Point 12.2: Structural
Progression in Special Education

Arguments for Proposition One Special education is far from perfect, yet it has radically improved educational opportunities for children with all types of disabilities. The Forrest Gump days of administrative discretion via sexual favors as to who is allowed into mainstream schools are behind us, for it is now clearly established that no child may be denied an education on the discriminatory basis of disability. For those who did not witness the pre-IDEA exclusionary practices of the schools, it might be tempting to focus on the deficiencies and flaws of special education evident today, perhaps even call for its elimination. However, the dangers of failing to learn from the past are well-known and must surely be applied to this situation as well. Do we blame special educators for the inhumane conditions found in the 1960s and earlier in institutions so vividly depicted by Blatt (1966), or credit them with the deinstitutionalization movement? Do we cite the poor quality of instruction in some of the earliest self-contained special education rooms (Mercer, 1992), or point to the research-based practices and outcomes-based standards in place today?

Proposition One
Structure and social order are needed elements of educational communities. Today, special education is a critical component of our educational foundation. The field must continue evolving and seeking its own improvement to better serve the students and families whose educational needs are not addressed without such alternatives. It must never become stagnant or allow itself to be eliminated. It has become the voice for a group that previously had no power and, as such, is critically needed as a social structure regardless of the particular models of service delivery that are currently popular or internal disagreements that are a necessary part of the field's development.

Historical Development A review of the historical development of special education offers evidence on the progressive nature of the field and clearly lends support to the important role it has played in improving educational opportunities for persons with disabilities. Any introductory special education text offers a litany of court cases that were necessary precursors to the federal legislation that finally affirmed the basic right to an education for all children. Typically, these historical reviews begin with the classic Supreme Court case that focused on the inequities of racially segregated schools, *Brown v. the Board of Education*. Concurrent with the litigation movement, special education as a profession began expanding—developing a research agenda to accompany its advocacy role and forming collaborative partnerships with parent and self-advocacy groups in the pursuit of improved educational services for the community of disabled students. The evolution of the field from an apologetic philanthropy to a basic right afforded to all citizens requiring it is evidence enough to confirm its worthiness. Leaders in the field have demonstrated their dedication, perseverance, flexibility, and determination. A group that not only had no power base but also had no opportunity to create one through the most effective avenue open to other citizens—self-improvement through education—has become a force not to be taken lightly or ignored. The Americans with Disabilities Act and the Individuals with Disabilities Education Act both reflect the strength of a power base that was virtually nonexistent in 1970.

The Present and Beyond Inclusion is the reformation cry of the present. Not all see it as a positive advance for the field. Just as the debate within the country was strong as to whether the precepts of the 1995 Republican newcomers in Congress had a "contract with America" or a "contract on America," special educators disagree over the merits of this latest trend. The great debates within the field today center predominantly on the soundness of the inclusion movement and exactly who should be included. Parents, teachers, and administrators alike hold widely differing views. The debates include virtually all children who have traditionally been served by special educators, from those with the most severe disabilities to those who experience specific learning disabilities as well as those considered to be intellectually gifted. Constitutional rights, educational appropriateness, and the needs of normal children to develop sensitivity and understanding are all used to support both sides of the debates. However, even the most extreme conception of full inclusion for all is not a call to end special education, but rather to reform it. The only likelihood of inclusion programs being successful will be if they incorporate extensive support services provided by highly trained special educators. Full inclusion is not a cry to end special education as a field, but a call for change and improvement. Regardless of the final outcomes associated with the current inclusion movement, special education as a field must maintain a solidarity and identity on the behalf of all students with special needs and their families.

Postmodernists could argue that the development of special education enabled regular education to avoid any real reformation. As the argument goes, for the child unable to succeed in the educational mainstream, excuses could be found attributable to the child or his family. As a result, a referral to special education was all that was needed, and the regular education program could remain unchallenged and unchanged by that child's failure. However, such an argument is of little consequence when considered from the perspective of those actually served by special education. The greatest flaw in the argument is that it is based on the presumption that these students should have remained within the mainstream educational community to create a tension and, therefore, a solution. In fact, no reformation of general education would have taken place, because many of these children were being specifically excluded from the educational system and even considered unable to profit from an education. Certainly, many were not challenging the regular classroom teacher to find effective instructional techniques for them but were at home, in institutions, or in church basements, having been rejected as unworthy. There could be no worse educational option than total exclusion, which was what many of children faced prior to the creation of special education programs. Others with milder disabilities who remained within the educational system were considered to be deficient as pupils, deserving of the poor grades that they received rather than triggering an investigation into the appropriateness or effectiveness of classroom instruction. Special education was created as the result of exclusion and rejection, and is the product of the hard work and efforts of a powerless group to have their needs met, not a duping by those in power.

Argument Summary The present focus is on the very existence of the structure of special education and its worthiness as a valid response to the educational needs of children with disabilities. Although special education has been inappropriately used as a means of removing challenging students from the mainstream, such past abuses do not warrant its destruction. Rather, it must continue, as a unified body of professionals and parents use it as a means to allow all students to pursue the most appropriate educational opportunity for them as individuals. It is up to the field to reestablish its parameters and limitations without its annihilation. Special education must be reconstructed, not deconstructed.

Arguments for Proposition Two Power is the ultimate principle of social reality (Sarup, 1993). Education today cannot be assumed to have progressed and improved, although it has changed. Nor can the continuing work of specialists in the field be assumed to be leading us toward some improved version of education. Specialists exploit their positions and pose as the educational conscience of their age. They evoke power by securing the public assent not by threatening

---

Proposition Two
Special education has been created and maintained by those in power as a means to avoid making real change. Concurrently, those with the power have convinced professionals who enjoy working with students described as having dis-

abilities, the students, and their parents that they do need and have a right to it. All special and compensatory educational programs should be dismantled and no longer allowed to function as an escape valve for the education community to avoid its responsibility for all children.

punitive sanctions, but by persuading society to internalize their norms and values, to accept their world view. This pattern is particularly evident in relation to special education and its very existence. Special education provides a means by which the education community can disassociate itself from the students who do not fit in and whose presence might disprove the effectiveness of accepted practices and values, while claiming to be just the opposite. The system has been created and is now led by persons who believe that it represents progress and improvements in the educational opportunities available to students with disabilities. In fact, it is an effective means for general educators to avoid confronting the challenges presented by students who do not readily comply with the existing theories of education or who are physically or mentally unable to learn from the standard teacher repertoire. Those in power acquiesced, only after much hard-fought litigation, that they could no longer bar such children from a publicly supported education, and they would now have us believe that the model of special education in place today is indeed a well-intended, effective means of serving students whom they have had us label as disabled. Both the historical development and current trends in the field are, in actuality, not what those of us in the field have accepted them to be—increased power and access to education for a group previously excluded from public class rolls.

Historical Development Special education has developed around four assumptions that run parallel to ones shared with general education and educational administration (Skrtic, 1995b). When these assumptions are questioned, the need for the specialized system of education that is in place for a select portion of the population faces serious challenges. The first assumption is that student disability is a pathological condition. We have accepted as a given that student failure is often directly attributable to characteristics within the child rather than conditions within the environment. Second, we assume that differential diagnosis by category is objective and useful. The distinctions between our various categories are treated as precise, valuable realities, as evidenced by the expenditures and emphasis placed on the diagnostic process. The third assumption is that special education is rationally conceived and benefits the children served by this coordinated system of services. To believe anything less is considered heresy. The final assumption is well grounded in the basic modern belief in progress. It is that progress in special education occurs as a rational–technical process of incremental improvements in conventional practices. Rejection of these assumptions as universal truths opens many alternative paths for understanding the historical development of special education.

The notion that children with deficiencies in learning must be remediated to bring them to a point of readiness for learning is arbitrary, yet such remediation plans have developed as the heart of special education practice. These plans now serve as the new gatekeepers to protect the general educational programs from the detrimental effects of children perceived to be unworthy of the time and efforts of general education teachers. The process of diagnosing children and issuing prescriptions for them has been treated as though it were simple and accurate. To define, label, and treat pathological conditions present in children has become the focus. The real meaning or fairness of this approach has long since been abandoned. For example, the practice of labeling a child as emotionally disturbed because he is acting out, disruptive in class, or destructive to himself and others seems rather absurd when over his short life he has perhaps known no father and has watched as his mother repeatedly gave her loyalties to a series of unreliable alcoholic boyfriends. It is the greatest lie our "scientific" special education system could perpetuate. Of course the young child is striking out, not because he is mad, but because he isn't mad and must face living in a world that neither accepts nor loves him. Not only has the child been rejected and mistreated, but he has also become the culprit through the diagnostic and labeling process. Indeed, many in the system have seen such systemic flaws as our present system has evolved and have chosen to turn their heads, accepting rather than questioning these assumptions and their implications for our practices.

The Present and Beyond How can general education become a humane place for every student when not every student is welcome or even considered to belong? Today, some children have to prove their worthiness for a place in the mainstream of education, and many never make it. There are arbitrary standards set by those who possess the power to grant children perceived to possess flaws that "fit" our equally arbitrary definitions of disabilities their opportunity to participate in general education. Until general education is challenged by the presence of such children, it can never become an appropriate setting for them. Yet the counterargument that general education must change before students with disabilities are placed in mainstream classes perpetuates the current system of disassociated systems, an imbalance of power, and a sense of gratitude expected from those perceived as disabled for having been allowed into a system that was rightfully theirs in the first place. Whereas decoupled programs, such as special and general education, have provided a means through which to avoid problems and the presence of undesirable students in general education, they have not led to solutions to these problems.

Today, inclusion is the cry coming predominantly from special educators. Yet inclusion's wholesale value and merit as a solution to the inequities in place today must be questioned as well. The current decoupled systems that are in place today are inordinately expensive. The power base of general education has watched as a greater and greater share of education dollars has shifted over into the special education arena. The dilemma such a situation creates is real—the programs that have been established as if in the best interests of the students labeled as disabled and supported by the special education community have proven too burdensome to the education machine that allowed them to come into being. The dismantlement of a system that has proven too difficult to control, without undoing the benefits it has afforded to general education, is the present unspoken task of those holding the real power. Inclusion has become the new cry, but to whom will the greatest benefit accrue?

How can special educators, whose professional identities are at stake, be expected to call for the dissolution of themselves if such were in their students' best interests? Special educators must confront the realization that "there is nothing inherently true or correct about their knowledge, practices, and discourses" (Skrtic, 1995c, p. 38). It is no longer possible to think that everyone accepts the tenets of functionalism, historically the prevalent paradigm for special education. Special educators have championed the practices in which they were trained, hesitant to notice flaws and deficiencies in these accepted practices. Failures could always be attributed to their students' pathology, the inaccuracy of an original diagnosis, school placement, or any number of other rationalizations rather than the validity and perceived objective truth of the field's accepted practices. The comfortable assumption has been that these practices "serve the best interests of their students and of society" (Skrtic, 1995c, p. 40). Skrtic (1995b) further emphasizes the role that student pathology has played in our approach to educational reform: "Redefining school failure as student disability prevents the profession of education from entering into a productive confrontation with uncertainty, the very sort of confrontation that it needs in order to move beyond its functionalist knowledge tradition" (p. 70).

The definition of *teacher* must change to eliminate the separateness of knowledge, teacher, and learner, as if these were disparate entities. In a postmodern world they become integrated aspects of a fluid, dynamic relationship, each influencing and constructing the other. The teacher's role might be more aptly characterized as one of visionary, participating in self-critical reasoning and negotiated constructions of meaning with other human beings in the school community (Stone as cited by Danforth, Rhodes, & Smith, 1995). Visionary teaching brings together a multitude of elements in the meaning-making process, addressing values, ethics, power, culture, beliefs, relationship, context, negotiation, agreement, and disagreement intertwined within the languages of art, math, science, play, history, drama, and on and on.

Argument Summary   From the postmodern perspective it is far easier to deconstruct our current structures than it is to make recommendations on how to proceed for the future. Although we must avoid and reject universals in a postmodern world, we also must use language and narratives to convey the directions that antifoundationalism[2] would lead. Skrtic (1995a) describes the particular irony for special education in that the necessary elimination of it cannot occur until we make our schools humane places for every student.

The ability to deconstruct the field of special education is essential to make it morally and politically viable in a democracy, necessitating a move away from beliefs in universal truths. The special education knowledge tradition must be evaluated for its ability to serve the best interests of its students and their families and those of society, not its truth according to one paradigm. Lack of universal truth does not imply a lack of responsibility, moral commitment, or pursuit of the best we have to offer (Kiel, 1995). Since there is no real, true world to experience, we have the obligation of choosing which world of appearances we wish to create. The neutralization and exclusion of individuals who are different from what

---

2. Skrtic uses this term to mean the inability of any of the four modern paradigms to prove itself superior to the others, whereas those adhering to the principles of each argue from their own biases of their own truth.

educational institutions want children to be like have been occurring as a legitimate "scientific" approach through special education (Danforth, Rhodes, & Smith, 1995). When children are seen as constructors of knowledge rather than recipients of it, the notion of them as categorical entities, deficient along finely structured definitions, is absurd. Brain damage is real, genetic defects do occur, and mental illness is present in children as well as adults, but all persons construct themselves from experience, not a textbook.

Teachers become defined through the interactions that take place between themselves and children, parents, fellow teachers, administrators, and members of the community. If even one child were absent from last year's roll, the teacher would not have had the same experiences and constructed the same meanings about teaching and children as she has done with the child present in her class. Similarly, an individual encounter with a single parent can become the basis of elaborately constructed beliefs about parents and how teachers should interact with them. These beliefs are surely the truth for the individual teacher who has constructed them, but may in no way resemble the truth for all teachers. Concurrently, children are constructing their own meanings—about themselves, teachers, friends, the world. Let us strive to have schools that accept as a vision the validity and significance of these constructed worlds that represent the many truths without the burden of categories of children, categories of teachers, and the implied valuing of some over others.

CLOSING THOUGHTS

The points of discussion in this chapter present hard choices. In both issues, strong advocates on each side of the debates hold to the moral and ethical principles in which they are grounded. Poverty and the harshness of life are a reality that seems to have grown beyond meaning for all except those who are living it. The young children who are victims of this harsh life grow to become the next generation's members who seem unable to offer any better for their children but who are now held accountable for their inabilities. Certainly, the schools seem unable to intercede to stop these patterns of failure and desperation. Yet we continue to research and expand our knowledge base, reaching such broad conclusions as whole language is not the way to teach reading, and we must restore phonics to its proper place in the primary grades, because some test scores went down. Is the truth ever this simple?

Postmodern influences abound in our society—in our dress, our vocabulary, our standards of behavior, our political practices, the curriculum in our schools, the financial decisions we make, and our personally held beliefs about "what is wrong in our society today." Whereas the esoteric theory might be dismissed without a second thought, this evidence of postmodernism in our daily lives cannot. Nor can we ignore its implications for the field of special education. Do we honor and cherish our traditions, fighting to maintain our identity and separate professional organizations as the true advocates for children with special needs, or reject them as a great lie perpetrated on us by those in power?

REFERENCES

Blatt, B. (1966). *Christmas in purgatory: A photographic essay on mental retardation.* Boston: Allyn & Bacon.

Bredekamp, S. (1987). *Developmentally appropriate practice in early childhood programs serving children from birth through age 8.* Washington DC: National Association for the Education of Young Children.

Bredekamp, S., & Copple, C. (Eds.). (1997). *Developmentally appropriate practice in early childhood programs* (rev. ed.). Washington, DC: National Association for the Education of Young Children.

Brophy, J. (1987). Synthesis of research on strategies for motivating students to learn. *Educational Leadership, 45,* 40–48.

Brophy, J., & Good, T. (1986). Teacher effects. In M. C. Wittock (Ed.), *Handbook of research on teaching* (3rd ed., pp. 328–375). New York: Macmillan.

Chubb, J. E. (1990). *Politics, markets, and America's schools.* Washington, DC: Brookings Institution.

Comer, J. (1988). Educating poor minority children. *Scientific American, 259,* 42–48.

Crosby, E. A. (1993). The at-risk decade. *Phi Delta Kappan, 74,* 598–604.

Danforth, S., Rhodes, W., & Smith, T. (1995). Inventing the future: Postmodern challenges in educational reform. In J. L. Paul, H. Rosselli, & D. Evans (Eds.), *Integrating school restructuring and special education reform* (pp. 214–236). Orlando: Harcourt Brace.

Davis, W. E., & McCaul, E. J. (1991). *The emerging crisis: Current and projected status of children in the United States.* Orono, ME: Institute for the Study of At-Risk Students.

Elkind, D. (1994). *Ties that stress.* Cambridge, MA: Harvard University Press.

Gitlin, A. D. (1990). Educative research, voice, and school change. *Harvard Educational Review, 60,* 443–466.

Goodlad, J. I. (1994). *Educational renewal: Better teachers, better schools.* San Francisco: Jossey-Bass.

Hatch, J. A., & Wisniewski, R. (1995). Life history and narrative: Questions, issues, and exemplary works. In J. A. Hatch & R. Wisniewski (Eds.), *Life history and narrative* (pp. 113–135). Briston, PA: Falmer.

Hodgkinson, H. (1993). American education: The good, the bad, and the task. *Phi Delta Kappan, 74,* 619–625.

Irwin, C. E., Brindis, C. D., Brodt, S. E., Bennett, T. A., & Rodriguez, R. Q. (1991). *The health of America's youth: Current trends in health status and utilization of health services.* San Francisco: University of California at San Francisco.

Janko, S. (1994). *Vulnerable children, vulnerable families: The social construction of child abuse.* New York: Teachers College Press.

Kiel, D. C. (1995). The radical humanist view of special education and disability: Consciousness, freedom and ideology. In T. M. Skrtic (Ed.), *Disability and democracy: Reconstructing (special) education for postmodernity* (pp. 135–149). New York: Teachers College Press.

Kozol, J. (1995). *Amazing grace.* New York: Crown.

Lawson, H. A. (1994). Toward healthy learners, schools, and communities. *Journal of Teacher Education, 45,* 62–70.

McCoy, K. M. (1995). *Teaching special learners in the general education classroom: Methods and techniques.* Denver: Love.

Mercer, J. R. (1992). The impact of changing paradigms of disability on mental retardation in the year 2000. In L. Rowitz (Ed.), *Mental retardation in the year 2000* (pp. 15–38). New York: Springer-Verlag.

National Commission on Excellence in Education. (1983). *A nation at risk.* Washington, DC: Government Printing Office.

Pallas, A. M., Natriello, G., & McDill, E. L. (1989). The changing nature of the disadvantaged population: Current dimensions and future trends. *Educational Researcher, 18,* 16–22.

Pinnell, G. S. (1989). Reading recovery: Helping at-risk children learn to read. *Elementary School Journal, 90,* 161–182.

Reynolds, M. C., Wang, M. C., & Walberg, H. J. (1992). The knowledge bases for special and general education. *Remedial and Special Education, 13,* 6–10, 33.

Ruenzel, D. (1995). Is the education crisis a fraud? *Teacher Magazine, 7,* 29–33.

Sailor, W., & Skrtic, T. (1995). Modern and postmodern agendas in special education: Implications for teacher education, research, and policy development. In J. L. Paul, H. Rosselli, & D. Evans (Eds.), *Integrating school restructuring and special education reform* (pp. 418–432). Orlando: Harcourt Brace.

Sarup, M. (1993). *An introductory guide to post-structuralism and postmodernism.* New York: Harvester Wheatsheaf.

Schorr, L. B. (1989). *Within our reach: Breaking the cycle of disadvantage.* New York: Anchor.

Schrag, J. A. (1993). Restructuring schools for better alignment of general and special education. In J. I. Goodlad & T. C. Lovitt (Eds.), *Integrating general and special education* (pp. 203–227). New York: Merrill.

Skrtic, T. M. (1991). The special education paradox: Equity as the way to excellence. *Harvard Educational Review, 61,* 148–206.

Skrtic, T. M. (Ed.). (1995a). *Disability and democracy: Reconstructing (special) education for postmodernity.* New York: Teachers College Press.

Skrtic, T. M. (1995b). The functionalist view of special education and disability: Deconstructing the conventional knowledge tradition. In T. M. Skrtic (Ed.), *Disability and democracy: Reconstructing (special) education for postmodernity* (pp. 65–103). New York: Teachers College Press.

Skrtic, T. M. (1995c). Power/knowledge and pragmatism: A postmodern view of the professions. In T. M. Skrtic (Ed.), *Disability and democracy: Reconstructing (special) education for postmodernity* (pp. 25–62). New York: Teachers College Press.

Slavin, R. E., Madden, N. A., Dolan, L. J., Wasik, B. A., Ross, S., Smith, L., & Dianda, M. (1986). Success for all: A summary of research. *Journal of Education for Students Placed at Risk, 1,* 41–76.

Streissguth, A. P., Aase, J. M., Clarren, S. K., Randels, S. P., LaDue, R. A., & Smith, D. F. (1991). Fetal alcohol syndrome in adolescents and adults. *Journal of American Medical Association, 265,* 1961–1967.

U.S. Department of Education, National Center for Educational Statistics. (1994). *The condition of education, 1994.* Washington, DC: Author.

Wang, M. C., Reynolds, M. C., & Walberg, H. J. (1995). Introduction: Inner-city students at the margins. In M. C. Wang & M. C. Reynolds (Eds.), *Making a difference for students at risk: Trends and alternatives* (pp. 1–26). Thousand Oaks, CA: Corwin Press.

Index

Amniocentesis, 320–21, 324, 328
A Nation at Risk, 70, 250–62, 258, 381
Annual Report to Congress on the Implementation of IDEA, 216
Antifoundationalism, 374, 394–95
Applied behavioral analysis, 180
Apprentices, teacher, 253
Appropriate education, 182
Asian Americans
    ethnicity of, 44
    in higher education programs, 368
    increasing population of, 39
    ethic identity of, 43
    values of, 336
Assessment
    authentic, 141
    alternative, 143–44
    bias, 45–46
    for diagnosis, eligibility, and placement, 144–63
    dynamic, 140
    eligibility, costs of, 170
    functional, 150, 157–58, 162
    outcomes–based, 143
    practices, 51, 135–74
Assimilation, 43–44
Assistive technology, 304–05
Authentic assessment, 141
Autism, 192, 373
Autonomy, 211–13, 217–18, 221–23, 233

Baby Doe, 339
Behavioral goals, 187
Benefits-cost analysis, 286
Best practices, 377
Bias
    assessment practices, 51
    potential IQ test, 47–48, 51, 144
    social, 208
    in teacher referral process, 148
Bilingual children, 40–44
Binet-IV, 146
Biological intelligence, 140
Black-white achievement gap, 60
Brain injury, traumatic, 30
Bush administration, 74

Career counseling, 215
Cash validity, 192
Categorical labeling
    educational efficacy and, 8–20
    expense of system, 17
    flaw in system, 15.
    See also Classification system; Labeling
Categories, retention or elimination of, 13–20

Caucasian Americans
    population, 39
    teachers, 59
    See also European Americans
Center for the Future of Children, 313
Center for Special Education Finance (CSEF), 270, 275–76, 284, 286–87
Cerebral palsy, 348–49
Chapter One, 12, 89
Child abuse, 371
Child Abuse Amendments of 1984, 339
Child care, technology and, 310–11, 314–15
Choice system, 164–65, 167–70
Chorionic villus biopsy (CVS), 328
Civil rights protections, 342
Classification, eligibility and, 2–36
Classification system, 6–8
    changes in, 10
    eligibility and gaps in, 20–32
    See also Categorical labeling; Labeling
Classism, 115
Classroom
    computers in, 304
    as research-replication site, 193
Cochlear implant, 337
Cognitive processing tests, 152
Cognitive stimulation opportunities, 305–06
Cognitive strategy training, 193
Collaboration, 246, 249
Collaborative prevention/services model, 285
College
    community, 231
    developmental instruction in, 225–33
Communication
    family-professional, 44–47
    skills, 214
Community integration, 341
Compensatory training, postsecondary level, 227, 230, 232
Computers, 304–05
Conduct disordered students, 22
Congential abnormalities, 328
Constructivism, 177–80, 193
Contextualism, 179
Continental perspective, 374
Cooperative Integrated Reading and Composition model (CIRC), 121
Cooperative learning (CL), 193
    effectiveness of, 122, 125–126
    gifted children and, 120–28
    heterogeneous groups, 123–24
Cooperative teams, 11